The Intimate Environment

Exploring Marriage and the Family

FOURTH EDITION

Arlene S. Skolnick
UNIVERSITY OF CALIFORNIA, BERKELEY

Little, Brown and Company

BOSTON   TORONTO

Library of Congress Cataloging-in-Publication Data

Skolnick, Arlene S., 1933–
   The intimate environment.

   Bibliography: p.
   Includes index.
   1. Family—United States.   2. Marriage—United States.
I. Title.
HQ536.S56   1986   306.8'0973   86-20964
ISBN 0-316-79744-8

Library of Congress Catalog Card Number 86-20964

ISBN 0-316-79744-8

9 8 7 6 5 4 3 2

MV

Published simultaneously in Canada
by Little, Brown & Company (Canada) Limited

Printed in the United States of America

Produced by R. David Newcomer Associates

FOR MY PARENTS,
ROSALIE CHAIKEN SILBERSTEIN
AND THE LATE HAROLD SILBERSTEIN

ACKNOWLEDGMENTS

Excerpt from Nadine Brozan, "Parley Asserts U.S. Undercuts Family," *The New York Times*, July 28, 1982. Copyright © 1982 by The New York Times Company. Reprinted by permission.

Excerpt from William Martin, "Two Cheers for the Moral Majority," *The Texas Humanist* 7:4, p. 13. Reprinted by permission of the publisher.

Excerpts reprinted from "Fun Morality: An Analysis of Recent American Child-Training Literature," by M. Wolfenstein, in M. Mead and M. Wolfenstein, eds., *Childhood in Contemporary Cultures*, by permission of The University of Chicago Press. © 1955 by The University of Chicago. All rights reserved.

Excerpt from T. Lidz, *The Family and Human Adaptation* (New York: International Universities Press, Inc., 1963), pp. 51–53, reprinted by permission of the publisher.

Excerpts from *The Rise of Anthropological Theory: A History of Theories of Culture* by Marvin Harris (Thomas Y. Crowell Co.) copyright © 1968 by Harper and Row, Publishers, Inc. Reprinted by permission of the publisher.

Excerpts from William J. Goode, "Force and Violence in the Family," *Journal of Marriage and Family* 33:4, pp. 624–636, reprinted by permission of the author.

Excerpts from *Centuries of Childhood* by Philippe Ariès, translated by Robert Baldich, copyright © 1962 by Jonathan Cape Ltd. Reprinted by permission of Alfred A. Knopf, Inc., and Jonathan Cape Ltd.

Excerpts from William J. Goode, *World Revolution and Family Patterns*, copyright © 1963 by The Free Press. Reprinted by permission of the publisher.

Excerpts from Edward Shorter, *The Making of the Modern Family*, copyright © 1975 by Basic Books, Inc.

Excerpts from Talcott Parsons and Robert F. Bales, *Family Socialization and Interaction Process*, copyright 1955 by The Free Press, a Corporation. Reprinted by permission of the publisher.

Excerpts from Lillian Breslow Rubin, *Worlds of Pain: Life in the Working-Class Family*, copyright © 1976 by Lillian Breslow Rubin.

Excerpt from F. Hilliker in W. F. Mondale, "Government Policy, Stress, and the Family," *Journal of Home Economics* 68:5, p. 14, reprinted by permission of the publisher.

Excerpts from Richard Udry, *The Social Context of Marriage*, Second Edition (Philadelphia: J. B. Lippincott Co., 1971), reprinted by permission of the author.

Excerpts from Jay Haley, *Strategies of Psychotherapy* (New York: Grune & Stratton, 1963), reprinted by permission of the publisher and the author.

Portions of chapter 10 originally appeared in "The Social Contexts of Cohabitation" by Arlene Skolnick, *American Journal of Comparative Law* 19:2, Spring 1981, pp. 339–358, and are used by permission of the publisher.

Excerpt from *Lines on Reading D. H. Lawrence, Sher-*

wood Anderson, et al. by John Haynes Holmes, reprinted by permission of Roger Holmes.

Excerpts from Robert Ryder, "A Topography of Early Marriage," *Family Process* 9, pp. 51–68, reprinted by permission of the publisher and the author.

Excerpt from Robert O. Blood and Donald M. Wolfe, *Husbands and Wives*, copyright © 1960 by The Free Press. Reprinted by permission of the publisher.

Excerpt from Robert J. Samuelson, "In Praise of Children," *Newsweek*, January 13, 1986, p. 49. Copyright 1986, by Newsweek, Inc. All Rights Reserved. Reprinted by Permission.

Excerpt from Dr. Haim Ginott's King Features Syndicate column, "Being a Parent," which appeared in the *San Francisco Sunday Examiner and Chronicle*, Feb-

ruary 11, 1973, reprinted by permission of Dr. Alice Ginott.

Excerpts from E. H. Pohlman, *Psychology of Birth Planning* (Cambridge, Mass.: Schenkman Publishing Co., Inc., 1969), reprinted by permission of the publisher.

Excerpts from J. W. Macfarlane, "Perspectives on Personality Consistency and Change from the Guidance Study," *Vita Humana* 7, pp. 115–126, reprinted by permission of the publisher.

Portions of chapter 15 which originally appeared in "The Family and its Discontents" by Arlene Skolnick are published by permission of Transaction, Inc. from *Society*, Vol. 18 #2. Copyright © 1981 by Transaction, Inc.

Each new edition of *The Intimate Environment* has faced the task of describing the changing state of both the family and family scholarship. When I began work on the first edition of this book more than a decade ago, there was already widespread concern about the family. During this period, traditional family and sex role arrangements were being challenged by feminists, unmarried people living together as couples, people living in communes, and the gay movement. Some worried about these changes. Others used the issue of "the family" to bring home messages about policy—poverty programs, day care, health care, tax reform. But for many people this was a time of liberation, of new possibilities, of an end to hypocrisy. It was a time that seems very far away from the present, when disillusion, gloom, and nostalgia have spread all across the ideological spectrum.

Family textbooks then had little to say about the changes that were taking place. By and large, they presented the traditional nuclear family with a breadwinner husband and full-time wife and mother as a univer-

sally necessary, functional, and relatively changeless institution. In contrast to that abstract, idealized image of the family, I argued that families were much more diverse than generally recognized and that there was a dark side to family life. Conflict and ambivalence are as intrinsic to the family as intimacy and love, and relations among individuals, families, and society need not always be harmonious. Although some people mistook the earlier editions of this book as "antifamily," the critique was directed at the prevailing idealizations and myths about the family. As I wrote in the preface to the first edition:

Paradoxically, by emphasizing the problematic nature of the family, this book is able to be unpessimistic about the future of the family. If there is no definition of the family that will hold across all cultures and periods, and if the family is a concept rather than a biological reality, then novel forms of the intimate environment may be equally valid. If conflict between the generations and the sexes is part of human history, then today's situation is not such a radical departure from the past. If the normal family is a myth, then perhaps the craziness we observe in family life is also part of the human condition. What we are witnessing may not be so much the breakdown of the family as an institution, as the destruction of myths and assumptions about family living that were never true in the first place.

By the third edition pessimism about the breakdown of the family had become the new conventional wisdom. The notion of family decline had been linked to a host of changes and social problems: not only the demographic trends of recent years, such as rising divorce rates and the movement of women into the labor force, but also alienated youth, teenage pregnancy, welfare dependency, pornography, and child abuse and neglect. I believe that it is a mistake to lump all of these issues together. It is also a mistake to attribute these problems to the deterioration of the family.

Public concern about the family does, however, provide a useful framework for discussion of the family. The notion of family breakdown involves a tangled mass of myths and unexamined assumptions about the family in the past, its relation to the larger society, its psychological relationships.

The 1980s witnessed the rise of conservative "new right" perspectives on family life and the increasing prominence of "the family" and family-related issues on the political scene. For conservatives, the solution to the crisis of the family was the restoration of the traditional family, headed by the male breadwinner and with the wife at home. By the middle of the decade, however, public attention started to turn away from ideological debates between the conservatives and their opponents toward a more realistic assessment of the current problems afflicting family life—the impact of no-fault divorce, the feminization of poverty, the difficulties of combining parenthood with work, and the

implications for family life of the economic changes of recent years.

Given the level of public concern, the study of family life is of more than personal or even academic interest. It is fortunate that in recent years research on the family has been flourishing as never before. The "new" historical studies of the family provide an especially useful framework for examining the widespread notion that family life today has declined from some former golden age of stability and harmony.

No new chapters have been added to this edition, but the book has been revised and updated throughout to reflect recent research and changing public issues. Among the newer topics discussed are the declining economic situation of women and children as a result of the "divorce revolution," the shrinking of the middle class and the emergence of a two-tiered economic structure, the Yuppie lifestyle and stereotype, the Hispanic family and its changing images in social science research, recent psychological research on infancy, the history of sexuality, and so on. The graphs and charts presenting demographic data have been updated, and there is more detailed information about current public opinion in relation to family issues.

Since the first edition of this book came out, I have had many helpful conversations with friends, colleagues, and acquaintances. It is hard to list all of them. For this edition I have benefited especially from talks with Nancy Chodorow, William J. Goode, Arlie Hochschild, Karen Paige, Lillian Rubin, Judith Stacey, and Lenore Weitzman. I have also benefited from the lively discussions of the members of the Seminar on Family Dynamics and Personality at the Institute of Human Development, organized by Guy Swanson and Philip and Carolyn Cowan. The Faculty Woman's Research Forum has been a continuing source of intellectual stimulation and support. I am also indebted to the reviewers who made suggestions for revision. Donna Schuele helped to find necessary materials and provided critical comments on various chapters. I am grateful to Sarah Dorrell, who assisted in many ways with the preparation of the manuscript.

Finally, I thank my husband, Jerome H. Skolnick, for his continuing support for what has turned out to be like another addition to the family—this book. He has been, as always, a tough critic as well as lover and best friend.

CONTENTS

CHAPTER 1

Introduction: The State of the Family and the Study of the Family

American families are in trouble—trouble so deep and pervasive as to threaten the future of the nation.

Report to the White House
Conference on Children, 1970

The family is, as far as we know, the toughest institution we have. It is, in fact, the institution to which we owe our humanity.

Margaret Mead
*"The Impact of Cultural Changes on
the Family"*

Far from being the basis of the good society, the family, with its narrow privacy and its tawdry secrets, is the source of all our discontents.

Edmund Leach
A Runaway World?

The American family and its public image have been remarkably transformed in recent years. During the 1950s—the period when the parents of many of today's college students were entering adulthood—the American family seemed to represent the latest model of a timeless unit. It was the era of "togetherness," the baby boom, and the growth of suburban living. No one denied that there were family problems, such as illegitimacy, marital unhappiness, divorce, and conflicts between parents and children, but most people, including most family scholars, thought of these as exceptions to the usual state of family life.

A Rip van Winkle who went to sleep in the 1950s and awoke in the late 1980s would be astonished at how much marriage, family, and sexual arrangements have changed. Probably the first thing he would notice is the great frankness about sexual matters. Behavior that was taboo is commonplace today—unmarried couples openly moving in together, teenage girls showing up pregnant in high school, homosexuals marching in Gay Pride parades and running for office, abortion a widely practiced legal right.

A 1980s Rip van Winkle would also be surprised at the changes in women and in the relations between the sexes. A majority of women are now in the paid labor force, although most still work at the kind of jobs they had in the 1950s—as teachers, secretaries, nurses, and so on. Further, women can now be found in traditionally male occupations—they are police officers and fire fighters as well as doctors and lawyers.

These observable changes in the social landscape are confirmed by statistical evidence. The following are some of the most striking demographic trends reported by the U.S. Bureau of the Census and illustrated in the figures here:

People are marrying later than they did in the 1950s and 1960s. In 1983, 56 percent of American women between the ages of 20 and 24 had not yet married, compared to just 36 percent in 1970.

Birth rates declined dramatically from 1960 to 1979, reaching the lowest level ever recorded in 1975–1976. Recently, they have increased slightly as couples began having the children they had postponed.

The proportion of married women in the labor force has tripled in 4 decades—from 17 percent in 1940 to 53 percent in 1984. The changes have been most dramatic among women with young children.

Divorce rates have tripled.

Single-parent families have increased dramatically.

Increasing numbers of people live alone.

Births out of wedlock have increased in proportion to all live births.

As a result of these changes, the traditional or "typical" family consisting of a bread-winning husband, a full-time housewife, and two children has become a statistical rarity; in March of 1983, only 6.2 percent of American families fit this description (Thornton & Freedman, 1983).

To many observers, all these changes seem to signal that the family is falling apart.

Percent in labor force

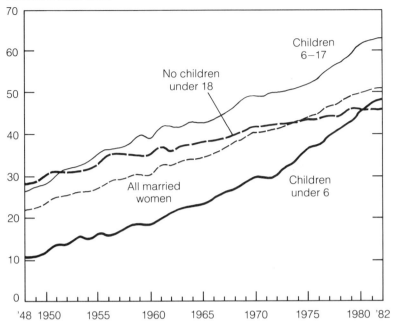

From A. Thornton and D. Freedman, *Population Bulletin: The Changing American Family*,
a publication of The Population Reference Bureau, Vol. 38, No. 4, October 1983, p. 5.

FIGURE 1.1
Labor Force Participation Rates of Married Women, by Presence and Age of Children: 1948–1982

By the early 1970s, the breakdown of the family was a familiar theme in newspapers, on television, on the covers of *Time* and *Newsweek*. At the same time, the media lavished attention on alternative life-styles—hippie communes, swinging singles, married swingers, open marriage, cohabitation. It seemed as if marriage and the nuclear family were going the way of the horse and buggy. A few writers celebrated the death of the family (D. G. Cooper, 1970; R. D. Laing, 1971). Some feminists denounced the family as a trap that turned women into slaves. Most people, however, were anxious or at least ambivalent about the changes. Many people were deeply worried that the family might be an endangered species.

These prophecies of doom did not go unchallenged. In 1976, Mary Jo Bane published a highly influential book arguing that the family is here to stay. Bane looked at demographic and public opinion data and concluded that the family is not only alive but well. Contrary to the myth of the decaying family, she argued, Americans have a greater personal commitment to family bonds than ever before; today's children are not less well cared for than those in the past, and today's adults have not abandoned ties to their own parents and kin. Bane concluded that "the facts—as opposed to the myths about marriage, childrearing, and family ties in the United States today—provide convincing evidence that family commitments are likely to persist in our society" (p. 141).

Most family scholars and social scientists have tended to agree with Bane that the family is here to stay. But the debate about the survival of the family continued throughout the 1970s. After the middle of the dec-

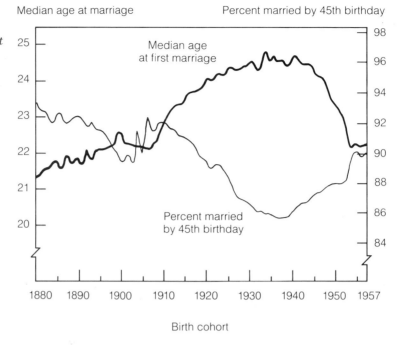

FIGURE 1.2
Median Age at First Marriage and Percent Married by Age 45, Birth Cohorts of White Women: 1880–1957

From A. Thornton and D. Freedman, *Population Bulletin: The Changing American Family,* a publication of The Population Reference Bureau, Vol. 38, No. 4, October 1983, p. 5.

ade, social critics noted an increasing preoccupation with self that seemed incompatible with family ties. Tom Wolfe (1976) wrote of the growing popularity of awareness and personal growth therapies and new religious cults. He labeled the 1970s "the me decade"—a name that stuck. Christopher Lasch (1977, 1978) popularized the term *narcissism* to describe American culture. A new character type had emerged, he claimed, incapable of deep and lasting relationships, seeking instant intimacy but fleeing from commitment. Pollster Daniel Yankelovich stated that a revolution in values had transformed the rules of American life. In place of the old values, "we now find people who refuse to deny themselves *anything*—not out of bottomless appetite, but on the strange moral principle that 'I have a duty to myself'" (1981a, p. xviii).

THE NEW POLITICS OF THE FAMILY

In the 1980s discussions of the family took a new direction. Instead of arguments about whether or not the family was dying, an intense debate about family policy erupted. Since the election of Ronald Reagan, discussions of family policy have been dominated by a conservative point of view, which differs in major ways from the liberal perspective that dominated the 1960s and 1970s.

It was the liberal side, ironically, that first put the family on the national agenda. In the presidential campaign of 1976, Jimmy Carter promised that if elected he would convene a special White House conference to explore the problems of families and what government policies could do to help. It seemed an uncontroversial idea at the time. But the conference soon became a battleground over such issues as abortion, the equal rights amendment, sex education, and gay rights.

The definition of the family provoked a major debate. The conference planners wanted to recognize that there are many types of American families; in fact, they called it the White House Conference on *Families*. Conservatives argued that there is only one true family: the traditional one with a breadwinner father and a full-time mother. In short, instead of bringing people together, the conference revealed that Americans are deeply divided in their beliefs and values concerning the family. Observing the controversy, a conservative columnist predicted that the family would be to the 1980s what the Vietnam War had been to the 1960s.

THE GOOD NEWS AND THE BAD NEWS: ALTERNATIVE VIEWS OF FAMILY CHANGE

This prediction was accurate. The debate over the family grew in intensity as the decade wore on. There were even street demonstrations and bombings—this time not the work of war protestors, but of antiabortion activists. There was another reminder of the Vietnam era: once again, hospital wards were filled with sick and dying young men, only this time the cause was AIDS. Strictly speaking, of course, neither abortion nor AIDS is a family issue in itself. But both issues reflect deep disagreements about the nature of the family, sexual morality, and the proper roles of men and women.

In the middle to late 1980s, there appear to be three major points of view in the debate over the family. The first is that of the New Right conservatives who adopt the pro-

family label, as if to suggest that those who differ from them are antifamily. The second view is that of family scholars and others who argue that the family is here to stay and that the notion of a crisis in the family is a myth. The third viewpoint is that of many family scholars and other family professionals, who see the family as a durable but troubled institution. Although agreeing that the family is here to stay, these writers believe that the family is beset with serious problems and that public policies have a role in alleviating them.

In addition, there is a fourth view which is more often attacked than defended these days. As we saw earlier, in the 1950s and 1960s some radical feminist theorists did denounce the family and celebrate reports of its death. Not all radical feminists took this extreme view even back then, and feminist and radical positions on the family have evolved a good deal since them. However, the media at the time devoted considerable attention to the more extreme positions— and they still serve as a convenient target of attack for the New Right.

Who Are the New Right?

The conservatives who adopted the pro-family label are a coalition of diverse groups: traditional political conservatives, religious groups such as the Moral Majority, anti-feminists such as Phyllis Schlafly's Eagle Forum, and groups concerned with particular issues, such as abortion and sex education, or with censoring school textbooks and banning the teaching of evolution. These groups are united in the belief that there has been a breakdown of moral values in recent years that is revealed as much in high divorce rates and working mothers as in pornography and prostitution.

The villains responsible for these ills are feminists, the media, the "experts," and

An Arkansas farm family in the 1940s. Family photographs reveal two aspects of family life—families as sets of personalities and relationships, and families as people living in a particular time and place. [Michael Disfarmer/ Archive Pictures Inc.]

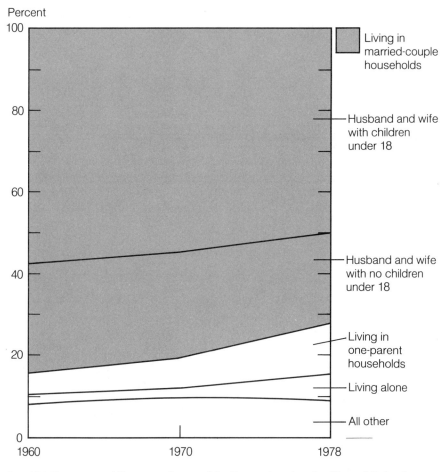

Percent

- Living in married-couple households
- Husband and wife with children under 18
- Husband and wife with no children under 18
- Living in one-parent households
- Living alone
- All other

1960   1970   1978

FIGURE 1.3
Living Arrangements of the Noninstitutional Population: 1960, 1970, and 1978

Despite recent changes, three of every four persons in the United States live in married-couple households. This proportion declined from 85 percent in 1960 to 75 percent in 1978. Fifty percent of the 220 million people lived in married-couple households with young children present, and nine percent lived in one-parent households. Among the others, 2.7 million persons in 1978 lived in households of unmarried couples of opposite sex, twice as many as in 1970.

From U.S. Department of Commerce, Bureau of the Census, *American Families and Living Arrangements.* Current Population Reports, Special Studies, Series P-23, No. 104, May 1980.

above all, Big Government—the modern welfare state. All of these have undermined family values and promoted permissive attitudes toward divorce, sexuality, and child-rearing. According to the New Right, the social programs of the welfare state have taken over family responsibilities and thereby eroded the strength of the family. By protecting people against the risks of joblessness, disability, and poverty in old age, the welfare state also undermines the work ethic. Further, according to the New Right, federal spending eats up family income, thereby driving mothers into the work force and depriving fathers of their authority.

The New Right is united in its goal of dismantling government social programs. It believes that as a result women will remain in the home as full-time homemakers, men will become responsible providers, divorce rates will drop, and America will be revitalized at home and abroad. The economic part of the argument is developed most fully in George Gilder's *Wealth and Poverty* (1981), a book President Reagan gave to his cabinet members at the beginning of his first term.

Despite its current influence, the New Right does not reflect the mainstream of American thought. Opinion polls show that far from accepting the father-dominated home as an ideal, most Americans believe a more equal relationship between husband and wife promotes a healthy family. They also support the idea of equal pay for equal work. Further, a majority of Americans still support the equal rights amendment and the right to choose an abortion. Nor do most Americans favor the dismantling of the welfare state; in fact, polling data show that public support for government social policies has *increased* over the Reagan years (Ferguson & Rogers, 1986).

Nevertheless, many people are anxious about the recent changes in family life. They resonate to the New Right's perception that the family is in trouble and that the troubles of the family have serious implications for individuals and the whole of society. William Martin (1985), for example, does not identify with the Moral Majority, but he does give two cheers for it. He paints a grim landscape of American society; after citing the familiar litany of statistics on divorce, single-parent families, and illegitimacy, he goes on to state:

Eleven million unborn children . . . have been aborted since the Roe vs. Wade decision in 1973. Twenty million Americans have herpes, three million have gonorrhea, new strains of syphilis and other venereal diseases have appeared, and the AIDS epidemic is causing a panic among homosexuals and heterosexuals alike. Hundreds of thousands of children are sexually abused. . . .

Sixty per cent of women with school children work, leaving millions of children in day-care centers and more than two million latchkey children without adult supervision for long periods each day. . . . Alcohol problems trouble 22% of American homes. . . . More than half the population has used marijuana and 20% has used harder drugs. Crime and violence—in the streets, in the schools, in the media—have stripped us of

the freedom and peace of mind that characterized the lives of our childhood and that ought to be characteristic of the lives of our children. So it goes. (p. 13)

The Family Is Alive and Well

In sharp contrast to Martin's dark vision of the American social landscape, Ben Wattenberg insists that Americans "never had it so good." Wattenberg states his case in *The Good News Is the Bad News Is Wrong* (1985). As far as the family is concerned, he makes three points: there has been *less* change than generally assumed; many of the changes that have occurred are for the *better*; to the extent that harmful changes have occurred, they are correcting.

Wattenberg applies his less–better–correcting analysis to all areas of family change. For example, with regard to premarital sex, he cites evidence to show that virginity was far from universal before the sexual revolution of the 1960s; Alfred Kinsey's data showed that 36 percent of American women born between 1900 and 1920 experienced premarital intercourse by the age of 25. Almost one out of five first births in the 1950s were conceived before marriage. Further, he argues, permissive sexual standards have some beneficial effects: less sexual guilt and no more marriages based mainly on sexual need—a poor reason to marry. Finally, a variety of statistics indicate that casual or promiscuous sex has been decreasing in recent years.

What about drugs, alcoholism, incest, runaway children, and child and spouse abuse? Wattenberg argues that there is little evidence that these distressing problems are any more common than they used to be; rather we are much more aware of them than in the past. Drug addiction—to opium—was a problem in the early years of this century, and alcoholism was rampant on the American frontier. "The fact that human beings live in a world with some very ugly aspects —and always have—does not establish the case that our values are eroding" (p. 292).

At the core of the optimistic side of the debate is evidence that despite all the changes, the family remains the primary value in the lives of Americans. Public opinion data confirm consistently that Americans value a good family life above work, religion, and health. Between 1973 and 1981—the infamous "me decade"—pollster Daniel Yankelovich found that about three-fourths of those interviewed said that family life was their most important value (1981a, 1981b). The Gallup Poll and other survey data report similar findings (Gallup Poll, 1985). Furthermore, surveys reveal that Americans not only value family life, but also report they derive great satisfaction from it. Family contact is frequent as well. A 1983 survey found that 53 percent of Americans spend a social evening with relatives several times a month, compared to 19 percent who go to a bar or tavern over the same period (cited in Wattenberg, 1985, p. 282). A 1985 study found that "most Americans are involved in close-knit families that get together several times a month" (Rubenstein, 1985, pp. 24ff).

Studies of well-being provide additional evidence of the importance of marriage in American life. Surveys consistently find that married people are happier and enjoy better mental and physical health than those who are single. And Bane sees even the grief and emptiness that people experience when they divorce as evidence of the importance of marriage. People do not change spouses the way they trade in cars. We are "very far from being a society of casual liaisons rather than permanent families" (1976, p. 36).

The frequency of remarriage is further evidence for the continued importance of family ties. In the 1980s, five out of six divorced men and three out of four divorced women will remarry, typically a few years after divorcing. In fact, remarriage rates for divorced people are higher than they were 40 years ago (Cherlin, 1981c).

What about the new values of sexual equality, self-fulfillment, and personal development—don't these undermine family bonds? Bane and others point out that these new values have been *added* to traditional commitments to the family; they do not replace them. Thus, the Gallup Poll (1985) finds that the ideal life-style of a majority of American women continues to be marriage with children. But lately that ideal has come to include a full-time or part-time job outside the home. Similarly, Gallup reports that sexual attitudes have changed dramatically— in 1969, 68 percent of U.S. adults said premarital sex is wrong and in 1985 only 39 percent held that view—but that Americans have continued to place a high value on the family, hard work, and religion over the entire 50 years the Gallup organization has been polling.

The Middletown Studies

Another highly optimistic view of the current family scene was put forth by Theodore Caplow and his associates in a book entitled *Middletown Families: Fifty Years of Change and Continuity* (Caplow et al., 1982). Middletown is the fictitious name given to a midwestern community (actually Muncie, Indiana) immortalized in Robert and Helen Lynd's classic studies (1929, 1937). Between 1976 and 1978 a team of social scientists returned to Middletown to gauge the changes that have taken place in a typical American town in the past 50 years.

The major finding was that while nearly everybody in Middletown was worried about the crisis of the modern family, the Middletown family itself seemed to be in surpris-

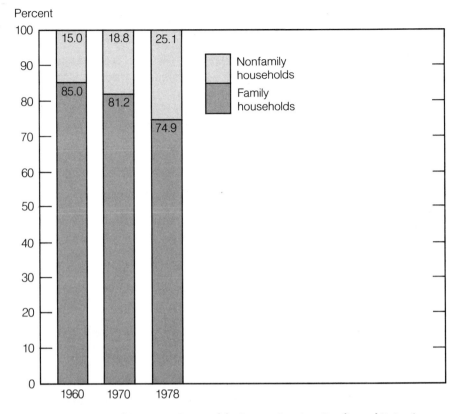

FIGURE 1.4
Family and Nonfamily Households as a Percent of All Households: 1960, 1970, and 1978

One-fourth of all households include no family group. As more elderly wives outlive their husbands and as more young adults establish separate homes before marriage or after separation or divorce, a growing number of adults live apart from relatives, usually alone.

From U.S. Department of Commerce, Bureau of the Census, *American Families and Living Arrangements.* Current Population Reports, Special Studies, Series P-23, No. 104, May 1980.

ingly good condition: "Tracing the changes from the 1920s to the 1970s, we discovered increasing family solidarity, a smaller generation gap, closer marital communication, more religion, and less mobility" (p. 323).

The deepest concern of those who worry about the state of the family, however, is children. The studies of Bane and Caplow and his associates dispute the common belief that today's children are less well cared for than children in the past. Bane and others have pointed out that children are more likely to be living with at least one parent than children of earlier generations. Caplow's Middletown study found that parents spend more time now with their children.

Much of the improvement in the quality of family noted by the Middletown researchers can be attributed to improvements in the standard of living. For blue-collar families in the 1920s, family life was often bleak and dreary because of long working hours, too little income, and poor housing. Improvements in material well-being—such as shorter working hours, more leisure time, higher incomes, better health care, and housing—have also improved the quality of family life.

Moreover, comparisons of Middletown in the 1920s and 1970s reveal how much the sexual revolution has improved the quality of family life. Fifty years ago, marital sexuality

The kind of intimacy that goes on in families is precious in a large-scale, impersonal society. [Joan Liftin/Archive Pictures Inc.]

was constrained by ignorance, a general lack of communication between husbands and wives, and fear of pregnancy. Prostitution flourished in the Middletown of the 1920s. Contraception and greater knowledge about sexuality have improved not only marriage but also the lives of children, who are more likely to come into the world as wanted and planned additions to the family.

A Durable but Troubled Institution

As we have noted, there is a third group of observers who disagree with pessimists (who believe the family is a declining institution) as well as with the optimists (who insist that family life has never been better). This group sees the family as a durable and resilient institution, yet one beset with a number of serious problems. Some of these problems—child neglect, runaways, domestic violence, teenage pregnancy, and other adolescent difficulties—have been on the

public policy agenda for decades (Steiner, 1981). It's a mistake to see all these issues together with such problems as crime, prostitution, and pornography as part of a breakdown of the family that started in the 1960s. But it is also a mistake to ignore the fact that the family has been afflicted with a number of persistent dilemmas.

Moreover, while many of the changes in recent years have been beneficial, they have also created some very real difficulties. Thus although divorce, working mothers, and single-parent families do not necessarily spell the doom of the family, they do create problems: divorce can be emotionally devastating for all family members, especially children, and economically devastating for women and children (Weitzman, 1985). Single parents do face enormous hardships in raising children and supporting them without the help of another adult. Women who work, although they are now in the majority, still face persisting inequality in the workplace and the burden of the double day or second shift at home. Further, there are the difficulties faced by men and women trying to construct family lives according to new ideals of gender equality. Finally, poverty and unemployment persist with devastating effects on family life.

Thus, Cherlin and other family researchers who take the "durable but troubled" position do believe public policies have a role to play in improving the quality of public life. They differ from both the conservatives who would try to turn the clock to some idealized version of the traditional family and from the optimists who deny that there are serious problems in American family life.

Consider, for example, the issue of latchkey children. Conservatives—as well as others—are appalled by large numbers of children at home alone after school, unsupervised by their parents. The conservative remedy is to get women out of the workplace and back into the home. Optimists like Wattenberg, however, deny that latchkey children pose a problem. "There is little evidence of damage done," he writes, "and some data suggest benefits for the children" (1985, p. 298).

The third camp recognizes that being left alone can pose difficulties for many if not all children. But it sees the problem as arising not because working mothers are uncaring, but because they have few alternatives. In this view latchkey children, to the extent there is a problem, reflect the unresponsiveness of other institutions of the society, such as schools and business, to adapt to the new realities of family life.

Despite the difficulties brought about by the recent changes, this school of thought on the family does not believe, as the New Right does, that these trends can be turned around. They are an inevitable part of our country's economic and social development. As Andrew Cherlin puts it, "We can no more keep wives at home or slash the divorce rate than we can shut down our cities and send everyone back to the farm" (1983, p. 429).

MAKING SENSE OF THE CHANGING FAMILY

Each of the contrasting positions outlined above embodies a whole set of assumptions about the nature of family life, the relations between parents and children, the individual and the family, the family and society, and the family in past times. Which view is right? Is it possible to arrive at objective answers about the family? Even the researcher most dedicated to standards of scientific objectivity cannot avoid having deep emotional and moral responses to family issues. Yet social science can help to sort out facts from myths and armchair speculations from interpretations backed up by empirical evidence. Fortunately, we now have more information about the family, its past history, its relation to the rest of society, and its innermost emotional workings than has ever been available. While public debate has raged over the past decades, a great deal of quiet scholarship has been revealing new insights into the family, past and present.

Once something of an intellectual backwater in the field of sociology, the study of the family has now excited the curiosity of scholars in a variety of disciplines—history, economics, psychology, and psychiatry. Ironically, much of the new scholarship is at odds with the public perception that the family is in crisis as well as with the idea that families were more stable and harmonious in the past than they are today.

Although historians of the family differ in various ways, they agree that many of the

Question: Do you think that people who have con-tracted AIDS are unfortunate victims of chance or do you think they are offenders getting what they deserve?

Question: How about "AIDS is a punishment God has given homosexuals for the way they live"—do you agree with that statement? (If agree or disagree) Is that (agree/disagree) strongly or (agree/disagree) somewhat?

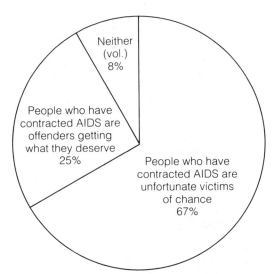

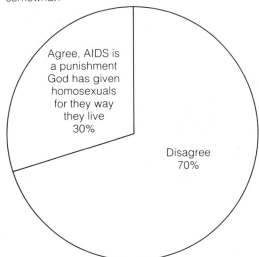

Note: Agree = "Agree strongly" + "Agree somewhat," Disagree = "Disagree strongly" + Disagree somewhat."

From "Opinion Roundup," *Public Opinion,* December/January 1986, p. 37.

FIGURE 1.5
AIDS: Not a Punishment

widely held ideas about family life in the past were mistaken. Because so much of our thinking about the current state of the fam-ily is based on comparisons with our notions of the past, the new research provides us new insights into the nature and problems of today's family life.

Above all, the new research undermines one of the persistent myths about the fam-ily: the myth of the "good old days," that golden age sometime back when families were strong, warm, and loving.

The basic contribution of the new his-tory of the family is, as Michael Anderson (1980) observed, to reveal that these images of the past are distorted.

Perhaps the most basic of the de-mystifying ideas which come from knowledge of the past is also the most simple: "change has occurred be-fore; almost no generation has got by without public debate over family crisis"; most problems of our time have, in fact, also been problems in the past. (p. 39)

The Family Observed

We have also learned a great deal in re-cent years about the inner psychological world of family life. While the new history of the family has undermined the sentimen-tal image of family life in past times, recent studies of the emotional dynamics of family

A greater proportion of children in the twentieth century know their grandparents than children in the past. [Christa Armstrong/Photo Researchers, Inc.]

life have demythologized the contemporary family. Studies of families with troubles of various kinds—violent families, families with mentally ill children, or simply families with more run-of-the-mill problems—suggest that such families are not a breed apart from ordinary ones. Rather, they seem to show in exaggerated form the kinds of tensions that can exist in any family. A major breakthrough in understanding the family came about when clinicians and researchers began to observe live family interaction from behind the looking glass—the one-way screen that is a mirror on one side but transparent on the other.

Family life is the place where, as family therapist Carl Whitaker once put it, "you're dealing with life-and-death voltages" (quoted in Framo, 1972, p. 3). From Greek tragedy to the latest soap opera, writers have always portrayed the intimacies of family life in terms of love and anger, sacrifice and selfishness.

The dark side of family life has also emerged into public awareness in recent

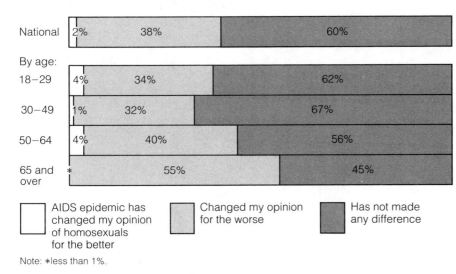

Question: Would you say the AIDS epidemic has changed your opinion about homosexuals for the better, for the worse, or has it not made any difference in the way you feel?

FIGURE 1.6
AIDS and Opinion of Homosexuals

National	2%	38%	60%
By age:			
18–29	4%	34%	62%
30–49	1%	32%	67%
50–64	4%	40%	56%
65 and over	*	55%	45%

☐ AIDS epidemic has changed my opinion of homosexuals for the better

☐ Changed my opinion for the worse

☐ Has not made any difference

Note: *less than 1%.

From "Opinion Roundup," *Public Opinion,* December/January 1986, p. 37.

years with increased concern with previously ignored topics: husband–wife violence, child abuse, and incest. The increased focus on such matters and on such other previously taboo topics as abortion and homosexuality may have contributed to the widespread sense that the family is falling apart. But what has actually happened is that public attention is now focused on matters that used to be shameful secrets. Thus, the fact that child abuse and other forms of family violence were "discovered" in the 1960s doesn't mean that they didn't exist before— or even that they have increased. Rather our awareness of them, as well as our understanding of them, have changed.

The Discovery of Complexity

All in all, the new research on the family has led to a greater awareness of how complex and ambiguous this seemingly simple, universal institution actually is. Glen Elder (1981) summed up the contribution of the new historical studies of the family as "the discovery of complexity," but the term applies to all aspects of the study of the family. The discovery of complexity is not unusual; research in any field often reveals that previous ideas or theories about the topic in question were too simple.

It has become clear, for example, that it is very difficult to define the word *family.* Of course, you know what I mean when I talk about "the family" or "my family" or "the Jones family." But, in fact, each of these terms has a variety of different meanings. The term *the family* is particularly vague. One social worker complained about a meeting of family therapists she attended:

I sat there during the whole time listening to talks about THE family, studies of THE family, arguments about THE family, until I couldn't stand it any longer. I got up and said, "What on earth do you mean . . . THE family? There is no such thing. There are two-parent families, one-parent families, no-parent families, three- or

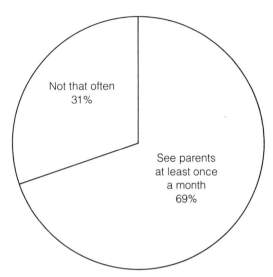

Question: Would you say you see your (parent/ parents) at least once a month or don't you see (them/her/him) that often?

Not that often
31%

See parents
at least once
a month
69%

Note: Asked of those who have one or both parents still alive and who don't live with parent(s) = 68%.

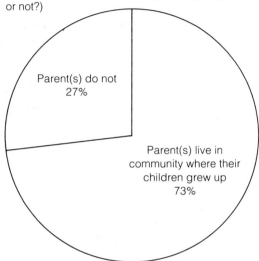

Question: (Do they/does she/does he) (parent/ parents) live in the community where you grew up, or not? (If respondent says parents are separated or divorced, say: Then thinking only of your mother, does she live in the community where you grew up, or not?)

Parent(s) do not
27%

Parent(s) live in
community where their
children grew up
73%

Note: Asked of those with one or both parents alive = 69%.

From "Opinion Roundup," *Public Opinion*, December/January 1986, p. 34.

FIGURE 1.7
Parents and their Grown-up Children

four-parent families, families without children"—there was a burst of applause when I finished. (Westoff, 1977, p. 3)

Even when I talk about "my family," the meaning is still unclear. I could be referring to the family I grew up in, or to my husband and children, my mother and brother, my aunts and uncles, my husband's parents and relatives, or any combination of these. I might even be talking about long-dead people: "My family came to the country around the turn of the century." We will discuss the problem of defining the family at great length in a later chapter.

In addition, statistics about the family are not as simple or self-evident as they might seem at first glance. We often hear statistics that compare the number of divorces in a particular year to the number of marriages. Thus we might learn that in 1982 there were twice as many marriages as divorces or that in a certain county in California there were almost as many divorces as marriages. But these statistics would not really be a valid measure of divorce. Because they depend on the number of people who happen to be getting married that year, they don't tell us about the rate of divorce for the married population as a whole. Nor do these

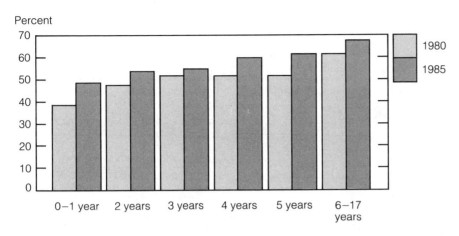

Percent

FIGURE 1.8
Labor Force Participation Rate of Married Women, by Age of Youngest Child

1980

1985

From C. Russell and T. G. Exter, "America at Mid-decade," *American Demographics*, January 1986, pp. 22–27. © January 1986, Ithaca, New York.

statistics give us the most personally meaningful measure of divorce: the likelihood that individual marriages will break up. We will discuss divorce rates in greater detail in a later chapter.

Even if we do arrive at more valid measures of divorce, interpreting them is still tricky. Most people assume that a rising divorce rate, which we have had in recent years, means that marriage is a decaying institution. Divorce rates, however, must be placed in context. If we compare today's divorce rates with those of an earlier era, we must ask how accurately marriage and divorce records were kept in those days. How many people were getting the proverbial "poor man's divorce" through desertion or separation? How many people in that earlier era remained in failed marriages because divorce was expensive, hard to get, and scandalous? We must also ask what life expectancy rates were then. How likely is it that some couples were parted by death before they could be by divorce? Finally, we must also ask how recent changes fit in with long-term trends. Were divorce rates low and con-

stant for many decades before their recent rise, or is there a long-term historical trend towards higher divorce rates?

The answers to all these questions show that we cannot use divorce rates to conclude that marriages were better in the good old days than now or that the current divorce rate represents a sharp break from a stable past. Divorce records were more unreliable in the past, desertion and separation were widespread, and a large proportion of marriages that end in divorce today would have been ended by death in previous eras (Weitzman, 1981b). Moreover, the divorce rate has been climbing at least since the Civil War.

In spite of all the complexities involved in comparing current divorce rates with those of earlier times, most family researchers agree that divorce rates have been climbing in recent years. Our image of the past as a time of long-term stable and happy marriages may be distorted, but divorce is rising. The question still remains: Is this a symptom of breakdown in the family?

Here we come to even more tricky problems of interpretation. Most researchers

FIGURE 1.9
Marriage and Divorce
Rates, United States:
1930–1984

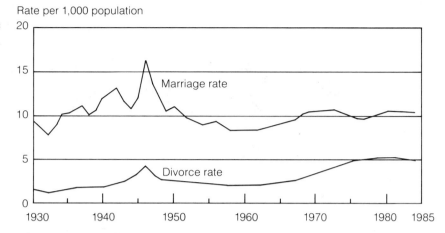

Rate per 1,000 population

From U.S. Department of Health and Human Services, National Center for Health Statistics
Monthly Vital Statistics Report, *Annual Summary of Births, Marriages, Divorces, and Deaths:
United States, 1984.* Vol. 33, No. 13, September 26, 1985.

agree that there has been a major change in the values surrounding marriage. In the past, the expectation was that a couple would stay married unless one of the spouses committed some gross offense against the marriage—adultery, cruelty, extreme neglect. Now most people see the purpose of marriage as personal fulfillment. But does this change mean that people are becoming more selfish and narcissistic, to use the fashionable term, and that the norms concerning marriage have broken down? Or does it mean that the norms have changed—that people no longer regard it as admirable for a couple to put up with the kinds of unsatisfactory or empty shell marriages previous generations were willing to tolerate?

Similar questions can be raised about other changes in the family. Falling birthrates can be taken to mean that people are too selfish to want to have any or many children. Or they can mean that people are no longer having children by accident, without thought or because of social pressure, but because they truly want children. High rates of remarriage could mean that people are giving up, not on marriage but on unsatisfactory re-

lationships. Or these rates can be thought to mean that the strain of living in contemporary society drives people into marriage but makes marriage difficult to sustain.

Is the rise in illegitimacy a sign of moral breakdown? Or does it simply reflect a different set of moral norms, reflecting a society no longer eager to punish unmarried mothers or to damage a child's life chances because of the circumstances of its birth?

The Family, Science, and Values

How one answers these questions depends on personal values. For example, which is more important: marital stability or the personal happiness of the spouses? Although empirical studies can provide a great deal of information about the family in the past, they cannot tell us how we should evaluate these developments.

One of the greatest difficulties in studying the family is the closeness and emotional significance of the subject to our everyday lives. It is not possible to study the family in the same way that natural scientists can study chemical reactions or the

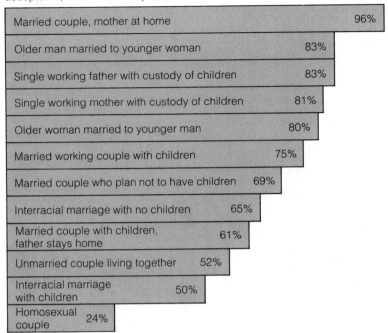

A majority of Americans find most types of families acceptable, with a few exceptions:

Family type	Percent
Married couple, mother at home	96%
Older man married to younger woman	83%
Single working father with custody of children	83%
Single working mother with custody of children	81%
Older woman married to younger man	80%
Married working couple with children	75%
Married couple who plan not to have children	69%
Interracial marriage with no children	65%
Married couple with children, father stays home	61%
Unmarried couple living together	52%
Interracial marriage with children	50%
Homosexual couple	24%

FIGURE 1.10
The "Normal" Family

What is a "normal" family? There is a new tolerance toward all kinds of families— extreme variations on the traditional working-father/stay-at-home mother—that might have been heartily condemned a few decades ago.

From *Family Circle*, October 15, 1985, p. 25. Copyright © 1985, The Family Circle, Inc.

movements of the earth's crust—or even in the same way that social scientists can study such social institutions as schools and factories. The family touches on our deepest feelings about ourselves, our own family, society, and nature. It touches our deepest moral and political convictions.

Until recently, family research tended to be inhibited by the sensitive nature of its subject matter. The family researcher, observed Waller and Komarovsky, "is shackled by taboos and ancestral superstitions, which he has the more trouble in combating because they are in his mind as well as his environment. We are able to see only what the social norms permit us to see" (cited in Christensen, 1964, p. 970).

Because of these taboos, the study of the family has lacked a critical tradition. As D. H. J. Morgan (1975) points out, the field of family sociology has not had the same tradition of theoretical debates or argument about basic assumptions as other areas of sociology. Instead, much about the family was simply taken for granted: that family is pretty much the same everywhere, that families are basically harmonious institutions, that families are good for society and for the individuals in them, that society needs the family and could not survive without it, that parents mold their children, and that men's and women's traditional roles in the family are necessary and inevitable. Above all, the lack of a critical tradition meant researchers tended to assume that the daily realities of family life pretty much corresponded to the norms describing the way the family was supposed to work; the rich

Old woman in nursing home. Contrary to the stereotype, only a small proportion of old people live in such institutions. [Leslie Starobin]

variation in the way different families live was ignored, as was the darker side of normal family life.

In recent years, fixed ideas about the family were challenged by feminists, radical psychiatrists, Marxists, and other social critics; by historians and scholars from other disciplines; and by the great changes in behavior and attitudes in recent years. Child abuse, marital incest, violence, and the problem of family stress have also been "discovered" in recent years. As a result of these changes, the field that was once a dull backwater has now become more intellectually exciting and rigorous. And the family that is discussed in the research literature and the classroom is not so remote as it once was from the family as people experience it in everyday life.

This is not to say that we have reached some neutral, scientific position that en-

ables us to look at the family in a completely value-free way. Researchers may now regard many different forms of the family as equally legitimate, but this pluralism involves no less of a value judgment than the insistence that only the traditional model of the family is legitimate. We may try to shift the argument to the more neutral ground of how well the different family patterns work, but here too we run into value differences. In the older pattern, many people, especially women, led lives of quiet desperation. You may argue, "Yes, but the older pattern gave people a sense of security and made for a more stable society." Ultimately, in discussing the family, there is no way we can completely escape our own values.

New Questions

Although we may never achieve a totally value-free position, the new social and intellectual climate has made it possible to ask some intriguing new questions. For example, in the past researchers tended to look into the causes of divorce but paid little attention to the nature of ongoing relationships. What are the essential properties of marriage and other close relationships? How do they differ from other kinds of relationships? Now there is greater interest in exploring the processes that bring people together and sustain relationships—attraction, attachment, intimacy, commitment—as well as the processes that lead to the breakdown of relationships. Indeed, as will be seen in more detail later, the more we come to understand the bonds that hold people together, the more insight we have into the difficulties of close relationships. The greatest frustrations and disappointments of family life arise out of the same sources that produce the greatest joys and satisfactions. The paradoxical, ambivalent nature of close relationships forms one of the major themes of this book.

A second major theme is the embeddedness of the family in social, economic, and political conditions. To understand family life, we have to look in two directions at once: inward into the intimate, psychosocial interior of family life and outward into the wider society. The family does not exist in a social vacuum—there are only families living in particular times, places, and circumstances. It matters a great deal whether the family is the unit of economic production, whether the society is a relatively affluent one or hovers on the brink of starvation, and what the level of mortality is. Ironically—and this is another theme we shall pursue here—many of the most vexing problems we face in family life today result from historical changes few of us would want to undo if we could.

For example, the fall in mortality rates in the twentieth century has had profound effects on family life and on the life course of individuals. Children have a much greater chance to survive to adulthood and to grow up without experiencing the death of brothers, sisters, and parents. Orphans and orphanages have virtually disappeared. Children now are much more likely to have living grandparents than children in earlier generations.

Demographer Peter Uhlenberg (1980) has calculated the impact of mortality rates on the family experience of individuals, based on data from 1900 and 1976. Under 1900 mortality rates, half of all parents would lose a child; by 1976, only 6 percent would. More than half of all children surviving to the age of 15 would have lost a parent or sibling by that age. Today's children almost never experience the death of a close relative, except that of elderly grandparents.

Because of these mortality rates, life in the past had a precariousness we can scarcely imagine today. Babies and children were the most vulnerable, but death could take anyone at any time. The young widow or widower was as common a figure on the social landscape as the divorced person is today. Before antibiotics, it was not unusual for young adults to die of infectious diseases, such as tuberculosis or pneumonia. A common theme in nineteenth-century literature was a young person dying "a beautiful death" (Ariès, 1981).

Ironically, these changes in mortality and fertility rates are responsible for many of the problems facing families and society today. The most obvious problem is the graying of America: the increasingly large proportion of old people in the population. In the past, the aged were not a problem because there were so few of them.

In a less direct way, lowered mortality rates have led to other problems, such as rising divorce rates. People who marry in their 20s can look forward to 50 years together, mostly without young children to care for. Many researchers believe that current high

FIGURE 1.11
Divorced Persons per
1,000 Married Persons
with Spouse Present:
1960–1984

From U.S. Department of Commerce, Bureau of the Census, *Marital Status and Living Arrangements: March 1984*. Current Population Reports, Series P-20, No. 399, 1985.

divorce rates are in part a compensation for the fact that the early breakup of a marriage by death is now such a remote possibility. As Kingsley Davis (1972) observed, "As the probability of escaping a bad marriage by death approaches zero, the willingness to consider divorce must surely rise" (p. 246).

Other beneficial changes of modern life have also brought problems in their wake. Few people would want to go back to an era when children started to work as early as they could and school was reserved for a wealthy few. But the removal of children from participation in productive work has produced its own problems. Adolescence was less often a difficult stage of life in the days of child labor, no public high schools, and little choice about one's future occupation. And education often changes people psychologically; it is not just a matter of learning basic skills or being trained for an occupation. The more educated a population is, the more likey it will be to take a critical and questioning stance—toward society, family life, and the self.

SUMMARY AND CONCLUSIONS

This chapter has examined the state of the family from several perspectives: from the point of view of the general public, the media, and some social critics who feel that the family is breaking down; from the conservative New Right, from those who feel the family is here to stay, and those who feel the family is a durable but troubled institution.

Recent research on the family does not lend support to the notion that the family is in danger of imminent collapse. Fears about the decline of the family do have some basis in fact: divorce rates are rising, increasing numbers of children are being raised in single-parent homes, and record numbers of women are entering the labor force. In addition to changes in the major statistical indicators of family life, sexual norms have changed dramatically, and people seem to be increasingly preoccupied with their own self-fulfillment. Researchers most closely in-

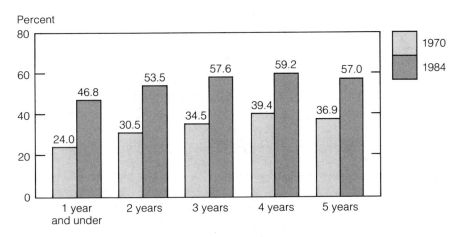

Percent

FIGURE 1.12
Labor Force Participation Rates of Married Mothers by Age of Youngest Child

From *The United Nations Decade for Women, 1976–1985: Employment in The United States.* U.S. Department of Labor, Office of the Secretary, Women's Bureau, July 1985.

volved in the study of the family, however, do not take these changes as evidence of decline and erosion.

The belief that the family is now in a state of decline rests on a set of assumptions that do not hold up very well in the light of recent research. Above all, it rests on the assumption that the family has had a long history of stability and harmony until it began to break down in recent times. This nostalgic view of family life in the past is a major casualty of one of the most exciting new areas of the study of the family: the study of family history. Despite massive research in recent years, historians have not located "the good old days" when families were strong and stable and family members behaved unselfishly and followed all the norms of family life. Instead, for as far back into the past as there are historical records, it appears that people have always been concerned about the future of the family and the failure of the current generation to live up to the standards of its ancestors.

The new historical studies of family life are part of a major upsurge of interest in the family on the part of scholars in several disciplines. The outcome of all this research may be summed up as the discovery of complexity. Family life either in the past or in the present is not as simple to understand as it appears at first glance.

One of the problems of the study of the family is the lack of a critical tradition. The family is an emotionally charged topic that touches on our deepest feelings about morality as well as those about ourselves and our own families. Researchers in the past tended to be more respectful of the norms and taboos surrounding family life than researchers in other areas. As a result, the dark side of family life has been underresearched or studied only as a separate problem having little to do with normal happy families.

Recently social scientists and the general public seem to be taking a more realistic view of the family. Rather than seeing the family as a haven of peace and tranquility, they have begun to recognize that even normal families often fall far short of the mythical idea of "the happy family."

Another important theme in recent research on the family and of this book is the embeddedness of the family in the social, economic, and cultural circumstances of particular times and places. Some social critics have argued that contemporary Americans are simply more selfish and less moral than their ancestors. If only we had the will to return to earlier patterns of family behavior, we would have strong, happy families and a strong society.

The trouble with this argument is that we cannot return to the demographic and economic conditions that shaped family behavior in the past, nor would we want to. We pointed out, for example, that the reduction of mortality rates in the twentieth century has changed family life profoundly. There have been problems along with the benefits, however. We now have very few orphans, and parents can raise their children without the realistic fear that at any moment a child or spouse might die. But we now have a large and growing population of old people, and we have not devised ways of giving them a useful role in society or of supporting them without imposing a burden on younger generations. And marriage has been transformed from a time when the odds were against a couple's surviving into old age together, and when a young spouse might be here today and gone tomorrow.

In sum, then, to understand family life today it is necessary to understand the society around it and the historical changes that have transformed it. At the same time, we must also focus on the inner emotional life of family members and their relationships with one another. Here, in the psychosocial interior of the family, we see the imprint of particular times and places as well as the more universal themes of family life and its discontents that seem to be part of the human condition.

CHAPTER 2

The American Family in Our Time

> *To study the history of the American family is to conduct a rescue mission into the dreamland of our national self-concept. No subject is more closely bound up with our sense of a difficult present—and our nostalgia for a happier past.*
>
> John Demos
> *"The American Family in Past Time"*

In this chapter we take a deeper look at the current changes in American family life. The only way to understand these changes is to look in the rearview mirror of recent history. In particular we examine the postwar era—the time between the end of World War II and the early 1960s. Although the period extended into 3 decades, the 1950s are often used to symbolize the whole period.

There are several reasons why an examination of the postwar era is crucial to understanding the current state of the family. For one thing, it is the time that many people regard as the golden age of American family life. Confronted with the difficulties of the present, they look back with longing for the era of togetherness and the affluent society, of the baby boom and the suburban way of life. As Morris Dickstein (1977) put it: "The lure of the fifties . . . speaks to our wish to have done with these problems; it tells us we can return unscathed to an idealized time before life grew complicated" (p. 27).

The nostalgia began in the early 1970s. In 1972 *Newsweek* carried a feature story entitled "Yearning for the Fifties: The Good Old Days." Movies like *American Graffiti* and such television shows as *Happy Days* recreate a simpler and more stable time. Nor is this nostalgia confined to pop culture. Writing in the intellectual journal *Com-*

mentary, John Mander (1969) proclaimed the 1950s to be "the happiest, most stable, most rational period the Western world has known since 1914." Thus our images of the 1950s represent the stable norm from which the current changes in family life have sadly deviated. And this tendency is encouraged by the fact that when statistical trends in family life such as marriage, birth, and divorce rates are described, the starting point is usually somewhere in the 1950s.

The postwar era is also significant because it shaped two important generations (or, to use the technical term, *cohorts**) of today's adults. Today's 45–65-year-olds, born between 1920 and 1940, were the people who married early, created the baby boom, bought the houses in the suburbs and the large cars, and believed in the feminine mystique. These people have been called the "lucky" generation (Masnick & Bane, 1980) because they entered adulthood in a time of expanding economic opportunity. This generation is now in command of our major institutions, and their views therefore constitute an important influence on public and private policy.

The younger generation of adult Americans are the baby-boom babies themselves, ranging in age from their early 20s to 40, depending on how one dates the onset of the baby boom. Because there are so many of them, they have had a profound influence on American life since the time they were born (Bouvier, 1980). Fascinated by members of the baby-boom generation since its infancy, the media have portrayed them as Yuppies— young urban professionals. The image, however, fits only a small percentage: the 5 percent with $30–$40,000 annual incomes necessary to fit the mold of the Yuppie life-

---

*A *cohort* is a group of people who experience a common event, such as being born in the same year.

day. Middle-class women tended to have carefully done hair and makeup. Pants were inappropriate for all but the most casual occasions. Being well dressed meant matching shoes and purses, high heels, gloves, and often hats. Similarly, the normal dress of the middle-class man was suit and tie—"the man in the gray flannel suit" became a symbol for the times. It was also the era of the "organization man" and the "silent generation" of young people. One 1957 survey of college students concluded that their dominant characteristic was to be "gloriously contented" about their current lives and their futures (Morison, 1958, p. 163).

"The Counterfeit Decade"

There was more to the national mood than celebration, however. The 1950s were a paradoxical period. Despite the country's prosperity and power, Americans were deeply divided among themselves and fearful of conspiracies both home and abroad. As John Conger (1982) observes, "It was an era of suppressed individuality, of national paranoia, and of largely unrecognized discrimination against minorities, women, the poor, 'foreigners,' homosexuals, and indeed, most of those who dared to be different—the era that came to an end with the onset of the 1960s was a time bomb waiting to explode" (pp. 1477–1478). The literary critic Frederick Karl (1983) labels the 1950s "the counterfeit decade." Not only was there a contrast between the sunny, affluent surface of life and the social tensions and hostilities that lay just below, but also a widespread concern with fakery and pretense—with "innocent" appearances concealing "subversive," "un-American" motives.

Today, *McCarthyism* is a term of political insult, but in his heyday in the 1950s McCarthy was an admired, feared, and above all powerful figure. He was a master of the "big lie"—accusations of treason and conspiracy in high places that were so astounding "they might just be true" (Siegel, 1984, p. 17). Suspicion poisoned all levels of American life. Libraries were searched for subversive books; *Robin Hood* was considered communistic because it tells of stealing from the rich and giving to the poor; the Cincinnati Reds changed their name to the Redlegs. Although these results of McCarthyism seem funny today, McCarthyism had a tragic impact on thousands of lives as teachers, writers, scientists, actors, union members, and government workers were driven from their jobs.

Along with the witchhunts, blacklists, and fears of political subversives, there was a kind of McCarthyism of marriage and the family toward anyone who dared deviate from prescribed sex roles—the single adult, the working woman, the childless wife or husband, the "weak" male. Singleness was regarded almost as a contagious disease (Miller & Nowak, 1977). One of the influential books of the time, *Modern Woman: The Lost Sex* (Farnham & Lundberg, 1947), argued that bachelors over 30 should receive psychotherapy and that all spinsters should be forbidden by law to teach children on the grounds of emotional incompetence.

Homosexuality was seen as an extreme form of deviance, even mental illness; often the homosexual served in literature and real life as a symbol of evil and corruption. In this hostile climate, before the days of gay liberation, homosexuals kept their identity a secret. Ironically, with no visible group of men admitting homosexuality, any man could be suspected of being a latent or hidden homosexual. As Barbara Ehrenreich points out, "It was a diffuse possibility that haunted every man, a label that could be hurled against the man who was 'irresponsible' as well as the one who was overtly 'effeminate'" (1983, p. 129).

The Paradox of Female Roles

The culture of the 1950s abounded in contradictions, and the whole area of women and work contained several. What Betty Friedan later described as the "feminine mystique" (1963) was an accurate description of the prevailing mood of the times. People were marrying in greater numbers and at younger ages than ever before. Young women told pollsters they looked forward to having four or more children. The mass media, especially women's magazines, celebrated domesticity, motherhood, togetherness, and femininity. Freudian ideas about women's biological nature were widely influential. For a woman to be considered normal, according to psychoanalyst Helene Deutsch (1944/1945), she had to find fulfillment in devotion to husband and children. Any inclinations toward independence, involvement in work outside the home, or dissatisfaction with her roles as wife and mother, were signs of neurosis and penis envy.

And yet there was something "counterfeit" about all this rhetoric. As William Chafe has recently observed (1986), "The effort to reinforce traditional norms seemed almost frantic, as though in reality something very different was taking place" (p. 125). In fact, at the same time as they were celebrating togetherness, the women's magazines were also writing about women's discontents. Articles appeared about the struggles of young women coping with 24-hour-a-day domesticity after college or work experience, of the increasing use of tranquilizers and alcohol by suburban housewives, and of rising divorce rates during the era of "togetherness."

Indeed, despite the image of the normal woman as the happy housewife with no commitments outside the home and the corresponding image of the working woman as a deviant, more women than ever joined the work force during the 1950s. The rise in women working is now recognized as one of the most obvious and widespread changes in the American family since World War II. Actually, women's participation in the labor force has been climbing since the nineteenth century. But the most rapid increase occurred during the postwar era. Thus the percentage of women working doubled from 1900 to 1940, but then it tripled from 1940 to 1970.

Before World War II most working wives had come from the lower class; by the late 1950s women of all classes were working or looking for jobs. As historian Peter Filene (1975) observed, the large influx of women into the labor market effectively closed the question that had been debated for a hundred years: should a woman, particularly a mother, work outside the home? The issue had become as obsolete as the debate over whether women should attend college. The "startling news" (Kaledin, 1984) that large numbers of married women, even mothers of preschool children, were working outside the home was uncovered by a number of conferences and government commissions in the 1950s. Books and reports spoke of revolutionary changes in the pattern of women's lives. Nevertheless, such findings had little impact on the prevailing feminine mystique. To the extent that awareness did seep into public consciousness, it was cause for alarm that women were neglecting their families and violating their femininity. A 1956 article in *Life* (Caughlan, 1956) denounced the "disease" of working women.

Typically, however, women's jobs were secondary to family. Women worked before they got married, and they went back to work at convenient points in the family cycle—after the youngest child started school and in the empty-nest period after the children left home. Sometimes they went to work at other times—when there were young children at home—if the family finances seemed to demand it. Most women have worked in "the pink-collar ghetto" (Howe, 1977)—in jobs at the bottom of the work hierarchy, such as clerical or sales work. At every level of work, however, from the most unskilled to the most technically demanding job, women were paid less than men.

Despite the image of "the affluent society," few families felt that they had enough money to cover all their needs and wants. Working-class women took jobs to make ends meet, to cover the gap left when the husband's paycheck went to pay last month's bills; middle-class women went to work to pay for the remodeling of the garage or for the children's braces and music lessons.

Three decades later, in the aftermath of the women's movement, we have learned that even jobs with low pay and low prestige can provide some degree of satisfaction (L. B. Rubin, 1976). Contributing to the family budget by bringing home a paycheck and showing that one's hours have a cash value can give women a feeling of usefulness and self-esteem. Many find the companionship of co-workers a relief from the isolation of the household.

Women have felt free to say these things to researchers in recent years, but in the 1950s most working women denied they were working for any other reason than to serve family needs. To have hinted at finding fulfillment in one's work would be to open oneself to the charge of being an unnatural woman. Some women did manage to follow careers or to find and admit satisfaction in work, but the majority of women, whatever they have thought inwardly, conformed outwardly to the feminine mystique.

The general hostility toward the idea of women working was focused on two particular kinds of women: working mothers and career women. Working mothers received the most criticism. There were more of them, and, more importantly, their working raised questions about their children's well-being. Not only the mass media but also the combined voices of psychiatry and social science, citing case histories and statistics, warned about the harm that could come to children if mothers worked outside the home. Dr. Spock, in his book that was the bible of child care in the postwar era, repeated the warnings. Worried mothers wrote the Children's Bureau asking, "Am I making my child into a juvenile delinquent because I have to work?" Despite the agonies of guilt this literature undoubtedly produced, there is now, according to one recent review of the research literature, a remarkable consensus among investigators that the mother's outside employment is not a crucial variable in the child's well-being and development (Herzog & Sudia, 1973).

But the poorly designed research studies that "documented" the harmful effects of the working mother were not the basis of the popular prejudice; more likely the studies themselves reflected the prejudice. The notion that woman's place was in the home was so ingrained in the culture of the 1950s that it would have been unreasonable to think that such a deviation from natural femininity could fail to harm children.

Some writers of the time allowed that women could work without violating their natures if they took jobs that had little prestige, made few demands on their time, and conceded authority to men. A woman who pursued a career was denying her femininity and trying to be a man—an obvious case of penis envy. Hostility to the "unnatural" career woman was expressed in viciously direct terms. Writing in *Esquire* in 1954, Merle Miller, later to emerge from the closet as a homosexual, denounced "that increasing and strident minority of women who are doing their damnedest to wreck marriage and home life in America, those who insist on having both husband and career. They are a menace and they have to be stopped" (cited in D. T. Miller & Nowak, 1977, p. 164).

Thus women were caught in a double bind: if they took their work seriously, they were condemned as unwomanly deviants; if they failed to take work seriously, they were open to the charge of being frivolous. Their lack of commitment could be used to excuse low pay and exclusion from responsible jobs.

But that was only one of the tightropes women had to walk in the 1950s. There was also the sexual tightrope: women were supposed to make themselves attractive to men but were not supposed to "tease"; they were not supposed to be "frigid," but they were not to go "too far" or "all the way" lest they lose their status as "nice girls." Alix Schulman (1977) has written of "the war in the back seat" that went on between young men and women in the 1940s and 1950s. Boys demanded sex while making it clear they would never marry a girl with a "reputation." Petting was the major form of sexual activity among the unmarried in the 1950s, and it embodied the contradictory demands of the time. Although the activity is alive and well among today's teenagers, the "petting culture" (Petchesky, 1984) with its peculiar mixture of permissiveness and restraint was a distinct part of the sexual climate of the 1950s. Today, the word has practically disappeared from our sexual vocabulary.

Contradictory Male Roles

Male roles were also caught in a tangle of contradictions. On the one hand, the Victorian patriarch was held up as a model for husbands and fathers, although few living examples were ever observed. Mostly, it was his disappearance that was lamented. Psychi-

atrists warned about the dire effects of the "passive" or "ineffectual" male. The "weak" father and his partner in psychiatric crime, the dominant mother, were blamed, as one critic put it, for "everything from homosexuality to ingrown toenails" (Levenson, 1972, p. 73). Comic strips and television made millions laugh by poking fun at the emasculated male in the form of Dagwood Bumstead, Ozzie Nelson, and George Gobel.

On the other hand, the ideology of male domination was contradicted by the ideology of the democratic family. The marriage and family literature, as well as the popular media, reported that the happiest marriages were equal partnerships. The doctrine of "togetherness" prescribed that the wife share in the husband's job by discussing his problems and entertaining his associates.

Leisure time and sexual satisfaction were also to be shared. In fact, the bedroom was the scene of the most complete equality; the marriage manuals of the time most decidedly did not call for the return of the Victorian patriarch, who inflicted his animal need on his sexless wife. Rather, the good husband must see to it that his wife got satisfaction, preferably at the same moment he did. This was a difficult demand for both partners because of the widely held view that a vaginal orgasm, produced by the husband in attaining his satisfaction, was the only legitimate kind.

The ideology of togetherness also applied to housework. Family-life author Paul Landis (1955) found in the increased sharing of housework by both spouses evidence for the "twentieth century democratizing of the American home"; studies of household decision making and task responsibilities reported high levels of male participation.

The ideal of household democracy conflicted with the patriarchal ideal *and* reality. Studies purporting to show such household democracy reveal actually little time put in

The black population has remained disproportionately poor. [Danny Lyon/ National Archives]

by males and great selectivity in what tasks they performed. Men's share of the household chores tended to consist largely of "male tasks," such as fixing things and yard work; even here, males participated only about half the time. Women did more of the time-consuming daily chores that must be done repeatedly and are never finished because they are always being undone by the family—making beds, doing the laundry, washing dishes, and so on. Sometimes male participation consisted of little more than "helping" the wife at tasks defined as her responsibility. At any rate, various studies found that male participation was less than equal. Men did seem to participate more in child care, but mostly they gave bottles to babies or played with older children; they tended to avoid diaper changing and the messier and more tedious aspects of caring for children. Nevertheless, fathers were providing more affection and companionship to their children than men in their father's generation.

Even though men were not living up to the ideal of the democratic division of labor in the home, their participation in any but the most "masculine" of household tasks was outside the traditional male role. Washing the dishes even occasionally, or helping one's wife do them, did not fit the image of the Victorian patriarch retreating from the dinner table to relax with pipe and slippers. Even the advocates of togetherness and equality seemed to be uncomfortable with the idea, and the solution they proposed could have come from Orwell's *Animal Farm:* husband and wife were equal, but one was more equal than the other. Thus *McCall's* magazine, in a 1954 issue proclaiming the new era of togetherness, warned: "For the sake of every member of the family, the family needs a head. This means Father, not Mother" (cited in Friedan, 1963, p. 43). In 1958 the singer Pat Boone wrote a best-selling book in which he described his family as "the happy home corporation." "I do believe marriage is a fifty-fifty deal," he noted, "but every corporation has to have a president who, when the chips are down, can say, 'it's going to be this way'" (pp. 83–84).

Still another contradiction of the 1950s was a strong undercurrent of male resentment of women and marriage. This sort of resentment has a long history in Western culture. It has traditionally been expressed in the form of jokes about henpecked husbands, ball-and-chain wives, and nagging mothers-in-law. George Orwell (1946), in a study of such humor, once suggested it served as a kind of safety valve, a harmless rebellion on the part of men deeply committed to stable marriage. In American literature, the theme of male escape from marriage and responsibility has persisted since the time of Rip van Winkle.

In the 1950s, despite the mystique of togetherness, the traditional male view of marriage as a trap for men was elaborated in some new ways. Barbara Ehrenreich, in her book *The Hearts of Men* (1983), describes how *Playboy* joined the battle of the sexes. From its first issue in 1953, *Playboy* offered a vision of good living in which man could keep his earnings for himself and enjoy sex without being married.

Playboy was not alone in the 1950s in portraying the traditional male role as a kind of slavery. "Conformity," which Ehrenreich sees as a code word for male discontent, was a national concern. Novels such as Sloan Wilson's *Man in the Gray Flannel Suit* (1955), nonfiction books and articles, and William Whyte's *The Organization Man* (1956) complained that white-collar work in giant corporations was turning men into "corporate robots," robbing them of their masculinity as well as their individuality. By the end of the 1950s a more extreme version of male protest appeared in the form of the Beat rebellion. The Beats (for *beatitude*) or Holy Barbarians rejected both marriage and work. Led by writers such as Jack Kerouac and Allen Ginsberg, they celebrated individualism and spontaneity, indulged in alcohol, pot, and casual sex, and practiced Zen Buddhism. Though they were a tiny minority, the media were fascinated by them. The Beats, wrote

Life, were "against virtually every aspect of current American society: Mom, Dad, Politics, Marriage, the Savings Bank, Organized religion" (O'Neill, 1959, p. 114).

Hollywood, too, glamorized male rebellion. While the bland films of Doris Day and Rock Hudson were popular, the big stars of the decade were James Dean and Marlon Brando, both macho individualists. In sum, then, the family ideology of the 1950s created difficulties for both men and women. Each was faced with contradictory demands on the self and contradictory expectations of the other. Moreover, a significant minority were asking hard questions about American culture and family life. The heresies of the 1950s would become mass movements in the following decade.

The Big Boom

If the tensions in family life and in the larger society in the 1950s escaped notice at the time, it may have been because of the seemingly miraculous abundance of the postwar economy. During the Great Depression one-third of the country was ill-housed, ill-fed, and ill-clothed. At the start of the 1940s, millions still faced seemingly endless unemployment and relatively few had any hope of owning a new house or car or sending a child through college.

World War II ended the depression and started a boom that lasted well into the 1960s. The war put an end to hard times for many families. During the war years the proportion of families living on less than $2,000 a year dropped from three-quarters to one-quarter of the population. Family income more than doubled between 1939 and 1969.

For the first time a majority of Americans no longer had to worry about being able to obtain the basic necessities of food, clothing, and shelter. Instead, they could take these for granted and indulge in expenditures on a spectacular scale for items that had once been luxuries: new homes, television sets, wall-to-wall carpeting, cars, boats, hi-fi sets, travel. Coming after 4 years of war and 12 years of depression, the boom set off a mood of celebration and hope; it was as if, as one writer put it, "milk and honey appeared suddenly to a people who had been trudging across an economic Sinai for a decade and a half" (Hodgson, 1977, p. 52).

Since the beginning of the nineteenth century, the single-family detached house had been considered the ideal setting for family life and had great influence on architects and designers. But it was not until the postwar suburban era, supported by the massive government financing of Veterans Administration (VA) and Federal Housing Administration (FHA) programs as well as by private financing, that the dream of the single-family home came to be realized on a large scale.

The general prosperity overshadowed in both popular awareness and the social sciences the poverty of a considerable minority of the population. The eye of the social scientist was firmly focused on the middle-class majority and its remarkable affluence. Admittedly all social problems had not been solved. There were still slums, bigotry, and sudden eruptions of violence. But in the 1950s these seemed to be peripheral matters. Compared to the problems of the past—scarcity, mass unemployment, ethnic and class conflict, political instability, epidemics—these difficulties seemed trivial.

Even when poverty was "discovered" in the early 1960s, the answer to it seemed obvious and easy: to incorporate the disadvantaged and "culturally deprived" into the general affluence and well-being. The middle-class family pattern was held up as the model for the disadvantaged to follow. Indeed, the "inadequate" family life of the poor, particularly the black poor, was held to

be the major reason why those groups had not yet made it into the great middle class. Looking to the future, social scientists saw more of the same—an extension of affluence and middle-class life-styles to those left out or left behind in their pockets of poverty, more technology, more economic growth—all leading to a more stable and balanced social order.

The key to it all was continued abundance. Until the late 1960s, it looked as if economic growth could go on forever. Even the counterculture rebels of the 1960s, who rejected most of the assumptions of postwar America, took continued abundance for granted. Indeed, for mainstream opinion leaders during the 1950s and early 1960s, prosperity was in the process of solving all social problems. Social harmony would be guaranteed, as Geoffrey Hodgson (1977) put it, "by distributing the consumption of goods so lavishly that it would not seem urgent to distribute them equally" (p. 51).

THE EXPLOSIVE 1960s

The decade or so that followed the middle of the 1960s was probably the most turbulent period in the nation's history. The country has experienced wars, social upheavals, and times of rapid change, but no period contained as many sudden shocks to the nation's sense of moral and political order. After the sluggish years of the 1950s, events followed one another with bewildering speed.

The decade began on a note of youthful idealism; John Kennedy took office announcing "the passage of the torch to a new generation." In the same year a handful of young blacks began "sitting in" at a dime store in Greensboro, North Carolina, to protest segregation. By the end of the decade, the nation had witnessed the assassinations of a president and two other major public figures, the growth of black militancy, the emergence of student dissent, the antiwar movement, the rise of the counterculture, and riots and fighting in the streets. The following years were to bring still more shocking events—the collapse of the American war effort in Vietnam and a hasty retreat, the scandal of Watergate and the forced resignation of the vice-president and then the president.

All of these events had a profound effect on family life. The generation gap was not as wide or widespread as was proclaimed by the media, but still many families were divided, as was the society as a whole, by the Vietnam war, by the race question, and by personal and moral issues, such as sex, drugs, and hair length. In a way not foreseen by President Kennedy, the torch had been passed to a new generation. On the major issues of the time—especially the issue of the war—young people served as moral leaders for their elders, pioneering in views that were later to become widespread among the rest of the population.

In the tranquility of the 1950s no one had foreseen anything like these developments. Even more unlikely in those days than the "politics of protest" was the emergence of a politics of the family. The cultural critics and Beat writers of the 1950s who had questioned the dominant values represented a tiny minority of the elite or the disreputable. By 1970 virtually every assumption of the family and sex-role ideology of the 1950s was under atack. Their validity was challenged by rebellious students, the commune movement, women's liberation, gay liberation, and the spread of nonmarital cohabitation. In a relatively short time such notions as the "obsolescence" and "crisis" of the nuclear family passed from being heresies of the counterculture to mass-media clichés.

In retrospect, the whole postwar way of life—not just its assumptions about women, the family, and home—was founded on illusion and contradiction. First, the image of America as an affluent society was seriously flawed: some parts of the population were excluded altogether from the American dream of affluent suburbia, and others had only a precarious hold on it. Second, the affluent society produced new sources of discontent in many of those who had been its most favored beneficiaries. Finally, there was a fundamental flaw at the very heart of the postwar life-style, in the economic engine that drove it through a decade and a half of prosperity.

As is true with most myths, there was some basis in reality for the myth of the affluent worker. During the postwar era, American workers enjoyed a level of material well-being that contrasted dramatically with the standard of living of workers in other countries and with American workers in previous decades. In the ideology of the times, however, this rise in living standards was elevated to the mythical notion that class differences and inequality had been abolished.

Furthermore, although living conditions did improve in the postwar era for a majority of middle- and upper-income families, they deteriorated for millions of poor and low-income families. The growth of the suburbs that benefited the nonpoor majority imposed heavy costs on the less advantaged. In fact, the process tended to worsen existing social, economic, and family inequalities.

Most people tend to think of the mass migration to the suburbs in the postwar decades as being due to some unplanned social force or simply to individual families making decisions to move. In fact, however, government policies played a large role in both the growth of the suburbs and the erosion of the cities.

One set of policies helped millions of Americans move out of large cities to the spacious environments of the suburbs: the

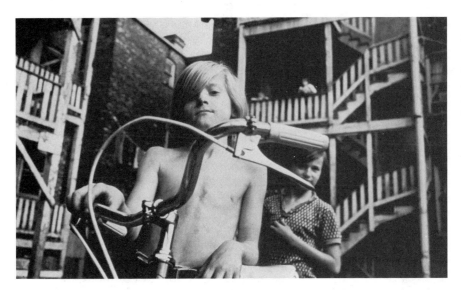

Children in poor white neighborhood in Chicago. Large numbers of white families are also poor. [Danny Lyon/National Archives]

provision of FHA insurance and mortgages for suburban development (but not inner-city housing), federal support for highways connecting suburbs to the central cities, and the tax advantages given to homeowners but not renters.

Meanwhile, the inner-city environment was being worsened by another set of policies. The flight of the middle class in itself led to the deterioration of the cities, since it resulted in a greater concentration of the poor and the traditional correlates of poverty—crime, drug use, and other forms of delinquency and despair. Adding to the problem was the large influx of blacks and other poor who were being driven off the land by the mechanization of southern agriculture (Gutman, 1976).

Very low income families were concentrated still further by the big public-housing projects that were being built in most major cities. These now are widely recognized as the most dangerous and unhealthy environments for children and families, yet millions had no alternative but to live in them. Further, urban-renewal and highway-construc-

tion policies led to even more concentration and isolation of the poor. Meanwhile, these same policies were breaking up poor and working-class neighborhoods that had contained cohesive communities and strong social ties. Finally, welfare policies were encouraging the breakup of families by providing support only to women and children.

By the 1960s American society had become more sharply segregated than it had been in the past; it had become two societies: a black inner city ringed by white suburbs. Further, in addition to the more obvious racial segregation, there was increasing separation of people by income level, age, and life-style. Retirement communities for the elderly were a postwar innovation; and by the end of the 1960s real-estate developers all over the country were offering housing exclusively for singles and childless couples.

In short, during the postwar era the environments for poor and low-income urban families, especially minorities, had worsened "precisely *because* middle- and upper-income households—especially whites—had deliberately excluded the former from sharing in the improved quality of the neighborhood environment" (Downs, 1977, p. 176). Few of those who joined the great postwar exodus to the suburbs realized that they were the beneficiaries of government policies. Still less did they realize that they had contributed to deterioration of family environments in the inner city.

While poor black families trapped in the inner cities bore the brunt of the urban crisis, white ethnic and working-class families bore a disproportionate share of the costs of the changing urban landscape. Working-class and lower-middle-income neighborhoods were more likely than upper-middle-class ones to lie in the path of the expanding black population, an urban-renewal project, or a new highway. For most lower- and middle-income families, their home is the biggest investment. Further, as Andrew Levison (1974) pointed out, workers' homes are not simply a piece of property, "but something which has absorbed so much of their income, so many hours of work, and closed out so many alternatives, that losing it is like making all the sacrifices futile" (p. 106). Thus the "changing" of a working-class white neighborhood could provoke fury and even violence. Often housing did lose its value as neighbors rushed to sell after a black family moved in. In short, the transformation of the American landscape in the postwar era resulted in a white backlash as well as the black uprisings of the 1960s.

THE 1970s: SCARCITY AND "THE ME DECADE"

In spite of violence and turmoil, the 1960s were a remarkably optimistic time. The dissenters of the 1960s agreed with their establishment opponents about the basic assumption of unlimited economic growth.

Both left and right believed that the end of scarcity was at hand. The only problem was what to do with all that abundance.

The Kennedy–Johnson years were an era of great enthusiasm for social reform. At the same time as he presided over a major war, President Johnson launched the Great Society—a collection of government programs aimed at eliminating some of the worst immediate effects of poverty, such as poor nutrition and health care, and also at helping people rise up out of poverty by providing them with skills.

The programs of the Great Society resulted in a tremendous sense of disillusion. By the end of the 1960s many people were persuaded that "throwing money at problems," as Richard Nixon had put it, not only doesn't do any good, but only makes things worse. Welfare, some said, makes people irresponsible; trying to help families only makes them weaker. The programs of the 1960s had not, in fact, failed as badly or been as wildly expensive as most people believe, but people had been oversold by Johnson's own rhetoric that the end of poverty and its attendant social ills was at hand.

It was, however, the stunning, unexpected reversal of the economy in the 1970s that soured the optimism of the 1960s. The disastrous combination of inflation, the energy crisis, recession, and unemployment that hit the country in the mid-1970s put a final end to the postwar era. It became dramatically clear that the expectation of growing abundance, taken for granted in both the 1950s and the 1960s, was fundamentally wrong. The postwar era and its life-styles had been based on three basic assumptions about the economy: that unlimited economic growth was good, that it was possible, and that economists possessed the technical know-how to control both inflation and unemployment.

By the late 1960s, there was increasing awareness that growth brought costs as well as benefits. The automobile was a prime example. It polluted the air and damaged the physical and social environment of both the city and the country. A luxury in the 1920s, it had become a necessity in the 1950s. The early dream of driving freely through the countryside gave way to the reality of the daily morning and afternoon traffic jam. Each year more people were killed in traffic accidents than during the entire Vietnam war. Other forms of technology had similar built-in problems. Perhaps the ultimate insult of technology was the announcement by scientists in the spring of 1977 that human mothers' milk had become so polluted by chemicals in the environment that if it were sold in stores it would have to be banned as carcinogenic.

By the 1970s it became clear that untrammeled growth not only was causing problems but could not go on even if we wanted it to: the image of boundless abundance was replaced by the image of scarcity. Wants and technological ingenuity might be infinite, but natural resources were limited; people began to talk of "the spaceship earth," of "small is beautiful," of "survival," of "lifeboat ethics."

Finally, during the 1970s economists lost confidence in their ability to control and even predict the national economy. They fell into warring camps disputing what went wrong and how to solve it, and the latest editions of the leading textbooks on economics talked of doubt, change, disaffection, and uncertainty.

Self-Fulfillment

If one major theme of the 1960s—the hope for reform—died in the 1970s, another theme—the search for self-fulfillment—grew. It expanded from a minority of young people who emphasized "doing your own thing," exploring consciousness, and sensuous awareness of the immediate moment to become a major cultural revolution that is transforming American life. After the 1960s, it spread beyond the college campus to the wider society, where it was expressed in a variety of ways—in challenges to traditional sex roles; in a greater acceptance of sexuality, both within marriage and outside of it; and in a new interest in physical well-being, in jogging, fitness programs, and concern for good nutrition. Yankelovich (1981b) found in his surveys that about 80 percent of Americans are now engaged in a search for self-fulfillment to one degree or another. The new cultural rules clash with the new set of economic conditions. "In a matter of a few years," observes Yankelovich, "we have moved from an uptight culture set in a dynamic economy to a dynamic culture set in an uptight economy" (p. 43).

In the 1980s, the dynamic culture was no longer at odds with an uptight economy. It was not just that the New Right had come to power with Ronald Reagan. People from all parts of the political spectrum had become disillusioned with the rhetoric and the excesses of the 1960s and 1970s. The changed climate was partly due to the sobering realities of herpes and AIDS; to one writer, it seemed as if nature has a bias against promiscuous sex (Barone, 1985). But even apart from the threat of disease, casual sex and the ethic of self-fulfillment itself had lost some of their appeal. Terms like *liberation* and *do your own thing* began to sound old-fashioned. The new watchwords were *intimacy, community, relationship,* even *commitment.*

Nevertheless, a large change has taken place in American culture, in the way Americans think about themselves, their families, their work, and what they want out of life. The question is how to describe and understand this change. Is it really "the new narcissism"?

The problem with this kind of social criticism is that it generalizes on the basis of limited information:

Facts are observed correctly: the divorce rate has increased; women have left families in order to realize their individual talents or needs; the best seller lists are dominated by books on self improvement, personal growth, narcissistic preoccupation. But the facts are then interpreted too broadly, accorded a centrality and power in the broad population which they may in fact hold only for a part, for a highly articulate, "leading," powerful subgroup—but a subgroup all the same. (Veroff, Douvan, & Kulka, 1981a, p. 16)

Such terms as *narcissism* and *the me decade* are simple, negative labels for describing a social change that is very complex. Moreover, they characterize that change in terms of its most extreme, even pathological forms. Lasch (1979) does this quite literally in his use of the term *narcissism*—a clinical term referring to a severe personality disorder—to describe a broad social trend. In fact, the symptoms that clinicians use to identify patients with narcissistic personality disorders have nothing to do with self-preoccupation, worrying about sexual fulfillment, jogging, or eating health foods (Satow, 1979).

It is true that Americans seem to be more concerned with themselves now than in the past, but it does not seem accurate to describe this concern as a demand for constant "emotional titillation," nor does it imply that people have abandoned their commitments to the family and other intimate relationships. Perhaps the best way to understand the cultural revolution of recent years is to contrast it with the older cultural values it replaced. Daniel Yankelovich (1981a)

gives some examples of this older way of life from statements by people between the ages of 55 and 70 interviewed about their lives in the post–World War II era:

Even though we no longer had anything in common we stayed together. We didn't break up even though the children were grown.

We lived on his salary even though I was making good money at the time. He said he would not feel right if we spent the money I earned for food and rent.

Sure it was a rotten job. What the hell. I made a good living. I took care of my wife and kids. What more do you expect? (pp. 8–9)

The unspoken assumptions in these statements might be summed up as follows: "We do what is expected of us and go along with the rules society has laid down concerning work and family. We swallow our frustrations and disregard our impulses to do what we would enjoy rather than what we are supposed to do." The first quotation illustrates in a particularly vivid way how the norms surrounding marriage have changed in recent years. It expresses an unstated view of marriage that may be paraphrased as follows: "Marriage is a lifelong commitment. Divorce is justified only under the most extreme circumstances."

Today the norms surrounding marriage have changed drastically. Couples are no longer expected to stay married to one another if their emotional relationship has flaws—such as a lack of intimacy, understanding, companionship, or a satisfying sexual relationship. Fewer people consider it admirable to stay in a marriage like the one just described. Some writers criticize the fact that rising expectations for marriage and the quest for the perfect relationship paradoxically doom most marriages to dissatisfaction. But this situation is very different from the widespread notion that people have rejected marriage or no longer think it is important.

The Michigan Studies

A major study of the recent changes in American life documents the shift away from traditional definitions of work, marriage, and parenthood and at the same time suggests a useful way of interpreting them. The findings of this study are reported in two books, *The Inner American* (Veroff, Douvan, & Kulka, 1981a) and *Mental Health in America* (Veroff, Kulka, & Douvan, 1981b). Both books report the results of national surveys conducted in 1957 and 1976 by the University of Michigan's Institute of Social Research. In 1957 a random sample of over 2,000 people were asked a broad range of questions about themselves, their families, and their work, as well as about their troubles, fears, and sorrows. Each interview lasted for about 90 minutes. The 1976 survey asked the same questions, plus a few new ones, of a matched sample of about the same size.

Comparing these two surveys yields many insights into the ways Americans have changed over 20 years. Although the analysis of the data and the findings is complex, the best summary of these studies is a theme emphasized by the authors themselves: between 1957 and 1976, American culture underwent a "psychological revolution"; that is, there has been a fundamental shift in the way people look at their lives. In 1976, people were much more likely than they had been in the past to speak about their satisfactions and problems in psychological terms—whether they were speaking of work, marriage, or parenthood. They had become more introspective, more attentive to their inner experiences. In 1957, people were more likely to attribute their satisfactions or problems to external or material conditions, such as money, health, or the outward signs of success.

Another facet of the change is a greater willingness to admit to having problems. As the authors point out, there were remarkable decreases in the number of people who said they never had any problems in their marriage, with their children, or at work. "We do not interpret this to mean that the problematic nature of these roles has necessarily increased, but that denial of problems was more common in 1957" (Veroff, Douvan, & Kulka, 1981a, p. 532).

Perhaps the most fundamental change is in the way people think about and define themselves. In the past, people tended to define themselves in terms of their social roles and statuses—for example, a man might define himself as an American, a lawyer, a husband and a father, a Catholic, a Democrat. Today people are less likely to see their "true selves" (Turner, 1976) as contained completely in their social identities. They are more likely to define themselves in terms of their personal qualities, styles, and inner experience.

The change is reflected in the themes of the mass media, especially the rise of a new kind of cultural hero—for example, Woody Allen:

In earlier eras, the cultural hero was the man of action taming the West; in our era he is more likely to be presented as the individual searching for meaning and self definition. . . . Woody Allen gives us a hero who has all the success and achievement, the money and fame a person could dream of, and who at the same time, struggles with unsatisfactory relationships and a twenty year psychoanalysis. (Veroff, Kulka, & Douvan, 1981a, p. 6)

An Oklahoma farm family hitchhiking to California after their car broke down, 1936. [Dorothea Lange/ Reproduced from the Collections of the Library of Congess]

But in some ways Woody Allen is a misleading image of the psychological revolution. The data show that people were more satisfied with their marriages in 1976 than they were in 1957, in spite of their willingness to admit to having marital and other problems. The authors interpret this finding as a result of the increased divorce rate. People are now freer to move out of relationships that are not personally gratifying, and we now have many fewer marriages that are unhappy over long periods.

One of the major findings of the study was of an increase in sensitivity to the quality of interpersonal relationships, not only in the family, but also at work. People want friendly, warm relationships at work and increased intimacy and closeness in the family. The new emphasis on warmth and closeness may put new burdens on relationships and create discontents in many that would otherwise be fairly satisfying. Overall, however, the results of this study do not suggest that Americans have become a nation of narcissists, unable and unwilling to form close, long-term attachments. Summing up their results, the authors conclude that Americans are still a family-centered society and still committed to work, although family roles are more important than work roles to self-definitions. There is no evidence here that the family is anywhere near the verge of extinction.

The Gentrification of America

Although the psychological revolution seemed to grow out of the counterculture of the 1960s, with its emphasis on feelings, immediate enjoyment, the expansion of consciousness, and encounter groups, in fact it was rooted in deep changes in American society as a whole. Affluence was one of the most powerful forces bringing about change, but it involved more than an increase in living standards. Affluence not only meant that goods once considered luxuries were now available to masses of people; it also meant that, through education and the mass media, ideas that were once held by relatively small groups of the privileged were also spread to middle and working classes. A concern with inner psychological experience and the quest for identity is not a new cultural invention; rather, it is a traditional preoccupation of aristocrats, artists, and bohemians. It is likely to become a concern whenever people do not have to devote their lives to simple survival—to meeting basic needs for food, clothing, and shelter. People brought up in relative economic security, political freedom, and affluence simply take these for granted as facts of life, rather than as goals or values to organize their lives around. It is then that the search for meaning and self-definition is likely to emerge, especially if affluence is accompanied by some degree of "higher" education.

In a sense, the changes in American life we have been describing might be described as the "gentrification" of American culture. *Gentrification* is the term that describes the change that occurs when middle- or upper-middle-class people move into a poor or lower-class neighborhood, restyling it to middle-class tastes. The process of gentrification is a metaphor for what has happened to American culture: the "psychological revolution" is not so much a revolution as a spread of formerly avant-garde, elite ideas to large segments of the population.

Several observers have noted similarities between the ideas that were popular in the 1960s and 1970s and earlier cultural styles. Daniel Bell (1976) pointed out that the counterculture was a warmed-over version of the attack on puritanism that had been launched by avant-garde intellectuals in the first decades of the twentieth century. Centered in Greenwich Village, the group included John Reed and Emma Goldman, and others. The Young Intellectuals preached an ethic of hedonism, free love, and unmarried monogamy. This group and their ideas are vividly portrayed in the 1981 movie *Reds*. And Michael Harrington (1981) observes that

one of the most fascinating aspects of the contemporary world is the speed with which ideas diffuse from a cultural vanguard to the mass of people. The emotions felt by the Lost Generation in Paris in the twenties were known to hordes of college students by the sixties; the Cubism which shocked the middle class before World War I inspired wallpaper patterns after World War II. And the sexual mores of the Freudian Left and Bohemia between two world wars became commonplace for almost all youth by the seventies. (p. 27)

The process of psychological gentrification is documented statistically in the University of Michigan surveys. In 1957, the psychological approach to life and the concern with warm, intimate relationships had been almost exclusively a characteristic of the highly educated. By 1976, this way of looking at the world had become "common coin" (Veroff, Douvan, & Kulka, 1981a, p. 25).

Psychological gentrification is not to be explained simply as a change in consciousness, important though that is, nor even as a result of higher education—which certainly resulted in the spread of avant-garde ideas. But it is unlikely these ideas could have spread so far and so deeply among the American population were they not rooted in some of the basic economic and social trends of American society.

The New Capitalism

During the twentieth century the United States underwent a transition from an older form of capitalism that stressed hard work, savings, and the repression of impulse to a new capitalism based on mass consumption, spending, and immediate gratification. Credit and advertising were key instruments of the transformed economy.

Although credit cards are now a taken-for-granted part of American life, the whole notion of buying something without having saved up for it first was, as Daniel Bell (1976) has pointed out, "a revolution in moral habit" (p. 69). "Buy now, pay later" became the watchword of the new consumer economy. In the past, being a respectable person meant savings, abstinence, and living within one's means. If you wanted something, you paid cash for it. Going into debt was wrong and dangerous. Only the poor who could not afford major expenditures bought things on the installment plan. During recent years, credit cards have almost replaced cash as the basic currency in which things are bought and sold. These cards offer the consumer the constant temptation to regularly go into hundreds, if not thousands, of dollars into debt.

The other major instrument of a mass-consumption society, along with easy credit, is advertising. Our major corporations, through their advertisements, have for dec-

ades preached an ethic of pleasure, instant joy, self-indulgence, and self-fulfillment. Long before "the me decade," advertisers promoted the idea of change and personal transformation. Advertising, Michael Schudson (1984) suggests, may be viewed as a kind of "capitalist realism." Like "Socialist realism," the official art of the Soviet Union, its aim is to picture life not so much as it is, but as it should be. Where socialist realism glorifies labor in the service of the state, American advertising "glorifies the pleasures and freedoms of consumer choice in defense of the virtues of private life and material ambitions" (p. 218).

Advertisers preach that the meaning of life and the definition of self are to be found in our leisure activities, our personal styles, and the brand of clothes, cars, and cigarettes we wear, drive, and smoke. Thus there is, as Bell observes, a "cultural contradiction" at the heart of the new capitalism; on the one hand, to get its factories and offices to produce, it promotes an ethic of hard work and productivity; on the other hand, to sell the goods it produces, it encourages self-expression and self-indulgence.

Ironically, while promising to satisfy needs and wants, the consumer economy offers a powerful stimulant to discontent on a mass scale. Advertising constantly bombards us to be dissatisfied with what we already own and tries to stimulate appetites for more, bigger, better, and newer things. Modern advertising focuses less on the product itself and more on the mind of the consumer—particularly on his or her self-image. In 1929 Helen and Robert Lynd noted that the new type of ad tried "to make the reader emotionally uneasy, to bludgeon him with the fact that decent people don't live the way he does" (1929, p. 82).

More recently, Schudson points out, advertisements stir uneasiness with their moving but sentimental portrayals of happy, loving couples, families, and friends. Commenting on AT&T's "Reach Out and Touch Someone" commercials for long-distance phone calls, he notes that such ads provide models of sentiment that real experience cannot often match. "Most of our phone calls, even with loved ones, are boring or routine" (p. 231).

But the discontents that advertising stimulates are not always directed at the self. The other side of consumerism is a deep skepticism concerning all advertising claims and a "scrutinizing, evaluating, and questioning [of] all areas of life from the environment, to education, to automobiles, and . . . even to politics" (Gartner & Reissman, 1974, p. 9). Further, advertising, as Schudson (1984) and others have pointed out, is not nearly as successful at selling goods as is widely believed. Yet even though we reject its messages as false and silly, its symbols have a "special cultural power" to pick up and reflect back to us some of our deepest wishes and discontents.

Fun Morality

Another reason affluence fails to satisfy is that it is based on a "fun morality," as Martha Wolfenstein (1954) describes it, that contains a paradoxical injunction: one is obligated to have a good time. Although the Protestant ethic could give rise to feelings of guilt and worthlessness, it offered the possibility of trying to satisfy one's conscience through hard work. Fun morality is more elusive. Play becomes permeated by the work ethic; one asks, Am I having enough fun, a good-enough orgasm, a happy-enough marriage? Not only does happiness tend to elude such introspection but being permitted to satisfy impulses may weaken the pleasure of anticipation:

In the past when work and play were more sharply isolated, virtue was associated with one and the danger of sin with the other. Impulse gratification presented possibilities of intense excitement as well as of wickedness. Today we have attained a high degree of tolerance of impulses, which at the same time no longer seem capable of producing such intense excitement as formerly. (Wolfenstein, 1955, p. 75)

Knowledge and Dissent

Still another source of contradiction and discontent has been the spread of higher education to large masses of people. The very dependency of the key institutions on an intelligentsia of educated professionals makes for a less stable society. Along with providing the trained manpower, this same intelligentsia is just as likely to provide the major critics and rebels of the social order. The critical faculties required by highly educated professionals lead them to question the very legitimacy of the order they serve.

Lipset and Dobson (1972) present some dramatic statistics documenting how the occupational structures of such advanced countries as the United States and the Soviet Union have changed in recent years. Between 1930 and 1965, for example, while the general work force in the United States increased by half, the number of engineers almost quadrupled and the number of scientists increased almost ten times over. In addition, there has been expansion in the numbers and influence of other kinds of knowledge and cultural workers—teachers, artists, writers, journalists, and people in the media.

Why are there such strong tendencies for intellectuals to constitute a dissenting force, to bite the hand that feeds them? The answer seems to be that creative work of any kind—scientific or artistic—seems to call for a certain skepticism, a critical detachment from prevailing ideas. Moreover, when existing knowledge changes rapidly, it is not possible to train young persons with skills that will last a lifetime. An engineering student, a computer programmer, a student of business administration—none of these can simply be taught a set of techniques that will remain valid from then on. Rather, they must be taught to be flexible—there have been different ways of looking at the problem in the past, and the future will bring still more innovation. The more broadly a people have been educated, the easier it will be for them to change occupations or skills several times over.

The Transformation of the Self

The spread of higher education in the postwar era has created not only a different kind of citizen—a more critical and skeptical one—but also a different kind of personality. Although the lack of money, education, and success can produce unhappiness, having these things doesn't guarantee happiness. Education, in particular, seems to change people's desires, values, and self-perceptions. A number of studies dealing with the impact of income and education on people's sense of well-being have discovered what one writer calls a "Richard Cory complex" (Tavris, 1976). Richard Cory was the subject of a poem by Edward Arlington Robinson; he had looks, social status, and money, but one day he went home and put a bullet through his head.

Angus Campbell and his associates (1976) surveyed people about how satisfied they felt, whether they regarded their lives as interesting or boring, enjoyable or miserable, and so forth; they discovered a surprising interaction effect between education and income. They found that the people who gave themselves the highest happiness ratings were those who did not finish high school but were earning more than $12,000 a year. College graduates, however, were not very happy regardless of how much they earned. But college graduates with low incomes were happier than other people in that income category. In the group of people making the most money, however, the college graduates were the least happy.

The reason for this discontent seems to be that education doesn't merely impart skills but transforms the way people feel about themselves and the world. Education seems to make people more introspective—more able and willing to look inside themselves and thus more likely to find weaknesses (Gurin, Veroff, & Feld, 1960). Further, education changes values. College graduates value economic security less than other people do; they also feel that having an important or exciting life is more important than having money. And they care more about the psychological aspects of their jobs than the economic ones. Since these values are more intangible than the size of one's paycheck, it is harder to measure one's success or failure.

Bringing Up Father: Adulthood as a Stage of Development

The increased emphasis on the psychological needs of adults has resulted in a new view of adulthood. The idea of development, once applicable only to growing children, is applied to adults as new stages of adult life are "discovered." Indeed, the psychological revolution of recent years—the tendency to look at life through psychological lenses—can be understood in part as the extension of ways of thinking about adults that were once confined to children.

During the postwar era, the advice of childrearing experts, such as Dr. Spock, came to be enormously influential. This advice, promoted through best-selling books as well as the other mass media, had a strong psy-

A woman mechanic in Beaumont, Texas, 1943. During World War II, it was considered patriotic for women to do men's jobs. [John Vachon/Reproduced from the Collections of the Library of Congress

chological flavor. In earlier times, parents had been concerned with raising children to be healthy and obedient; they did not pay much attention to children's inner psychological worlds. After World War II, American parents came to be increasingly preoccupied with their children's psychological motives and potential.

Earlier generations of parents had viewed children's behavior and misbehavior in moral terms; parents now began to look at children's behavior in terms of "needs" and "stages." In the past a young child's temper tantrum would be seen by parents as wilful disobedience and treated accordingly. The modern child is likely to be seen as going through a difficult stage or as having some unfulfilled need.

Now we have learned to apply this way of thinking to adults; a 40-year-old man or woman who leaves a spouse, changes career, or dresses in a new style is now regarded by many people as showing signs of a "normal" stage in adult life—the mid-life crisis. Although there is much debate among scholars as to whether there really is such a thing as a "mid-life crisis"—that is, a stage of life that everyone goes through—there is little doubt that adulthood has become a more distinct and problematic time of life in recent years (Smelser & Erikson, 1981).

More than a change in consciousness, the new way of thinking about adulthood is rooted in changes in the adult life in the twentieth century. Modern adulthood has become both more age graded—more divided into distinct periods with different life tasks—and more flexible and open to choice.

FIGURE 2.1
Fertility Rates, United
States, 1930–1984

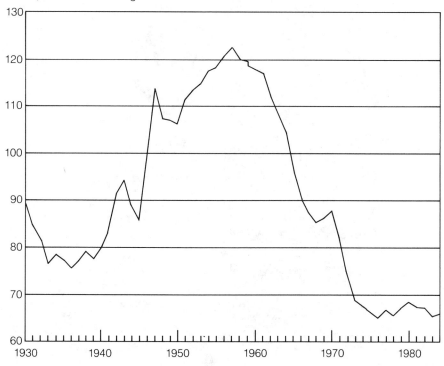

From U.S. Department of Health and Human Services, National Center for Health Statistics, *Monthly Vital Statistics Report, Annual Summary of Births, Marriages, Divorces, and Deaths: United States, 1984.* Vol. 33, No. 13, September 26, 1985.

In the past, for example, when people had many children and died in middle age, work and childrearing occupied most of life from adolescence on. Now people have a few closely spaced children and live longer lives. The result is that couples face the empty nest at a younger age and remain in it for a much longer time. Today's couples face a much longer period of time together as a couple without major child-care responsibilities than their ancestors did. Retirement is also a distinct, formally marked off period of life, and the period of semiadulthood that people experience in college and graduate school is another phase of adulthood that did not exist on a mass level in earlier eras.

At the same time, adults today have more options than in the past. Basic life decisions, such as what to study, what kind of career to follow, who and when to marry, and so forth are now up to the individual, while in the past these life events were determined by the needs of the parental family (Hareven, 1982). Today's adults have the privilege—and the burden—of making these choices for themselves and of revising them later in life. Above all, modern adults have the historically novel privilege of actually having a reasonable expectation of surviving into old age and of being able to contemplate living out a complete life course. As late as the end of the nineteenth century, less than half the population actually had lived out a full lifetime (Uhlenberg, 1980).

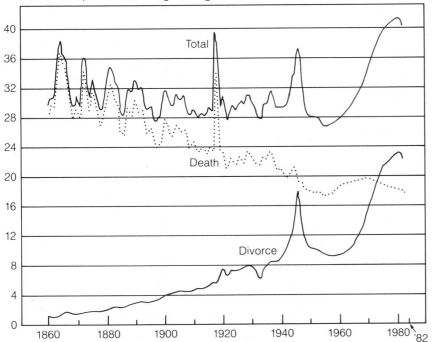

Dissolution rate per 1,000 existing marriages

FIGURE 2.2
*Marital Dissolutions
per 1,000 Existing
Marriages, by Divorce,
Death, and Total:
1860–1982*

From A. Thornton and D. Freedman, *Population Bulletin: The Changing American Family*, a publication of The Population Reference Bureau, Vol. 38, No. 4, October 1983, p. 7.

THE POSTWAR ERA IN DEMOGRAPHIC PERSPECTIVE

In the past section, we looked at the psychological and cultural revolution of recent years and concluded that these changes were both a reaction against the conformist culture of the 1950s and a reflection of a mass-consumption society. In this section, we turn away from culture and ideas to look at demographic data on family life in the past several decades. We examine some long-term trends in family life, reaching back before the 1950s to the beginning of the twentieth century. When we do so, we arrive at the surprising new insight into the 1950s we mentioned at the beginning of this chapter: far from the postwar era's being the last era of normal family life from which the current state of the family is a deviation, it is rather the family patterns of the postwar era, the time between the late 1940s and the mid-1960s, that are deviant.

This is the unavoidable conclusion that emerges from carrying the leading statistical indicators of family life back into the past. Thus the low marriage, high divorce, and low fertility rates of today's young adults may differ from patterns of their parents' generation, but the young adults' behavior is consistent with long-term trends. One study of these trends concluded, "Had the 1940s and 1950s not happened, today's young adults would appear to be behaving normally" (Masnick & Bane, 1980, p. 2).

Until the 1940s, fertility rates had been falling steadily (Figure 2.1) while divorce and women's employment had been rising

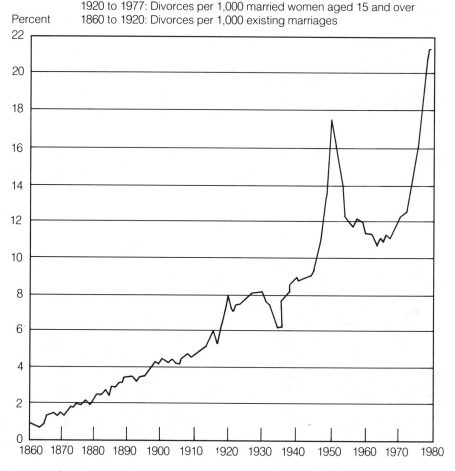

FIGURE 2.3
Annual Divorce Rate
for the United States:
1860–1977

1920 to 1977: Divorces per 1,000 married women aged 15 and over
1860 to 1920: Divorces per 1,000 existing marriages

From A. Cherlin, *Marriage, Divorce, Remarriage.* Cambridge, Mass.: Harvard University Press, 1981, p. 22. Reprinted by permission.

steadily. During the depression and the baby boom, the age of marriage was earlier than before or since. The trend that has been most worrisome is the rising rate of divorce in recent years. Yet the divorce rate—the number of divorces per 1,000 existing marriages—has been going up since at least the middle of the nineteenth century. During the postwar era, however, the annual rates were lower than would be predicted from the long-term rise (Figures 2.2 and 2.3). Thus, if we contrast today's divorce rates with those of the post-

war era, the current rise looks larger than if we look at the long-term trend.

A more useful gauge of the significance of current divorce rates is to look at the lifetime divorce experience of adults (Cherlin, 1981c); that is, instead of looking at annual divorce rates, we can look at the proportion of marriages begun in succeeding years that end in divorce. Andrew Cherlin (1981c) has drawn a graph showing the proportion of marriages begun in every year between 1867 and 1973 that have ended, or are likely to

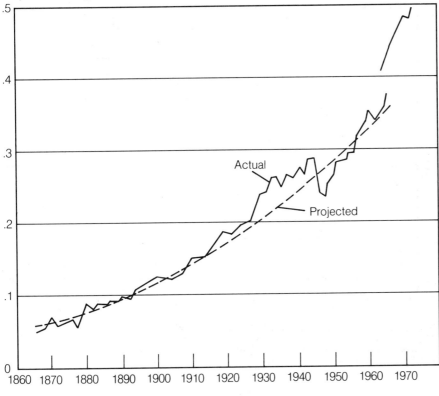

FIGURE 2.4
Actual and Projected Proportions of Marriages Begun in Each Year Which Will End in Divorce: 1867–1964 and 1963–1973

Year marriage was begun

From A. Cherlin, *Marriage, Divorce, Remarriage.* Cambridge, Mass.: Harvard University Press, 1981, p. 23. Reprinted by permission.

end, in divorce (Figure 2.4). The graph also shows a smooth curve that most closely fits the data.

Cherlin summarizes his findings as follows: despite yearly fluctuations, the proportion of all marriages in a given year that end in divorce has been rising steadily since the middle of the nineteenth century. The only variations from these trends were the somewhat lower than expected levels of divorce of those who married in the decade after the war, and the higher levels of those who married in the depression and in the early 1970s. Although the lifetime divorce experience of

today's young adults will be higher than the current historical trend predicts, the rise in divorce is not nearly so sharp as most people assume it is.

Another trend that has alarmed many people in recent years is the decline in virginity. Yet here, too, we are dealing with a trend that originated long before the 1960s. In fact, in 1938 one researcher, Lewis Terman, predicted that if the then current trends continued, no girl born after 1940 would enter marriage a virgin. However, his prediction was off the mark; even in the late 1970s about 20 percent of women between 18 and

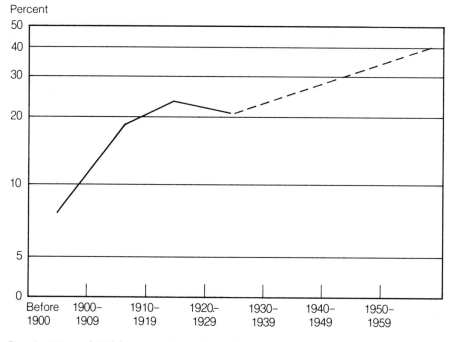

FIGURE 2.5
Proportion of Young Women Who Had Sexual Intercourse by Age 20, by Decade of Birth

From Jessie Bernard, "Adolescence and Socialization for Motherhood" in S. E. Dragastin and G. Elder (Eds.), *Adolescence in the Life Cycle*. New York, Hemisphere Publishing Corporation, 1975, p. 239. Reprinted by permission of Hemisphere Publishing Corporation, 19 West 44th Street, New York, N.Y. 10036.

24 were estimated to be virgins (Adams, 1980, p. 219). Researchers disagree about whether we have even had a sexual revolution in recent years. Some believe that the sexual revolution actually started in the 1920s, when there was a sharp rise in the rate of premarital intercourse (Figure 2.5). Others prefer to avoid the term *revolution* altogether but rather see a steady trend toward more premarital sex with each succeeding generation.

A Cultural Earthquake

The long-term trends we have described were like the silent, unnoticed underground forces that erupt into earthquakes. On one side of a fault line the earth remains fixed in place while the other side creeps steadily past. On the surface nothing seems to be

happening until the strain grows too great and the two sides jolt with alignment. The recent changes in the family were like a cultural earthquake.

The situation fits the model of what anthropologists call a cultural lag—there was a discrepancy between the images or norms of family life and what people were actually doing. All during the postwar era of domesticity and the feminine mystique, trends in divorce, remarriage, premarital sex, and women's labor force participation were either rising or on a temporary plateau. There was much more diversity in family life than was recognized. Yet the mass media and most social scientists seemed to assume that all brides were virgins, women's place was exclusively in the home, and all marriages were first and only marriages. When variations

TABLE 2.1   *Changing Social Norms*

Question: Today there are many different kinds of life-styles that people find acceptable, such as a husband staying home and caring for the children while the wife goes to work. How do you feel about this? Do you find it acceptable for other people but not for yourself, acceptable for other people and yourself, or not acceptable at all? (Respondents were then asked a series of questions about other behavior, as shown below.)

	Not acceptable at all (a)	Acceptable for others but not for self (b)	Acceptable for others and self (c)	(b + c)
A single woman having and raising a child	26%	40%	34%	74%
The husband staying home and caring for the children while the wife goes to work	26	36	38	74
Premarital relationships	36	23	41	64
A mother of young children going to work for career purposes and self-fulfillment when the money is not needed	39	27	34	61
Enrolling very young children in day-care centers or nursery schools to give the mother more leisure time	49	24	27	51
Young people with children living together in what they call the "extended family"	54	34	12	46
Homosexual relationships	59	35	6	41
Divorced women asking their parents to raise the children while they build a new life	71	19	10	29

Source: Ruth Clark and Greg Martire, "Americans, Still In A Family Way," *Public Opinion* October/November, 1979, p. 19. Used by permission.

were noticed, they were considered deviant exceptions to the norm. Then in the 1960s the two sides of the cultural fault line jolted into alignment, and what had previously seemed deviant became recognized as commonplace and even typical (Table 2.1).

Using a somewhat different metaphor, Jessie Bernard (1975) has applied the concept of "tipping points" to the moment when significant numbers of people engage in a formerly atypical pattern of behavior. The concept of a tipping point seems to fit what happened to the norms about women working outside the home. After being denounced in the 1950s the career woman is now idealized. Many women feel coerced by this image; those who prefer to be homemakers feel they have become second-class citizens—that it has become "slightly less than respectable" for a woman to be "just a housewife" (N. Rubin, 1982).

Something similar has happened to divorce. While divorce is not idealized in the way that the career woman sometimes is, divorce has been "normalized" in the sense that it is no longer rare or regarded as a sign of deep personal failure. Rather, it has become a life event many people expect to encounter.

The sudden realization that long-held assumptions about the family were out of line with social reality provoked great anxiety and concern. The family, as we have seen, was said to be in crisis, on the way to extinction. But there are other reasons for the sense of strain and uncertainty many people feel today about the family.

Changes in family norms and behavior are always difficult. Family change does not imply deterioration or decline, but it does call for a great deal of rethinking and adaptation. The old rules and customs no longer apply. People feel awkward as they try to figure out such seemingly trivial issues as how a man and a woman should go through a door

together or how to refer to the person someone lives with but isn't married to, and they feel uncertain as they face major choices about marriage, work, and children. The two-paycheck couple who are trying to share the housework, the single parent raising a child alone, or the remarried couple who are trying to raise children from both marriages are like pioneers in new territory with no guides to follow.

Even those most committed to the new ways may find their feelings lagging behind their beliefs and actions. A feminist woman may want her mate to be a "new man"—sensitive, caring, and willing to do his share of the housework. But deep down she may also want him to be bigger, stronger, and smarter than she is. A man may believe in the principle of sexual equality, but feel uncomfortable in a marriage where housework and professional success really are equal (L. B. Rubin, 1983).

Another major source of strain is the fact that our social institutions—schools, businesses, and medical facilities—and, indeed, our cities and suburbs are not geared to the needs of changed family patterns. There is a shortage of child care for young children, schools assume a parent is in the home at all times, and businesses run on an inflexible nine-to-five schedule that does not take their employees' family needs into account. The economic disadvantage women have always faced in the labor market used to be based on the assumption—not true even in the past—that women didn't need to work because they were supported by men. Today, those traditional disadvantages add enormously to the stress of divorce and single parenthood.

The kinds of changes we have been witnessing in the family would have been troubling even in a time when the rest of society was stable. But, of course, they are taking place in a time of economic dislocation and uncertainty, when some of the most fundamental assumptions of American life are being questioned. For the first time in recent history, Americans have had to face the prospect that their children may not lead better lives than themselves. And for the first time in a generation, young adults can no longer count on those staples of middle-class family life—a good job and owning their own home.

The unsettled state of the economy and the world in general is having contradictory effects on family life. Surveys reveal that to a greater extent than in the past people expect family life and individual needs to take priority over careers as a way of retaining feelings of self-worth, self-determination, and self-fulfillment. On the other hand, the very economic and social uncertainties that encourage this turn toward domesticity put strains on close relationships. Further, at a time when there is greater need than ever for family support services, such as child care and counseling, as well as new ways to balance the demands of work and family, the fiscal crisis and the new conservatism create demands for cutting back and retrenchment.

In this climate it is little wonder that the changes in the family seem to be a source of further unwelcome instability. It is easy to understand the lure of nostalgia. But as we saw in the last chapter, there is no golden age of the family to long for. Nor can we look to some past family pattern as the solution to today's problems. We cannot look to the past for solutions to the problems facing American families because they grow out of the circumstances of this particular moment in history. As we saw in this chapter, many of the family changes of recent years were a continuation of long-term trends that began generations ago.

The patterns of marriage and childbearing in the 1950s did not typify the family in its normal state, nor even the family in modern society. Rather, these patterns were a historical aberration brought about by a period of sustained prosperity that followed years of depression and wartime austerity. Nor was the postwar era the idyllic period that its nostalgic image suggests. The seeming calmness of the times was fragile as well as deceptive.

SUMMARY

In times of change and uncertainty people often look nostalgically back to the good old days of some earlier period. Many feel that the post–World War II era, especially the 1950s, was an era of contentment, prosperity, and family stability. It is important to examine the realities of family life and attitudes during that era because it often serves as a baseline against which we measure current changes.

Despite the idealized image of the era, the postwar life-style was both fragile and contradictory. The revolts that broke out in the 1960s—of blacks, young people, and women—were a product of tensions that were either created or repressed during the 1950s. Three flaws undermined the postwar American way of life. First, a majority of American families did not enjoy the level of affluence that was portrayed in the mass media as typical. Blue-collar or working-class families struggled to maintain a modest level of material comfort, while the poor and minorities were excluded altogether. In fact, the growth of the suburbs during the postwar era imposed heavy costs on the disadvantaged. America became a society divided between angry, despairing inner-city ghettos and the surrounding white suburbs. Working-class, white, ethnic families also suffered from the changing urban landscape. The result was an increase in racial, ethnic, and class tensions by the end of the 1960s.

A second flaw appeared in another set of

tensions that arose paradoxically from affluence itself. The chief beneficiaries of the postwar life-style, the educated upper-middle class, discovered that once basic survival needs could be taken for granted, new sources of striving and discontent arose. Many of the young people who had experienced the greatest advantages as children came to be the most dissatisfied with American society. They created a counterculture based on both political opposition and alternative life-styles. Eventually, these attitudes spread from the fringes to influence the mainstream of the American population.

Women rebelled against the feminine mystique of domesticity that had prevailed during the postwar era. The influence of the women's movement also spread well beyond its original middle-class origins.

The final flaw in the postwar way of life lay in the economic forces that drove it. Economists, policy makers, and social theorists during the 1950s assumed that economic growth could go on forever and that abundance and technology could solve all problems. By the 1970s it had become clear that there were limits to growth, that technology produces disastrous side effects, and that many serious problems—inflation, unemployment, the energy crisis, and so on—seem to have no quick and easy solutions.

Further, the postwar era, when Americans were marrying early, having lots of children, and getting divorced infrequently, turns out to have been a deviant period. Recent changes in marriage, divorce, childbearing, and women's participation in the labor force are all consistent with long-term historical trends reaching back to the turn of the century, and even earlier.

Although the economic crises of the 1970s and 1980s put an end to the easy optimism of the 1960s, the cultural themes of the 1960s—the emphasis on self-fulfillment and self-expression—spread to a majority of the American people. This new national mood is best understood as a "psychological revolution," an increased tendency to take a psychological perspective in interpreting other people as well as one's own psychological experience. The psychological revolution reflects the spread of ideas formerly held only by a segment of the highly educated to the masses. It also is the product of the affluent consumer society of the postwar era; affluence released people from preoccupation with survival, and the new consumer economy emphasized self-fulfillment and immediate gratification through buying. Whatever the causes of the psychological revolution, it has created new sources of discontent as well as new possibilities for intimacy. In the years to come, we will be grappling with the problem of responding in both private and public ways with changing family patterns.

CHAPTER 3

In Search of the Family

One difficulty in the psychological sciences lies in the familiarity of the phenomena with which they deal. A certain intellectual effort is required to see how such phenomena can pose serious problems or call for intricate explanatory theories. One is inclined to take them for granted as necessary or somehow "natural."

Noam Chomsky
Language and Mind

Nobody knows what really goes on in a family.

"Betty Neumeyer," in Paul Wilkes
Trying Out the Dream:
A Year in the Life of an
American Family

In Chapter 1, we discussed some of the reasons why studying the family turns out to be a more problematic enterprise than it might seem at first glance. We pointed to some of the difficulties in defining the family and in interpreting statistical evidence. We also pointed to the ways in which the family touches on deeply personal issues of values, morality, and private experience.

In this chapter, we explore these complexities in more detail. It is necessary to emphasize the complexities of studying the family because otherwise our discussion will be clouded by unexplored notions of what the family "really" is. However, to point out the difficulties in studying the family is not to state that research on the family cannot be done or that the family cannot be studied scientifically.

There is a widespread misunderstanding about how science actually works. Dr. Lewis Thomas (1982), who writes for the general public as well as for his fellow scientists, complained about the way science is taught these days. Biology, chemistry, physics, and the other "hard" sciences, he observed, are taught as if each field were a vast collection of solid facts and unchanging laws.

In reality, Thomas argues, science doesn't work this way. The conclusions scientists reach are far more tentative than nonscientists realize. "Next week's issue of any scientific journal can turn a whole field upside down, shaking out any number of immutable ideas and installing new bodies of dogma," which may sooner or later no longer look so convincing. Further, every field of science, no matter what its achievements, is incomplete. There is a "wilderness of mystery" to explore—vast areas of ignorance about the universe, the atom, the cell.

Thomas is not trying to debunk science. Rather, he is arguing for a change in the way science is taught. He feels that science would be more interesting to most people if they understood how many questions remain to be answered. It is, he argues, the very "strangeness of nature" that keep scientists working. In a similar way, the complexities of the family should not discourage us from trying to understand it.

OBSTACLES TO UNDERSTANDING

We approach the study of the family with a great handicap: we know both too much and too little. In no other field of study is there such a great temptation to use one's own experience as a basis for wide-ranging generalizations. Rather than being the easiest of subjects to study, however, the family may be one of the hardest. Anthropologists often find their own culture harder to study than an exotic one; perhaps only a person who has never lived in a family is really qualified to study them. As R. D. Laing (1971) puts it:

The first family to interest me was my own. I still know less about it than I know about many other families. This is typical. (p. 67)

And, even more surprisingly, he admits:

The most common situation I encounter in families is when what *I* think is going on bears almost no resemblance to what anyone in the family . . . thinks is happening. . . . Maybe no one knows what is happening. (p. 77)

The anthropologist Ray Birdwhistell (1966) argues that the family is an extremely difficult form for social scientists to study, not only in their own culture but in other cultures also. He concludes that everywhere family processes are both idealized and camouflaged. Social scientists look out through the blinders and filters imposed on them as members of a particular culture. They deal with people who may hold unrealistic assumptions about their own family systems. As an anthropological field worker, Birdwhistell was struck by the discrepancy between the actual behavior of people in their family life and the accounts people gave of their family systems:

What even the most sophisticated interviewer gets when he asks about the family is a set of personalized stereotypes—the stereotype obscured by anecdotes which purportedly report personal experiences, but which are no less banal by virtue of this pseudo-individuality. (p. 211)

Families, like governments or organizations or even individuals, do not find candor a necessary ingredient for their day-to-day functioning. Quite the opposite. One of the discoveries of recent family research is that families have myths, secrets, and information-processing rules that determine the kind of communication that goes on—what can be said and, more important, what can't be said. Families filter information not only about the wider culture, but also about their own functioning. Or, as Laing puts it, families practice mystification: they have complicated stratagems for keeping people in the dark about what is going on, and in the dark that they are in the dark.

Sanctity and Secrecy

Besides familiarity and mystification, other obstacles handicap the study of the family: it is morally sacred and it is secret. The family in America includes two moral dimensions, a religious one based on Judeo-Christian family ideals and a legal one relating to the laws of marriage, economic obligations between husband and wife, parents and children, and so on (Ball, 1972). Thus the happenings of family life are the concern of others besides the family members themselves; they have a public dimension.

Paradoxically, however, because privacy is also a cherished value, the family is perhaps the most secret institution in American society. To a greater extent than in other societies and in our own historical past, American family life goes on behind closed doors (B. Laslett, 1973). The home is a "backstage area" (Goffman, 1959) where people can be relaxed, informal, and off guard precisely because they cannot be observed by outsiders.

As a result of this privacy, family life in America is marked by what sociologists call "pluralistic ignorance," a term usually applied to sexual experience. We know what goes on in our own household or bedroom, but we have little or no direct knowledge of what really goes on in other peoples'. Thus we know where our own family life falls short of the *ideal* norms—the way family life is supposed to be—but we do not know where it fits in *statistical* norms—the extent to which other families also may be departing from prescribed behavior. As Goffman (1959) puts it, people are aware of how their own "backstage" behavior differs from how they act "in public," but they are not in a position to come to the same conclusion about others (p. 132).

Until very recently family scholarship has paid relatively little attention to the

Family Resemblances: the Problem of Defining the Family

Most dictionaries offer several different definitions of the term *family* (see Figure 3.1).

Social scientists also define the family in several different ways. Some see the marriage bond as the central element in the family; others see the mother–child unit as the central element. Biologically, the family consists of people who are related by mating and birth. But the human family is a psychological and social unit that may not always fit the biological "facts."

Adoption removes children from their biological parents and makes them legally and socially members of a different family. Adoption is found in many cultures, and in at least one part of the world—Tahiti and the other islands of the South Pacific—it is a very widespread practice (R. I. Levy, 1973). Divorce, working in the opposite direction, removes the sociological and legal definition of family from a biological one. "Illegitimate" children are not socially recognized as the children of their biological fathers, although sometimes they have been granted such recognition. In recent years legal systems around the world have been reducing the distinction between children born inside and outside of legal marriage. Then there are "fictional" kin—unrelated people who come to have the status of family members.

In our society, although we speak of "the family" and "the nuclear family," sociologists have traditionally pointed out that people usually belong to two families: the *family of orientation*, the family we grew up in, and the *family of procreation*, the family we form by marrying and having children.

Defining the family has always been problematic, and it has grown more so in recent years. Cohabiting couples in long-term relationships as well as gay couples have in some places gained the legal right to be recognized as families. "Blended" or "reconstituted" families, created by remarriage after divorce, are a common new type of family. They raise interesting new forms of relationship; for example, there are children with eight "grandparents." Marriage traditionally creates ties between two kin groups;

backstage aspects of family life. Despite the vast literature on family life spreading across several disciplines, practically everything social scientists knew about the family was derived from questionnaires and interviews obtained from family members seen alone. Often only one member of a family, usually the wife, served as an informant about the rest of the family.

There are, of course, some very good ethical reasons for respecting family privacy. Keyhole peeping and eavesdropping, electronic and otherwise, would be hard to justify as research methods. In recent years, however, researchers have found a compromise between privacy and research. They have begun to observe family interaction live with the consent of those being observed. Although these glimpses of family life do not give a view that is truly backstage or unobserved, they nevertheless have led to new conceptions of what families are. Viewing live family interaction has reclaimed for social science some of the insights into family life that previously had been found only in the writings of novelists and playwrights. We shall explore these insights later.

The Definition Problem

In much of this chapter we are going to explore what people mean when they speak with remarriage making more ties between families, one observer recently joked that before too long, everybody in California will be related to everybody else.

Some family scholars believe that the problem of defining the family can and should be resolved. Yet as a concept "the family" may not be that different from other concepts. Recent research in information processing suggests that all complex concepts and categories may be "fuzzy sets" (McCloskey & Glucksberg, 1978). The notion of fuzzy sets argues that no single set of features defines a category such as *bird*, *chair*, or *fruit*. Rather, knowledge about a category consists of an ideal *prototype* plus a number of other less typical examples. For example, robins, penguins, and turkeys are all birds, but the robin fits the prototype of the *bird* concept better than the other two. Similarly, a plain wooden chair with four legs fits the prototype of the chair concept, but we can also recognize rocking chairs and bean-bag chairs as chairs.

As the philosopher Wittgenstein (1953) pointed out, people use "family resemblances" to decide whether an object belongs to a certain category. We often see resemblances among family members, but they do not all resemble one another the same way. For example, you might have your father's eyes and your mother's nose, your sister might have your grandmother's hair, your brother might have your grandfather's walk. The more features a person shares with other family members, the easier it is for an observer to decide whether or not the person belongs to the family. But not all the members of the family—or category—share the same rigid set of features.

The notion of fuzzy sets clearly applies to the concept of the family. Thus, the standard definition of the family as a married couple and their children who live together is the prototype of the concept, at least in our culture. But other groups can be considered families if they share one or more of the features of the prototype. As with any other concept, however, the fewer features the group shares with the prototype, the harder it is to decide whether it fits the category of family and the less agreement there is among observers.

of families and "the family." The family has proved to be an elusive concept, in spite of our conviction that we know what families are all about. Trying to pin down the meaning of the term is not just an intellectual game. There is, as we shall see, genuine doubt among those who have thought about the matter just what it is that distinguishes families from nonfamilies and whether there is a single definition of family that applies to all times and places.

Definitions of the family have important consequences in people's lives. Government agencies, for example, often have to define what a family is in order to carry out their programs. These definitions often determine who benefits, and who fails to benefit, from such programs. Further, if only one particular pattern of family life is held out as the only normal and desirable form, people with different life-styles may be stigmatized as deviants (see box).

Conceptions of the Nuclear Family

There is a widespread belief, encouraged by popular writings on the family as well as by some scholars, that the nuclear family is universal, found in every known human society. Many people interpret this belief to mean that the family as we know it or would like it to be in our society occurs every-

FIGURE 3.1
Some Definitions
of the Family

fam·i·ly \ ˈfam-(ə)lē\ n, pl -lies [ME familie, fr. L familia household (including servants as well as kin of the householder), fr. famulus servant; perh. akin to Skt dhāman dwelling place] (15c) **1** : a group of individuals living under one roof and usu. under one head: HOUSEHOLD **2 a** : a group of persons of common ancestry: CLAN **b** : a people or group of peoples regarded as deriving from a common stock: RACE **3 a** : a group of people united by certain convictions or a common affiliation: FELLOWSHIP **b** : the staff of a high official (as the President) **4** : a group of things related by common characteristics: as **a** : a closely related series of elements or chemical compounds **b** : a group of soils that have similar profiles and include one or more series **c** : a group of related languages descended from a single ancestral language **5** : the basic unit in society having as its nucleus two or more adults living together and cooperating in the care and rearing of their own or adopted children **6 a** : a group of related plants or animals forming a category ranking above a genus and below an order and usu. comprising several to many genera **b** in livestock breeding (1) : the descendants or line of a particular individual esp. of some outstanding female (2) : an identifiable strain within a breed **7** : a set of curves or surfaces whose equations differ only in parameters **8** : a unit of a crime syndicate (as the Mafia) operating within a geographical area

Source: Webster's Ninth New Collegiate Dictionary. Copyright © 1986 by Merriam-Webster Inc., publisher of the Merriam-Webster® Dictionaries. Reprinted with permission.

where. Thus in every society we expect to find family groups with the following characteristics: a man and woman and their children, recognized as distinct social units set apart from other such units, who share a living space, and who are bound to one another by affection.

This view of the family as a universal social institution was first stated by the pioneer anthropologist Bronislaw Malinowski. In 1913, Malinowski published his book *The Family Among the Australian Aborigines*, which refuted the idea that primitive peoples were incapable of having families. Nineteenth-century scholars believed that primates were sexually promiscuous and had not yet "evolved" far enough to have families. Malinowski showed that the Australian aborigines had rules about who might have sex with whom even during orgies and that they also distinguished between marriage and casual sexual relationships.

At the heart of Malinowski's argument was the contention that the family had to be universal because it filled a universal human need—the nurturing of infants and young children. Pointing out that human infants need care and protection for a longer time than even the highest apes, he concluded that

no culture could endure in which the act of reproduction, that is mating, pregnancy, and childbirth, was not linked up with the fact of legally-founded parenthood, that is, a relationship in which the father and mother have to look after the children for a long period, and in turn, derive certain benefits from the care and trouble taken. (Malinowski, 1944, p. 9)

A later and highly influential statement as to the universality of the nuclear family was made by Murdock in 1949:

The nuclear family is a universal social grouping. Whether as the sole prevailing form of the family or as the basic unit from which more complex familial forms are compounded, it exists as a distinct and strongly functional group in known society. (p. 2)

In addition, Murdock postulated the following characteristics of the family: common residence, economic cooperation, socially approved sexual relationships, reproduction, and childrearing.

Since Malinowski first asserted that the nuclear family is a cultural universal, an imperative found in all societies, anthropologists have been debating the statement. In general, even those who argued for the idea of a universal nuclear family were well aware that family life as a day-to-day reality was not the same everywhere. In many societies, for example, husbands and wives are not expected to be emotionally close to one another and may not even eat or sleep together.

Murdock actually argued that the nuclear family is one of three distinct family organizations found in human society. The other two are the *polygamous family*, formed by the marriage of one man to two or more women, or one woman to two or more men, and the *extended family*. The extended family forms when a married couple joins the parents of one of the spouses, and three generations live under one roof or close to each other. Murdock argued, however, that the nuclear families are still separate units in these complex forms of the family. Other scholars disagreed that these larger family organizations could be viewed as being made up of nuclear families; the nuclear families are not marked off in any special way (M. Levy, 1955).

More recently, some anthropologists have challenged the idea that the father defines the basic family unit and have argued that a mother and her children form the basic family. However, these anthropologists often ascribe the other features of the universal family to the mother–child unit (Collier, Rosaldo, & Yanagisako, 1982).

Although it is possible for an outside observer to find mother–child units and married couples plus their children, it is not clear that these groups have the same meaning in other societies that they do for us. For example, many languages do not have a separate word to identify what we would call a family. The Zinacantecos of southern Mexico identify the basic social unit as a "house," which may include from one to twenty people (Vogt, 1969). In fact, this notion is not so far from our own cultural tradition. One of the earlier meanings of the word *family*, which is still listed in our larger dictionaries, is a group of persons who form a household, including parents, children, servants, and others.

Families in other cultures vary in other ways from the pattern identified by Malinowski and Murdock. In many societies, husbands, wives, and children do not live together under the same roof. Nor do family members necessarily have affectionate bonds with each other. In some cultures in which people retain strong ties to their kin groups all their lives, close bonds between husbands and wives may be seen as a threat to kinship loyalties and are frowned on if they occur.

The emphasis on the universal nuclear family has taken attention away from the fascinating variety of ways people have arranged their family lives. It is true that the basic biological facts of family life are universal and that family members have strong feelings about one another. The variation in the ways families think and feel and act, however, is no less significant than any resemblances we might find.

David Schneider and Raymond Smith (Schneider, 1968; Schneider & Smith, 1973) have tried to clarify the confusion surrounding the concept of the nuclear family by pointing to three different ways of talking about it. It is necessary to distinguish the nuclear family as a *cultural symbol*, as a *set of norms or roles*, and as a *residential or domestic unit*.

The Family as a Cultural Symbol

The nuclear family as a cultural symbol is deeply rooted in Western culture. The nuclear family is what people in these cultures mean by the term *family*. It is represented in images of the Holy Family, in family photographs, and in mass-media depictions of family life. Thus, for family textbook writers, many social scientists, and the American public, "the family" is a married couple and their children. Society seems to be divided into nuclear-family groups, each living in a home of its own. Any deviation from the parent–child unit living together is not quite a family and needs explanation. It may be a broken home or some other variation from the expected pattern.

One of the striking features of the way Americans think about the family, Schneider (1968) noted, is the emphasis on the family as natural. The underlying image of the family is of a man and a woman united in physical love, whose children are seen as the "flesh and blood" of both parents.

Other cultures define the family differently. The traditional Chinese family, for example, is defined as a long line of fathers and sons, including remote ancestors and unborn descendants. A man remains a member of his family throughout his life. "He is identified with the family from birth, and every action concerning him, up to and including his death, is in the context of that group" (Wolf, 1972, p. 32). Women provide the links in the male chain of descent, but they are not included in anyone's genealogy. A woman is not a member of her husband's family, and although she is a temporary member of her father's household, she is not a member of his family either.

The Nuclear Family as a Normative System

Although all Americans share the cultural symbolism of the nuclear family described above, there is great variation in how different segments of the population define their obligations to various family members. Schneider and Smith (1973) distinguished between two broad codes of family conduct: a middle-class one in which the husband and wife are the "solid core around which the whole system revolves" and a working-class, ethnic, or black pattern with an emphasis on help, cooperation, and solidarity with a network of kin, centering around a parent and his or her grown children.

The book and the movie *The Godfather* portray one version of the kin network and the rich, extended-family culture of Italian-Americans. Although the film perpetuates the myth that Italians have a special propensity toward crime, it presents a fairly accurate picture of this family culture (Gambino, 1975).

More often, however, kin networks in American families are focused on the mother. Although much has been written about the "matriarchal" black family, working-class white families often have an equally strong emphasis on ties between mothers and grown children, even where there are few female-headed households. The same is true of English working-class families. Thus one English mother of five reported to an interviewer: "I couldn't get on without me mother. I could get on without me husband—I don't notice him" (Kerr, 1958, p. 40).

These descriptions, it should be noted, are greatly oversimplified. Not all working-class or ethnic families follow the pattern ascribed to them, nor do all middle-class families follow the middle-class style. The obligations and attitudes of a son toward his mother, for example, may vary with the kind of work he does, how old he is, the region of the country they live in, the particular ethnic group they belong to, as well as personal and familial idiosyncrasies. Further, at the high end of the socioeconomic scale, upper-class families often emphasize the continuity of generation and have less emphasis on the independent nuclear family. Finally, people's beliefs about their kin obligations do not necessarily predict their behavior, a problem we shall examine in more detail in the next chapter.

The difficulties of describing American family life in terms of one or even two typical patterns is illustrated by the work of John Spiegel. Spiegel and his associates decided to learn as much as they could about the structure and function of family life in the United States, in order to define "the normal American family." Spiegel (1971) described a remarkable search for "the family" amid the welter of real families in their varied day-to-day existence. Instead he found "the most astonishing variance in their structure and function" (p. 144). It was difficult, for example, to know where to draw the boundaries around the family. Some families seemed to extend laterally—that is, to include such relatives as aunts, uncles, and cousins—whereas others extended vertically to include grandparents and great-grandparents.

The complexities reached into the very heart of the nuclear unit itself—the relations between husbands and wives and between parents and children. Spiegel (1971) wrote:

Not only were various and differing functions assigned to the family in different social milieus, but even those functions which were apparently

Sharecropper's home, Hale County, Alabama, 1936. [Walker Evans/Reproduced from the Collections of the Library of Congress]

universal, such as the socialization of children, the satisfaction of sexual needs, or the biological and material maintenance of the members of the family, were carried out in such various ways with such differing implications that it proved impossible to obtain meaningful patterns without reference to the surrounding social system. (p. 144)

But the complications did not end there. Beyond the occupational structure, Spiegel wrote, was another level of human behavior: the level of cultural and subcultural values. Middle-class families in the United States, for example, emphasize planning for the future, hard work, and individual initiative.

The United States, however, has a mixed cultural heritage that complicates the picture. Each ethnic group seems to relate to the dominant value system in its own way.

Misunderstandings can arise between people who grow up in different kinship patterns. Some of Birdwhistell's (1966) Kentucky subjects, for example, who lived in extended families, had very different conceptions and definitions of family from their friends, neighbors, and even spouses who had grown up in more nuclear or, as Birdwhistell calls them, segmented families. The interdependent or extended-family members seemed to define family in terms of blood kinship. They expected to continue all their lives the intense involvement with kinfolk they had known as children. They would not expect this involvement to be affected by reaching maturity, marrying, or work. In fact, the main purpose of Birdwhistell's research was to learn why some rural Kentuckians would migrate to other areas of the country and try to be "successful," while others who seemed much like them would remain behind in their hometowns. He believes he found the explanation in the different family patterns of the movers and nonmovers.

The family in the extended-family pattern is a very different entity from the series of separate units in space and time that make up the nuclear family. The traditional family is continuous in space and time, unbounded by household walls, and immortal. Marriage, birth, maturity, even death do not reduce the central unit. The genetic family tree defines not only genetic connections but ongoing obligations and involvements. Rather than the marriage of grown children leaving behind an empty nest, the in-law line may add additional family members:

If the marriage is, in family terms, a good one, the affinal relatives/in-laws of the family member become one's own "almost like family." And as these affinal relatives meet at funeral, church, and family gatherings, they gain kinship status and are called by kinship terms. (Birdwhistell, 1966, p. 209)

Yet Birdwhistell's interviewees did not perceive the unique quality of their family life. When asked directly about their family relationships, the interdependent family people talked in the stereotyped terms and imagery of the nuclear-family model. It was as if the nuclear-family imagery had blotted out the experiences of those who had a very different life-style from the standard husband–wife, parent–child unit. And if there was any awareness of being different, it was stated with a sense of shame.

People who hold to one of the foregoing family patterns are likely to see people in the other family model as not quite healthy or normal psychologically. For example, Birdwhistell (1966) notes that his nuclear-family subjects tended to define people with extended-family ties as immature, dependent, and lacking in ambition. The traditional people, on the other hand, were likely to feel that people with the nuclear-family emphasis were cold, selfish, and too driven by ambition.

The Nuclear Family as a Domestic Group

So far we have discussed two ways of talking about the nuclear family. The first deals with the nuclear family as a cultural symbol—a set of images and definitions of what the family is. Second, we discussed the nuclear family as a normative system, a code of conduct concerning how particular family members should act toward one another, what obligations they have to each other, and so on. We contrasted two different patterns of family norms: one was a middle-class pattern centered on the husband–

wife–children unit, with grown children emotionally and economically independent of their parents; the other pattern—generally found among working- or lower-class, ethnic, or black families—emphasizes ties between extended-family members, especially between grown children and their own parents, particularly the mother, and places less emphasis on the husband–wife bond. The issue that concerns us here is the third way of talking about the nuclear family—the nuclear family as a household unit.

House, home, and family One of the main assumptions in the middle-class definition of family is that a family lives together in a home. The terms *home* and *family* are used almost interchangeably; we know, of course, that in reality some families do not live together and some people live together who are not families.

Until recently most social scientists also tended to assume that home and family were equivalent. Common residence was one of the defining attributes of the family. Households were thought of as containers or shells for family members, not as something to be considered separately.

Including the notion of households as part of the definition of the family, however, has created many problems. For one thing, home and family are logically different, as Bohannan (1963) has pointed out. Family has to do with kinship relations, whereas home is a place, a spatial concept. Bohannan argues that households or homes perform the functions usually ascribed to the family—they provide food and shelter and raise children. The distinction between household and family must be made because in many societies around the world families do not usually form households, and households may not be composed of families. Nuclear-family members often do live together, but it is also very common for husbands and wives

and even for children not to live together under the same roof. Thus situations regarded as unfortunate, if not unusual, in our society turn out to be regarded as the usual and normal way of living in many other societies.

The confusion between households and families has sometimes made it difficult to understand how the family in the past differed from today's families. Studies have shown that for the past 400 years in England, most households have consisted of nuclear families, not large groups of kin (P. Laslett & Wall, 1972). The meaning of this finding is unclear, however. Household composition may not reflect obligations, emotional ties, or the exchange of money, goods, and services. Parents, for example, may *expect* to live with their married children, but if the children marry late and the parents die relatively young, the extended-family household may exist for only a short time in the life cycle (Berkner, 1972).

Schneider and Smith (1973) observe that even though the lower-class or ethnic family pattern does not emphasize the nuclear family, most households consist of the nuclear-family unit. In these families, however, household boundaries do not define who is considered "close family." Often it is hard to tell which household a given individual belongs to at any particular time.

The composition of lower-class households can be more diverse without being considered unusual, there can be more coming and going on the part of those who live together, and ties maintained across household boundaries may be as intense as those between persons who live together. (p. 53)

Although Schneider and Smith, among others, argue that there is nothing inherently abnormal or disorganized in the family patterns of the poor and working classes,

This household consists of a mother, her four natural children and one adopted child, and a housekeeper who is considered "a member of the family." The father lives up the street, and the children spend several nights a week at his house. Both parents are physicians. [Helen Nestor]

and that the differences between them and middle-class families should not be interpreted as deviations from a "normal" standard, much family research has been conducted using American middle-class patterns as the norm.

Variations in Residence Patterns

We have seen that in other cultures it may not be the custom for nuclear-family members to live together. Recently, American society has had its own version of separate living in the form of "commuter couples"—husbands and wives who have jobs in different cities. Of course, there have always been couples where the husband's work took him away from home—as in the case of sailors and military men. What is

novel in the present situation is the fact that it is the work of both spouses that keeps them apart. For most couples, living apart is not a permanent way of life, as it is in other cultures (Kirschner & Walum, 1978). When nuclear-family members live apart, most often it is the father-husband who lives apart from the rest of the family. Among some peoples—the Iroquois, for example—households consisted of mothers and daughters and daughters' children, while the men engaged in hunting or warfare. In some societies, adult men may live in men's houses, apart from their wives and children; and sometimes all-male households consist of brothers.

In most of these male living situations, the father lives nearby his wife or wives and their children and visits fairly often. Such an arrangement would be considered "common residence" by many anthropologists. But Stephens (1963) raised this question: how close must the father be in order to be counted as living with a wife and children? Fifty feet? A mile? Perhaps the extreme of distance is that found among a people in Kenya, where the mother–child households are located on widely separated farms. Among the Navaho also, a man may marry unrelated women who live at considerable distances from one another (Bender, 1967).

Another question can be raised: how often must a father visit, and how long must he stay, in order to be considered part of the household? Or, to put it another way, how long must he be gone in order not to be counted as a member of the household? Sometimes work or warfare take the father-husband away for years at a time. Is he then to be considered as "living with" his wife and children? It is also unclear whether the father should be counted in the household if his job requires him to live away from the rest of the family and maintain a separate residence.

Besides those instances when the father lives apart from the rest of the family, there are many cases of children normally living separate from their parents. The Israeli communes (kibbutzim) are probably the best-known example. But in societies in which the mother–child household prevails, boys usually move away from home at or before the onset of sexual maturation. The boys may merely sleep out and eat at home or move to the village of another relative (Stephens, 1963).

Even younger children sometimes live away from home. Among the Ibo, boys of 5 or 6 leave their mothers' houses and live with boys their age from the same compound (Bender, 1967). Samoan children wander around from one relative's household to another, choosing where they will stay and for how long (M. Mead, 1928). Closer to home, in Europe and America in past centuries it was a common practice for children past the age of 7 or so to leave home to become apprentices or servants in other households (Demos, 1970). And, of course, 7-year-old boys in upper-class British families are to this day sent off to boarding schools.

Finally, there are instances in which infants do not live at home. During most of European history, when of course there were no feeding bottles, many babies were sent off to wet nurses or to baby farms to be nursed; they returned home, if they survived, after weaning, during the second or third year. Stephens notes two societies in which infants leave home after weaning; among these two African peoples, the Hehe and the Thonga, the grandmother typically takes the child to her home after it has been weaned and returns it to its parents several years later (Stephens, 1963).

Nonkin in the home Another reason for analyzing family and household separately—besides the *absence* of nuclear-family members—is that the household can also *include* people who are not members of the immediate family. The idea of outsiders living in the family is alien to most contemporary Americans. Even such relatives as in-laws tend to be defined as outsiders. It is taken for granted that households should consist only of husband, wife, and their minor children. Recent census data reveal an increasing tendency for unmarried adults of all ages to live alone. As Margaret Mead (1949) described some time ago:

The belief that every family should have a home of its own seems like a truism to which almost every American would assent without further thought. . . . Furthermore, each family should consist only of a husband, wife, and their minor children. All other forms of living are seen as having great disadvantages. (p. 300)

The feeling that the nuclear family should occupy its own home without outsiders appears to be relatively recent, historically speaking. According to Peter Laslett, one of the major features of the Western European family over the past several centuries has been the presence of servants in the household. Until the early 1900s, for example, servants were the largest single occupational group in England. Four-fifths of all young people would have the experience of either growing up with or being servants—the vast majority, of course, were the latter.

Households of European peasant and craftsmen families in the distant and recent past commonly contained servants, apprentices, and lodgers. Servants, usually young people employed by the family with whom they lived, shared the family's food and shelter as part of their wages. They were not a distinct social class; being a servant for several years during one's youth could be part of the experience of the most respectable and well-off families (Berkner, 1972). Laslett labels these as "life-cycle servants," to distinguish them from people who would be servants all their lives (1977).

Lodgers typically worked outside the family with whom they lived. In peasant households these servants and lodgers were considered part of the family rather than "employees" or "tenants."

The legal definition of the household was very precise in Austria; it meant all the people living in the same house under the authority of the head of the household, whether or not they were members of the family. Moreover, as Otto Brunner has pointed out in his marvelous essay on the concept of the household in European history, *the word "family" was not commonly used in German until the eighteenth century—before that people spoke of belonging to a house or a household.* (Berkner, 1972, p. 411, italics added)

In preindustrial England the households of craftsmen also included more than the immediate or nuclear family. In the year 1619 the bakers of London described a typical bakery and its expenses. The bakery was a household as well as a workshop; it contained thirteen or fourteen people, including the baker and his wife and children, plus paid employees, apprentices, and servants. This group too was called a family.

The only word used at that time to describe such a group of people was "family." The man at the head of the group, the entrepreneur, or the manager, was then known as the master or the head of the family. He was father to some of its members and in place of father to the rest. There was no sharp distinction between his domestic and his economic functions. His wife was both his partner and his subordinate. (P. Laslett, 1965, p. 2)

The key to the size of the household in preindustrial times was economic need. Homes were workplaces. When the farm or the craft needed and could support more hands, the household group expanded. In hard times, it contracted.

In America, also—well into the twentieth century, in fact—servants, boarders, and lodgers were found in a sizable proportion of families at some point in their lives. Although taking in boarders was more common among poorer families, the practice could be found among the affluent also. Young people in transition to adulthood could live as boarders in the homes of families whose children had moved out, and old people could remain in their own homes without being isolated. Historian Tamara Hareven (1982) has argued that the most important change in American family life has not been the decline of the extended family but rather the virtual disappearance of the practice of taking strangers into the home. Because of this change, the family has lost some of the flexibility and adaptability it once had.

The decline of boarding seems to have been associated with the rise during the twentieth century of a belief that the household should contain only the nuclear-family group, and the practical condition that enabled this value to be acted upon—the availability of private homes and apartments and the widespread ability to pay for them. Sociologist Barbara Laslett (1973) has argued that family privacy, in principle and practice, distinguishes the modern nuclear family from its counterpart in the past.

A house is not a home Recently some of the same problems that plagued the concept of the family have been raised with regard to the household. Consider, for example, the situation of a group of college students who share an apartment or a house, but have all their meals out and send all their dirty clothes to the laundry. Should this group be called a household? Or consider this situation: among the Ashanti, an African people, husbands and wives do not live together (Bender, 1967). Each partner lives with his or her relatives on the mother's side. The wife, however, prepares meals for the husband and children, and the husband provides his wife and children with clothes. The nuclear family doesn't form a household, yet they seem to be involved in household activities in a way that the college roommates are not. Then there is the situation in which households carry on domestic functions but are not composed of families. The arrangement of the two divorced men on the *Odd Couple* television show illustrates this kind of household.

In order to deal with distinctions like these, Bender (1967) has suggested that we ought to distinguish between "coresidence"

—the roommate or dormitory situation— and "domestic" functions or activities, which have to do with the basic day-to-day necessities and trivia of living—the provision and preparation of food, the cleaning and mending of clothing, and the care of children:

One is dealing, then, not with two distinct social phenomena—families and households—but with three distinct social phenomena: families, coresidential groups, and domestic functions. All three frequently correspond, both ideally and in fact (this is reflected in at least one meaning of our folk term "home," which implies a family residing together functioning as a domestic unit). The three also can and sometimes do vary independently. (p. 495)

In sum, then, Bender proposes that the term *family* be reserved for kinship relations. Family members may or may not live together and may or may not engage in domestic relations. People can live together and carry on domestic functions without being families. Or people can simply live together without sharing in domestic activities.

In modern societies, of course, domestic functions need not be performed by the family. Indeed, this is one of the most important features that set off modern societies from traditional or preindustrial ones. P. Laslett (1965), for example, describes how institutional life in preindustrial England was almost unknown; most people spent all of their days in small familial groups: "There were no hotels, hostels, or blocks of flats for single persons, and very few hospitals and none of the kind we are familiar with, almost no young men and women living on their own" (p. 11).

The concept of domesticity, however, seems to capture an important part of the essence of what we mean by family, and it is useful to distinguish it from kinship on one side and living under one roof on the other. Domesticity involves both intimacy and trivia. Sharing meals, for example, appears to represent a higher degree of intimacy—of communion—than merely living together under the same roof. Berkner (1972) notes that servants in peasant households usually ate with the family, out of the same pot. Later, when the relation between master and servant became less patriarchal and more like that of boss and worker, the practice of eating together stopped (p. 412).

Finally, the concept of "home" as a place of intimacy, comfort, and privacy for the members of a family is a relatively modern notion. It emerged with the rise of the rich commercial middle class in early modern Europe. Comfortable homes became a reality for ordinary families only in the late nineteenth and early twentieth centuries, with the invention of household machines and use of electricity (Rybczynski, 1986).

THE MEANING OF KINSHIP

Perhaps at this point the reader is bothered by all this scholarly nit-picking about the definition of the family and household. Surely the family and kinship are based on the solid bedrock of biology: parenthood and sexual intercourse! But the social facts of family life often violate the biological facts in various ways. In some societies, for example, it is necessary to distinguish between the *genitor*—the biological father—and the *pater*—the man who plays the father role. Thus, among the Tallensi, an African society, any child a woman bears belongs to her husband's descent group. Even though he knows he is not the biological father of the child, the husband is said to experience all the emotions of true fatherhood, while the *genitor* is said to feel no fatherly emotions at all (Zelditch, 1964, p. 465).

Kin relations also violate biology through fictional relationships, such as adoption and godparenting. Such relationships are common in many societies, although only recently have they been studied to any great extent. Two kinds of fictional relationships occur. In one kind the fictionalization is so complete that everybody involved "forgets" the relationship isn't real. An orphan, for example, might join the household of a relative, treat its members as parents and siblings, and be treated as a "real" child. The other kind of fictional kinship maintains the distinction between fictional and real, as in the godparent relation, which was widespread in Mediterranean Europe and Latin America. Such fictional relations may tell us more about the true nature of kinship than those instances in which the biological facts and the social facts coincide.

David Schneider (1968), for example, has argued that kinship has as much to do with real biological facts as supernatural beliefs have to do with the real nature of ghosts and spirits. Both kinship and religion, he argues, are systems of cultural beliefs that originate in people's heads, rather than in some reality out there.

To be sure, there are biological facts, but kinship systems make use of these facts in various symbolic ways. The biological relationships involved in kinship and marriage

represent something other than what they are. . . . They represent diffuse, enduring solidarity. They symbolize those kinds of interpersonal relations which human beings as biological beings must have if they are to be born and grow up. They symbolize trust . . . they stand for the fact that birth survives death, and that solidarity is enduring. (p. 116)

Schneider does not suggest that actual family life is characterized by perfect love, trust, and solidarity, only that the family *symbolizes* these ideal qualities. The symbolic meaning of kinship, for example, is shown when people in social movements call them-

Households, particularly among the poor and minority groups, are often quite diverse. [Dick Swartz/ Office of Human Development Services]

selves brothers and sisters, and people in communes call themselves "families."

THE POLITICS OF FAMILY DEFINITIONS

Much research in the social sciences, especially that about the family, is guided by concern with social problems of one kind or another. What one defines as a problem, however, depends greatly on what one defines as normal and what as problematic. The definition of the normal family as a married couple with their children residing together leads to conceiving of any variation as a social problem—for example, common-law unions, husband and wife living apart, illegitimacy, homosexual unions, bachelorhood, spinsterhood, and even childlessness (Ball, 1972). In the same way, definitions of age and sex roles dictate what is to be defined as normal and what as problematic. The family literature is full of concern about such "problems" as broken homes, working mothers, illegitimacy, dominant wives, weak fathers and husbands, and children being given too much or too little love, independence, or discipline. Many of these problems derive from what are essentially political assumptions about how people should live.

Definitions of the family, as we mentioned earlier, have important consequences in people's lives, and government agencies must define what a family is, to carry out programs and policies. For example, in 1977, the Supreme Court was called on to decide two definitions of the family. Mrs. Inez Moore shared her "single-family home" in East Cleveland with her son and his son, and a second grandson whose mother had died. The problem was that a zoning ordinance allowed only one family for each house. It defined "family" to mean a head of household, a spouse, only one of the couple's parents, the couples' unmarried children, and the minor children of only one of the children. Mrs. Moore was given a 5-day jail sentence and a $25 fine because she had taken in the children of *two* of her children. After 4 years of litigation, a slender majority of the court—5 to 4—struck down the law as hostile to the family itself.

The difficulties of defining the family were dramatically illustrated by the controversies that arose over the planning of a White House conference on the family. As a Democratic presidential candidate in 1976, Jimmy Carter made the family a public issue and proposed convening a White House conference on the American family shortly after becoming president. However, the administration was unable to stage the conference throughout almost all 4 years of Carter's term (Steiner, 1981). In the end, during the summer of 1980, three regional conferences were held, far away from the White House.

One of the major problems plaguing the conference planners was how to define the family. On one side were conservatives and family traditionalists who defined the family as the stereotypic nuclear family—breadwinner husband, housewife, children—and on the other side were liberals, feminists, blacks, and other minority group members who saw strong families as possible in forms other than the traditional family. The conference planners were never able to resolve the differences between those who saw only one kind of family as "the family" and those who emphasized diversity and pluralism in family life.

The planners also vacillated about their own position. On the one hand, 6 weeks after Carter's inauguration, the conference became a conference on families, rather than a conference on "the family." The president and conference planners said they wanted to give clear recognition to the pluralism of family life in America. On the other hand, being divorced turned out to be enough of a deviation from the stereotypical family pattern to disqualify a person from serving in a high-level position on the conference staff. When conservatives protested against the appointment of a divorced mother of three as executive director, the government planners gave in. The woman, who also happened to be black, was asked to accept a co-director who was white, male, married, and Catholic. She resigned from the conference staff.

The problem of defining the family reveals in a vivid way the deep divisions within American society about what families are, what problems they face, and what the goals of public policies should be. To conservatives, the diversity of family patterns is evidence that something is wrong with family life in America, and the goal of public policies should be to somehow make families conform to the traditional ideal. To liberals, how well a family functions does not depend on its form, and government policies should be sensitive to the needs of different kinds of families. Everyone is for "the family," but consensus dissolves when specific social policies are proposed.

There may indeed be much that is problematic about atypical family situations. But the assumption that the heart of the difficulty lies in deviations from the usual family forms and norms obscures what the real problem might be. Rodman (1965) discusses the prevailing assumptions concerning family problems as follows:

Are interfaith marriages the problem or is it organized religion and its demands that is the problem? Are "illegitimacy," "desertion" and "common law" unions problems of the lower class, or are they solutions of the lower class to more basic problems? (p. 450)

Similarly, we can ask whether some of the current "problems" of the family, such as single-parent families or working mothers, are inherent in those kinds of families or stem from difficulties such families must face because of inflexible work schedules, the lack of child-care programs, and inadequate incomes.

The Rise and Fall of the Legitimacy Principle

The issue of illegitimacy provides a particularly useful instance of the way value judgments enter into social-science concepts and methodology. At first glance illegitimacy would seem to be an easy concept to define and measure. A child is either legitimate or not at birth, and the fact enters into the birth records. Most people define a child as illegitimate at birth if its mother is unmarried,

as do the public agencies who calculate illegitimacy rates. Actually, however, illegitimacy can come about in other ways. For example, the mother may be married to one man, but have a child by another. Or the mother may be separated or divorced at the time of birth. A child is also illegitimate if the parents live together as a stable couple but are not married. Some researchers have argued that illegitimacy statistics are not as "hard" and accurate as they are generally supposed to be. Teele and Schmidt (1970, p. 144), for example, argue that official statistics tend to underreport illegitimate births to white women and to married women, and thus to overestimate the degree to which illegitimate births occur among blacks and the unmarried. They also questioned the practice of labeling children as illegitimate. Philip Hauser (1970), himself a demographer, argued that demographers and statisticians use "inherited and probably inaccurate conceptual frameworks." He stated:

I think it is important to remember that the standards we employ are based on our own categories of legitimate and illegitimate births. According to our standards, half the population in Latin America is illegitimate, and all of the population with whom I lived for two years in Burma is illegitimate and I'm not sure what that means. (p. 148)

What *does* "illegitimacy" mean? Is it a social problem, and if so, why? Is illegitimacy itself the problem, striking at the very basis of the social order and jeopardizing the "continuity of society"? Or is illegitimacy only a symptom of other social problems, such as poverty and discrimination? Or is the problem of illegitimacy located in those who label children as illegitimate in order to "punish" unwed mothers and their children?

For many years, a so-called principle of legitimacy, set forth by Malinowski (1930), was considered to be a universal social law. The principle states that in every society a child must have a socially recognized father to give the child a status in the community. The principle naturally leads to the assumption that illegitimacy is a sign of social breakdown.

Over the years, sociologists and anthropologists built an extensive literature trying to show that the numerous exceptions to Malinowski's law were only apparent and not real. There has been, for example, a debate concerning woman-headed households, particularly in the countries in the Caribbean. In these areas, illegitimate births are as high as 70 to 80 percent of total births. On one side of the argument, the proponents of the universal nuclear family and the principle of legitimacy argue that these woman-headed or matriarchal households are abnormal, incomplete, or disorganized forms of the family. Further, the argument goes, the people who live in such arrangements think so too because they value the nuclear family as an ideal in spite of their inability to live up to it.

Although the principle of legitimacy had been treated by many social scientists almost as a law of nature, the argument has been overtaken by changing social realities. Illegitimacy has become increasingly irrelevant as a social status. Far from a law of nature, the principle in fact is based on certain prior assumptions about society (Blake, 1979; W. J. Goode, 1964). Chiefly, it assumes that children inherit their economic and social status from their fathers. In modern democratic societies, a person's place in society in theory, at any rate, is supposed to be based on achievement. A child's future is not supposed to be determined solely by who its father happens to be or the circumstances of its birth.

In recent years, legal systems around the world have been systematically doing away with the distinctions between children born inside and outside of legal marriage (Glendon, 1977). Further, the significance of traditional forms of wealth and property has diminished as a new kind of property has arisen in the form of benefits and entitlements from private employers and the state—not only salaries, but health insurance, pensions, Social Security, and so on (Reich, 1964). Finally, the social norms surrounding illegitimacy have changed drastically. Women's magazines feature articles on the hows and whys of motherhood, and a *Time* magazine poll carried out in 1978 found that 74 percent of Americans found it acceptable for a single woman to have and raise a child (cited in Clark & Martire, 1979).

The rise and fall of the illegitimacy principle illustrates once again the besetting danger of family studies: imposing one's own customs and categories on other peoples' experience. As one anthropologist put it, in arguing against the legitimacy principle, the first job of science is, after all, to study what *is*, not what might be or could be (Adams, 1968, p. 67). Rather than assume at the outset that a given family form is pathological, we should assume that any variations we find are equally viable alternatives, at least until the contrary is demonstrated. In addition, the meaning of the family varies from one historical period to another, from one culture to another, and among different social groups within the same culture.

SUMMARY

The most familiar subjects are often the most difficult to study because we take them for granted. This statement is especially true of the family. In America the nuclear family—two parents and their minor children—in a home of their own is defined as *the family*. Variations from this pattern have usually been seen as unfortunate and abnormal.

It also has been widely believed that the middle-class American family pattern is universal.

When we look at family life in other societies, however, at our own historical past, or at different ethnic groups and social classes in America, we find that variations in family form and living arrangements are rather common. Nuclear-family members are often found living apart. The household may contain nonkin living together as a family. Households themselves may only be places where people sleep, whereas eating, child care, and other domestic functions occur elsewhere.

In recent years, family scholars have paid increasing attention to the diversity and complexity of family life. In contrast to such family scholarship in the past, there is now less of an insistence on the notion that the family is a universal social institution or that variations from the nuclear family must be unworkable or pathological. The family remains a difficult subject to study, but that fact does not mean it is impossible to do so. Natural phenomena, such as cells and atoms, are complex and elusive, and the conclusions scientists reach about them are more tentative than nonscientists realize.

CHAPTER 4

Theory, the Ideal, and Reality in Family and Society

The family we discuss in lectures . . . —the family with its functions, its roles, its kinship and networks—often appears to be remote from the family we experience outside the lecture room or even the family we experience through the novel, through the drama and through the cinema.

D. H. Morgan
Social Theory and the Family

How many people, surrounded by their real rather than their imaginary relatives, have ever experienced a Norman Rockwell Thanksgiving?

Michael Arlen

HUMAN NATURE, SOCIETY, AND THE FAMILY

Every theory of the family implies a set of assumptions about human nature and society. Many people, for example, would agree with such statements as the following: the family is the basic unit of society; a civilization cannot "survive" if its family system does not work well; it is "natural" or "instinctive" for people to form families. Thus the family seems to represent both social necessity and individual desires.

This duality has led one writer to describe the family as "a slippery concept":

It is slippery not only in definition, but also in focus. It is rare to complete an article or book whose title indicates it is about the family without finding the discussion sliding away from the family either to the individual or to the society, or even both. (Troll, 1969, p. 22)

The family is a slippery concept in part because it can be discussed in terms of individuals, families, and societies. Although family scholars have argued for decades about how to define the family and other matters, all would agree with the following three statements: First, in every known society

family groups, in one form or another, are an observable part of social reality; second, family relations have a highly charged emotional meaning for individuals; third, the family, in one or several of its various forms, is a key institution in the society as a whole.

Yet social scientists have had difficulty in going beyond these observations to the construction of a strong theory of the family. As one sociologist confessed, "I am . . . not sure what a 'theory of the family' would look like even if it were to be developed" (Morgan, 1975, p. 7). There are theories about particular aspects of the family, such as kinship or the socialization of children. There are also a number of theoretical perspectives on the family, such as *exchange theory, social role theory,* and *systems theory.* These suggest models or metaphors that help organize findings about the family and show relations among them (see box). But none of these integrates or explains the three observations stated earlier. To do so, a theory would have to be at once a sociological theory of society, a social psychology of groups, and a psychological theory of the individual—a tall order indeed.

Functionalism and the Family

One theorist did propose such a comprehensive theory. Talcott Parsons's *functionalist approach* was, until the 1970s, the dominant theory of family (Parsons, 1964; Parsons & Bales, 1956). Parsons and his followers tried to bring together the various aspects of the family—the relations between the family and the larger society, relations between men and women and between parents and children, and the development of the child. Parsons's theory provided the framework in which the family was, and often still is, analyzed. Although in many ways his view of the family has been dis-

Theories and Perspectives

Facts have little meaning outside some theory or framework of interpretation. A "good" theory should explain and predict a great deal using a few simple principles. With three simple principles Newton was able to explain the tides, the movements of the planets, and falling apples. Theories of human behavior can never be as abstract and general as theories that explain the movement of physical bodies. Rather, the social sciences offer contrasting frameworks of interpretation.

Family scholars use several different theoretical approaches. Each represents a different way of looking at families, societies, and individuals.

1. *The structural-functional approach.* In this framework, the family is viewed as part of the larger social structure. The theory emphasizes the functions the family serves for the maintenance of the social order and for the survival and well-being of individuals. This approach is also called *functional theory* or *functionalism.*

2. *The social conflict approach.* While functional theory focuses on harmony and stability, conflict theory assumes conflict and change are normal features of social life. The interests of families and the wider society are not necessarily harmonious, nor do the interests of family members necessarily coincide. The family contains two kinds of power imbalances—those based on gender and those based on age. Thus, the husband's experience of the family is not the same as the wife's, and the parents' view is not necessarily the same as the children's.

3. *Symbolic interaction theory.* Social scientists who take this approach argue that families, or any other aspects of social life, cannot be understood as abstractions. Social reality, they insist, is to be found in the behavior of particular people interacting in particular social settings. Further, the observer cannot understand a particular situation unless he or she understands what it means to the individuals involved. Symbolic interactionists stress that we interact as selves in relation to other selves.

4. *Social exchange theory.* This approach is based on the idea that people generally try to balance the costs and benefits of any particular course of action. People in relationships exchange benefits and stay in relationships only as long as cost–benefit ratio is satisfactory and fair. Social exchange theory emphasizes the resources each person brings to the relationship, such as money, social status, attractiveness, or personality. Social exchange theory predicts that people whose resources balance one another are more likely to marry than others and that, when they occur, imbalanced relationships are likely to be more uncomfortable and unstable.

credited, the language and concepts of functionalism seem to be almost unavoidable in discussions of the family.

Parsons's theory was in part an answer to an earlier generation of critics who argued that in urban industrial societies the family had "lost its functions" and was declining.

Parsons countered that the modern family was a streamlined, more highly evolved, and specialized version of the family. Far from having lost its importance, the modern family was more important than ever. Independent of kinship groups, and with work, education, and health care carried on by other

In portraits, families often present idealized images of themselves. [Michael Hayman/ Photo Researchers, Inc.]

specialized institutions, the family had become stripped down to two vital functions: childrearing and providing emotional support to adults.

No single theory replaced Parsons's; his approach to the family was undermined by the social changes of the 1960s and 1970s as well as by the criticism of other sociologists. Parsons had assumed that the ideal middle-class family of the 1950s represented a universal, necessary social institution. He assumed that it fulfilled the needs of both the individuals in it and the larger society. The theory emphasized stability rather than change, harmony rather than conflict, function rather than dysfunction.

The upheavals of the past 2 decades, especially the changes in women's roles, made many of Parsons's assumptions obsolete. For example, he had assumed that highly contrasting gender roles within the family were essential; society required that men be "instrumental" and women "expressive." That is, the man is to be the breadwinner, the manager, and leader of the family. The wife-mother is to take care of the emotional well-being of the family and provide nurture and comfort.

Further, Parsons's general theory was attacked by numerous critics and no longer dominates the field of sociology. Now that the dust of battle has settled, however, it is useful to examine the merits both of the functional approach to the family and the views of its critics. Parsons's theory, despite its limitations, remains a useful framework for understanding the family.

Functionalist models   If we were to examine the body of an animal, we could assume that any organ we found would play some vital role in keeping the animal alive. In the same way a functional analyst assumes that social customs or institutions persist because they serve a necessary social function, some ongoing usefulness to the society as a whole. Further, a living organism tends to be in a state of dynamic equilibrium or homeostasis: for example, a warm-blooded animal maintains a constant body temperature in spite of changes in the surrounding temperature. The Parsonian functionalist sees society as also maintaining such a dynamic equilibrium; the society is not static, but changes are adjusted to smoothly.

This brand of functionalism, as we have seen, has come under increasing criticism in recent years. For example, the habit of thinking of society as an organic system has been attacked as arbitrary and misleading. The assumption that certain practices and institutions are like vital organs predetermines that they are both necessary and sound.

If a social institution is as necessary to society as the liver is to the body, it would be dangerous to change it or remove it. By ignoring alternatives to existing social structures, functionalism tends to assume that things *must* be as they are, especially in the area of familial and sexual statuses and roles. Moreover, by implying, without arguing the point, that the fundamental goal of society is the same as that of an individual organism— that is, surviving and maintaining a steady state—functionalism lends support to a conservative political stance.

Perhaps the most pointed criticism of functionalism was offered by sociologist Ralf Dahrendorf (1958), who argued that functional sociology employs a utopian vision, in the tradition of a long line of writers beginning with Plato. Dahrendorf's point-by-point comparison of utopia with the social system as posited by functional sociology is important in two respects: First, it enlarges our understanding of the relation between the institution of the family and society; second, it suggests what is basically wrong with the functional understanding of family life.

Utopia and Its Discontents

Most utopias, whether "good" ones like Plato's Republic or "bad" ones like Orwell's *1984*, tend to have a number of common features. First, nothing ever changes. They have no past, or only a vague one, and no future. Utopias are isolated not only in time, but also in space. Often they are located on islands or remote planets. Outside influences are simply irrelevant.

Second, there is nothing to argue about in utopia. Everybody agrees on goals and values and on the ways and means for reaching these goals. Most utopian writers, says Dahrendorf, make it clear that in their society, conflict about values and institutional arrangements simply cannot arise or is just unnecessary. Thus there are no strikes or revolutions, or even parliaments in which opposing groups compete for power. Equality is not a feature of most utopias; in fact, they are often caste societies—for example, some people in *Brave New World* were genetically engineered to be the working drones of the society. But again, everyone accepts the power arrangements as they are.

It is something of a problem for the utopian writer to explain how a dissident can arise in a "perfect" social structure. In some of the literary utopias, such as *Brave New World* or *1984*, the plot centers on a nonconformist who does not go along with the system. This nonconformist is often an outsider of some kind, such as a survivor from a previous society.

Everything that happens in utopia serves to uphold the existing state of affairs. Since utopias consist of mortal beings, they face the problem of producing and training new generations of utopians. This creates a major risk to the stability of utopia, and utopian writers have given a good deal of attention to such matters. Inventors of utopias could solve all these problems in one stroke by making people immortal, but they usually avoid this solution. Nevertheless, the utopian world operates *as if* people were immortal—that is, new generations replace their parents just as body cells replace each other, preserving the intactness of the body.

Dahrendorf embarked on his travels in utopia to advance a major critique of functionalism, particularly the work of Parsons in *The Social System* (1951). Dahrendorf argues that the vision of society in this brand of sociology corresponds point by point with all the elements of utopia. In the social-system model, society is based on consensus. Change is not absent but is seen as abnormal or unusual, something that has to be explained. Dahrendorf (1958) and other critics take functional sociology to task for generating a conservative complacency about society and its problems, and also for being boringly unconcerned with "riddles of experience."

Conflict Models

Along with a number of others, Dahrendorf has suggested a conflict model of society. Utopian definitions of the normal and expectable, as opposed to the unusual and in need of explanation, should be turned on their heads. Thus change and conflict are to be seen as constants in society. Instead of assuming that social organizations remain the same until something happens to change them, Dahrendorf suggests we assume that change is constant unless something intervenes to stop it. The task of the sociologist should be to try to determine what is interfering with the normal process of change.

In the same vein, Dahrendorf argues that conflict is always present in social life. We should become suspicious or curious to find a social organization or society that exhibits no conflict, although the conflict need not be violent or uncontrolled.

Finally, the conflict model of society is based on the notion of constraint. Rather than being held together by consensus, societies and social organizations are based on the coercion of some by others. This is the source of conflict and change. Constraints lead to conflict, and conflict leads to change. Dahrendorf acknowledges that the idea that conflict is always present in social life is not a pleasant one, but it is indispensable for an understanding of social problems.

The essential elements of the conflict model of society that Dahrendorf suggests can be summarized as follows:

1. Every society is subjected at every moment to change.

2. Every society experiences social conflicts.

3. Every element in society can contribute to change.

4. Every society rests on the constraint of some members by others.

Functionalists tend to think of societies as total systems with needs of their own, apart from the individuals and groups that make up the society. Conflict models, on the other hand, view societies as settings within which struggles between classes, factions, interest groups, and individuals are acted out. These conflicts and the conflicting factions, not the social system, are the focus of interest (Lenski, 1966).

There is also an important difference in how the two models handle conflict and change. Functionalists do not deny that conflict and change exist, but they assume that social systems adapt smoothly to such disturbances, or else that conflict and change actually make the society more stable and integrated. Conflict theorists generally recognize that both conflict and cooperation are pervasive and normal features of human life. Unlike the functionalists, however, they do not see conflict as an unusual or pathological condition (Chamblis, 1973).

Critical Approaches to the Family

Closely related to conflict theories are critical approaches to family and society. Although one writer has offered a "critical theory of the family" (Poster, 1978), many observers have offered critical perspectives on the family even if they have not adopted that label (see Morgan, 1975). Those with a critical perspective share several characteristics. First, they are critical of the taken-for-granted explanations and justifications for social institutions and practices, focusing instead on questions of power and domination. Thus, they reject functional explanations of family roles and examine inequalities between men and women and between parents and children.

Second, critical writers are sensitive not only to conflicts in social systems, but also to dysfunctions, contradictions, and dilemmas. For example, where Parsons emphasized the "fit" between family and society, critical theorists see dysfunctions in the relation between the family and society as well as within the family itself. Thus, although the family is supposed to be a "haven in a heartless world" and make up for tensions in the workplace, those tensions can be brought home to strain family relations.

Critical theorists also share an emphasis on human subjectivity and the self. Ironically, however, some critical theorists, such as R. D. Laing, see people as helpless pawns in the grip of powerful social forces—in a sort of dark version of Parsons's theory. Some critical theorists, however, deny that humans are totally controlled by biological or social forces. They recognize that people are constrained in all sorts of ways, but still have the ability to think about their situations and even to say no (Morgan, 1975).

The Family as a Little Utopia

We devoted so much space to the issue of utopia because of its direct relevance to the study of the family. The traditional view of the family fit the utopian model in two distinct ways: as part of the utopian social system as a whole and as a miniature utopia in itself. As part of the social system, the family carries out vital functions: it helps maintain the equilibrium of the system by replacing and training new generations. As we saw earlier, utopian writers from Plato on have been preoccupied with the family and education. The introduction of children into the social system brings with it an element of risk. There is always the possibility of a generation gap to threaten the stability of the system. Social theorists have also been strikingly preoccupied with the family and with the "problem" of socialization, including both education and assignment of people to occupational slots. Like the utopian writers, functional sociologists speak in terms of the survival of the society.

In short, the functional view of the family fits the utopian model of regulated, orderly change: "Children are born and socialized and allocated until they die; new children are born, and the same thing happens all over again" (Dahrendorf, 1958, p. 121).

As a little world unto itself, the family has also been portrayed as a utopia. The family is suspended in time and isolated in space; it is outside of history and not deeply affected by social surroundings. Major historical changes, such as the industrial revolution, do have their effect on the family, but these are only a matter of changing the relative importance of one of the basic functions. The family, like society, is assumed to adapt to change.

The family as a little social system also fits the model of utopian harmony and consensus. Like most utopias the family is a system of unequal statuses, a hierarchy in which the order of priority is men/women, adults/children. Yet in the conventional assumptions this class or caste system does not give rise to conflict, nor is it even recognized as such by the family members. For in living up to their prescribed roles, they are presumed to be carrying out their natural functions. Thus in acting out the roles of male, female, and child, each person acts out his or her own biological and psychological predestination. Further, mother and father are also acting out the cultural rules learned in their own families: they are replacing their own parents.

The infant's need for care matches the mother's need to mother. The needs of mother and children for economic support match the need of the husband-father to fulfill his masculine nature by providing for his family. In short, the family is envisioned as a system of perfectly interlocking needs.

Perhaps an example will illustrate the way these ideas are usually presented. The following description of the nuclear family comes from a book by a well-known professor of psychiatry, one of the leading theorists of the family in that field. This description of the normal nuclear family serves to introduce the author's theory of the family origins of schizophrenia, which he assumes results from a failure to live up to the following norms:

1. The nuclear family is composed of two generations, each with different needs, prerogatives, and tasks. . . . The parents . . . seek to merge themselves and their backgrounds into a new unit that satisfies the needs of both and completes their personalities in a relationship that is permanent for them. . . . The parents serve as guides, educators, and models for the offspring. They provide nurturance and give of themselves so that the children can develop. . . .

2. The family is also divided into two genders with differing but complementary functions and role allocations as well as anatomical differences. The feminine role derives from the woman's biological structure and is related to nurturance of children and the maintenance of a home, leading to emphasis upon interest in interpersonal relations and emotional harmony—an expressive-affectional role. The male role is related to the support and protection of the family and leads to an emphasis upon instrumental-adaptive leadership characteristics. . . .

3. The bonds between family members are held firm by erotic and affectional ties. . . .

4. The family forms a shelter for its members within the society and from the remainder of society. . . . However, the family must reflect and transmit the societal ways. (Lidz, 1963, pp. 51–53)

The family system outlined above can in no way give rise to serious strain or conflict. It contemplates no conflict over age, sex roles, or power relations. There is no room for any distance between the person and the role. Dissent from these role norms places the dissident outside the system as it normally functions. And, in fact, that precisely is Lidz's theory of schizophrenia: it arises from parental failures to observe their proper age and sex positions. For Lidz and many other psychiatrists, it is all perfectly clear: there are sick families over here and well families over there. Thus, surprisingly, clinical work with troubled families seems to reinforce, rather than challenge, the utopian image of family life. We will return to this paradox later.

Psychoanalysis and Utopia

We noted earlier that utopian stories often center around a nonconformist who rebels against the system. But how can a perfect social system give rise to a nonconformist in the first place? The writers of utopian fiction solve the problem by making the rebel an outsider—a visitor from another society or a survivor from a previous era. Thus the outsider is not a product of the social structure of utopia, but a deviant "infected with some unique disease" (Dahrendorf, 1958, p. 117).

How does the functional model of society deal with the problem of deviance and nonconformity? One way is by pointing to the hidden functions performed by seemingly dysfunctional behaviors, such as conflict and criminality—some sociologists have argued that society needs deviants to remind the rest of us what moral rules are. But a more basic way functional models deal with deviance is to attribute it to the dark depths of human nature. Following the eighteenth-century philosopher Thomas Hobbes, these models assume that human beings are at heart so murderous and anarchic that strong societies are needed to prevent a war of all against all. The most recent and influential version of the Hobbesian view is found in some of Freud's work, particularly his later writings.

Psychoanalysis has contributed to utopian views of family life from two directions: its conception of society or "civilization" and its conception of human nature. Freud's notion of civilization corresponds to the utopian social system of sociology, with one exception: Freud's civilization has as its fatal flaw innate sexual and aggressive drives. These drives, which Freud referred to as the libido or the id, play the role of original sin in the fall from paradise. "Every individual is virtually an enemy of culture," wrote Freud in *The Future of an Illusion* (1898, p. 4).

Thus psychoanalysis abets the conservative thrust of the functional view of society in two ways. First, it accounts for social conflict and pathology in a way that does not challenge the legitimacy or perfection of the social system. And, second, it suggests that, since the troubles that beset us arise from dark, unruly forces in human nature, there is little use in trying to change social conditions.

Freudian ideas have been used in another way to support the idea of a balanced social system. Parsons finds in Freud's concept of *internalization* an explanation of how the social system perpetuates itself smoothly from one generation to the next. In Freudian theory, a major step in the development of the child is its identification with the parent of the same sex. The moral dictates taught by the parents, according to Freud, are taken into the child's own personality, where they become the superego or conscience. Parsons expanded the concept of internalization. Instead of just moral dictates, the child incorporates all of the culture, including values, roles, and knowledge. The child's personality becomes a mirror image of the social world around him or her. Thus the requirements of the society are translated into individual motivation; people come to want to do what they have to do, and the society functions smoothly (Parsons & Bales, 1955).

This view of internalization has been criticized as a distortion of Freud's own thinking. As Dennis Wrong (1961) puts it, "The concept of internalization as it is used by many social scientists presents an oversocialized view of human nature, one that is infinitely malleable and capable of accepting the demands of any social system" (p. 192).

NORMS AND BEHAVIOR

The relationship between people's values and attitudes on the one hand and their actual behavior on the other is one of those perennial problems that plague the social sciences. Are people's ideals reliable guides to their behavior? Or are norms and behavior two separate realms that have nothing to do with each other? Or are norms a kind of smokescreen that obscures what is really going on?

Social scientists have disagreed on their answers to these questions. Some, in particular those functionalists who assume society tends toward a state of balance, assume that there must be a close fit between norms and behavior.

The defects of such assumptions about the relation between ideal and reality are pointed out by Marvin Harris (1968). Warn-

ing anthropologists to avoid the temptation to write descriptions of exotic cultures in terms of their ideals, he offers the following ethnography of American life, written in ideal terms:

If permitted to develop unchecked, the tendency to write ethnographies in accord with the . . . rules of behavior will result in an unintentional parody of the human condition. Applied to our own culture, it would conjure up a way of life in which men tip their hats to ladies . . . unwed mothers are a rarity . . . chewing gum is never stuck under tables and never dropped on the sidewalk; television repairmen fix television sets; children respect their aged parents; rich and poor get the same medical treatment; taxes are paid in full; all men are created equal; and our defense budget is used only for maintaining peace. (p. 59)

People may give lip service to such values as honesty, faithfulness in marriage, or not losing one's temper with one's children, but circumstances may override commitment to such behavior in practice. There may even be counternorms that may turn out to be stronger in practice than the ideal. What is a counternorm? Jules Henry (1963) illustrates one with his observations on cheating in American high schools. In spite of the lip service paid to the idea that cheating is wrong, there is a great deal of pressure to cheat from the grading system, from the students as a group, and even from the teachers who seem to be indifferent to the cheating going on under their noses. Henry notes that a student who refuses to share test answers with a classmate would be the real deviant in the social system of the high school he observed.

Likewise, Goode (1971) observes that the family *preaches* nonviolence but *teaches* violence:

Parents and other moral authorities constantly exhort young children against violence, but their own behavior belies that advice. We are all trained for violence. The child does learn that force is very effective at stopping others, and that force or its threat can change other people's calculations of profit and loss. The child experiences this directly, and watches it in others—the fright of his mother when his father is furious, arguments and threats among the neighbors, battles with his own siblings, and so on. (p. 630)

Similarly, the norms of marital faithfulness have a highly problematic relation to actual behavior. Again, the rules and pressures against observing the norms often seem to dominate those in favor of the norms. Extramarital sex seems to be an institutionalized part of American life that coexists, however uncomfortably, with the monogamy principle. Morton Hunt's (1969) book *The Affair* describes the social system of extramarital affairs and the discomforts caused by the discrepancy between people's beliefs and behavior.

Hunt's book and such works as the study of upper-middle-class marriages by Cuber and Harroff (1965) reveal considerable social and environmental pressure on people to have extramarital affairs. Advertising and the mass media eroticize everyday life in America. Flirtation games are played in work settings as well as at parties. Travel and business provide the opportunity for liaisons with minimal risks of embarrassment and entanglements. In some social and business circles, an insistence on strict monogamy would render one as deviant as the high-school student who refused to offer examination answers to a classmate.

The reader should not leap to the conclusion, based on these examples, that American society is necessarily marked by a greater discrepancy between norms and behavior than that found in other societies. There is little evidence anywhere of a culture whose ideal norms are reliable guides to what people actually do. Harris (1968)

pointed out that even the kinship rules of "primitive" peoples, sometimes described as the most binding of social norms, often fail to be carried out in practice. For example, a rule may dictate that a young man has to marry his mother's brother's daughter. Some anthropologists, however, when actually tabulating who was married to whom, have found more exceptions to the rule than cases in which it seemed to have been followed. And in one culture in which the divorce rate approaches 100 percent, people still express the wish at every wedding that the marriage be a permanent one. Because of social science and the mass media, however, we may be more *aware* of discrepancies between our ideals and our behavior than are other cultures.

As a research strategy and a general approach to the family, asking What is actually going on? will generally lead to a different set of findings and a different view of the phenomena than asking What are family norms and roles? Questions about norms and roles are important, but they should not be taken as descriptions of observable behavior.

The sociological concept of role—as, for example, "the mother role," "the father role"—may be similarly misleading as a guide to understanding actual behavior. The term *role* was utilized to emphasize that people often seem to follow cultural scripts, rather than merely expressing their particular personalities. Thus one can analyze the roles of mother, salesperson, college president, police officer, and so on as something apart from the individual personalities of the particular people who occupy those roles. Accordingly, societies and cultures may be described as being made up of "role relationships."

Like many other valuable constructs in the social sciences, however, the idea of role is sometimes overextended. People may play

Family dinners are supposed to symbolize the family's unity. In reality, however, mealtimes often become the occasion for scolding children or airing grievances, or family members may find they have little to say to one another. [Mitchell Payne/ Jeroboam, Inc.]

several and conflicting roles. Does the role of "mother" accurately describe actual mother–child interaction in a culture?

As D. H. J. Morgan (1975) points out, sociologists who use the role metaphor tend to overemphasize constraint and conformity. They imply that human behavior is determined by the social scripts people are assigned to and overlook the ways in which people negotiate around and change their roles. Further, the role metaphor may be less useful in explaining behavior than it is generally assumed to be:

As I write a woman passes pushing a pram and carrying a shopping bag. Is she carrying out her role as a wife, a mother, a woman, a housewife or as a consumer? Were I to do the same would I be seen as enacting the role of a father, a housewife, a husband or a consumer, or would I be seen as some kind of deviant, someone departing from my role as a father, husband, man breadwinner, etc.? And if we apply the "correct" or "agreed" label, would it make any difference, would it really explain anything? (p. 135)

In the studies that have observed and measured what goes on between parents and children in households—that is, in the natural habitat of family life—a very different picture emerges of the mother role. A child may receive its mother's undivided attention no more than a half-hour or an hour a day. The rest of the time the mother is busy with other things. What goes on between mother and child seems to be a by-product of the horde of small and seemingly trivial events and pressures that make the parent's day a good or a bad one, a harried or a calm one, a tired or an energetic one. To those investigators who have been observing the complex realities of family life—from such events as the preparing and eating of meals, putting children to bed, greetings and leave-takings, to such patterns as the organization of household time and space—norms and roles are, as concepts, simply too broad and abstract to be useful.

Although ideals and images and role definitions cannot be taken at face value as guides to behavior, they cannot be ignored either. Looking at behavior only, without some idea of what the behavior means to the participants, is misleading also. Consider a parent spanking a child. To understand the meaning of this event, one would have to know its context—why it occurred. If the parent were a modern, permissive parent who did not believe in spanking, the situation would have a different meaning for both parent and child than if, say, the parent belonged to a culture teaching that physical discipline was good for children and that a parent who did not spank children was neglecting his or her duty. The modern family differs from its historical counterparts in its ideals and images of family life. The beliefs in close emotional bonds between husbands and wives and parents and children and in personal happiness as the chief justification for marriage enter into people's perceptions and experience of the daily events of family life. So these beliefs and norms cannot be ignored. They influence relationships even if they do not accurately describe them.

PSYCHIATRY AND THE IDEALIZATION OF FAMILY LIFE

At first glance it would seem that psychiatrists and other clinicians who help troubled families would be unlikely to make utopian assessments of family life. In fact, one might expect that coming into daily contact with family miseries kept private from the rest of the world would lead clinicians to exaggerate the dark side of family life. Paradoxically, however, clinicians have contributed to the utopian model of the family: experiences with troubled families often seem to reinforce idealized conceptions of the family rather than challenge them.

Thus the idealized model of the family remains the standard by which the "sick" families are judged:

Studies of the family have, with a few memorable exceptions, accepted the sentimental model—statistics are made of units derived from this model; anecdotes are collected; and formalistic abstractions are derived from it. . . . Focusing upon the family's pathologies serve(s) to *reinforce the sentimental model by the assumption that the pathologyless family has the shape of the sentimental model.* . . . The pathologies are defined as variations from the sentimental model, and the sentimental model is reinforced in its supposed shape by the shape of its supposed pathologies. (Birdwhistell, 1966, p. 211)

The Medical Model

The medical model of pathology stands behind the psychiatric assumption that normal families differ considerably from the families whose children become psychiatric patients. In recent years there has been a great deal of debate about the value of applying concepts of physical health and illness to matters of thoughts, feelings, and personalities. The issue has many ramifications, but the aspect that concerns us here has to do with the kind of thinking the medical model leads to—the kinds of inferences the psychiatrist draws about normality by observing patients. Suppose, for example, a patient (child) were to describe a parent as acting in some way that parents are not "supposed" to act—for example, cruel, irrational, neglectful, bizarre, impervious to what the patient says. What conclusion can the psychiatrist make about the normality of these parents? Assuming that the psychiatrist believes the child, can the psychiatrist infer that the parents are very different from most parents, only a little different, or typical?

Actually, no conclusion about prevailing childrearing practices and parental behavior can be derived from patients. There is no way of knowing whether and how much and in what ways patients differ from the general population. The question is a matter for scientific investigation. To answer it, a study would have to be carried out comparing families having children in psychiatric treatment with families having children who had never been psychiatric patients. As a matter of fact, several such epidemiological studies have been carried out. They generally conclude that people who become psychiatric clients or patients represent only the tip of an iceberg:

Studies from many countries confirm the picture of a high and persistent burden of neurosis in the population, the differences in rates between different studies probably reflecting differing criteria, rather than real differences in prevalence. (Ryle, 1967, p. 135)

Even if one did find differences between the families of schizophrenics and other families, there would be no way of knowing whether the differences came after the schizophrenia or before unless the family had been studied before the patient got "sick."

When using a model of thinking borrowed from physical medicine, the psychiatrist may fail to perceive any problem in comprehending the normal family world. Thus the medical model leads to utopian conceptions of family life without any help from social theories! Medicine is based on the popular opposition of health and disease: if a patient comes to a doctor complaining of a symptom, such as an itchy rash, the doctor easily understands "normality"—it is the absence of the symptom. In the realm of behavior, such thinking can lead to the erroneous conclusion that normal behavior and family life must be the exact opposite of what the psychiatrist confronts:

The diagnosis of normality is made by exclusion, and if a psychiatrist can label a feature it is by implication pathological and undesirable. Therefore anything that is called by a name is implicitly abnormal. . . . Since the psychiatrist's attention is focused upon deviation, and since he has little or no training in normal psychology, he tends to construct a hypothetical norm by averaging the exact opposite of those features he sees in his patients. (Ruesch & Bateson, 1968, p. 71)

Freud and Family Psychology

Freud and his followers have made an enormous contribution to the understanding of the family. Freud's discoveries of the impact and lasting significance of early experiences must be included in any serious understanding of the family. Freud's discoveries derived from his invention of a new social situation—a new form of human interaction and communication.

In psychoanalysis the patient talks at length about whatever comes to mind to a fully attentive and sympathetic listener who will not interrupt or censure, no matter how outrageous the thoughts expressed might be. Using this method, Freud opened up a strange new inner world, just as Columbus opened up new portions of our outer world. Freud explored large areas of inner life that had seemed too disturbing or too unimportant to study: dreams, fantasies, slips of the tongue, seemingly irrelevant—and irreverent—thoughts.

In these explorations, Freud discovered that the impact of the family on the child was much greater than anyone had suspected. Most important, perhaps, was his discovery of the child as a person, capable of sensuous feelings, fantasy, and suffering. The prevailing view during the nineteenth century was that the child was essentially a nonperson, someone whose view of things should not be taken seriously. As women were placed on a pedestal, the child was sentimentalized as an adorable innocent. Such sentimentalization coexisted with economic exploitation of children in mines and factories and savage disciplinary measures in homes and schools (Coveney, 1967).

Freud destroyed Victorian illusions about childhood innocence and family serenity. His discovery of infantile sexuality was perhaps the most shocking of all his findings; it aroused the most indignation. Yet Freud also discovered—or rediscovered—passions in adults that had been denied by idealized conceptions of family life. Freud was fond of stating that the essential themes of his theories were based on the intuitions of poets and playwrights. The conflicts and strivings Freud found lurking beneath the surface of ordinary family life were the same passions dramatized by Shakespeare and the Greek tragedians. The lustful, murderous impulses between husbands and wives and parents and children that one could see acted out in *Hamlet, King Lear, Oedipus Rex, Medea,* and other classic works are ever-present, but secret, undercurrents in ordinary family life.

The Freudian theory of the family is thus a conflict theory, with conflict not only between family members but also within them. Freud's most important concepts are those of *repression* and *ambivalence*. Repression is the mechanism by which people keep wishes and fantasies outside their awareness; it explains why we may not be aware even in ourselves of the passions we see acted out overtly on the stage. The concept of ambivalence points to the duality of many of our wishes and fantasies. We not only love *or* hate, we can love *and* hate at the same time. We want intimate relationships, but we want our freedom and individuality; we want deep sexual intimacy with one person, but at the same time we want to sample sexual experiences with as many people as possible.

Despite Freud's antiutopian vision of family relations, psychoanalysis often has reinforced the sentimental model of the nuclear family because Freud and his followers tended to ignore the everyday realities of family life in favor of inherited instincts—this despite Freud's stress on childrearing in the formation of personality. Nathan Ackerman (1958), himself a psychoanalyst, has pointed to such incongruities in Freud's approach to the family:

The Freudian theory focuses attention on the role of the family in the shaping of personality, but it gives priority to inborn instincts. . . .

Child-parent relations are the core of the psychoanalytic view of human development. . . . Yet in psychoanalysis direct observations of family interaction have not been carried out until recently, and only now is their importance beginning to be recognized. (pp. 27–30)

Freud's lack of concern for the everyday realities of family life may stem from his emphasis on the child as a biological organism. He defined development as a progression through a series of innate maturational stages. These stages Freud conceived to be universal, hence only partly influenced by differences in individual experiences or social conditions. Parents, in Freud's theory, also have a relatively fixed part to play; they are the tamers of the child's instincts.

Freud conceived the family as the instrument for disciplining the child's biologically fixed instinctual urges and enforcing repression of their spontaneous release. He described the child as a polymorphous, perverse little animal. The child epitomizes animal pleasure. The parent personifies reality and the restraints of society. (Ackerman, 1958, p. 28)

The emphasis on parent–child relations as the taming of impulse has several implications. For one thing, it implies that a certain amount of suffering on the part of children is inevitably part of growing up. Psychoanalytic writers often argue against the notion that childhood can ever be a happy, conflict-free time of life. Even the most loving and beloved parents can be transformed in the child's imagination into witches and monsters:

So there are no ways in which a child can avoid anxiety. If we banished all the witches and ogres from his bedtime stories and policed his life for every conceivable source of danger, he would still succeed in constructing his own imaginary monsters out of the conflicts of his own life. (Fraiberg, 1959, p. 15)

The problem with this point of view is that it assumes that all the witches and monsters in a child's life are imaginary. It implies that in family government the virtues are with the rulers, and the vices with the ruled. The assumption of parental virtue, however, was wryly challenged by Herbert Spencer (1946/1858), the nineteenth-century philosopher whose career overlapped Freud's:

Judging by educational theories, men and women are entirely transfigured in their relations to off-spring. The citizens we do business with, the people we meet in the world, we know to be very imperfect creatures. In the daily scandals, in the quarrels of friends, in bankruptcy disclosures, in lawsuits, in police reports, we have constantly thrust before us the pervading selfishness, dishonesty, brutality. Yet . . . we habitually take for granted that these culpable persons are free from moral delinquency in the treatment of boys and girls. (p. 87)

The psychiatric idealization of the family in fact contradicts the analyst's clinical knowledge of parental behavior. It also contradicts the psychoanalytic view of persistent human nature. Thus the witches and monsters of the child's imagination may reflect accurate perceptions of veiled or not-so-veiled parental hostility.

Freud seems to have been curiously uninterested in the daily realities of family life. Far from blaming his patients' families for their children's disorders, Freud overlooked or rejected much negative information, even in his own published case histories. He blamed his patients' troubles on their own wayward impulses rather than on parental treatment.

During the early part of his career, Freud thought that his adult patients had become neurotic because they had been seduced by their parents. Later he realized that his patients' reports of seduction were fantasies rather than real events. Impressed with the power of unconscious, conflicting wishes, he came to view neuroses as a "pathology of desire" (Ricoeur, 1973) rather than as a product of family life.

Freud and his followers came to focus most of their theoretical and clinical attention on the inner psychological world of their patients and regarded their actual family life as having only limited significance. Some of Freud's most famous case histories reveal a striking lack of interest in family relations.

The case of Little Hans, for example, is considered the classic statement on the Oedipus complex. It describes Freud's analysis of a phobia in a 5-year-old boy. Erich Fromm (1970) uses the published case to show Freud's bias in favor of parental figures. Freud, he argues, attributes qualities to Hans's parents as models of enlightened parenthood that contradict the facts he presents. Both parents were among Freud's closest adherents. Little Hans was treated by Freud, with his father as an intermediary, because he de-

Regardless of the actual quality of family relationships, the family is a source of meaning and identity. [Arthur Siegel/Reproduced from the Collections of the Library of Congress]

veloped a strong fear of horses. According to Freud, the boy's parents were determined to raise him without coercion, bullying, or ridicule. They were, in short, rebelling against the prevailing childrearing practices of their time and place—turn-of-the-century Vienna.

As often happens when people set out to raise their children by new principles, the old ones have a way of persisting. For example, Little Hans's mother, according to Freud, told Hans the following at various times: that she would have his penis cut off, that she would abandon him, and that she had a penis. She also threatened to beat him with a carpet beater. At the same time Hans's mother was described as being seductive in various ways. Yet none of what the mother did entered into Freud's diagnosis of what troubled Hans. Freud attributed the phobia only to Oedipal wishes that arose from Hans's inner depths. His amorous feelings toward his mother and his fear of castration were not related by Freud to his mother's seductiveness or actual threats! The case is a remarkable demonstration of how concrete incidents in day-to-day family life can be at odds with the professed beliefs and values of the parents, as well as with professional estimates of the parents as people.

Similar observations have been made of the case of Dora, an 18-year-old girl who was brought to Freud for treatment of hysteria (Chesler, 1971). Once again Freud overlooked the family situation as a source of Dora's troubles and attributed her problems solely to her unrecognized sexual wishes toward her father and toward her father's friend and his wife. This family situation was more extreme than Little Hans's. Dora's father was having an affair with the friend's wife and was trying to offer Dora to this man so his own affair could continue. Freud was aware of this situation but considered it irrelevant to Dora's problems and to her treatment. He was concerned only with tracing her hysterical symptoms to their presumed origins in sexual wishes.

THE DISCOVERY OF COMPLEXITY

New trends in the study of the family suggest some profound changes in our assumptions about ordinary family life. Each of the new trends in its own way is undermining traditional concepts of family normality. As we noted earlier, both the average person and the family expert tend to think of family problems as a kind of pathology attacking an otherwise healthy system, like a germ invading the body. This way of looking at the family forces us to think of problems as separate from normal family life and of normal families as separate from pathological families. Tolstoy wrote, "Happy families are all alike, but each unhappy family is unhappy in its own way." Like Tolstoy many observers put normal families in one pile and schizophrenic or child-battering families in another. Then they develop a theory of what goes on in normal families and a different theory to explain what goes on in pathological families. They keep the two or three kinds of families in airtight, logical compartments, paying little or no attention to the similarities, as opposed to the differences, between the types of families or to the process by which one type changes into another.

Studies in family history, family interaction, and family violence have undermined this polarized way of looking at families. In different ways they suggest that definitions of family normality and pathology are much harder to draw than had been thought. Further, these new approaches emphasize variations among families rather than similarities.

As we mentioned in an earlier chapter, the study of the family has been a major growth industry in the field of history since the 1960s. The amount of knowledge that has been gathered about family life in the past is spectacular, and much of it challenges long-held notions. Above all, the new work amounts to what Glen Elder had called "the discovery of complexity" (1981). The family has turned out to be much more complex and varying an institution than anyone had believed.

Not only is there no such thing as "the family," there is no such thing as a national family type at any particular period. As Lawrence Stone, summarizing the outpouring of new historical studies, says, "There never has been a French family or an English family or an American family, but rather a plurality of families" (1981, p. 81). There is also no such thing as a New England family or a Provençal family. Stone points out that there are not only regional differences, but differences within regions due to social class and religious difference.

The new historical studies also provide important glimpses into the emotional lives of people in past times, even though this is the most difficult kind of information to document. One of the major contributions of the new historical studies is to show that the kinds of close emotional bonds we tend to think are universal and "natural" to the nuclear family are in fact a relatively recent invention in Western society. The nuclear family as a household unit may have existed for many centuries, but people's ideas about family life have changed only in the past couple of centuries. Historians disagree among themselves as to precisely how to describe the change, and how it came about, but they agree that a major revolution in family feelings and ideology took place. Phillipe Ariès (1962) traced the withdrawal of the nuclear family from the "torrent" of public sociability that surrounded it in the Middle Ages. For Ariès, the change centered on a new preoccupation with childhood.

Jean-Louis Flandrin (1979) traces the development of a "new family morality" in mid-eighteenth-century England and France. The nuclear family detached itself from kin, servants, and neighbors and came to be more emotionally intense. A central part of the new family morality, according to Flandrin, was the expectation that husbands would be less brutal and more considerate of their wives. There was less approval of wife beating and of husbands insisting on their sexual "rights."

For Lawrence Stone (1977), the revolution in family emotions concerned the whole family, as relationships between husbands and wives and between parents and children became warmer and more individualized. Stone labels the change the rise of "affective individualism." Beginning in the upper middle class, according to Stone, it eventually seeped upward to the aristocracy and downward to the lower classes. Stone suggests that this change in "mentality"—in the ideas and values regarding the family—may be the most important cultural change in the last thousand years of Western history.

The idea that the psychological bonds between husbands and wives have changed over time is a familiar one. Most people know, for example, that in the past in our culture, and in many other places today, marriages were not based on love but arranged by families. It is more surprising to learn that parental feelings toward children may be equally variable.

When infant- and child-mortality rates are extremely high, as they were in the early years of the modern era, parents are unlikely to invest a great deal of emotion in infants. No one claims, observes Lawrence Stone, a "direct and crude correlation" between infant mortality rates and the attachment of parents to children (1981). But a child-centered society is not likely to develop in a society in which a third of infants are dead at 1 and half of all children fail to survive into adulthood. That children were born to die was taken to be a fact no one could do much about. "'All mine die,' said Montaigne casually, as a gardener might speak of cabbages" (Plumb, 1972, p. 156).

Even more incomprehensible to us in modern society is the mounting evidence that premodern parents contributed to infant mortality rates. Poor parents used infanticide, neglect, or abandonment as a substitute for birth control and abortion, which were unavailable. In France, upper- and lower-class parents sent their children off to be wet-nursed on "baby farms," with lethal results. These findings, argues Stone, undermine the "argument of those who believe that maternal love is a historical constant in all cultures, as well as a biological given" (1981, p. 59).

The Violent Family

Nothing could be more opposed to the image of the loving and happy family than the idea of physical violence between husbands and wives and parents and children. If such cases are brought to our attention, we tend to assume that the violent individual must be deranged and disreputable. Yet, according to a number of recent studies, force and violence may be a fundamental part of family life. One major study concluded that the family is "the most violent institution in American society except the military, and only then in time of war" (Straus, Gelles, & Steinmetz, 1980).

Some of the findings on family violence are not new, but they had not previously been included in a general analysis of ordinary family life. Studies of murderers and their victims, for example, reveal that the single most frequent category of murderer-victim relationship is that of family members. More policemen are killed or injured dealing with family fights than with any other kind of crime.

Rather than considering the more sensational cases as abnormal exceptions to the usual state of family life, these researchers argue that they represent just the tip of the iceberg:

Underneath the surface is a vast amount of conflict and violence—including bitter feelings, anger, hatred, much physical punishment of children, pokes and slaps of husbands and wives, and not altogether rare pitched battles between family members. (Steinmetz & Straus, 1974, p. 3)

Although the family traditionally is viewed as a place of love and solidarity, the family in fact is one of the few groups in society empowered by law and tradition to use physical force and restraint on its members. In every state, for example, it is legal for parents to strike their children; many Americans see physical punishment as the most desirable form of punishment, and even more believe that parents are morally obliged to use it if their children cannot be controlled in any other way (Stark & McEvoy, 1970). There is also widespread support for the idea that husbands are "entitled" to use physical force to keep their wives in line and that the wife who is beaten by her husband must have provoked him (Gelles, 1972). As Straus observes, "the actual or implicit threat of physical coercion is one of many factors underlying male dominance in the family" (cited in Gelles, 1972, p. 14).

Although it can be argued that there is a big difference between a spanking and the kind of beating that comes to the attention of police, in practice it has proved difficult to define the dividing line between legitimate and illegitimate acts of family violence. Gelles (1972) concluded from a study of both violence-prone and ordinary families that violence is more widespread and more severe than the image of the happy family suggests:

Neither the 57% violent figure for the entire sample nor the 37% violent sample for the neighbor [control group] families can serve as definitive estimates of the extent of the family violence in society. But taking into account the figures on the extent of conjugal violence, it is indeed common in American families. Furthermore, these incidents . . . are not isolated attacks nor are they just pushes and shoves. In many families violence is patterned and regular and often results in broken bones and sutured cuts. (p. 192)

Similarly, the research on child battering points to a continuity rather than a sharp break with normal childrearing methods. Some battering parents seem only to have exaggerated notions of obedience and of the capacities of very young children to respond to commands. Such parents are likely to be righteous about their acts, arguing that they were only trying to teach their child not to be spoiled or disrespectful. For other parents the injuries that bring in the authorities are more like momentary outbursts of anger in the course of "normal" discipline.

In looking for the causes of child abuse, research points beyond the motives and weaknesses of the particular parent and toward the physical and social environment surrounding parents and children. What happens to the child in the course of a day often seems to be a by-product of what happens to the parent in his or her adult life outside the realm of parenthood—a fight with the spouse, troubles with the boss, money worries, the household workload, illness. If stresses mount too high, the parent may be overwhelmed and explode at the child. In short, a host of actors apart from the child determine the parent's mood and the time and energy the parent has for child care. All this seems obvious—we see it even in television commercials: "I'm not going to let a headache MAKE ME SCREAM AT MY KIDS!" Yet this knowledge tends to be ignored in most family research and in the sentimental mythology of family life as a refuge from the stresses of the outside world.

Rather than being a refuge from the stresses, strains, and irrationality of the outside society, the family often seems to transmit or even magnify these strains. The contemporary family seems to be a particularly efficient magnifier of strain because so few people are involved. Husband and wife look to each other to make up for whatever deprivation they have suffered in their social and work lives, and the adults have absolute power over the children. A good deal of truth appears in the comic strip showing the boss yelling at the husband, the husband coming home and yelling at the wife, the wife yelling at the child, and finally the child kicking the dog. Periods of unemployment are usually accompanied by increases in child abuse and wife beating (Steinmetz & Straus, 1974).

Anthropologists have pointed out how American culture is extreme in letting parents and children be alone together, shut off in their own houses and away from the watchful eyes and sharp tongues that regulate parent–child relations in other cultures. This isolation sets the stage not only for physical abuse but also for the more usual and common psychological abuse.

Madness and the Family

Like the studies of family violence, the studies of families of schizophrenics began with a group of people in a category clearly labeled "pathological" and "not like other families," and they have concluded with a set of concepts that make the line between the normal and the pathological—"them" and "us"—harder than ever to draw. The studies of the families of schizophrenics form one part of an important shift in psychiatric thinking that has taken place in the past 20 years. The issues surrounding schizophrenia, its nature, and causes remain unclear. But the concepts that have come out of these studies have produced profound and revolutionary implications for understanding family life as well as human behavior in general.

These studies developed a new therapy, a new methodology, and ultimately a new set of concepts that have been hailed as major scientific discoveries. The new therapy was family therapy. Rather than seeing the individual patient alone, psychiatrists started to observe and to treat whole families. The new methods of research grew out of the new therapy. With whole families coming together in hospitals and clinics, it became possible to observe the intimate conversations and interactions of family members in ways that had never before been available to researchers. Furthermore, a whole new technology was now available to record and preserve the record of what people said and did. Movies, tape recorders, videotape, and so forth caught the words, looks, and gestures of family members, so it was no longer necessary to depend on anyone's memory. "Instant replay" became possible in the study of family interaction. Researchers could study a family scene again and again, picking up the more subtle aspects that had been missed the first time, or changing their definitions of what had gone on.

The new techniques transformed the family psychiatrist into a kind of anthropologist. Each family was like a newly discovered tribe, with its own language, rules, roles, and rituals. In looking at families this way, the researchers discovered that they lacked a vocabulary to describe what they saw. Psychiatry and psychoanalysis had many terms to describe the behavior and inner states of the single person, but very few terms to describe the interaction between two or more people.

To fill this information gap, concepts were borrowed from many fields, some seemingly far removed from psychiatry—information theory, logic, ecology, general systems theory, sociology, existentialism, and Marxism. Oddly enough, no name has yet emerged for this new science. Several have been suggested, but none has stuck. "Communication theory" is perhaps used most

This is obviously not a formal family portrait. Does it, however, portray something of this family's emotional reality? [Bob Adelman/Magnum Photos Inc.]

often, but it refers mainly to one particular version of the new approach, that of Gregory Bateson and his associates (Bateson et al., 1956). Other suggested names are "clinical sociology" (Lennard & Bernstein, 1969), "social psychiatry" (Rabkin, 1970), and "interpersonal psychiatry" (Sullivan, 1953).

"Communicational psychiatry" failed to prove its initial assumptions: it did not discover a set of behavior patterns unique to schizophrenic families. Rather, it seems to have discovered patterns common to many families. The following features are some of those first found in families with a schizophrenic member:

the "politics of experience": struggles over definitions of what is really going on, over whose experience is to be defined

as real, and whose experience is to be invalidated

imperviousness: ignoring what the other person says

mystification: doing something that is really in your own interests, but insisting you are doing it for the other person's good—for example, a parent tells a child "You're sleepy, dear—go to bed" when in fact the child is not tired, and the parent merely wants the child out of the way

parent caring for a child only as an extension of himself or herself, not as a separate person

mother and father as enemy camps; a cold war in the household

mother and father united in a "holy alliance" against the rest of the world double-bind or paradoxical communications, such as glaring at a child and ordering him or her to kiss you at the same time; saying such things as "Don't take me seriously" or "Be spontaneous"

too great a boundary between the family and the rest of the world—everyone outside the family is a suspicious character

too little boundary between the family and the rest of the world—outsiders or other relatives constantly intruding on intimate family matters

family secrets that everyone is aware of but doesn't dare discuss

a parent being preoccupied with the child's inner state—his or her moods, feelings, and general happiness

a parent mislabeling the child's inner states—stating that the child is hungry or sleepy when he or she is neither

a parent reacting to a child's statements or acts by belittling the child with sarcasm: "You can always depend on John—to do the wrong thing"

These findings were not so much discoveries as a rediscovery of what intuitive observers of the human scene had known all along: most families have small and large skeletons in their closets; the most mature-seeming people have foibles and weaknesses that emerge only in the presence of members of their family; family members conspire together to create a favorable impression for the outside world; family members may say one thing but imply another—"Don't worry about leaving me with all the dinner dishes—go and enjoy yourselves"; every family has its own unique set of rules, myths, communication networks, secret alliances, loves, and hates (Framo, 1965, 1972).

Accordingly, the concept of a psychiatrically "normal" family is coming to seem as abstract and empty as the concept of a "universal" nuclear family that is the same everywhere. The more family interaction was studied, the harder it became to think that there was a normal "type" of family that could be contrasted with an abnormal "type."

The enthusiasm engendered by the new research gave way to disillusionment among those who had been hoping for an answer to the riddle of schizophrenia. But the less the new findings tell us about what is unique to schizophrenic families, the more they tell us about family life in general.

Jules Henry (1971), an anthropologist who studied families of schizophrenics by living in their homes, raised the question as to how far these newly discovered patterns reach among families never labeled as "sick." Are they the inevitable result of people living together? Are they peculiar to Americans? Are most families "pathogenic"?

A somewhat different way of looking at family interaction has been suggested by Lennard and Bernstein (1969). Rather than defining most families as "pathogenic," these researchers suggested that though ordinary family life can often be a difficult interactional environment, most people can cope with these difficulties most of the time. Just as our bodies have immune systems enabling us to live in a germ-filled environment without being sick constantly, so most of us are psychologically robust enough to deal with the emotional ups and downs of family interaction. Pathology, such as schizophrenic reactions, may occur when the level of interactional difficulty in a family exceeds the ability of a family member to cope with it. Some persons may be especially vulnerable to conflict, hostility, or emotional demands, and some families are more difficult interactional environments than others. When a vulnerable person finds himself or herself in a particularly difficult family, chances are that he or she will either try to withdraw from the family or develop symptoms that will lead to becoming a psychiatric patient.

Lennard and Bernstein were led to their conclusion concerning the difficulties of the family context by research comparing small-group interaction in families and other groups. They looked at "schizophrenic families," "normal families," and a variety of groups of unrelated people—for example, small groups that had participated in psychological experiments or therapy or discussion. One of their major measures was the ratio between positive interactions—agreeing, supporting, affirming—and negative interactions—disagreeing, contradicting, criticizing. As anticiapted, they found that the "schizophrenic" families had lower ratios of positive to negative interactions. But to their surprise, the differences between the "normal" families and those with a schizophrenic member were not as wide as previous clinical descriptions had led them to believe. Furthermore, family groups, whether with a schizophrenic member or not, contrasted with the groups of unrelated people:

Family contexts as a whole, whether or not they involve families with a mentally ill member, exhibit lower concordance ratios than any other form of social context on which we had data available. Moreover, family interaction process does not meet the criteria set forth by Bales for a viable, task-oriented system. . . . The family interactional environment then must be considered as a difficult context for interaction—an observation that is, needless to say, not inconsistent with common experience. (p. 185)

CONCLUSION

We began this chapter with a critical look at the functional approach to the family, especially Parsons's functionalism. We also noted that despite its limitations Parsons's theory provides a useful framework for looking at the family as a unit in itself and in relation to the wider society. Indeed, there is actually a good deal of overlap between the functionalist perspective and conflict or critical approach; both attempt to understand the social groups and institutions that make up society and the relations among them. However, it is not necessary to assume, as Parsons did, that the system "works" to benefit all of its parts and maintain social stability. The relations among various groups and aspects of society can be marked by contradiction and conflict.

It is also possible to discuss the functions of the family without making utopian assumptions about its nature and without assuming that the family must take any particular form. Thus, W. H. Goode (1982) discusses the advantages of the "familistic social package." He notes that people form familistic relations under a wide variety of conditions; not only do all societies have some kind of family arrangement, but these arrangements even emerge often in prisons (in the form of homosexual couples). Why?

Goode suggests that in essence the family consists not so much of a particular cast of characters—husbands and wives, parents and children—but rather of a particular kind of social relationship. Familistic relation is marked by a continuing process of sharing and exchanging. Family members share such things as food, houses, goods, and social activities. They also carry out a continuing series of exchanges of help, nurturance, affection, protection, and economic goods.

The familistic package, Goode points out, offers a number of advantages as a way of living. People can cooperate with one another to do what would be hard or impossible for one person to do alone. The continuity of familistic relations means that family members have a "much longer line of social credit" than do unrelated people.

People in families can do things for one another without having to be concerned about being "paid back" right away; they know that in the long run the other person, or some other family member, will reciprocate. The anthropologist David Schneider has made a similar point in arguing that the essence of kinship is "enduring diffuse solidarity" (1968).

Another advantage of familistic living is one shared with any informal, small group. Members can communicate easily, respond quickly in time of need, and adapt to one another's idiosyncrasies. Finally, whatever the advantages of the familistic package to family members, the institution of the family is supported by the wider society by means of norms, values, laws, and social pressures. Other members of society generally assign to families the task of raising the next generation and taking care of the sick and dependent.

Viewing the family as a particular kind of social relationship with a particular set of advantages helps to explain many of the observed facts about the family: its universality, why it can take so many forms, why familistic social relations often appear in unlikely settings such as prisons, and why they tend to emerge again after people have tried other arrangements. On the other hand, this view of the advantages of the familistic package does not imply a utopian image of family relations. Nor does it imply a fit among the needs of individuals, families, and societies. Indeed, some of the problems that plague family life grow out of some of these very same advantages.

Continuity, as we have seen, means that people can give more than they get at any particular time, expecting that eventually the favor will be returned. Yet, as we know, families don't always work this way; many family arguments, grudges, and feuds arise when one family member feels that another has not made good on a social debt.

Another problem arising out of the continuity of family relations is what Robert Merton (1976) has called the "accumulation of ambivalence": people who are in long-term relationships of any kind, not just familial, will tend to experience dissatisfactions. Further, the intimate knowledge that family members have of one another can, as Goode points out, be used to please or to create misery. Overall, for most of the people most of the time, the advantages of familistic social relations outweigh the disadvantages. That is why, despite all the changes of recent years, we are unlikely to become a society of rootless, disconnected individuals.

SUMMARY

The family often has been studied from the point of view of either the society as a whole or the individual. Both of these approaches can lead to idealized conceptions of family life. The view of society as a balanced social system leads to a utopian vision of family and society as conflict-free and harmonious. Clinical work with individuals and families often leads the clinician to assume that the patients are troubled only by personal failings rather than by social strains besetting families in general. Recent work in history, family interaction, and family conflict is undermining such idealized models of family life.

CHAPTER 5

Social Change and the Intimate Environment

We have come to know that every individual lives, from one generation to the next, in some society, and that he lives it out within some historical sequence. By the fact of his living he contributes, however minutely, to the shaping of this society and to the course of its history, even as he is made by society and by its historical push and shove.

The sociological imagination enables us to grasp history and biography and the relations between the two within society.

C. Wright Mills
The Sociological Imagination

The past is a foreign country.

D. Lowenthal

How does our own family life compare with family life in other times and places? Leaving aside for the moment that we actually know little about family life as it is lived in contemporary families, what can we say about the experience of motherhood and fatherhood in the Middle Ages or of being a child in a band of hunters? Is family life essentially "the same everywhere" or does it vary significantly from time to time and place to place? What is the connection between family change and changes in the rest of society?

In the course of this chapter, we shall see that there are no simple answers to these questions and, as was noted in the first chapter, no agreement among scholars as to the best way to describe current and past changes in family life. In spite of the confusions and uncertainties in the historical study of the family, however, recent research has produced some extremely important findings and laid to rest some long-held assumptions about the family.

Also, in spite of the various debates among family scholars today, they agree on some fundamental issues. One of these points of agreement is that there have been some major turning points in history; two major watersheds are the invention of agriculture and the great change from traditional to modern society. Another point on which

most scholars would agree is that these changes have been accompanied by profound changes in personal and family life.

It has become clear that family life as we experience it today has been shaped by the transition to the modern world. As Lawrence Stone (1981, p. 82) observes, Western society in the early sixteenth century was sparsely populated, with high birth and death rates; it was also "poor, rural, agrarian, illiterate, small-scale, communitarian, hierarchical, pious, weakly governed, and amateurish." Late twentieth-century society, in contrast, is "dense, with low birth and death rates, and is rich, urban, industrial, literate, large-scale, individualistic, depersonalized, egalitarian, democratic, agnostic, bureaucratized, and professional. There is hardly a single one of these transformations in which the family has not played a key role as an agent, subject, catalyst or transmitter of changing values and experience."

Until recently, the changes just described were widely assumed to represent "progress." Faith in the idea of progress—the belief that in the future life would be better for oneself, one's children, and one's children's children—has been part of Western culture since the eighteenth century (see Almond, Chodorow, & Pearce, 1982). The concept of progress was a reaction against the nostalgic idea of a past golden age from which time things have gone downhill.

Since the 1970s, it has become increasingly hard for anyone to hold to a belief that each generation will inevitably enjoy a richer, happier, more enlightened life than the previous one. People now look backward nostalgically once again to the past. At the center of this new nostalgia is a longing for a more stable, ordered, and harmonious family life. Would we find it if we could return to premodern times? The new history of the family can provide some insights into "the world we have lost."

THE NEW HISTORY
OF THE FAMILY

The study of family life in other places, of course, is very different from the study of family life in other times. No matter how remote or exotic an existing group, it is possible to study their family behavior firsthand. The historian, by contrast, faces the task of reconstructing history. Until fairly recently, there was a great deal of skepticism about trying to reconstruct family life and family change in past eras. In 1964, William H. Goode asserted that "not a single history of the U. S. family would meet modern standards of historical research" (p. 105).

Until the 1960s, most historians avoided studying the family, leaving the topic to anthropologists and sociologists. This avoidance can be attributed in part to the practical problems mentioned by Goode: the scarcity of documentary materials and the hesitancy of historians to venture into the alien territory of the social sciences. More important perhaps was the general tendency of historians to focus on public events rather than private experience, and on elites rather than on the bottom 90 percent of the population. Since the 1960s, however, there has been a massive outpouring of studies on the family life of past times.

New Methods

For the new scholars of the family in history, reconstructing past family life does not appear to be an impossible task. As Tamara Hareven (1971) pointed out, historians neglected the family not only because materials were lacking but also because they failed to ask the right questions.

Now new ways of using existing materials have been discovered. A number of important techniques have been borrowed from the field of demography, enabling historians to trace population changes, mobility, fertility, birth control, infant mortality, illegitimacy, and even marriages with pregnant brides. One highly significant development is a technique known as family reconstruction: using records of births, deaths, marriages, land transfers, and wills, the historian can reconstruct the family and household patterns of large numbers of ordinary people who had previously been considered lost forever in the depths of time.

Using the family-reconstruction technique, for example, Philip Greven (1970) was able to trace the structures of individual families in Andover, Massachusetts, beginning with the first settlers and continuing through four generations. Greven emphasizes the role of the land in the family lives of farmers—the subtle ways in which inheritance patterns and the availability of land influenced relations between fathers and sons.

John Demos's (1970) study of the Plymouth colony presents another attempt to reconstruct the intimacies of everyday family life in the colonial era. Demos tries to depict the concrete realities of the family by a detailed study of colonial houses, who lived in them, their furnishings, clothing, child-rearing methods, the tasks carried out in the households, and the relations between households and the larger community. More recently, the new methods have been used to document the nature of black family life during slavery and the post–Civil War era.

New Controversies

Not surprisingly, the further such studies get from such facts as births, deaths, and household arrangements in making interpretations about the experiences of family life, the more debate their conclusions elicit. Demos and Greven, for example, disagree about the quality of emotional life in colonial households: Greven sees life in the first generation of Andover settlers as harmonious, in part because of the abundance of land; Demos suggests that the crowded households built frustrations and resentments that were expressed in disputes with other families.

There is similar debate about the emotional quality of family life in premodern Europe. Peter Laslett (1965) has argued that in the "world we have lost" all of life took place in the midst of the family, "in a circle of loved, familiar faces." In contrast, Edward Shorter (1975) has portrayed premodern times as "the bad old days" in which the family was more a reproductive and economic unit than an emotional one, and there was little love between husbands and wives, or parents and children.

In a relatively short span of time, however, the recent work of historians has revised many notions about the family that had been held by family scholars as well as by the public. We have learned that the typical household in centuries past was not necessarily filled with large numbers of kin; sexual behavior was not frozen at a constant level until the sexual revolution of the 1920s; and people did not have the same ideas and emotions about children that they have now. As noted in the last chapter, the new historical studies have also blurred the line between normality and pathology. Historians have analyzed nonmarital sexuality, illegitimacy, and generational conflict as part of family life itself, rather than as a separate category of deviance.

In spite of its achievements, however, the new history of the family has probably raised more questions than it has answered. Much of this research has been concerned with the impact of modernization on the family. Research began to look for this impact in changes over time in the size and composition of the average household. At first, historians were attracted to the study of household structure for several reasons: First, it is easy to obtain quantifiable data about it, since the household is the basic unit used by census takers in many countries; second, the prevailing social-science generalizations seemed to suggest that the history of the family should be viewed as the decline of the great extended patriarchal household and the rise of the isolated nuclear family. Further, to many historians, household structure seemed to be the key to the emotional environments of family life— an extended-family household seemed to create a radically different emotional atmosphere than that of the nuclear family.

One of the earliest studies of the new family history was Peter Laslett's research showing that the nuclear family was the prevailing household unit well before modern times (Laslett & Wall, 1972). Since then, other historians have taken issue with Laslett. Jean-Louis Flandrin (1979), for example, has argued that in the past the nuclear unit was embedded in a network of kin, domestic servants, and neighbors, creating a far different emotional climate than the more intense, isolated families of more recent times. Nevertheless, despite the disagreements about household structure, historians agree that the modern family differs profoundly from its historical counterpart.

On the other hand, the image of family change from traditional to modern has become more complicated. When we talk about the transition, we are apt to have a linear image, with family life becoming more modern the closer it comes to our own time. However, there is growing evidence that family patterns and beliefs may follow a more cyclical course. Research on the nineteenth century suggests, for example, that certain trends actually reversed themselves. In the Victorian era, there was a retreat from the

A family around the turn of century. Notice how widely the ages of the children vary. [Charles Van Schrack Collection, State Historical Society of Wisconsin]

growth of gender equality and positive attitudes toward sex that had been prevalent in the eighteenth century (Stone, 1977). Further, in countries that are just now undergoing modernization, the changes are more complicated and diverse than they are portrayed in the prevailing image (S. LeVine & LeVine, 1985). In the rest of this chapter, as we review the broad shifts in family life that have occurred through time, it is a good idea to keep in mind there is more variation than we can describe.

SOCIETAL DEVELOPMENT AND THE FAMILY

Economic and technological development have a profound influence on family life. Modern theorists, however, do not assume a mechanical sort of economic determinism; instead, they realize that how a society provides for basic needs and the abundance it can produce set off a chain of influential consequences. The sheer amount of food a society is able to produce, for example, determines how many and how densely people can live together. Further, more surplus frees people from agriculture and permits specialization in crafts and other occupations.

Modern scholars, as noted earlier, see the agricultural revolution as a major turning point in human history. The transition from hunting and gathering to the invention of agriculture made possible a settled way of life, the birth of individual and family property in land, herds, houses, and other objects, and the rise of unequal social classes and the state. Although the nuclear family tends to be the major family unit in hunting societies, the extended-kin group characterizes agricultural societies.

A second major transition is the shift from agrarian to industrial society. In industrial societies the nuclear family once again emerges as the dominant household form. R. L. Blumberg and Winch (1972) have documented this pattern for more than 900 societies. Not only does the structure of the family vary, but also the psychological quality of life. In general there are marked contrasts in the relations between men and women and parents and children over the range of societal development. Let us consider the family more closely under these major shifts in technology.

HUNTING-AND-GATHERING SOCIETIES

For 99 percent of human history, hunting and gathering was the major means of subsistence.

To date, the hunting way of life has been the most successful and persistent adaptation man has ever achieved. . . . It is still an open question whether man will be able to survive the exceedingly complex and unstable ecological conditions he has created for himself. If he fails in this task, interplanetary archeologists of the future will classify our planet as one in which a very long and stable period of small-scale hunting and gathering was followed by an apparently instantaneous efflorescence of technology and society rapidly leading to extinction. . . . The origin of agriculture and thermonuclear destruction will appear as essentially simultaneous. (Lee & Devore, 1968, p. 3)

Recent anthropological research has placed less emphasis on hunting as the key feature of early human social life. Today's hunter-gatherers, except for those who live in the Arctic, get more of their daily calories from plant foods gathered by women than from meat obtained through hunting (Lee & Devore, 1968). Some anthropologists emphasize food sharing as the central element in early human evolution, the feature that separated early humans from their great-ape relatives (Isaac, 1978; Lancaster, 1985).

About 175 contemporary hunting-and-gathering cultures have been studied in detail, including Eskimos, Bushmen of the Kalahari Desert in southern Africa, forest Pygmies, and many Canadian and South American Indian groups (Gough, 1971). These living groups of hunters cannot be regarded as fossils—precise replicas of human society as it existed ten to fifteen thousand years ago—but they do offer clues to earlier family and social organization.

Although the technology of hunters is rudimentary, they are not primitive in mentality. Nor do hunting societies live up to the image of "bloodthirsty savages." Nineteenth-century anthropologists erroneously concluded that people in simpler societies were less intelligent than people in "civilized" societies. Eighteenth-century philosophers thought hunters epitomized a simple "state of nature."

But in religion, morality, art, and etiquette their culture is at least as elaborate as ours, and in one respect it is more elaborate. Some hunting groups possess enormously complex kinship systems. Moreover, there is no primitive language; the languages associated with primitive technologies may be more elaborate than the languages of some advanced societies. Still, the underlying structure of all human languages is identical, and any human infant placed in any group at birth will grow up a native speaker of whatever language prevails.

Although hunters live in many different environments with varying cultures, anthropologists consider it useful to analyze hunting societies as a major societal type:

In spite of their varied environments, hunters share certain features of social life. They live in bands of about 20 to 200 people, the majority of bands having fewer than 50. Bands are divided into families, which may forage alone in some seasons. Hunters have simple but ingenious technologies. Bows and arrows, spears, skin clothing, and temporary leaf or wood shelters are common. Most hunters do some fishing. The band forages and hunts in a large territory and usually moves camp often.

Social life is egalitarian. There is of course no state, no organized government. Apart from religious shamans or magicians, the division of labor is based only on sex and age. Resources are owned communally; tools and personal possessions are freely exchanged. Everyone works who can. Band leadership goes to whichever man has the intelligence, courage, and foresight to command the respect of his fellows. Intelligent older women are also looked up to. (Gough, 1971, p. 765)

Marriage and sex practices in hunting societies in some ways resemble those in modern societies more than those in the agrarian states at the middle range of societal complexity. Hunting societies tend to be relaxed sexually; there is premarital sexual freedom, special times of sexual license for people not married to each other, and a "pragmatic" approach to adultery. The best-known example of the relaxed sexual customs that tend to prevail among hunters is the Eskimo custom of the wife's sleeping with male guests as part of normal hospitality.

Kathleen Gough (1971) notes that although group marriage does not exist among hunters, mating has more of a group character than in agrarian or industrial societies. There is less differentiation between the band and the nuclear family than in our society—the band is as much part of everyone's daily environment as the family.

Although elders arrange marriages, couples usually know each other and have some choice.

Both sexual and companionate love between individual men and women are known and deeply experienced. With comparative freedom of mating, love is less often separated from or opposed to marriage than in archaic states or even than in some modern nations. (Gough, 1971, p. 765)

Relations between parents and children also appear to be more relaxed in hunting societies than in more complex ones. Stephens (1963) suggests this may result from the greater authoritarianism of stratified states with central political leadership. When society is organized as a pyramid, with a king or chief at the top and social groups arranged in layers beneath him, children and women are likely to be at the bottom.

Furthermore, children may be better treated in hunting societies because hunters seem to enjoy their work and life more than farmers or workers in industrial societies. Although the productivity of hunters is low, they do not work at hunting endlessly. They are not harried; indeed, many hunting peoples are extremely leisured. One anthropologist calls hunting society "the original affluent society" (Sahlins, 1968). Children in hunting societies, as part of their socialization, do the kinds of things that are intrinsically enjoyable for small children in any culture. Turnbull (1961) describes the way children's play in one hunting society imperceptibly changes into adult work.

At an early age, boys and girls are "playing house."
They will also play at hunting, the boys stretching out their little bits of net while the girls beat the ground with bunches of leaves and drive some poor tired old frog in toward the boys. . . . One day they find that the games they have been playing are not games any longer, but the real things, for they have become adults. Their hunting is now real hunting; their tree climbing is in earnest search of inaccessible honey, in the pursuit of elusive game, or in avoiding malicious forest buffalo. It happens so gradually that they hardly notice the change at first, for even when they are proud and famous hunters their life is still full of fun and laughter. (pp. 128–129)

Finally, obedience is not a major value among hunters and gatherers. A study by Barry, Child, and Bacon (1959) compared child-training practices and child behavior in societies having different types of subsistence economy. They found that hunting-and-fishing societies emphasized achievement, independence, and self-reliance, whereas agricultural societies stressed compliance and obedience. If crops and animals must be tended regularly, disobedience or even innovation can endanger the food supply for months. Thus farmers and herders must be cautious and responsible. Since hunters cannot store food, cautiousness and responsibility are not so crucial.

In recent years hunting-and-gathering societies are coming to be viewed in a new light. In the nineteenth century, peoples with low levels of technological development were considered savages, living fossils with mental capacities between civilized people and apes. Civilization was regarded as progress up the ladder of human perfection. If, as nineteenth-century "false Darwinism" had it, evolution was the survival of the fittest, then simple societies obviously were unfit. Now, however, assessing the alienation of modern life and the environmental crises, anthropologists and others are coming to reevaluate the relative advantages of civilization and the oldest form of human society.

AGRARIAN SOCIETY

The agricultural way of life that came to predominate several thousand years ago is still followed by a majority of the world's population. The agricultural revolution represented a major step in the advance of "civilization" or, to use a less value-loaded term, societal complexity. Hunting-and-gathering societies depend wholly on what nature provides for food, clothing, and shelter. Since they are always on the move, possessions are a burden, and even infants, the very old, and the very sick may have to be abandoned in times of short supply.

Agriculture made it possible for people to settle in one place, and enormous consequences followed. The ownership of property and its hereditary transmission appeared on the scene. Surplus wealth led to the growth of population, increased population density, and a greater division of labor: people could specialize in crafts and trade. With the increase in population, larger social units began to appear, resulting in the rise of cities and the emergence of the centralized state ruled by kings or other hereditary monarchs, about 4000 B.C. (Gough, 1971; Rapp, 1977). Military conquests of one people by another became possible, and they contributed to the increasing stratification of society into different social classes.

The characteristic form of the family in agrarian societies is the large kin group, whether the unilineal descent groups of preliterate peoples or the extended families of European peasants (R. L. Blumberg & Winch, 1972). These kin groups are also hierarchically organized along patriarchal principles.

The agricultural revolution ushered in a way of life with its own social and psychological characteristics. The first farmers had more in common with modern peasants than with the prehistoric hunters who preceded them.

It might be said that for the individual, the revolutionary psychological change was the substitution of routine and hard work for excitement and uncertainty, while the social counterpart was a new stability demanding greater discipline and more government. (Hawks, 1963, p. 354)

The other important contrast between agrarian societies and those at either end of the scale of societal complexity is the importance in them of the extended patriarchal family.

The Patriarchal Family Observed

"Traditional" family systems, although differing among themselves, contrast sharply with the Western industrial family. In each, the role of the individual is defined by heredity and long tradition: the extended family group, whether or not it lives in the same household, is an economic unit tied to durable property of some kind, and deviation from community norms is severely sanctioned.

Societies at the middle of the scale of societal complexity tend to exhibit the most extreme patterns of age and sex subordination within the family. S. LeVine and LeVine (1985) point to four major features shared by all agricultural societies:

1. A sharp distinction between the sexes, rooted in reproduction but affecting all aspects of social life and subjective experience. The essential female function is motherhood. With food production requiring intensive labor, best supplied by a large family, women are expected to produce babies from marriage to menopause. The notion of "enough" children is "irrelevant in societies where the hazards of disease, drought, and pestilence can make maternal success ephemeral" (p. 32). The contrast between male and female is sharpened by cultural ideologies and by the widespread practice of women moving to their husband's residence and kin group after marriage.

2. An age hierarchy within each gender, with younger people subordinated to older ones.

3. The expectation of lifelong loyalty to parents. "Agrarian parents feel entitled to expect obedience from their offspring while they are children, loyalty from them when they are young adults, and increasing respect and support from them as they grow older" (p. 31).

4. Kinship as the main determinant of identity. Whatever their particular qualities as individuals, agrarian adults continue to define themselves and are defined by others by their gender, their age, and their location in the kinship system. The concept of a personal identity separate from social ties is rare.

In some agrarian societies, patterns of age and sex subordination are so marked that they have been described by William Stephens (1963) as "deference societies," characterized by ritualized expressions of respect, submissiveness, and obedience. Defer-

ence customs between sons and fathers involve such behavior as the following:

1. not addressing father by his first name
2. using verbal restraint when speaking
   to father; speaking in a low voice; not
   arguing
3. kneeling or bowing when greeting father
4. not touching father
5. not being permitted to eat with father
6. father has a seat of honor
7. father and son not supposed to laugh and
   joke together
8. strict obedience rules for children

Deference behavior demanded of wives is
similar to that demanded for sons. Wives
may also be excluded from gatherings attended by husbands.

In studying deference customs cross-
culturally, Stephens discovered an all-or-
none effect: if there is one deference relationship, there tend to be others. The hub of it all
is the child-to-father relationship. If the children must defer to father, there are usually
deference rules for elder male relatives, as
well as wife-to-husband deferences.

Patterns of subordination are illustrated
in a classic study of the Irish peasant family
system by Arensberg and Kimball (1968).
Children in these families begin their work
lives very early and attain sociological adulthood very late. A man remains a "boy" ver-
bally and socially until his father dies or retires and he inherits the family farm or his
share of it. Thus some men of 45 and even 50
are still "boys." Even though the sons do the
major work of the farm, they have no control
over the spending of farm income.

Thus, the . . . farmer and his sons are often seen
at fairs and markets together, but it is the farmer

father who does the bargaining. Once when one
of the authors asked a countryman about this at
a potato market, he explained that he could not
leave his post for long because his full-grown son
"isn't well-known yet and isn't a good hand at
selling." . . . Even at forty-five and fifty, if the old
couple have not made over their farm, the countryman remains a boy in respect to farm work
and in the rural vocabulary. (pp. 53–55)

Along with a subordination of the young,
there is a sharp differentiation between sex
roles and derogation of women. Farm duties
are divided into men's and women's work.
Some tasks are divided according to heavi-
ness of the labor, but many divisions are
arbitrary, although those involved do not
consider them so. They assume that the distribution of tasks corresponds to the natural
propensities of the sexes. Thus selling eggs
and milking cows are "natural" for women,
and plowing is "naturally" a male activity.
"There is . . . an entire body of popular belief
and superstition surrounding the dichotomy
in farm labor" (p. 40).

Cernea (1970) has provided a similar description of the Rumanian peasant family.
About the position of the woman in the family he writes:

The inequality between husband and wife in the
traditional Rumanian peasant family was enormous. Both societal and family values and rules
reinforced that inequality. . . . unwritten but
very powerful village norms required that the
woman should bow to the man and greet him
first. A wife should not walk beside her husband
but follow behind him; when he stopped to chat
with another villager, she should stop at a defi-
nite distance behind him, not interfere with the
conversation, wait, and start again only after her
husband starts walking. At home she was "the
humble servant of her husband, for all his needs,
under the penalty of being beaten" (Negrea, 1936,
p. 45). Out in the agricultural field, she had to
perform a considerable share of the hardest activities, side by side with her husband. Advanced

pregnancy was not a reason to discontinue work, and giving birth to a child in the field was reported as a common occurrence. (p. 55)

In cultures in which deference roles apply in the family, they appear to generate an emotional climate of reserve, lacking in spontaneity. Not only is the behavior of the deferent person inhibited, but so is the behavior of the person in the superior position. Extreme power inequality seems to generate stiff, formal behavior from everyone in the family and may even result in family members avoiding each other; indeed, some societies prescribe patterns of apartness and estrangement (R. A. LeVine, 1965). In the most patriarchal societies, in which the father is all powerful over his children, he is often quite inhibited in his dealings with them. He may order them around, but he doesn't play or laugh with them or let them sit on his lap. Here is an example of such a family climate from a study of Tepoztlan, Mexico:

The husband avoids intimacy with members of his family [in order] to be respected by them. He expects them to demonstrate their respect by maintaining a proper social distance. His contacts with the children are brief and reserved. The Tepoztlan husband expects his wife to see that the children are quiet when he is at home, and it is her obligation to teach them to fear him. Men are generally not talkative at home and contribute little to family conversation, nor do they seek or expect their children to confide in them. When the husband is at home during the day, he sits apart from the rest of the family; at night, he eats alone or with his grown sons and goes out, or retires soon after. (O. Lewis, 1951, pp. 322–338)

What accounts for such family patterns? Scholars have offered political explanations based on the structure of authority in the larger society, as well as economic explanations based on the control over resources within the family. Stephens (1963) attributes the authoritarianism of traditional family life to the autocratic state. He examined family customs in fifty-one societies: Those with extremely high deference patterns were parts of kingdoms; tribal groups tended to be low in deference. Stephens describes the difference between tribes and kingdoms as follows:

These are the defining attributes of the kingdom: a state, nobles and commoners, an agrarian economic base, exploitation of commoners by nobles, and a state religion.

The other type of society—the tribe—is a society without a state. It is not subject to "a centralized organ of political control, with coercive power over the populace," with an army and tax collectors. Although the tribe may evince some rudimentary form of social stratification, it does not have "nobles" who have the power to economically exploit "commoners." (p. 329)

Between the time the first centralized states developed—about 4000 B.C.—and about 200 years ago, the history of the world was made by kingdoms. (Tribes may have histories, too, but these are unrecorded.) Traditional European societies that preceded the modern democratic state belong to this same general cross-cultural type—that is, kingdoms.

Others explain the family patterns of traditional societies differently. Cernea (1970) suggested that the economic infrastructure of the peasant family accounts for the extreme subordination of women and children. The father not only exercises power as head of the household, but also owns and manages the family's labor and property. Further, agriculture, unlike industrialism, encourages caution and conservation rather than innovation. When social change is slow and traditional ways are rewarded, the elders are thought to possess superior wisdom, heightening still further their position vis-à-vis the young.

The patriarchal family was not restricted to peasants cultivating the land; it appeared in other preindustrial settings in which the whole family group was an economic unit.

The household of a property-owning family in seventeenth-century England was a complicated economic enterprise that included not only children and relatives but servants, apprentices, and journeymen from different social classes. At its head was the *paterfamilias* who worked alongside his wife, children, employees, and wards. He was solely responsible for the economic and spiritual welfare of his family and represented in his person the supposed unity and independence of the family. (Zaretsky, 1976, p. 39)

Even during the early stages of industrialism, during the domestic or putting-out system, whole families working in their homes could be part of the manufacturing process:

Weaving had offered an employment to the whole family, even when spinning was withdrawn from the home. The young children winding bobbins, older children watching for faults, picking over the cloth, or helping to throw the shuttle in the broadloom; adolescents working a second or third loom; the wife taking a turn at weaving in and among her domestic employments. (Thompson, 1963, p. 306)

It should be noted that not all scholars agree with the idea that women occupied a very lowly status in the preindustrial family. Some historians have argued that in the family-based economy women enjoyed some degree of autonomy and were respected because of their direct contributions to the family's work (Tilly & Scott, 1978).

The Patriarchal Family Idealized

In this book so far we have dealt at length with the familiar idealizations of the nuclear family in our contemporary culture. We have seen in the previous chapter how the nuclear family, in the writings of some students of the family, is presumed to be a harmoniously balanced social system providing for the satisfaction of human needs and societal stability. But the other family systems have also been justified in exactly the same terms. Since the nineteenth century, critiques of the modern family have been made from the right and from the left, contrasting the nuclear family with an idealized version of a different family system.

The conservative defense of the patriarchal family was developed by scholars who mourned the passing of the old monarchial regimes based on hereditary status, religion, tradition, and blood ties. They combined a utopian vision of feudal society with an acute insight into the strains of modern industrial ones. In traditional society people knew their duty and their place, and life was stable and cohesive. To these scholars the traditional family seemed to symbolize the principle of "authority without resentment."

For the scholars in this tradition the modern family is a disastrous social form. In fact, the popular cliché that the decline of family life leads to the downfall of civilization originated with this group of scholars. People who state the cliché today believe they are talking about the nuclear family, but it was the decline of the traditional family that was lamented in the original formulation of the idea. Thus Zimmerman (1947) wrote that the decline of patriarchal authority in the Roman family led to the demoralization of society and ultimately the downfall of Rome. Zimmerman argued that familistic values, which dictated that people subordinate their own needs to those of the family, gave way to individualism, leading to the breakdown of morality, authority, and social cohesiveness. Zimmerman thought the same process might be happening in the United States during the twentieth century.

Zimmerman's work was influenced by that of Frederic Le Play (1866/1935), a nineteenth-century French scholar. Like a number of other French scholars of the family and the old regime in France—that is, of France before the French Revolution—Le Play contrasted two extreme forms of the family, the patriarchal and the "unstable" or conjugal family, with an intermediate form, the stem family, which Le Play thought of as ideal. In the patriarchal family, sons and sometimes daughters remain in their parent's home after marriage. When the household grows too large, some members leave to create a new patriarchal unit. Le Play saw the patriarchal family as a more primitive form and emphasized that most of these families would be found in agriculture.

In the stem family only one heir inherits and lives in the ancestral home and lands. The others are given dowries and can become independent, although the ancestral home remains a permanent center for all the members of the family. The direct heir usually inherits the same profession as the father. Le Play thought the stem family "answered all the legitimate instincts of humanity. This is why public order prevails everywhere it exists in strength" (cited in Farber, 1966, p. 20). The patriarchal system was too limiting, since all the sons were confined to the father's household and occupation, but Le Play saw it as a sound system nevertheless. But for the "unstable" family he had not a single good word to say.

Le Play saw the "unstable" family prevailing among factory workers as well as among the wealthy classes of France. He noted that the individual under the new family regime could rapidly reach a high social position because he could dispose freely of his inheritance and his income. He need no longer provide for the needs of relatives. For Le Play, however, mobility and achievement were not particularly attractive values.

The detachment from the larger family that made mobility possible also made the "unstable" family vulnerable to disorganization as a result of illness, death, and financial need. People not only could rise but also could rapidly fall into misery and pauperism. Le Play believed that happiness in private life was guaranteed in the stem family because it balances tradition and novelty, liberty and restraint, individualism and association. As for the individualism of the new family system, Le Play had this to say:

The advantages which certain people derive from the unlimited extension of individual desires appear greater than they are in reality. Where individualism becomes dominant in social relations, men rapidly move towards barbarism. (cited in Farber, 1966, p. 20)

Le Play disregarded the strains within the traditional society and family, but his analysis of the weaknesses of the modern family is still valid: its vulnerability to crisis and its replacement of duty and obligation with individual freedom.

Another idealization of traditional or feudal society may be found in Philippe Ariès's *Centuries of Childhood* (1962). Ariès described medieval society as a big, happy, sociable mixture of young and old, rich and poor, from which the middle classes came to withdraw over the centuries of their rise to social power. His glossing over of the social inequalities of the medieval society places Ariès in the conservative tradition; class distinctions were sharply marked by dress and manner, but people of different ranks were physically and emotionally close to each other:

The valet never left his master, whose friend and accomplice he was, in accordance with an emotional code to which we have lost the key today. . . . The haughtiness of the master matched the insolence of the servant and restored, for

Irish father and son at a sheep market. [Henri Cartier-Bresson/Magnum Photos Inc.]

better or worse, a hierarchy which excessive familiarity was perpetually calling into question. (p. 414)

Although Ariès's praise of medieval times and his rejection of modern society and the whole modernizing process—mass education, industrialism, achievement motivation—places him in a conservative camp, the value he placed on individualism puts him on the opposite side from such writers as Le Play.

The conservative historians denounced individualism because it opposed the hereditary duties and customs of the traditional family. Ariès argued that individualism has triumphed over the family. In his view, the increasing power of the intense, tightly knit nuclear family has flourished at the expense of the individual and also has destroyed the richly textured communal society of medieval times.

Strains in the Patriarchal Family

Considerable evidence indicates that the traditional family system was never as harmonious as its defenders would have us believe. It is interesting to contrast the idealized versions of traditional family life in Le Play and others with actual studies of European peasant families showing the household and inheritance patterns of the patriarchal and stem family. Wherever studies of peasant families have been carried out, one finds the same picture of individual subordination to the demands of the land and a patriarchal authority structure. As Berkner (1972) pointed out:

The peasant's entire household may have looked like a big happy family, but it was held together by legal restrictions imposed in the peasant community and by the limited opportunities offered by the rural economy. (p. 418)

Among peasants the father's parental authority is enhanced by his economic roles as manager, owner, and decision maker. The demands of the peasant father for obedience and discipline are strengthened to the extent that the children have no choice as to what they will be or where they will live: they will be farmers or farmers' wives. In short, the traditional peasant family imposes a life of toil and obedience and raises "virtually insurmountable barriers to possible attempts at escape" (Cernea, 1970, p. 55).

The chief source of strain appears to have been in the father–son relationship. For the son the hardest time was when he was full grown, waiting to inherit the farm in order to marry and achieve a man's status. For the father the hardest time was the retirement period, when the farm was transferred to the son during the father's lifetime. Such strains could be deduced from the prevalence of separate living quarters for the retired couple and of detailed legal contracts setting forth the specific rights the father retained after relinquishing the farm to the heir:

When, for example, Joseph and Anna Maria Pichler decided to retire in October 1784, they drew up a contract with their son Johann and his bride Gertraud, selling them their house and fields for 100 florings. Joseph deducted 20 florings from the price as a wedding gift . . . and

asked that the rest be paid in installments of 20 florings every . . . September 29. . . . They reserved the right to live in *Stubl* [retirement room] rent-free for the rest of their lives, the use of a small piece of meadow and a section of garden to grow cabbage and potatoes and a yearly supply of seven bushels of wheat, thirty-two batches of hay, and two piles of wood. (Berkner, 1972, p. 401)

The prolongation of the lifespan in relatively modern times obviously increased this source of strain:

The dutiful son mourned the day when his parents passed promptly to their reward. . . . That was as it should be and he inherited their place. But there were no attitudes proper for the situation in which the old people lived on and on while their successor waited impatiently. (Handlin & Handlin, 1971, p. 8)

Patriarchal Marriage

Marriage in this system was part of the family business rather than an individual affair of the heart. Stone (1960) described the bitter family struggles in the English nobility that led to the acceptance of the woman's right to a veto over marriages arranged by parents. During the early part of the period, marriages among the nobility were arranged as important business transactions, without regard to the wishes of the marrying couple. It was common, for example, for small children to be bartered in advance by their families. Stone argued that these practices were supported by an ideology of strict parental control over children. These beliefs in the natural subjugation of children paralleled the political doctrine of the divine right of kings. In addition, noble sons as well as daughters were totally dependent economically on their parents—another instance of similarity between the extreme ends of the social scale. In trying to account for the modification of parent–child relations that resulted in the right of a child to say no to the parent's choice of a spouse, Stone referred to the several ideological currents at the time that favored individualism in religion, economics, and politics: the rise of the Protestant ethic, the growth of capitalism, and the growing challenge to the institution of absolute monarchy.

Besides the influence of new ideas, however, transportation affected the social lives of young people. The opening of roads and of a coach service between London and the countryside led to the development of a social season in London. The nobility from all over England would come together every year for the balls and other events of the season. The increased social contacts resulting from the festivities may have made the old obligation to marry someone picked out by one's parents more objectionable. It was one thing to marry a stranger chosen by father when you didn't know any other young men and women; it was something else to have to do so after having met the entire field of eligible young people during the season.

Some scholars have argued that whenever the process of breaking away from traditional kinship patterns occurs, it tends to go along with a sense of personal liberation. When a shift toward modernization takes place in underdeveloped countries, W. J. Goode (1963) notes, the resentments generated by traditional family systems play an important role in enhancing change. Both modernization and the conjugal family appeal to intellectuals, to the young, to women, and to the disadvantaged in general:

The ideology of the conjugal family is a radical one, destructive of the older traditions in almost every society. . . . Its appeal is almost as universal as that of "redistribution of the land." It asserts the equality of individuals, as against class, caste, or sex barriers. (Goode, 1963, p. 19)

Recently, S. LeVine and LeVine (1985) described the pressures on traditional family systems in agrarian societies now undergoing modernization: "Children know more than their parents; they are less compliant, less obedient, more troublesome. The old social structure that had defined an individual's position almost exclusively in terms of age and gender is no longer functional" (p. 37).

Tradition and Change

The appeal of the conjugal family does not mean, however, that people in patriarchal families constantly chafe under their restrictions. These family structures can remain stable for centuries, sustained by duty, law and lack of other opportunities. Like most revolutions, the revolution in family patterns requires that some alternative vision, some other way of doing things, becomes available or necessary to large numbers of people. Such change can be facilitated by a number of factors—literacy, improved transportation, access to market towns and outside jobs, a poor harvest, or too many sons for the land to support. All these factors promote migration of sons and brothers from the family farm, while illiteracy and isolation perpetuate traditional family structures (Parish & Schwartz, 1972).

Some scholars have taken issue with the notion that the shift from traditional to more modern forms of family life imply personal liberation. They have pointed out that the rise of individualism, as well as the shift of work out of the home, had different effects on men than on women, as well as on different social classes. Louise Tilly and Joan Scott (1978), for example, argue that women were better off in "the family economy"—when work went on in the home—than they were later on under industrialism because they had more control over their working conditions. Tilly and Scott argued that the working class did not absorb the upper-class value of individualism but rather tried to retain their traditional values under the new economic conditions. These authors also reject the idea, put forth by Edward Shorter (1975), that new notions of sexual freedom and romantic love arose among the working classes in the eighteenth century and led to an increase in illegitimacy. Instead, Tilly and Scott argue that industrialization led to a breakdown in parental control; parents could no longer watch over their daughters as carefully as in the past, nor force young men to marry them if they got pregnant.

These contrasting views reflect different assumptions about family life and its cultural and economic context. Where Goode, Stone, and Shorter point to the impact of changing values and political ideas on the family, Tilly and Scott stress economic change. As Mary Shanley (1979) has pointed out, to understand how the family has changed, we need to look at changes in ideas as well as changes in the ways people make a living. Study of the family that leaves out any of the forces that shape it can only be misleading.

"MODERN" SOCIETY, "MODERN" FAMILY

We realize that the world we live in and the lives we lead differ from those of the past. Modern Western societies of Europe and America seem to contrast both with their own past and with non-Western societies. Social scientists, including economists and historians as well as sociologists and anthropologists, have been much concerned with describing and analyzing such changes. Societies are often divided into two contrasting types: industrial/preindustrial, modern/traditional, advanced/underdevel-

oped, complex/simple, urban/folk, literate/preliterate. Each term accents a different aspect of the contrast between two types of society. None of the terms is completely satisfactory to the scholars involved.

We noted earlier that there is widespread agreement among social scientists that great changes occurred in the European world over the past several centuries—changes that affected the rest of the globe as well. It is also agreed that these changes involved all realms of life—political, economic, social, and psychological. There is, however, intense debate about the meaning and usefulness of the term *modernization* to refer to these events.

The term seems least objectionable as a simple description of a historical process. The problem, however, is that *modernization* has acquired a host of additional meanings. It has, for example, been associated with the idea of "progress," implying that modern societies are necessarily superior to traditional societies. The term *development* has been used as a synonym for modernization, adding evolutionary notions of natural progress to the idea of superiority. In the work of many scholars, "development" is abstracted from its European origins and viewed as an irresistible force affecting all people in the same way.

Stripped of these additional meanings, however, modernization can be studied as a historical phenomenon like any other. Despite the controversies, the concept of traditional versus modern societies seems a useful one. As Peter Stearns (1980) observes, although there have been various critiques of the concept, no valid alternative has been advanced, and "the definitive academic burial has not taken place" (p. 189). Stearns pointed out that modernization is a useful concept because it points to the huge change that transformed Western society in the past 2 centuries—a change that is larger than the usual historical transition. To speak of the industrial revolution is not enough because some of the changes occurred before industrialism took place and also involved much more than modes of production. Modernization implies a basic shift in the human context, as well as in the family and emotional lives of individuals.

Traditional societies may not resemble one another, and modernization may or may not have increased the sum total of human well-being, but the concept does point to significant differences between societies. In short, it seems useful to regard a society as traditional if ways of behavior in it continue with little change from one generation to the next. If behavior continues unchanged, certain other characteristics usually occur. Custom, rather than law, tends to regulate behavior. Social relations tend to be hierarchical rather than "democratic," and occupations and social positions are inherited. As Hagen (1962) observed, a society could not continue to be traditional unless these conditions prevailed. Finally, it should be noted that although modernized societies are also marked by custom, hierarchy, and the inheritance of social position, "the differences in degree and scope are such that without undue distortion of reality they may be thought of as differences in type" (Hagen, 1962, p. 56).

The preceding cautions should be kept in mind when using Table 5.1, which summarizes some of the major contrasts that scholars have drawn between the modern and the traditional family. It should be noted that different scholars have emphasized different contrasts. Further, on several of the items they disagree as to whether traditional and modern families do differ from each other.

The categories in the table represent ideal types—broad patterns rather than firm and certain distinctions. In any particular country, historical period, or social class, however, everything does not change all at once. In general, the modern family pattern is found more completely and is more widespread in the middle class. Even today some aspects of the traditional pattern occur in families at the extreme ends of the socioeconomic class scale. Kinship, for example, is more important among American families in the social register and among the poor than it is in middle-class groups. And Japanese society has combined an advanced economy with a traditional patriarchal family system.

Industrialism and the Family

Despite the possibility of citing major contrasts between the modern and traditional families, scholars still disagree on the essential difference between modern and traditional social organization as well as between these types of family. Is it the presence of large factories, the growth of cities, widespread literacy, the spread of democratic ideas, the separation of kinship from other aspects of life? Or is it all of these taken together? It is similarly difficult to offer definitive answers to questions about the relation between social change and family life: does family life really change drastically in the transition to modern society? In what aspects is there an underlying stability and continuity? Finally, what aspects of family life do change—household living arrangements, who lives with whom, the quality of emotional relationships, the economic functions of the family, the ideas people have about marriage and family?

One source of confusion in discussions about the family and industrialization is the assumption that in modern societies all families are nuclear, whereas in the past all families were large, extended-kin groups. W. J. Goode (1963) described as a myth the "classical family of Western nostalgia": the

TABLE 5.1   *Traditionalism Versus Modernism in Family Form, Function, and Ideology*

Traditionalism	Modernism
1. Kinship is organized principle of society; almost everything a person does is done as a member of a kinship group.	Kinship is differentiated from economic, political, and social life; recruitment to jobs is independent of one's relatives.
2. Sons inherit father's status and occupation.	Individual mobility based on merit.
3. Low geographic and social mobility.	High geographic and social mobility.
4. The extended or complex family may be basic unit of residence and domestic functions—e.g., meals and child care.	Conjugal or nuclear family is basic unit of residence and domestic functions.
5. Most adults work at home; the home is workshop as well as school, hospital, old-age home.	Separation of home and work; household consumes rather than produces.
6. Dominance of parents over children, men over women.	Relatively egalitarian relations within nuclear family in ideals and practice.
7. Kinship bonds override economic efficiency and maximization of individual gain.	Advancement and economic gain of individuals prevail over kin obligations.
8. Ideology of duty, tradition, individual submission to authority and to fate.	Ideology of individual rights, equality, freedom, self-realization.
9. Little emphasis on emotional involvement within nuclear family; marriage not based on love; predominant loyalty of individual is to blood kin, rather than spouse; children are economic rather than emotional assets, but subordination and dependency of children on parents may continue as long as parent lives— in Europe parent–child bonds may be reduced further by practice of apprenticing children to other families at an early age.	Intense involvement of spouses, parents, and children with each other; ideologies of marital happiness and adjustment; great concern with child's development, current adjustment, and future potential, but sharp break with parental authority on attaining adulthood.
10. Little or no psychological separation between home and community; broad communal sociability; no large-scale institutions.	Sharp line of demarcation between home and outside world; home is a private retreat and outside world is impersonal, competitive, threatening.
11. High fertility and high death rates, especially in infancy; rapid population turnover—death a constant presence in families.	Low, controlled fertility and low death rates, especially low in infancy; death a phenomenon of old age.

stereotype of a happy life down on the farm, where lots of kinfolk and their children live in a big, rambling house.

The myth of the large extended family household in times past was laid to rest by Peter Laslett and his associates (P. Laslett & Wall, 1972). Analyzing census data, they concluded that families in former times were small. In England and Europe, the average household size in the sixteenth through the eighteenth centuries was between four and six people, and extended families were even less common than in our times.

However, these findings set off a controversy that is still not resolved. Some historians argue that Laslett and other demographic historians focus too much on household size, ignoring ties with kin outside the home. Flandrin (1979) has pointed out that although the average household size may have been small, there was actually a great deal of variation, not only by class and region, but in the same village. The households of the elite—landholders and gentry—were larger than those of people lower down on the social scale. Such households contained kinfolk and servants who were considered part of one large family. Also, he argues, people may have preferred to live in extended families but were prevented from doing so by poverty and high mortality rates.

Despite the controversy, most scholars agree on several crucial points. The typical household in past centuries was not a large one filled with kin; further, they agree that a major change in family behavior and attitudes took place roughly during the eighteenth century. During this time the mother–father–child unit came to be seen as separate from the larger kin group, and emotional bonds between husbands and wives and parents and children intensified. Recent work by historians has shown that the nuclear family form predominated in Western Europe and America long before the coming of industrialism.

Another misleading assumption, found not only among laymen but also among family scholars, is the belief that the coming of factories destroyed the large kin group down on the farm. The correlation between industrial society and the nuclear family is often interpreted, in a simplistic way, to mean that the nuclear family comes about *only* in an industrial society and that the presence of factories leads in some inexorable way to the breakup of large kin groups. Often studies use literal models of industrialism to attack the idea that technological change leads to family change: thus, for example, a study might be done in country X to show that large industry moved in and did not at once destroy all existing kin ties. Or a study might attempt to show that working in factories did not destroy the kin ties of a group of nineteenth-century immigrants to America who came with extended family structures. Or a study might argue that the nuclear family existed in Europe and America before industrialization, and therefore technology does not cause family change.

The problem with such studies is that they attack simplistic and mechanical versions of the relation between economic and family change. Most scholars now recognize that the relations among social, economic, and cultural change are a complex tangle of interacting forces. The presence of large factories is only one of a number of factors that set off a modern or advanced society from a more traditional one. "Industrialism" is a convenient metaphor, a shorthand reference to a host of social changes that occur when a society modernizes: cities grow in size and importance; population size and density increase; demands arise for literacy and other trained skills; communication and transportation systems improve; and the rate of social change increases. Each of these changes by itself could have profound effects on family life. The term, however, may be misleading in its emphasis on factories as the essential ingredient of modern life and the most important factor in family change.

Indeed, some scholars have argued that industrialization is not even an essential part of modernization. The historian E. A. Wrigley (1972), for example, argued that a society might become modernized before becoming industrialized and that this in fact occurred in Europe beginning in the sixteenth century. The essence of modernization in this view is the existence of commerce and trade, a money economy, and the values of economic self-interest and rationality—rationality being defined in a narrow sense as "that which maximizes economic returns either to the individual, the nuclear family, or the state" (p. 229), as opposed to the larger kin group. Such rationality also implies that people are recruited to jobs on the basis of ability rather than hereditary status. Once kinship is no longer the basis of economic life, social, occupational, and geographic mobility tend to increase. All these changes together weaken kinship bonds by making them less necessary and less enforceable.

Finally, the most far-reaching impact of industrialization on the family came from its effects on mortality and fertility rates. We have seen earlier how the lives of people in agrarian societies are shaped by the strategy of high reproduction in the face of a precarious supply of food and high mortality rates. The industrial revolution brought about a revolution in population known as the *demographic transition*.

Despite the horrors of life in the industrial working classes, realistically portrayed by Dickens, Zola, Marx, and Engels, mortality rates in the nineteenth century fell dramatically in the industrializing countries of Europe, especially among children and teenagers. As Wrigley observes, "The age-specific death rates of the nineteenth century are amongst the most important and impressive testimonies to the economic benefits which came in the wake of the industrial revolution and which took place among the mass of people in spite of the rapid growth of population" (1976, p. 177).

Falling mortality rates made it possible for fertility rates to drop also. Eventually, lower death rates led to much smaller families and the spread of contraception. Further relieved from the burdens of unrestrained fertility, people could give freer expression to sexuality. In sum, the control over birth and death brought about by the industrial revolution would have seemed an impossible dream to people in earlier times. The demographic transition immeasurably changed our assumptions about life, death, family relationships, and the way we think about ourselves. Ironically, the partial conquest over death is also responsible, in part, for some of the problems besetting contemporary society—the growth of the aged population, divorce, and the rise of what many see as a narcissistic degree of individualism.

The Emergence of the Nuclear Family

The economic and psychological separation of individuals and the nuclear family from the larger kin group can occur in preindustrial or primitive societies as well as in modern and industrial ones. Thus, in a survey of 250 societies, Murdock (1949) noted that the development of the nuclear (neolocal) family is favored by any influence that emphasizes the individual:

Individualism in its various manifestations, e.g., private property, individual enterprise in the

FIGURE 5.1
Societal Complexity and Family Form

This chart indicates that the percent of societies with extended family households reaches highest in agricultural societies.

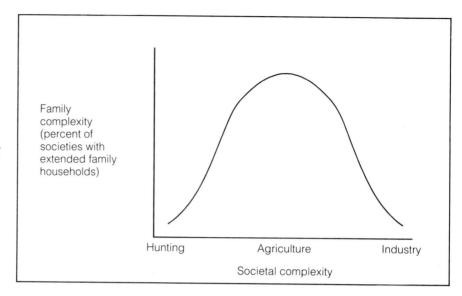

Based on "Societal Complexity and Familial Complexity," R. L. Blumberg and R. F. Winch, *American Journal of Sociology* 77:5, 1972, pp. 898–920, by permission of The University of Chicago Press. © 1972 by The University of Chicago.

economic sphere, or personal freedom in the choice of marital partners, facilitates the establishment of independent households by married couples. A similar effect may be produced by individual migration, or by pioneer life in the occupation of new territory, or by the expansion of trade and industry, or by developing urbanization. . . . Even a change in architecture might exert an influence, e.g., the supplanting of a large communal house by a form of dwelling suited to the occupancy of a single family. (pp. 203–204)

Another seemingly paradoxical finding about the nuclear family is that it appears in the most advanced, modern countries as well as in the most technologically simple. The nuclear family appears as the dominant form in hunting societies, such as the Eskimo; the extended family predominates in agricultural societies; and the nuclear family then reappears in modern conditions (see Figure 5.1). In other words, if all known societies were listed in the order of their "complexity" along the horizontal part of a graph

and family type were plotted on the vertical part of the scale, the relationship between societal development or complexity and family form would be curvilinear, as indicated in Figure 5.1. Why should this be so?

To answer this question, Nimkoff and Middleton (1960) examined more than 500 societies for which detailed ethnographic information existed. They concluded that modern industrial societies in some important ways resemble simpler hunting-and-gathering societies. Both hunting and modern societies tend to individualize the worker.

The modern industrial society, with its small independent family, is then like the simpler hunting and gathering society . . . for some of the same reasons, namely limited need for family labor and physical mobility. The hunter is mobile because he pursues the game, the industrial worker, the job. (Nimkoff & Middleton, 1960, p. 225)

The variables associated with the appearance of the extended family were the reverse of the foregoing ones: an ample and stable food supply, the use of the family as the unit of labor, geographic immobility, and family-owned property, especially in the form of land. Payment in money also has individualizing effects. In peasant societies labor tends to be unpaid family labor. Property in the form of money rather than family-owned land or durable goods also favors the nuclear family over the extended family.

Winch and Blumberg (1968) found some striking parallels between Nimkoff and Middleton's variables and the correlates of extended families in American society today; that is, geographic mobility, family property, and the family as a unit of labor also account for variations in the extent to which American families are involved with extended kin. Winch and Blumberg also found that certain ethnic groups in American society, particularly Jews and Italians, tend to have stronger extended family ties than others; they account for these differences in terms of length of time since immigration, social class, and occupational traditions. Thus the closer a group is to its immigrant roots, the stronger the extended family ties. Also certain occupations, such as storekeeping, tend to encourage the maintenance of extended family ties. In short, family patterns vary within industrial societies, and this variation can be explained in much the same terms as variation in family form among different kinds of societies.

The work of Winch and Blumberg also sheds light on the relationship between industrialism and the nuclear family. When they arranged 933 industrial societies in order of their complexity, they found that the nuclear family began to emerge *before* industrialism. In other words, the curve of extended familism took a downward turn in societies that were still mainly agricultural but complex, as indicated by their having irrigation, towns with more than five thousand people, and three or more levels of political hierarchy. These are indicators of societal complexity because they are complicated kinds of social organization, requiring specialized skills. They also show that the society is producing enough food to release some people from agriculture. These cross-cultural findings parallel the historical findings that the nuclear family emerged in Europe before the industrial revolution.

Psychological Quality of the Intimate Environment

What is it that sets the modern family off from its historical counterparts? We have seen that the classical family of Western nostalgia—the large household bursting with kin—is largely a myth. In America and Western Europe the nuclear family was the prevailing unit, although peasant families were extended during part of the life cycle, and the household often contained nonkinspeople in the form of peasants and servants. How then was family life different in the past?

The answer, now emerging in the work of a number of scholars, lies in the psychological and emotional aspects of family life, not household structure. What seems to have changed are the psychological quality of the intimate environment of family life and the relation between the family and the larger community. Within the home the family has become more intense emotionally, while the ties between home and the outside community have become more tenuous.

Lawrence Stone's (1977) term *affective individualism* sums up the change in family sentiment. "People within the nuclear family in certain circles treated one another quite differently in 1780 from the way their great grandparents had done in 1660, and

Mexican father and son at work. [Helen Nestor]

their attitude towards outsiders, whether kin or neighbors, was also substantially different" (p. 658). The term makes clear that there are two distinct aspects to this change, which is part of a transformation in the larger cultural system.

One aspect of the change is a new view of the individual in relation to society—the rise of individualism. By individualism Stone is referring to a growing introspection, a new interest in individuals as unique personalities, as well as to the new political emphasis on individual rights. The second aspect of the change—the growth of affect—refers to a change in the ways people acted toward

their spouse and children on the one hand and their parents and kin on the other. The change included a greater degree of emotional closeness among nuclear family members as well as a greater appreciation for the individuality of each person in the family.

In the past the line of demarcation between the family and the outside world was not marked as in our time. Edward Shorter (1975), in his book *The Making of the Modern Family*, compared the family in traditional society to a ship moored in a harbor:

The family . . . was held firmly in the matrix of a larger social order. One set of ties bound it to the surrounding kin . . . who dotted the regime's social landscape. Another set fastened it to the wider community, and gaping holes in the shield of privacy permitted others to enter the household freely and, if necessary, preserve order. A final set of ties bound this elementary family to generations past and future. Awareness of ancestral traditions and ways of doing business would be present in people's minds as they went about their day. Because they knew that the purpose of life was preparing coming generations to do as past ones had done, they would have clear rules for shaping behavior within the family. (p. 3)

The modern family has broken these ties to the surrounding community and the chain of generations. The home has become a private retreat, and ties to family members within the home have intensified as ties to outsiders have weakened. Above all, it is domesticity—"the family's awareness of itself as a precious emotional unit that must be protected with privacy and isolation from outside intrusion" (Shorter, 1975, p. 205)—that distinguishes the modern family.

Economic Change, Ideology, and Private Life

It seems clear that there has been a major change in attitudes and feelings about family relationships since the eighteenth century. It is less clear how and why the change came about. One question debated by researchers is: In what social class did the new family pattern originate—in the aristocracy, as Trumbach (1978) believes, or in the upper gentry, as Stone (1977) argued, or in the working class, as Shorter (1975) contended? Or was the rise of the new domesticity a cultural phenomenon that affected people in all social categories at roughly the same time? Carole Shammas (1980) has found evidence of such a widespread cultural change by looking at the kinds of things people had in

their homes at various times in the past, as recorded in probate inventories. She found that in the middle of the eighteenth century all social classes experienced a change in living habits; even working-class households now contained expensive tools of domesticity, such as crockery, teapots, eating utensils, and so on. Thus, according to Shammas, the home was becoming an important center for social interaction, and family meals had come to occupy an important place in people's lives.

The reasons why the change occurred are even less well understood. There is general agreement that the change had something to do with the rise of capitalism—not industrialism, but market capitalism: the production and exchange of goods for money. But the rise of capitalism is part of a complex cultural change that involved changes in political and religious ideas and values as well as an increase in literacy, and major changes in the social landscape, such as the growth of cities. The links among these various dimensions of change, as well as the links between family life and its economic and cultural context, are still being worked out.

Scholars have pointed above all to individualism and a certain kind of individualistic rationality when trying to define the essential difference between modern and traditional societies. As Wrigley (1972) put it, it is not that traditional societies are irrational, but that they define rationality differently. Traditional rationality may mean working only enough to supply one's minimal wants, or it may mean staying together in larger kin groups even though the family lands can scarcely support everyone. In modern Western terms, however, rationality has come to mean maximizing economic gain. Wrigley argues that, once begun, modernization sets off a chain reaction of psychological effects that further increase the momentum of change; rationality and individualism "eat like acid" into the fabric of traditional society, destroying the web of rights and obligations as well as the structure of traditional authority.

But individualism has other meanings in addition to the economic one. It involves a heightened awareness of the self as a separate, unique individual. A person living in an unchanging, traditional social world, where there are no alternatives to the influence of kin and community, can take that world for granted and live with a minimum of self-awareness. The individual remains embedded in the family of origin—the family he or she is born into—just as the family is embedded in the community. From the very beginning, however, the rise of capitalism in the West was associated with a heightened self-awareness:

Christianity has always encouraged a certain degree of self-consciousness in the form of the conscience. . . . But Puritans and other Protestants viewed social behavior as a sign of inward grace and argued that no church ritual or other outward act could determine for certain whether an individual was "saved." One indication of the expansion of self-consciousness was the proliferation of diaries in the seventeenth century. More broadly, the same period saw the invention of silvered mirrors, the spread of autobiography, the building of chairs instead of benches, the spread of private lodgings, and the rise of self-portraits. In this period sincerity became a dominant social ideal. (Zaretsky, 1976, p. 43)

The coming of large-scale industry, bureaucratic organizations, and, above all, the separation of work from family life caused by these developments resulted in further increases in the sense of the separateness of the self. The awareness of discrepancy between our inner selves and the roles we are playing in work and public life creates the need for intimate relationships—a private world where we can express our real and whole selves. Thus the family comes to have a whole new set of demands placed on it in advanced industrial societies. Whether the family can in fact meet these demands is a theme we shall be pursuing throughout this book.

Literacy

Another major individualizing force in modern life is the widespread ability to read. Some scholars have suggested that the spread of literacy is the most meaningful feature of modernization, antedating industrial development (Goody & Watt, 1962). Parsons (1965), for example, considered the invention of writing the dividing line between primitive and intermediate societies and the extension of literacy from elite groups to the whole population a major distinguishing feature of modern societies. The growth of commerce and industry would be almost unthinkable without the existence of written records, bookkeeping, and accounting systems.

Though literacy spreads because of economic need, it has profound psychological consequences. Literacy fosters the same tendencies toward rationality and individualism that are encouraged by the economic aspects of modernization. Preliterate people are not unsophisticated, simple, or at a lower stage of intellect; rather, they are skilled in a different medium of communication—the oral tradition. Using human memory capacities that remain undeveloped where literacy prevails, people who live entirely in the oral tradition can store enormous amounts of information, experience, and entertainment, and they can reproduce this information with astonishing accuracy.

Literacy is a decisive dividing line in individual development also. There is by now an impressive body of research evidence showing that many psychological changes once thought to represent the unfolding of the innate capacities of the human mind may actually be the result of literacy (R. A. LeVine, 1970, p. 585). Such skills as the capacity for abstract thought and the ability to make logical inferences, for example, now appear to develop from the outside in rather than from the inside out. Or, as Jerome Bruner (1964) put it, cognitive development may be to a large degree the internalization of technology. David Reisman (1960) has summarized some of the consequences of the transition from the oral tradition to literacy. Writing tends to foster hierarchies of skill rather than age. In the oral tradition the status of the old is enhanced by their role as storehouses of experience and lore.

Another effect of literacy is to individualize the person, separating him or her from the primary group of family and kinspeople and the world of immediate experience. Books permit detachment and a critical attitude. Just as the ability to write improves the conversation one carries on with oneself, so the ability to read makes it possible to "converse" with people in distant times and places. Reading a book in the presence of others is an isolating act. We noted earlier the finding that geographic and social mobility is associated with the breakdown of extended kinship relations. Reisman has emphasized that reading is the mental equivalent of mobility—you can leave home in your imagination:

Thus the book helps liberate the reader from his group and its emotions, and allows the contemplation of alternative responses and the trying on of new emotions. . . .
    At the same time, while the book helped people break away from family and parish, it linked them into noncontiguous associations of true believers. The Polish peasant who learned to read and write became identified with the urban world of progress and enlightenment, of ideology and Utopia, even while still in the peasant world. (Reisman, 1960, p. 113)

If literacy is used as an indicator of modernity, Western Europe began to change centuries before the first factories appeared on the scene. The growth of cities, trade, and, perhaps above all, the growth of empire during the age of exploration accelerated demand for people who could read and write (Cipolla, 1969).

The Industrial Revolution

Industrialization did not create the nuclear family structure in Europe, but it did change the quality of family life. It destroyed, as Peter Laslett (1965) put it, the "familial texture" of society. The transformation of the world outside the home from a small community into a place of impersonal, large-scale institutions transformed the home itself and the family. There began to be a sense of a gulf between the home and the society at large; each came to be perceived as a separate sphere of life. The home came to be idealized as an "Edenic retreat" from the harsh realities of nineteenth-century industrial society, a place of perfect love, companionship, and moral regeneration (Jeffrey, 1972). Demos (1970) described the kind of gulf that separates the modern American family from society, in contrast to continuity between family and community in colonial times:

The family becomes a kind of shrine for upholding and exemplifying all of the softer virtues— love, generosity, tenderness, altruism, harmony, repose. The world at large presents a much more sinister aspect. Impersonal, chaotic, unpredictable, often characterized by strife and sometimes by outright malignity, it requires of a man that he be constantly "on his guard." (p. 186)

In the next chapter we explore some of the issues scholars have raised concerning the paradoxical place of the family in modern society: as it has lost its economic functions, it has come to loom larger psychologically.

SUMMARY

In recent years scholars have become increasingly interested in family change. Rather than considering the family as essentially the same everywhere, they have been looking at how broader aspects of society affect family life. The relation among the family, technological change in general, and industrialism in particular has been the subject of much confusion and debate. Rather than being a product solely of modern society, however, the nuclear family emerges whenever the individual is set off from the large family group. Thus hunting societies also have the nuclear family. Further, in Western societies the nuclear family structure appeared before the industrial revolution of the nineteenth century. It emerged in early modern times when towns grew in size and number, trade and handicrafts increased in importance, a monetary economy replaced barter, and literacy spread, along with other indicators of societal complexity. In short, the nuclear family structure in Europe seems to have emerged in the context of mercantile, rather than industrial, capitalism. Industrial capitalism, however, altered the quality of family life by separating the workshop from the hearth and the family from society, leading to the enhancement of the psychological over the social and economic functions of the family.

CHAPTER 6

Families in Modern Society

The word alienation is part of the cant of the mid-twentieth century and it began as an attempt to describe the separation of the worker from his world of work. We need not accept all that this expression has come to convey in order to recognize that it does point to something vital to us all in relation to our past. Time was when the whole of life went forward in the family, in a circle of loved, familiar faces, known and fondled objects, all to human size. That time has gone forever. It makes us very different from our ancestors.

Peter Laslett
The World We Have Lost

Around the turn of the century it was a sociological truism that the coming of the urban industrial society was causing the family to lose its functions and wither away. Not just the extended family but also the nuclear unit was included in predictions of decline.

The ideas of such scholars were paralleled in the arguments of feminists of the period, but with a different emphasis. Whereas the scholars regretted or had mixed feelings about the passing home and family, the feminists applauded it:

The family, they thought, once the most important unit of production, had gradually surrendered its functions to institutions outside the home—manufacturing to the factory, control over property to the state, the education of children to the public schools. . . . The tasks formerly performed by the housewife and the family in general were now performed elsewhere, and the function of the housewife in consequence was reduced to the passive role of consumption. The feminists did not regret the passing of the family; on the contrary, as staunch evolutionists, they regarded it as highly desirable. (Lasch, 1965, p. 47)

In 1903 Charlotte Perkins Gilman saw in the kindergarten and the day nursery the liberation of both women and children:

There is no more brilliant hope on earth today than this new thought about the child . . . children as citizens with rights guaranteed by the state; instead of our previous attitude towards them of absolute personal ownership—the unchecked tyranny, or as unchecked indulgence, of the private home. (p. 335)

During the period under discussion the issues raised by the feminists preoccupied the leading intellectuals as well as the pages of the women's magazines, just as today. During the 50-year eclipse of the feminist movement, however, the idea that the demise of the family was a mark of progress passed from popular consciousness, remaining alive only on the fringes of society in bohemian and socialist groups.

ASSESSING THE FAMILY IN MODERN SOCIETY

Until recently much social science literature on the family in modern society was written as an attack on scholars who had predicted the death of the family as a result of urban industrialism. Unlike the feminists, the social scientists who believed the family would wither away were not happy about the prospect. Some of these writers, most notably Le Play and Zimmerman, argued that "civilization" itself was threatened by the breakup of traditional paternalistic authority. They felt that the conjugal family, which Le Play called the "unstable family" and Zimmerman called "atomistic," was only a way station on the road to the total collapse of family life and civilization. Once individualism replaced tradition and filial duty as the ruling principle of life, people would ultimately reject the burdens of family responsibility.

Another group of writers—notably Louis Wirth and Ralph Linton—agreed that urban-industrial society presaged the demise of the family, but they did not go along with the idea that the quality of civilization would also decline. Wirth acknowledged that city life was accompanied by a more impersonal and superficial level of human relations, but he also credited the city with the production of cosmopolitan tastes and sophisticated ideas.

All these writers recognized that modernization and urbanization introduced profound transformations in culture and personality. In traditional societies, although there are many differences among them, ways of behavior continue with little change from one generation to the next. Individual attitudes and behavior are shaped by norms and customs governing familial obligations. Persons of a particular age, sex, and family status are supposed to behave in prescribed ways toward others occupying particular sex, age, and kinship categories. The individual's position in the society is inherited rather than achieved, and he or she usually has little say in the choice of a marriage partner. In any event, marriages are not based on "love" (W. J. Goode, 1963).

Although, as we've noted earlier, there are debates about the concept of modernization and its applicability to non-Western societies, there seems little doubt that an industrialized economy—and all that it implies for education, the mass media, urbanization, and so on—tends to undermine the traditional pattern of customary kinship practices, patriarchal authority, and inherited status. In Western societies the modern emphasis on the conjugal family and marriage for love has been accompanied by an ideology of individualism and personal freedom. In socialist countries, such as the U.S.S.R. and China, however, the values of equality and the subordination of the individual to the state and community have also undermined traditional family obligations.

Parsons's Assessments

Despite these changes, most sociologists have argued that the family remains as important as ever in modern society. The leading advocate of this view is Talcott Parsons, the most important modern theorist of the family (1949, 1951, 1955, 1965). Although Parsons's notions have been under attack in recent years, he remains a major influence. He has provided the major framework for discussions of the family, even though many writers discuss him only to criticize him. His model of the family analyzes the links between the family and the wider society, as well as the inner emotional environment of the family—the relations between husbands and wives and between parents and children. No one has yet provided an alternative theory of the family that attempts to be as comprehensive as Parsons's.

Parsons and his associates agreed that the traditional family, linked by economic and residential rights and obligations as well as kinship bonds, was undone by industrial society. But, in contrast to earlier writers, Parsons argued that an industrial society still requires a stable family system to socialize children and to maintain the psychological balance of the men who face the pressures of competition in their work life.

As evidence for the separation of the nuclear family from kinship groups, Parsons pointed to the rise in jobs not based on kinship and the decline in family-operated economic units, such as farms, small retail shops, and the like. Further, he pointed out that households were increasingly limited to nuclear family members.

He found further support for the importance of the nuclear family in the high rates of marriage and remarriage after divorce, the drop in the average age of marriage, and the increase in the birth rate during the postwar era—the time of Parsons's major statements

In the twentieth century, the home became a more private place than it had been in earlier times. [Joan Liftin/Archive Pictures Inc.]

on the nuclear family. Thus, Parsons argued, rather than having lost its importance, the nuclear family under industrialism is more vital than ever, in both senses of the word. It has become specialized as part of the general process of social change.

Parsons and his followers argued that the relative isolation of the nuclear family from the kinship group and its loss of functions made the family *more* rather than *less* important:

The family has become a *more specialized agency* than before, probably more specialized than in any previously known society. This represents a decline of *certain* features which have traditionally been associated with families, but whether it represents a "decline of the family" in a more general sense is another matter. . . .

The family is more specialized than before, but not in any general sense less important, because the society is dependent *more* exclusively on it for the performance of *certain* of its vital functions. (Parsons & Bales, 1955, pp. 3–9)

Parsons emphasizes the home as a place to escape from the pressures of work. It is the only place in urban-industrial society where a person can find love and trust—the only place, that is, where a person can find affection and acceptance for the self, apart from particular achievements and accomplishments. The family remains the only dependable primary group in modern society—that is, a group involving regular, face-to-face contact over a long period of time in a mood of intimacy and informality.

Parsons's Critics

Many criticisms can and have been made of Parsons's analysis, and some have been mentioned earlier in this book. He tended to disregard the diversity of family life and to concentrate on the "normal American family" as a middle-class urban couple with young children and reduced kin ties; the husband plays an "instrumental" role as the breadwinner and the wife follows an "expressive" domestic role. Deviation from these patterns implies social disorganization, or personal psychopathology, rather than an alternative life-style.

Parsons also confounded the meaning of the term *function;* for example, he asserted that the two functions of the nuclear family—the socialization of children and the psychological security of adults—are more important than ever, because now the nuclear family is the only place where such nurturing can be found. In this statement Parsons used the term *function* to refer to both a need and the fulfillment of the need. He assumed that if a social need exists, it must be satisfied. This assumption flows from the general concept of Parsons and many other sociologists that societies are neatly organized and balanced social systems.

As noted in a previous chapter, however, not all sociologists hold to such a utopian model of social systems. Any society can give rise to contradictory functional requirements. Thus, although Parsons has offered a convincing explanation of why the family is desperately needed in modern society, he was overly optimistic about the ease with which the "psychological gold" of warmth and affection can be created, stored, and circulated in an urban-industrial society. (Parsons actually used money as a metaphor for solidarity.) His argument overlooked the possibility that the same social changes generating the need for a stable and secure family life may also undermine society's capacity to fulfill the need.

Parsons's writing on the nuclear family gave rise to a wave of critical articles. Some writers questioned Parsons's treatment of the psychological aspects of family life, in particular his theory of role differentiation. Parsons had theorized that for a child to develop a normal personality, the roles of its parents had to be sharply different from one another—the mother "expressive" or nurturant, the father "instrumental" or demanding. Philip Slater (1974) questioned this notion, pointing out that, in reality, both parents often act in both ways. Further, Slater argued that extreme differentiation between the parents would have a negative effect on personality development—for example, by making it harder for a son to model himself on a father who was never warm and loving.

A major debate centered on Parsons's emphasis on the isolation of the nuclear family from kin groups in modern society. The critics opposed both Parsons and the earlier writers who had predicted the decline and fall of the extended family, and they asserted that kinship groups remained alive and well in urban and industrial settings. Thus, the argument went, people are not isolated from their kin groups: they visit their relatives, speak to them on the telephone, write letters, exchange Christmas cards, celebrate happy occasions, and help in emergencies. What's more, parents often help their married children, and children help support their aged parents.

The debate between Parsons and his critics has passed into the literature as a victory for the critics. For example, many reviews in textbooks agree with the verdict of Sussman, one of the leading critics of Parsons:

The isolated nuclear family is a myth. This has already been conclusively demonstrated. It does not merit any further attention of the field, and I for one refuse to waste any more time even discussing it. (cited in Rosow, 1965, p. 341)

Instead of the isolated nuclear family as the typical family structure of modern societies, the critics offered such concepts as the "modified extended family" and the kin network.

Criticizing Parsons's Critics

Despite widespread agreement that the critics won the debate with Parsons, their own arguments are riddled with conceptual and methodological flaws. A fairly mild critique of the nuclear family critics was offered by B. N. Adams (1968), and a more devastating one has been published by Gibson (1972).

First, the critics make Parsons appear more extreme than he actually was. Parsons did not insist that the isolated nuclear family never saw any of its relatives. Indeed, as Parsons himself pointed out, his emphasis on the psychological importance of parent–child relations would suggest that people would not be likely to break off completely from their parents when they marry. It is worthwhile to look at Parsons's original statement about the isolation of the contemporary nuclear family:

This "isolation" is manifested in the fact that the members of the nuclear family, consisting of the parents and their still dependent children, ordinarily occupy a separate dwelling not shared with members of the family of orientation (parents) of either spouse, and this household is in the typical case economically independent, subsisting in the first instance from the occupational earnings of the husband-father. It is of course not uncommon to find a surviving parent of one or the other spouse, or even a sibling or cousin of one of them, residing with the family, but this is both statistically secondary and it is clearly not felt to be the "normal" arrangement.

Of course, with the independence, particularly the marriage, of children, relations to the family of orientation are by no means broken. But a separate residence, very often in a different geographical community, and separate economic support, attenuate these relations. . . .

A particularly significant aspect of the isolation of the nuclear family in our society is again the sharp discrimination . . . which it emphasizes between family members and nonmembers. (1955, pp. 3ff.)

Obviously, then, Parsons was not talking about "isolation" in the sense of no social interaction, but rather about such structural issues as living in separate households (often in a different community from one's parents), about being economically independent, and about being emotionally as well as ideologically more focused on one's spouse and children than on parents and blood relatives. One problem of Parsons's analysis, however, is that the isolated nuclear family is presented as a type, an either/or matter, rather than as a continuum along which different families can be arranged.

The problem of many of his critics is similar: they also approached the issue in an either/or fashion. Asserting that Parsons had said there was no kin interaction at all among married couples, the critics point to family visiting and helping in times of need as evidence that the typical city dweller in modern society lives in close-knit kin networks. Gibson (1972), however, points out that these critics often use "absurdly low levels" of interaction between members of different households to show that the nuclear family isn't isolated, and they have overestimated their own statistics. Their assertions that kin networks play a major role in urban society show more enthusiasm than accuracy. For example, data showing that people turn *more* to banks than to relatives in times of financial need and *more* to clergymen and doctors in times of trouble, get *more* from

Mexican women doing the family wash. [Helen Nestor]

friends and neighbors during illness, and so on are interpreted as showing the strength of kinship ties in contemporary society!

Some writers, such as Litwak (1965) and Sussman (1965), argue that the basic family system of the United States is "the modified extended family," consisting of coalitions of nuclear families; yet they never specify precisely what it takes for a group of families to become such a coalition. How much interaction or exchange of services is needed? What are the boundaries of such systems? Such questions are not answered by the proponents of the "modified extended family" notion. As Gibson (1972) stated:

Unlike the classical extended structure, or the isolated nuclear family, for which clear identifying characteristics may be developed (i.e., household composition), the modified extended family is not clearly defined for either conceptual or research purposes. If the case is to be made of the primacy of kin relations over non-kin relations, much clearer definitions need to be provided. . . . It is hard to avoid the conclusion that the concept of the modified extended family is intended more as an ideological device to refute Parsons than as a meaningful research tool to describe reality. (p. 17)

Whether or not the modified extended family exists as a reality, it is important only if it fosters a "radically different set of emotional arrangements" from those created by a more isolated nuclear family—for example, if it is associated with different childrearing arrangements, such as multiple mothering, or with a diluted husband–wife relationship (Demos, 1972, p. 562). The proponents of the concept, however, do not make this claim. And, paradoxically, by applying the concept of the modified extended family to the society as a whole, they overlook those class and ethnic situations in which extended family structures do actually create a radically different set of emotional arrangements—such as the kin networks in poor black communities.

Even if the modified extended family does not alter relationships with the nuclear family, it would still be significant if it could be shown to have the same functions as kin and community groups in traditional society. Nobody argues, however, that kinship plays the same role in modern society as it did in the past. Parsons and the earlier writers who saw a withering away of the family were not discussing family interaction, such as visits, so much as the role of kinship in the larger society. In comparison to other societies, relations between adult relatives in industrial society are peripheral to the functioning of the total society. That relations with all relatives, even close ones, are largely optional and voluntary places kin relations in industrial society on an entirely different plane from the obligatory roles found in traditional society.

Unlike kin relations in traditional societies, those in industrial society are not clearly prescribed. No strict rules dictate how often you should see your mother's brother or your father's sister's son, how you should act in his presence, or what precisely your mutual obligations are to each other. Rather, kinship in America and other indus-

trial societies is much like friendship—people often interact with their relatives according to how they feel about them. W. J. Goode (1963) calls such kin relations "ascriptive friendship."

Another source of confusion in the debate over kin relations in modern society centers around the meaning of the term *kinship*. As D. H. J. Morgan (1975) has pointed out, when anthropologists use the term they are referring to a wide network of relatives. In discussions about modern urban families, however, the focus is on the relationship between grown-up, married children and their parents. For Morgan, this means that the core of the debate disappears—all Parsons's critics have proved is that the nuclear family remains important well into adulthood (p. 69).

Thus, modern kin relations are not a replacement for the intense community life that enmeshed families in previous eras. Although it is tempting, observed Edward Shorter (1975), to regard the kin network, with its seemingly enhanced importance in the contemporary world, as a replacement for the web of community relations, the temptation should be avoided. The intensity of such contact, he observes, bears little resemblance to the intense sociability of traditional times:

As often as people nowadays see their kin, the intensity of such contact bears no resemblance to the intensity of sociability in traditional times. In terms of viewing oneself as part of a larger social unit, no number of visits with Mom and Dad will add up to the annual cycle of Carnival, Easter, St. John's Day, the harvest home, and so forth. . . . So, quantitatively, one would have to live with one's kin—and a wide circle of relatives at that—to get anything like the frequency of interaction achieved in village society.

Qualitatively, kin contacts are no replacement for community contacts either. . . . Kin-

TABLE 6.1   *Behavioral and Attitudinal Characteristics Hypothesized to Occur in Family Systems Organized Around Extended-Kin-Oriented Versus Nuclear-Kin-Oriented Familism*

Extended-kin-oriented familism	Primary-kin-oriented familism
1. Individuals will be immersed within a web of secondary relatives who live within close geographic proximity.	Individuals will be cut off geographically from secondary relatives.
2. Individuals will emphasize remaining within their geographic area in order to remain close to secondary kin even though mobility may be perceived to result in better economic conditions.	Individuals will not be inhibited from moving away from geographic area if mobility is perceived as leading to better economic conditions.
3. Sentimental ties and attitudes of closeness should remain strong for both primary and secondary relatives.	Sentimental ties and attitudes of closeness should be strong for nuclear family members, but should weaken extensively for secondary relatives.
4. Sentimental ties and attitudes of closeness should lead to a high incidence of marriages among secondary kin.	Lack of sentimental ties and feelings of closeness should lead to a seeking of mates outside the secondary kinship group.
5. Individuals should manifest attitudes and behaviors in line with ascriptive criteria, emphasizing the obligatory nature of familism regarding secondary relatives.	Individuals should manifest attitudes and behaviors in line with achievement criteria, emphasizing the voluntary nature of relationship between both secondary kin and nonrelatives.
6. Nuclear family members will not participate in social and community activities as a nuclear family unit, because nuclear family and family member identities are maintained through extended-kin support.	Nuclear family members will participate in community and social affairs as a nuclear family unit because nuclear family, and individual family member identities are maintained through community support.

Source: P. G. Heller, G. M. Quesada, D. L. Harvey, and L. G. Warner, "Familism in Rural and Urban America: Critique and Reformulation of a Construct," *Rural Sociology 46:3*, 1981, pp. 446–464.

folk today extend and complement the conjugal family's egotistical emotional structure. They don't rival it, or threaten to break it down.

There is research evidence supporting Shorter's observations. A study by Heller and his associates (Heller, Quesada, Harvey, & Warner, 1981) found that the kinship involvements of people in a "middle American" urban sample did not come close to matching the traditional kinship orientation of families living in the Blue Ridge mountains of Virginia. Among the mountain dwellers, the identities of nuclear and extended families were fused. Kin were the major sources of social support, and involvement with relatives was obligatory regardless of personal feelings. Heller et al. called this pattern "extended-kin-oriented familism." In contrast, the kin relations of urban dwellers fit Goode's description of "ascriptive friendship." Heller et al. call this pattern "primary-kin-oriented familism" (see Table 6.1). Despite the strong kin ties of the Blue

Ridge mountain dwellers, however, it is doubtful that they duplicate the conditions described by Shorter.

HOUSEHOLDS AS INTIMATE ENVIRONMENTS

The key symbol of the "physical and spiritual isolation" of the modern nuclear family is the single-family home. In a previous chapter we noted the confusions about the universality of the nuclear family that resulted from failing to distinguish among kinship, living together, and domestic functions, such as child care. Households do not always consist of family members, and family members do not always live together. Stephens (1963), for example, noted that one of the problems with the idea of the universal nuclear family is that, in many societies, husbands and wives do not live together, and it is also common for children to live with someone other than their own parents.

The advocates of the modified extended family fail to make crucial distinctions between degrees of interaction. They do not distinguish exchanging cards and telephone calls from face-to-face interaction, nor do they consider the significance of different amounts of interaction—daily, weekly, monthly. Above all they fail to take into account the differences between domestic functions and visiting. This is also the reason why it is important to know about who lives with whom—households are intimacy-producing environments.

Household structures are important in two senses. First, knowing about the typical household structure in a society tells us something about the kinds of relationships and experiences that a society encourages. Bohannan (1971), for example, argued that the kind of houses people build, or would like to build, is an excellent indicator of the particular relationship emphasized in a kinship system. Mother–daughter, father–son, and husband–wife are the three relationships around which households most often are built. In the second sense, the household is the basic intimate environment in every society, and the process of living together, rather than the facts of kinship or marriage bonds, produces intimacy. Parsons (1971) observed that there is a

central complex of privacy that seems to exist everywhere which consists of the sharing of "residence" in the sense of premises of daily living, perhaps above all sleeping, and . . . the privilege of eating in company with others. . . . Similarly, lines are drawn between clothing appropriate for public contexts and dress appropriate only to intimate occasions and company. (p. 428)

An element of eroticism always exists in intimate environments, but the eroticism is neither the central feature nor the basis of intimacy. We tend to exaggerate the erotic aspects of intimacy because our own household structures are most often based on sexual relationships. When the household is built around the husband–wife bond, however, the eroticism of that relationship seems to intensify the intimacy already generated in any household through the mere fact of living together. Slater (1963) has analyzed the tendencies to "dyadic" withdrawal when two people are deeply attached to each other; he included mother–child relationships as also subject to dyadic withdrawal. Thus the nuclear family household is more likely to withdraw from other relationships than any other kind of household structure. Gibson (1972) reported data showing that nuclear family households are more isolated from kin in comparison with other types of households—for example, those with single people and/or extended families.

It is a mistake to think that the intimacy of the household results only from deep emotional or sexual attachment. Much of the emotional atmosphere of households arises from the fact that they are what Goffman (1959) has called a "backstage area." Goffman used the terms "backstage" and "backstage behavior" to describe the way people act when they are relaxed, informal, and just being themselves rather than acting a role, such as worker, teacher, host or hostess, and so on. Goffman gave the example of waiters who switch back and forth from scowling to smiling as they pass through the door from the kitchen to the dining room. Another example is the scene from a domestic comedy on television or in the movies in which a husband and wife smilingly say good-bye to the last guest, close the door, scowl at each other, and resume the argument they were having before the guests arrived.

Family secrets are not unique to families; all backstage regimes have them. Restaurant kitchens again serve as a prime example. The household also shares with other such backstage regions a kind of informality that permits a regression to "childish" ways. Goffman noted that backstage behavior has a certain uniformity whether it takes place in a worker's locker room, the backroom of a store, or in a home. "Polite" or public behavior requires certain styles of speech and posture indicating self-control and an appropriate distance from the other person. Backstage areas have their own code or "language" of behavior:

The backstage language consists of reciprocal first naming, cooperative decision making, profanity, open sexual remarks, elaborate griping, smoking, rough informal dress, "sloppy" sitting or standing posture, use of dialect or substandard speech, mumbling and shouting, playful aggressivity and "kidding," inconsiderateness for the other in minor . . . acts, minor physical self-involvements such as humming, whistling, chewing, nibbling, belching, and flatulence. The frontstage behavior can be taken as the absence . . . of this. In general, then, backstage conduct is one which allows minor acts which might easily be taken as symbolic of intimacy and disrespect for others. . . . It may be noted here that backstage behavior has what psychologists might call a "regressive" character. (p. 128)

Goffman warned against concluding that backstage is full of the pleasant things in life such as warmth and generosity:

Often, it seems that whatever enthusiasm and lively interest we have at our disposal we reserve for those before whom we are putting on a show and that the surest sign of backstage solidarity is to feel that it is safe to lapse into an asociable mood of sullen, silent irritability. (p. 132)

Because family behavior is a backstage kind of interaction, it is, of course, extremely hard to observe. As Goffman noted, people in backstage regions know about their own unsavory secrets, but they are not in a position to know about those of other people. Thus families may think of themselves in terms of their backroom knowledge, but judge other families by their onstage performances. This may be why the discoveries of the new family interaction studies are at one and the same time so shocking and so familiar. By observing backstage family behavior, these studies have opened up for public discussion aspects of family life that could never be reached by means of questionnaires and formal interviews.

Rise of the Private Family

Although a distinction between public and private contexts may exist everywhere, the degree of family privacy in modern societies vastly exceeds that available elsewhere. Thus, as Parsons notes, although the places where people sleep and eat together seem always to be defined as intimate, private places, in most cultures and in our own historical past households have been more open and accessible to outsiders. Furthermore, as we noted in the last chapter, the sense of a gulf between the home and the outside society seems to exist only in advanced industrial societies.

Indeed, there is reason to believe that the concept of the home as a sanctuary and retreat is a relatively recent cultural feature of the United States and, to a lesser degree, of England. In these countries we find not only the ideology but also the practice of family privacy. Sebastian de Grazia (1962) contrasted the "at-home-ness" of Americans with the more extensive out-of-the-house leisure life that exists in Europe. Citing a 1954 survey showing that at 6:00 P.M. of any workday three-quarters of the American male population from age 20 to 59 had arrived home from work to stay for the rest of the evening, he wrote:

The . . . separation of home and work . . . and the growth of cities into sprawling, black, transportation maps are two factors that help make the home a refuge against the impersonality outside. The trend seems to have begun in the reign of Victoria. Massive, comfortable chairs and sofas appeared in solidly appointed houses. By now the home as a sanctuary has legal and constitutional support in both England and the United States. (p. 184)

Grazia noted that on the Continent, however, the concept of home as distinct from house is lacking. Particularly for men, the café and the bistro provide an out-of-the-house environment where they can "eat, drink, write letters or poetry, discuss women, and argue about politics and literature" (Grazia, 1962, p. 184).

The separation of the home from public life reflects not only a set of values, but also the technological self-sufficiency of the modern American home. The telephone, televi-

Mexican women hanging laundry. [Helen Nestor]

sion, refrigerator, freezer, washer, dryer, air conditioner, and backyard swimming pool all increase the privacy and isolation of the household by reducing the need to go out for the necessities of life or for entertainment.

The less the household is a self-contained unit, the more family life goes on in the presence of nonfamily members. For example, in the Mexico City *vecindad* described by Oscar Lewis (1965), individual dwellings surround a central patio. People do most of their work in the patio and share a common toilet and washstand. This type of housing brings individuals from different and not necessarily blood-related households into intense daily interaction and enables people to maintain in an urban setting the extended family pattern of the rural village. On the other hand, Lewis noted, such intense interaction also leads to problems of privacy and quarrels among neighboring children and parents.

To an American the unappealing aspects of the lack of family privacy in the *vecindad* do not need to be spelled out. But the drawbacks of too much family self-sufficiency and privacy are only beginning to be realized. Sociologist Barbara Laslett (1973) argues that only in contemporary America has the ideology of the private nuclear family actually been put into practice, and hence only in America are its problematic aspects becoming apparent. The chief difference between the traditional family and its modern counterpart, according to this analysis, is the public–private dimension. The family of the past was a much more public institution:

When it is common practice for family life to occur elsewhere than within the confines of the [home], such as in parks or front stoops, when it is common for nondomestic activities—such as political and economic—to be pursued within the domestic context, when it is common for nonfamily members—such as servants, apprentices, and boarders—to constitute part of the household, the family can be described as having a public character. (p. 70)

By contrast, family privacy increases when most of family life goes on within the home, and when family activities are purely domestic rather than economic. Laslett sees the significance of the public–private distinction in the social-psychological effects of being observed while acting out family roles. Following Goffman's concept of backstage interaction, she argues that the increase in family privacy in recent years may result in less social control over what goes on in families, as well as less social support for family roles.

The Great Transformation

Of all the changes in family life brought on by the emergence of the industrial society, the most dramatic and clear-cut was the separation of home and work. In preindustrial societies, the family is the basic economic and productive unit. Family life takes place in the midst of the daily cycle of labor, to which all members contribute except for the very young and the physically disabled. Thus, although the traditional family system was patriarchal, the "head" of the family was as dependent on the contribution of wife and children to the family enterprise as they were on his.

In the modern industrial system, however, the head of the family leaves home to work elsewhere, and the rest of the family comes to depend on the father's wages for their support. Instead of sharing in the family's productive tasks, men exchange their wages for emotional support. The care of small children can no longer be carried out along with what society considers "real" work. Women, children, and older adults come to occupy a limbo outside the labor force. Given the demands of the factory or office—the time clocks, impersonal relationships, and monotonous work routines—people look to family life to ease the stresses of the outside world.

These changes, along with the other social and cultural changes that have accompanied the emergence of mass industrial society, have had a profound impact on the daily realities of family life and the experiences of family members. Yet the questions raised by the decline-of-the-family school have never been dealt with in a detailed and serious way by students of the family. Le Play, Zimmerman, Wirth, and Linton had seen in urban-industrial society forces inimical to all family ties, both of marriage and of blood. Parsons turned the issue aside by declaring the nuclear family the basic unit. He separated its fate from that of the traditional family by arguing that while modern society was undermining extended family ties, it rendered the nuclear family more necessary than ever. Parsons's critics confused the issue still further by arguing that the traditional family never died.

By assuming that the nuclear family was either the norm or nonexistent, both the Parsonians and the anti-Parsonians failed to come to grips with the contradictions of modern family life. They did not consider the possibility that modern social conditions unglue family ties and at the same time make them more needed. What happens to family life when the household stops being a workplace and father and older children leave for most of the day? What happens to women when they are "freed" from working on the family farm or trade and are left alone in isolated households with young children? What happens to the quality of family relationships when home becomes a refuge from the rest of society, and the family is the main place for people to enjoy intimate sociability?

Both Parsons and his critics share an optimistic view of family functioning in contemporary society. The "structural-differentiation" model of Parsons and his associates assumes that changes are adaptive:

When a social organization becomes archaic under changing historical circumstances, . . . it differentiates . . . into two more roles or organizations which function more *effectively* in the new historical circumstances. (Smelser, 1963, p. 2)

But why make the assumption that the changes are adaptive? W. J. Goode (1963) suggested that the fit between industrialism and the conjugal family may be one-sided: the nuclear family may suit the needs of the industrial economy, but urban-industrial society may not serve the needs of the family. Further, the nuclear family may not be as ideally suited to a complex industrial society as is usually thought. Like the early generation of writers, Goode asked whether the ultimate thrust of advanced societies is to do away with the family altogether, making the individual the basic unit of society.

Conflict and Contradiction in the Family

Despite the general optimism of Parsons and his followers, they do recognize that there are strains and tensions in the modern family—or to use the jargon term, *dysfunctions*. However, sociologists have traditionally viewed such strains not as general problems of family life itself, but rather as something that may occur in some families some of the time. Also, strains and dysfunctions suggest something that can be removed or relieved. Some family scholars prefer to use the term *contradiction* when talking about the general problems of the modern family (D. H. J. Morgan, 1975). A contradiction is a built-in, unavoidable difficulty—a demand, not necessarily conscious, that one act in two opposite ways. An example of a contradiction in the modern family is that parents are supposed to love their children intensely and yet prepare them to break away from home and be independent.

Until recently very few social scientists have ever argued that the modern family itself contained built-in flaws. C. Wright Mills (1959) was one such critical voice. He used marriage as an example of how personal troubles could be viewed as social issues. Mills wrote that though a man and a woman could have personal troubles inside a marriage, when 250 out of every 1,000 marriages ended in divorce (the rates are now approaching 500 out of 1,000 in some places), there had to be a "structural issue having to do with the institutions of marriage and the family and other institutions that bear upon them" (p. 10). He suggested, as some of these structural strains, a "crisis of ambition" for men in a corporate economy, and the stultifying role prescribed for women within the family:

Insofar as the family as an institution turns women into darling little slaves and men into their chief providers and unweaned dependents, the problem of a satisfactory marriage remains incapable of purely private solution. (p. 10)

Another critical sociologist writing during the family-togetherness celebration of the 1950s was Barrington Moore (1958). At a time when it was axiomatic among social scientists that the family is a universally necessary institution in all societies, past, present, and future, Moore asked: "To what extent may we regard the family as a repressive survival under the conditions of an advanced technology?" (p. 409).

With a frank cynicism Moore struck out at the "barbaric nature" of the duty of family affection. Parent–child relations were included in Moore's dim view of all kin bonds. He wrote that if people were to talk to each other about the "sufferings brought on by raising a family today, the birth rate would drop to zero" (p. 410).

Moore argued that the home of today is less effective than it was in earlier times as a place to rear children. The family was once an economic unit in which all members worked together, but the separation of home and work brought on by industrialization removed the father from the household during the day. This separation meant that the children could have no direct experience of fa-

ther's work, but even if they did, it was no longer an automatic model for their own careers. Also, the father would spend part of the day in a separate world of social interaction. More recently, mass media and peer groups have come to compete with parents in shaping children. The loss of work ties between family members, involvement in outside interests, and the intrusion of the media into the home all make it harder for family members to form genuine emotional ties with each other.

Like Mills, Moore saw through the popular myths that the woman's place in the contemporary family was one of privilege and dominance as well as instinctual fulfillment:

Is she, perhaps, the happy person whose face smiles at us from every advertisement, and whose arts justify the sociologists' case? A more accurate assessment might be that the wife suffers most in the modern middle-class family, because the demands our culture puts upon her are impossible to meet. (p. 411)

Moore took his argument to its logical conclusion: The family is already a part-time thing for most people; in the future it would become more so. The trend toward more efficient technology and a greater division of labor would be extended to the home and its tasks. The childrearing function would be carried on by specialized agencies, developing from today's play schools, boarding schools, and so on. Moore recognized that infants have a special problem: they need affection, fondling, and the "illusion of being the center of the universe." But, he reasoned, mechanized and bureaucratized childrearing could be made warm and supporting, often more so than a family ridden by problems and conflict.

This analysis of the future of the family sounds even more chilling to many people now than it did during the togetherness era.

Our sense of values has changed. Moore criticized the family of the 1950s in terms of the values of the 1950s: technology, efficiency, rationality. These are, of course, the very values against which there is so much protest. Moore could hardly have foreseen that the direction of value change would be opposite to the one he predicted: rather than technology and bureaucratic efficiency taking over home tasks, the family-togetherness principle moved out beyond the family into the commune movement, encounter groups, political protest groups, the reawakening of religion, and so forth.

Moore, nevertheless, had pointed to strains in the mid-century American family that would shortly reach crisis proportions: the fact that, despite the ideology of "togetherness," mother, father, and children lived in different worlds of experience, values, and information. Moore also recognized the paradoxical quality of the emotional ties between family members—the obligation to love when the day-to-day relationship may not generate any feelings of warmth. Moore, however, also reiterated the concern of Le Play, Zimmerman, and other traditionalists: would not reduction of family burdens in the interests of individualism result in a world of "shallow and fleeting erotic intrigues"? He acknowledged that Hollywood might be the "ugly prototype" of such a world:

The most that might be claimed by any future apologist for such institutions . . . is that they give greater scope to the development of the creative aspects of the personality than did the family. (p. 417)

Moore in effect presented the dark side of "structural differentiation." Parsons and his students saw the nuclear family stripped down to its basic psychological functions as an effective supplier of security for family members as well as the producer of new re-

cruits to industrial society. The nuclear family was now the only source of the pure gold of solidarity. Moore, on the other hand, argued that the stripping away of work, education, and other functions from the nuclear family had left the members with little or nothing on which to base their relationships. The specialized function of the nuclear family amounts to a heightened emotionality, a pure togetherness paradoxically harder to achieve as a goal in itself than as a by-product of working together on some task.

Parsons as a Critical Theorist

Actually, despite the fact that Mills and Moore are critics of "establishment" sociology while Parsons and Goode, the latter to a lesser extent, are the establishment, the analysis of the family made by the four writers does not differ very much. The differences lie in the implications drawn from the analysis. Where Parsons and Goode saw tensions and points of strain in an otherwise stable and functioning social system, Mills and Moore saw fatal flaws, contradictions that call into question the viability of modern family arrangements and the social system that supports them.

Yet the built-in strains noted by Goode and Parsons are fundamental ones; they exist for the old and the young, for men and women, at work and at home. In Goode's (1963) analysis of the human costs of both industrialism and the conjugal family, the first and most obvious "cost" of the conjugal as opposed to the extended family system is to the elders. Viewed as a power struggle, the rise of the conjugal system represents a victory of youth over age. Years of experience make one obsolescent rather than wise.

Parsons (1949) saw the plight of older people not so much in terms of power but as a by-product of modern kinship, residential patterns, and occupational structures:

An immigrant family making suspenders, New York City, about 1910. [Lewis Hine/National Archives]

In such fields as farming and the maintenance of small independent enterprises, there is frequently no such thing as abrupt "retirement," rather a gradual relinquishment of the main responsibilities . . . with advancing age. So far, however, as an individual's occupational status centers in a specific "job," he either holds the job or does not, and the tendency is to maintain the full level of functioning up to a given point and then abruptly to retire. In view of the very great significance of the occupational status and its psychological correlates, retirement leaves the older man in a peculiarly functionless situation, cut off from participation in the most important interests and activities of the society. (p. 231)

Yet work in industrial society also has strains built in. But Goode, like Parsons, believed that the industrial system, based on competition and achievement, creates great psychological tension. Security and satisfaction in work are almost impossible, no matter whether one is janitor of the building or president of the corporation:

The modern technological system is psychologically burdensome on the individual because it demands an unremitting discipline. . . . Lower-level jobs give little pleasure to most people. However, in higher-level professional, managerial, and creative positions, the standards of performance are not only high but are often without clearly stated limits. The individual is under considerable pressure to perform better than he is able. (W. J. Goode, 1963, p. 14)

This recognition of strains built into male roles does not diminish Goode's and Parsons's estimates of the strains in women's roles in modern society. The values embodied in the conjugal system—freedom, individualism, sexual equality—contradict the daily realities of the housewife in a modern society. Ironically, the woman is liberated from the extended family only to find that her domestic burdens are increased rather than lightened:

The modern woman is given little relief from child care, which is typically handed over to one person, the wife, rather than to several women, some of them elders, who are part of the family unit in the more extended systems. . . . Even the substantial development of labor-saving devices and technology has not lightened labor in the modern United States home. . . . Most of these devices merely raise the standards for cleanliness and repairs, and allow the housewife to turn out more "domestic production" each day. Every study of the time allocation of mothers shows that housewives work extremely long hours. (W. J. Goode, 1963, p. 15)

Parsons's analysis of the strains in women's roles focused not so much on the contrast between family structures—extended versus conjugal—but rather on the effects of the modern occupational structure on the family. The principal source of strain in women's roles, he noted, derives from the fact that the wife is no longer a partner in a common economic enterprise. When the home was also a workplace, economic roles were not differentiated from family roles. Women—and men—could combine child care and reproduction with economic activi-

ties. Industrialization, however, moves work, and the father too, out of the home. Men acquire the status that once was attached to the family as a group. The husband's occupation, more than any other factor, determines the status of the family in terms of prestige as well as standard of living.

The common enterprise is reduced to the life of the family itself and to the informal social activities in which husband and wife participate together. (Parsons, 1949, p. 223)

In a society with a strong emphasis on individual achievement, the woman is left with the unstable, "pseudo-" occupation of housewife and no claim to status in her own right. The instability of the housewife role, especially in the middle class, Parsons noted, is indicated by the prevalence of women's varying strategies for escaping it—by hiring maids, by dissociating their personality from the role of domestic drudge and emphasizing glamor or cultural activities, and so forth. But because none of these is clearly defined, there tends to be a rather "unstable oscillation" between them, along with a considerable degree of neurosis in women.

The child does not escape built-in strains either, in Parsons's view. In the small modern conjugal family, the emotional intensity of family bonds is increased at the same time that a greater necessity to become emancipated from them is imposed. Thus adolescence is a particularly difficult time in advanced societies.

SUMMARY

The turn-of-the-century feminists and social theorists who predicted the end of family life as the inevitable result of urbanization and industrialization were both right and wrong. They were right in predicting the demise of the traditional preindustrial family pattern in which the whole family was an economic unit. But they underestimated the continuing, and even increased, needs of people in industrial societies for the emotional supports that can be provided only by intimate relationships.

Similarly, the sociologists who argued that the family was more important than ever in modern society were both right and wrong. Whether they stressed the nuclear or the modified extended as the typical contemporary family form, they too easily assumed that family life could fulfill the new demands that were placed on it. They overlooked the possibility that the same social conditions that create the need for the emotional support of the family—the impersonality and competition of the work and public life—make it difficult for the family to fulfill its emotional tasks. Family ties have become more intense than they were in the past and, at the same time, more fragile and conflictive.

Families in contemporary society differ from preindustrial families in at least two major ways: they are more private than families in the past and they are no longer held together by their dependence on each other's labor. In the past, the family was embedded in the community, and outsiders, such as neighbors and kin, could supervise relations between parents and children and husbands and wives. Now the family is a backstage area where family members can express themselves with more freedom, more emotionally and irrationally, than they can in public. While privacy permits the family to be more loving and intimate, it also permits the expression of more negative feelings.

When the family stopped being a productive unit, relationships among family members were transformed in other ways. Women, children, and old people were placed in an ambiguous position outside the world of productive work. The wife and children came to be dependent on the husband's wages, and his ability to fulfill his masculine role came to be defined by his success in the economic marketplace.

CHAPTER 7

Class and Caste in the American Family

It is after all this division into working class and business class that constitutes the outstanding cleavage in Middletown. The mere fact of being born upon one or the other side of the watershed roughly formed by these two groups is the most significant single cultural factor tending to influence what one does all day long throughout one's life: whom one marries; when one gets up in the morning; . . . and so on indefinitely throughout the daily comings and goings of a Middletown man, woman, or child.

Robert S. Lynd and Helen Merrill Lynd
Middletown

In the last chapter, we took a bird's-eye view of the historical transformation of the family brought about by industrialization. That family breadwinners go out of the home to work for wages seems an obvious fact of life. As a way of life for the majority of the population, however, it is scarcely a century old. The impact of this change on families varies according to their places in the social order. American families share the same culture, but they confront marriage, child-rearing, work, and relations with kin and others in very different ways according to their resources and their class, racial, and ethnic experience.

BLUE-COLLAR AND WHITE-COLLAR FAMILIES: THE REDISCOVERY OF SOCIAL CLASS

In the decades after World War II, America was widely celebrated as an affluent society unique in human history. The mass media portrayed a way of life in which practically every family lived on a tree-lined suburban street with two cars in every garage. Social scientists viewed America as a "middle-class society in which some people were simply more middle class than others" (Bottomore, 1966, p. 105).

There was, as we mentioned in an earlier chapter, a firm basis in reality underlying the notion of the affluent society. By the middle of the 1950s, 60 percent of the American people had attained a middle-class standard of living, in contrast to only 31 percent during the last year of prosperity before the onset of the Great Depression (Chafe, 1986). There was a growing "democratization of life's pleasures" (Siegel, 1984, p. 107), which included the growth of home ownership and the spread of television sets, washing machines, and other amenities to a majority of American homes. The social structure of America, with its greatly expanded middle class, came to resemble a diamond rather than pyramid. Many people, however, mistakenly believed that the growth of mass consumption meant that economic inequality had been eliminated.

The first challenge to the image of America as a uniformly affluent society came with the "discovery" of poverty in the 1960s. Suddenly the government, the media, and social scientists realized that significant numbers of Americans were suffering from economic deprivation and even malnutrition. The War on Poverty, the crisis of the inner cities, and the welfare problem became major public issues. Yet the discovery of poverty did not really discredit the image of widespread affluence; economic deprivation was widely viewed as a problem confined to urban ghettoes and backwoods shacks.

Thus, the discovery of poverty in the 1960s obscured the persistence of class and ethnic differences among white Americans. There is no agreed-upon way to refer to these millions of people who probably constitute a majority of the American population. Working class, blue collar, and lower middle class are some of the terms used by professional observers, but the people referred to are more likely to label themselves as "average," "ordinary," or "plain" people (Coles, 1971). It

The upper tier of the emerging two-tiered economy is exemplified by the young, urban professionals ("Yuppies"). [Book cover: Piesman, M., and M. Hartley (1984). The Yuppie Handbook. *New York: Long Shadow Books] [Photo: COMSTOCK, Inc./Tom Grill]*

is easier to describe them in terms of what they are not: not black, not brown, not poor, not on welfare, not intellectuals, not rich or even affluent. They include the people who emerged to prominence on the national scene in the early 1970s as hardhats attacking student protesters and as white backlashers protesting school and neighborhood integration. Conservatives hailed them as the vanguard of an emerging right-wing majority; most liberals denounced them as violence-prone bigots, while others argued that they had legitimate grievances and were no more racist than other groups in America.

The social divisions revealed in the 1960s and 1970s deepened in the 1980s. Americans witnessed scenes reminiscent of the depths of the Depression: factories and whole industries closing down, soup kitchens, and homeless people—not just skid-row bums

and crazies, but families and others who had recently had homes and jobs. Indeed, the recession of the early 1980s was the worst since the 1930s. Although the economy recovered in 1984, many of the same scenes remained. Unemployment rates dropped, but to a level that would have been regarded as high in the 1960s. Poverty rates also declined, but to levels that were higher than those of the 1970s.

Behind the stubborn persistence of economic hardship in the midst of prosperity, observers noted disturbing long-term trends in the American economy. The job structure has been shifting from a diamond to an hour-glass shape. The number of middle-level jobs has been shrinking, and upper and lower occupations have been expanding. We are becoming a two-tiered or dual economy.

The division has transformed the social

landscape of American life. The affluent top tier contains the Yuppies—young, urban professionals—and their not so young or urban counterparts. These are people trained to market their skills in the postindustrial "information" society. They are electronics engineers, lawyers, doctors, other professionals, financial analysts, high-level managers, and skilled workers in high-tech industries. They have gentrified large areas of American cities and brought computers and condominiums to small towns and the countryside.

The lower tier of the economy consists of an expanding array of low-paying service jobs—waiters and waitresses, fast-food servers, dishwashers, janitors, nurse's aides. It contains a disproportionate number of minorities and women.

Despite the economic difficulties of recent years, some observers argue that American living standards in general have not only not declined, but have continued to rise, albeit at a slower rate than in the boom years of the 1960s. Ben Wattenberg (1984), for example, pointing to statistics on education, life expectancy, infant mortality, and sales of videocassette recorders, new cars, and exercise bicycles, claims that "we never had it so good."

Yet the terms of making a decent living have changed. For most of American history, especially in the post–World War II era, the assumption was that "someone whose only credential was a willingness to work long and hard with his hands could earn a good wage" (Siegel, 1984, p. 274). The sharp decline in blue-collar jobs since the 1970s has largely done away with that promise. Increasingly, it is only in the upper postindustrial tier that one can find jobs that pay enough to support a family in middle-class style. It is this change in the economy that has propelled many married women into the work force.

Social Scientists Look at Social Class: A Brief Review

With some exceptions, the study of social class over the past several decades tells us more about shifting ideological fashions in scholarship than it does about the experiences and living conditions of people in different social strata. Many social scientists have been preoccupied with making comparisons between classes. In the 1940s, the comparison favored the lower class, which was portrayed as warm and indulgent towards its children, while the middle class was described as repressive. More recently, the comparisons have favored the middle class; however, the two classes are always seen in a "contrapuntal and judgmental relationship" (S. M. Miller & Reissman, 1964, p. 26).

Furthermore, the traditional social-science treatment of social class has emphasized emotional and motivational differences between the classes, rather than differences in life conditions and perceptions of reality. For example, working-class and poor people are often described as passive, lacking in the ability to delay gratification, and fatalistic—believing that luck rather than hard work leads to success. Rather than reflecting deeply rooted inadequacies of personality, however, these differences may reflect realistic assessments of the opportunity structure and the amount of control lower-income people actually have over their lives.

Despite the large amount of work that has been done, social scientists do not agree on terminology or a set of concepts defining social classes in America. There is disagreement about whether occupation, income, education, life-style, subjective perception, community reputation, or some combination of these should be used as the major indicators of social class (L. Otto, 1975). Perhaps this lack of consensus is to be expected in a topic with such obvious ideological and political implications. Yet even sociologists trying to apply Marxist conceptions of social class disagree among themselves (see Wright et al., 1982).

Surprisingly, income differences have received relatively little attention in the social class literature. As Rainwater (1974) notes, it is odd that in a mass-consumption society, in which money buys not only the necessities of life but also identity and status, so little attention has been paid to the "social psychology of materialism":

One would think that a principal activity of sociology and psychology would be to chart the intimate connections between access to economic resources and possibilities for self-realization. . . . Instead, sociologists have sought to stake their claim as interpreters of human reality on variables that are somehow more "social." In the area of stratification this has meant a preeminent emphasis on occupation and education and ultimately on "values." It is amazing how many sociological studies do not even present data on income as an independent variable or when they do measure income much more sloppily than other social structural variables. (pp. xi–xii)

Given the lack of consensus about how to define social class, it is not surprising that there is also disagreement about where to draw the dividing lines between classes. Many social scientists, as noted earlier, have contrasted "the middle class" with "the lower class." This practice not only applies an invidious label to a large part of the American population, but it also creates a good deal of conceptual confusion. S. M. Miller and Reissman (1964) argue that it is important to make a distinction between the working class—the stable blue-collar worker —and an underclass of the irregularly

employed and the unskilled. Some observers would place certain white-collar workers in the working class, while some radical sociologists would count as working class anyone who works for a large business or other organization even if he or she makes a high income and has a managerial title (C. H. Anderson, 1975).

Some observers have argued that the term *working class* is inappropriate for Americans. In contrast to many European countries, America is often described as a "classless" society in which class does not form a significant part of people's identity. A study by Mary and Robert Jackman (1982) challenges these assumptions about class awareness. In probing interviews with over 1,900 people, they found that 97 percent of their respondents identified themselves with one of five socioeconomic class labels. Eight percent identified themselves as poor, 37 percent working class, 43 percent middle class, 8 percent upper middle class, and 1 percent upper class. Occupation was the most important basis for this identification, but the traditional distinction between blue- and white-collar work did not hold; half of all clerical workers and craftsmen identified themselves as poor. People were sensitive to distinctions in occupational prestige, education, skill, income, and authority on the job, as well as to differences in life-styles and beliefs.

The Jackmans also found that class differences play an important role in social life, people feel closer to people in their own class, friends tend to be closely matched in class position, and most people prefer to live among people like themselves. All in all, these researchers conclude that class is a major source of group identity for Americans, rivaling even race in importance.

Despite these debates, it seems reasonable to suggest that a realistic image of American life would contain at least two classes or social layers between the very rich and the poor. An upper group, consisting mainly of professionals, managers, executives, and businessmen, fulfills the image of the affluent society. The lower group, consisting of blue-collar workers and white-collar workers at the lower levels of income and status, is vulnerable to economic anxiety in a way that the upper group is not.

At the very top of the social hierarchy is a relatively small number of extremely wealthy families. This elite group sends its children to prestigious prep schools and universities and encourages them to follow the family traditions by marrying the right sort of person and entering the family business or profession. It maintains close kin ties to perpetuate its property and power and associates with its own kind in neighborhoods and clubs. Despite the great changes in American society in recent decades, this elite has remained remarkably intact. As P. M. Blumberg and Paul (1975) observe,

It is perhaps the most untouched group in American life. It is significant, for example, that despite the civil rights tidal wave which engulfed the country in the 1960's, it is the upper-class territory of school, neighborhood, club, and blue book which remains the most racially segregated turf in America. (p. 75)

At the opposite extreme is the lowest strata of society, the poor and near poor. An "official" poverty line is set by the federal government. Thus in July 1981 a family of four with an income of $8,400 or less was considered poor. In 1979, according to the official poverty thresholds, 12.5 percent of the American population, or about one out of eight people, lived in poverty.

Regardless of where the official poverty line is drawn, however, poverty means high rates of infant mortality, poor nutrition and housing, and higher rates of mental illness and family disruption. Poverty is most prevalent among blacks and households headed by women. However, in terms of total numbers, the majority of America's poor are white, and about half consist of male-headed households.

Contrary to the widespread notion that the poverty programs of the 1960s were a failure, the poverty level in America was reduced during the 1960s. During the early years of the programs, the results were dramatic—the number of poor Americans dropped from 40 million in 1960, before the War on Poverty, to 24 million in 1969, or from 22 percent of the population to around 12 percent (Light & Keller, 1982). Food programs, created when it was discovered that millions of Americans suffered from malnutrition and even outright hunger, sharply reduced those conditions. Social Security, Medicare, and Medicaid greatly reduced abject poverty among the elderly. After the initial drop in poverty, however, the decline over the following decade was much less. From 1969 to 1977, the drop was only half a percentage point. In the 1980s, because of unemployment and the Reagan administration's cutbacks in social programs, the population of poor and near poor rose again. In 1983, the official poverty rate rose to 15.2 percent, the highest level in 18 years. By 1985, after 3 years of economic recovery, it had declined only to 14 percent—by historical standards, still a very high level (Rose, 1986).

As we noted earlier, the poverty population is not an unchanging one. People who are poor at any one point are likely to climb out of poverty sooner or later. But, on the other hand, many people who do not start out poor fall into poverty. A University of Michigan study (Duncan, 1984) found that over a 9-year period about 25 percent of Americans—about 55 million—can expect to fall below the poverty line for at least 1 year.

Lower Class Versus Working Class

The lower class is set apart from the working class by its lack of education and marketable job skills. Although members of the working class may find themselves out of work and in desperate economic straits—an increasing trend in the 1980s due to the recession and decline of major industries, such as auto, steel, and rubber—many in the lower class never really made it in the industrial job market in the first place. They are marginal to the mainstream of stable working-class and lower-level white-collar workers and their families.

This economic marginality of the lower class often leads people to adapt special ways of countering their situation. As Rainwater (1974) pointed out, many of the "social pathologies" associated with low income, such as marital disruption and illegitimacy, can be seen as products of these special adaptations. Lower-class people share many of the values of the working and middle class, such as a belief in the desirability of stable marriage, but circumstances do not encourage them to act on these values. Men who have few hopes of becoming breadwinners, for example, may take part in street life as a way of salvaging their self-esteem. Involvement in street life, however, may further discourage marriage and contribute to a high rate of marital disruption.

The Social Psychology of Economic Well-being

Poverty, of course, is a complex concept with several meanings. At an absolute level, poverty implies a lack of food, shelter, and other necessities of life. People on welfare, however, are still poor relative to others even though they have the basic resources needed for survival. The poverty line is drawn at the level of income that provides a minimal food budget, indoor plumbing, a double bed for every two people, and a few other essentials. It does not provide for much clothing, meat or fresh produce, nor does it provide for dental care or entertainment.

It is a curious fact of American life that almost anyone can feel poor, regardless of income. The images of affluence portrayed in advertising and the media can make people feel deprived in comparison. A family may not be poor according to some objective standard of income, but its members may feel poor if they can't keep up with the Joneses. For one family, keeping up with the Joneses may mean getting a second car; for another, it may be getting a second home.

The idea that economic well-being is relative, above some minimal level of income, was stated by Karl Marx (1850): "Our desires and pleasures spring from society; we measure them, therefore, by society and not by the objects which serve for their satisfaction. Because they are of a social nature, they are of a relative nature" (p. 87). More recently, economist James Duesenberry (1967) developed a theory of consumption based on the idea that the satisfaction people derive from consumption is a function of what they know about other people's consumption.

Along the same lines, some sociologists have suggested that people have a conception of a going standard of living—a "standard package" of goods and services the American family can and does enjoy (Rainwater, 1974). In addition to the mainstream "standard package," people also have images of lower and higher standards of living. For most people, however, the most important judgment they have to make about their economic well-being is how close they are to the mainstream standard package. These conceptions have profound implications for family life. Discrepancies between a family's idea of what its standard of living should be and what it actually is can influence the self-esteem of individual family members and create tensions between them.

The dramatic turnaround in the American economy during the 1970s resulted for many people in both absolute and relative deprivation in economic well-being. Inflation cuts across class lines, but it hits particularly hard at people at the bottom. David Caplovitz (1979) found, in a survey of 2,000 people, that 81 percent of those with incomes under $7,000 a year reported being worse off because of inflation, compared with only 38 percent of those earning over $20,000. Since unemployment also strikes harder at the lower and working classes than at the middle class, these changes suggest that the gap between the haves and the have-nots in this society may be growing ominously wider.

At the same time, the middle class is undergoing significant deprivations in both an absolute and relative sense. It has been a premise of middle class life since the end of World War II that a young man who did reasonably well in school could count on getting a fairly decent job. Another such premise has been that a couple starting out in married life could count on owning their own home before too long. But in the 1980s jobs are harder to find, and the costs of housing have risen so high that owning a home now seems an impossible dream for many people whose parents could take home ownership for granted.

Between Rich and Poor

Despite the discovery of poverty and the economic crisis of the 1970s and 1980s there is a persisting image of America as a basi-cally middle-class society. In between the extremes of extreme wealth and poverty there lies a vast, homogenous, comfortably well off middle-class majority. Much of this imagery is due to advertising and the media, which still portray the average American family as living in a tree-lined suburb with a two-car garage.

The image also persists, however, because in one sense it is true. America really is a middle-class society in that the overwhelming majority of Americans label themselves as middle-class whether they work on an assembly line or in an office, or wear blue collars or white ones. We may talk about "working-class families" as social observers, but unlike their European counterparts, Americans do not often apply that term to themselves. The notion of a single homogeneous middle class, however, is misleading because it obscures the wide disparity of lifestyles that pass as middle class—from the family that is just over the official poverty line to families whose prosperity shades off into wealth.

The image of widespread affluence was inaccurate even during the postwar boom years. It is refuted by the statistical evidence on the distribution of income and wealth as well as by studies of how people at different income levels actually live their daily lives, and how they perceive the world and their place in it. The economist Paul Samuelson (1967), for example, warns in his introductory economics textbook against the assumption that a majority of Americans share an affluent way of life:

In the absence of statistical knowledge, it is understandable that one should form an impression of the American standard of living from the full-page magazine advertisements portraying a jolly American family in an air-conditioned mansion, with a Buick, a station wagon, a motor launch, and all the other good things that go to make up comfortable living. Actually, of course, this sort of life is still beyond the grasp of 90 percent of the American public. (p. 12)

The realities of sharp differences in income and opportunity among white Americans remain obscured, however, by the persistence of the myth of affluence. Despite rising unemployment, the myth of the affluent worker persists, as the following quotation by Tom Wolfe (1976) illustrates:

In America, truck drivers, mechanics, factory workers, policemen, firemen, and garbagemen make so much money—$15,000 to $20,000 (or more) per year is not uncommon—that the word *proletarian* can no longer be used in this country with a straight face. So one now says *lower middle class*. One can't even call workingmen *blue collar* any longer. They all have on collars like Joe Namath's or Johnny Bench's or Walt Frazier's. They all have on $35 Superstar Qiana sport shirts with elephant collars and 1940s Airbrush Wallpaper Flowers Bunchagrapes & Seashell designs all over them. (p. 31)

Perhaps the best way to illustrate what is wrong with applying the notion of affluence to those at the middle of the economic scale is to examine the "intermediate" or "adequate" budget constructed by the Bureau of Labor Statistics for an urban family of four. This budget clearly has a "no frills" character—shabby, but respectable. It assumes, for example, that the family will buy a 2-year-old car and keep it for 4 years, that the husband and wife will go to the movies together once every 3 months, and that the television set will last for 10 years. The budget leaves nothing for savings and, although it sets aside some money for medical care, it does not provide for serious illness.

The tenacity of the image of the affluent society and of blue-collar workers as overpaid fat cats derives in part from the lack of communication between different locations in the class hierarchy. For most college stu-

Men who enjoy respect and power at work may have less need than others to dominate wives and children [Cornell Capa/Magnum Photos Inc.]

dents, professors, and others of the professional and managerial middle class, working-class people are shadowy figures. If we live in a middle-class suburb and work in an office, we may rarely see blue-collar workers. Our contact may be limited to a glance at construction workers eating lunch on the sidewalk or a few words exchanged with a letter carrier, guard, or telephone installer.

It is likely that more students have walked through the slums of Mexico with a copy of

Oscar Lewis in their hands than have ever done so in the working-class neighborhoods of Hammond, Indiana, or Flint, Michigan. In fact, there is no comparable book for middle-class people to read. (Levison, 1974, p. 43)

More is known about families of the very poor or those with known problems, such as delinquency or mental illness. Thus, as Lillian Rubin (1976) observed, when hardhats and white backlashers appeared on the national scene, the nation was caught off guard:

We knew almost nothing of the forty million American workers—just under half the total work force—who are employed in blue-collar jobs, most . . . of them steady workers living in stable families; most of them asking nothing and getting nothing from government programs that give welfare to the rich and the poor.

Seeking to redress the oversight, the media gave us such caricatures as Archie Bunker on television and Joe on film. Social scientists went back into the field to see what they had missed. (p. 5)

Making Ends Meet

The great increase in consumer goods available to lower-middle-class blue- and white-collar workers since the end of World War II has obscured basic differences between them and the upper-middle class. The gap between the two groups has often been considered merely a matter of differences in life-style and quality of possessions—smaller houses and yards, less stylish cars, bowling and motorboats rather than skiing and sailboats, beer rather than wine, spanking rather than Spock. The acquisition of consumer goods, however, is a misleading indicator of economic security. As Shostak (1969) observed, blue-collar prosperity is precariously supported, maintained largely by heavy installment debt and steadily declining purchasing power. What is seldom realized by

upper-middle-class observers is that payments for the house, the car, appliances, and so on take a large chunk out of the worker's paycheck, leaving almost nothing for savings or leisure. Savings and other liquid assets provide a family with a cushion against disaster and enable it to invest in the future, as in college education for the children. But in 1969 nearly half the population had less than $500 in savings, and less than a third had more than $2,000 (Parker, 1972).

A more fundamental difference between upper- and lower-middle-class families concerns the main earner's lifetime income patterns. Most upper-middle-class jobs are "careers": the manager or doctor or professor may start out at a low level of income and responsibility, but over the course of time, he (or more rarely she) will experience a series of advances that bring greater economic rewards. By contrast, most working-class and many lower-middle-class jobs lead nowhere: they involve doing the same routine tasks in the factory or the office throughout one's entire working life, even assuming that one can count on continuous employment.

Thus the typical working-class career has a rather "tragic fate" built into it (Hamilton, 1972). Although life generally gets better and better over time for the upper-middle-class family—at least financially—the working-class or white-collar family very early reaches a plateau as the breadwinner reaches the limits of his capacity to earn by promotion or advancement. The young single male worker may make enough to support himself in style—recall Tom Wolfe's affluent workers in their fancy sport shirts—but by the time he has reached his earning peak, family needs may have greatly exceeded his ability to provide for them. Even though his income may have increased, expenses continue to rise as the last children are born, older children enter their teens, and support may be needed for aging parents.

Thus working-class and lower-middle-class families often live on the edge of financial crisis. A single economic setback—a father's loss of a job, a cutback in overtime, an illness or injury requiring an operation or long-term care—can wipe out a family's savings. The realistic fear of unexpected economic danger imposes a heavy psychological burden in the form of nagging anxiety and a loss of sense of freedom. In Robert Coles's (1971) book *The Middle Americans,* a man who works in the loan department of a bank provides insight into the difficulties of his own relatively comfortable and secure white-collar family, as well as into the more desperate situations of the people he interviews for loans:

Like my father used to tell us, it's a mean rotten world if you don't have any money. And there I am in the bank, deciding if people will get money—but I myself don't have very much! We're always behind on bills; and we run a tight ship, my wife and I—no waste and no luxuries except what we can pay for. I hate borrowing money, maybe because I can see what happens to people who do. It's like quicksand; they fall into it, and they nearly die trying to get out. And the banks and finance companies are whispering in everyone's ear that they can have money . . . and the commercials on television are telling you every half minute to buy this and buy that or else you'll really be behind the times and left out. (p. 91)

The economic insecurities experienced by nonaffluent families create a vast psychological gulf between them and the more advantaged. For example, upper-middle-class women, when asked what they value most in their husbands, are likely to mention such things as emotional intimacy, sharing, and communication; working-class women are likely to say, "He's a steady worker; he doesn't drink; he doesn't hit me (L. B. Rubin, 1976, p. 93). It is not that middle-class women do not consider financial security and support important, or that working-class women are unconcerned about the emotional aspects of marriage. Rather, each group of women states goals that seem to be more problematic; when economic security is uncertain, it comes to be defined as a dominant issue in marriage. When financial security can be taken for granted, the emotional quality of the relationship comes to be a primary concern.

Childrearing, husband/wife relations, and everything else in the family are influenced by financial problems. When money runs short, each spouse may blame the other; the wife may criticize the husband for bringing home an inadequate income, while he can argue that the blame lies with her overspending and inadequacies as a household manager. The quality of a family's leisure-time activities is especially likely to suffer when paychecks don't stretch far enough. Levison (1974) noted that much that seems "parochial and limited" about working-class life stems from these restrictions:

Many workers, in the elation of the first days after their honeymoon, lock themselves into a lifetime of debt when they buy a house and furniture to add on the payments they are already making on their car. From then on, their freedom to travel, or to try a new job, or just engage in a range of activities outside work is taken from them by the structure of debt in which they are enmeshed. (p. 106)

Hiring a baby-sitter and going out to a restaurant and a movie, taking a family vacation, or going off for a weekend by themselves are activities taken for granted by upper-middle-class couples. To working-class families these things seem like major investments. Such little luxuries, though, help to make life interesting, provide relief from daily routines, and ease the inevitable tensions of family life. Particularly for housewives with small children, the lack of such activities can make them feel as if the house is a prison. Little wonder that many working-class women "attribute their major problems in life to their lack of sufficient money for the necessities of life as well as such 'luxuries' as an occasional baby-sitter or a visit to the hairdresser" (Shostak, 1969, p. 130).

Working Wives

In recent years, as economic pressures on families have worsened because of inflation and unemployment, working-class women have responded by getting jobs. Thus the recent great influx of women into the labor market has been due not only to middle-class women seeking liberation, or divorced women trying to support themselves and their children, or single career women, but also to working-class wives pushed by economic necessity. With only 46 percent of all jobs paying enough to sustain the average family at a reasonable level, the two-worker family is rapidly becoming the national norm (Ginzberg, 1976; Oppenheimer, 1979). Of all the changes in family life that have occurred in the twentieth century, this may be the most profound. It is producing pressures for changes in marital roles, the division of labor in the family, and child care. And it is creating new perceptions of self in both men and women.

Although the problems of adjusting to the new pattern cut across class lines, the change in female roles creates the most problems in working-class families. Middle-class men have traditionally been more willing to accept the ideology of sexual equality than working-class men, even if in daily life they have failed to act accordingly. For working-class men, sharing the breadwinner role

with one's wife poses a serious challenge to self-esteem and masculinity:

Despite the enormity of the burdens they carry, many men still feel they must go it alone if they are to fill their roles successfully. Often they cannot, as the soaring proportion of women who work attests. For the working-class man, that often means yet another challenge to his already uncertain self-esteem—this time in the only place where he has been able to make his authority felt—the family. For his wife, it means yet another burden in the marriage—the need to somehow shore up her husband's bruised ego while maintaining some contact not only with her own desires but with family needs as well. (L. B. Rubin, 1976, p. 184)

Love and Money

The impact of economic realities on the quality and structure of family life is not restricted to hard times. Though poverty and deprivation have received the most attention from family researchers, there is impressive evidence that variations in economic resources above the poverty line are also related to variations in family satisfaction and stability. However, the notion of a direct link between love and money flies in the face of some of our most cherished beliefs.

Similarly, sociological theory—the functionalism that has been predominant until lately—has postulated that the chief task of the family in industrial societies is to compensate for the harsh world outside the home by supplying a warm refuge where people are treated as whole and valuable persons independent of their value in the market place. Much of the literature on marriage stresses personality factors—maturity, stability, or compatibility—as the chief ingredients in marital success. Clinicians often view marital conflicts over money as a reflection of presumably more basic personality problems. Those in the marriage-and-family field who specialize in giving advice on "how to do it" also present an image of marriage as an emotional and sexual relationship in which all problems can be solved through open communication.

Although communication and sexual issues are important, marriages are also based on economic realities. As Scanzoni (1970) points out, preparation for marriage should also include an understanding of how "the realities of an acquisitive society . . . impinge on marital interaction" (p. 196). Although economic well-being does not guarantee marital happiness, economic insecurity is likely to have a profound impact on family relationships.

Our popular mythology, however, often seems to consider money somehow harmful to love. Thus there is an image of working-class families as warm and stable, while the well-to-do are supposed to have brittle, cold relationships that often end in divorce. The evidence, however, suggests the contrary: the distribution of rewards and resources in the economic world outside the family seems to be faithfully reflected within it. This is not to say that working-class and poor families cannot be loving and protective, or that affluent families do not have their own problems. But the trends are clear: studies of poor and working-class families do not reveal the warmth and stability extolled in the myth (Blood & Wolfe, 1960; L. B. Rubin, 1976; Scanzoni, 1972).

Indeed, there is impressive cross-cultural and historical evidence of an inverse correlation between socioeconomic status and marital instability—that is, the higher a person's occupation, income, or education, the less is the likelihood of divorce. (The inverse correlation seems not to hold for women—having a higher income seems to make for greater rather than less marital instability in

women [Ross & Sawhill, 1975]. Evidently deviation from the traditional pattern of male breadwinning increases marital tension and instability.) The popular belief that divorce is more common among the rich and fashionable probably arose during the era when divorce was expensive or difficult to obtain; during such times, legal divorce would be confined to the well-to-do, while less advantaged would have to remain in unhappy marriages or else resort to legally unrecorded separations and desertions. Another reason for the mistaken notion that wealth and status are associated with divorce is the publicity that attends the divorce of the rich or famous. Whenever there is a free market in divorce, however, the greater marital instability among the lower social strata reveals itself.

In short, economic resources come to be converted into emotional responses within the family. How this conversion takes place has been described in theoretical detail in survey studies by McKinley (1964) and Kohn (1963) for parent–child relationships, and Scanzoni (1972) for marital relationships. And Lillian Rubin's (1976) study of working-class families portrays the conversion process with the insight of a novelist. All of these studies confirm that the contemporary American male's occupational success or lack of it may set off a chain reaction of emotional responses within the family.

Beyond the question of income and making ends meet, which affect everyone in the family, there are the tensions and frustrations created by working conditions on the job, which also affect what happens at home. A husband whose every day at work is a bad day comes home grumpy, withdrawn, and uncommunicative—his family may even seem like the enemy at times. Unable to assert himself at work, he may insist on his traditional male prerogatives at home, demanding service and deference from wife and children. Even within the same occupation, as McKinley found, fathers whose jobs provide more autonomy, satisfaction, and power tend to be more supportive of their children, while those who suffer greater frustrations tend to be more severe.

Work and the Family

A study by Chaya Piotrowski (1978) looks at the "psychological interface" between work and the family. Through interviews and home observations with thirty members of thirteen working- and lower-middle-class families, she examines how the working conditions of wage earners influence the emotional lives of families. She identifies three patterns.

In the first, called "positive carry-over," the job is enjoyable, but not totally absorbing. An example of this pattern is a technician in charge of an animal laboratory in a large hospital. The enjoyment and gratification this man derives from his work extend into his relationship with his family. When he arrives home after work, he is emotionally available to other family members—the whole family comes together to greet him, and his arrival introduces warmth and energy into the household. (The author found that observing the wage earner's arrival home yielded striking insights into the quality of family life and the impact of the job on family relationships.)

In the "negative carry-over" pattern, more common in the sample, a stressful job that offers little control over working conditions produces anger and frustration that spill over into family relationships. When the father returns home, the family scatters, not wanting to deal with his bad mood. Needing time to "recover" from work, he is emotionally unavailable to other family members. The mother has to act as "gatekeeper" of the father's mood, keeping the children away and quiet. Often, the father displaces his anger onto his wife, resenting the fact that she does not have to experience the stress of his job.

Piotrowski called the third pattern one of "energy deficit," and it was the most common one. Here, the father finds his job so boring and monotonous that he arrives home drained of energy, describing himself as physically exhausted. His tiredness leads him to withdraw from the other family members on arriving home, but the families in this pattern did not see any connection between the job and home life.

This study should be interpreted cautiously, since the sample is so small. Also, it intentionally did not include families in which both husband and wife worked (in order to see the effects of the one worker's job more clearly). Further, the reader may wonder whether personality differences may be causing difficulties on the job as well as in the family.

But Piotrowski does not suggest that these are the only possible patterns, or that the particular families studied were always consistently in one pattern. And she denies that personality differences are responsible for the three patterns, since many of the families reported that things were different when the job was different. For example, the lab technician and his family fit into the "negative carry-over" pattern when he held a different, more stressful job, with less control over his working conditions. In general, along with the work of the other researchers mentioned here, this study suggests that the family does not function simply as a "haven in a heartless world" (Lasch, 1977).

Apart from working conditions that may be unpleasant in themselves, there is also what Sennett and Cobb (1974) refer to as the "hidden injuries of class"—the bruises to self-esteem suffered by men at the lower ranges of the status hierarchy. In America, a man's personal worth both in his own eyes and those of others is tied to his success in the job market; his wife's "success" and self-esteem as well as her material well-being have traditionally been derived from her husband. It is little wonder, then, that his self-esteem and the respect he receives from the family are tied up with his occupational status. Ironically, the upper-middle-class father, who needs less ego-bolstering respect and submission from his wife and children, is more likely to find family members going along with him in everyday decision making. The frustrated lower-status father, more demanding of deference and obedience, is likely to find his wife and children less willing to accede to him; the less the father's occupational success, the less legitimate does the rest of the family regard his authority. Thus the stage is set for power struggles between husbands and wives and between parents and children, resulting in strains, tensions, and ultimately the instability that is reflected in differential divorce rates.

Unemployment and the Family

The strongest impact of economic realities occurs when the family breadwinner loses his job. Historically one of the major distinctions between the upper-middle and the blue-collar class has been vulnerability to unemployment. The two classes differ not only in level of income and type of work done, but also in the likelihood of having no work and no income. Although the loss of income is the most visible effect of unemployment, it also places severe strains on the psychological functioning of families.

Although families may be drawn closer together as they struggle to get by, more often it appears that lengthy unemployment places strains on family relations, sometimes to the breaking point. Unemployment can be devastating to a man's self-esteem; men tend to blame themselves rather than the "system" for their lack of work, and their families may do likewise. Even during the Great Depression of the 1930s, when unemployment was massive and recognized as a national emergency, out-of-work men still felt guilty about their plight. The symbolic importance of work is reinforced by the daily realities of household life for the unemployed man; his presence around the house all day with time on his hands creates problems for the whole family.

A dramatic illustration of the effects of unemployment on family life is provided by the city of Flint, Michigan, a major auto-manufacturing center. When unemployment hit 20 percent, alcoholism and child-abuse rates also soared. A social worker describes exactly how unemployment damages the fabric of family life:

The story has become so common in Flint, it would be a cliché if it wasn't so terribly sad. A man has been employed for maybe ten years. He had a decent income, a modest house, perhaps a camper, and lots of payments. He had debts, sure, but he also had hope. Then came the layoffs. Still, he didn't worry. He had unemployment compensation and union benefits and felt he would be called back before long.

But he didn't get called back and the special benefits ran out. He lived by the skin of his teeth even in good times, because there was always something to pay for. And it gets worse and his optimism fades. He's around the house almost all day and he has fixed everything in sight. Something goes out of the family because he's around. He sees the kids when they are dirty and noisy and misbehaving. And they don't pay him the same attention they used to when they greeted him at the door when he came home from work.

A Tennessee miner and his daughter. [Jack Corn/National Archives]

He had always had the disciplinary role around the house. He was the boss, the bread-winner. So his relationship with his wife changes. He bosses her around and demands she bring him a beer because he has to prove that he's still the man of the house. In a situation like that, everybody in the house gets bent out of shape.

I don't know how many cases I've had where the father admits that what his child did would normally not have been cause for reprimand. Or it would have been overlooked. But in the house of the unemployed, there is so much tension it's like striking a match in a room full of gas fumes. The child misbehaves, the father loses his temper, and smacks him harder than he intended.

There is no evidence of sadism or serious emotional illness in most of the child-beating cases we have been seeing. . . . The hospital or the doctor shows me a child covered with bruises and when I ask the parents what happened, the father breaks down and tells me he did it. He says over and over again that he's sorry, that he simply lost control, that if he could only find a job he would make it up to the child.

I may sound crazy, but most . . . child beaters are concerned and loving fathers, and in a way they are driven to child beating because they are. (Hilliker, 1976)

A growing body of statistical evidence also documents the effects of unemployment on the family. A major study by Harvey Brenner (1976) found significant correlations between unemployment and seven measures of stress-related pathology: suicide, homicide, admission to mental hospitals, admission to prisons, mortality from heart and kidney disease, and mortality from all causes. The data were from the United States, England, and Sweden, and covered the period from World War II to 1973. The correlations between unemployment and all the pathological indices held steady across age, sex, and racial groups in different states and three different countries.

Of course, most families manage to cope with the hazards of unemployment and do not contribute to the statistics on suicide, child abuse, or mental-hospital admissions. But the correlations reveal the kinds of stress that, with less dramatic outcomes, affect the families of the unemployed. As one economist puts it:

For every case of child abuse to which unemployment might have contributed, there are many more where parents no longer have the psychological resources to respond warmly to their children; for every divorce, there are several more lifeless marriages; for every admission to a mental hospital, several more individuals whose abilities to function as worker, spouse, and parent have been broken down. (Grubb, 1977, p. 29)

BLACK FAMILIES: MYTHS AND REALITIES

In January 1977 the television dramatization of Alex Haley's book *Roots* became a national event. Appearing for eight consecutive nights, it told the story of seven generations in an American black family, beginning with the capture of a young African man and his enslavement in America and ending with the birth of his descendant, the author Haley. The dramatization of *Roots* made history for a number of reasons. It attracted and held an enormous audience for the whole eight days, at the end exceeding previous viewing records set by the Superbowl and *Gone with the Wind.* Further, these records were set by a program presenting black history from a black point of view; *Roots* destroyed the myth that the mass television audience would not sit still for dramas with serious social content, especially if presented from a black perspective.

Finally, and perhaps most significantly, *Roots* challenged the stereotype of black family life that had prevailed for decades in both popular opinion and the social sciences. This stereotype held that blacks had no family life to speak of: slavery had "destroyed" the black family, and the descendants of the slaves had never been able to overcome this damaging legacy.

Before the 1970s family scholars tended to deal with black family life in one of two ways: the first was to ignore it altogether, the second was to treat the black family only as a social problem. The term *black family* came almost to be a synonym for family instability, disorganization, and pathology. Most research dealt with middle-class white families; the smaller number of studies on blacks and other minorities dealt with lower-class populations, who were found wanting in comparison (Staples & Mirande, 1980).

In recent years there has been a great deal more research on black family life, past and present, much of which has challenged the traditional stereotypes. Walter Allen (1978) has pointed to three different ideological perspectives on black families. The first is the traditional approach, which regards black families as culturally deviant and pathological. The second, the cultural-equivalent approach, argues that black families do not differ greatly from middle-class norms. The cultural-variant approach depicts black families as different from white families, but strong and resilient.

Underlying the debates about the black family is a question that is important for both theory and social policy: Is family life to blame for the social and economic hardships of a disadvantaged minority group, or are that group's family patterns best understood as responses or adaptations to those hardships and disadvantages?

Probably the best-known presentation of the problem theory of the black family is Daniel Moynihan's *The Negro Family: The Case for National Action* (1965). He described the black family as the center of a "tangle of pathology," perpetuating itself from generation to generation.

Like many previous writers, Moynihan traced the present disorganization of the black family to the heritage of three centuries of slavery. White America broke the "will of the Negro people by destroying the Negro family." Thus slavemasters had encouraged promiscuity to increase the slave population, had prevented slaves from marrying, and had broken up families on the auction block. The slave household was fatherless and matrifocal (mother-centered).

Emancipation created still more disorder and disorganization. E. Franklin Frazier, a black historian and one of the leading scholars on the black family several decades ago, had written about how black-family life disintegrated still further after the Civil War:

When the yoke of slavery was lifted, the drifting masses were left without any restraint upon their vagrant impulses and wild desires. . . . Promiscuous sexual relations and constant changing of spouses became the rule. . . . Marriage as a formal and legal relation was not part of the mores of the freedman. (1948, p. 89)

Migration to the North, according to the Moynihan report and the writings on which it is based, reinforced the social and familial disorganization among southern blacks. Black women were forced to become breadwinners and the men became emasculated dependents or tried to assert their manhood in the bedroom and the streets. Family discipline broke down, producing juvenile delinquency and other forms of crime.

Although the Moynihan report acknowledged that decades of "catastrophic unemployment" rates have undermined black-family structures, it did not conclude that ending unemployment will cure the "tangle of pathology." Rather, it argued that the black family is so damaged that its children, especially sons, are unable to profit from school and job opportunities. Until the "damage" to the black family is repaired, "all the effort to end discrimination and poverty and injustice will come to little" (1965, p. 5).

The Moynihan report was greeted with a storm of protest and criticism. Although it expressed concern for the victims of racism and discrimination, critics perpetuated racial stereotypes, substituting sociological and psychological explanations for crude racist ones. William Ryan (1976) charged that the report constitutes the classic case of "blaming the victim": attributing the cause of social problems, such as poverty and discrimination, to defects within the victim.

Billingsley (1968) and others complained that by referring to "the problem of the Negro family," Moynihan ignored the fact that the majority of black families were stable and responsible. Other critics complained that the report overlooked class differences among black families. Hylan Lewis (1968) and others pointed out that when the effects of both income and race on family structure are examined, the income differences are more striking than the color differences. Poverty among whites is also correlated with family instability and illegitimacy, while higher income and status among black families goes along with more stable and conventional family arrangement.

For black families, the problem of poverty is compounded by the problem of racial discrimination; the castelike barrier makes it difficult to compare black and white families at similar income levels. Poor black people are not simply poor white people with black skins; they face additional hardships due to discrimination. Even when black and white families match on income, education, and occupation, they are not wholly comparable. The black group "must reflect its experience with the caste barrier as well as its distinctive history, both of which set the conditions for growing up black in America" (Billingsley, 1968, p. 201).

Social Class and Black Family Life

It makes as little sense to talk about "the black family" as it does to talk about "the white family." Black families may be upper class (about 10 percent), middle class (about 40 percent), or lower class (about 50 percent), with additional subgroupings within these categories (Billingsley, 1968). They may be urban or rural or suburban, northern or southern or western; and they vary in child-rearing practices, values, and family roles.

Even within the lower class, distinct groupings exist. There are stable blue-collar families, comparable to the stable white working-class families described earlier. The working poor with marginal incomes, employed in unskilled and service occupations, constitute the largest sector of the lower class. The third segment of the lower class, which has attracted the most public and scholarly attention, includes the unemployed and people living on welfare. According to Billingsley, this group constitutes about a quarter of all lower-class black families. Even within this category, there are wide variations in family values and practices.

Charles Willie (1981) has described the everyday lives of black families in three different class situations—affluent or middle class, working class, and poor. Living mainly in nuclear households with one or two children, middle-class black families, he observes, "manifest probably better than any population group the Puritan orientation towards work, success, and self-reliance so characteristic of the basic values of this nation" (p. 50). Education is a major means of mobility in this group; both husband and wife are often college graduates, there is a strong emphasis on children's education, and both boys and girls are encouraged to strive for high-level professional careers.

The second type of family Willie describes is working class. Here, households are also nuclear, but they are likely to be larger than in the middle class because four or more children as well as relatives or lodgers may be living in. These families are more likely to be broken, with illness and death prominent reasons for the absence of the male spouse. These families live just above the poverty line; all members work, and wages of the older children are often an important part of family finances. Parents' aspirations for their children's education does not exceed their own level by very much. The goals they wish for their children require only a high school or junior college degree: secretary, nurse, or skilled manual worker.

Poor families are the third group described by Willie. These people adapt to poverty through "necessary, clever and sometimes foolish arrangements" (p. 55), ranging from extended family households to taking in boarders and foster children. There is a great deal of distrust between men and women, marriages are unstable, but there is "fierce loyalty" between mothers and children and other kin. Parents, however, often hold themselves up as negative examples, of what not to do—that is, not to marry too young, not to have children too soon. Despite the seeming deviance of the poor, Willie maintains that they are not isolated from American values.

Recently, there has been much discussion of the emergence of a black "underclass." The notion of an underclass is not new; Marx wrote about the *lumpenproletariat*—a class of disreputable and dangerous poor people who were incapable of functioning in early capitalist society or of making a revolution. A 1982 book by journalist Ken Auletta called *The Underclass* popularized the term. Auletta used it to describe a small minority of poor people made up of long-term welfare recipients, drifters, hustlers, drug addicts, and street criminals.

However, the notion of "underclass" has come to be used to characterize a large proportion of the black population and also to explain its problems. Actually, Auletta did not argue that the underclass was either

huge or specifically black. He observed that an underclass can be found in any group facing severe social and economic conditions—for example, in white Appalachia. Oscar Lewis (1951) had described a similar population in the slums of Mexico City; he coined the term *culture of poverty* to describe the phenomenon. Nor did Auletta argue that a majority of black poor are permanently dependent on welfare or fall into the category of the underclass.

Indeed, Auletta's own conclusions about the extent of the underclass were called into question by a landmark University of Michigan study (Duncan, 1984). This study, which tracked the economic fortunes of 5,000 families over a decade, found that a large majority of poor people move in and out of poverty. The proportion of poor people might remain the same, but the individuals and families who make up the poor are constantly changing. Relatively few people remain on welfare for long periods of time or pass on the habit of welfare dependency to their children. There is a segment of the black poor that fits the description of the underclass, but it is a small minority of the black population.

A Tangle of Pathology?

The debate about the Moynihan report and the concept of an "underclass" or a "culture of poverty" is not about whether poverty, family disorganization, and social pathology are correlated. Rather, the debate is about how these correlations should be interpreted. Moynihan insists that the family plays a central causal role in sustaining poverty and disorganization in the black community. Family deviance, he argues, is at the "center of the tangle of pathology," the crucial intervening variable between socioeconomic discrimination and community pathology.

Thus, poor families do not suffer simply from a lack of money or opportunity; they also supposedly suffer from a number of personality defects and deviant values that keep them from getting ahead. This package of deviant attributes, the theory goes, constitutes a "culture of poverty" that is passed along from parents to children, thereby ensuring that the children of the poor remain poor.

At the heart of the debate between Moynihan and others of the "culture of poverty" school on the one hand and their critics on the other is how to interpret observable differences between lower-income people and the advantaged. There is empirical evidence of inadequacy and incompetence among people living in slums and ghettos. Living in poverty is decidedly much worse for one's physical and mental health than living at an adequate economic level. Further, nobody doubts that economic stress can impair the ability of parents to provide for the physical and emotional well-being of their children. But the central issue is this: Are these "disabilities" passed on from parent to child as a set of deeply ingrained values and personality traits? Or are they learned anew in each generation in response to the conditions of life in slums and ghettos?

There is a good deal of evidence that the differences and disabilities that set the poor apart from the middle classes can be attributed to the realities of living at the bottom of the economic hierarchy (Valentine, 1968). For example, Elliott Liebow (1967), in a participant-observation study of lower-class, unemployed black men, found little evidence of a self-sustaining cultural system set off from the rest of society. The men he studied were painfully aware of their failure to meet the dominant American standards for success. Because they shared the standards of the larger society, they saw themselves as failures.

Liebow's analysis of the "delay of gratification" idea is particularly useful because

this presumed defect is one of the central components of the culture of poverty. To be unable to delay gratification means to be impulsive, to spend rather than save, to do whatever you feel like doing right now without regard for the future. Supposedly induced by lower-class or black childrearing practices, it is said to account for the poor child's failure to succeed in school and the poor adult's inability to get ahead. One of the problems with this concept is that the middle classes, who are supposed to exemplify the virtues of delayed gratification, have been described in recent decades as increasingly hedonistic, impulsive, and devoted to spending rather than saving.

Despite the dubious existence of the delayed-gratification pattern in the middle class, Liebow argued that the current realities of life in lower-income populations are sufficient to cause what appears to be an inability to delay gratification. What appears as a "present-time orientation" to the outside observer, he argued, may actually take the future very much into account:

The young streetcorner man has a fairly good picture of [the future]. . . . It is a future in which everything is uncertain except the ultimate destruction of his hopes and the eventual realization of his fears. The most he can reasonably look forward to is that these things do not come too soon. Thus, when Richard squanders a week's pay in two days, it is not because, like an animal or a child, he is "present time" oriented, unaware of or unconcerned with his future. He does so precisely because he is aware of the future and the hopelessness of it all. (pp. 64–68)

Although some of Moynihan's critics dispute the extent of pathology in the black community and attribute whatever pathology does exist to economic stress and discrimination, other critics refuse to take a completely negative view even of lower-class family patterns. Without denying the pain-

Chicano teenagers. [Danny Lyon/National Archives]

has developed her personality out of the necessary role adjustments required to withstand the oppressive odds against her family's survival in an admittedly racist society. (p. 132)

Since the Moynihan report appeared in 1965, the bias implicit in the concept of male dominance and female submission as the norm for marital "health" has become starkly apparent.

Other critics have pointed to the fact that adult women have traditionally played strong roles in the families of oppressed groups. For example, the Jewish family, the Irish family, and the working-class English family could be caricatured as matriarchal, yet these families have also been regarded as "strong" and "cohesive," not as part of "a tangle of pathology." Schneider and Smith (1973) observed that there is nothing inherently disorganized or abnormal about "matrifocal" families. Mother-centeredness is not confined to any particular cultural tradition but derives from the relationship of individuals and families to the economic system:

Steady employment for males, with involvement in a range of welfare plans such as medical and unemployment insurance, savings and life insurance, and home-purchase schemes, provides a stabilizing effect upon marriage and reinforces middle-class normative stress upon the nuclear family. Unemployment and irregular employment, coupled with high rates of female participation in the labor market, has the opposite effect. In neither case is this relationship to economics determinative in any simple way of familial structure at the behavioral level. For the lower class, it often results in the emergence of the perfectly normal configuration of domestic units based on a stable female core, to which males are related in a variety of supportive, dominant, or dependent ways. (p. 107)

Although such adaptations of people living under oppressive conditions may appear to

ful social and psychological costs that have been inflicted on black Americans, they nevertheless insist that lower-class black family life is not necessarily "disorganized." They argue that many of its features are sources of strength that have helped the black community cope with its enormous burdens. For example, the supposedly matriarchal character of poor black families may have been an important contributor to black survival. As Robert Staples (1971) observed, rather than being a "matriarchal villain," the poor black woman the surrounding culture as excessive or pathological, once the social pressure that created it is removed, a new adjustment develops.

Carol Stack's (1974) anthropological study *All Our Kin* provides vivid insights into some of the adaptive strategies of black families at the lowest income levels. Like the work of Elliott Liebow, it reveals that observations of how people actually live yield a very different picture of reality than census or survey data.

What census records, for example, indicate as a fatherless or female-headed household does not necessarily mean that a woman is isolated and alone. Also, ethnographic studies like these reveal that if you look closely at so-called disorganized families and communities, you may find distinct forms of social organization. Stack described how networks of kin and quasi-kin—good friends who can be relied on—meet daily needs:

Black families living in the flats need a steady source of cooperative support to survive. They share with one another because of the urgency of their needs. Alliances between individuals are created around the clock as kin and friends exchange and give, and obligate one another. They trade food stamps, rent money, a TV, hats, dice, a car, a nickel here, a cigarette there, food, milk, grits, and children. . . .

Without the help of kin, fluctuations in the meager flow of available goods could easily destroy a family's ability to survive. (pp. 32–33)

The adaptations to poverty described in Stack's book do not lock people into a cycle of poverty or prevent the poor from marrying. But her work does show that trying to become more middle class through marriage or employment involves a dubious risk. For a poor black woman to withdraw from the kin network means sacrificing the security gained through the system of exchange, and giving up her welfare payments as well, to depend on the precarious employment of an unskilled black man. It is a dubious proposition indeed. The kin group also has a vested interest in keeping its members loyal and avoiding marital commitments. Ironically, official welfare policies also discourage social mobility and formation of nuclear families and encourage the maintenance of domestic networks. They do so by rewarding only fatherless families and preventing the poor from inheriting even small amounts of cash or from acquiring investments typical for the middle class, such as home ownership.

The women Stack encountered in the course of her study provide vivid evidence of the futility of trying to live up to middle-class family standards under these conditions:

Julia Ambrose estimated the man she married to be a good provider and a reliable risk. After her husband was laid off from his job, Julia was forced to apply for welfare benefits for her children. Ruby Banks returned to the flats without her husband within a year of marriage, embarrassed, disappointed, depressed. Her pride was injured. She acquired a bitter resentment toward men and toward the harsh conditions of poverty. After the separation, Ruby's husband moved into his older sister's home in a neighboring town. His spirit and optimism towards family life had also been severely weakened. (p. 126)

The Heritage of Slavery

Although the critics of the Moynihan report disputed his analysis of the "pathology" of contemporary black families, few of them disagreed with his description of slavery, or the view that slavery had "destroyed" the black family. In recent years, however, this traditional view of black families under slavery has been radically revised by new historical discoveries. Herbert Gutman's (1976) book *The Black Family in Slavery and Freedom* is the most important work in this line of research, but other scholars have also contributed to the new view. The book and television version of *Roots*, with its vivid emphasis on the strength of family bonds among slaves, dramatizes the findings of the new scholarship.

Gutman's work was originally inspired by the Moynihan report. Trying to evaluate what has been called the "slavery-specific hypothesis" presented in the report—the view that contemporary black family disorganization is a legacy of slavery—Gutman looked at census data for a number of cities between 1880 and 1925. He discovered that two-parent households were the norm among blacks during this period and that single-parent households were no more common than among comparable whites. There was no evidence among lower-class blacks of the "tangle of pathology."

Trying to explain how this stable family pattern could have arisen, Gutman used a variety of statistical and other evidence to explore the structure of the black family during Reconstruction and slavery. He discovered that the two-parent household prevailed among slaves and continued to do so after emancipation. He found that slave unions tended to be remarkably long-lasting, forced separation through sale being the major reason for family break-ups. The various letters and statements made by ex-slaves reveal the strength of the attachments of slave families and the deep and lasting grief caused by these separations.

The nuclear family, however, was not the only kind of family structure discovered by Gutman. He also discovered evidence of a strong extended-kinship structure. The existence of distinctive slave-marriage rules, such as taboos against blood-cousin marriage, and the fact that slave children were often named for blood kin, such as aunts, uncles, and grandparents, provide part of the evidence for the importance of slave kin groups. This kinship structure, and the sense of community and interdependence that this structure fostered, may have been the chief means by which African cultural traditions were preserved, as well as an important survival mechanism of black people under slavery.

The major conclusion of Gutman and the other historians who have contributed to the new black history is this: to the extent that contemporary black families are matrifocal or disorganized, it is not a legacy of slavery but a result of the destructive conditions of northern urban life encountered by a massive number of migrants from the rural South. Gutman compared the twentieth-century migration of blacks to the Enclosure Movement in eighteenth-century England, when millions of farmers were driven from the land when landowners turned to sheep herding.

The modern enclosure movement was caused by the mechanization of southern agriculture, particularly by the cotton-picking machine. As a result, the migration from American rural areas between 1940 and 1970 was equal to the century of European immigration between 1820 and 1920. In 1940 half the black population lived on the land; by 1965 it was four-fifths urban. The Moynihan report acknowledged that black employment rates in northern cities have continued at disaster levels for 35 years. Yet the report preferred to blame the black family rather than the economic conditions that had uprooted millions from the land and failed to provide jobs in the cities. It is much easier "to lament the sins of one's forefathers than to confront the injustices of more contemporary socioeconomic systems" (Furstenberg, Hershberg, & Modell, 1975, p. 233).

Recent Changes in Black Family Life

As a result of the historical work of Gutman and others, it seems clear that current differences between black and white families cannot be traced to slavery but have a much more recent origin. As Andrew Cherlin (1981c) observes,

The family patterns of urban blacks differ today from the patterns among whites in large part because of differences in the current experiences of city-born-and-bred blacks and whites. Instead of looking back to slavery or to the rural, post-bellum South, we need to look at life in the cities today. (p. 104)

Indeed, the differences between black and white families do not extend far back into the past, but rather seem to have started during the depression years of the 1930s. And since 1960 the divergence has become wider. Some observers have noted a growing class distinction within the black community. Julius Wilson (1978), in his controversial book *The Declining Significance of Race*, has argued that while educated blacks have been able to find steady, well-paid work, the condition of unskilled, uneducated blacks has grown worse. Wilson has been criticized for underestimating the continuing importance of racial discrimination. Willie (1981), for example, points out that there are striking differences in income between blacks and whites in the same age, sex, and occupational categories. But other observers agree that many of our central cities are experiencing the growth of a black population for whom unemployment and poverty are taken for granted as the facts of life.

In some ways, the debate over the black family seems to have come full circle. Few scholars accept the old pathological model of the black family based on the heritage of slavery. But there seems to be a greater willingness to accept a new pathological model based on the grim realities of inner-city ghetto life. A surprising aspect of recent discussions of black family problems is that black leaders and organizations are calling attention to them. In the spring of 1984, a number of black organizations convened a Black Family Summit. The principal issue on the agenda was the plight of teenage girls with babies, and to a lesser extent the problems of older single mothers (Hulbert, 1984). While not denying that unemployment, poverty, and racism play a large role in the problems of the black family, these leaders were arguing that teenaged parenthood is a problem to be addressed in its own right.

In the end, as Staples and Mirande (1980) have suggested, researchers may "have to go back to the drawing board on black family research" (p. 503). Before the 1970s, we have seen, the black family was viewed as a tangle of pathology. The research of the 1970s emphasized the stability of middle-class black families and the resilience of lower-class ones. Now we hear talk of "crisis" and "catastrophe." Yet the statistical picture is more complicated than it seems at first glance, and the social realities of black family life in the 1980s have not yet been documented by researchers. Some of the social indicators on young black people are up: for example, the black high-school dropout rate has declined, and the disparity between black and white educational levels has almost disappeared. According to the Census Bureau, the median years of school completed by people who were between the ages of 25 and 29 in 1982 was 12.9 for whites and 12.7 for blacks. Even statistics on unwed motherhood are complicated. It is true that more than half of all black babies today (56% in 1981) are born out of wedlock, but teenaged parenthood is not a sudden development in the black community; in fact, birthrates among unwed black women, including teenagers, have

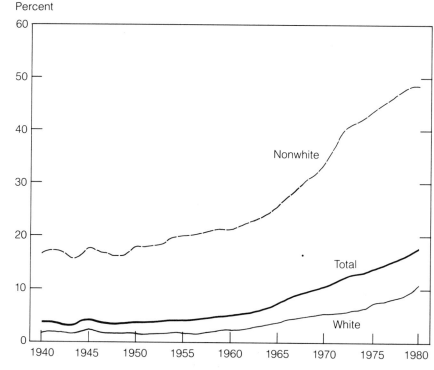

FIGURE 7.1
*Percent of Children
Born out of Wedlock:
1940–1980*

From A. Thornton and D. Freedman, *Population Bulletin: The Changing American Family*, a publication of The Population Reference Bureau, Vol. 38, No. 4, October 1983, p. 20.

declined since 1970. Further, overall birthrates among blacks have dropped dramatically. Although teenaged parenthood is a serious and unfortunate situation, it cannot be understood apart from conditions in the black community as a whole.

THE MEXICAN AMERICAN FAMILY

In recent years, the Mexican American or Chicano family has come to the attention of both researchers and the general public. This interest reflects the growing importance of Hispanic Americans in the United States; Mexican Americans have become the fastest growing and largest ethnic minority

in the United States. In 1982, the Census Bureau counted about 15 million people of Spanish ethnic origins in the United States (U. S. Department of Commerce, Bureau of the Census, 1982). In addition, there are about a million or more uncounted illegal immigrants. Not all of these are Mexican, of course. There are also Puerto Ricans, Cubans, and Central and South Americans. Spanish-speaking peoples are much more diverse than other groups with a common native tongue—for example, those who speak Italian or Yiddish.

Despite their rural origins, Mexican Americans today live mainly in urban areas, mostly in ethnic enclaves or *barrios*. Although they have spread to other areas of the country, they remain concentrated in the

Southwest. Chicano families tend to be larger than mainstream American families, with higher fertility rates than both whites and blacks. They are less likely to be divorced than other groups. Economically, Mexican Americans are substantially less well off than the population as a whole, but about a fifth to a quarter enjoy middle class incomes and occupations (U. S. Department of Commerce, Bureau of the Census, 1982).

Stuart Queen and his associates (Queen, Habenstein, & Quadagno, 1985) suggest that the farm labor history of Mexican Americans is as important to an understanding of them and their culture as slavery is to an understanding of black Americans. Traditionally, Mexicans worked as wage laborers on Anglo-owned land. Although they are today a largely urban population, their agricultural history made it difficult to become as mobile and assimilated to mainstream American society as European immigrant groups.

There is, of course, no such thing as "the Chicano family," any more than there is "the American family." Nevertheless, within Mexican American culture there is a distinct set of values centering on the family. Indeed, the family, not the individual, has traditionally been an overriding value and the basic social unit. Families are large and kinship bonds are strong. Nuclear families are part of kinship networks on both sides; parents and grandparents, brothers and sisters, aunts, uncles, and cousins remain the individual's most important ties throughout life. In addition to their emphasis on familistic values, Chicano families have also tended to have more sharply polarized gender and age roles than middle-class Anglo families. The meaning and extent of this difference has been the subject of a good deal of controversy.

Until the 1970s, most writing on the Mexican American family describes it in negative, even pathological terms. In the early 1970s researchers, including a number of Chicano scholars, began to dispute the earlier descriptions and present a sympathetic view of la familia (Staples & Mirande, 1980). Some of these researchers tended to idealize and romanticize the Chicano family. Recently, more balanced studies have appeared, appreciating Chicano family and culture but recognizing the existence, as in any family system, of diversity, change, and strain.

The negative views of the Chicano family focused on its machismo authoritarianism and its tendency to make the family, rather than the development of the individual, the central purpose in life. While the black family was seen as pathological because of its presumed female dominance, the Mexican American family was viewed as unhealthy because of its patriarchy. In contrast, the ideal, middle-class Anglo family was seen as egalitarian and democratic and as promoting the values of achievement, independence, and self-esteem. In the Mexican family, the man was portrayed as the lord and master of the household, dominating his wife and children, often with physical violence.

The assumption was that Chicano child-rearing fostered a passive, dependent personality, ill equipped to achieve mobility. Further, the familistic values of Chicanos and their obligations to relatives on both sides of the family were also seen as hampering individual achievement. More recently, the same qualities that seemed to be defects in the past have been portrayed as virtues. The Chicano family has been seen as warm and nurturing, a family that provides emotional security and a sense of belonging to its members (Murillo, 1971). Machismo no longer means power and violence, but is now seen as benevolent authority. The strong extended family ties are now an admired source of social support, rather than a hin-

Middle-class black families have traditionally upheld the puritan ethic of hard work and success. [Charles Harbutt/Archive Pictures Inc.]

drance to individual mobility. Indeed, in a reversal of earlier values, it is now the middle-class Anglo family that is described as a "not particularly praiseworthy model of the family" (Queen et al., 1985, p. 328).

In addition to being viewed differently by researchers, the Chicano family is also turning out, in recent empirical studies, to differ from earlier stereotypes. Chicano families are much more egalitarian in husband–wife relations and more permissive in childrearing than expected on the basis of traditional descriptions. Chicano families have been affected by the recent changes in American life, both economic and social, and will undoubtedly experience more change in the future, especially as women find more opportunities out of the home and more individu-

als of both sexes experience educational and occupational mobility.

SUMMARY

The removal of work from home to factory transformed the family from a productive unit to a group of consumers dependent on the income of the family breadwinner. The impact of this change differs according to the family's location, hierarchy of occupation, and income. Although the effects of the husband's occupational situation can be seen most clearly in working-class families living with economic uncertainty, or among black families coping with chronically disastrous employment levels, the dependency of the wife and children on the breadwinner's income affects all families.

Above all, the exchange of the husband's money for the wife's service creates the potential for each to feel exploited by the other. We live in a mass-consumption society in which money buys not only the necessities of life but also identity and status. People are encouraged to have limitless appetites for goods and services, making most people feel that their incomes are inadequate. Thus family members must compete with one another in the allocation of the family's limited resources. Further, when income seems insufficient, the family breadwinner, traditionally the husband, may feel his dependents are squandering his hard-earned money, while the wife and children may blame the husband for failing to be more successful.

In recent years, women have entered the labor market in massive numbers, in part to help fill the gap between the husband's income and the family's needs and wants. Once again, a shift in the economic functions of the family seems to be changing the nature of family relationships and producing a redefinition of family roles and obligations.

Race and ethnicity add another dimension of variation in family experience. The black family experience in America is unique because of the heritage of slavery, discrimination, and massive unemployment persisting for generations. Many social scientists, however, have tended to blame black family life for the continuing poverty of much of the black population—the classic case of blaming the victim. The view of the black family as a "tangle of pathology" not only ignores the role of economic and social discrimination in perpetuating the disadvantages of racial minority, but also overlooks the diversity of black families. Further, many features of poor, urban, black family life are ways of coping and surviving in a difficult environment.

After black Americans, the largest U.S. ethnic minority is Mexican Americans or Chicanos. It is also the fastest growing. Chicanos have a distinct set of family traditions, centering on strong bonds with kin. Like the black family, the Chicano family has sometimes been described in negative terms. More recently, it has been seen in a much more positive, even idealized, way. However, the Chicano family seems to be experiencing the same changes, especially in women's roles, that are affecting the rest of the country.

CHAPTER 8

Sex and Gender

If we have come to think that the nursery and the kitchen are the natural sphere of a woman, we have done so exactly as English children come to think that a cage is the natural sphere of a parrot—because they have never seen one anywhere else.

George Bernard Shaw
The Womanly Woman

In the past 2 decades America has experienced dramatic changes in both sexual behavior and sex roles. Researchers may debate about whether there has been a sexual revolution or just a steady liberalization of our sexual norms and behaviors, but no one doubts that the sexual climate has changed dramatically from what it was in the 1950s and early 1960s.

Sex roles—the social scripts that define how males and females are supposed to act—have also changed. Women are entering the work force in increasing numbers, and a large majority of Americans (63 percent) prefer a marriage of shared responsibility in which the husband and wife cooperate on work, childrearing, and homemaking; only 29 percent prefer a traditional marriage in which the man is the breadwinner and the wife stays home (Ladd, 1981).

The sexual and sex-role revolutions, however, have in many ways made life more complicated, even for people who eagerly embraced them. A large opposition has developed to both sexual liberalization and equality for women. Many people feel the recent changes have gone "too far," upsetting a "natural" order between the sexes, with dire consequences for social and individual stability. Many others feel that change has hardly begun. They point to women's persistent inequality in the workplace and their continuing to shoulder most of the burden of childcare and housework in the family, as well as to the 1982 defeat of the Equal Rights Amendment.

In this time of intense and polarized debate about sexual equality it is extremely difficult to carry on scholarly discussions objectively. Researchers themselves are equally polarized; some find evidence of psychological or behavioral differences between the sexes and use their findings to justify traditional sex roles. Others argue that all differences between males and females are learned and that the only biological differences between the sexes are the obvious physical ones. Meanwhile, findings about sex differences have news value; unlike other topics that appear in scientific journals, a study of sex differences in mathematics or brain chemistry is likely to appear on the evening news. But a study that finds no sex differences will not be reported and, indeed, would not likely be published, even as original research.

Not all feminists object to biological interpretations of sex differences. One prominent feminist, Alice Rossi (1977), has argued that women's greater involvement in parenting is based on hormonal differences between women and men. Others argue that while there may be some biologically based behavioral differences, these do not justify social inequality between men and women.

There are still other complications in discussing sex differences and sex roles. One concerns the very terms to use. Some writers have recommended making a distinction between *sex* and *gender*. These writers use *sex* to refer to the biological differences between males and females and *gender* to refer to social and psychological distinctions, such as having an identity as male or female, or acting in "masculine" or "feminine" ways. But others object to this terminology, arguing that it prejudges important questions about the origins of sex-linked behavior. Thus, Eleanor Maccoby (1980) comments, "In point of fact, we cannot yet be sure about the mix of social and biological differences between males and females. The nature of the causal factors should be investigated rather than implied at the outset through the choice of terminology" (p. 203n).

Further complicating matters is the fact that few writers on sex differences are willing to say that they completely discount either biological or social explanations of sex differences. Most writers state that they are interactionists—that is, they claim to believe that both biological and social factors work together. In practice, however, many pay only lip service to interactionism and in their actual writings discount one side or the other. We have not yet exhausted all the complexities of dealing with biological differences. We will pursue the issue in the rest of this chapter.

THE STUDY OF SEX AND SEX DIFFERENCES

In speculating why the social sciences have lagged behind the natural sciences such as physics and chemistry, some writers have argued that the social sciences are too new; they are only now at the point that physics was when Galileo was dropping balls off the leaning tower of Pisa. Others who have thought about the matter come to the opposite conclusion: the social sciences have lagged because they are too old. People always had theories about what social life is all about, and these folk psychologies and folk sociologies get in the way of, and even get mixed up with, the more scientific models (Murphy, 1971). Still others have argued a third position: that the social sciences can never attain the precision and predictability of the natural sciences for the

simple reason that the subject matter is so different; the physicist, watching a ball roll down an inclined plane, does not have to worry about the ball's reactions to being observed—that it might be too embarassed to roll at all or, just to be contrary, might decide to roll uphill.

Prudery and Patriarchalism

Besides sharing in the general difficulties that beset the study of human behavior, the study of sexuality has been hampered by cultural attitudes surrounding sexuality with anxiety, making it a taboo topic for private or public discussion, and by cultural biases defining women as the natural subordinates of men because of biological and intellectual inferiority.

Thus, in approaching the study of either the physical or the social relations between the sexes, it is important to understand how the prevailing assumptions of male dominance and female submissiveness may have influenced both popular and professional conceptions of sexuality and sex differences. Feminism has made us aware of how deeply entrenched sexist attitudes are in men and women, even in our language and habits of expression. It is difficult for students of sexual biology and behavior to escape the patriarchal image of the passive egg waiting for purposeful, active sperm to impregnate it, or of female animals during their periods of sexual interest as being "receptive," when in fact their behavior shows them to be the initiators of the sex act (Hershberger, 1948). Anthropologists have applied male–female stereotypes to the study of human evolution, emphasizing the importance of "man the hunter" and overlooking the contributions of "woman the food gatherer" in prehistoric times (Martin & Voorhies, 1975).

As John Stuart Mill and later feminists have argued, the history of relations between the sexes is analogous to those between different races, classes, and castes. All such relationships have involved the domination of one group, defined by birth, by members of another group, also defined by birth. Thus patriarchy—the rule of men over women—must be placed alongside feudalism, despotism, slavery, aristocracy, and racism. In practice, however, such power arrangements appear natural and inevitable, and alternatives to them unthinkable. When religion is given as the major justification for behavior, subordination of one group by another is explained in religious terms. More recently, domination is usually justified in terms of biological necessity, irrevocable instincts, and inherent inferiority.

Images of Sexuality

In popular thought, sexuality is said to represent the instinctive, "animal" side of human nature, separate from and opposed to the higher forms of human behavior that are learned and cultural. The prevailing ideas about sex and sex differences are that sex is a powerful natural drive, necessary for reproduction, but one that must be socially controlled. Learning and culture enter into the process only as controls, not as influences on the patterning or development of sexuality.

Sexuality in the folk model includes more than the urgency of lust. It accounts for masculine and feminine behavior, the choice of sex partners, and the differences between the father's and mother's role in child-rearing. Thus the natural model of sexuality implies that the person intuitively knows whether he or she is male or female. His or her behavior follows naturally the patterns laid down by the body's biological gender. And, in the same way, a person will naturally be sexually attracted to and fall in love with members of the opposite sex.

Sex is used to mark off humanity into two separate species. At birth children are divided into males and females, with the assumption that everything else about them is secondary to, or flows from, that basic distinction. If the child is a boy, he will be active, assertive, aggressive; he will go out into the world and seek his fortune. If the child is a girl, she will be gentle, passive, dependent, intuitive; her place will be at home. The notion that maleness or femaleness necessarily determines social role and behavior runs deep in many cultural traditions. Ancient Chinese sages divided the world into male and female qualities: yang is bright, hot, active, and positive; yin is dark, moist, cold, and passive. The essential feature of the folk beliefs about sex differences is duality, with gender being a matter of either/or rather than both/and or more/less. Some social-science theorists similarly have held that the biological division of labor between the sexes and a sharp differentiation between men and women are necessary to the functioning of any society.

SEX ROLES AND BIOLOGY

Biological determinism often seems more compelling than the notion that sexual destiny is also based on culture and learning. For the layman, it is relatively easy to believe that innate biological forces transform boy babies into men and girl babies into women, because most men and women until very recently have lived up to the prescribed sex roles. Such exceptions as obvious homosexuals could also be accounted for on biological grounds.

Although biologically men are men and women are women, sex roles—that is, definitions of masculine and feminine behavior—differ widely from one culture to another. The discovery of cross-cultural variation in

Women as sex objects. [David Hurn/Magnum Photos Inc.]

sex roles was one of the earliest kinds of evidence against the idea that each sex has a "natural" temperament and set of interests. In American culture, for example, it is considered "feminine" to be artistic and emotional, but in other cultures men are supposed to be more emotionally expressive and artistic than women. Margaret Mead's (1935) classic study of sex and temperament in three cultures was the earliest study of the variability of sex-role patterning. In one of the New Guinea tribes, the Arapesh, both men and women were found to be cooperative, unaggressive, and gentle. In contrast, the Mundugumor prescribed what would be a masculine temperament in our culture for both sexes—ruthlessness, aggressiveness, and severity. Neither the Arapesh nor the

Mundugumor emphasized a contrast between the sexes. In a third New Guinea tribe, the Tchambuli, however, there was such a contrast, but it was the reverse of sex-role temperament in our culture. Tchambuli women tended to be aggressive, domineering, and managerial, whereas the men tended to be dependent, artistic, and sensitive. In short, the study concludes that sex differences are arbitrary and do not reflect any underlying predisposition.

The Maccoby and Jacklin Review

The most complete review of evidence regarding sex differences was published in 1974 by Eleanor Maccoby and Carol Jacklin. *The Psychology of Sex Differences* undertook the enormous task of reviewing over 2,000 articles and books on the subject, most of them published between 1966 and 1973. Although the book has some weaknesses (Block, 1976), it is the classic reference on the subject. Maccoby and Jacklin found that many widespread beliefs about sex differences were unfounded—there was simply no evidence that males and females differed in the expected ways. On the other hand, they did find evidence of some interesting differences.

To sum up a large study all too briefly, Maccoby and Jacklin found the following common assumptions about sex differences to be without foundation: that females are more social than males; that females are more suggestible and open to the influence of others; that females excel at simple repetitive tasks, while males are better at more complex ones; and that females have less achievement motivation and creativity than men do.

The following are sex differences for which Maccoby and Jacklin did find some evidence: males are better, from adolescence on, in visual–spatial tasks—tasks involving the manipulation of objects in space, either visually or mentally; similarly, boys pull ahead of girls in mathematical performance at adolescence; and at all ages, males show more aggression—physical, verbal, fantasy and play. This finding does not mean that females are submissive or lacking in assertiveness. Rather, it reflects the tendency of males to be more rambunctious, violent, and antisocial—as evidenced by the fact that men have higher rates for crime, accidents, and fights.

For some traits, the evidence was inconsistent: women are traditionally thought to be more empathic—that is, sensitive to other people's feelings, more emotional, more dependent, and more nurturant and "maternal," but data did not yield clear-cut answers as to whether these differences exist.

As Maccoby and Jacklin themselves admit, findings of sex differences should be interpreted very cautiously. Where differences are found, they are often only small differences in the average behavior of large numbers of males and females. There is a great deal of overlap between the two sexes. Second, there is no reason to assume that any differences found are "natural" or biological. The finding of a difference implies nothing whatever about how it came about. Finally, the studies are based on observations of children and adults whose sex is obvious. There is evidence that observer's reports are influenced by knowing the subject's sex (Maccoby, 1980).

In general, the differences between the sexes are smaller than the prevailing stereotypes imply. There may be some biological bases for some of the differences—the evidence seems to be strongest for aggressiveness and spatial abilities, though some researchers would strongly disagree that the case for a biological basis for these differences has been established. In most instances it is impossible to determine how much of the difference between the sexes is due to biology and how much is due to social influences. In any case, knowledge of group averages tells us very little about individuals.

Roger Brown (1965) argues that although there may be a natural biological tendency for males to be rougher and tougher than most females, there is also considerable overlap between the sexes: some women are bigger and stronger and rougher and tougher than some men. Most cultures, however, subscribe to sex-role stereotypes that force people into predetermined molds regardless of their individual inclinations. Thus a tough, dominant woman is regarded as a deviant female in our culture, but among the

Tchambuli she would be considered a normal female. In Mundugumor society she would be regarded as merely a normal person, but in Arapesh society she would be regarded as a deviant human being, not merely a deviant from a sex role. In similar fashion the fate of a temperamentally gentle, sensitive male would vary from culture to culture. Brown concludes that the sex difference is an inadequate method of assigning people to roles.

The essential difficulty is this: temperaments, tastes, and attitudes are usually prescribed on the basis of biological sex when they actually reveal an imperfect natural linkage with sex. Men aren't always big, tough, and logical; women aren't necessarily small, gentle, and flighty. If you want your furniture moved, you would be better off with a heavyweight woman than a bantamweight male. Or, to use one of Brown's examples, if you want to hire a door-to-door salesperson, you'd be wiser to hire a determined, aggressive woman than a shy, retiring male.

A similar difficulty often arises when roles are assigned on the basis of other inherited attributes:

Not all brahmans have a religious "vocation"; not all elderly men are wise; not all sons of kings are equipped to lead a nation. . . .
   The answer must be to detach leadership, aggressiveness, aestheticism, wisdom, and the like from irrelevant ascribed attributes and incorporate them in pure achievement roles. (R. Brown, 1965, p. 171)

As noted earlier, all theories about sex and sex roles agree that there is some interaction between biological determinants and social factors. But they disagree over the source of the patterning of sexuality. Are sex roles biologically determined, is biology tempered by social learning, or are the learned factors the means by which undirected biological capacities are shaped?

Freudian Biological Determinism

To Freud, "anatomy is destiny." He also believed in one prototype for humanity—the male. This "sexual monism," as one writer described it (Shainess, 1971, p. 14), is not unique to Freud. Indeed, it is built into the English language. Thus "man" or "mankind" is used to describe the human race, and "he" is the generalized term for person. But Freud went further: he presented an elaborate psychological theory based on the idea that the female constitutes a defective or incomplete male. For Freud there were not really two sexes, but only one. Freud believed that the little girl thinks of herself as a little man until she discovers, to her horror, that she is castrated. This discovery represents the crucial point in her development, according to Freud and his followers. She can either accept her biological destiny, transform the wish for a penis into the wish for a child and become a passive female as nature intended her to be, or she can persist in the misguided belief that she is really a man and can do things men can do.

In the perspective of the 1980s it seems remarkable that psychoanalytic writers of the 1940s and 1950s—even women—could confidently interpret departures from wifely and maternal roles as abnormal. Helene Deutsch (1944/1945), a leading psychoanalytic authority on the psychology of women, believed that an "overgrowth" of a girl's intellect was a form of masculinization; it could only impoverish her own emotional life, wreck her marriage, and ruin her children. She believed that a healthy woman would renounce her own claims to accomplishment and originality, realizing herself instead through identification with her husband and sons:

They are the loveliest and the most unaggressive of helpmates and they want to remain in that role; they do not insist on their rights, quite the contrary. They are easy to handle in every way—if only one loves them. (p.192)

The belief that the anatomical distinction between the sexes has the most fateful influence on a person's destiny persists among many writers in the psychoanalytic tradition. Anatomy is destiny, not only for Freud at the turn of the century, but also for many psychologists, sociologists, and biologists down to the present time. Even Erik Erikson, who has changed Freud's libido theory in major ways, persists in the belief that anatomy is destiny; men are directed by their bodies to an interest in "outer space," whereas women will be forever focused on "inner space" (1964).

Despite the biologism and bias against women in much psychoanalytic writing, it contains many insights into male and female psychology and the relations between the sexes. Recently there have been a number of attempts to disregard the obvious biases in order to extract these insights from Freudian ideas. Juliet Mitchell (1974), Nancy Chodorow (1978), and others have advanced social and cultural interpretations of the sex differences Freud describes. While accepting the Freudian account of sexual development—the Oedipus complex and so on—they argue that these psychological reactions are not biologically determined but reflect the social and cultural realities into which children are born.

A major social reality emphasized in these writings is the dominance of the mother in early infancy; every infant's "first love" and "first boss" is a woman (Dinnerstein, 1976). By different routes, boys and girls must extricate themselves from this early relationship and find their proper places in a world divided into masculine and feminine roles and a hierarchical order in which adults rule over children, and men rule over women.

Dorothy Dinnerstein (1976) argues that one of the outcomes of a mother-dominated infancy is that both males and females grow up repudiating femininity and resenting female authority. Nancy Chodorow (1978) argues that women's mothering produces contrasting personalities in sons and daughters. Girls never really gain a sense of complete separation from their mothers because they do not have to deny their attachment to her in the course of finding their own identity. Boys have to propel themselves out of the close mother–child bonds of early infancy, and as a result their ability to form intimate relations with others is stunted. These differences produce "heterosexual knots": both men and women seek nurturance from one another in love relationships, but men are in a better position to have their needs met because men's capacities to get close to others are not as developed as women's. Both Chodorow and Dinnerstein argue that until men participate fully in the care of babies and young children, it will be difficult to overcome the present malaise between the sexes and achieve genuine equality. One need not agree fully with the diagnoses or prescriptions of the new approaches to Freudian writings to appreciate their usefulness; they help us understand our current sexual predicaments and some of the obstacles standing in the way of solving them.

Man as Ape

In recent years, in the writing of such men as Konrad Lorenz, Desmond Morris, and Lionel Tiger, a new version of biological determinism has arisen. These writers have put forth a number of books arguing that human behavior can be understood as the result of powerful instincts or rigid patterns genetically programmed during the course of evolution. They offer a version of what is supposedly "natural" human nature by using primate societies as models of the earlier stages of human evolution. They argue that man evolved as a killer ape. He is genetically programmed, they assert, with implacable instincts to make war on his fellow man, to seize and defend territory, and to exclude and dominate females. Females, in this theory, are obviously programmed to attract males and to bear and nurture the young.

Although the books of Morris and the others have proved extremely popular, for the most part they are not taken seriously by other scholars. Because of the popularity of the man-is-an-ape school, a number of detailed rebuttals have appeared. As David Pilbeam (1972) argued, "The fashionable view of man as naked ape is . . . an insult to apes . . . simplistic . . . male-oriented . . . rubbish." The basic flaw consists of exaggerating the similarities between man and other primates (as well as the similarities among the primates themselves) and ignoring the crucial differences between human beings and apes.

The naked-ape school of popular writing represents an exaggerated version of what was, until recently, accepted scholarly wisdom about the importance of man the hunter in human evolution. Recent anthropological studies suggest that the economic role of women in hunting societies was more critical than had previously been assumed. In fact, the gathering and sharing of plant food rather than hunting may have been the critical invention in human evolution. Instead of viewing women as passive creatures dependent on men for meat and protection, women emerge, in these theories, as central economic and social actors:

Females gathered plant food and shared it with their young, and mother-centered units may have been the most enduring segments of the larger group. An important selective agent may have been the preference of females in mating with nonaggressive males whose presence in the mother-centered unit was least disruptive. In this model, hunting as an important economic activity, and the sexual division of labor, emerge late in hominid evolution. (Stack, Caulfield, Estes, et al., 1975)

Other authors argue that hunting and gathering emerged together as the critical innovation in human evolution. Whatever the final version of human evolution turns out to be, it seems clear that the androcentric—that is, male-centered—model stressing male economic dominance overlooks important archeological and cross-cultural evidence.

The naked-ape school also represents in exaggerated form a kind of biological reductionism that has been stated somewhat more respectably by others. For example, Harlow (1962), a psychologist, reports on some of his findings on the play behavior of infant macaque monkeys and generalizes his observations to humans:

Males threaten other males and females but females are innately blessed with better manners; in particular, little girl monkeys do not threaten little boy monkeys. . . .
I am convinced that these data have almost total generality to man. Several months ago I was present at a school picnic attended by twenty-five second graders and their parents. While the parents sat and the girls stood around or skipped about hand in hand, thirteen boys tackled and wrestled, chased and retreated. No little girl chased any boy, but some little boys chased some little girls. (pp. 3–6)

Ironically, Harlow's most notable contribution to psychology is to have shown that certain kinds of behavior that had always been believed to be instinctive have large learned components. In the same article from which the preceding quotation is taken, Harlow reported on the sexual and maternal behavior of rhesus monkeys who have been raised in total isolation. These isolated monkeys did not know how to have sex relations when they grew up. When, after many attempts to teach them, some of the isolation-reared females became pregnant, they did not know how to "mother" the infants born to them, and even attacked them.

In any event, the range of sex-role behavior among primates is actually much more diverse than is generally recognized. In some species, for example, females are more aggressive than males, and in some males participate in child care more than females (G. D. Mitchell, 1969).

The sexual behavior of female primates provides an interesting example of data that do not support either popular intuitions or the earlier assumptions of male-biased scientists. For some time, it was assumed that female mammals tend to be selective in mating, if not monogamous, while males tend to be promiscuous, trying to impregnate as many females as possible. Each of these patterns was assumed to represent the best "reproductive strategy" to ensure the survival of one's genes. Sociobiological writers were fond of quoting the following rhyme:

Higamous, hogamous, women (are)
    monogamous,
Hogamous, higamous, men are polygamous.

The only problem with this assumption is that female primates have turned out to be quite promiscuous and sexually aggressive, displaying behavior that would be considered "nymphomaniacal" in humans (Lancaster, 1985). Sarah Hrdy (1979) has suggested that this behavior is also a reproductive strategy; its aim may be to enmesh as many males as possible into involvement with the offspring, in the hope of gaining their protection and preventing them from attacking the infant.

Regardless of whether primate sex-role behavior is varied or rigid, its relevance to human beings is highly dubious. What does it mean to say that primate behavior shows what human behavior "naturally" is? Does it mean that humans are biologically incapable of acting in any other way? If that were the case, "unnatural" sex or sex-role behavior would never occur, and there would be no need for writers to argue against women violating their natural sex roles. For example, a single instance of a little girl chasing a little boy would be enough to disprove Harlow's generalization that children's playground behavior is determined by innate biological differences.

Another way "natural" is used in talking about sex differences is to point to the way things ought to be, not the way they necessarily are. Thus Harlow might argue that it is "unnatural" for little girls to chase little boys, and therefore they shouldn't. But in that case the burden would be on him to explain why it is "better" for human beings to act like certain species of monkeys. As another psychologist, Naomi Weisstein (1971), put it:

There are no grounds to assume that anything primates do is necessary, natural, or desirable in humans, for the simple reason that humans are not nonhumans. . . . Following this logic, it would be as reasonable to conclude that it is quite useless to teach human infants to speak, since it has been tried with chimpanzees and it does not work. (p. 218)

Sex Roles in Cross-Cultural Research

Cross-cultural research demonstrates that a division of labor by sex occurs in all currently known cultures. Women's work centers on preparing food and caring for children; men's work varies according to the economy of a particular culture, but it is more likely to involve being away from home—as in hunting, herding, traveling, and fighting—and is more often strenuous (D'Andrade, 1966).

The conclusion often drawn from such findings is that sex roles and the division of labor by sex are innate and biologically necessary. The critical questions are: What is "biological necessity"? Do the "biological necessities" similarly prevail in advanced industrial societies? The cultures in the cross-cultural surveys differ in three crucial ways from modern ones: they lack the technology of contraception and bottle feeding; they have high infant-mortality rates; and they highly value children's labor. Given these circumstances, the lives of women in pre-industrial societies are often dominated by an endless cycle of pregnancy, nursing for 1 to 3 years, then another pregnancy, and so on, until the end of fertility, which often coincides with the end of the woman's life itself (Lancaster, 1985). It makes sense, then, that while women are thus preoccupied, the tasks of hunting, herding, and so forth are carried out by the men.

Given the necessity for women to bear and nurse children, women's "nature" can be explained as part of the requirements of women's work. Their working role requires them to be giving, nurturant, responsible, unaggressive. Men's work may or may not require the opposite of such traits. In some cultures, as Margaret Mead pointed out, both sexes have "feminine" personalities, whereas in others both sexes are "masculine."

These differences in cultural emphasis, however, seem to depend to some extent at least on the type of work that is done in the economy. Where agriculture or herding represents the means of subsistence, both boys and girls are socialized to be compliant; but in hunting societies children are socialized to be independent and assertive (Barry, Child, & Bacon, 1959).

Hormonal Effects

The primate analogy represents one form of the argument that sex behavior is biologically determined. Another version of the biological theory of sexual behavior is based on hormones. Females and males differ in the kinds and amounts of hormones their bodies produce. Hormones shape the bodies of men and women and cause the secondary sex characteristics to take their distinctive form—body and facial hair, voice depth, and fat and muscle distribution. Hormones also enter the brain.

Research on rats and other animals shows that sex hormones seem to have an "organizing" effect on the body and behavior (S. Levine, 1966). Thus a male rat fetus can be feminized and a female fetus can be masculinized by manipulating hormones during the prenatal period. Further, hormones given early in development can affect adult behavior; thus a female rat given male hormones in infancy will tend to fight more than other females and to use male mating postures. The variety of behaviors that show hormonal effects suggests that sex hormones affect large areas of the mammalian brain and are not confined to the lower centers.

The evidence from hormonal studies in animals has led some researchers to extend their findings to human behavior. Even the animal research, however, tells a more complicated story than this description implies. As Ford and Beach (1951) point out, the dominant fact with regard to human sexuality is the evolutionary trend away from hormonal control over behavior and toward control by the higher centers of the brain—in other words, control by learning and by symbolic social meaning. Studies of the actual effects of hormones reveal that no simple relation exists between the amount of sex hormones in a person's blood and erotic arousal or aggressiveness. Further, attempts to cure sexual problems, such as impotence or frigidity, with hormones generally have been unsuccessful (Hardy, 1964). In fact, social learning and experience can override and even influence biological factors: environmental events can affect physiological happenings such as menstruation and level of male hormone in an animal (H. H. Lambert, 1978), and as we shall see a little later on, a normal infant of one sex can be transformed psychologically into a member of the other.

Sexuality: Life Force or Appetite?

The alternative to the life force or hormonal view of sexuality emphasizes the role of learning and the social context in the shaping and patterning of sexual experience and behavior. This concept of sexuality has been put forth by a number of social psychologists, sociologists, and anthropologists. Basically it conceives of sexuality, or any human biological motive for that matter, as a two-step process at least, involving a biological capacity that is shaped, directed, and amplified by social learning as well as individual cognitive processes. In other words, sex is in the head and in the social environment, as well as in the genitals.

Sexuality can begin in infancy. Hardy (1964) has noted that there are two distinct constitutional bases around which sexual "appetites" can form: mild local stimulation of the genital area and the more intense excitement—relaxation of orgasm. Although some children are capable of genital climax, cross-cultural evidence shows that sexual interest and behavior does not depend on the maturation of the sex glands or the ability to experience orgasms. Hardy notes that mild stimulation of the genital regions is pleasur-

able from infancy, and even in the preschool years may lead to orgasm. The cultural shaping of sexual appetites and sexual behavior, he argues, is built upon this constitutional basis. Thus some cultures encourage young children to masturbate and play at having intercourse. In such societies sexual behavior is continuous from childhood to adulthood.

Stephens (1963) reports on a number of societies around the world in which sexual stimulation is used as a pacifier for infants and as an aid in weaning older babies from the breast. In a number of cultures children play at intercourse during childhood, and "real" intercourse may begin at the age of 8 or 10. Some societies believe that children will not mature properly or be able to produce babies when they are adults unless they have regular sexual practice early in life.

American parents typically discourage masturbation and any other form of sexual behavior in children, and try to keep them from observing sexual behavior. Most American children, therefore, do not develop a sex interest until their teens, at which time it is expected of them. The male peer group encourages boys to have sexual interests in girls, but the girls' peer group, as well as parents, inclines girls toward a more social interest in boys.

Learning thus plays a role in the development of a general appetite for sex, as well as specific tastes. As with food, everyone needs to eat in order to stay alive, but beyond the minimal caloric requirements a great deal of individual variation is possible in what people like to eat, which is often what they have learned to like as children. As there are different cuisines in different cultures, with different tastes and styles of food preparation, there are varying symbols of sexual attractiveness and types of sexual behavior among cultures.

Even within one culture, such as ours, some people think about food often even when they are not hungry; other people express particular tastes in food and will refuse to eat certain dishes even when very hungry. Both obesity and an interest in gourmet cooking represent in different ways psychological approaches to food irrelevant to tissue needs.

Ultimately, however, the analogy between sex and food breaks down because there is little evidence that sex fulfills any tissue need. There is no sexual counterpart to starvation. As Beach (1956) put it:

No genuine tissue or biological needs are generated by sexual abstinence. It used to be believed that prolonged sexual inactivity in adulthood resulted in the progressive accumulation of secretions within the accessory sex glands, and that nerve impulses from these distended receptacles gave rise to sexual urges. Modern evidence negates this hypothesis. . . . What is commonly confused with a primary drive associated with sexual deprivation is in actuality sexual appetite, and this has little or no relation to biological or physiological needs. (p. 4)

Physiological states alone are never enough to produce emotional arousal and behavior. As Silvan Tomkins (1965) has put it, the "oomph" of biological drives is an illusion. The "oomph" comes not from physiology but from the person's response to a physiological state. Tomkins offered the example of oxygen deprivation. What motive could be more urgent than that of a drowning or choking person for air? Yet, Tomkins noted, the tissue need for oxygen, by itself, does not create a psychological need for air. In fact, when oxygen deprivation is gradual, people become euphoric. Some pilots in World War II refused to wear their oxygen masks at high altitudes and died with smiles on their lips. In the same way, argued Tom-

kins, sexual arousal is a state of conscious excitement, which amplifies the physiological arousal. No one, he wrote, "has ever observed an excited penis."

One is excited and breathes hard, not in the penis, but in the chest, the esophagus, the face, and the nose and nostrils. Both the sexual urge and the sexual pleasure of intercourse are ordinarily amplified by excitement as anoxia is amplified by panic. . . . To be fully sexually aroused and satisfied, one must be capable of excitement as well as tumescence. (pp. 118–119)

Tomkins noted that the concept of amplification helps explain how couples can report that they have orgasms and yet complain of the lack of sexual satisfaction:

Sexual intercourse repeated with the same partner is vulnerable to such attenuation of satisfaction whenever the decline in novelty of the interpersonal relationship is such that excitement can no longer be sustained. Those who are generally bored with each other may also be unable to become sexually excited even when they are capable . . . of orgasm. (p. 119)

Further, the experience of orgasm can even be perceived as a burden. Lillian Rubin (1976) reported that among the working-class couples she studied, the sexual revolution has been a mixed blessing, especially for women. Once these women were expected to submit passively to sex. Now, however, new standards of sexual performance teach women—and their husbands—that if they don't have orgasms they are impairing their husbands' pleasure. Once an unexpected and pleasing occurrence, orgasms have become a requirement.

The women in Rubin's study not only worry about their ability to achieve orgasms at all, but they also worry about having them at the right time—at the moment of their husbands' ejaculation. They also worry about the possibility of their husbands leaving them for women who can produce more and better climaxes. Many women feel that their orgasms are for their husbands, not for themselves. Thus, although the new sexual freedom has brought increased satisfaction, it has also brought new anxieties and new demands. Human sexuality remains, as always, a complicated psychological and social process, and not a simple physiological response.

SEXUAL DEVELOPMENT

Challenges to the innate-determinism view of sexuality and sex-role development have also been emerging in recent years from research on the sexual development of normal children, as well as on people with sexual anomalies of various kinds. Probably the most striking illustration of the ambiguities of sex and gender is the phenomenon of transsexualism—the belief of a seemingly normal male or female that he or she is actually a person of the opposite sex. In recent years several such cases have made headlines; for example, a male tennis player who underwent a sex-change operation stirred up a controversy when she tried to enter a women's tennis tournament. In the San Francisco Bay Area, a popular woman gym teacher who became a man was fired by the school board and sued to be reinstated, setting off a community controversy. Most sex-change operations are done confidentially, however. Although it is difficult to know how many people have changed their sex, it has been estimated that by 1975 approximately 1,500 such operations had been carried out in the United States (Gagnon & Henderson, 1975).

Why would anyone want to undergo the pain and humiliation of a sex-change opera-

Early in life, children begin to identify with masculine or feminine sex roles. [Dick Swartz/ Office of Human Development Services]

tion? Although it's not possible to answer the question in a final way, thanks to one gifted transsexual we do have some insight into what it is like to grow up believing that one was born into the wrong body. James Morris was a distinguished British newspaperman and writer of nonfiction books before he underwent a sex-change operation at the age of 46. He was the most prominent person to have had such an operation, and he seemed a highly unlikely candidate for one.

He had climbed Mount Everest, had served 4 years in the army, and had married and become the father of five children. Yet since the age of 3, he had felt that he really was a girl.

After the operation, Jan Morris (1974) replaced James Morris and told the story of her life and transformation in an extraordinary book, *Conundrum*. It begins with the moment she "knew" she was a girl trapped in a boy's body:

I was three or perhaps four years old when I realized that I had been born into the wrong body, and should really be a girl. I remember the moment well, and it is the earliest memory of my life.

I was sitting beneath my mother's piano, and her music was falling around me like cataracts, enclosing me as in a cave. The round stumpy legs of the piano were like three black stalagmites, and the sound box was a high dark vault above my head. My mother was probably playing Sibelius; . . .

What triggered so bizarre a thought I have long forgotten, but the conviction was unfaltering from the start. (p. 1)

For more than 40 years after that, Morris lived what was outwardly a man's life, all the while tormented by "the tragic and irrational ambition . . . to escape from maleness into womanhood" (p. 8).

James Morris and other transsexuals illustrate the problematic nature of sexual identity. Maleness and femaleness do not spring automatically from anatomy or hormones: possessing a penis or a vagina does not necessarily make us a man or a woman. Jan Morris's female identity was clearly her own creation. The rest of us also construct sexual selves through experience and over time, but if the final outcome is in accord with our anatomical equipment, the temptation is to attribute our destiny to biology.

Some of the most dramatic evidence for the ambiguity of sexuality has emerged from studies of "sex errors of the body": people born with physical characteristics of both sexes. Studies of such people, generally referred to as hermaphrodites or intersexed individuals, have provided new insights into the development and patterning of sexuality. They have revealed that these processes are more complex than anyone had thought. These studies have also shown that popular discussions tend to use sexual terms in a confused and imprecise way, and some scholarly writing does so also. Thus D. G. Brown and Lynn (1966) pointed out that the following terms are often used synonymously:

male and masculine

female and feminine

homosexuality, sexual transvestism, inversion, and transsexualism

Actually, most contemporary sex researchers agree that it is important to distinguish between the biological aspects of sexuality and the psychological aspects. *Male* and *female* are the terms used to refer to biological aspects of sex, but *masculinity* and *femininity* are psychological and behavioral characteristics. We are so accustomed to thinking of all the aspects of sexuality as hanging together that it is difficult to get used to the idea that anatomy may be independent of the sense of gender identity ("I am a boy" or "I am a girl"). Table 8.1 presents the physiological and psychological aspects of sex differences.

Masculinity and femininity are not to be confused with gender identity. Thus a tomboy is a girl with boyish interests in, say, sports, tree climbing, and playing with soldiers, but there is no doubt about what gender she belongs to. A boy may have an interest in the things the culture places in the feminine world but he is still a boy. People may worry about their femininity and mas-

TABLE 8.1 *Male/Female Characteristics*

Characteristic	Male	Female	Explanation
Physiological:			
1. Chromosomal composition	XY	XX	At the moment of conception the unborn child's sex is determined by whether the father's sperm cell contains an X or a Y chromosome; if it is a Y chromosome, child will be a boy.
2. Gonads	Testicles	Ovaries	
3. Hormonal composition	Androgen, etc.	Estrogen, progesterone, etc.	These hormones operate before birth to differentiate male and female fetuses and again at adolescence to produce secondary sex characteristics— e.g., deep voices, beards, and body hair in men; breasts and menstruation in women.
4. Internal accessory organs	Seminal vesicles and prostate gland	Vagina, uterus, and fallopian tubes	
5. External genitalia	Penis and testicles	Vulva	
Psychological:			
1. Gender identity	I am a male	I am a female	The basic sense of one's social identity.
2. Masculinity-femininity	I am a masculine or effeminate male	I am a feminine or mannish woman	This refers to the person's conformity to the sex-role standards of the particular culture; it involves certain interests, attitudes, fantasies, ways of moving and speaking.
3. Sex-object preference			Whether one is aroused by members of one's own sex or the opposite one.

culinity but, with rare exceptions such as Jan Morris, they have no doubts about their gender identity. Further, there appears to be very little relationship between being worried about one's masculinity or femininity and the actual degree of discrepancy between one's behavior and the cultural standards. Thus a male who seems very "masculine" to other people may go through a crisis of doubt about his masculinity during adolescence, whereas an "effeminate" male may go through life without any such worries at all.

Gender identity and masculinity-femininity are also to be distinguished from the third aspect of psychological sexuality, sex-object preference. Whether a person is sexually aroused by a member of his or her own or the opposite sex is independent of gender identity and masculinity-femininity. Homosexuals are not confused about their gender identity. Nor do homosexual men and women necessarily differ from their "straight" counterparts in masculinity and femininity. Some homosexual men view themselves as masculine and take the masculine role in sexual encounters. Others view themselves as feminine and take the feminine role, whereas still others see their masculinity as independent of homosexual roles (Hooker, 1965).

The argument that the psychological aspects of sexuality—gender identity, masculinity and femininity, or sex-object choice—are learned rather than innate comes in two versions. The first is a social-learning model of sex development.

The Social-Learning Model

According to the social-learning approach, the child learns sex-typed behavior the same way he or she learns any other type of behavior, through a combination of reward, punishment, and observation of what other people are doing. Proponents of this view include psychologists, such as Mischel,

Bandura, and Walters, and anthropologists, such as Margaret Mead in her early writings. In essence, proponents argue that it is unnecessary to invoke innate biological drives or tendencies to account for sexual behavior, particularly sex-role behavior, since learning can and does account for whatever behavioral differences are found between the sexes. Bandura (1969), for example, described sex-role learning as a process of indoctrination that begins at birth:

Sex-role differentiation usually commences immediately after birth, when the baby is named and both the infant and the nursery are given the blue or pink treatment depending upon the sex of the child. Thereafter, indoctrination into masculinity and femininity is diligently promulgated by adorning children with distinctive clothes and hair styles, selecting sex-appropriate play materials and recreational activities, promoting associations with same-sex playmates, and through nonpermissive parental reactions to deviant sex-role behavior. (p. 215)

Besides direct indoctrination, the view of sexual development includes modeling as a way of learning: the boy will be rewarded for imitating his father and discouraged from using his mother as a model for his own behavior; the girl will be rewarded for the reverse. Eventually the child will find imitating the appropriate models rewarding in itself.

The Cognitive-Development Model

Unlike the social-learning model of sex-role development, which reflects a general approach held by a number of psychologists, sociologists, and anthropologists, the cognitive-development model of sex typing is mainly the work of one scholar, Lawrence Kohlberg (1966). Kohlberg's approach is largely an elaboration of the theories of Piaget, applied to the area of sexual development. Like the social-learning theorists, Kohlberg argues against the notion that gender identity is instinctually patterned. Nevertheless, he does not believe that sexuality and sex-role learning are based on learned conformity to cultural patterns. Rather, he argues, children's concepts of sexuality arise in the same way as all their other concepts about the world and the things in it. Sexual ideas and sex-role concepts result from children's *active structuring of their own experience*, rather than from something directly taught by other people.

The key cognitive event is the categorization of one's self as male or female. Once this recognition of self is acquired, between the ages of 1½ and 3, it organizes the way the child perceives and categorizes the rest of the world and his or her place in it. For example, other people are defined as belonging to one category or the other, male or female. The child places himself or herself in one of these categories, and begins the process of "cognitive rehearsal"—the lifelong accumulation of memories and fantasies in which he or she acts out the appropriate sex roles. A little boy will dream of being a fireman or a policeman or an astronaut when he grows up, and when he thinks of his future family life he will imagine himself as a daddy with a wife and children. A little girl will dream of having breasts and wearing grown-up clothes and lipstick and attracting men, and her fantasies of family life will feature her in the role of mother. The learning is gradual and changes with the child's stage of thinking—that is, young children may think that one's sexual identity is something that can change, like one's age.

Kohlberg also shows that genital anatomy plays a surprisingly small part in young children's thinking about sex differences. Clothing styles and social-role differences,

such as the fact that males are policemen and firemen, are more impressive to childish minds. In short, learning to be male or female seems to be a process of understanding and interpreting the rules, both explicit and implicit, defining sex roles.

Kohlberg cites evidence showing that bright children tend to be ahead of their age-mates of average intelligence in the maturity of their sexual attitudes. Between the ages of 4 and 8, for example, boys tend to show a number of changes in preference for masculine toys and toward affiliation with male figures rather than female. Bright boys show these shifts earlier than average boys.

Kohlberg cites the work of John Money (1961) and his associates as further evidence for the theory. These were studies of hermaphrodites, children born with genital abnormalities that make it hard to tell whether the child is a boy or a girl. Certain tests now make it possible to tell whether the child is "really" male or female—that is, whether the chromosomes are male or female in pattern. In previous years the doctor simply had to guess. Sometimes the doctor would find out later that he had assigned the child to the wrong sex. In such a case the child might be reassigned to the appropriate gender.

Body, Mind, and Gender

Money and his associates undertook a series of studies of children and adults with sexual abnormalities of one kind or another. The most striking discovery of this research was the finding that children with the same anatomical structures could be assigned to either sex and grow up to be a psychologically "normal" member of that sex. These researchers argued that the biological aspects of sexuality are independent of the psychological aspects—that is, the sex category to which one is assigned at birth and reared in, one's own sense of gender identity, and one's preference in sex objects. Thus, not only can intersexed or hermaphroditic children be raised successfully in either sex, but children erroneously assigned to the wrong category can grow up to be psychologically normal members of the sex to which they were assigned.

Money ultimately concluded that every child is "psychosexually neutral" at birth. In his more recent research, Money has moved away from the concept of complete psychosexual neutrality at birth. One study (Money & Ehrhardt, 1972) examined a group of genetic females who had been born with enlarged male-appearing genitalia because their mothers had taken male hormones to avert miscarriage. After corrective surgery they were raised as girls. When interviewed during childhood and adolescence, these girls considered themselves female, but they were "tomboyish" girls—preferring boys' activities, such as sports and games, to more "feminine" pursuits, such as playing with dolls. Money and Ehrhardt speculated that this tomboyism might be due to the masculinizing effects of prenatal hormones.

But there are many methodological problems with this study. For example, the parents knew that these girls had been masculinized in the womb and born with genital abnormalities. This knowledge might have affected how the girls had been raised. Although Money acknowledges that prenatal hormone levels may influence behavior to some degree, he does not subscribe to the notion that sex-role differences are determined in a simple and direct way by biological forces. He argues that while sex-typed traits such as tomboyism may be influenced by sex hormones, gender identity arises mainly from social experience.

Money and Ehrhardt (1972) describe a particularly dramatic case that shows how the gender label a child is given can override even normal anatomy and hormones. The story begins with the birth of two identical twin boys. At the age of 7 months, during a routine circumcision by electrocautery, one of the boys had his penis burned off. After some months of agonizing, the parents agreed to transform the little boy surgically into a little girl and raise her accordingly. By the age of $4\frac{1}{2}$, the little girl was a model of traditional femininity, in dress, interests, and activities.

Because of such mistakes of medicine or nature, we assume that gender identity is a natural unfolding of innate biological inclinations. The psychosexual neutrality concept argues that we assign children to one sex or the other on the basis of their anatomy and then believe that the psychological aspects of sexuality are caused by anatomy and physiology.

The child does not, however, remain psychosexually neutral for very long; once the child has established a gender identity (during the period of language mastery, $1\frac{1}{2}$ to 3 years), it seems to be irreversible. Before that age a child can be reassigned to the other sex; after that age it becomes much more difficult. Money compares the process to "imprinting" in birds. In certain species of birds there is a critical period during which a young bird will follow any moving object it sees, and later will try to mate only with something that resembles the imprinted object. Usually the baby bird will see its mother and so become imprinted with appropriate responses. Experiments carried out by Lorenz and others, however, show that the baby birds can become imprinted on humans or vacuum cleaners or any moving object. Money suggests that sexual imprinting is something like that in humans. Kohlberg warns, however, that the notion of imprinting is only a metaphor in human sexuality. He argues that early sexual identities are difficult to reverse later because they are basic to other learning. They constitute the cognitive categories around which experience and memory have been organized, and any such categories learned early in life are hard to reverse.

Sex-Role Learning in Infancy

Regardless of whether one uses a social-learning or a cognitive model to explain the development of sex-role identity, the observational facts are that sex-role learning begins at birth. Researchers have found that parents describe and interpret their newborn's behavior along sex-stereotyped lines, handle boy infants more roughly and touch them less than girls after 6 months, and talk to girls more, particularly in the first 6 months (M. Lewis & Weinraub, 1979). Some of these differences may be elicited by infant behavior, but researchers have found the sex differences in infants are very slight compared to later differences. It is not surprising that sex differences begin so early when we consider that gender is such a basic social status, and the first one announced at birth.

As the infant grows, the parent's behavior continues to be guided by traditional sex-role conceptions. Hoffman's review (1972) of the literature reveals that girls are protected more than boys and given less encouragement for independent, adventurous, exploratory behavior. As a result, little girls do not develop skills in coping with the environment, but remain dependent on adults, particularly their mothers. Hoffman argues that these early childhood experiences help to explain how girls are turned away from the kinds of experiences that lead to achievement striving in later life and develop an overemphasis on emotional relationships. In boys the emphasis is reversed. She suggests that a better balance of love and achievement would be desirable for both.

SEXUALITY

Sex in History

In this section we focus on the erotic aspects of sexuality, especially the question of how sexual experience is modified by its social and historical context.

Until recently, the sexual history of Western culture was an unexplored territory. It was known that views of sexuality had changed dramatically in the past. There had been Roman orgies and bawdy Elizabethans on one hand, and early Christian ascetics, Puritans, and Victorians on the other. But there was little detailed knowledge of these patterns of belief and behavior and their relations to one another. Thanks to careful research by many scholars in the past decade or so, we now know vastly more about the history of sexuality in Western society than ever before. The new research contains many surprises.

For one thing, the new findings are hard to reconcile with the sociobiological notion that sex is simply a pattern of responses that evolved to ensure the reproduction of the human species. If so, we would find little variation in other times and places. Instead, the new research shows that sexuality has had a long and complicated history. Summing up the recent findings, Lawrence Stone observes: "What is absolutely certain . . . is that over the long history of Western civilization, there has been no such thing as 'normal sexuality.' Sexuality is a cultural artifact that has undergone constant and sometimes dramatic changes over time" (1985, p. 37).

Two of the most drastic changes concern homosexuality and the place of sex in married life. Several recent studies suggest that homosexuality as we know it is an "invention" of the nineteenth century (Ariès, 1985). This is not to say that there were no homosexuals. Rather, the evidence suggests that in the past those with homosexual tastes were likely to be heterosexual also. Thus, in ancient Greece and Rome it was considered normal for men to be bisexual. The important distinction was between the active and passive roles in sex. Those who penetrated others were considered superior; those who were penetrated—women, boys, and slaves of both sexes—were considered inferior. In Greece, the most idealized form of love was the bond between a man and a preadolescent boy. It was also considered proper and moral for male citizens to use the bodies of male or female slaves for any kind of sexual pleasure without their consent. With the rise of Christianity, homosexuality became a sin, but no more so than any other form of sexual sin. It was only around the end of the eighteenth century that homosexuality came to be seen as a distinct and pathological condition.

The second great change concerns attitudes towards marital sex. For many centuries, Christian theologians held that passionate love between husband and wife was immoral. Today, of course, sexual love is central to marriage, and a lack of sexual adjustment is an accepted reason for divorce.

Using a variety of Church records and writings, Jean Flandrin (1985) has described the Church's attitudes toward sex in marriage in the Middle Ages. He has also tried to find out how much this literature reveals about actual behavior. Two aspects of the Church's teachings may seem odd to us today. The first, as just noted, is the condemnation of passion in marriage. All sex was considered immoral, except for the purpose of producing a child. St. Jerome argued in the fourth century that a man is who is too passionately in love with his wife is guilty of adultery.

Even writers outside the Church, who did not adhere to a strict morality, thought there was something indecent and unwholesome about a sexual passion in a married couple. Passion was for mistresses. The other odd aspect of Church teachings is the later notion of sex as a debt that the couple owed to one another. By the fifteenth century, some theologians agreed that sex between husband and wife was not sinful if it was done to relieve sexual drives and protect against worst temptations. Husband and wife "owed" one another this service.

The word *love* did not enter into these writings. Flandrin observes that this lack is not surprising because marriage was not mainly a love relationship, but rather an arrangement between families to advance their own fortunes and produce heirs. The rules surrounding sex, he suggests, may actually have been helpful to people thrown together under such circumstances.

The history of sexuality is not simply a succession of moral codes, one after another. At any particular time, a variety of sexual cultures and ideas have coexisted. Stone (1985) observes that all cultures have displayed competing tendencies toward repressing and controlling sexuality on the one hand, and expressing it on the other. Every high civilization from ancient Egypt onward has produced erotic art, handbooks of sexual practices, sexual toys and pornographic literature. They have also developed ascetic codes and religious and legal prohibitions directed toward limiting and controlling sexuality. The strength of these opposing tendencies varies from one period to the next and across social classes. Usually it is the wealthy and elite who cultivate their sensuality. The middle classes have tended to be the most restrained and working class sexuality has tended to be direct and casual.

Further, there is often a wide gap between the rules of proper sexual behavior and what people actually do. For example, while the Church was insisting on marital fidelity for both husbands and wives, a double standard prevailed in reality. For centuries, extramarital relationships have been tolerated and even expected for men. Today, although premarital sex is widely approved, adulterous relations are widely condemned (Wattenberg, 1985). Nevertheless, they are practiced by large numbers of both men and women (Lawton, in press).

In general, the recent studies suggest that the distinction between modern and premodern family patterns makes little sense when talking about sex. A linear model of increasing progress or liberalization does not fit the evidence. For example, the Victorian morality of the nineteenth century is further away from the spirit of our own times than the morality of the eighteenth century. The Victorians retreated from the earlier trends, which had been toward a more positive attitude to sex and closer and more equal relations between husbands and wives.

Trying to explain this nineteenth-century reversal, Stone sees parallels to an earlier wave of sexual repression in the sixteenth and seventeenth centuries: "The causes of the second tidal wave of moral regeneration and repression," he observes, "seem to be very similar to those that caused the first between 1550 and 1660. There was a sense of social and political crisis, a fear that the whole structure of social hierarchy and political order were in danger" (1977, p. 677).

The earlier period was a time of religious wars, peasant revolts, and increased unemployment. The nineteenth century was also a time of social unrest. There was panic in the upper and middle classes that the impoverished industrial workers would rise up in a bloody revolution. Further, Stone and others have suggested, the Victorians' repressive attitudes were in keeping with the middle-class emphasis on frugality and saving. However, these hypotheses are difficult to prove.

Whatever the explanation, it is clear that the history of sexuality in Western society is the history of cyclical change rather than linear development. Periods of liberalization follow periods of repression or restraint, which then give way to greater toleration. In our own times, the pendulum has swung very far in the direction of liberation. It seems now to be swinging in the direction of restraint; the free spirit of the 1960s and 1970s—the spirit of "do your own thing" and "whatever turns you on"—is out of keeping with widespread fear of AIDS and herpes, concern over teenage pregnancy and pornography, and the more general concern about what many people see as the disintegration of the family. Yet the historical records suggest that the pendulum is likely to swing again.

The Legacy of Victorian Morality

In spite of the sexual revolution, we have not escaped from the long shadow of Victorian morality, the so-called civilized morality that prevailed in Europe in the nineteenth century.

In recent years some scholars have been pointing out that Victorianism was not so monolithic as has usually been assumed. It was not so dominant on the Continent as in England, and even where it was most authoritative and repressive—in America—there were inconsistencies and ambivalence in people's attitudes toward sex. Historian Carl Degler (1980), for example, has found evidence showing that at least some upper-middle-class women in the nineteenth century enjoyed sex and experienced orgasms. The evidence so far, however, does not suggest that we should stop regarding "Victorian" as a synonym for "repressive." There does seem to have been a "more or less unified nineteenth-century style in sexual theory" (Robinson, 1976, p. 2) that has persisted, in some segments of the population, until very recently.

Above all, the Victorians believed that sexual experience was a threat to moral character and a drain on vital energies. If you were a woman, the leading medical authorities and their popularizers would have assured you that it was normal to have no sexual feelings at all—to have any would have marked you as a degenerate or a whore. It would have been wrong, however, for you to refuse your husband his "marital rights" because this would harm his health. Although men were acknowledged to have sexual desires, sex was dirty and dangerous for them also. Many doctors of the Victorian era warned against "excess" and its dire consequences to mental and physical health. One of the leading authorities warned married men that they should have intercourse no more often than every 7 to 10 days, and that often only if they were very strong and healthy (Comfort, 1967, p. 111).

The most notorious example of the tendency of Victorian doctors to mix morality with medicine is the concept of "masturbation insanity." A number of medical writers have described the rise and fall of this concept. Alex Comfort (1967) showed how the promotion of sexual anxiety came to be practiced by the medical profession. Comfort argued that sexual anxiety is an *iatrogenic* malady—a disorder produced as a result of medical intervention. He compared the history of masturbation insanity with the outburst of witch hunting that occurred in earlier periods of European and American history.

Although masturbation had always been considered a sin by the Catholic Church, it was not regarded as a worse sin than any other form of disapproved sex, and medical authorities showed no particular concern with the subject. Some writers before the eighteenth century regarded masturbation as a useful form of sexual relief. The notion that masturbation not only is sinful but the leading cause of insanity, blindness, and epilepsy was put forth in the eighteenth century and reached its peak in the middle of the nineteenth. The preoccupation led to numerous devices for controlling masturbation, such as chastity belts and even surgical intervention.

Perhaps the most widespread and pernicious effect of the concern about the practice was its effect on childrearing. From the mid-nineteenth century to the first half of the twentieth, mothers were warned by childrearing manuals to be ever watchful lest their children touch their genitals. As late as 1928 an English childrearing manual was still recommending "untiring zeal" on the part of the mother to prevent masturbation, and suggesting that it might be necessary to put the child to bed with the legs in splints. The fear of masturbation insanity did not really end until the Kinsey reports of the late 1940s, showing that masturbation was practically universal for both sexes.

Ironically, the very prevalence of masturbation made it possible for the proponents of masturbation as the cause of insanity to give the appearance of proving their point: they found if they were to interrogate any mental patient, he or she would confess to being a masturbator.

The current sexual climate in many ways appears to have been shaped by the previous era of repression. For one thing, our very preoccupation with sexuality may be a backlash phenomenon, a sudden outpouring of all the questions that couldn't be asked, all the words that couldn't be said, all the sights that couldn't be seen. But the present sexual atmosphere is more than an outpouring of blocked impulses. The assumptions of Vic-

In recent years, women have become increasingly involved in sports. This girl and her parents won a lawsuit that enabled her to play on her school soccer team. [Helen Nestor]

torian morality provide much of the framework for today's liberal morality and for research into sex. For example, the view of sexuality as a powerful, natural force that civilized society holds in check was the prevailing model of sexuality for the Victorians and for Freud and is also for *Playboy* magazine and the liberal morality it represents. The Victorians believed in taming sexuality and banishing it even from thoughts; Freud believed that people should control their sexuality consciously and direct sexual energy into useful work. *Playboy* and other advocates of liberal morality believe it is healthy and natural to follow the dictates of nature and act on one's sexual impulses. All agree with the life force model of sexuality.

Freud was an outspoken critic of the excesses of "civilized" morality, particularly the silence and secrecy that prevented even doctors and patients from discussing sexual problems. Yet he shared many of the assumptions of the most extreme representatives of sexual conservatism. The historian Nathan Hale (1971) has pointed out the parallels between Freud and Anthony Comstock, the guardian of American purity who campaigned for censorship and obscenity laws:

Despite enormous differences Freud, Hall, and Comstock reflected 19th-century "civilized" morality and they agreed on certain fundamentals. They believed that civilization and progress depended directly on the control of sexuality and on the stable monogamous family. They believed in different ways that "mind" should govern the "sensual nature." Even Freud displayed some of the reticence Comstock would enforce by public censorship. It was only after greater inner resistance that Freud brought himself to publish the sexual histories of his patients. These broad similarities between men so unlike testify to the strength of the common elements in European and American versions of "civilized" morality. (p. 25)

Freud, too, in his earlier years, believed in a version of masturbational insanity. Neurasthenia, a common psychiatric complaint of Victorian times involving weakness, weariness, and lassitude, was attributed by Freud to masturbation. At the same time, however, Freud believed that the guilt and anxiety caused by the taboos on masturbation might cause more harm than the practice itself.

THE SOCIAL CONTEXT OF SEXUALITY

Not only do the past theories about sexuality and sex differences influence present theories; in addition, the social context surrounding sexuality may influence sexual experience and behavior itself. Thus the common notion that the sexual drive is pretty much the same everywhere and only the openness of talking about it varies is probably wrong. Whether or not one can talk about sex or think about it, who can talk to each other about it, and how one learns about sex—all of this may have an enormous influence on the experience itself.

Most discussions of sexuality focus on sexual behavior itself, or the content of people's information and beliefs, or their attitudes, rather than on the context in which sex is learned and acted out. A number of researchers have suggested that it is also useful to look not only at what people say and do but also at the context of the interaction. Lennard and Bernstein (1969), for example, suggested that when a patient goes to see a psychotherapist, the patient may be helped as much by the form of the interaction as anything the therapist may say. In this perspective, therapy is a process of going to a place once or several times a week where you speak your innermost thoughts in confidentiality with the complete interest and attention of another person and with the assurance that you will not be criticized or scolded.

Lennard and Bernstein use television as another example of the contrast between content and context. They note, for example, that people tend to worry a great deal about the effect of the content of television programs on their children—whether watching violent programs will make children act aggressively. But few people worry about the effects of television as a medium or context—the fact that television turns experiences on and off arbitrarily, that reports of serious real-life events such as wars, disasters, and human tragedies are interrupted by cheery advertisements.

What is the medium or context in which information about sex, and sexuality itself, is exchanged? The most important of such features are secrecy; the aura of shame and anxiety; the transmission of information via childhood peer groups rather than by adults; the preoccupation with health, morality, and normality; the taboos about discussing sexuality; the assumption that any statement by an individual is related to the sexual preferences and desires of that individual; and, as a corollary of the latter, the assumption that talking about sex is an act of seduction (Gagnon, 1965, p. 215).

Until very recently sexual knowledge in America was in a state sociologists call "pluralistic ignorance"—everybody knew about his or her own sexual behavior, but nobody knew what anyone else was doing or feeling. Thus everyone had a backstage or undressed view of his or her own sexuality, and a frontstage, dressed-up view of other people's. The Freudian revolution had made sexual feelings more acceptable than previously, but this loosening up was accompanied by rather strict notions of normality. For many people the old concern with the sinfulness of sex was replaced by a concern with normality.

For women the change from Victorian sexuality to Freudian was like jumping from the frying pan into the fire—or, more aptly, from the freezer into the refrigerator. The Freudian revolution discoverd that women have sexual feelings after all, but it created the myth of two orgasms: the notion that the clitoris transfers its sensitivity to the vagina in "mature," nonneurotic women. Actually, as Kinsey and later Masters and Johnson have shown, all orgasms center on the clitoris, although the stimulation that leads to

orgasm can come from any erogenous zone or from the imagination.

From the perspective of the 1980s it appears that the truly revolutionary event in the social context of sexuality was the publication of the Kinsey reports in 1948 and 1953. Kinsey's statistics not only broke through the curtain of pluralistic ignorance, but also made it permissible to discuss sexuality in conventional social situations. They revealed widespread deviance from conventional moral standards and upset previously held notions of rigid distinctions between normality and deviance in sexual matters. For example, Kinsey found considerable evidence of childhood sexual activity, homosexual experiences in the sex histories of "normal" heterosexual men, premarital and extramarital sexuality, and deviations from presumably "normal" patterns of intercourse in marriage.

The Effects of Secrecy

The secrecy previously surrounding sexuality has had profound effects. For one thing, it set the stage for guilt and anxiety. Masturbation is the classic instance of a practice that is practically universal, yet so taboo that countless millions of people have been tortured by the thought that "I must be the only one to have done this." One of the reasons the notion of masturbational insanity seemed plausible was that people were indeed driven crazy by guilt and worry over having ruined themselves physically and mentally.

Another effect of secrecy is to call attention to whatever the secret is about. Georg Simmel (1950), one of the classic sociologists of the nineteenth century, described the secret as a sociological form. Any secret, he noted, creates a great atmosphere of tension. Does the other person know my secret? What would happen if I told?

The secret is surrounded by the possibility and temptation of betrayal; and the external danger of being discovered is interwoven with the internal danger, which is like the fascination of the abyss, of giving oneself away. The secret creates a barrier between men but, at the same time, it creates the tempting challenge to break through it, by gossip or confession—and this challenge accompanies its psychology like a constant overtone. (p. 334)

Adding sexual guilt and anxiety to the general tensions of any kind of secrecy results in a very potent mix. The context of prudery and repression may well have had the effect of heightening the excitement and "oomph" of sexuality.

Freud and Secrecy

Breaking through the knots of secrecy that surrounded sex was one of the major achievements of the Freudian revolution. Part of the "miracle" cures of the early analysts—severe symptoms clearing up after only one session—may have been due to the fact that the early analysts were able to attack the social context surrounding sex.

The discoveries of Freud have transformed emotional life itself. There is a vast difference between a psychoanalytic patient in 1899 learning of his romantic attachment to his mother and the same occurrence in the 1980s. The novelist Mary McCarthy once wrote about the banality of the insights she had gained from her psychoanalyst. She was disappointed to learn how unoriginal her neurosis was; she suffered from the same conflicts as everybody else.

For several decades now sophisticated parents have been watching their offspring for the first stirring of sexual attachment to mother, Oedipal hostility to father, and sibling rivalry for the little sister with the same parental interest as other milestones of development, such as the first tooth, the first word, and the first step. In short, the Freud-ian revolution transformed what had been a private, unthinkable torment—What kind of monster must I be to have such thoughts and feelings?—into a problem common to everyone. As the mama in the joke put it, "Oedipus, shmedipus, as long as he loves his mother."

Another aspect of the Freudian revolution was to legitimize thinking previously forbidden thoughts. Freud drew a sharp line between having a fantasy and acting it out. Victorian morality did not make this distinction. It was almost as much a sin to have unclean thoughts as to do unclean things. Much of the torment of Freud's patients as well as of their contemporaries must have come about through struggles with their own thoughts as well as reactions to them—the knots of Western conscience, as Laing has described them.

When Freud began his psychiatric career, it was unheard of for patients to discuss their sex lives with physicians. Patients tried hard to conceal any information about the subject, and doctors were as prudish and lascivious as any other respectable people of that time.

Freud argued that every nervous illness could be traced to a sexual origin. As Freud freely admitted, this idea did not originate with him. But Freud's method of treatment, "the talking cure," was original, and it required that the doctor and the patient communicate with complete openness. In one of his early papers (1898) he pleaded that it should be possible to discuss sexual matters "without being stamped as a disturber of the peace or as a person whose aim is to arouse the lower instincts" (p. 221).

Childhood Sexuality

Before the nineteenth century, as we noted earlier, European culture was not nearly so repressive as it was to become.

Before the Protestant reformation of the sixteenth century, it was even less so. It is instructive to look at this pattern of sexuality because it contrasts both with the "civilized" morality of Victorian times and with our own. Anyone who has read Chaucer or Boccaccio or Rabelais is aware of the bawdiness of early modern literature. The evidence is that people's everyday behavior was more openly sexual than even today, in the sense that there were fewer taboos on sexual talk, and sexual horseplay was a usual part of adult interactions. Even more surprising than the ribaldries of adult life was the fact that adults felt no need to shield children from these goings-on. Ariès (1962) wrote:

One of the unwritten laws of contemporary morality requires adults to avoid any reference, above all, any humorous reference, to sexual matters in the presence of children. This notion was entirely foreign to the society of old. The modern reader of the diary in which Henry IV's physician, Heroard, recorded the details of the young Louis XIII's life is astonished by the liberties which people took with children, by the coarseness of the jokes they made, and by the indecency of gestures made in public which shocked nobody and were regarded as perfectly natural. . . .

There is no reason to believe that the moral climate was any different in other families, whether nobles or commoners; the practice of associating children with the sexual ribaldries of adults formed part of contemporary manners. (pp. 100–103)

In the fifteenth and sixteenth centuries there began to be a new concern with protecting childhood innocence, but the new attitude was slow in separating children from adult sexuality. "Broad talk," wrote Ariès, "was so natural that even later on, the strictest reformers would introduce into their sermons to children and students comparisons which would seem shocking today" (p. 109).

He also pointed out that sixteenth-century textbooks for schoolboys often included sex jokes and riddles as well as conversations about sexual matters in order to illustrate points of grammar and so forth. "The coarsest jokes, as well as topics of anything but educational value, are to be found in these dialogues."

The campaign to desexualize childhood eventually succeeded in building the taboos we are familiar with today, taboos so firmly entrenched as to have been practically untouched by the sexual revolution. Even the educational discussion of sex in schools is extremely controversial today, in spite of, or perhaps because of, the fact that parents find it extremely hard to teach their children the facts of life.

The campaign for childhood innocence did not succeed, of course, in eradicating children's sexual interests; it only succeeded in driving them underground. On their side of the sexual generation gap, children created their own cultural traditions of sexual lore and misinformation. Such works as the Opies' (1959) *Lore and Language of Schoolchildren* and Martha Wolfenstein's (1954) study of children's jokes document the pervasiveness of sexual interest in children, as part of a "subversive" (i.e., anti-adult) culture passed on through generations.

The result of the taboos against adult–child sexual communication has resulted in a system of sex education in which the vast majority of people learn about sex from their peers. It is a system of negative teaching and nonteaching from parents and positive learning from peers. As the students of human communication point out, not communicating about sex is one form of communicating about it. This context of sexual learning has profound consequences for individual experience and for the relations between men and women.

Sexual Learning and Nonlearning in the Family

The sexual attitudes and feelings learned in early childhood have a way of persisting even in people who have reevaluated or rejected their parents' attitudes and values in politics, religion, and other matters. Thus changes in adult behavior and the liberalization of public attitudes may obscure the persistence of traditional patterns of parent–child communication—and noncommunication—about sexual matters. One rather dramatic bit of evidence on this point is the study of Leah Shaefer (1964) of a group of middle-class women in their 20s and 30s whom she interviewed in the early 1960s. These women had all rebelled against the sexual Victorianism with which they had been brought up. Yet many or most of them seemed to be raising their daughters in the same way they had been raised. They were able to overcome the feeling of shame and guilt as far as their own sexual feelings were concerned, but found it difficult to think of their children as having sexual feelings.

John Gagnon (1965) provided a cogent analysis of why early sexual learning tends to be so heavily negative and persistent. First, he noted that American parents tend to respond to children's sexual behavior—handling the genitals, sex play, and so on—in one of two ways. One way is to tell the child not to do that—that the behavior is wrong or bad. This type of response from the parent will not surprise the child because he or she has heard many don'ts before—don't touch the stove or knife, don't step into the street. The other way is to avoid saying anything to the child, but to try to distract the child by pointing to something more "enjoyable" to do, or by pointing out some other reason than the sexual one to stop the behavior—"it's too cold to have your pants down" or "kissing can spread germs." Both the negative injunction—"It's wrong"—and the distraction technique—nonlabeling or mislabeling—may have much the same effect. The child learns that there is something vaguely wrong with sexuality. Further, as a result of the parents' reluctance to label sexual parts and activities and acts of excretion, the child is left with an infantile vocabulary that will later be filled in by terms learned from other children.

Parent–child relations are influenced by the lack of a vocabulary for matter-of-fact discussions of sexuality: the four-letter words have been tainted by their long use as curse words. Adults are beginning to use them more easily, but they are not felt to be a proper medium of instruction for children. Medical terms are too forbidding and polysyllabic.

In any event, nonlabeling or mislabeling may result in profound consequences. First, early sexual negative learning is never corrected. Gagnon points out that the parents modify their early *no's* and *don't's* about many things as the child grows older—thus the child later learns how to cross the street and how to use knives and manage stoves. But the primitive early learning about sexuality is rarely, if ever, corrected in the same way.

Further, the child's lack of a vocabulary to describe what he or she sees and feels and the difficulties of communication with parents permit fantasies to flourish for long periods of time without correction.

The mysterious penis that must exist behind the female pubic hair, the feeling that females have been castrated, and other childhood fantasies are common because there has been no system of naming which will adequately control the child's nascent interest in his own or others' bodies. (Gagnon, 1965, p. 222)

To point out the problems in early sexual education of children is not, however, the same as suggesting a solution. The sexual instruction or noninstruction of children in families is part of a complex cultural pattern. The concept of childhood innocence is deeply rooted in our culture, even though we can trace its beginnings in relatively recent historical times. It may well have arisen as an intensified form of the incest taboo, made necessary by the intimate emotional climate of the modern nuclear family. Despite the sexual revolution and today's frank movies, television, and rock lyrics, parents and children still find it hard to talk about sexual matters. A recent national survey of teenagers found 45% reporting that their parents taught them nothing at all about sex (Coles & Stokes, 1985).

Sex and Sex-Role Socialization in Peer Groups

Because parents and other adults provide little in the way of sex education for children, the information gap is filled by the growing child's friends and acquaintances—his or her peer group. After a child becomes of school age, both sex education and sex-role learning are carried out in large part by sex-segregated groups of children of comparable ages. Evidence indicates that elementary-school children are no longer as rigidly separated into same-sex groups as they once were, but for many generations the existence of separate male and female subcultures among schoolchildren has had profound effects on definitions of masculinity and femininity, as well as on relations between the sexes.

As far as sexuality is concerned, the exchange of sex information by children is guilty and clandestine. It generally tends to reinforce the negative attitudes the child has acquired at home as a result of the parents' direct teaching or silence.

Although communication about sex is much more open in child and adolescent peer groups than in the family, much of what is said is not very informative. Male sociologists report that the sexual emphasis in the male subculture is both pornographic and achievement-oriented. As Udry (1971) observed:

Since status results from convincing other boys of one's heterosexual escapades, most early adolescent heterosexual activity is discussed in male groups. There is considerable fabrication and elaboration of experience, and boys learn to discount one another's tales of prowess. The emphasis in the descriptions is on anatomical and manipulatory detail and erotic responses. . . . Sex emerges as something which boys "do to" girls. . . . Accounts of boys' early coital experience with girls show the boys to have been unconcerned with and largely unaware of the girls' own behavior. Among unattached adolescent boys, sex is sex, and it is divorced from emotional involvement, love, or romance.

Recent surveys show this picture is still valid. Discussions of sex among boys are still marked by boasting and exaggeration, and teenagers of both sexes are often reluctant to reveal doubts, worries and uncertainties, lest they be thought weird or ignorant.

Udry noted that the male orientation to sex acquired in child and adolescent groups persists into adulthood and does not disappear at marriage. He suggested it accounts for the man's greater interest in and participation in extramarital affairs and pornography, and is the cause of much misunderstanding between husbands and wives.

In the girls' subculture the order of priorities is reversed. If boys like sex more than they like girls, little girls like boys much more than they like sex. Girls have more trouble arriving at an image of a sexual self. There is often a huge gap between the images of love and romance and thoughts of direct sexual activity. The girl has no role models for sexual behavior such as those provided by male pornography or even male-oriented literature. In adolescence the girl tends to be caught in a bind between the wish and need to be popular with boys and the fear of losing her reputation or being taken advantage of by giving in to male sexual demands. Parents often contribute to the bind by pressuring the girl to be popular and have lots of dates, but not be "cheap" or to let boys go "too far." The anthropologist Jules Henry (1963), in a perceptive analysis of teenage culture in the 1950s and 1960s, saw the American girl as living on a "razor edge of sexual competition":

Thus, beneath the gaiety of any teen-age party throbs the anxiety of being left out next time, of losing a boy tomorrow that one has today or not getting the right one, of not getting the one you really want, of not getting the popular one, and so on. (p. 181)

Since those words were written, America has experienced the sexual revolution and the women's movement. For teenagers, the whole pattern of dating, going steady, and early marriage has altered. Fewer and fewer adolescent girls are thinking about their futures exclusively in terms of husbands and babies. Also, peer-group sex standards have changed. Boys may still boast about sex, but the double standard has declined in both word and deed. For most teenagers, intercourse has become an acceptable part of being in love and going together. Thus, love has become a prerequisite for intercourse, rather than marriage—a dramatic change in sexual standards (Sorenson, 1973).

Teenage Pregnancy

One unwelcome by-product of the increase in sexual activities is an increase in teenage pregnancies. An "epidemic" of teen-age pregnancies has captured the attention of the media, the general public, and government policy makers. Nearly 1,000,000 teenagers become pregnant every year, and almost 600,000 of them have babies. Estimates vary, but between 31 and 40 percent of all teenage girls will become pregnant if present rates continue. Because early childbearing usually has unfortunate consequences for both mothers and children, it is a social problem that deserves serious attention.

The idea, however, that there is an epidemic of teenage pregnancies and that this is a crisis in need of immediate and drastic government action is misleading. As demographer Maris Vinovskis (1981) has pointed out, the rate of childbearing among young adolescents has actually remained constant over the past 2 decades—in spite of the great increase in adolescent sexual activity.

Why then the perception of an epidemic of teenage pregnancies? Vinovskis lists several reasons. While the rate of teenage pregnancies has remained constant, the size of the teenaged population has increased. So in absolute terms, there are more teenage mothers in the population. Even more important, girls who get pregnant today act differently from their counterparts in the past. A teenage girl who got pregnant 10 or 20 years ago would be likely to do one of two things: get married or give the baby up for adoption. In recent years this pattern has changed drastically. The number of births legitimized by marriage declined from 65 percent in the early 1960s to 35 percent in the early 1970s. In other words, young people are no longer willing to be forced into early, unwanted marriages as an alternative to having a child out of wedlock.

The change in adoption has been even more striking: A decade ago, more than 90 percent of babies born out of wedlock were given up for adoption; today, almost 90 percent are kept by the mother. As a result of

In recent years, many men have begun to share in meal preparation. [Pat Todd for the Office of Human Development Services]

these trends, the financial costs of teenage pregnancy for the general public has increased dramatically. The high costs of welfare payments to teenage mothers are one reason that government policymakers came to be concerned over the problem.

Although it is easy to denounce teenage sexuality and illegitimacy, it is hard to suggest ways of dealing with it. Eliminating sex education or access to contraception is unlikely to reduce either sex or out-of-wedlock pregnancy. Controlling teenage sexuality would probably involve controlling adult sexuality also, and would require a great deal of government intrusion into private lives. As one study concludes:

Teen-aged sexuality might recede if we could bring ourselves to accept greater censorship of movies, television, books and magazines, including the advertising therein . . . combined with greater restrictions on the daily movements of teen-agers . . . a drastic reduction in unchaperoned social activities . . . social sanctions against open displays of affection by young people, combined with the imposition of punishment in some form for those who stray from clearly marked "paths of righteousness." . . . For ourselves, we prefer to cope with the consequences of early sex as an aspect of an emancipated society, rather than pay the social costs its elimination would exact. (Zelnick, Kanter, & Ford, 1981, p. 182)

On Sexual Revolutions

As we saw earlier, the history of sexuality has followed an uneven course, with periods of sexual freedom alternating with periods of greater strictness. Also, at any one time there was great variation in sexual mores according to social class; the classes at either extreme of the social scale have traditionally been freer than the middle classes.

The sexual revolution of the past decade or so represents the continuation of a trend that began around the turn of the century. The decisive break with Victorian morality was the Freudian revolution.

To those scholars who have studied the rise and fall of sexual moralities, the Freudian contribution was only part of a larger revolution in attitudes toward sexuality and toward the family. These social attitudes in turn seem to have been part of still wider changes in the society, especially in the economic and religious order. These changes accompanied the beginnings of the mass consumption economy and the decline of the Protestant ethic with its distrust of idleness and pleasure. Thus Hale (1971) noted:

The change in attitudes, however, does coincide with profound alterations in exactly those factors that caused the nineteenth-century addictions to "civilized" morality. The decline of religious controls over sexuality has been noted. By 1900 American observers had become aware of decisive changes in the economic system. The American sociologist Simon Pattern argued in 1907 that America was moving from an economy of deficit and saving to one of surplus and abundance. A new kind of character had to emerge, no longer dedicated to austerity and sacrifice but to leisure and rational enjoyment. Repression would give way to release. The new economy was giving a new place to women outside the home and family. (p. 476)

It would be a mistake, however, to think of the sexual revolution as simply a liberation of previously repressed impulses. Like Victorian doctrines about the danger and ugliness of sex, modern ideas about sex as healthy and good are, above all, just that—a set of ideas with a complicated relationship to behavior and experience. There is no denying that for many people the sexual revolution as brought greater freedom, pleasure,

and mutuality in sex. At the same time, however, the new legitimation of sex and the new standards of sexual performance can create new tensions and anxieties.

For example, the working-class women described earlier illustrate how the new sexual freedom can be experienced as a kind of oppression; many of these women not only felt burdened by their husbands' demands for oral sex, but also felt alienated from their own orgasms. Some of these women's problems can be blamed on lingering Victorianism, as well as distrust of their husbands' commitments to sexual liberalism. But liberated attitudes do not necessarily lead to uninhibited joy. Lillian Rubin (1976) also interviewed upper-middle-class women in her study. These women and their husbands were much more relaxed and accepting in their attitudes toward sex. Yet they often felt guilty about their inability to overcome their inhibitions and live up to their beliefs. While the working-class women wished their husbands would be less demanding, their middle-class counterparts blamed themselves for what they saw as inadequacies in their own personal sexual adjustment.

Paradoxically, the new sexual freedom may have decreased people's enjoyment of sex by raising the standards of satisfaction. Rather than unleashing wild and insatiable instincts, the sexual revolution reveals that for many people a lack of sexual desire is a major problem; the number one complaint of people who go to sex clinics is an inability to get "turned on" as much as they would like.

A survey of young adults, carried out by *Psychology Today* (Shaver & Freedman, 1976), reveals the extent to which the new expectations have ironically increased dissatisfaction. More than half of the men and over one-third of the women were dissatisfied with their own sex lives, but they believed that the average person of their sex had more sexual partners and greater satisfaction than they did. About one of five unmarried men and women had never had intercourse, but only 1 percent of the men and 2 percent of the women thought their peers were virgins. Pluralistic ignorance persists despite the sexual revolution. Now, however, people worry about having less sex than other people, not more.

There are still other contradictions and tensions in contemporary attitudes toward sex. As Paul Robinson (1976, p. 3) pointed out, the sexual revolution has not yet solved "the most vexing problem of human sexual psychology: the paradoxical need for both companionship and variety in erotic life." The modern revolt against Victorian prudishness has taken two inconsistent directions. One approach argues for a liberation of sex, but only in the context of a deep emotional bond between the partners. The other approach to sexual modernism emphasizes the sensuous, bodily aspects of sex and separates sex from love.

The first point of view, which has been called "romantic" or "person-centered," is exemplified in the work of Freud, Havelock Ellis, and Van de Velde. The second point of view, "anti-romantic" or "body-centered," is best exemplified in the writings of Kinsey. He believed that the idea of restricting sex to persons who were truly in love was as absurd a notion as the idea that masturbation causes insanity. In the work of Masters and Johnson, both tendencies coexist in an almost schizoid fashion. On the one hand, Masters and Johnson unromantically manipulate sex in the laboratory, treating it as a physiological response; on the other hand, they insist on the need for emotional closeness and communication in sexual relationships.

This kind of ambivalence applies to many people today. Robinson observed, "As moderns, we remain permanently divided be-tween a romantic past, whose repressions we would gladly rid ourselves of, and a deromanticized future, whose emotional emptiness we fear even while we anticipate its greater freedom" (p. 195).

By the mid-1980s, there was clear evidence that body-centered casual sex was losing the glamor it had had in the 1960s and 1970s. The outbreak of new and seemingly incurable venereal diseases such as AIDS and herpes brought fear and guilt back to sex. A decade earlier, it had seemed that medical progress, in the form of penicillin and the pill, had transformed sex into a risk-free pleasure.

By 1982, before AIDS became widespread, fear of herpes had already produced marked changes in sexual behavior. One poll found that 22 percent of single people between the ages of 18 and 37 said they had changed their behavior to avoid the disease (E. Goodman, 1985). Many people saw the diseases as punishment from God or nature. It had happened before. Epidemics of syphilis, the most dreaded sexual disease, had help to end periods of sexual liberalism in earlier centuries. Religious reformers saw sexual disease as evidence of God's anger.

Not all disillusion with casual sex was due to fear of disease. After casual sex had passed from being taboo to relatively acceptable, its limitations could be seen more clearly. Most people, it seems, prefer longer and more intimate relationships to one-night stands. Indeed, during the 1980s there was so much talk and writing about "relationships" that one writer complained that the "R-word" was becoming a cliche.

Looking back at the changing cultures of the past several decades, a pattern emerges. As Sharon Brehm observes:

Perhaps the most interesting aspect of the sexual revolution we have had in this country is the way we have gone from a rule-bound culture, where as in every age, plenty of people broke the rules, to a relatively rule-free culture where many people are looking for new rules. If the 1950's was a decade of sexual oppression and the 1960's and 1970's an age of sexual liberation, the 1980's can be considered an age of sexual questioning. (1985, p. 118)

Scientific and Technological Changes

The recent changes in sexual attitudes and behavior and in sex roles are not due to ideological changes alone. The first half of the twentieth century witnessed three advances with profound implications for sexuality, the family, and the roles of women—the demographic revolution, the contraceptive revolution, and the technological revolution.

The demographic revolution resulted from medical advances that reduced infant mortality and extended the lifespan. Before the nineteenth century a married woman could expect to devote the greater portion of her adult years to reproduction. In the United States, for example, the average number of births per woman around 1800 was seven. Infant-mortality rates varied over time and place, but until the twentieth century many, and at times most, infants could be expected to die. Thus high fertility rates were "needed" to offset the high death rates.

The reduction of infant mortality, as well as the invention of contraception, made it possible to separate sexuality from reproduction. The invention, development, and widespread acceptance of contraception—and of abortion—will probably prove to be the decisive advance in women's liberation. At least some of what we take to be sexist thinking today reflects the realities of women's lives in the past. The idea that "all women are mothers" was not much of a distortion during the centuries when women could exercise slight control over their own reproductive capacities.

Finally, the industrial revolution may, after a century and a half, enhance the freedom of women and encourage the development of their mental capacities and talents. Whether women can match men in brute strength has sometimes been an issue, but in a technologically advanced society it is irrelevant.

In short, the demographic revolution, the contraceptive revolution, and the technological revolution have radically altered the potential role, status, and the very destiny of women in society. The current ferment over sex, sex roles, and family life may accordingly be interpreted as a form of "cultural lag"—a process of bringing social practices into cohesion with already existing biological and technological realities.

SUMMARY

In both popular thought and many social-scientific writings, thinking about sexuality and sex differences has been dominated by biological imagery. Sexuality has been defined as a life force pressing for release, and sex-role differences are assumed to reflect innate temperamental inclinations. Obviously, males and females differ in anatomy, physiology, and perhaps even in temperament to some degree. Neither sexuality nor sex differences, however, can be understood as being independent of background, such as learning, culture, and the historical context.

Anatomy is destiny largely because children are assigned at birth to two different worlds of experience and self-definition on the basis of the genital difference. Further, the biological capacity of women to bear children is much more fateful in societies without contraception and with high rates of infant mortality.

As a human motive, sexuality fits the model of an appetite or craving rather than a life force. In general, then, our sexual selves are not simple reflections of the animal side of human nature; in our sexual lives as elsewhere, we are shaped by our time, place, and situation.

Recent studies of the history of sexuality in Western society have revealed that dramatic changes have taken place in beliefs and behavior. Among the most striking contrasts with our own times are the acceptance of bisexuality among men in ancient times and the disapproval of sexual pleasure in marriage for many centuries of the Christian era. The new studies also reveal that the sexual culture of any particular place and time is a complex mixture of expressive and repressive codes.

In general, the pattern of sexual change over time has followed a cyclical rather than a linear model. There has been an oscillation between periods of restraint and repression and periods of liberation. The recent sexual revolution was a reaction against Victorian restraints, which followed a more relaxed period in the eighteenth century. In the 1980s, the tide seemed to be turning back toward greater restraint, due in part to the emergence of new and deadly sexually transmitted diseases.

CHAPTER 9

The Ultimate Human Connection: The Love Relationship

Anyone who has seen the film Casablanca will not have forgotten its theme song and the memorable line from it which declares: "the fundamental things apply, as time goes by." . . . But do they? . . . For instance, when two lovers woo, do they still say, "I love you"? Or are they more likely to say, "I'm not really ready for an involvement at this stage in my life"?

William Kilpatrick
Identity and Intimacy

Despite the fact that I could live alone for years at a time, support myself in banal as well as curious ways, travel alone all over the world, drive a motorcycle at 70 miles an hour, have sex with whomever I chose, I was still capable of sitting by a telephone, unable to think of anything beyond whether or not a man I loved was going to call and feeling the most common hurt and frustration when he didn't.

Ingrid Bengis
Combat in the Erogenous Zone

Despite the great changes in attitudes toward sex, marriage, and family life in recent years, the vast majority of Americans eventually marry. Most people experience one or several love relationships in the course of their lives, and love remains the only legitimate reason for marriage. Even more than in the past, such relationships are based on the choices of the two individuals themselves. What is it that attracts people to one another in the first place? Why do some relationships end at the first encounter, while others develop into emotional attachments and permanent commitments? What keeps people together in enduring relationships? Why do some relationships decline and dissolve over time?

The rapid social changes of recent years seem to have made people even more concerned with love and intimacy than they were in previous decades. One sign of this increased interest is the flood of books offering advice on how to find and manage intimate relationships. Another is the current boom in social-science research on love.

Some people look to science to tell them how they can make a person fall in love with them, or to tell them what kind of person they should choose as a mate. Others fear that the scientific study of love will destroy and dehumanize it. Senator William Proxmire, for example, criticized a grant for re-

search into love by stating: "200 million Americans want to leave some things a mystery and right at the top of those things we don't want to know is why a man falls in love with a woman and vice versa" (1975, p. 3).

Neither the hopes nor the fears are justified. Although social scientists have offered explanations of love and attraction, they have not, as yet, been able to predict in advance which individuals will fall in love with one another. And although we know a good deal about the processes that lead to problems in relationships, we still don't know which ones will succumb to the difficulties and which ones will survive in spite of them. Nevertheless, the study of love relationships may, as one researcher put it, "make a positive contribution to the quality of life" (Z. Rubin, 1977, p. 59) at a time when rapid changes in attitudes and behavior concerning sex, love, and marriage have caused great confusion.

THIS THING CALLED LOVE

Writers on the subject of love agree on only one thing—that love is an elusive concept; otherwise they contradict one another about its nature and significance. As one writer put it almost a century ago: "Love is such a tissue of paradoxes, and exists in such an endless variety of forms and shades, that you may say anything about it that you please and it is likely to be correct" (Fincke, 1891, p. 244).

Disagreement exists, not only among poets and novelists, but among scholars as well. To some people, love is a trivial notion concocted by Hollywood movies and popular songwriters, and therefore hardly worthy of serious discussion. To some biologists and ethologists, love is part of our evolutionary inheritance, comparable to the pair bonding found in certain mammals and birds.

Traditionally, many sociologists of the family have scoffed at love as a kind of irrational frenzy, typical of teenagers and the early stages of some adult sexual relationships, but having little to do with marriage. In this view, the American idea of love is dysfunctional because it encourages people to believe that "love and marriage go together like a horse and carriage" and thus sets them up to be disillusioned by the discovery that they don't. Others believe love is functional because it brings people together, saving the institution of marriage from disintegration in modern societies where marriages are no longer arranged by kin.

To some radical critics, love is a kind of "opiate of the people"—an ideology that leads people to seek happiness in personal relationships and to ignore the problems of the larger society. Some feminists have argued that love is a trap leading women to be exploited by men. But not all radicals disapprove of love; some feminists argue that when men and women are able to relate to each other as equal human beings and no longer use each other as objects, love will flourish. One Marxist writer has argued that love and fidelity, far from being abolished in a socialist culture, "only need to be freed from their narrow bourgeois existence" (Reiche, 1971, p. 27).

Psychologists who have examined love tend also to disagree. To some, love is a kind of selfishness, a preoccupation with one's own feelings rather than a genuine concern for the other person. In this view, lovers are more in love with love than with one another. To others, love is a giving of the self, ennobling and enriching. Freud defined the healthy person as one who could love and work. Erikson made ability to love a major developmental stage in adulthood.

What are we to make of these inconsistent views? Perhaps, like the six blind men and the elephant, each writer on love has seized on a different aspect of love and declared it to be the essential nature of the beast. As Morton Hunt pointed out, something is wrong with the question What is this thing called love? because it implies that love is a single entity. The word *love* is used to refer to many things:

There is making love and being in love, which are quite dissimilar ideas; there is love of God, of mankind, of art, and of pet cats; there is motherly love, brotherly love, the love of money, and the love of one's comfortable old shoes. (1959, p. 5)

The Experience of Romantic Love

Recently the issue of "what we talk about when we talk about love" (Carver, 1982) has been considerably clarified by two books. One is by a philosopher and the other is by a psychologist. Although they approach the topic in very different ways and were not influenced by one another, there is remarkable agreement between the two about what romantic love is and is not. The philosopher Robert Solomon (1981) analyzes the concept of love in its philosophical and historical context. He also describes the experience of love "from the point of view of an enthusiast." Love was one of the great themes of classical philosophy, but it has been neglected in recent years. Solomon resumes the philosophical discussion of love, attempting to get through the "myths" and misconceptions that have surrounded the concept.

The psychologist Dorothy Tennov (1979) would label Solomon a "limerant." Tennov coined the term *limerance* to distinguish the experience of being in love from other ways of loving. Using a variety of sources—interviews, formal and informal questionnaires, diaries—Tennov explored the love experiences of over 500 people. Although each individual had a unique tale to tell, the emotional experience each described contained elements that were strikingly similar—certain basic components to the process of being in love. She also discovered that while some people were in love much of the time and others some of the time, others had never experienced romantic love. Like a blind person trying to understand what colors are, these individuals couldn't understand what an intense romantic love must be like. And yet these nonlimerants usually enjoyed close relationships with people they loved and cared for.

Besides those who loved but had never been in love, Tennov also found many people in long-term relationships that had begun with romantic love and who still described themselves as being in love, but who did not currently exhibit the major symptoms of limerance. (Others in long-term relationships did show these symptoms, sometimes for decades.) She also found people who had experienced being in love, but had no interest in doing so again or in building a relationship on romantic love. For these reasons, Tennov felt she had to have a distinct term to separate love from being in love: "It appears that love and sex can coexist without limerance . . . any of the three may exist without the others" (p. 16).

What then is this thing called romantic love or limerance? How do these two writers, coming at the question from very different directions, answer it? The first major point made by both Solomon and Tennov is that romantic love is essentially sexual, but it is not merely sexual. The love may never be consummated, but the object of romantic love is always someone who is a potential sexual partner. They also insist that the love object need not be a person of the opposite sex; homosexuals also fall in love, and the experience is no different from that of heterosexuals.

Although sexuality lies at the core of romantic love, what is yearned for is something more than sexual satisfaction. Indeed, satisfaction in romantic love is far from guaranteed. Tennov reports that although some of her informants felt that sex with the loved one was the greatest pleasure known to human existence, others found that shyness and emotional intensity often interfered with sexual functioning.

While sex may be the medium of love, it is not the whole message. What the message is, though—what the "more" is that the lovers strive for—is hard to define. Writing of his own experience, Solomon observes:

If there was one thing that was utterly obvious to us, it was the *sanctity* of sex. . . . The more we had, the more we wanted, the more dissatisfied we became, the less sex was "sex" and the less we even knew *what* we wanted . . . not sex but something *through* sex. (p. xv)

By insisting that sexuality lies at the core of romantic love, Solomon and Tennov contradict a long line of philosophers and some psychologists who make a sharp distinction between sexuality on the one hand and "spiritual" or "pure" love on the other. Since the twelfth century, the ideal of love without lust has been called "platonic love," although as Solomon points out, Plato is not totally responsible for the idea. Plato in fact recognized the link between sex and more spiritual forms of love. In his *Symposium* he wrote:

The intense yearning which lovers have towards each other does not appear to be the desire for sexual intercourse, but for something else which the soul of each desires and cannot tell, and of which he/she has only a dark and doubtful presentiment. (Cited in Solomon, 1981, p. xv)

Another way in which Solomon and Tennov show that the sexuality of romantic love

is more than sex is their insistence that the eyes, not the genitals, are the organs of love. Tennov found that love begins with a look—two people find their gaze meeting and locking. In couples who are in love relationships, the length of their mutual gaze is correlated with their reported depth of feelings for one another (Z. Rubin, 1970). Solomon emphasizes the mutuality of gaze.

To be in love (even unrequited) is to be looked *at,* not just to look. . . . One supposedly looks "into" the lover's eyes; I never could. One no more looks into them than at them, for what one sees is always their looking back at you. The eyes, only the eyes, are the organs of love. (p. 131)

Love as an Emotion

Both writers agree that romantic love is best understood as a complex psychological state involving both thoughts and feelings. For Tennov, "limerance is first and foremost a condition of cognitive obsession" (p. 33). Persistent intrusive thinking about the loved one is the characteristic that most sets it apart from other kinds of love. Past words, gestures, and actions of the loved one are reviewed, scanned, and examined for alternative interpretations. Intricate scenarios of future meetings are invented.

No matter where I am or what I am doing I am not safe from your spell. At any moment, the image of your face smiling at me, of your voice telling me you care, or of your hand in mine, may suddenly fill my consciousness, pushing out all else. . . . Everything reminds me of you. I try to read, but four times on a single page some word begins the lightning chain of associations that summons my mind away from my work . . . my imagination constructs long and involved and plausible reasons to believe that you love me. (Tennov, 1979, p. viii)

For Solomon, love is an emotion like any other. The obsessiveness of love, he argues, is a characteristic of all emotions. Emotions are not simple feelings, but "intelligent constructions"—complex structures of experience, "like theatrical performances in which we are both the leading actor and the director." Each emotion changes the way we view the world. The depressed person lives in a depressed world. For the person afraid of some dread event—such as losing a job, or fearing a diagnostic test will reveal cancer—fear is part of the structure of experience, from waking up in the morning to going to bed at night. Similarly, to be in love is to live inside a special world—the "loveworld"—centered around a single relationship, with all else pushed to the sidelines. It is a world both familiar and grand:

It is a world we know well, of course—the world of *Casablanca, Romeo and Juliet,* and a thousand stories and novels. It is a world in which we narrow our vision and our cares to that single duality, all else becoming trifles, obstacles or interruptions. It is a magical world, in which an ordinary evening is transformed into the turning point of a lifetime. (p. 128)

Reciprocity

Although love is an emotional state of one person, it is, as W. J. Goode (1959) observes, the most projective emotion: it reaches out toward the other person, seeking reciprocation. Tennov finds that the objective the limerant person longs for and daydreams about so persistently is a return of feelings—some clear sign that one is loved by the loved one. The goal of limerance is not possession, not copulation, not even marriage, but "the ecstatic bliss of mutual reciprocation" (p. 120).

Similarly, Solomon writes that an essential element of love is a sense of shared identity—a transformation of two selves into a double being. He cites the ancient Greek myth that the first human was a double creature who was cut in two by Zeus, and ever since the two halves have yearned to get together.

Instability

Alas, the yearned-for goals of perfect reciprocity and oneness turn out to be elusive, or else, like King Midas's golden touch, no longer so wonderful when you get them. The instability of romantic love is another major theme of both writers. Tennov describes it as "an emotional roller coaster" that carries a person from the peaks of joy to the depths of despair, and back again (1979, p. viii). The process of limerance is one of constant oscillation of feelings, both within each individual and between the couple. Even in a seemingly mutual relationship, there is a constant shifting back and forth of which one loves the most.

Love is not only a roller coaster, it is also a seesaw. As we have seen, the chief goal of limerance, the blissful moment that is endlessly dreamed about, is reciprocity—the return of feelings. Once that happens, however, the intensity of feelings may drop. To the extent that limerance is fueled by uncertainty and fear of rejection, it may be reduced when these conditions no longer exist. Indeed, if the loved one responds too quickly or too blatantly, the state of limerance can be killed off completely.

For Solomon, romantic love is also unstable. The goal of shared identity, of two selves merging into one, is impossible. Or at least impossible to sustain over any length of time. For Solomon, love is not a state of union but the very process of yearning for union, seeming to reach it, and then moving apart.

No sooner do we approach this goal [of a shared identity] than we are abruptly reminded of our differences. Perhaps you dislike a movie I love, or maybe I'm bored or insulted by one of your friends. Even in our most trivial differences, we are thrown back on our individuality. . . . But then, as we move apart, the self we have already formed together pulls us back. . . . We *want* this, whatever the differences. (p. 269)

Misconceptions About Romantic Love

Despite their different methods, there are some striking agreements between the two writers about certain misconceptions concerning love. The experience of romantic love, for example, is not a necessary or universal experience, even in this culture, which so emphasizes it. Solomon observes that it is a luxury, not an essential emotion.

Similarly, Tennov observes that a relationship that includes no limerance may be far more important in a person's life than one that is full of passionate striving.

They also agree that certain other assumptions about romantic love are mistaken. Love does not necessarily happen at first sight—people can fall in love after any amount of prior acquaintanceship. The notion of the "one and only love" is a myth: people are able to experience full-blown romantic love with more than one person, although not at the same time. Tennov notes, however, that in the milder stages of limerance it is possible to be limerant about more than one person.

The Value of Romantic Love

One major difference between the two writers, apart from their different methods, is how they evaluate romantic love. Solomon, as we've noted, describes himself as "an enthusiast." Romantic love, he argues, provides us with the most powerful kind of intimacy and a sense of self-worth.

Tennov is more ambivalent. She shares our culture's schizoid attitude toward romantic love. On the one hand, it is considered the most intense form of happiness, almost a religious experience, as well as the ideal kind of relationship between man and woman. On the other hand, romantic love is often dismissed as a kind of foolishness, a symptom of emotional weakness and even madness. She contrasts limerance with "affectional bonding"—based on concern for the other person, compatibility of interests, pleasurable sex, and companionship. At times, Tennov refers to affectional bonding as the ideal form of a couple relationship. Also, she points to the costs of limerance: it can be full of pain and misery. A majority of Tennov's respondents had experienced depression in connection with romantic love. A considerable number (17 percent) had considered suicide after a failed love affair. Many of her informants regretted the time and energy they now felt they had wasted on romantic love—they had neglected their work and other more precious relationships.

Perhaps the differences in how these two authors evaluate romantic love arises from their difference in methods: Tennov's is an empirical study, which, although not based on the most rigorous survey techniques, nevertheless considers the experiences of a large number of people. Solomon's book is based on conceptual analysis and his own necessarily limited but happy experience. There is also a difference in value: Tennov ultimately regards affectional bonding as the most reasonable form of relationship; limerance is something to be understood and controlled, not idealized. Solomon chooses the opposite way. He would, however, find little to disagree with in Tennov's summary statement: "Limerance is not in any way preeminent among types of human attractions or interactions, but when limerance is in full force, it eclipses other relationships" (p. 16).

LOVE IN CROSS-CULTURAL PERSPECTIVE

One of the persistent puzzles about romantic love concerns its relationship to Western culture. Is the capacity to fall in love built into human nature and hence found in all times and places? Or do Americans and Europeans experience a different set of emotions than people in other cultures?

The answer seems to be that both statements are partly true. Although there has been a great debate about the subject, no one who argues that love is universal denies that it occurs more widely and is more elaborate in Western society than elsewhere. In most of the world's cultures, marriages are arranged by kin, not by the bride and groom. Those who emphasize the uniqueness of love in the West admit, however, that love *can* bloom anywhere, even if it rarely does so. Thus the anthropologist Ralph Linton (1936), often quoted as a proponent of the notion that love is a trait peculiar to our culture, conceded "all societies recognize that there are occasional violent emotional attachments between persons of the opposite sex" (p. 175). On the other hand, he goes on to argue that our present American culture is practically the only one that makes them the basis of marriage. The rarity of such attachments in most cultures, he wrote,

suggests that they are psychological abnormalities to which our own culture has attached an extraordinary value, just as other cultures have attached extreme values to other abnormalities. The hero of the modern American movie is always a lover just as the hero of the old Arab epic is always epileptic. (p. 175)

Arguing against Linton's position, William J. Goode (1959) points out the potential for falling in love is universal. Even in societies in which romantic love plays no role in the decision to marry, individual love relationships may appear in literature and myth, and in real life also. The Bible contains several descriptions of love: David and Bathsheba, the Song of Solomon, and the love story of Jacob and Rachel. The classical literatures of India, Japan, and China also include tales of romantic passion and tragedy.

Goode noted that because strong love attachments can occur in any society, those societies that do not allow free choice in marriage partners must control love. Typical strategies of love control range from child marriage to constant chaperonage, to the isolating of young people from potential mates. Nevertheless Goode concedes that although the potential for love is universal, the belief that falling in love is the only proper basis for marriage is peculiar to Western culture. In most traditional cultures, the emphasis is on congeniality rather than love between marital partners. Young people are brought up to believe that any reasonably well-adjusted man and woman will be able to live contentedly.

Yet even in those cultures in which the spouses have no say in the marriage, personal preference can enter the picture, if only to make the person miserable. Anthropologists have recorded numerous instances of people complaining bitterly about having been pushed into marriages with people they detested. On the other hand, many cultures with arranged marriages do offer escape routes for people with strong feelings about one another. Thus in many of these societies, a couple can disobey their elders and elope, hoping that the parents will eventually approve the marriage.

Love and Labeling

The question of whether people in different cultures feel the same emotions is hard to answer because emotions are not simple reactions to events or people, but complex mixtures of feelings and ideas. Feelings acquire meaning only in relation to a specific social and historical context. In other words, emotional words such as *love* do not have a fixed meaning corresponding to a fixed set of human feelings. As one writer put it, "Hunger is hunger, pride is pride, and love is love—but these feelings, while universal, are evoked, expressed and experienced differently in different societies" (Shanley, 1979, p. 750).

Work in the psychology of emotion suggests that thought processes play a large role in emotional experience. We are not passion's slaves, in the sense that emotions are not events that "happen" to us. Rather, we construct emotional experience on the basis of culture, learning, and bodily responses. Currently, the most influential explanation of emotions has been advanced by Stanley Schacter, a social psychologist. Schacter (1964) suggested that emotional experience consists of two parts: physiological arousal, as manifested in a pounding heart, breathlessness, weakness in the knees, and so on; and an interpretation or labeling of the experience. Various kinds of strong emotions—fear, anger, and love—are not clearly distinguished from one another physiologically. In a well-known experiment, Schacter injected research subjects with a drug that induced physiological arousal; the subjects experienced their arousal as either elation or anger, depending on the circumstances Schacter placed them in. Thus, Schacter argued, when people experience the symptoms of arousal, they look around for an explanation.

Other researchers have applied Schacter's two-part theory of emotion to love. One study (Dutton & Aron, 1974) compared the reactions of men to a young woman encountered in the middle of either of two footbridges. The men on a high, rickety, swaying bridge were more likely to express sexual and romantic interests than were men on a more solid structure. Two thousand years ago, Ovid observed the same principle. In the *Art of Love,* he advised that a man could easily arouse passion in a woman by flirting with her at the arena where gladiators were disembowling one another.

If Schacter's theory is correct, then social and cultural influences play a large role in determining how people label their emotions. And, as Judith Katz (1977) pointed out, culture helps to determine when people will become emotionally aroused in the first place because it shapes our desires and goals. Our culture encourages the experience of love in many ways. It teaches that practically everyone will fall in love, and it leads people to apply the label *love* to a wide range of feelings. An elaborate set of images presented in literature, movies, and other mass media provides images and ideas of what love is like.

Arlie Hochschild (1975) has noted the various ways people process the inner stream of thoughts and feelings in terms of such cultural symbols. The first step is to attend to feelings. In a culture in which the love ideology is lacking, a boy and girl could be attracted to each other and yet pay little attention to such feelings.

Children in our culture, however, are primed for love from an early age. The little boy or girl who plays with a member of the opposite sex may be teased about his or her boyfriend or girlfriend and about being in love. Even before children are old enough to read, they will hear such fairy tales as "Cinderella," "Snow White," "Sleeping Beauty," and many others.

Hardly any child *believes* the tales, but they all have the same message. A handsome prince overcomes obstacles to marry the poor maid with whom he has fallen in love; they are married and live in bliss. Alternately, the handsome but poor peasant boy overcomes obstacles to marry the princess, with whom he has fallen in love; they are married and live in bliss. Always beauty, always obstacles, always love, always a class barrier . . . always married bliss. The unsaid last line of each story is, "Someday this may happen to you." Parents set the proper example for their children by relating to the child their own prince-and-beauty story. "Why did you marry Daddy?" "Because we fell in love." (Udry, 1971, pp. 162–163)

Once attended to, feelings are codified in accord with cultural understandings. Thus many people would label the following set of feelings as love: a sense of excitement at first meeting someone; daydreaming and preoccupation with the other person; yearning to be with him or her; jealousy of rivals; a feeling that this is the one and only love and that the feeling will last forever. On the other hand, a person experiencing a mild, nonphysical attraction with no sense of urgency and no jealousy would not be likely to label it as love.

Romantic love in Western culture seems to be a unique compound of many elements: not only a strong emotional attachment with sexual overtones, but also elements of tenderness and idealization of the beloved. What looks like love in another culture may have a different quality than Western love. Thus Margaret Mead (1928) observed that although Samoan love making has a superficial resemblance to our own, Samoan love songs and flowery love letters are merely conventionalized rituals that may have little to do with feelings or behavior. Other anthropologists have reported similar ritual declarations of love in other cultures.

Finally, feelings, once codified and labeled, are managed. That is, we may do "feeling work" to help bring our feelings in line with "feeling rules" (Hochschild, 1975). For example, feeling rules tell us that we should feel sad at funerals and happy at weddings and christenings. If we don't feel the way we are supposed to, we may feel guilty and try to make ourselves feel the "proper" emotions. Thus we may try to suppress feelings of love if we feel that they are inappropriate, or stir them up when they seem to be lagging behind the situation. In students' reports of emotional experience, Hochschild found many examples of feeling work. Several people, for example, reported trying to make themselves love another person to justify sleeping with him or her. Others reported trying to make themselves stop loving people.

In sum, then, love is a constructed experience built with feelings, ideas, and cultural symbols. In addition to knowing about the inner psychological processes involved in love, it is necessary to understand something of the historical roots of the idea of love in Western culture.

The Ideology of Love
in Western Culture

Twentieth-century American attitudes toward love are a distillation of themes that have been evolving through many centuries of Western civilization. Although most of the ideology of romantic love was derived from courtly love—the formalized love relationships celebrated by the troubadours of the twelfth century—certain ideas about love reach back to the Greeks and Romans. Sappho listed symptoms of lovesickness that have lasted for 25 centuries: a faltering voice, blushing, heart palpitations, erratic eye movements, muscle tremors, faintness, and pallor.

Love in ancient times, however, was very different from what it was to become later. Love was not part of courtship or marriage, but occurred between married men and prostitutes or between men and young boys. It is paradoxical, as Morton Hunt (1959) observed, "that modern love began with Greek love and owes so much to it, although the forms and ideals of Greek love are considered immoral and, to a large extent, illegal in modern society" (p. 16).

Because of the inferior social position of women in Greek society, little importance was attached to heterosexual love. Because women were not educated, even the upper-class Greek wife had more in common with servants and slaves than with her own husband. Many of the traditional antiwoman jokes about nagging wives originated in Greek times. The leading Greek philosophers praised love and friendship between men. And Sappho's original description of

lovesickness depicted the love of one woman for another.

Among the Romans, love tended to be heterosexual rather than homosexual, but, as among the Greeks, it occurred outside marriage and applied only to adulterous affairs. As codified in Ovid's first-century *Art of Love*, love was an elegant game of deceit, not the basis of serious or long-lasting relationships. It is impossible, of course, to state how widespread extramarital affairs actually were among the Roman upper classes, but other writers of the period suggest that Ovid's textbook of flirting and adultery had educated his entire generation in the game of love. Like the modern-day advisor, Ovid argued that personal hygiene and good grooming were essential for lovers: the man was to wear spotless, well-fitting clothes, keep his hair and nails trimmed, and avoid body odor and bad breath. Women were advised to shave their legs and underarms and to avoid getting tanned.

Deception played an important role in Ovid's love games: flattery was to be used, preferably in conjunction with expressions of tender concern. It was permissible to fake the symptoms of lovesickness to advance an affair. In one of his poems, Ovid describes how lovers at a party can secretly communicate through intense looks, subtle gestures, a special code, and the secret touching of feet under the table.

The American ideology of love owes more to the courtly love ideal of the Middle Ages than to the cool and sensual games described by Ovid. Courtly love is based on the idea that love between the sexes is a supreme value of life on earth. It included the following beliefs: that love is an overwhelming passion inspired by the beauty and character of the loved one; that it strikes suddenly and uncontrollably at the first sight of the beloved; that the lovers are fated for one another; that love leads to perfect bliss or utter misery; and that it uplifts and ennobles the lover. Courtly love included profoundly contradictory elements such as adulterous passion and Christian religious devotion, stereotyped flirtation games and serious moral purpose, betrayal and faithfulness, joy and suffering.

The great courtly love romances—for example, Tristan and Isolde, Lancelot and Guinevere—are tales of adultery. Some of the writers who propounded the doctrine of courtly love argued that it was impossible for love to occur in a marriage, while others insisted that it was still possible, although rare. Marriages were still being arranged according to the family's interests, on the basis of property and status considerations; hence love was likely to be found outside of marriage.

One of the most significant contributions of courtly love was the social elevation of the woman to an object of devotion. The knight's worship of his lady, scholars generally agree, paralleled religious devotion to the Virgin Mary. The traditions of chivalry have survived in the codes of etiquette that still persist in diminished form. The customary signs of deference toward women—holding the door for a woman, lighting her cigarette, and so on—are not done in other cultures, such as India and Japan. Rather, women are expected to show deference to men (Stephens, 1963).

Women have rightly protested that being placed on a pedestal represents a stifling denial of their needs and capacities; further, the idealization of some women as ethereal beings puts others in the category of impure beings who can be treated disrespectfully. Nevertheless, the Western tradition of respect for women, however much it has interfered with the achievement of sex-role equality, has made the goal of equality seem closer to reality than in other cultures in which

women have been, and still are, treated as not quite human; as property to be traded, exchanged, and used; and as servants, child-bearers, and sex objects. Courtly love invented the novel idea that love must be a mutual relationship, involving respect as well as passion.

Courtly love has remained part of the cultural tradition of the West since it began in the eleventh century. The theme of romantic love has dominated Western literature for 800 years, from the legend of Tristan and Isolde to Romeo and Juliet, to Love Story, The Graduate, and even Annie Hall. Regardless of how this or that feature of the myth has been changed, passionate love between a man and a woman has preoccupied the Western mind and woven itself in the fabric of daily life. It sets us apart from the other cultures of the world and from the early stages of Western culture. C. S. Lewis (1958) observed that courtly love and the troubadours who celebrated it "effected a change which has left no corner of our ethics, our imagination, or our daily life untouched, and they erected impassible barriers between us as the classical past and the oriental present" (pp. 3–4).

From its origins as an adulterous love game played by the feudal aristocracy, the code of romantic love came to be grafted onto the institution of bourgeois marriage. Later still, with the coming of industrialization and urbanization, the ideology of love spread to the working class. And, in ways that we shall examine in more detail later, the ideal was transformed again by the sexual and cultural revolutions of the twentieth century.

The link between love and marriage came early in England, and has remained ever since. By contrast, continental European literature continued to maintain the courtly tradition that love occurred outside marriage. Writing of the French novel, for ex-

Passion does not always require a romantic setting. [Susan Rosenberg/ Photo Researchers, Inc.]

ample, Denis de Rougemont (1956) observed, "To judge by its literature, adultery would seem to be one of the most characteristic occupations of Western man" (p. 3).

This was not true in England, where the Puritan bourgeoisie sanctified marriage and the family and condemned the adultery and other sexual excesses of the aristocracy. The Puritans, contrary to their reputation, were not against sex; rather they argued that it should be contained in marriage. The Puritans redefined marriage as a partnership based on companionship, trust, fidelity, and premarital chastity. The joining of love and marriage was foreshadowed in such works as Chaucer's "Franklin's Tale" in *The Canterbury Tales* and Spenser's *The Faerie Queene*, but it received its supreme expression in Milton's *Paradise Lost*, one of the few works of world literature that include praise of married love.

The ideology of romantic love, however, did not merge completely with marriage until the eighteenth century and the emergence of the middle class as a major factor in society. In *The Rise of the Novel*, Ian Watt (1957) described how the new social and economic order gave rise to a new literary form, the novel, which placed the search for love and social mobility at the center of the plot, with marriage providing the happy ending. Samuel Richardson's novel *Pamela*, in which a servant girl comes to marry her master, is the first example of this genre. This basic plot has served as the prototype of the love stories that have dominated our popular culture.

Some people have suggested that the romantic love myth functions as a religion in Western culture. It is not necessary to believe literally in a religion to be influenced by it; the lapsed Catholic or the unobservant Jew is still, in deep ways, a variant kind of Catholic or Jew. Ann Swidler (1981) pointed out that the symbols of love in our culture, like religious symbols in more traditional societies, provide models that shape the experience and the course of individual lives.

Although love in real life is not like love in the movies or in literature, the images of love in our culture provide a background, a language, a set of symbols within which people frame the meaning of their own lives. In loving and being loved, people give themselves for brief periods to a more intense level of experience, and achieve a new awareness of self and others. (p. 12)

Is Love Necessary?

The theme of love could not have persisted through so many centuries were it not linked to other basic themes in Western culture and, in turn, to social structure. At the core of the myth is the image of two individuals set apart from all others, obsessed with their own inner feelings and striving to communicate these thoughts and emotions to each other. In short, the love myth includes the themes of individual self-awareness and the need for communion with a unique and freely chosen loved one. As Heer (1962) observed, courtly love began a long tradition of self-discovery that culminated in psychoanalysis.

The individualism that lies at the heart of romantic love has deep roots in the religious, economic, and political life of the West. It is widely recognized that Western culture values individualism to a unique degree and that two of its major historical sources are the rise of capitalism and the spread of Protestantism, particularly Puritanism. Christianity, as noted in an earlier chapter, has always encouraged attention to inner feelings as a form of religious duty to cleanse the mind from evil thoughts. Protestantism emphasized individualism and self-awareness by attributing supreme spiritual importance to the direct relation between an individual and God.

Capitalism is the other major source of individualism in the West. In feudal society, the individual's place was fixed from birth. The rising bourgeoisie overthrew these restrictions in the name of freedom. The new concept of individualism was based on the idea of each person as a free agent—independent of tradition, society, and even other people—with the right to rise or fall through one's own efforts. The right to choose a marriage partner oneself, rather than submit to a marriage arranged by parents, was an important step in the growth of individual freedom in Western Europe (Stone, 1964).

The rise of industrialized mass society increased the practical possibilities of individualism still further. As S. J. Greenfield (1969) has pointed out, there is no rational reason for anyone to marry in the contemporary United States: the division of labor between the sexes is not so extreme that people cannot survive without the services of a mate, and all needs, from food to clothing to sex, can be satisfied in the marketplace. Although it is not necessary for individuals to marry, set up households, and have families, the social system would cease to operate if they did not do so. Therefore the ideology of romantic love performs a vital function by driving people together to form families.

What appears to be necessary for the maintenance of American culture in its present form, then, is a special mechanism that would induce these generally rational, ambitious, and calculating individuals—in the sense of trying to maximize their personal achievement—to do what in the logic of their culture is not in their own personal interest. Somehow they must be induced—we might almost say, in spite of themselves—to behave emotionally and irrationally and to desire and to occupy the positions of husband-father and wife-mother. (p. 360)

This account, although it recognizes the importance of love in American society, overlooks the psychological processes that form a missing link between social structure and the individual's wish to enter into love relationships. The notion that the ideology of love is necessary to make people do what they would not otherwise want to do misses the point: the very technological advances that have made it possible to live as an unattached individual have created a cold, impersonal world that makes us crave intimate relationships. At the same time, these conditions make it hard to find and sustain them.

Paradoxically, individualism seems to foster not only a preoccupation with the self, but also an emphasis on close personal relationships. As Murray Davis (1973) observes, a preoccupation with friendship and love emerged during every period of urbanization in Western culture: in ancient Greece, in the Roman empire, during the Renaissance, and, most recently and extensively, since the eighteenth century. Without the traditional bonds of kinship and community, the urban individual must construct a more consciously chosen social life to replace the world that was lost.

Love and Loneliness

According to John Bowlby (1969), all human beings have an innate terror of solitude inherited from our history as primates. Fears of darkness, of strangers, and of being alone, he argues, are natural responses to what were high-risk situations for primates and early humans, and still are even in the modern world. Throughout life, people need "attachment figures": In each phase of our lives we tend to make strong bonds to one or more special and particular individuals; as long as these bonds remain intact, we feel secure in the world, and when they are broken by separation or death, we become anxious and distressed. Infants may experience separation distress when they are out of sight of the attachment figure; older children and adults can tolerate separation without distress when they know the attachment figure is available.

Other psychological theories have argued that attachment is a learned behavior—

that the child comes to depend on the mother and later on other people because the mother or other caretaker fulfills the child's basic needs for food, warmth, and so on. Whatever theory is ultimately correct, the end result is the same: people tend to need people. Few of us would accept the offer of a life in which all material needs were met, but which had to be spent alone. Although individuals differ in the amount of social contact they need, and some can get by with very little, the experience of extended isolation, even under optimal circumstances, seems always to be stressful. The picture of isolation that emerges from many accounts and studies is

one of a difficult experience that frequently produces fantasy and anxiety-like symptoms. There may be indications of nervousness, of depression, of a general going-to-pieces. . . . People seem to need contact with others to continue functioning in a healthy manner. (Middlebrook, 1974, p. 215)

In most times and places, attachment needs are fulfilled continuously throughout life because people remain rooted to the communities in which they were born. Relationships with parents do not undergo a major change at adolescence or marriage. The necessities of daily life make people dependent on one another, and there may be few or no occasions for being alone, much less lonely.

Many of the conditions of modern life conspire to make loneliness a potential problem for large numbers of people. First, as noted earlier, it is possible to supply all one's material needs without entering into close or committed relationships. Second, individuals in contemporary Western cultures are required to give up their original attachments to their parents. Willingly or not, the adolescent must withdraw emotionally from his or her parents and transfer attachment to peers: a best friend, a girlfriend or boyfriend, or a group of peers. Eventually, attachment feelings merge with sexual strivings, so a person of the opposite sex comes to fulfill both needs.

The conditions of modern life make social relations problematic because the individual must construct his or her own set of intimate and friendly relationships: they are not supplied automatically by economic necessity or the kinship system. As Robert Weiss (1973) observed:

The relinquishment of parents as attachment figures . . . provides the opportunity for there to be a total lack of attachment figures; . . . it becomes possible for there to be no figure in an individual's life whose accessibility would provide the comfort and security associated with attachment. The parents will not serve, and no replacement may have appeared. The adolescent can now experience all the symptoms of separation distress, but without an object. This is *loneliness.* (p. 92)

How frequent is the experience of loneliness? Social theorists, such as Eric Fromm and David Riesman, have argued that loneliness is inescapable in modern society, and Robert Weiss estimates that it is about as frequent as the common cold. Surveys that have asked people if they often feel lonely have come out with positive responses ranging from 10 to 80 percent.

It is not surprising that there is such variation in responses to the question; people in some situations—such as students away from home for the first time, widows, and people who have just moved—are more vulnerable to loneliness. And there are personality differences in susceptibility. Moreover, many people may be unwilling to admit to being lonely. Finally, people who have been driven into relationships out of loneliness would not show up in the typical survey.

Ironically, even when we find someone to love, we may find that love is not enough.

Weiss's research suggests that there are two kinds of loneliness: *emotional* isolation, resulting from the lack of intimate ties with a spouse or lover, and *social* isolation, resulting from a lack of a network of relationships with peers, such as fellow workers, neighbors, relatives, or friends. Without such ties, people may feel lonely and depressed even though they are deeply in love with their spouses. Yet for many people, particularly those in the economically and geographically mobile middle classes, social networks may be harder to find and to sustain than intimate relationships. As Suzanne Gordon (1974) observes, America is a "couple culture": love becomes the only thing of real importance, and people make or break other social bonds with friends, kin, and community in its interests.

Modern mass societies generate loneliness not only because they do not provide automatically for intimate or friendly relationships, but also because of the peculiar kinds of impersonal relationships they provide in abundance. Much of the person's daily life in modern society is spent in narrow roles, such as worker, student, customer, client. People begin to experience themselves in a double way—as anonymous and replaceable players of such roles, and as unique and whole individuals with distinct thoughts and feelings. The discrepancy between the public roles we play and our "real" inner selves creates the need for a private world, a set of relationships in which we can express those aspects of ourselves that must be denied at work and elsewhere.

LOVE IN THE MODERN WORLD

Until very recently much of the literature in marriage and the family was fond of pointing to research data contradicting one or another tenet of the romantic love ideology. Thus, to counter the romantic idea of the one and only love, writers would point to findings showing that people typically fall in love several times before they marry.

Nor does research support the idea that love happens suddenly, one enchanted evening, when two strangers look at one another across a crowded room and their hearts stand still. There is much evidence that falling in love is usually a gradual process, coming after a period of acquaintanceship and repeated encounters. Many people report growing to love someone whom they did not find overwhelmingly attractive in the first place, but with whom they develop deep rapport and enjoyable companionship. Burgess and Wallin (1953) found that more than half the married men and women in their survey said they had no strong physical attraction until at least 2 months after they had met. Contrary to the idea that love is blind, that lovers idealize their beloveds so much that they cannot perceive any faults in them, Burgess and Wallin found that among the 2,000 engaged people they studied, two-thirds of the men and three-quarters of the women were able to mention defects in their loved ones.

Finally, to counter the notion that love overcomes all obstacles and transcends class barriers, sociologists point to well-established findings that the vast majority of marriages take place between men and women in the same class, race, religion, educational level, and even the same level of physical attractiveness.

Such debunkings of love could be found in much of the marriage-and-family literature of the 1930s, 1940s, and 1950s. People married for practical reasons; whether anyone believed in the love myth or not, it had little effect on the choice of a marriage partner, and mates might just as well have been selected by parents or matchmakers. In recent years many people have assumed that the sexual revolution must have killed off whatever remained of romantic love in America.

Such people had been persuaded by Freud's theory that the emotion of love is aim-inhibited sex; that is, they believed that a person experienced love as a result of the blocking of the sex drive. Courtly love seemed to fit this model perfectly, and the conventional norm against premarital sex seemed to ensure that couples would fall in love and marry to fulfill that love. Thus it seemed that the new sexual freedom, which permitted people to go to bed together shortly after meeting one another, would surely prevent the growth of love. And with sex so easily available, most people, it seemed, would certainly prefer instant intimacy with an endless series of new partners to the dullness of monogamous marriage, or even to old-fashioned love affairs.

These reports on the death of love seem to be greatly exaggerated. It is true that marriages in America were rarely based on blind, heedless passion. And it is true that the sexual and cultural revolutions of recent years have revised the rules and meaning of love, sex, and marriage. But for most Americans in the twentieth century, love has been a strongly felt emotion, and intimate relationships continue to occupy a central place in people's lives.

Nor does the sexual revolution seem to have interfered with the capacity to form love relationships. There is little evidence to support the Freudian idea that love can flourish only if the lovers abstain from sex. In fact, recent research evidence suggests the opposite; among unmarried couples, sex can become the basis for the deeping of love relationships. And Morton Hunt (1974) argues that sexual liberation may have had the strongest impact within marriage itself; he found a great increase in the frequency and variety of sexual relations within marriage— a change that seems to be associated with a deepening of the emotional attachment between the spouses.

In the Shadow of Love and Marriage: Being Single

Another recent change that many see as a sign that people are avoiding love relationships is the growth of the single life-style. Recent statistics reveal a striking increase in the number of unattached individuals and an increasing tendency for the unattached to live apart from families.

According to the U. S. Census Bureau (U. S. Department of Commerce, Bureau of the Census, 1981), single-person households represented 23 percent of all households in 1980. Between 1970 and 1980 the number had grown from 10.9 million to 17.8 million. Most of the increase has been among people under 35 and the divorced. In 1980, three times as many people under 35 lived alone as in 1970. The number of divorced people who lived alone grew from 1.5 million to 3.4 million during the same decade. Although the increase in the number of people living alone was most dramatic among younger age groups, a majority of the population living alone—65 percent—was over 45.

What are the implications of the growth of singleness for love and marriage? Does the new life-style mean that large numbers of people are giving up the ideal of romantic love? Or are they merely giving up the idea of marriage? Or are they giving up neither?

There are several images of what it is like to be single in America today. One image is that of the swinging single as idealized by *Playboy* and *Cosmopolitan*; life is a continuous round of exciting sex partners, discotheque dancing, gourmet dining, ski weekends, and vacations to exotic places. Another image is suggested by television's Mary Tyler Moore: the single person as a self-contained, independent individual, finding satisfaction and contentment in work and a circle of good friends. Finally, there is an image derived from the stereotype of the single person as a lonely, rejected loser at the game of love, the single life as a desperate search for love and escape from singleness.

There probably is some truth in all these images. People categorized as single include those in very different social and psychological situations: young unmarrieds, the divorced, the widowed, the elderly, and the unmarried young person. Included are people committed to remaining single as well as those eager to marry at the first opportunity, and also people who, though officially single, are involved in love relationships of varying degrees of commitment. Because there has been very little research on singlehood— apart from studies of the widowed and the divorced—it is difficult to state with any certainty what the nature of the single experience is for different kinds of people. The rise of the singles life-style, however, can be attributed to the increase in the age of first marriage, the increase in the divorce rate, and the tendency of the divorced to postpone remarriage longer than divorced people in the past. The growth of singles-only housing complexes and recreational facilities has made singles a visible part of the population.

Although there is an emerging ideology of singleness, relatively few single people seem to be committed to singleness as a permanent way of life. A 1974 survey of young Americans aged 14–25 found that only 17 percent of women thought the single life was the most desirable life-style, and only 5 percent expected to be single in 5 years. The corresponding figures for young men were 24 percent and 9 percent (Institute of Life Insurance, 1974).

Other evidence for a lack of commitment to singlehood may be found in the appeals offered by the various facilities and establishments catering to singles. Advertisements for such activities often suggest that singleness is a lonely state and that the advertised activity can lead to love or marriage.

Thus singleness in America appears to be an ambivalent and contradictory status. On the one hand, the single life offers extraordinary appeal in an individualistic society. Single people can spend their money as they like and do what they please when they please. They can live in cities or suburbs, often in housing complexes designed to provide them with recreational facilities and social activities. They can throw themselves into their work without having to worry about neglecting the family, or they can reduce their work commitments to a minimum without worrying about mortgage payments on the house or savings for the children's braces and college educations. Single people can enjoy the sexual freedom made possible by the pill and the new permissive morality. Or they can involve themselves in romantic attachments to be enjoyed as long as they last, without the commitment to permanence or marriage.

Yet the loneliness-making conditions of American society that previously drove people into early marriages have not vanished; rather than having found a way to avoid them, single people seem to be in a constant struggle against them. As Peter Stein (1977) observes in a study of singles: "The greatest need single people feel is for substitute networks of human relationships that provide the basic satisfactions of intimacy, sharing, and continuity" (p. 496).

It is often hard to find such substitute networks. Single people often look back nostalgically to high school, college, or graduate school days as a time of easy friendship, when an institution brought large numbers of young people together and provided a setting for relationships. The cities to which singles flock usually don't encourage easy sociability, and most work settings seem to provide fewer candidates for friendship and love than did the college campus.

Single people often turn to other single people for friends. They tend to feel uncomfortable around married or living-together friends, and the feelings tend to be reciprocated. Single friendships, however, are often undermined by the search for love and romance. It has been traditional for women to give priority to male relationships—that is, to drop a date with a female friend if a man invites her out. It is sometimes difficult even for liberated women to overcome this habit.

In fact, looking at the various studies of the single life-style, it oftens seems as if single people are caught between two standards of behavior—the stereotypes of previous decades and the new images of swinging singleness. Thus single people sometimes find themselves feeling as if they are missing something by not being part of a couple and that feeling lonely or not having a date on Saturday night means one is a misfit and a failure.

This attitude is reinforced by the still-prevailing assumption that marriage is the only desirable and natural state. Unmarried people are continually pushed toward marriage by parents, relations, co-workers, and married friends. One of the single women in Stein's study described the meaning of being single in this way:

There is a whole part of me that sees as freedom the possibilities of meeting different people and having different kinds of relationships, which is the exciting part. And then, there is the part of me that looks at where I'm not doing what I'm supposed to be doing, where I'll ultimately end up lonely, where something is the matter with me because I'm not in love with somebody, whatever that means. (p. 528)

On the other hand, single people may feel inadequate because they are not living up to the image of the swinging single. Writer Suzanne Gordon (1974) observes that there seems to be a new expectation that if you don't have somebody to love, then you should at least have somebody to have sex with. If you don't, then "something's really wrong with you." After interviewing many single people, however, she concluded it's a myth that this is an age of easy sex. The myth suggests that you don't have to be married or in love or involved with one person to have sex.

All you have to do is have the right attitude and step outside your door and there it is—sex. But according to hundreds of people I have interviewed, "easy sex" is painfully at odds with reality. As one young man in Berkeley succinctly put it, "Everyone I know is horny." (p. 83)

Morton Hunt's (1974) survey presents more systematic information about sex and the single person. Although he did not deal with the issue of how people perceive the availability of sex, he found relatively few swinging singles and little evidence that a "recreational" as opposed to a "romantic" view of sex is becoming a widespread philosophy among singles. Although there has been a dramatic increase in premarital sex and swinging singles do exist—more among older divorced people than young unmarrieds—there has not been a violent overthrow of the traditional link between love and sex. Hunt concluded:

The new sexual fredom operates largely within the framework of our long-held cherished cultural values of intimacy and love. Even while it asserts its freedom from marriage, it is an apprenticeship for marriage, and is considered successful by its participants when it grows, deepens, and leads to ever-stronger commitment, and unsuccessful and a wasted effort when it does not. (p. 154)

Contemporary Love: Research Findings

Despite the sweeping changes in sexual morality and life-styles in recent years, most people have not abandoned their belief in some form of love as an important value. We can get some insights into the contemporary meaning of love from social-psychological studies of love and love relationships. Zick Rubin (1973) has constructed a paper-and-pencil love scale to assess the kinds of feelings that constitute love relationships. Obviously, a paper-and-pencil scale cannot measure real feelings, but simply what people say their feelings are. But there is some behavioral evidence that supports the scale's validity. For example, couples with above-average scores on the love scale tended to spend a great deal of time gazing into each other's eyes, an activity that both folk wisdom and social scientists regard as one of the supreme expressions of intimate communication between two individuals.

Rubin's research revealed that couple relations seemed to have several components. His love scale is divided into two separate scales, a love scale and a like scale. The love scale contains three components: intimacy (I feel I can confide in _____ about virtually everything); attachment (It would be hard for me to get along without _____); and caring (If _____ were feeling bad, it would be my first duty to cheer him/her up). The liking scale dealt with admiration and respect for the other person on grounds of competence, good judgment, intelligence, the high regard of other people, and also the feeling of being similar to the self. The pattern of correlations within and between the

items on each scale supported the idea that loving and liking are different phenomena. Although the love scale itself does not ask couples if they are in love, when Rubin asked them this question, two-thirds of the men and women in his sample of 182 dating couples indicated that they were. Further, the correlation between the love scale and saying one was in love was reasonably high.

Rubin's data show that different kinds of love can propel people into more intense relationships and marriage. Although the people who scored high on the love scale thought themselves more likely to marry than those who scored high on the liking scale, when the actual progress of relationships was followed over time, liking was almost as good a predictor of marriage as love.

Along with the lovers for whom respect and admiration were sufficient grounds for marriage, Rubin found a large number of people who seemed to subscribe to the full-blown ideology of romantic love. These

people obtained high scores on a romanticism scale by agreeing with such items as "To be truly in love is to love forever" and "A person should marry whomever he or she loves regardless of social position," and disagreeing with such statements as "Most of us could sincerely love any one of several people equally well" and "Economic security should be carefully considered before selecting a marriage partner."

Since Rubin's work on liking and loving, other social psychologists have been exploring the terrain. For example, Robert Sternberg and his colleagues (Sternberg, 1986) asked subjects to describe their relationships to lovers, parents, siblings, and friends, using Rubin's loving and liking scales and other measures of interpersonal relationships.

Factor and cluster analyses of the data revealed three components of close relationships. The first is an intimacy component, encompassing feelings of closeness, mutual understanding, and social support; Sternberg also identified a passion component and a commitment component reflecting the decision to maintain the relationship. He found that the intimacy component forms the common core in all close relationships, with the passion and commitment components experienced more selectively. Thus, romantic relationships have a passion component as well as the core intimacy component. What Sternberg (1985) calls "consummate love" results from the combination of all three components; it represents the ideal many people strive for. "Empty love" is a relationship high in commitment but lacking intimacy and passion. "Fatuous love" is a relationship based on passion and commitment but no intimacy, such as that of a couple who meet one day and get married a few weeks later. Each of the components has a different course over time: Passion is high at the start but tends to decline over time; intimacy and commitment develop more slowly and are maintained longer.

Other recent research parallels that of Sternberg and his colleagues. For example, Davis (1985), using questionnaire data, also found that there is a common emotional core in friendship and love consisting of enjoyment, acceptance, mutual assistance, and so on, but that love relationships combine friendship with passion and a deeper level of caring. In addition, Davis found that love relationships had a greater potential for stress, ambivalence, and conflict.

The romantic male One surprising but persistent finding in love research is that, contrary to the stereotype of women as starry-eyed romantics, men turn out to be more romantic than women. Thus, Zick Rubin (1973) found that men scored significantly higher than women on the romanticism scale. He also found that although men seemed to fall in love more quickly and easily than women, women seemed to fall

out of love more quickly and easily, at least in premarital relationships. Also, women were more likely to be the ones to end relationships, to disengage themselves emotionally, to do what Arlie Hochschild (1975) calls "feeling work." Men tended to experience more grief and despair after a breakup than women.

In an earlier study, Kephart (1967) had found a similar sex difference. He asked college men and women the following question: "If a man or woman had all the other qualities you desired, would you marry the person if you were not in love with him or her?" Although 65 percent of the men said no, only 24 percent of the women said they definitely would not marry such a person. Two-thirds of the women and one-third of the men were undecided. One woman remarked, "It's rather hard to give a yes or no answer to this question. If a man had all the other qualities I desired and I was not in love with him—well, I think I could talk myself into falling in love" (p. 473).

In short, while men can be romantic, women have a more practical, realistic approach to love and take a more managerial attitude toward their own feelings. The difference is understandable in terms of sex-role inequality, particularly the contrasting social and economic positions of sexes. Women are more economically dependent on marriage than men are. As sociologist Willard Waller (1938) once observed: "A man, when he marries, chooses a companion and perhaps a helpmate, but a woman chooses a companion and at the same time a standard of living." Thus women stand to lose more than men by falling in love with the wrong person.

Also, as Hochschild (1975) pointed out, there has been a patriarchal etiquette governing the courtship process; if a man is attracted to a woman, he has the right to initiate a relationship with her, to call her for a date, to pursue her, and to propose to her. Women have traditionally engaged in flirting and other strategies to get men to court them. But when a woman cannot directly pursue a relationship with a man who attracts her, and when she may be courted by men she might not have chosen in the first place but who have other desirable qualities, she is likely to try to manage and control her feelings. When women and men approach economic equality, these differences are likely to vanish.

COMING IN OUT OF THE COLD: THE DEVELOPMENT OF LOVE RELATIONSHIPS

In the past the development of a relationship not only was something to be worked out between the individuals, but it also followed socially defined steps. Thus marriage used to be the endpoint of a series of distinct stages, each involving a greater degree of commitment—dating, keeping company, going steady, a private agreement to be married, a public announcement of the engagement, and finally marriage, presumably for life. A different level of sexual intimacy was permitted at each stage of the relationship.

In recent years this whole system has collapsed. One by one, the various stages began to sound old-fashioned; *courtship* and *keeping company* were obsolete terms by the 1950s; in the 1970s both *dating* and *engagement* were no longer appropriate to describe the development of relations between the sexes. The whole sequence of ever-increasing commitments have given way to a series of "involvements" that may or may not evolve into marriage.

Noting that marriage no longer implies monogamy and permanence, and that couple relationships outside marriage no longer exclude sex and a sense of commitment, Farber (1964) has suggested that the American system of mate selection and marriage is best described as one based on the "permanent availability" of all adults as potential marriage partners, whether they are currently married or not. As McCall (1966) has pointed out, there is a paradox in the new pattern of couple relationships. Marriage has become less exclusive and permanent, but in what used to be courtship there is an emphasis on deep personal intimacy or some kind of commitment. Neither type of involvement, however, is expected to last if it turns out to be dissatisfying. Couple relationships are both more intensely personal and less stable and enduring. The notion of the "one and only love" has faded.

Although a love "involvement" no longer follows set, socially defined stages, it does follow a developmental course. It seems obvious that because in modern societies most lovers start out as strangers, their relationships must proceed through at least three different stages: First, the couple must have the opportunity to meet and be attracted to one another. Second, they must explore one another's interests and attitudes to see if they are compatible and whether they enjoy one another's company. Third, they develop a set of expectations and commitments about the relationship, or decide whether there is to be a relationship at all. Later, if the relationship is to be a long-term one, it will enter a more routinized and committed phase.

There have been several attempts to conceptualize this process. Murstein (1971) has developed a theory of marital choice based on three stages: (1) a *stimulus stage* in which people are attracted to one another on the basis of physical appearance and other obvious traits; (2) a *value stage* in which the couple discovers whether they are compatible; and (3) a *role stage* in which they consider how they will fit together as long-term partners.

Alternatively, Reiss (1960) has proposed a "wheel theory" of relationship development. Different interpersonal processes form four spokes of a wheel: rapport, self-revelation, mutual dependency, and need fulfillment. The four spokes work together so that as the relationship moves in a positive direction, a sense of rapport will lead the couple to confide in one another, which will lead to mutual dependency and thus to the fulfillment of interpersonal needs. The wheel can also run backward; a loss of rapport will make people reluctant to confide in one another, and so on.

Although these explanations seem to be reasonably accurate descriptions of many, if not most, relationships, they seem to portray those based on liking and companionate love more than those based on passionate love. As Dorothy Tennov (1979) and others have argued, passionate love may be very different from liking someone, even liking him or her a great deal.

Liking is a very sensible emotion. As in the models just described, we tend to like people who are similar to us in interest and values, who offer us affection, and who reward our acts of self-revelation with approval and correspondingly intimate disclosures. We reject those who reject us. Although passionate love sometimes operates in this reasonable way, often it does not. As Elaine Walster (1971) observed:

Individuals do *not* always feel passionate about the person who provides the most rewards with the greatest consistency. Passion sometimes develops under conditions that would be more likely to provoke aggression and hatred than love. (p. 87)

It would be reasonable, for example, to reject lovers who reject us or give us cause to be jealous, but experiences such as these often make people love even more passionately.

Walster presents an array of anecdotal and experimental evidence suggesting that negative emotions such as fear, anger, and frustration can enhance passionate love.

The Complexities of Love: Mixed Emotions

Although the connection between love and negative emotion is clearest in excited states, such as anger, fear, and jealousy, there is reason to believe that an undercurrent of negative feelings accompanies love in all stages of its growth, from casual acquaintance to deep commitment. Theories suggesting that the development of a love relationship is based on the accumulation of rewards and satisfactions underestimate the complexities of human emotions. Freud theorized that all important human relationships are inherently ambivalent, and the insight that love and hate are closely related has been portrayed in literature throughout history.

Several other theorists have elaborated this view. As we saw earlier, some writers have suggested that rather than a direct increase in positive feelings, the growth of love is marked by an oscillation between positive and negative feelings, or a series of crises and resolutions. Theodore Reik (1944) suggested that the prospect of love is actually frightening: "The person whom love approaches does not welcome it as a gift, but tries to chase it away as an intruder. . . . It is as if the ego were afraid of a danger, of a threatening loss" (p. 85).

What is this mysterious fear: What have we got to lose in loving? The answer seems to be "several things." We dread loneliness, but we also fear being trapped in relationships in which we are more committed than our feelings justify. We want love, but seeking it makes us run the risk of humiliation and rejection. Involvement with one person usually means giving up the opportunity to be involved with others. More fundamentally, perhaps, we fear the growing dependency that falling in love brings with it.

Several theorists have believed that an "anxiety of dependency" (Klein & Riviere, 1964) is an inevitable component of love. As Berscheid and Fei (1977) observed, to become dependent on someone is to

give a portion of ourselves away as hostage. . . . As our dependency grows, we relinquish more and more control over our fate. . . . Love involves a loss of freedom and independence. . . . As our happiness becomes more and more vested in another, our awareness—and dread—of the conditions and circumstances which may take the loved person away from us, and threaten our happiness, may grow also. (p. 104)

Getting Together

For many people the first step in a relationship—meeting and attracting other people—is the most painful. At this stage a person's fantasies of love and his or her sense of self-worth confront the often brutal realities of the love market. The relationship market does not fit the model of a just world in which rewards follow inner virtue. Although the "rating-and-dating" game may not be as snobbish and rigid as it was found to be in the studies of college social life in the 1930s and 1940s, social hierarchies have not disappeared. Writing of the rating-and-dating complex that prevailed in the 1930s, Waller (1938) noted that certain men and women were at the top of the social hierarchy. These Class A men and women tended to date each other. The men's prestige depended on belonging to the right fraternities, having a large supply of spending money, and being smooth in manners and appearance. Women students gained their Class A status by dating Class A men. The class system was

recognized by students, creating problems of adjustment for those below the Class A category. Thus some Class B individuals could challenge the system by dating Class A women. Class D men developed a series of rationalizations putting down the women above them in the campus hierarchy, who usually rejected them. Class D women tried to rationalize going out with Class D men, but not very successfully, so that they often felt uneasy.

Although fraternities and smooth manners may no longer serve as criteria of prestige on today's campus, people still tend to rank one another in desirability. Recent social-psychological research suggests that physical attractiveness is still extremely important in forming impressions of other people. Further, there is little tendency for people to be attracted to partners whose desirability matches their own; everyone seems to prefer the most attractive date possible.

The collision between the matching principle—seeking out people like oneself—and the desirability principle produces what might be called the "Groucho Marx effect": Groucho once observed that he didn't want to belong to any club that would have him as a member. Those at the lower reaches of the rating-and-dating hierarchy are often faced with the choice between having no relationships or having one with a person less attractive than one would ideally like. Thus Burgess and associates (1953) observed that dating often presented severe problems to those outside the minority of the very attractive. They quoted a typical college student:

One of the greatest troubles is that men here, as everywhere, I guess, are easily overwhelmed by physical beauty. Campus glamor queens have countless beaux flocking around them, whereas many companiable, sympathetic girls . . . go without dates and male companionship. . . . I will never understand why so many men (even, or maybe particularly, those who are the least attractive themselves) seem to think they may degrade themselves by dating or even dancing with a girl who does not measure up to their beauty standards. (pp. 163–164)

The singles bar provides the best and clearest example of the contemporary rating-and-dating complex. Most people seem to find going to these places an alienating experience. People are under pressure to give the most favorable impression of themselves as they can, and to assess very quickly the social desirability of possible partners. Surface characteristics count for a great deal—how pretty or handsome one is, how much money and status one has, what kind of car one drives, and what neighborhood one lives in.

A man who had been a bartender at a singles bar told a reporter that the waiters think of the place as a "zoo."

I used to stand around the bar and watch people, and the sense of values there is so incredible I used to just stand in awe, because I didn't believe people were actually like that. You'll hear a regular income rap, "Where did you go on your last vacation, what kind of car do you drive?" . . . Nobody actually cares who someone is, but what they have and where they come from. (Gordon, 1974, p. 226)

The chance of rejection is great for both men and women, and people are under pressure to make snap decisions in the first minutes of a conversation as to whether to end the encounter or indicate an interest in seeing the person again.

A demonstration of the importance of a good appearance was provided in a field study by Elaine Walster and her associates (1966). They recruited 752 college freshmen to attend a "computer dance." Although the students were led to believe that they had been matched by a computer on the basis of similar interests, actually couples had been paired randomly. The study was intended to test the matching principle—the hypothesis was that people would like, and prefer to see again, people who were close to themselves in social desirability. Each student was assessed in terms of intelligence, intellectual achievement, personality, and appearance. During an intermission, the students were asked how they liked their dates. Although the researchers expected that intelligence and personality would have a lot to do with how well a person was liked, they discovered that for both men and women, the physical attractiveness of the other person was the most important determinant of how much students liked their dates.

This correlation between good looks and being liked contrasted strikingly with what college students say they are looking for on dates. Both men and women mention intelligence, friendliness, and sincerity as more important than appearance. In real-life situations, however, these traits seem not to be the ones people are looking for.

Although it might be argued that attractiveness would have played a lesser role if the students had had time to get to know one another better, or that physical attractiveness becomes less important as individuals get to be older than the 18-year-olds interviewed in the study, the evidence suggests otherwise. Numerous studies have shown that people of all ages and sexes are inclined to believe that physically attractive men, women, and even children possess more desirable personality traits as well. Although most people would deny it, they seem to act on the assumption that "what is beautiful is good" (Patzer, 1985).

Eventually, however, most people find some way of reconciling their idealized images with reality. The vast majority of average people who do not look like models or movie stars, and even the majority of unattractive people, also meet, fall in love, and marry. There is strong evidence that people choose romantic partners who are comparable to themselves in looks and other desirable traits. Yet as Elaine Walster (1973) pointed out, people often do not submit to reality gladly; they may persist in trying to attract partners more "desirable" than themselves. "Thus, romantic choices seem to be a delicate compromise between one's desire to capture an ideal partner and one's realization that one must eventually settle for what [one] deserves" (p. 6).

The Dilemmas of Commitment

Attractiveness may bring people together for a first encounter, but it cannot sustain a relationship in the absence of common interests and values. Once they have found each other and have entered into a continuing relationship, a couple is likely to encounter a new set of difficulties. The classical love stories of Western culture typically end with death or the decision to marry. It's hard to imagine Romeo and Juliet growing old together. We lack an imagery that portrays enduring relationships in a romantic way.

The arbiters of courtly love believed that love was incompatible with marriage. In 1174, Marie, Countess of Champagne, wrote that "lovers give each other everything freely, under no compulsion of necessity, but married people are in duty bound to give in to each other's desires and deny themselves to each other in nothing" (Hunt, 1959, pp. 43–44). Andreas Capellanus (1968), who wrote the major treatise on love, observed that too many opportunities to see the beloved and too much chance to talk to one another would also decrease love.

The traditional criticism of romantic love made by sociologists and marriage counselors also assumes the incompatibility of passion and marriage, of feeling and commit-

ment. They argue that by generating impossible expectations, the myth of romantic love creates untold misery, dooming most marriages to disillusion and frustration and thus contributing to divorce. Although this view underestimates the normal human capacity to reconcile wishes with reality and to relinquish impossible dreams, it is true that there is a contradiction in the idea of a freely chosen commitment to a love relationship. Once the decision has been made, there is no more freedom of choice. Before the point of choice, feelings guide action; after the choice is made, feelings may lag behind the commitment to love.

A tension between emotion and commitment is implicit in any ongoing couple relationship—most obvious in legal marriage but not eliminated in a "living-together" couple. As Jay Haley (1963) observed:

When a man and a woman decide their association should be solemnized by a marriage ceremony, they pose themselves a problem which will continue through the marriage: Now that they are married, are they staying together because they wish to or because they must? (p. 122)

In recent years, the tension between commitment and individual feeling has taken a new form. Now that divorce is so easy and common, people have to justify staying together. A study by Robert Bellah and his associates (Bellah, Madsen, Sullivan, Swidler, & Tipton, 1985) found that many Americans have come to adopt a "therapeutic language" to describe their relationships—they talk about "openness," "self-development," and "change." They accept a therapeutic ideal of love in which the partners offer each other empathy and psychological understanding. This leads to a paradox, however. They want committed, enduring relationships, but they have difficulty with the idea that commitment implies obligation and possibly sacrifice. They cannot find a language to justify their wish for a relationship based on something other than their own wishes. "They long for the unquestioning commitment their parents seemed to have, yet they are repelled by what they take to be the lack of communication, the repression of difficulties, and, indeed, the resigned fatalism such commitment seems to imply. These respondents both envy their parents and vow never to be like them" (p. 103).

The Green-Eyed Monster

Insecurity often takes the form of jealousy. Until very recently, social scientists gave little research attention to the subject of love, and still less to jealousy. Now, however, as the study of love and attraction has become an important area of social psychology, there is beginning to be serious interest in love's frequent companion, jealousy.

Before the most recent sexual revolution, many people thought of jealousy as a normal part of love and marriage. Other people argued that jealousy was something rather easily controlled if recognized as bad, rather than as the expression of a just moral indignation. Albert Memmi (1968) observed that "great minds of left and right agree that jealousy is an outmoded emotion" (p. 148). For many people, however, it just isn't as easy as that. It is difficult to imagine a firmer intellectual commitment to the total liberty of each partner than that of Simone de Beauvoir and Jean-Paul Sartre, two of the leading French intellectuals of the past 3 decades. Yet, according to Beauvoir's own writing, she suffered during his liaisons with others.

I often wondered if he did not care for M more than for me. . . . According to what he told me, M shared completely in his reactions, his emo-

tions, his desires. . . . Was this perhaps the sign of a profound harmony between them—a harmony at the very well-spring of life, present in the rhythm of its ebb and flow—that Sartre did not sense with me, and which was more precious to him than our understanding? (Cited in Memmi, 1968, p. 147)

There are other instances of people without commitments to conventional morality who still suffer pangs of jealousy when their partners enter into liaisons with others. A fictional example is the revolutionary hero in Malraux's *Man's Fate,* who on the eve of the Shanghai uprising is devastated to learn from his wife of her fleeting affair with a colleague of hers. Jan Myrdal, the son of the famous Swedish sociologist and radical, writes in his autobiography of a fateful quarrel with the young woman he had been living with. He finds a letter in her coat pocket from a lover. He himself is also having an affair with someone else, but this does not prevent him from being overwhelmed by jealousy.

I read the letter. I find it strange that such a letter—I myself have also written them—has such a totally different effect when you yourself are neither sender nor receiver but only the third party. It would be sane and reasonable to put it back again in its envelope and stick the envelope back in the pocket. Reasonable and calm. . . . But I don't do so. I know that I won't do it. Anyway, everything is unavoidable. . . . I will stage a scene of jealousy. The consciousness of this disgusts me. (1968, p. 159)

The statements by Beauvoir and Myrdal correspond to some recent findings about sex differences in response to jealousy. Studies by Gregory White (1977) suggest that women are more likely to feel depressed if their partner has an affair with someone else, while men are more likely to feel angry and aggressive. These results seem due not to tem-

The first stage of a relationship has been called the "stimulus" stage. All that people know about each other is what they can see. [Alan Carey/The Image Works]

peramental differences between the sexes but rather to the imbalance of power between men and women. Generally, the partner with fewer alternatives outside the relationship is more likely to experience jealousy, even when no cause exists. Usually, but not always, the man holds the powerful position in a romantic relationship or a marriage because he is likely to have more economic resources and can more easily go out and find another partner. Thus the woman may respond to jealousy with feelings of loss and powerlessness, while the man may be responding to a sudden threat to his power position within the relationship.

A peculiarity about the psychology of jealousy and betrayal comes through clearly in the Myrdal passage cited. There is often a lack of parity in the perception of each member of a couple about the relations of each with another party. That is, consider any couple A and B (these could also be close friends of the same sex): A may feel that he or she can enter into a relationship with any third party X without taking anything away from the relationship with B; A may well even feel that he or she can love X without reducing the love for B. The relationship between A and X looks very different from B's point of view, however. No matter how uninvolved this relationship may be, it is likely to be magnified in B's perspective. And the same is true for a relationship between B and another person from A's viewpoint.

Carl Rogers (1972) presents a clinical case study showing these mechanisms in action. He describes how a sexually liberated couple returned to monogamy as a way of resolving conflicts over jealousy and openness. Both partners had love affairs with others, and each was willing to accept the other's outside relationships. But it turned out that this willingness was more intellectual than emotional.

Eric experiences a full measure of primitive jealousy when he knows she is having sexual relationships with another man. And Denise, though ashamed of her feeling, is hurt when he is sexually involved with another woman, a hurt she feels even though she has been similarly involved with other men. . . .

So they have come to a somewhat peculiar accommodation. If either feels such attraction to another person that he/she wants it to come to a climax in a sexual relationship, so be it. But they will keep these matters private from each other, simply because openness brings too much pain and hurt. But since they are accustomed to an astonishing degree of complete openness with each other, such deceit does not come easily and the result is to make them monogamous. (pp. 195–196)

Anthropologists have had more to say about sexual jealousy than the psychologists. William Stephens (1963) observes that though there seems to be great variation in the jealousy potential of different societies and social arrangements, in no society is jealousy absent or incomprehensible. The peoples with the least amount of jealousy live in polyandrous societies—those very rare cultures in which women can have several husbands at the same time. Usually the cohusbands are brothers or other relatives. Yet even in these societies, some husbands experience jealousy and some do not.

One reason for the relative absence of extreme jealousy in polyandrous groups, according to Stephens, is the fact that husbands are given some say in whether the wife will take a cohusband, and, further, there is usually an economic benefit in bringing another man into the household. Although men's feelings in polyandrous societies are spared, women's feelings in polygynous societies are not. In most cases in which men can take several wives, at least some of the wives suffer intensely from jealousy, and many polygynous families are strife-torn. Again, there is a great deal of individual variation.

Although the cross-cultural literature does not show monogamy to be a common human disposition, in only a few societies is adultery a permitted and expected form of behavior. Perhaps the most extreme example of institutionalized adultery occurs among the Lesu, a Pacific people. A woman's lover gives her presents—tsera—that are to be passed along to her husband. Yet even in this culture, jealousy is still a problem. Another anthropologist reports that among the Kaingang, "people are sexually promiscuous; yet they still wish—rather pathetically—for marital fidelity" (Jules Henry, cited in Stephens, 1963, p. 253).

The societies with the most extreme expression of jealousy are those Latin cultures in which the ideals of machismo prevail. In Tepoztlan, Mexico, for example, husbands try to prove their virility by seducing other men's wives, but worry obsessively about other men seducing theirs. And in the United States there has been something called "the unwritten law"; if an irate spouse, especially a husband, were to shoot his wife's lover, a jury would be likely to let him off.

There are reports in the literature of couples who are able to maintain a close relationship with each other and tolerate affairs on the part of each other. Cuber and Harroff (1965), for example, wrote that some very close couples were also adulterous:

To some of them, sexual aggrandizement is a way of life. Frequently the infidelity is condoned by the partner and in some instances even provides an indirect (through empathy) kind of gratification. The act of infidelity in such cases is not construed as disloyalty or as a threat to continuity, but rather as a basic human right which the loved one ought to be permitted to have—and which the other perhaps wants also for himself. (p. 63)

Another context in which jealousy may be controlled is in "swinging" groups, or mate-swappers. These couples try to control their jealousy, however, by submitting their behavior to strict rules—for example, not engaging in certain sexual practices with others, not meeting sex partners outside the group setting, and so on. In effect, each spouse has veto power over the sexual behavior of the other.

The first studies of swingers in the early 1970s suggested that this life-style did not harm marriage, and perhaps actually improved marital satisfaction. Later research revealed that many people dropped out of swinging, and that many were troubled by jealousy, guilt, and fear of the neighbors finding out (Macklin, 1980). Some people are able to live comfortably with this life-style, others are not (Gilmartin, 1977).

During the 1970s the idea of sexually open marriage—a life-style in which a couple mutually decided to permit the partners to have open relationships with others—gained wide popularity. Research revealed that these couples also had considerable difficulty with jealousy (Knapp & Whitehurst, 1977). Many people began to have second thoughts about this life-style, including Nena O'Neill, one of the authors of *Open Marriage* (1972). In 1977 she wrote a new book entitled *The Marriage Premise*, emphasizing the importance of the marriage bond and arguing against the individualistic values that she had promoted in the first book.

Explaining Jealousy

Why should jealousy be such a deeply rooted—and hard to control—emotion? One obvious reason is that it is realistic to be jealous when a lover or spouse has an intimate relationship with someone else; people who try another partner are more likely to fall in love with the new person than those who do not get involved with third parties. But jealousy does not always seem to be based on realistic considerations. Jealousy can exist even when a person believes the partner's involvement does not involve a threat to the relationship. Nor are people jealous only of potential romantic competitors; one social-psychological experiment found that people were likely to be jealous when a same-sexed friend became interested in a third person. And as writer Judith Viorst (1977) put it, women can be jealous of their husband's families, business partners, psychiatrists, and bowling teams.

Several psychological and sociological explanations of jealousy have been advanced. The psychological explanation would trace jealousy back to infancy and the nearly universal fact that infants are nurtured by, and form a primary attachment to, one person. An intimate attachment to someone later in life may bring back some of the earlier feelings—the sense of dependency and the wish to be the exclusive recipient of the loved one's love. Thus jealousy in adult life might be the equivalent of sibling rivalry in childhood. There is some recognition of this possibility in the often-heard advice to parents about what to say when a new baby is brought home. The parent is warned not to tell the older child: "We love you so much we decided to have another baby." How would the parent feel if his or her spouse came home and said: "I love you so much I decided to have another one just like you"?

One sociological explanation of jealousy is based not on individual emotions but on the structural properties of the two-person group. Georg Simmel (1950) pointed out that the dyad differs from groups of all other sizes from three on up in a fundamental way. In groups larger than two a sense of groupness exists apart from the individual members. Even in a triad, for example, one person can leave and there is still the sense of a group carried on by the other two people. But in a dyad there is no group independent of the two people. If one person leaves or dies, that is the end of the relationship. Thus, argued Simmel, the peculiar properties of the dyad make it the most intimate of groups, and hence the most vulnerable to jealousy. The addition of a third party to a two-person group results in a very different social structure and changes the relationship between the original two. Where there was a relationship only between person A and person B, now there are three dyads: A and B, B and C, and A and C. This complication results in a certain instability:

No matter how close a triad may be, there is always the occasion on which two of the three members regard the third as an intruder. . . . It may also be noted how extraordinarily difficult and rare it is for three people to attain a really uniform mood—when visiting a museum, for instance, or looking at a landscape—and how much more easily such a mood emerges between two. (pp. 135–136)

Sasha Weitman (1973) proposed a different sociological explanation of jealousy. According to this argument, sexual jealousy is just a specific instance of a general human tendency to feel excluded when witnessing other people engaged in acts of intimacy or friendship. Weitman argued that all acts of "social inclusion"—that is intimacy, love, and friendship, as well as membership in clubs or religious groups—are at the same time acts of exclusion as well. Thus if a person invites friends A, B, and C for dinner, he or she is thereby excluding D and E. If a person confides in one friend, he or she is excluding others. Weitman contended that witnesses to acts of social inclusion are likely to feel as if they had been subjected to aggression. Or as Judith Viorst (1977) put it: "The everyday kind of jealousy has less to do with a fear of overt sexual betrayal than it does with a fear of intimacy that excludes us." (p. 21)

Love and Conflict

Paradoxically, as we have seen earlier, intimate relationships are likely to experience more conflict than less intimate ones. Around the turn of the century, the leading social theorists, such as Simmel and Freud, recognized the ambivalence inherent in close relationships. Families and other close-knit groups deal with each other in many areas of life, so there are more occasions for conflict to arise. Also, intimate relationships involve deeper layers of the personality—the more private and vulnerable parts of the self—so disagreements are likely to arouse more passion.

The self-disclosure that sets close relationships apart from more casual ones makes it possible for intimates to hurt one another more deeply than other people. One of the major reasons people need intimate relationships is to share their innermost thoughts. Yet the secrets revealed in moments of closeness can become weapons during an argument; a person who confides a childhood unhappiness might be told in the heat of a fight: "Your mother was right not to love you—you are unlovable"; or "your father was right—you are incompetent."

Several studies have shown that people are likely to make the most intimate disclosures not to long-term intimates, but to strangers they don't expect to meet again—the "strangers on a train" phenomenon. There is also evidence of a curvilinear relationship between self-disclosure and satisfaction with relationships (Cozby, 1973). Up to a certain point, that is, the more openness and self-revelation between two people, the more content they are with the relationship. After that point, however, increased openness may lead to discontent; people may find out more than they want to know about one another.

Lovers betray one another in several ways—not only by using knowledge of weakness and soft spots in arguments, or revealing them to others, but by reducing their opinion of the other person after learning of his or her failings. Thus lovers become emotional hostages of one another. The current popular idea that intimacy brings only benefits and no cost is a myth. People can be hurt emotionally and even physically when intimate relations turn sour.

Another reason intimate relations are so prone to conflict and violence is that the signals we use to communicate love and affection are very close to the ones that signal aggression and domination. Thus although lovers stare at each other, so do enemies. Standing very close to a person, calling him or her "baby," remaining silent for long periods, or handling that person's possessions can signal either intimacy or hostility, depending on the emotional context of the situation. Because lovers are used to giving one version of these signals, it seems relatively easy for them to slip into the other mode.

In sum, then, many of the problems of love relationships are inherent in their very nature and hence are unsolvable. In fact, we may be on the verge of developing a new version of the romantic love myth that recognizes the basic tensions between love and hostility, passion and permanence. As Ann Swidler (1981) observed:

We hear of relationships in which "struggle" is the highest virtue, and in which loving means facing one after another crises in which two autonomous, changing individuals work to deepen communication, to understand each other, and to rediscover themselves. (p. 19)

The new version of love may be seen in Bergman's *Scenes from a Marriage* and Woody Allen's *Annie Hall*. The great love stories of Western literature, from *Tristan and Isolde* to *Romeo and Juliet* to *Anna Karenina* to *Love Story*, are based on obstacles keeping the lovers apart. In the new love stories, the obstacles are internal; the new love "requires heroic struggles with the self and the lover. Love must stimulate and absorb perpetual changes" (Swidler, 1981, p. 19).

The new version of love recognizes that love does not always last forever. But among some couples, there seems to be a renewed emphasis on marriage as a permanent commitment. For example, Jane Ferrar (1977) has described the phenomenon of "spiritual marriage," in which the right to divorce is voluntarily renounced by couples committed to the struggle for spiritual advancement in Eastern religions. Thus, although the new values of self-realization and personal fulfillment are placing new strains on relationships, there seems also to be a growing recognition that relationships can never be perfect. As Murray Davis (1973) observed:

It is my belief that the so-called crisis of intimate relations today is due to the increasing disparity between the rising expectation that all their problems can be solved and the intractable fact that many of them cannot be solved. Only by accepting the little tragedies of intimate relations as inherently necessary can the big tragedy of their breakup be avoided.

SUMMARY

The essential themes of this chapter may be summarized in two statements:

1. Love relationships derive from our unique individuality and most private sense of

self, and yet they are shaped by the time and place in which we live.

2. Close relationships are inherently problematic. In all stages of love and intimacy, there are psychological and social forces that pull the partners away from each other as well as forces that pull them together.

The ideology of romantic love has been part of Western culture for the past 800 years. It is deeply rooted in Western religious and economic traditions, and is strongly reinforced by the conditions of life in modern urban-industrial society. Although the potential for romantic love exists in all times and places, it is elaborated to a greater degree in Western culture than anywhere else. Also, some of the ideas in the romantic love tradition—deference to the woman, the mixture of sexual love and admiration, and the idea that love ennobles the lover—are uniquely Western.

In the course of history the idea of love has been redefined. Although it started out as adulterous passion, romantic love was joined to marriage with the rise of puritanism and capitalism. In recent years the connection between love and marriage has loosened once again; although love and sex are no longer necessarily linked to marriage, there is little evidence that large numbers of people are giving up the values of intimacy and love.

CHAPTER 10

Marriage: Tradition and Transformation

Boire, manger, coucher ensemble
Est mariage, ce me semble.

To drink, to eat, to sleep together,
Is marriage, it seems to me.

Old French Proverb

As I was writing this chapter, the following invitation came in the mail, from a couple I shall call Joe and Joan:

believe it or not . . .
we're getting married
flying off into the sunset
playing, working, loving together
down the path of life
we'd love to have you join us at our wedding.

The invitation was something of a surprise. About a year ago, we had been to a housewarming at the new home Joe and Joan had bought together. Both of them are professional people, well over 30. Each has been married before, and each has children who are now close to being grown up.

The invitation and the wedding it announces pose some questions that are highly relevant to the next two chapters. What is marriage? Aren't Joe and Joan already married, in some sense, even before the wedding? The housewarming itself is an example of the kind of conduct that anthropologists would classify as marriage: a heterosexual couple announces to the community or a social group (friends, or relatives, or neighborhood, or clan, or a larger society) that they intend to stay together for some time (not necessarily forever) (König, 1974).

Of course, in our society, legal marriage is one thing, social behavior that looks like marriage is another. But is that large distinction as sharp in the 1980s as it was earlier? Family law is now changing. The distinction between legal and social marriage, as well as the distinction between being married and being unmarried, is growing harder to discern (Glendon, 1977). The famous "palimony" case involving Lee Marvin and Michelle Triola Marvin is just one example of the increasing recognition the law is giving to cohabitation. (See photo spread pp. 266–267.) Returning to the story of Joe and Joan: whichever way we answer the question about whether they are married before the wedding, a further question must be raised. What will being legally married add to the relationship they and other couples like them already have?

In this chapter and the next, we will examine the nature of marriage and the ways it has changed in recent years. This chapter looks at marriage in its social and historical context. Chapter 11 examines marriage as a relationship between two people.

RECENT TRENDS

To many people the best evidence that the American family is falling apart is the seeming unpopularity of the institution of marriage. The divorce rate continues to rise, after reaching an all-time high point in the early 1970s with the biggest increases occurring among couples with children. Unmarried couples living together have become a commonplace and even accepted part of the social scene, especially among the upper middle class. Recent census data reveal a rapid expansion of the number of people living alone; although many of these people will eventually marry, and many are older widows who are willing to marry but unlikely to find mates in their age group, a small but growing number of people are developing a commitment to singlehood. Nor is marriage any longer the socially necessary prerequisite for home ownership or even parenthood. Despite the availability of abortion in recent years, many single women have chosen to continue their pregnancies and rear their children themselves.

Attitudes toward marriage have changed even more strikingly than behavior. In recent years marriage counselors have become concerned with saving the spouses rather than the marriages; feminists and social scientists have pointed out that for women, the legal, economic, and psychological costs of marriage often exceed the benefits. In Hollywood movies it has become a cliche to portray marriages as unhappy, particularly for middle-class or middle-aged partners. Even *TV Guide* published an article complaining about the lack of happy marriages on television (J. Greenfield, 1982).

Marriage, however, is not about to disappear from the American scene. Despite the statistics on divorce and increasing singleness among young people, the vast majority will eventually marry, and marriage remains a central part of American life. Some may celebrate the fact that marriage seems to be "here to stay"; others may lament it (see Figures 10.1 and 10.2).

Although young people have been postponing marriage in recent years, it seems likely that more than 90 percent will eventually marry (Cherlin, 1981c). In 1960, by age 26, 75 percent of men and 90 percent of women were already married. By the end of the 1970s, the comparable rates were 70 percent for men and 80 percent for women. By the time men and women reached the age of 34, however, their marriage rates were virtually the same at the end of the 1970s as in 1960 (Levitan & Belous, 1981).

As we saw in Chapter 2, it was the relatively young age at marriage during the 1950s that was out of line with the historical trend. In much of America's past, people married at relatively late ages, and many never married at all. As Andrew Cherlin (1981c) pointed out, it is only justified to say that young people are "postponing" marriage if we use the 1950s as the baseline.

Getting Married: Then and Now

The changes in the age of marriage are an indicator of deeper changes in the relations between young adults and their parental families, as well as in the economic functions of families. Today we take it for granted that getting married is a matter of individual choice. In the past, however, the timing of marriage was a collective, family decision.

Before the twentieth century most urban American families depended on the wages of their working children. Life was precarious, and there were no social safety nets to help families deal with such calamities as sudden death, accidents, unemployment, and sickness. Families needed to call upon their able-bodied members over a long period, well into the adulthood of their children. Whether or when a young person could marry depended on the needs of the family. Because marriage was based on family needs, there was great variability in the age of marriage and in the other steps to adulthood—such as setting up one's own home (Modell, Furstenberg, & Herschberg, 1973).

In recent times the family economy has been based on the husband and wife, not the children. Young people are economically dependent on their parents and in their 20s are expected to become independent of them—

*FIGURE 10.1
Number and Rate of
First Marriages,
Divorces, and
Remarriages of
Women: 1951–1977*

*The number of first
marriages rose during
the 1960s as persons
born during the baby
boom lowered the
average marrying age
but the marriage rate
per 1,000 never-
married persons
continued a longtime
downward trend.
Divorces surged
upward during the
1960s and early 1970s
but now the increase
has slowed.*

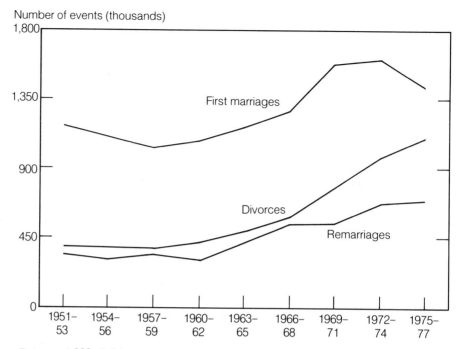

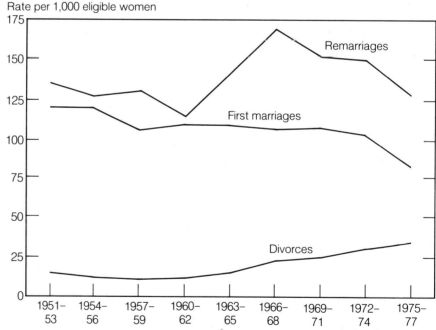

From U.S. Department of Commerce, Bureau of the Census, *American Families and Living Arrangements*. Current Population Reports, Special Studies, Series P-23, No. 104, May 1980.

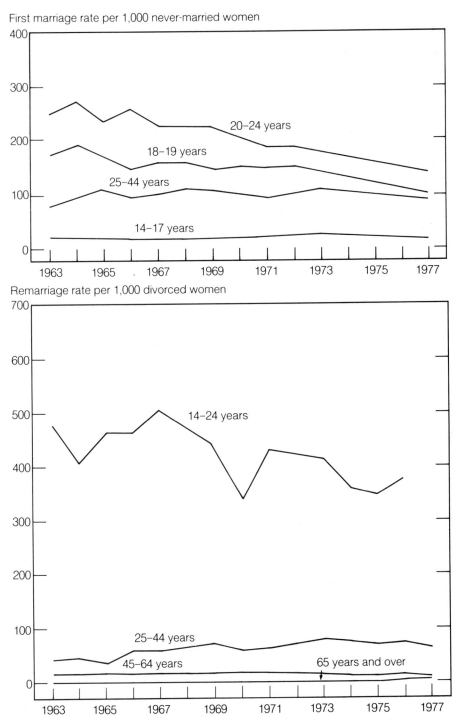

First marriage rate per 1,000 never-married women

20–24 years

18–19 years

25–44 years

14–17 years

Remarriage rate per 1,000 divorced women

14–24 years

25–44 years

45–64 years

65 years and over

From U.S. Department of Commerce, Bureau of the Census, *American Families and Living Arrangements.* Current Population Reports, Special Studies, Series P-23, No. 104, 1980.

FIGURE 10.2
First Marriage and Remarriage Rates Among Women, by Age: 1963–1977

Decline in marriage is greatest in late teens and early 20s. As more young adults continue their education at the college level and as more of them work and establish separate households, more first marriages and also more remarriages after divorce are being postponed, at least temporarily.

not contributors to their families of origin. The patterns of the nineteenth-century family are incompatible with our current notions of adult independence.

There is a temptation to view the older family pattern in the warm glow of nostalgia—"strong" families pulling together against adversity. The evidence, however, is that the subordination of individual to family needs did not take place without pain and conflict. In interviews with people who had lived under the older arrangements, historian Tamara Hareven (1978) found that many who had sacrificed personal preferences for family needs expressed long-repressed feelings of hurt and anger. Often, the burden fell unequally on the children in a family. One woman, for example, resented the fact that she had to start working at the age of 14 and postpone her own marriage long after her older sisters had all left home to marry.

By the middle of the twentieth century, getting married was a radically different process. Because of a host of social changes (including the increased level of affluence and the emergence of a social safety net), young people could make their own decisions about when to marry. They married younger, as a part of a tight package of transitions: finishing school, leaving home, setting up one's own home, having babies. Notions about the "right time" to marry, have children, and so on became much more rigid. Marriage became the key event in the passage to adulthood. In many ways, the postwar family pattern represented the fulfillment of a long-held ideal that until then had never been able to be put into practice. When it finally did become reality for larger numbers of people, it proved to be enormously problematic—culturally, economically, and psychologically (Furstenberg, 1981).

Thus the recent trend toward later marriage may be seen as a return to a more flexible pattern of timing, although for different reasons. People are now free to make marriage decisions according to their own needs and preferences. During the postwar era marriage was "freed" from the parental family, but there was great pressure to conform to the norms of marital timing—to be married and start childrearing in the early 20s. People who failed to do so were not only regarded as somewhat deviant, but were in fact at a disadvantage in the marriage market (Modell, Furstenberg, & Strong, 1978). Among the "costs" of the postwar pattern were people pressed into marriage and parenthood before they were ready, as well as those who were left out in the cold of singlehood in an era of marital togetherness.

The trend toward later marriage may have some other beneficial social effects besides the greater leeway individuals now enjoy about when to marry. For women especially, later marriage means more of a chance of getting an education, developing marketable skills, and even starting a career. Many men and women will enter marriage having had a chance to manage a household on their own or with peers. This situation represents a large change from a generation ago, when young people went directly from their parent's home to their own (Masnick & Bane, 1980).

Changes in sex norms and the rise in cohabitation have also contributed to later marriage. Between 1970 and 1980 the number of unmarried couples living together—as identified by the Census Bureau—reached 1,560,000, a threefold increase. During the 1950s, for middle-class young people getting married was the only way to become an independent adult—that is, to set up a household and have sexual relations.

When cohabitation first came to the attention of scholars and the general public, many people thought it was going to be a radical new life-style and a permanent substitute for marriage. Of course, cohabita-

TABLE 10.1   *Divorce Rates by Age*

	Divorce rates per 1,000 married persons with spouse present			
Year	Under 30 years	30–44 years	45–64 years	65 years and over
1978	91	108	84	59
1970	38	47	53	47
1965	28	41	48	45
1960	23	33	46	32

From S. A. Levitan and R. S. Belous, *What's Happening to the American Family?* Baltimore: Johns Hopkins University Press, 1981, p. 29. Used by permission.
Original source. Bureau of the Census (1979), *Marital Status and Living Arrangements. March, 1978,* Series 20, no. 338, pp. 3, 12.

tion was not invented in the 1970s. Men and women had lived together without formal marriage since time immemorial. In most times and places, marriage has been a matter of custom and religion, not of the legal system. And legal systems have often given some form of official recognition to couples who live together as man and wife (Glendon, 1977). But usually the practice has been confined to minority groups and the poor. The emergence of what used to be called "living in sin" or "shacking up" in the educated middle class was one of the most surprising aspects of the sexual revolution of the 1970s. It seemed at the beginning to pose a serious challenge to the institution of marriage.

Now, however, in the opinion of most researchers, it is simply a different route to eventual marriage. As Cherlin (1981c) suggested, cohabitation seems to be a new stage of intimacy that precedes or follows marriage. It has become a way of finding a compatible partner, rather than a permanent way of life for most people. While cohabitation is not necessarily a "threat" to marriage, it does reflect some profound changes in marriage itself. Not only cohabitation, but also

divorce and remarriage are part of this transformation of the meaning of marriage and its place in our lives.

The "Normalization" of Divorce

As we saw in Chapter 2, the annual divorce rate has been rising since the Civil War—but fairly slowly until World War I, when it doubled in the span of a few years. There was a divorce boom after World War II, and then a drop and leveling off in the early 1950s. Between 1963 and 1975 the divorce rate increased a dramatic 100 percent. In 1974 the number of divorces totaled 1 million for the first time in American history. The rise in divorce rates was highest for people under 30 and next highest for people between 30 and 44. All ages were affected. (See Figure 10.3 and Table 10.1.)

Annual divorce rates show large fluctuations in times of war or depression. Another way to gauge trends in divorce, as we saw in Chapter 2, is to look at the lifetime divorce experience of adults. One way of doing this is to look at the proportion of divorces in different marital cohorts—people who were

*FIGURE 10.3
Divorced Persons Per
1,000 Married Persons
with Spouse Present,
by Sex and Age, for
Selected Years:
1950–1978*

*The ratio of divorced
persons to married
persons has increased
at each age level.
The divorce ratio
has increased most
rapidly at ages under
45. Above age 30, the
divorce ratio for
women has risen more
rapidly than that for
men, as divorced
men continue to have
higher remarriage
rates than divorced
women.*

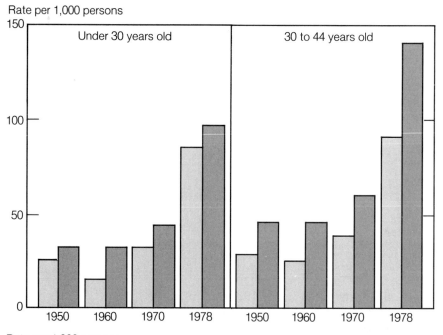

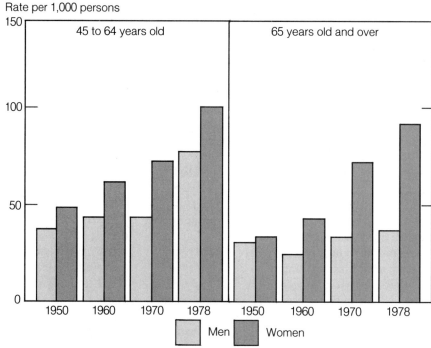

From U.S. Department of Commerce, Bureau of the Census, *American Families and Living Arrangements.* Current Population Reports, Special Studies, Series P-23, No. 104, May 1980.

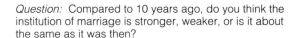

The institution of marriage today is stronger than 10 years ago   Weaker   About the same

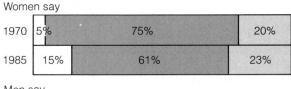

Women say

1970	5%	75%	20%
1985	15%	61%	23%

Men say

1970	5%	72%	22%
1985	16%	60%	24%

Note: Interesting differences exist among various subgroups. Those with less income, less education, blacks, and the elderly think the institution of marriage is weaker today, compared to 10 years ago.

From *Public Opinion,* December/January 1986, p. 25.

FIGURE 10.4
The Institution of Marriage

married in succeeding years (Figure 2.4, p. 51). (Another way of doing this would be to look at the lifetime divorce experience of birth cohorts—people born in different years.) Andrew Cherlin (1981c) has shown that the lifetime incidence of divorce for people married in a given year has increased at a faster and faster rate since the mid-nineteenth century. Those who married between the end of World War II and the later 1950s will probably end up with slightly lower levels than expected from the long-term trend, but still more of them will divorce than previous cohorts. Those who married in the 1960s and 1970s are likely to have rates higher than those predicted by the long-term trend. One estimate is that 48 percent of those who married in 1970 will eventually divorce. Scholars disagree about what will

happen to the divorce rate in the future—whether it will continue to rise, drop, or level off. Most of them, however, expect divorce rates to continue to be exceptionally high.

Disturbing as these trends may seem, they need to be put into perspective. When we look at the long-term trends in divorce, the recent rise looks less dramatic than if we compare it to the relatively low divorce rates of the 1950s. Actually the divorce rates of the 1950s were not as low as they appear at first glance. Increasing numbers of people were getting divorced during those years, but the growth in the divorce rate was concealed by the fact that growing numbers of people were also getting married. Moreover, an increasing proportion of marriages during that time of apparent marital stability were remarriages (Preston & McDonald, 1979).

Also, as we pointed out earlier in this book, today's divorce rates don't seem as high when we recall how often marriages were disrupted by death in the supposedly "good old days." Some scholars have observed that the total rate of marital dissolution—by either death or divorce—remained fairly constant between 1860 and 1970. Mary Jo Bane (1976) has shown that the percentage of women of different ages living with their husbands has remained stable during the twentieth century. Kinsley Davis (1972), as noted earlier, has interpreted the upward trend in divorce over time as compensatory: the less probability of escaping a bad marriage by death, the greater the willingness to consider divorce.

Since the mid-1970s, however, for the first time in American history more marriages ended every year in divorce rather than death (Cherlin, 1981c). Most scholars expect the divorce rate to continue to outpace the death rate. Death was not the only way marriages ended in the past, either. Divorce rates may have been relatively low. Desertion, however, the proverbial "poor man's divorce," or heading west were common ways for men to escape from unhappy marriages before 1900 (Freed & Foster, 1969).

While divorce has become commonplace, it is not, contrary to our media images, an inevitable event in every marriage. A majority of married couples are remaining together. Nor is staying together at all costs necessarily an indicator of good marriages in a good society. In many countries divorce is not permitted except in rare circumstances. Such countries are not notable for the happiness of their marriages or the faithfulness of their spouses. They are noted for other practices that are prevalent in the shadows of indissoluble marriage: mistresses, prostitution, and couples living together for years, unable to marry because one or both partners is married to someone else.

In our country in the not too distant past, many couples who no longer cared for one another would stay together for the sake of the children and their standing in the community, and also because divorce was expensive and hard to get. Rodney Dangerfield once expressed the spirit of such a marriage in his classic line: "We sleep in separate rooms, we have dinner apart, we take separate vacations—we're doing everything we can to keep our marriage together."

It may well be that couples today are doing too little to keep their marriages together. The evidence, however, does not support the idea that our high divorce rates mean that Americans are giving up on marriage, or going in for serial monogamy, Hollywood style—a la Mickey Rooney, Zsa Zsa Gabor, and Elizabeth Taylor. Rather, most people who divorce form new stable relationships. About half of all women and a somewhat greater percentage of men remarry within 3 years of their divorce decree; eventually three-quarters of divorced women and four-fifths of divorced men remarry. The rate of remarriage has tended to follow the divorce rate, but recently it has lagged behind. This change probably means that increasing numbers of divorced people are living together before they remarry (Glick, 1980, cited in Furstenberg, 1981).

The divorce rate for remarriages after divorce is slightly higher than for first marriages (Cherlin, 1981c), but relatively few people repeat the cycle of divorce and remarriage for a third time. Some researchers have suggested that the complexities of remarried life explain the higher probabilities of divorce after remarriage (Cherlin, 1978). Unlike couples getting married for the first time, remarried couples often have to deal with ex-spouses, children from both marriages, and even ex-in-laws. Other researchers have suggested that certain personality characteristics of people who have been divorced, plus their experience with the process, can increase the risk of their divorcing.

In any case, the prevalence of remarriage suggests that we are not witnessing the death of the institution of marriage. Rather, we are witnessing its transformation in a cultural system that includes cohabitation, divorce, and remarriage as intrinsic parts. It is a system that places a high value on individual choice and personal fulfillment. Cohabitation is becoming a way station en route to marriage for many people. Within the legal system, cohabitation is coming more and more to resemble marriage. Divorce is emerging as a mechanism permitting individuals to improve their marital situation.

The new system does not mean that marriage as an institution is on the rocks, or even withering away. The opposite is closer to the truth: marriage has probably never been more important to people than it is today. People break and remake marriages because they are not willing to tolerate relationships in which they are not deeply involved. There is a certain irony in this, as Frank Furstenberg (1981) has pointed out:

Divorce can be seen as an intrinsic part of a cultural system which values individual discretion and emotional gratification. Divorce is a social invention for promoting conformity to these cultural ideals. Ironically, the more it is used, the more exacting the standards become for those who marry. (p. 11)

Rising Expectations

The search for personal fulfillment in marriage and the use of divorce and remarriage as part of that search are not a product of "the new narcissism" or the "psychological revolution" of the past 2 decades. Rather, they are part of a longer historical drama in society that began over a century ago: the emergence of modern life and the transformation of America into an urban, industrial society (Griswold, 1982; May, 1980).

Beginning in the late nineteenth and early twentieth centuries, Americans began to divorce at an unprecedented rate; by the end of the 1920s, one in six marriages was ending in divorce. This increase was not due to liberalized laws; in fact, as the divorce rate began to accelerate between 1889 and 1906, divorce laws across the country were made more restrictive. Rather, Americans were more willing to dissolve marriages that did not live up to rising standards of personal happiness.

Public debate on the causes of divorce began over a century ago. Clergymen and moralists blamed individual depravity. Social scientists, newly emerging as professionals in the late nineteenth century, blamed the rise of the city for the breakdown of family ties. Some blamed the emancipation of women for destroying women's ability to keep a happy home—does this sound familiar? Meanwhile, feminists hailed the liberation of women from the chains of marital bondage.

However, as historian Elaine May (1980) has pointed out, the advances of women's rights during the twentieth century and increasing urbanization did not turn people away from marriage. Between 1900 and 1920 the proportion of people getting married increased, along with the divorce rate. May suggests that the two trends are two sides of the same coin—an increasing attraction to marriage and a growing difficulty in finding satisfaction in it. At the conclusion of her book May asks:

But is divorce really a liberation? Do people discard matrimony in favor of other alternatives— or do they merely move on in a perpetual quest for "the perfect relationship"? Personal life seems to have become a national obsession in 20th century America. It is not likely that the domestic domain will ever be able to satisfy completely the great expectations for individual fulfillment brought to it. (p. 163)

CONTINUITY AND CHANGE

It may seem strange to think of cohabitation, divorce, and remarriage as part of our family system, rather than as deviations from normal family life. It is true that they are not completely "institutionalized"— that is, we do not have clear-cut rules for dealing with the complexities of the new kinds of relationships, nor do we have habitualized patterns of daily living for dealing with them. For example, we still don't have a word to describe some of the common new forms of relationship. What do you call the person you live with, if you are not married? Your friend? Your lover? Your roommate? Or as Charles Osgood, the radio commentator, suggests, your posslque (person of the opposite sex sharing living quarters)?

This seemingly strange new world of relationships can, however, be viewed as the further development of trends in kinship, courtship, and marriage that sociologists had

Despite high divorce rates, a wedding still symbolizes the hope for a permanent relationship. [Abigail Heyman/Archive Pictures, Inc.]

noticed decades ago. These trends include the following:

1. the reduction of the role of parents and other relatives in marriage decisions
2. increasing changes in women's sexual behavior and a decline in the double standard
3. a blurring of distinction among the stages of courtship and between courtship and marriage
4. an increasing ability to rectify marital "mistakes" through divorce and remarriage
5. a shift in the individual and family life cycle resulting in an increase in the potential length of marriage and a reduction in the proportion of the marital life cycle spent in active childrearing

Most of these trends had been recognized by sociologists as part of the gradual evolution of traditional marriage. Over 40 years ago, Burgess and Locke (1945) described a shift from institutional to companionship marriage:

The central thesis of this volume is that the family in historical times, and the present, is in transition from an institution to a companionship. In the past, the important factors unifying the family have been external, formal, and authoritarian, as the law, the mores, public opinion, tradition, the authority of the family head, rigid discipline, and elaborate ritual. At present, in the new emerging form of the companionship family, its unity inheres less and less in community pressures, and more in such interpersonal relationships as the mutual affection, the sympathetic understanding, and the comradeship of its members. (p. vii)

Burgess and Locke described the companionship family as an emerging, not yet fully developed trend. Empirical studies of marriage during the 1950s and early 1960s found that it had still not arrived. One study suggested that many, if not most, marriages were utilitarian relationships, based on convenience, economic benefits and inertia (Cuber & Harroff, 1965). The recent increases in the divorce rate may reflect the wider spread of the companionship ideal and a corresponding intolerance for marriages that fall short of that ideal. And the rise of cohabitation may represent a working out of the logic of companionship marriage: a purely companionate relationship, without the institution of legal marriage at all.

Cohabitation and Sexual Bargaining

While most of the family developments of recent years may be viewed as continuations of earlier trends, one pattern does seem to represent a sharp break with the past. The emergence of cohabitation in the past decade or so was not so much a break with behavioral reality as with the rules of public decorum. It was one thing to have a secret sexual relationship—another for a woman to announce openly to the world that she was living with a man without benefit of marriage.

Publicly acknowledged cohabitation is symptomatic of a dramatic change in the patterns of relations between the sexes and in the social functions of marriage. Sociologists have often looked at courtship and marriage as a system of bargaining and exchange (McCall, 1966). Historically, parents and kin groups were the major bargaining agents in marriage. In more recent years women have used youth, good looks, and virginity to make their own bargains in the marriage market. A woman would try to strike the best possible marriage bargain, in terms of her future husband's potential earning power, prestige, and attractiveness, before her perishable assets had faded. Marriage was seen as a better deal for women than for men because of women's dependency, their need to wait for a proposal, and their inability to have sex outside marriage.

The morality of sexual restraint was an important part of the traditional bargaining process. Women withheld sexual favors before marriage to trade them, along with their other assets, for lifelong support. Men had to marry in order to receive sexual favors from "respectable" women. Under the double standard of sexual morality however, men could initiate sexual approaches, while women had the responsibility for controlling men. One of the persistent dangers of the system was the possibility for exploitation of women; a man might promise marriage in exchange for sexual favors, then fail to marry. The classical image of the exploited woman under this system was one who had been seduced and abandoned, her chances for marriage ruined. (The traditional system, like most others, did not always follow the prescribed norms, and it was not unknown for prostitutes to marry into respectable society. See Rosen, 1982.)

Recent social changes have affected both the rules of the sexual bargaining system and the payoffs for women inside and outside of marriage. Even before the recent sexual revolution, some sociologists perceived significant change in the courtship–marriage system. Thus Bernard Farber (1964) suggested that the United States was coming to have a "permanent availability model" of marriage in which all adults are in effect permanently available to marry, even if already married. Marriage was becoming a voluntary association in which the partners continue as long as their commitments to each other exceed their attachments to others. Divorce and remarriage are an integral part of this model of marriage, not separate phenomena.

Farber saw the then gradually rising divorce rates and remarriage as changing the

Actor Lee Marvin and Michelle Triola Marvin in 1967 and 1979. In 1977, she filed a lawsuit claiming she was entitled to half the community property accumulated during the six years the couple lived together without being married. Although Michelle Marvin ultimately failed to win the case, it resulted in a landmark decision by the Supreme Court of California. The court ruled that unmarried couples could make binding agreements about community property, thereby granting a degree of legal recognition to cohabitation. [Bettmann Newsphotos/UPI]

nature of *first* marriages. Getting married was no longer the once-in-a-lifetime, fateful decision it had earlier been. With no single propitious time to marry, the timespan of courtship widens; young people enter the marriage market extremely early, and older people make themselves available for marriage as long as possible. There is an increasing emphasis on glamour and youthfulness at all ages, as well as on the social skills involved in making and breaking relationships. Virginity loses its value as the rate of remarriage, where virginity is impossible, rises. Women's participation in the labor force rises, giving them a measure of independence and a means of keeping in touch with the outside world and the marriage market.

Farber also had some perceptive observations about the courtship process. Before the 1950s, marriage was the endpoint of a distinct series of stages—dating, keeping company, going steady, a private understanding between the couple to be married, and finally engagement. Each stage represented a deepening level of commitment and an increasing level of physical contact between couples, although intercourse was supposed to be reserved for marriage. Farber pointed out that this system of stages had given way to a "series of involvements." Courtship was

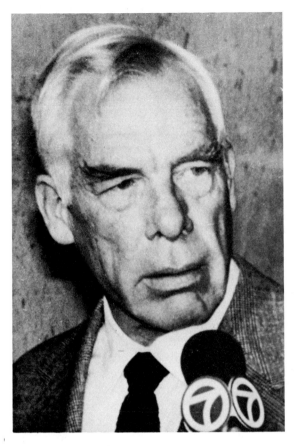

now a series of relationships that were both more intimate and more fragile than the later stages of courtship. In fact, there was now very little difference emotionally and sexually between married and unmarried couple relationships. Marriage was simply another involvement. The decision to marry reflected a more long-term, though still not permanent, commitment as well as the decision to have children.

The new marriage system also represented a declining role for parents. Once parents were active participants along with their children in the decision to marry. Their social position largely determined the eligibil-

ity of prospective mates, and thus they could attempt to veto their children's choices, using economic as well as personal pressure. In recent decades the role of parents has been reduced simply to being informed that their children were, or were about to be, married. But marriage was—and is—still a way of establishing kin ties. The woman's relatives recognize the husband as their kin, the man's relatives recognize her as kin to them.

With a few minor alterations, this picture of the courtship–marriage system in the 1950s and early 1960s seems remarkably applicable to the current picture of cohabitation–marriage. The major changes are that living together, rather than early marriage, constitutes the new emerging pattern for young couples. The role of parents and kin are reduced still further; there is no role for parents in the decision to live together.

The other difference is that the new pattern has been granted increasing public recognition as well as ideological justification. At the time Farber was writing, the "old" model of courtship and marriage was assumed to prevail, even though the reality was different. In the mass media as well as in sociological textbooks and scholarly writings, it was assumed that brides were virgins, wives were housewives, and marriages were first and only marriages. The changes of the past 2 decades, as we have seen, included both sharper increases in trends that had already been increasing as well as a demystification of sex, marriage, and women's roles that brought images more in line with reality.

It seems likely that the critical new element added to the situation in the late 1960s was an ideology justifying the new patterns of behavior. Changes in attitudes seemed to require a basic departure from the current ways of thinking about women's place. Although variation from traditional norms was widespread and increasing, variation was still regarded as deviation. The deviant individuals—whether they were nonvirgins, single women, working mothers or the divorced—remained on the defensive and discreet in their behavior. Historian Carl Degler (1980) has, for example, argued that there had never been an ideological basis for women to move into the labor force: during the 1950s increasing numbers of women worked after marriage, but they preferred to subordinate work to family life, or to say they did. The new ideology of feminism that arose in the late 1960s provided the crucial redefinition of women's place in the home, in the workplace, and in the bedroom.

The ideology of virginity persisted through the 1960s, although it was increasingly at odds with the fact that premarital intercourse for women was becoming both more frequent and more accepted. The cultural and sexual revolution combined with the revolution in contraceptive technology—the pill—to produce a sudden and massive shift in this ideology. Reversing the traditional stance, virginity was now a devalued state for adults of both sexes whether married or not. Sex was no longer an elusive prize or a bargaining resource, but a part of normal human experience.

The payoffs within marriage have changed also. The expansion of the female labor force has profound implications for both marriage and nonmarital relations between the sexes. While women are far from economic equality in terms of either pay or job opportunity, the increasing movement of women into the labor force gives women additional bargaining resources (Collins, 1971). As opportunities and wages increase for women, the opportunity costs for a woman remaining unemployed rise markedly. Not only does the full-time homemaker lose current wages, she loses the opportunity to develop her own human capital—her skills and capacity to earn. As one writer put it:

Earning power grows with seniority, with experience, with enhancement of the earning skill. Day by day and year by year in the homemaker role, the woman falls farther behind in earning power. When her full economic worth is eaten up by marital duties, she has neither property nor earning ability. (Krauskopf, 1977, p. 102)

At the same time as the opportunity costs of marriage have risen, the economic security of marriage has declined. Most male jobs do not pay enough to support families at an adequate level. Moreover, the rise in the divorce rate threatens all marriages with impermanence. With the likelihood of divorce approaching 50 percent or more, a woman who enters marriage assuming she will be supported for life and with no thought for how she might support herself is much more foolhardy in a statistical sense than someone who smokes three packs of cigarettes a day. Divorced women have typically been left in reduced and often extremely difficult financial circumstances (Weitzman, 1985). Alimony is largely a myth—rarely awarded, still more rarely paid. And no-fault divorce, with its assumption that women can be self-supporting from the moment of divorce, seems to have increased women's burdens, at least during a time of transition to economic equality (Weitzman & Dixon, 1980). Today's counterpart of the classic victim of the sexual bargaining system, the young woman seduced and abandoned, is the displaced homemaker, the divorced victim of a marriage system that promised, but did not deliver, lifelong support in exchange for services within the home.

Finally, in recent years, marriage has been losing one of its most important traditional benefits—that of making children legitimate. The distinction between legitimate and illegitimate offspring has been so widespread that it was raised almost to the status of a natural law in the form of Malinowski's principle of legitimacy (Malinowski, 1930). The principle stated that in every society a child must have a socially recognized father to give the child a status in the community. Traditionally sociologists have regarded illegitimacy as a symptom of social disorganization.

Illegitimacy has become increasingly irrelevant as a social status. The most direct attack on the principle has been carried out in legal systems around the world, which have been reducing the distinctions between children born inside and outside of marriage (Glendon, 1977). Further, the significance of traditional forms of family-based wealth and property has diminished. A new kind of property has emerged in the form of benefits and entitlements from employers and from the state—health insurance, pensions, death benefits, Social Security, and so on (Reich, 1964).

Finally, the social norms surrounding illegitimacy have changed so drastically that the word itself is coming to have an archaic ring. What once was the most stigmatized behavior a woman could engage in, or the most shameful secret, can now be openly practiced without fear of massive social disapproval. Women's magazines feature articles on the hows and whys of unwed motherhood, and a *Time* magazine poll carried out in 1978 showed that 74 percent of Americans found it acceptable for a single woman to have and raise a child (Clark & Martire, 1979).

Even when it was working as it was supposed to, conventional marriage still generated serious internal strains, particularly for women. In the nineteenth century, Tocqueville contrasted the social and personal freedom of young American women with the constraints of married ones. Even the post–World War II social theorists who argued for the functional necessity of the nuclear family recognized that women's roles were stressful. Talcott Parsons, for example, argued that the housewife–mother role was both a demanding job and a pseudo-occupation cut off from the economic structure of society. The dependency of women's traditional role is psychologically costly. Married women have higher rates of mental illness than single women, and most researchers believe the marital role itself is the cause.

The cultural notion that men don't really need or want strong attachments to women may make them uncomfortable when they do wish such attachments. In fact, the tradi-

An Arkansas farm couple in the 1940s. [Michael Disfarmer/Archive Pictures Inc.]

tional economic dependency of women on men in industrial society has obscured the extent to which men are emotionally dependent on women. Jessie Bernard (1972) speculates that "it might not be far-fetched to conclude that the verbal assaults on marriage indulged in by men are a kind of compensatory reaction to their dependence on it" (p. 19).

Ironically the evidence suggests that while men complain about marriage, they reap more benefits from it than women. Bernard amassed considerable evidence on the mental and physical health of married and unmarried Americans. Married men are healthier in all ways than single men. The rate of mental depression is 35 percent higher in single men, and married men are likely to get better jobs and pay.

Bernard recognizes that this conclusion might be putting the cart before the horse—maybe men who get married are mentally and physically better off to begin with. She tried to control for this factor by comparing married and unmarried men of the same general background and by comparing married men with widowers and divorced men. When other factors are considered, it is still marriage that seems to account for the difference. Further, once men have tried marriage, they seem to develop a craving for it. Most divorced and widowed men remarry quickly.

Wives, by contrast, not only get less out of marriage than men in terms of physical and mental health, but they are worse off than single women. Bernard and others have pointed to a paradox in these findings: wives give themselves higher happiness ratings than single women do, but on a long list of physical and mental symptoms of stress they do worse. She explains that women accept the cultural norm that says a woman should be married in order to be happy; so single women may think they would be better off married, even if they are doing very well, and married women may decide that since they have achieved the cultural goal, they must be happy. The changing norms about marriage may change the way people answer these questions in the future.

In general, Bernard's observations have been confirmed by other researchers. A study of middle-aged women by Pauline Bart (1970) revealed that the women who had made the deepest commitments to motherhood and domesticity were most likely to experience depression at the time of menopause. In a study comparing recent mental illness rates among men and women, as indicated by community surveys, admissions to mental hospitals, and so on, Gove and Tudor (1973) found women to have higher rates of "mental illness."

These higher rates of mental illness for women, however, are found mainly when married women are compared to married men. In studies of unmarried, widowed, and divorced people, the sex difference either does not appear or men may turn out to have higher rates. And among married women, full-time housewives seem to have more psychological problems than wives who work.

Gove and Tudor give several reasons why the housewife's role in modern industrial societies may be stressful for many women. First, the full-time housewife is restricted to a single social role, but most men have two major roles—worker and father–husband. If one of a man's roles is unsatisfactory, he can look to the other for gratification. The housewife has no such alternative. Second, because much of the housewife's work is repetitive and undemanding and does not call for a high degree of expertise, it is out of keeping with the educational attainments of many women. Third, the housewife's role is relatively unstructured. Her isolation and lack of structured job demands make it possible for her to brood over her troubles. By contrast, the person who has a job out in the world usually doesn't have the opportunity to be obsessed with worries. Finally, the expectations confronting women are unclear and contradictory.

Despite the fact that the benefits of marriage may be uneven for men and women, it is important to remember that many women are happily married. Also, in times of stress, such as a major illness, having a mate to provide support may make the difference between coping adequately and succumbing to

depression for both men and women (Pearlin & Johnson, 1977). Emphasizing the costs of marriage to women was a necessary antidote to the myth of the happy, fulfilled housewife that prevailed in the 1950s, as well as the myths of the happy bachelor and the henpecked husband. But we should not replace the old myths with a new one about the sad, mad, and miserable wife.

While many feminists in the early days of that movement regarded marriage as an inherently oppressive institution for women, many now recognize that it is the inequality of the sexes rather than marriage itself that is the problem. In recent years conventional legal marriage has changed. Particularly for the middle class, marriage has become more of a partnership, with wives sharing the breadwinner role and husbands sharing in child care and household work. There is a gap between the idea of equality and the practical reality, but a process of change has been set in motion.

SUMMARY

The current state of marriage seems to many people the best evidence that the American family is on the verge of extinction. The divorce rate is at the highest level in American history, and more than a million and a half couples are living together unmarried. Today's young people are remaining single well past the ages at which their parents were already married and starting to have children.

A closer look at recent trends and the historical record suggests that obituaries for the institution of marriage are a bit premature. There are several reasons why current statistics cannot be interpreted as a massive rejection of marriage on the part of the American people.

Some of today's trends are continuations of long-term trends that were interrupted or reversed in the 1950s, such as a rising divorce rate and a rising age at first marriage. Also, in earlier generations there was much more variability in the early stages of adult life than there was during the 1950s. In previous generations, decisions about when to leave home and marry were made by families in accordance with the needs of the family economy. During the postwar era, getting married was an individual decision on the part of the young person, but people who entered adulthood during that era did so in lock-step fashion. They married en masse during their early 20s and made marriage itself part of a package of life transitions: finishing school, setting up a household apart from parents, beginning a regular sex life, and having children. Among today's young people, getting married and taking these other steps to adulthood are discrete events that take place at a variety of times.

Marriage remains a central part of American life, and the vast majority of Americans— over 90 percent—will marry. But the meaning of marriage has changed. Cohabitation and divorce are best seen not as escapes from marriage, but as parts of a new system of courtship and marriage. Remarriage is also an integral part of the system. The continuing popularity of marriage and rising divorce rates are like two sides of the same coin: a search for personal fulfillment in marriage and an intolerance for marriages that are not emotionally involving.

Although the new marital system has emerged in the 1970s, it was foreshadowed by earlier trends that had been observed by sociologists: trends toward companionate marriage, a decline in the double standard of sexual morality, and the changing economic value of marriage to women. The changes do not mean that marriage is less important emotionally to contemporary Americans than to earlier generations; emotionally, it is more important, and therefore less stable, than in the past, when people had lower expectations of marriage.

CHAPTER 11

The Bonds of Marriage: Institution and Relationship

Above all, it must not be thought that the couple relationship is a simple one: a man and woman bound by some obvious contract.

Albert Memmi
Dominated Man

THE TWO FACES
OF MARRIAGE

Marriage has always had a dual aspect that has puzzled students of marriage as well as ordinary folk: marriage is a relationship between two people, but it is more than a couple relationship—it is an institution. Marriage is an intensely private affair, but it is public as well. "Marriage" seems to lead its own separate existence, quite apart from particular married couples.

In their study of American couples, Philip Blumstein and Pepper Schwartz offer the following definition of the term *institution:*

An institution is a way of life that is very resistant to change. People know about it; they can describe it; and they have spent a lifetime learning how to react to it. The *idea* of marriage is larger than any individual marriage. The *role* of husband or wife is greater than any individual who takes on that role. (1983, p. 318)

In the 1940s, as we noted in the last chapter, Burgess and Locke (1945) already saw marriage being transformed from an "institution" to a "companionship." The new emerging family was held together less by commu-

nity pressure, law, and tradition and more by affection, understanding, and sympathy.

In the 1960s and 1970s, many people rebelled openly against the institutional aspects of marriage—"who wants to live in an institution." The idea of conforming to rigidly defined roles, especially as the scripts for these roles had been elaborated in the 1950s, lost their appeal. Men rebelled against the good-provider husband role (Ehrenreich, 1983). Women rebelled against the gender inequalities written into the housewife role. Both men and women began to accord greater priority to personal growth and individual fulfillment than to obligation and commitment. Marriage counselors came to see their mission as saving the spouses rather than the marriage. "Open marriage" (O'Neill & O'Neill, 1972) proposed a new model of marital relationship, maximizing growth, minimizing permanence and conformity to established roles. Cohabitation offered couples a way to have a marriage-like relationship without any of the institutional trappings.

By the 1980s, many observers saw signs of a shift away from an extreme emphasis on personal fulfillment and gratification and of a yearning for commitment. Living according to the new values had given rise to new difficulties. Open marriage, for example, despite its wide appeal to middle-class couples, turned out to be hard to achieve in practice. Even Nena O'Neill, one of the authors of *Open Marriage,* expressed misgivings about the idea. In a later book, *The Marriage Premise* (1977), she confessed that in trying to correct the shortcomings of traditional marital patterns, she and others had ignored the "sharing aspects" of marriage: "once again the baby has been thrown out with the bathwater" (1977, p. 11).

If open marriage offered an ideal that was hard to live up to, unmarried couples living together face the problem of inventing their relationship as they live it. Blumstein and Schwartz (1983) have explored the meaning of marriage as an institution by comparing the experiences of cohabiting and married couples.

Paradoxically, they found that in some ways being married was more liberating than simply living together. They point out that roles and rules of conduct help interaction proceed smoothly. A couple does not have to deal with each issue that comes up as if no one ever dealt with it before. The rules enable the married partners to trust one another more. For example, one of the major differences they found between marriage and cohabitation centered on money. Cohabiting couples tend to do careful bookkeeping to keep track of who is spending how much for what. Most married couples have no need to do this. They can assume they will remain together, and if not, the rules of divorce would make for an orderly exit. The bookkeeping itself is alienating because it implies a lack of stability and trust in the relationship.

Although cohabitation has not replaced marriage, as many once feared it would, the line between the two, as we saw in the last chapter, has become blurred in recent years. The legal system has been recognizing cohabitation as a kind of partnership, if not exactly the same as a marriage. Further, the "divorce revolution" (Weitzman, 1985) of recent years has also led to a revolution in the institution of marriage. No-fault divorce laws have inadvertently undermined the traditional view of marriage as a permanent bond to be broken only by death or the severe misconduct of one of the spouses.

Many people are deeply ambivalent about the changes. They are disturbed at the fragility of marriage today. Yet there is little doubt that many couples find a degree of emotional satisfaction in marriage that was rare in the past. Few would tolerate the degree of marital disharmony that their parents and grandparents considered bearable for the sake of the children and their standing in the community (W. H. Goode, 1982).

An Ambivalent Tradition

Ours is not the first era in Western society to experience ambivalence about marriage. Indeed, hostility toward marriage has deep roots in Western culture. Usually, however, antimarriage attitudes have coexisted with respect for the institution and a sense of its inevitability.

This ambivalence toward marriage takes many forms, beginning perhaps with the statement of St. Paul that it is better to marry than to burn. Not marrying and not burning was better still, but was conceded to be beyond the capacities of most. Besides Christian ambivalence, the models of marriage put forth by the professionals in the field also have two faces. We shall look at the professional work on marriage later, but let us look first at what could be called the "classical ambivalence" of popular culture.

As Udry (1971) observed, there are two contradictory myths about marriage: one is cynical and the other romantic. Despite their inconsistency, many people hold to both.

The first myth—"and they lived happily ever after"—portrays marriage as a continuous courtship. The second myth is the picture of the domestic grind: the husband sits behind the paper, the wife moves about in the morning disarray; the husband leaves for work, the wife spends the day among dishes, diapers, and dirty little children. Although, as with most myths, no one *really* believes either one of them, they continue to affect the behavior of most people. (p. 270)

This popular ambivalence about marriage forms the basis of much of the humor on television and in the comics and cartoons, as exemplified in such fare as "Maggie and Jiggs," "I Love Lucy," "Dagwood and Blondie," mother-in-law jokes, and ball-and-chain jokes. George Orwell (1953) once took a long look at this kind of humor, in the particular form of obscene penny postcards. Orwell was writing of the English scene around the early 1940s, but the kind of humor he described persists; it is, as he said, "something as traditional as Greek tragedy, a sort of subworld of smacked bottoms and scrawny mothers-in-law which is a part of Western European consciousness." He listed the conventions of the sex joke:

Marriage only benefits the woman. Every man is plotting seduction and every woman is plotting marriage. No woman ever remains unmarried voluntarily. . . .

Sex appeal vanishes at about the age of 25. Well-preserved and good-looking people beyond their first youth are never represented. The amorous honeymooning couple reappear as the grim-visaged wife and shapeless, mustachioed, red-nosed husband, no intermediate stage being allowed for. . . .

Next to sex, the henpecked husband is the favorite joke. Typical caption: "Did they get an X-ray of your wife's jaw at the hospital?"— "No, they got a moving picture instead."

CONVENTIONS:

(i) There is no such thing as a happy marriage.
(ii) No man ever gets the better of a woman in an argument. (p. 107)

Orwell explained this humor in much the same way that some sociologists have explained the persistence of prostitution and pornography: as a sort of safety valve, a harmless rebellion against virtue, which protects a stable family life by giving some expression to otherwise disrupting impulses. This humor, said Orwell, implies that

marriage is something profoundly exciting and important, the biggest event in the average human being's life. . . . Jokes about nagging wives and tyrannous mothers-in-law . . . imply a stable society in which marriage is indissoluble and family loyalty taken for granted. . . . The working-class outlook . . . takes it almost as a matter of course that youth and adventure— almost indeed, individual life—end with marriage. (p. 109)

Orwell overlooked something else about such jokes: practically all are based on the male viewpoint, expressing male resentment of women. There are no male counterparts to the stock figures of the wife in curlers wielding a rolling pin, the nagging mother-in-law, and the crotchety old maid. Males appear only as victims of female domination— Dagwood Bumstead, Jiggs, Fred Flintstone, and others. There is no positive image of women other than the sweet young thing.

Such antifemale humor was encouraged during the Middle Ages when people who deviated from marital norms were publicly taunted. Historian Natalie Davis (1971) has described communal festivals in which all sorts of people were mocked, in something like the spirit of a school play making fun of the teachers. A prominent part of these festivities, or charivari, was the public humiliation of husbands who had allowed themselves to be henpecked or deceived, of widows and widowers who had remarried younger spouses, and newlyweds who had failed to produce a child in the first year of marriage. These customs were obviously an attempt to control family behavior, particularly women's. Davis noted, however, that they may have unintentionally encouraged the kind of rebellious behavior they mocked.

Sophisticated Ambivalence

Another brand of humorous ambivalence toward marriage occurs in the sophisticated tradition. This tradition includes the French bedroom farce and the humor of such magazines as *Esquire* and *Playboy*. Here the main source of humor is adultery, and the complications arising from deception and discovery.

This brand of humor reflects the moral order of the continental upper-middle class, in which separation of love and marriage is assumed, love affairs are expected of both spouses, but especially the husband, and conjugal love, particularly of long standing, is perverse.

I've been married 18 years,
And still adore my wife.
I have no hunger for other women,
I am content to be faithful,
I am resigned to decency.
I actually think I have found love and Life.
What's the matter with me?
—John Haynes Holmes (Cited in Klemesrud,
    1971, p. 23)

This poem, written in 1922, was quoted by a journalist who observed, "Even back in 1922, when those lines were written, people were asking themselves, albeit ironically, whether they were some kind of freaks because their marriages were happy" (Klemesrud, 1971, p. 23).

Cross-Cultural Ambivalence

Marital conflict and ambivalence toward marriage are not confined to Western European culture. William Stephens (1963), in his worldwide survey of family practices, has shown that divorce is as universal a custom as marriage. No known society forbids divorce—with the exception of Christian countries. Even here, however, escape can be found in the form of annulments and informal separations, as well as in approved ways of not marrying at all, such as joining religious orders. In spite of the widespread belief that marital disharmony is unique to modern industrial society, no culture has found the formula for perfect marriage.

Sexual Politics and Power Struggle

Two separate sources of marital strain are often inextricably bound together in real life, but should be kept separate for purposes of analysis. The first results as the inevitable by-product of any prolonged intimate association between two people, regardless of their gender: difficulties may arise from basic temperamental incompatibilities and differences in tastes and opinions or from changes in these. There are also momentary disharmonies of mood—one partner may feel tired while the other feels lively. Further, there is always the issue of whose wishes will prevail at a given moment, and how to decide whose wishes will prevail.

Legal Images of Marriage

We mentioned earlier that marriage always involves something more than just the relationship between people. The legal aspects of marriage are one of the important ways in which the institution goes beyond the interpersonal relationship. For most people the legal side of marriage is experienced only at the time of marriage or divorce, or when inheritance of property becomes an issue. There is more to marriage as a legal institution, however, than a series of procedures one has to go through to get married or divorced. The law defines what marriage is, what the relationships between the spouses should be, and the economic and social obligations of the spouses to each other

A California couple on their second wedding anniversary. Berkeley, 1979. [Helen Nestor]

and to their children, during the marriage and in the event of divorce.

In recent years there have been major changes in family law. Although the legal system has often lagged behind social reality, courts and legislators in many places have been trying to bring legal practices in line with recent changes in marriage and family patterns. The current reality is hard to describe. The traditional legal mode of marriage, which we will describe in more detail, is still on the books in many places, yet is being altered in significant ways.

Until the late 1970s getting married meant committing oneself to a detailed set of duties, rights, and obligations. Most people were unaware of the exact terms of contract implied by traditional legal marriage. Lenore Weitzman (1977) summarizes the four essential provisions in the traditional marriage contract. These assume that (1) the husband is the head of the household, (2) the husband is responsible for support, (3) the wife is responsible for domestic services, and (4) the wife is responsible for child care.

The historical traditions of Western law, from Roman times on, have defined women as inferior beings who must be under the protection of a man. The wedding custom of a father "giving" his daughter to the groom reflects this legal notion. Further, whatever women's status in general, they usually lost legal rights by marrying. In most countries there are two legal statuses for women: one for spinsters and one for married women.

The married woman's loss of legal rights can be traced to the feudal doctrine of coverture, the notion that the husband and wife are a unity.

Based in part upon Biblical notions of the unity of flesh of husband and wife, the doctrine was described by Blackstone as follows: "By marriage, the husband and wife are one person in law; that is, the very being or legal existence of the woman is suspended during the marriage, or at least is incorporated and consolidated." . . . The doctrine . . . has worked out in reality to mean . . . the one is the husband. (Kanowitz, 1969, p. 35)

The clearest symbol of the married woman's loss of an independent identity is her assumption of her husband's name; she also assumes his residence and his social and economic status. Although some women are trying to retain their maiden names, there are many obstacles in their way: they may have trouble voting, obtaining a driver's license, or securing credit. The woman's assumption of her husband's residence also affects a number of rights and duties, such as where she must vote, register a car, pay taxes, and so on.

In the United States today, married women also lose some of their rights to control property, and they cannot enter into contracts on the same basis as men or single women. In some states the husband controls the wife's earnings and property, and can dispose of it without her consent. The wife, on the other hand, has no right to a share of her husband's earnings beyond that necessary to run the household. She is not entitled to direct compensation for doing domestic work—her husband is merely obliged to "maintain" her. This distribution of obligations has been described by one observer as the economic relationship between an owner and his property, rather than between two free individuals (Crozier, 1935, cited in Kanowitz, 1969).

Discussions of family law can sound abstract and irrelevant for most people's lives, but family law is a part of an invisible web of forces maintaining family structures in the traditional forms. Family structures are backed in many ways that are not easily observable. As William J. Goode (1971) has pointed out, most people take the family structures they live in for granted and do not challenge them. We do not see the application of force to maintain family patterns, but its threat creates and maintains an imbalance of power:

For example, if in a patrilineal polygamous society an older woman were to announce that she is henceforth to be treated as the leader of her patriline, tried to sell its cattle, started to give orders, set dates for rituals, or chose a chief, very likely she would be beaten or treated as insane. Similarly, if a child in our society were to claim the headship of the family, give orders to his parents or siblings, try to write checks on his father's account, or trade in the automobile for a new one, the same result would occur. (Goode, 1971, p. 625)

The legal restrictions and obligations enter in subtle ways into the social exchange between marriage partners. Even if both spouses try to have a more egalitarian arrangement than the law allows, they may run into legal difficulties. Thus a couple may agree that the wife should keep her maiden name, or maintain a residence in another state, or buy a house on her own, or open her own charge account, but legal traditions and business practices may prevent them from carrying out these wishes or may cost the wife or the couple certain privileges. Or a couple may wish to challenge the legal precedent that a wife owes her husband household services and is not to be directly paid for them. The courts, however, may not grant a husband the right to pay for something he is entitled to free.

In a Texas case, David promised his wife, Fannie, that he would give her $5000 if she would stay with him while he lived and continue taking care of the house and farm accounts, selling his butter, and doing all the other tasks which she had done since their marriage. After David's death, Fannie sued his estate for the money which had been promised her. The court held the contract was unenforceable since Fannie had agreed to do nothing which she was not already legally and morally bound to do as David's wife. (Pilpel & Zavin, 1964, p. 65)

Recently there has been a growing trend for couples to write their own custom-designed marriage contracts, although alterations in the traditional contract face continued legal barriers (Weitzman, 1981b). An individual premarital contract could be expected to deal with such issues as the following: the aims and expectations of the relationship, the management and control of wages, the allocation of responsibility for support and household duties, relations with others outside the marriage, and plans for children. Such contracts may clarify the intentions and expectations of each partner, hence they may be useful even if their provisions may be legally unenforceable.

The idea of negotiated contracts between husbands and wives may seem to most readers an intrusion of business practices into an intimate relationship. It is not only women's liberationists, however, who have argued for such explicit bargaining; some marriage counselors have advocated this approach to dealing with the nitty-gritty conflicts of daily life.

The Divorce Revolution and the Transformation of Marriage

As we have seen, family law is changing now. The traditional model of marriage in the law remains on the books in some places and influences the behavior of judges and legislators. And in many ways, its sex-role assumptions reflect inequalities between men and women that are still part of social reality.

There is no doubt, however, that we are in the midst of a profound transformation in the legal definition of what marriage is and is not.

A legal scholar, Mary Ann Glendon (1977), has argued that recent changes in the law in America and elsewhere represent a "withering away of marriage." Her point is not that marriage is about to disappear, but that the state in the United States and Western Europe is gradually withdrawing from much of what it has previously done to regulate marriage. Legal obstacles to the formation and dissolution of marriage have lessened. Within the ongoing marriages, the individuality of the spouses is increasingly recognized, and cohabitation, as in the Marvin case, has emerged as a new legal institution that imitates marriage. The distinction between legitimate and illegitimate children is being erased.

The new divorce laws illustrate the law's changing image of marriage. Since 1970 there has been a major reform in divorce law, commonly referred to as no-fault divorce. It was first adopted in California and has since spread in one form or another to most other states.

The new laws have done more than change the rules of divorce; they also have transformed the meaning of legal marriage (Weitzman, 1985; Weitzman & Dixon, 1980). Historically the law has defined marriage as a lifelong permanent union that could only be dissolved by the death of one of the parties. Divorces or separations were granted only under extreme and rare circumstances. Even when divorce laws were liberalized around the turn of the century, the underlying model of marriage remained the same: a permanent union to be protected and preserved by the state.

Thus traditional divorce law permitted divorce only if one spouse committed a marital "offense." Because marriage was defined as a lifelong, permanent union, only such serious marital misconduct as adultery, cruelty, or desertion justified divorce. Traditional divorce proceedings centered on the issue of who was guilty of a marital fault and who was the innocent party. Child-custody arrangements and financial settlements were intended to reward the "innocent" and punish the "guilty." Divorce proceedings were often a charade in which couples took the roles of plaintiff and defendant and testified to "appropriate violations" of the marriage contract.

Many criticisms of the existing laws and practices led to the passage of no-fault divorce laws. These laws do away with the requirement of fault and of guilty and innocent spouses. They allow divorces on the basis of "irreconcilable differences" or "marital breakdown." In so doing, the new laws tried to bring divorce law more in line with the social realities of how marriages come apart.

Ironically, however, the new no-fault divorce laws, while eliminating much of the acrimony and hypocrisy from divorce proceedings, have turned out to be catastrophic for women and children. They are responsible for much of the "feminization of poverty" in recent years—the increasing proportion of poor families headed by women. Most of the country's poor and near-poor children are not the offspring of unwed teenagers, but the children of divorced mothers who have suffered the severe economic consequences of the new laws.

These effects have been documented in Lenore Weitzman's book *The Divorce Revolution* (1985). She shows that while divorce usually improves the economic position of husbands, it seriously reduces that of women and children, who remain with their mother in more than 90 percent of the cases. Thus, the husband's standard of living improves by 42 percent after divorce, while that of the wife declines by 73 percent.

The shocking effects of the new laws are a striking example of unanticipated consequences. The framers of the new laws, preoccupied with the defects of the traditional divorce laws, did not realize that they offered protection to women and children. If a woman had not given her husband grounds for divorce, such as adultery, she could agree to a divorce only if he provided adequate support for herself and the children. Further, judges would often divide property in accord with family need. The mother and children retained the family home and enough support to avoid sudden poverty.

More recently, the family's assets are split in half at the time of divorce, providing what Weitzman calls an illusion of equality. The man retains half the property, while the woman and the children split the other half. Often the family home must be sold to divide the proceeds in half. The husband, meanwhile, retains the major intangible assets of the marriage—his career assets, future earning power, education, pensions, insurance. The wife confronts a job market where women earn 64 cents to the dollar earned by a man. To make matters worse, the new laws usually fail to provide adequate child support, and even when they do, more than half of men fail to comply with them. Weitzman's findings are based mostly on California; in other states the situation is still worse. No one, however, advocates a return to the old divorce law; Weitzman and others have proposed changes to modify the worst effects of the new ones.

MODELS OF MARRIAGE: PARADISE AND PARADOX

"In every marriage more than two weeks old," playwright Robert Anderson once wrote, "there are grounds for divorce. The trick is to find and continue to find grounds for marriage." W. H. Goode (1982) makes a similar point when he observes that the ultimate cause of divorce is marriage. Any time two adults live together intimately, tensions are inevitable. Intimacy brings rewards, but it also has its costs.

In most societies, Goode points out, the inevitable tensions of marriage are contained in various ways. Couples are not led to expect happiness and fulfillment in marriage, and divorce may be difficult or impossible. Thus, we cannot conclude that where divorce rates are low, marriages are happy. Even forbidding divorce does not necessarily keep couples together. In many Catholic countries, before divorce was permitted, married couples would often separate informally. The men would often set up households with other women, in effect having a second marriage without benefit of the law.

Many studies of marital adjustment have accepted uncritically the high expectations of marriage that prevail in our culture. They have failed to recognize that even under the most stable social conditions, marriage is a complex and ambivalent form of human interaction. Orwell recognized this when he described sex and marriage jokes as a kind of collective jeer, a protest against marriage on the part of people who take it very seriously.

In modern urban societies marriage becomes even more problematic as tolerance for divorce and adultery arises, individuals change, and the need for intimacy and personal realization increases. Marriage studies typically overlook the large social forces altering marital relations, marriage, and the people in them. They perpetuate a utopian romantic mystique of marriage.

Marital adjustment—satisfaction, success, happiness, and so on—is the oldest and most studied variable in the field of marriage and the family (Spanier & Lewis, 1980). Yet it is beset with profound problems of defini-

tion and method. Recently, researchers have tried to resolve some of the difficulties by using the term marital *quality*, but the conceptual and methodological issues remain. Some researchers argue that the concepts of marital success, adjustment, happiness, and so on are so hopelessly vague and value-laden that they should be abandoned. Recently, Donohue and Ryder (1982) suggested that "Finally, it may be time to abandon the fundamental idea that there *is*, in any meaningful sense, a general dimension of marriage satisfaction, marital happiness, marital distress, or marital quality" (p. 747). Even researchers who accept the concept of marital quality find much to criticize in current research practices (Gilford & Bengston, 1979; Norton, 1983).

Nevertheless, despite all the controversy about defining and measuring marital quality, there is general agreement that the concept points to something real: some marriages seem to "work" very well, others generate stress and misery.

Utopian Marriage: The Adjustment Model

Traditionally, measures of marital adjustment were based on contentment with middle-class values, conservative definitions of sex roles, and a stress on harmony and absence of conflict. If there is any conflict at all, it is confined to the "period of adjustment," that stage between the bliss of the honeymoon and the mellow years of pure conjugal love.

The concept of marital adjustment used in the major studies, and in particular the prediction-of-success type of study, has been severely criticized on several grounds. One complaint charges that the studies rely too heavily on self-reports—that is, the individuals themselves rate how happy their marriages are and how happy their childhoods were, so the correlations may reflect nothing more than the tendency of some people to describe themselves and their families in favorable terms. This point has been documented in a series of studies by Edmonds (1967; Edmonds, Withers, & DiBatista, 1972). He put together a series of statements about marriage that would be too good to be true for anyone—for example, "If my mate has any faults, I am not aware of them"; "Every new thing I have learned about my mate has pleased me." Agreeing with such statements is an indicator of what Edmonds calls marital "conventionalization." He finds that conventionalization is widespared and that marital adjustment scales are heavily influenced by the tendency. Further, Edmonds's data show that, contrary to the prevailing views in the marriage literature, there is no connection between being conventional and conservative and having a happy marriage. He finds that when the distorting tendency of conventionalism is controlled statistically, people who hold traditional moral attitudes, who go to church regularly, and who abstain from premarital sex do not have a greater degree of marital adjustment than those who do not.

Edmonds's argument is with the measurement of adjustment in marriage rather than with the concept itself. Other critics have argued with the assumption that happiness is the criteria for a good relationship. George Simpson (1960) observed:

On the happiness schedule of Burgess and Wallin any person who gets very high scores may not be happy but slap-happy. . . . Their general satisfaction schedule is no less unsatisfactory. . . . Here we find the question: Do you ever regret your marriage? Answers and scores are as follows: frequently, 0; occasionally, 1; rarely, 3; never, 5. But a mature answer is: of course, but the very regret is the ambivalent aspect of my joy in it. All human satisfaction is tinged with dissatisfaction; by taking up one option, we surrender others.

The human psyche is not structured in such a way that answers to such questions give any indication of fundamental personality traits or make possible understanding of an individual's capacity for being interrelated with another. (p. 217)

Similar problems arise if happiness is defined as an absence of conflict and quarreling. One reason why a couple may not have any arguments is that they do not talk to each other very much in the first place. But as Simpson contended, quarrels and arguments are inevitable in marriage.

A Psychoanalytic Utopia: The Intimacy Model

Critics of the conventional adjustment notion argue that it is based on the wrong values, that it is superficial and does not deal with the quality of the couple's relationship and the kind of life they lead. Really "good" marriages, they say, focus on the qualities of openness, intimacy, trust, and personal growth. The classic statement on this ideal of marriage is provided by Erik Erikson (1963).

In this model of marriage the focus of marital success or failure rests squarely in the psyche of each spouse—more specifically, in the ego capacities. Marriage is seen as a critical developmental stage in the life of each individual, a sort of "maturity test" that a person must pass if he or she is to be a healthy, well-adjusted person. Erikson divides the lifespan into eight stages, each with its own point of conflict or encounter between the individual and the environment, and with its own distinctive outcome of personality "success" or "failure." Thus the first stage centers on how well the infant's need for "love" in the form of food and tender care is fulfilled, and the outcome is a basic sense of trust or mistrust. The most well known of Erikson's stages, the adolescent period, focuses on the "identity crisis"—the problem of finding one's own identity.

The next stage of life after adolescence is called the stage of "intimacy versus isolation," and one passes it, in part, by having a successful marriage. Erikson describes this stage as follows:

The young adult, emerging from the search for an insistence on identity, is eager and willing to fuse his identity with that of another. He is ready for intimacy, that is, the capacity to commit himself to concrete affiliations and partnerships and to develop the ethical strength to abide by such commitments, even though they may call for significant sacrifices and compromises. (p. 263)

Only during this period can "true genitality" develop, adolescent sexuality being dominated by searching for one's own identity or for a competitive kind of sexual combat.

The idea that marriage makes a unit of two people is, of course, an ancient one. "A man shall leave father and mother and shall cleave to his wife and the twain shall be one flesh," says the Bible. Within social science the idea of marriage as mutual identification also goes back a long time, relatively speaking. In 1926, for example, Burgess wrote of marriage as a unity of interacting personalities.

A different version of the intimacy model of marriage has been suggested by people connected with the human potential movement. Herbert Otto (1970), for example, wrote:

Marriage can be envisioned as a framework for actualizing personal potential. . . .
The New Marriage offers an ongoing adventure of self-discovery, personal growth, unfoldment, and fulfillment.

Another version of "the new marriage" is described in the O'Neills' book *Open Mar-* *riage* (1972). Criticizing traditional marriage for the limitations it imposes on the individual, the O'Neills proposed a model of marriage that stresses complete openness of communication, flexible roles, openness to outside contacts and interests, as well as "supportive caring" and the commitment of both partners to their own and others' psychological growth.

A major flaw shared by these models is their tendency to idealize marriage—to present utopian images of marriage rarely found in real life. The adjustment model, as we've noticed, leaves no place in marriage for conflict or disagreement between the spouses. Although the proponents of the intimacy model reject the idea that the marital relationship consists of only positive feelings, they do assume that conflicts are resolved through mature sacrifice and compromise. Each partner is conceived to be an individual with his or her own needs and wishes, and at the same time able to fulfill genitality. Marital problems are attributed to the unresolved neurotic tendencies of each spouse. Goethals and associates (1976) pointed out the difficulties in equating genital maturation with the capacity for intimacy.

Even the most cursory reading of the anthropological literature or an examination of non-middle-class standards suggests that sexual gratification per se is by no means related to or a predictor of an emotional relationship. Many cultures and subcultures . . . attach little if any emotional significance to adult sexual relationships. While tenderness and affection can be expressed toward children and while there can be extremely strong ties of family loyalty, the emotional overtones so characteristic of modern Western romantic attachment are entirely absent. (p. 231)

In short, the psychoanalytic model of marriage overlooks macrosocial and cultural influences on personal relationships. Furthermore, both the intimacy and the adjustment models overlook the strains that life in contemporary society places on marriage. Rather than the average or expectable state of married life, a "good" marriage may be a rare achievement or lucky accident. Both models fail to deal with the social changes that have transformed the urban scene and increased the pressures on marriage. The increasing acceptability of adultery and divorce, for example, may increase people's sensitivity to potential sources of dissatisfaction in their marriage. The emphasis on the nuclear family as the prime locus of intimacy may strain the marriage relationship by reducing the opportunity to satisfy needs for closeness and support within the larger community. As one writer observed:

It is ironic that sophisticated psychoanalytic theorizing tends to perpetuate the romantic mystique that Americans have always attached to marriage; nowhere is one able to find the vaguest hint of the ennui, the struggle over the minute details of existence, the hostility, and the sense of confinement that at *times* characterize the very best of marriages. (Shaffer, 1970, p. 173)

Finally, both models of marriage are unidimensional; they assume that all marriages can be lined up along a single dimension of adjustment, happiness, maturity, or else be clearly categorized as good or bad, healthy or pathological. A few studies, however, have attempted to explore the diversity that exists in marriage. Even during the 1950s there was much more diversity in marriage than social scientists recognized. As Elizabeth Bott (1957) has pointed out:

It is often assumed that there is a large measure of agreement on familial norms in the society as a whole. . . . Such a view implies that given individuals will recognize that these agreed-upon external standards exist, and that they will be

able to make the norms explicit without difficulty. (p. 194)

In her own research on marital roles in urban families, however, Bott found much more variation in the norms than is commonly assumed. Further, many of the people interviewed had a hard time generalizing about customary and proper behavior for husbands and wives. They were too much aware of variation among their acquaintances.

Marriage as Conflict: Exchange and Strategy Models

Although the prevailing models of marriage in the family literature have stressed adjustment, intimacy, and mutuality of interests between spouses, there has always tended to be a minority view stressing the competitive and conflictual aspects of marriage. Jessie Bernard (1964) has traced the history of this view of marriage.

The conception of the relation between the sexes as a bargaining situation is very old. Quite aside from the patent form of bride purchase or the dowry, the psychological give and take between men and women has long been viewed as essentially a duel of wits for advantage. . . .

It was Waller who formulated most elaborately and insightfully the bargaining model of the relations between the sexes. His application was primarily to the premarital period, but the fundamental processes are the same, although the specific "goods" involved in the exchange may vary greatly—love, mink coats, sex relations, approval, "freedom," etc. (p. 705)

In recent years the old insight that the daily events of social life could be compared to economic transactions or the dealings between hostile countries has been greatly systematized. Game theory, social-exchange theory, and strategic-bargaining theory all represent attempts to offer precise analyses or models of various types of competitive—and cooperative—behavior.

Classical game theory, based on pure competition and the assumption that any loss incurred by one side is matched by pure gain on the other, is not regarded as an appropriate model for international relations, much less marriage, so it need not concern us here.

The kind of model that is applied to marriage, one called a "mixed-motive" or "cooperative" model, is based, among other things, on a situation in which both sides can win and both can lose. Here is a rather simple situation: John and Mary, a married couple, have had a fight. They have said some harsh things to each other. Each would like to make up, but each is afraid of being the first to act friendly and being rebuffed by the other person. A similar situation: a young man and woman, strangers to each other, are deciding whether to act friendly or to ignore the other. Each party's preferred outcome is to smile and to receive a smile in return, but since each fears a frown, neither smiles! (Those who know something about the literature on mixed-motive models will recognize the outline of the Prisoner's Dilemma game.)

All exchange approaches share a cost–benefit-analysis way of looking at personal relations, but they differ among themselves in assumptions and detail. Here are some observations on love, based on Peter Blau's version of exchange theory:

The more an individual is in love with another, the more anxious he or she is likely to be to please the other. The individual who is less deeply involved in a love relationship, therefore, is in an advantageous position, since the other's greater concern with continuing the relationship makes him or her dependent and gives the less involved individual power. Waller called this "the principle of least interest." This power can be used to exploit the other; the woman who exploits a man's affection for economic gain and the boy who sexually exploits a girl who is in love with him are obvious examples. . . .

To safeguard the value of her affection, a woman must be ungenerous in expressing it and make any evidence of her growing love a cherished prize that cannot easily be won. . . .

The aim of both sexes in courtship is to furnish sufficient rewards to seduce the other, but not enough to deflate their value, yet the line defined by these two conditions is often imperceptible. (Bernard, 1964, pp. 78–80)

Beyond Exchange

Paradoxically, there is something both obviously right and obviously wrong about the social exchange model of relationships. People do tend to stay in relationships they find rewarding, and try to leave those that are ungratifying and even painful. On the other hand, the social exchange model of individuals as selfish calculators of the "bottom line" seems to be an inaccurate description of social reality.

There has been a good deal of dissatisfaction with social exchange models in the social science literature (Berscheid, 1985). As Levinger (1974) observed, the strength of the theory is also its weakness—"that which explains everything explains nothing." A major problem is determining what is a reward or cost to whom. Sometimes people's behavior seems to defy any clear notion of cost or benefit. For example, Berscheid observed:

What we see is people who love each other (or at least they say so . . .) literally beating each other about the head and shoulders, as those who investigate family violence are documenting. . . . We see people experiencing the most intense positive emotion in association with persons whom they indicate . . . to be neither "kind" nor "industrious," but rather thoroughly unreliable scoundrels, and conversely, we see persons giving

A couple in a family therapy session. [David M. Grossman/ Photo Researchers, Inc.]

the most glowing appraisals to a person they have just decided to dump in the divorce court— "a prince of a fellow," she says, "but I no longer wish to associate with him." (1982, p. 42)

In short, one person's reward may be another's cost, and people's feelings toward one another may not be consistent. Researchers have not found ways of measuring ambivalence, but it is an extremely important aspect of close relationships. Apart from the mixture of love and hostility that clinicians find in their patients, ordinary life supplies examples every day.

For example the sex-role changes of recent years have been confusing and difficult in part because people are ambivalent about them. Women complain that men expect them to be competent and successful on the job, but still feminine and "nice." Men complain that women want them to be loving, gentle and sensitive like a woman, but also strong and aggressive in the workplace. A man who is gentle and emotionally expressive may be regarded by both men and women not as a "new liberated man," but as a "wimp" (Brehm, 1985). Similarly, a woman who is competent and assertive runs the risk of being labeled a "bitch."

The same ambivalence about changing roles occurs within marriage, as Lillian Rubin observes in her book *Intimate Strangers*

(1983). She finds a staunch feminist confessing she sometimes feels angry at her husband for not supporting his wife and kids all by himself, as her father did. A man appreciates his wife's contribution to the family income, but longs nostalgically for the "good old days" when "a man was a man and a woman was a woman" (p. 35). Another woman voices the wish Rubin finds among most of the wives she interviewed—a wish for greater intimacy with her husband. Yet at the same time that she wants him to be interested in what she is thinking and feeling, she is also relieved that he doesn't know or seem to care what is in her mind. "There's a way it feels safer even though there's also a kind of loneliness about it" (p. 86).

Marriage as Paradox: Communications Model

The objection to game-theory and exchange models is not their portrayal of marriage as a conflict-prone institution or one in which bargaining takes place, but rather the qualities they ascribe to marital conflict. In these models conflict consists of the coldly rational sparring of two opponents simply trying to maximize their own gains.

A model that seems to fit better the daily facts of marital and family conflict is based on what has been called a "communicational" or "systems approach" to the family. It was originally developed by a group of psychiatrists and psychologists who studied the interaction in families with a schizophrenic member. As we noted earlier, the insights developed by this research have been extended to normal family life.

The basic tenets of communication theory may be contained in a short set of statements. These statements are more like assumptions of theorems in mathematics than hypotheses that can be tested and possibly rejected. Within the perspective of the theory, that is, they are self-evidently true.

The most basic principle is that it is impossible not to communicate—just as it is impossible not to behave. When two people meet, therefore, they have to decide how they are going to behave toward each other, and what kinds of messages they are going to exchange. They also must decide what sorts of things they will not say and do. This process is referred to as "defining the relationship."

Whenever one person speaks to another, the message either reinforces the ongoing definition or suggests a shift. One of the issues they can't avoid dealing with is that of dominance versus equality: will they deal with each other as equals, or will they assume complementary positions in which one will show respect for the other? These decisions will determine how they will address one another—whether they will use each other's first names, call each other "mister," or whether one will use "mister" and the other the first name. The other basic dimension of social life is what Roger Brown (1965) has called solidarity or affection. It also determines the content of messages as well as such things as how far the two people will stand from each other when speaking and whether one may put an arm around the other.

Another basic concept of communications analysis is that human communication always takes place at several levels. People not only say something, but they qualify what they say by their tone of voice, facial expressions, body movements, and by the context. A person, for example, can say yes to a request in an almost infinite number of ways, expressing anything from eagerness to extreme reluctance. Incongruity often occurs between these levels. Teasing and sarcasm are familiar ways of qualifying statements; in each instance the main message is disqualified by the speaker: "Don't take this statement seriously."

Finally, communications theory sees in any statement a person makes to another an attempt to control or define that relationship. This does not mean that one tries necessarily to be the boss or to advance one's self-interest in an obvious way. Consider the example of a person who acts helpless; such behavior is an invitation for the other person to take care of the helpless one. But the helpless person may control the relationship since he or she has been able to exert influence over the behavior of the other person. The more extreme the helplessness of the dependent one, as for example, a baby or a very sick person, the more the dependency may seem to be a form of domination. One cannot avoid communicating, or qualifying one's communication, or controlling the definition of the relationship.

How does the communication perspective apply to marriage? Marriage in these terms is seen as a situation in which two people must define their relationship to each other. That is, they must work out rules for living together as well as rules for making the rules. The couple need not necessarily be aware of the rules they are following, but they cannot, accordingly, avoid having them.

Whenever they complete a transaction, a rule is being established. Even if they should set out to behave entirely spontaneously, they would be establishing the rule that they are to behave in that way. (Haley, 1963, p. 123)

For example, couples must make rules about what kind of work each will do, how much say each one will have in the other's work, whose responsibility the various household chores will be, whether each can criticize the other, whether when one person makes a mistake the other is to comfort or criticize him or her, what topics are open for discussion and what topics are too sensitive to bring up, what roles outsiders are to play in the marriage, whether inlaws are outsiders, and so on.

Conflicts arise over the rules themselves, over who sets the rules, and over incompatible rules. One almost inevitable source of conflict results from the fact that the two spouses come from two different families. Each family would have impressed its child with its own set of implicit and explicit rules for dealing with people, for managing household finances and routines, and even for the proper distance one should stand from another person while talking to him or her. Disagreements over the rules themselves can often be settled by compromise. The really emotional battles occur over who is to make the rules. These have to do with the control aspects of the marriage.

For example, a wife could insist that her husband hang up his clothes so that she does not have to pick up after him like a servant. The husband might agree with his wife that she should not be his servant, and so agree to the definition of the relationship, but he still might not agree that *she* should be the one to give him orders on what to do about his clothes. (Haley, 1963, p. 226)

The communications approach helps to explain why talking things out doesn't always lead to a resolution of the problem and why heated arguments can arise over trivial matters. The proponents of this view do not argue that improved communication leads to improved relationships, or that interpersonal conflicts result only from failures of communication. Rather, they point out that talking things over and expressing feelings openly may make things worse between a wife and husband, or a parent and child, as often as it clears the air.

The communications perspective shows how anyone can become involved in irritating and disappointing hangups in the nitty-gritty struggles of daily life. It reveals how the interaction between two people has properties of its own, independent of their particular personalities. Consider, for example, the concept of paradoxical communication. A simple example of a paradoxical communication is the statement, "I command you to disobey me." The situation of the wife telling the husband to pick up his clothes also contains a paradox, but a more subtle one:

The communication of bids for two incompatible types of relationships can occur whenever there is an incompatibility between (a) the rule defining a relationship, and (b) the type of relationship implicit in *who* is defining the relationship. For example, if a wife tells her husband to pick up his own clothes. However, *when she tells him to do this* she is defining the relationship as complementary—she orders and he is to follow the orders. The husband is then faced with two different definitions of the relationship so that whichever way he responds, he cannot satisfy both requests. If he picks up his clothes, accepting the symmetrical definition, he is following her directions and so accepting a complementary definition. He cannot accept one definition without the other unless he comments on the situation in a way that redefines it. More likely he will erupt in indignation while uncertain what he is indignant about and his wife will similarly be indignant because he erupts over this simple request. (Haley, 1963, pp. 127–128)

A similar kind of paradox occurs when one spouse tells another to be more independent, or expressive, or assertive: "I command you to be spontaneous" or "I command you to love me."

Sexual relationships are full of such paradoxical messages, providing further examples of the problems of communication. Not only are there taboos about talking about sex matters in the first place, but there are taboos against talking about the taboos (Laing, 1969). Further, even if a couple does talk to each other about sex, talking may often lead to conflicts that are difficult to resolve:

For example, if a wife turns her back on her husband in bed, assuming that if he is interested in sexual relations he will turn her over, the husband might assume from her behavior that she is not interested in sexual relations and so he does not turn her over. Both spouses can then feel that the other is disinterested, and both can then feel righteously indignant. If this conflict is at the level of what kind of relationship to have, it can be resolved as a misunderstanding. Discussion and correction of the signals involved will lead to more amiable relations. However, if the couple is in a struggle over who is to define the type of relationship, discussion of the situation will not necessarily relieve the problem. After discussion, the wife may still feel that it is a law of life that only the man initiates sex relations, and she will not let him impose a different relationship upon her. The husband may continue to feel that he will not impose himself upon his wife until she has expressed some interest, and she is not going to tell him how to conduct himself. In this struggle, he might label her as frigid, and she might label him as unmanly. (Haley, 1963, p. 130)

Similar problems can arise over specific practices; one partner might define a satisfactory sex relationship as one that includes oral sex, whereas the other partner might define oral sex as unnecessary or even disgusting.

There are still other paradoxes in sexual interaction. For example, sex is supposed to be the ultimate refuge from the rat race, but achievement pressures exist as much in the bedroom as elsewhere. On the one hand, sex is supposed to be a free surrender to basic impulses and instincts; on the other hand, what you do and when you do it are supposed to be in tune with the needs of the other person. Each partner is supposed to let the other know what he or she wants. If a person doesn't communicate this information, he or she may be frustrated, and this frustration may spoil the partner's pleasure directly or indirectly. But the other horn of the dilemma is this: If one person communicates his or her own needs too clearly or too insistently, then the partner is likely to resent being *told* what to do; he or she may feel like a masturbatory tool of the other person, rather than a free sexual being.

Sexual hangups between couples probably result as much from communicational knots as from purely sexual problems. One of the attractions of affairs may be escape from the old knots, and the exploration of a new set of rules and metarules for talking about sex.

It is interesting that the Masters and Johnson (1970) therapy for couples having troubles in their sex lives is largely an attack on the couples' old communication or noncommunication patterns. This attack occurs at two levels. On the level of specifics, each partner is taught the preferences of the other by means of a hand-on-hand technique that eliminates the need for verbal communication. This technique and whole-therapy situation nearly disposes of the communications problem at the initial level. Now the therapists are telling the couple what to do and what not to do, thus extricating them from their impasse and presumably freeing them from their sex hangups by controlling their behavior and commanding that they be spontaneous.

Still another kind of communicational paradox occurs in the demand to be told what to do. Haley cited the example of a rebellious boy who says to his parents, "All right, tell me what to do from now on and I'll do it." If they tell him what to do, they are doing what the child tells them. The parents are likely to react to his statement of compliance with the same angry helplessness as they do to his demands. A similar situation is the following: a couple are trying to decide what movie to see or where to go on their vacation. After each one has suggested several alternatives and had them rejected by the other, one—say the husband—may say, "OK, *you* decide where we are going. Whatever you say, that's what we'll do." The recipient of such a message is likely to feel perplexed without knowing why. What has happened is that a symmetrical or equal relationship, deciding together what to do, has been changed to a complementary or unequal relationship in a paradoxical way. By demanding that the wife tell him what to do, the husband is in fact controlling her behavior, at the same time absolving himself of any blame if the movie or vacation spot turns out to be a dud.

In sum, then, the communication analysis of conflict, with its emphasis on ambivalence, paradox, and shifting emotional preferences, seems to do more justice to the complexities of marriage than the rational, cost–benefit analysis of game and exchange theory, or the face-saving of strategic-bargaining theory. One question that remains to be answered is whether paradoxical communication occurs in all human interaction or only in Western culture, and particularly in contemporary family life.

Types of Couples

In recent years a number of studies of marriage have begun to explore some of the diversity in outwardly conventional marriages. Most previous marriage studies tended to assume that all marriages could be lined up along a single dimension, with all the "good" marriages on one end of the scale and all the "bad" marriages on the other end.

The most well known of the descriptive studies is the one done by Cuber and Harroff (1965). These authors departed from the typical marriage study in several ways: They did not use the one-dimensional rationale of marital "adjustment"; they were more interested in collecting accounts of personal experience than in gathering statistics; they used no schedule of formal questions, but simply conversed with each person on the general subject of men and women for as many hours as the subjects felt like talking; and finally, they chose to study an elite group of subjects. Feeling that too many marriage studies had been done on families in crisis situations and too few on successful, "normal" upper-middle-class people, they chose their subjects from the top end of the income and occupation distribution: business executives, lawyers, government officials, and the like. They interviewed 437 such men and women, between the ages of 35 and 55.

One of the most widely quoted findings of this study is its description of five types of enduring marriage. The authors discovered enormous variation within a group of stable marriages among people of similar class positions, thus destroying the myth that "happy families are all alike."

Conflict-habituated marriage Cuber and Harroff described the "conflict-habituated marriage" as the type that is furthest removed from the notion of the happy/stable/conflict-free/adjusted couple as opposed to the unhappy/unstable/fighting/maladjusted couple. This type of marriage, though not the most prevalent, was the most dramatic one in the sample. In such marriages the couples simply fight with each other often. Being together usually suffices to trigger an argument, and the couple has a reputation for battling among the rest of the family. They do not, however, define the fighting as grounds for dissolving the marriage—to use communication terms, the husband and wife define it as acceptable to talk to each other that way. Cuber and Harroff speculated

that such spouses feel a lot of hostility that must be expressed, and the marital battles therefore bind them together.

Devitalized marriage In the second type, the "devitalized" marriage, the term applies to the relationship, not the individual wife or husband. Starting out their marriages romantically with love and closeness, these couples have drifted apart over the years but still get along with each other and want to stay married.

Passive-congenial marriage In the third type of marriage, called "passive–congenial," the couples differ from the devitalized couples in that they were never highly emotional about each other to begin with. Rather, they view being married as a convenient and comfortable way to live while directing one's true interests and creative energies elsewhere. Unlike the devitalized couples, these people do not regret the failure of their marriages to attain romantic stereotypes. Such a marriage can free the individuals to become absorbed in their careers or other social commitments. In other words these couples define their lack of intense involvement in each other as the way marriage ought to be—at least for them.

Although such a utilitarian version of marriage does not go along with popular romantic attitudes toward marriage or with the psychoanalytic intimacy model, it coincides with the European approach to marriage mentioned earlier. Moreover, it is not just upper-class or upper-middle-class circles in which this type of marriage is found. Elizabeth Bott (1957), in her study of English working-class and lower-middle-class families, found many marriages in which husband and wife led rather separate lives. Rather than having high-powered careers as did the Cuber and Harroff subjects, however, these people were involved in close-linked social networks of relatives, friends, and neighbors in relation to which the marriage tie was secondary.

Although all marriages must be understood in the context of their social and environmental surroundings, the dependency on outside forces is highlighted in the utilitarian type of marriage. If the strong involvement in career or community is missing, then such marriages can become drab cages of empty togetherness. Mirra Komarovsky (1962), in a sensitive study of blue-collar marriages, dealt with a group of white, Protestant, native-born American workers and their wives in a town she called "Glenton." These people do not hold romantic or psychological notions about marital companionship or intimacy, but—in contrast to Elizabeth Bott's Londoners and the Cuber and Harroff jet-setters—they also do not have many or strong outside associations and interests. Komarovsky argued that outside sources of stimulation, interest, and accomplishment may nourish a marriage while too much togetherness may overburden it, particularly for people who have not cultivated the skills of reflecting on and verbalizing their reactions to their experiences as daily life unfolds. She wrote:

Many couples in their late thirties, especially among the less educated, seem almost to have withdrawn from life. There they sit in front of the television set: "What's there to say? We both see it." "If you had two extra hours every day, how would you like to spend them?" asked the interviewer, and a man mused: "This would make the evening long and tiring if you're watching TV." (p. 107)

The passive–congenial or utilitarian marriage, though failing to live up to the ideal of what marriage should be, nevertheless confirms a common belief that a person must choose between work involvement and family involvement, that a hard-driving professional or successful executive must inevitably have an atrophied family life, and conversely that a man or woman deeply involved with spouse and children must lose out in the work rat race. There are, of course, plenty of examples of this stereotype. Most of the people studied by Cuber and Harroff fell into this category. But other findings by them and by Komarovsky dispute the notion that the more one invests in the family, the less time one has for work and outside friendships, and vice versa.

Komarovsky found that the people who were most involved in their work were the same ones who had more emotionally intense marriages. Similarly, the women who engaged in more leisure-time activities with their husbands also spent more time in club work and with women friends. The active, involved people had more education, which in this sample of blue-collar people meant having graduated from high school.

Vital marriage In the elite sample of Cuber and Harroff, there were also couples who belied the either/or stereotype about work involvement versus family involvement. The last two of their five types of marriage, the "vital" and the "total," conform more closely to the ideal image of what marriage is supposed to be. About one out of six of the marriages they studied fell into these two types. Again, the term *vital* refers to the relationship, not the personalities of the spouses. In the vital relationship the couple not only spend a lot of time together, but enjoy being together. The relationship itself is extremely important to each one, although the spouses do not lose their separate identities. Because the entire sample in this study was highly successful in work, there were of course no differences on that score between the vital couples and those with more utilitarian marriages.

Total marriage The last of the Cuber and Harroff types, the "total" marriage, differs from the vital marriages in that there are more aspects of life in which the couple participate together. The wife, for example, often is involved in various ways in the husband's work.

An interesting feature of these types of relationship, which the authors call "intrinsic," is the sense of being deviant among their friends and neighbors. Many of them felt that they had to hide their true feelings about their spouses for fear of being laughed at or doubted. That they were correct in judging how most people would react to them is shown by the comments of the Cuber and Harroff subjects in the more utilitarian types of marriage when the intrinsic types of marriage were discussed: some people doubted that there really were any such marriages, and some thought the people must be oddballs or immature. Others who knew people in such marriages disapproved of them—they felt that the spouses were so involved with each other that they weren't as devoted to their children as parents should be, or that they expressed too much affection in front of the children. The intrinsic couples, on the other hand, felt they did enough for their children and that many couples not that interested in each other often compensated by becoming overinvolved in their children's lives.

Other typologies Cuber and Harroff do not claim that their typology is the last word on marriages, or that their study is as high on methodological rigor as it is on human interest. They have presented suggestive findings and pointed out how some of the supposedly more scientific studies of marriage fall short as descriptions of real-life mar-

riages. Inevitably, however, their own study leaves many questions unanswered. Would different researchers, looking at the same sample of subjects, divide the subjects the same way and arrive at the same five types of marriages? Would another researcher perhaps have emphasized the sexual aspects less and considered other dimensions more—such as attitudes toward parenthood? Or, granting that the five types of marriage do have validity for the sample in the Cuber and Harroff study, would the same five types appear in a sample of people less affluent and of a different ethnic background?

Other researchers, looking at other families, have come up with different schemes for analyzing family life. A study of families by Hess and Handel (1959), for example, dealt with such matters as the images each family member has of the others, the ways each member establishes his or her separateness and connectedness and the way families deal with experience—how intensely they feel things and whether they evaluate their experiences and family themes. A family theme is a particular notion or motivation that determines how a particular family sees things, and all family members share it. For example, one family might be dominated by the theme of acquiring and displaying possessions, another by the theme of blaming and avoiding blame. One family might draw a tight boundary around itself in trying to maintain the home as a secure island in a threatening outside world; another family might see the world as its oyster, a place to explore and savor. Hess and Handel were dealing with whole families, but the same concepts could be applied to the study of married couples.

Still another way of looking at marriages is found in a study carried out by researchers at the National Institute of Mental Health. The original sample included 2,162 young, recently married couples in the Washington, D.C., area. To arrive at a typology of couples, one of the researchers, Ryder (1970), selected at random 200 interview abstracts, read them, and grouped together the couples who seemed to belong together. The basis for the similarity of the couples grouped together and their differences from the other types was certain combinations of husband and wife characteristics.

The husbands seemed to differ from each other in terms of their effectiveness in fulfilling middle-class male roles. Ryder calls these variables "potency" and "impulse control"; the former term is a bit misleading because it refers not to sexual performance but to some combination of occupational success, intelligence, and personal dynamism.

The women seemed to differ from each other in terms of their dependency, their attitudes toward sex, and their investment in marriage—the extent to which the wife's interests and satisfactions were bound up in the marriage. (It seems odd that the women differed from each other on this, but not the men.)

Twenty-one types of marriages emerged from this analysis. One recurrent pattern is called "competent husband/incompetent wife":

The husband is said to be highly intelligent, capable, planful, ambitious, but not very colorful, who is married to a woman seen by both of them as inferior: less organized, less attractive, unintelligent, etc. The wife wants and gets frequent reassurances that she is not worthless or unloved; but even with these reassurances the wife may feel that if she were more worthwhile her husband would be more attentive. (pp. 389–390)

This pattern seems to have validity as a description of some marriages. I have encountered quite a few couples like this among the Institute of Human Development sample (Skolnick, 1981a). It's surprising, though, that Ryder found this pattern among fairly young couples whom one might have expected to start out their marriages more nearly equal to each other in competence. The IHD sample couples were in their 40s and 50s, and the competent-husband/incompetent-wife pattern seemed to occur more often in that group of couples in which the husband has been very successful in business and the wife has had no career or major interest outside the roles of wife and mother.

A variation of this pattern, called "stern husband," differs from the first in that the husband does not reassure his wife:

They are more ostentatiously "masculine," i.e., stern, hard, unfeeling, and may find it desirable to be deliberately unkind or unsympathetic to their wives' distress. The wife . . . cries more and is more depressed than in the preceding pattern. . . . Further, she may have some private sorrow about which she cannot speak to her husband, since he would take it to be a sign of weakness. (p. 392)

Another type of marriage in which the husband rates high on the potency dimension is called "husband negative about children." The husband is not really impulsive in the sense that he can't or doesn't control his impulses and feelings or isn't dependable, but he is not as tightly controlled—uptight, some would say—as the previous types:

These husbands . . . tend to be exciting and active in physical ways. They may swim, boat, engage in contact sports, enjoy sports cars (and perhaps sell them). There is a fun emphasis, particularly on the part of the husband. He was not eager to acquire the restrictions of being married, and is less eager to be further restricted by having children. The wife may feel neglected, but wants to participate in her husband's active life. (p. 394)

There turned out to be more types of marriages in which the husband rated low on the potency dimension than ones in which he was both occupationally ambitious or successful and had a strong personality: "[These] husbands may be hard-working and ambitious, but their most salient characteristic is that they are, in a word, dull" (p. 394). One such type is called "second-choice husband." In this pattern the wife had lived an adventurous, sexually free life while single. Then, for some reason, perhaps pregnancy or an unhappy love affair,

she lowers her sights to select a sturdy, responsible, dependable husband, who is probably thought physically unattractive. The wife is pretty, impulsive, competitive with other women, and not very sexually interested in her husband. (p. 396)

We shall not describe all of the twenty-one types; there are several types in which, as Ryder saw it, the wife "pushes the husband around in various ways"; in another group of marriages the husband is violent, or footloose and irresponsible. In one rather large group, called "lonely spouses," both husband and wife have tended to have had lonely, frustrating lives, including job failures, mental hospitalization, suicide attempts, and so on. Very little interaction occurs between the spouses, but what does occur is positive.

At the very least this catalog of couples makes interesting reading, and seems to resemble couples that one encounters in real life. There are other types of marriages that did not seem to get into this catalog—marriages in which the couples are more nearly equal in competence and dependency, or the "intrinsic" or "total" kinds of relationships found by Cuber and Harroff. All of the twenty-one types of couples seem to be described in terms of some weakness or inadequacy, as if in trying to avoid the "happy marriage" concept Ryder leaned over backward and considered all marriages as bizarre in one way or

another. Actually, Ryder found he couldn't classify about one-third of the couples because they seemed to be "unique."

The task of making sense, scientifically, out of marriage as a phenomenon is an elusive one. The foregoing typological studies are certainly inelegant and difficult to use for predicting anything, but at least they describe couples, rather than fitting marriages into an abstract, unidimensional scheme.

Recently, Stephen Marks (1986) proposed a new framework for studying marriage that deals with everyday interaction as well as underlying emotional issues. He is especially concerned with the way each partner's sense of self influences, and is influenced by, the marriage. Marks conceives of each partner in marriage as a triangle and marriage as the intersection of the two triangles.

One corner of each person's triangle represents the inner self: the private, internal flux of thoughts and feelings. It also contains the personal history each partner brings to the marriage, as well as expectations, agendas, and scenarios for the marriage. The second corner of the triangle is the partnership, the relationship with the spouse. In this corner, the person attends to the other person's needs, moods, demands, and whereabouts. The third corner consists of all of a person's interests and involvements outside the marriage, including work, children, friends, relatives, recreation, religion, and hobbies.

Marks's approach provides a useful way of describing some of the emotional and behavioral dynamics of marriage. Each partner's triangle may shift its shape, develop over time, and mesh in a variety of ways with the other partner's. For example, in "romantic fusion" (see Figure 11.1), the couple is intensely involved with one another and withdrawn from all other involvements and commitments. This is represented by the closeness of each person's partnership cor-

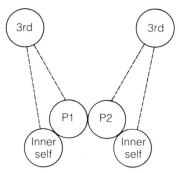

FIGURE 11.1
Romantic Fusion

Each partner's inner self and "partnership" corner are fused. The dotted lines indicate that the partners are weakly connected to the world outside their relationship.

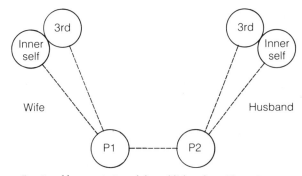

FIGURE 11.2
Marital Separateness

The members of the couple are emotionally distant from one another, and highly involved in outside activities.

ners, the closeness of each person's inner self to the partnership, and the distance and broken line between the third corner and the other two. Romantic fusion usually does not last very long; one or both partners, often the man, will feel stifled by the closeness of the relationship.

Another pattern described by Marks is called "dependency–distancing." In this kind of marriage, one person, usually the wife, is highly involved in the relationship and withdrawn from outside commitments. The other partner, meanwhile, is highly involved in work or outside relationships and relatively unconnected to the partnership.

"Marital separateness" is a pattern in which both partners are somewhat distanced from one another, and involved in outside interests (see Figure 11.2).

"Loose connection" is a pattern in which both partners require a great deal of "space," but remain closely attuned to one another and connect emotionally when they are to-

gether. Dual-career couples are the most likely to have this kind of relationship, but they can also drift into separateness.

In "family-centered connection," both partners are focused on the home and family, rather than on the couple relationship itself or outside involvements.

In "balanced connection" (see Figure 11.3), the partnership corners are close to one another but not fused. Each partner is involved in the relationship, but has an independent interest as well as one shared with the spouse. While this relationship pattern seems to be the ideal one, Marks points out that it is difficult to maintain and that other patterns can also provide satisfaction. There is no single formula for successful marriage.

In his book, Marks describes several other types of marriage. His scheme seems to offer a useful framework that can describe any marriage and yet is not one-dimensional. It is, however, a frankly exploratory approach that needs to be tested in further research.

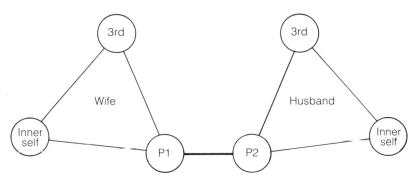

FIGURE 11.3
Balanced Connection

The "partnership" corners of each spouse are strongly connected, but each has a separate sense of self and separate outside involvements.

Reprinted by permission of the publisher, from *Three Corners: Exploring Marriage and the Self* by Stephen R. Marks (Lexington, Mass.: Lexington Books, D. C. Heath and Company, Copyright 1986, D. C. Heath and Company).

MARRIAGE OVER THE LIFE CYCLE

Ironically, during the "togetherness" era of the 1950s and 1960s, when the adjustment and intimacy models of marriage were idealizing it, empirical studies were revealing a dismal picture of what happens to marriage over time. Despite the fact that they are based on self-reports, which are heavily influenced by conventionality, the leading studies use as their key terms *disenchantment*, *disengagement*, and *corrosion*. An important study is one Blood and Wolfe (1960) made in the Detroit area. They conducted extensive interviews in the mid-1950s with 731 urban and suburban wives and with 178 farm wives. In contrast to many studies of marriage, the sample was not limited to middle-class people, but it did not include the husband's point of view. The authors summarize their findings on the course of marriage over time as follows:

The first few years of marriage are a honeymoon period which continues the romance of courtship. With the birth of the first baby, satisfaction with the standard of living and companionship decline. In subsequent years, love and understanding lag. If children do not come, their absence is an alternative source of dissatisfaction.

These trends do not involve all couples, but affect a very large proportion of the total. In the first two years of marriage, 52 percent of the wives are very satisfied with their marriages, and none notably dissatisfied. Twenty years later, only 6 percent are still very satisfied, while 21 percent are conspicuously dissatisfied. These figures suggest that a majority of wives become significantly less satisfied in later marriage than they were at the beginning.

Some of this decline involves the calming of enthusiasm into satisfaction as a result of getting used to the partner, no matter how fine he may be. . . . However, much of the decline in satisfaction reflects observable decreases in the number of things husbands and wives do with and for each other. Hence, corrosion is not too harsh a term for what happens to be the average marriage over the course of time. (pp. 87–88)

This study was cross-sectional—that is, at one point in time it looked at couples of different ages who had been married differing lengths of time. A number of other studies done in the same cross-sectional way found similar declines in marital satisfaction with length of marriage.

Studies, however, of the same couples over time—longitudinal studies—yielded essentially similar conclusions. In the best known of these longitudinal studies, researchers interviewed couples during their engagement period, again after 3–5 years of marriage, and a third time after they had been married 18–20 years. They found a decline over time in the following areas: companionship, demonstration of affection including both kissing and intercourse, common interests, common beliefs and values, belief in the permanence of the marriage, and marital adjustment. Feelings of loneliness increased. On the other hand, marital happiness, sex adjustments, and ratings of the spouse did not decline.

Using the term *disengagement* to describe these changes, one writer, Pineo (1961), saw them as the inevitable result of mate selection based on choice. Because the couple begins marriage at a high point of love and "fit" between their personalities, they have nowhere to go but down. According to this view, then, marital unhappiness is a normal operating feature of the institution. The description is rather far from the genital utopia that psychoanalysis offers as a model for marriage.

Some more recent studies have challenged this dismal view of what happens to marriages over time. In a cross-sectional study of 1,598 husbands and wives ranging in age from their 20s to their 70s, Rollins and Feldman (1970) found that the later stages of marriage have as high a satisfaction level as the earlier ones. The curve of marital satisfaction over time followed a U shape: satisfaction was highest in newlyweds, declined with the coming of children, and turned up again when the children left home. Similar findings appeared in a national survey of life satisfaction (Campbell, 1975).

Some studies show that couples in later life actually experience a new high in marital happiness. One found that a majority of middle-aged couples saw the later stages of marriage as a time of new freedoms: freedom from being economically responsible for children; freedom from housework and other chores; and finally, freedom to be oneself for the first time since the children came along (Deutscher, 1967).

In my own studies at the Institute of Human Development, there was no decline in marital satisfaction over time, nor did the older couples in the sample, who were in their 50s, differ significantly from the younger ones, who were in their early 40s (Skolnick, 1981a). The satisfaction ratings were made by psychologists on the basis of lengthy interviews. In comparing interviews that had been obtained from the same eighty-four people about 12 years apart, I was struck by the great variety of changes that had occurred in the marriages.

Although a little more than half the marriages stayed within the same range of satisfaction, almost half changed markedly in both directions. Situational changes seemed to have a great deal to do with changes in the marital relationship. The work situation of the husband and the childrearing burdens of the wife seemed to have the greatest impact on marriage. Money started coming in after a period of struggle, or finances became tight; the frazzled, overwhelmed mother of a young child would become calmer as the children grew up; conversely, teenage problems might emerge, causing friction between the parents; health problems came and went. In-law problems could lessen as the couple grew older, or aged parents could become a burden.

It was interesting that often what in the earlier interview looked like a deep-rooted personality incompatibility between the husband and wife had disappeared in the second interview, when circumstances had changed. For example, the overwhelmed mothers were likely to feel that their husbands were aloof and unsupportive. In the later interviews, when the children were older, the husband and wife had become closer. Here are some

examples of couples whose marriage improved over time. During the first interview, they were in their early 30s; in the second they were in their early 40s:

1958: John A. and his wife and child live in a cramped graduate-student apartment. He worries about how he will do in his finals, and whether he will find a good job after graduation. His wife works as a nurse and her salary supports the family, a fact that makes him very uncomfortable. He feels his wife is too reserved; she doesn't discuss problems. He also has a strained relationship with his father.

1971: John's family now lives in an expensive home. John has been very successful in his profession. Their teenage son is doing very well. His wife has become more outgoing and they are closer than they have ever been. His father has been dead for several years.

1958: Mary A. is overwhelmed with four small children under 5. She finds her husband noncommunicative and unavailable when she needs him. She expected married life to be a lot more fun than it turned out to be.

1971: Mary feels she and her husband have matured quite a bit. He is now a very involved father. The marital relationship is close and understanding.

1958: Joan J. reports her husband seems to be undergoing some sort of crisis or breakdown. He is under extreme tension at work; he drinks heavily, stays out late, and refuses to discuss his feelings with her.

1971: Joan's husband is now president of his corporation. They have become much closer to one another.

The marriages that declined in satisfaction over the years did not follow any consistent pattern, although alcohol seemed to be involved in one way or another in most of them.

1958: Ellen B. describes her husband as easygoing and very considerate. Their lives are centered on boating and fixing up their house. Her husband is on the verge of quitting his job to start his own printing business in partnership with another man.

1971: Ellen's next interview is dominated by her concern with her husband's drinking problem. She says it began several years ago when the partnership went sour. She recently gave him an ultimatum to quit, which he did, but he still goes on binges. Since he began to drink, he has lost all interest in sex.

In recent years there has been much talk of a "mid-life crisis." Unlike the slow corrosion of the marital relationship described earlier, the mid-life crisis is supposedly more sudden, and is centered in the individual rather than the marriage. It has been compared to adolescence, in that it involves a questioning of one's basic identity and a concern with sexuality. Only two of the eighty-four marriages seemed to be affected by anything like the mid-life crisis as it has been described. In one, a seemingly contented marriage of 17 years broke down when the husband became convinced he was a homosexual; after some experimentation, he decided he wasn't, but the relationship with his wife was seriously impaired. Another man reported he was vaguely dissatisfied with his marriage, although he couldn't figure out why, and thought about finding "a cute young mistress."

Probably the most important point about marriage over the life cycle is the fact that it has changed dramatically in recent years. Because people live together and have fewer children than in the past, today's couples will spend an unprecedentedly small number of years in their married lives taking active care of children.

According to Census Bureau estimates, we are entering a period in which marriages will follow a very different pattern than those of a century ago. A statistically average woman born in the middle of the nineteenth century, for example, would marry at 22 and have her first child a year and a half later. Her last child would be born when she was 36. She would be widowed at age 56 and her last child would be married 2 years later. By the 1930s, however, two-thirds of the married life of a couple would be free of the burdens of young children, and one-third would be free of children in the home. In the future, the length of time couples are likely to spend alone together, without children, will increase still more. Child-free marriage on a mass scale is a new phenomenon in human history with as yet unknown implications for marital stability and satisfaction.

THE FUTURE OF MARRIAGE

To many people, marriage as we have known it is a dying institution. As one recent writer put it:

All around me there is a marital turbulence. My editor has just remarried; an editor in the same firm has just separated from his wife; one of my doctors has left home and rented an apartment for himself and his mistress, leaving his wife with a flock of children to raise; one of my best friends is having an affair which his wife knows about; and another good friend is on the verge of divorce. My neighbor on the right is remarried, and the one on the left is also remarried. (Westoff, 1977, p. 143)

After viewing all this marital wreckage in her social landscape, Westoff concluded that "old-fashioned, once in a lifetime, till death do us part marriage" is "going on the rocks these days." As we have seen earlier, however, it is possible to look at the statistics on marriage, divorce, and remarriage and come away concluding, as Mary Jo Bane (1976) did, that "taken as a whole, the data on marriage and divorce suggest that the kind of marriage Americans have always known is still a pervasive and enduring institution" (p. 35).

The imagery of death and decay as applied to marriage may be too extreme; the marital turbulence described above certainly exists but it couldn't apply across the whole population, since the majority of marriages are still stable.

Rather than "dying," marriage is in the process of being transformed. Marriages are becoming, all at once, more varied, more equal, more intense, and more fragile. First, we are experiencing a major restructuring of sex roles both inside and outside the family. The pressure for change derives from both feminist ideology and the economic reality that a majority of women are now in the labor force.

Although women are still a long way from achieving economic equality, and many families with working wives still accept traditional sex-role ideologies, a wife's working tends to shift the division of labor and the balance of authority in the family. Studies of working wives show that they have more influence in major family decisions than full-time housewives. Husbands of working wives are more likely to participate in the housework and child care, even if it is only "helping" the wife in "her" tasks, rather than redefining the roles within the marriage. Most observers believe the trend toward female labor-force participation will continue into the forseeable future.

There is evidence that although working seems to be good for women—in terms of both physical and mental health (Bane,

1976)—it can create conflict and dissatisfaction in marriage. These findings can also be attributed to other factors, such as the money problems that lead to lower-middle- and working-class wives going to work in the first place. But because women's employment is a shift away from tradition and entails changes in family routines, it is little wonder that it creates tension and conflict. Some observers feel that problems created by women working are a temporary phenomenon caused by the transition from one pattern to another. Eventually, they feel, when expectations conform with the realities of the two-worker marriage, the level of marital satisfaction is likely to rise.

On the other hand, some observers feel that the demands of two outside jobs, caring for home and children, and coordinating the leisure-time interests of all the family members will continue to be a source of strain. Young and Willmott (1973), in *The Symmetrical Family*, argue that we have moved from an era when there was "one demanding job for the wife and one for the husband" into a time when there are "two demanding jobs for the wife and one for the husband." In the future, they predicted, the symmetry will be complete: there will be "two demanding jobs for the wife and two for the husband." Strains will be inescapable, and there will be more divorces, "because people will be seeking a more multifaceted adjustment to each other with the two outside jobs clicking with the two inside ones; and because the task will be harder, there will be more failures" (p. 278).

Another major transformation of marriage is the demand for personal fulfillment in marital relationships. In recent times the goal of personal growth and self-realization has come to be valued more than the obligation to fulfill social roles. As we noted earlier, most people have defined their "real selves" in terms of such roles—husband, wife, father, worker, student, and so on—whereas now feelings and impulses are more likely to be defined as the "true self" (Turner, 1976).

Looking back, the togetherness era of the 1950s seems to have been a transitional period. In the past, marriages had been what was called "institutional." Marriage was a matter of duty and obligation to family and community; maintaining the stability of the family took precedence over the happiness of the individual. The "companionate" marriage came to be the ideal of the twentieth century. The goal of marriage was a close and satisfying relationship between husband and wife. The psychoanalytic view of marriage, which was widely influential even among people who never would think of going to an analyst, argued that in marriage, a person could—or should—have it both ways: both conformity to social roles and the fulfillment of one's deepest emotional needs. Personal growth was defined as taking place *within* the roles of husband, wife, mother, father, and worker. The wish to leave a relatively satisfactory marriage or job to "find oneself" would have been considered a neurotic symptom.

In the 1970s this unity of social expectations and personal fulfillment split apart, with the latter taking precedence over all other considerations. In contrast to the psychoanalytic ethos of the 1950s, the new fulfillment ideology was promoted by the "new" psychologies—humanistic, gestalt, and so on.

In the future, as the trends toward sex-role symmetry and personal fulfillment follow the traditional path from the educated middle class to those lower down in the status hierarchy, we can expect a variety of sexual and marital life-styles to coexist. Most adults will probably continue to live as couples, either in marriage or cohabitation. Traditional marriage is likely to continue to exist as a widespread option. Legal marriage will also continue to perform as a more committed form of relationship. Remarriages, already amounting to one out of four of all marriages today, are likely to continue and even increase along with the divorce rate. The "blended" families that result from second marriage will become a more common and accepted part of the social landscape. Noncouple life-styles, ranging from singleness to communal households to group marriage, are also likely to continue.

Despite the proliferation of changes and options, the idea of marital commitment is a symbol if not a reality that will continue to hold its appeal. It is interesting to note that even the authors of *Open Marriage* stress the emotional significance of a one-to-one relationship, which

whether it is realized through monogamy or within other forms of marriage, fulfills man's profoundly human needs. . . . The relationship of two people to each other allows a closeness and psychological intimacy that no other kind of relationship offers. (N. O'Neill & O'Neill, 1972, p. 24)

Similarly, Jessie Bernard (1972), after a devastating feminist critique of traditional marriage, concluded:

The future of marriage is as assured as any social form can be. . . . For men and women will continue to want intimacy, they will continue to want to celebrate their mutuality, to experience the mystic unit which once led the church to consider marriage a sacrament. . . . There is hardly any probability such commitments will disappear or that all relationships between them will become merely casual and transient. (p. 301)

There is support for this prediction in the findings of anthropologists. Robert Murphy (1971) points out that expectations of permanence and faithfulness are almost universally held norms for marriage, even where the rates of divorce and infidelity are much higher than our own. Ronald Cohen (1971) reports on an African society, the Kanuri, in which the divorce rate approaches the theoretical limit of 100 percent—almost every marriage ends in divorce. Yet even here marriages are not entered into casually; furthermore, the Kanuri place a high value on marital stability and even perform a ritual at weddings to symbolize the desire of everyone that this particular marriage should be a lasting one. Cohen's research refutes the assumption that such a high-divorce society must be a "quagmire of instability" for people who live in it. A high divorce rate can become a stable aspect of a stable society. Even so, there are tensions as well as adaptations. He concluded with some implications for our own society:

If our own divorce rate is changing upward, we must prepare for widely ramifying effects in the society as a whole. I do not claim they would be the same as the ones described here, but I am certain they will be profound, and affect, in the end, the nature of the entire society and of the individuals who compose it. (p. 217)

SUMMARY

Although marriage is a relationship between a man and woman, it involves more than the sum of these two personalities. It is a social institution, a legally defined status involving legal rights and obligations, and a social group—the dyad—with its own interactional properties. In addition, the partners have been socialized to be different and unequal in status.

A great deal of ambivalence about marriage occurs in our culture, but in no culture anywhere is marital harmony the general rule. In the marriage-and-family literature, four broad models of marriage may be discerned. Two of these stress the positive, harmonious side of marriage; the other two emphasize the conflictual aspects. The adjustment model sees happiness, harmony, and stability as the hallmarks of marital success. Psychoanalytic models reject the adjustment concept as superficial and emphasize the attainment of intimacy and personality growth. Both of these models tend to assume that conflict indicates marital difficulty or failure.

By contrast, the conflict models assume that all social interaction involves conflict. Game theory or exchange theory tends to see marriage as a battle of the sexes, a rational struggle of two parties to maximize their own positions. The systems or communications approach emphasizes ambivalence and the paradoxes of human communication as the source of conflict in marriage.

All four models tend to view marriage largely as an interpersonal relationship in a social vacuum. They tend to ignore the ways in which social, economic, and cultural factors influence marriages.

CHAPTER 12

Parenthood

It may well be believed that if procreation had not been put under the dominion of a great passion, it would have been caused to cease by the burdens it entails. Abortion and infanticide are especially interesting because they show how early in the history of civilization the burden of children became so heavy that parents began to shirk it.

William Graham Sumner
Folkways

Until a year ago, I was one of those slobs who thought all infants ugly. But as I write, my first child, Ruth, born last January, is climbing the stairs. Is it the greatest thing ever? Hard to tell. Two weeks ago she mastered clapping. . . . Everything she says—for example—"ah-yee-dee-dee-dah"—makes more sense than all the people I interview. Don't get the idea that I like being a father; it's simply the best experience of my life.

Paul J. Samuelson
Newsweek

In some ways the romantic complex surrounding parenthood is even deeper and more unrealistic than that relating to marriage.

E. E. LeMasters
Parents in Modern America

"Looking back at the twentieth century," Robert Solomon (1981) observes, "historians, if there are any, will no doubt be impressed by the invention of the airplane, nuclear weapons, and frozen foods" (p. 91). But, he goes on, "the greatest revolution in our everyday lives has been brought about by the 'parasexual discoveries of the mid-century—effective birth control and penicillin.'" These inventions brought about two major changes in human life—sex without terror and the ability to control unwanted pregnancy. No method of birth control is perfect, and AIDS has brought terror back to sex. But most Americans take it as a matter of course that how many children we have, and when we have them, are a matter of choice.

Despite the nostalgia for the preindustrial "world we have lost," families before the age of contraception faced conflicts unknown today. The "conjugal rights" of the husband—the wife's duty by the law of church and state to have sexual relations with her husband—came into conflict with her own fears of pregnancy and death in childbirth—a serious danger in past times. The parents' interest in sex also came into conflict with the needs of nursing infants: a new pregnancy would stop the mother's supply of milk. Above all, as historian Jean Flandrin (1979) pointed out, "the demographic system of past times, based on uncontrolled fertility, was murderous to the children" (p. 216).

Children were often welcomed, however, as contributors to the family's work and as insurance policies for their parents' old age. Although affection between parents and children was not unknown in other times and places, parental love did not receive the emphasis it does in our culture. In contemporary Western cultures, parents are expected to love their children—to be "crazy" about them, as one psychologist recently put it—and children are expected to return that love. Maladjustment in later life is attributed to lack of parental love.

Parent–child relations in traditional societies were in many ways comparable to those between husband and wife. As noted earlier, the premodern bride and groom would not be expected to be in love when they married, nor would their failure to be in love several years later be considered a sign that the marriage was a failure. Unhappy marriages were regarded as a curse, but most people did not expect more than relative contentment with their spouse's performance of the traditional roles and duties (W. J. Goode, 1977, p. 382).

In the same way, parents and children in traditional societies and in our own past were expected to fulfill their obligations to one another; cruel parents and disobedient children would be condemned, but love was not considered the central element in relations between parents and children. Before the seventeenth century, the European child-rearing literature rarely mentioned parental love as a significant factor in the child's development. God's love, not the parents', was regarded as the major influence on the child's future. "The child needed a good education and a faith in God; parents provided physical care, consistent discipline, and a model for proper behavior" (Kagan, 1977, p. 42).

Viviana Zelitzer (1985) has traced the shifting economic and sentimental value of children over the past century. Her study shows that in the 60 years between 1870 and 1930, the economically useful child of the nineteenth century was transformed into an "economically worthless, but emotionally priceless child" (p. 3). Major institutions were reshaped by the changing value of children. Traditional forms of child work came to be seen as illegitimate child labor. In cases of the "wrongful death" of a child in an accident, nineteenth-century parents would be compensated for the value of the child's labor; twentieth-century parents are compensated for incalculable emotional pain.

Adoption is another institution that reveals the striking change in the value of children. In the 1870s, Zelitzer points out, there was no market for babies. A woman with an unwanted infant would have to pay a "baby farmer" to take the child off her hands. By the 1950s, would-be parents who could not adopt a child from a licensed agency were willing to pay as much as $10,000 for a baby on the black market. In the nineteenth century legal adoption was rare, but many families were eager to take older children into their home because of the value of their labor. In the twentieth century, it became almost impossible to find homes for children older than 6; they had become both economically and sentimentally "useless."

In recent years, children seem to have become even more emotionally priceless as their expense has increased. The cost of raising a child was estimated in 1980 to average between $100,000 and $140,000. People are having fewer children than in the past, but the ones they do have are more a matter of choice. The statement by economist and *Newsweek* columnist Paul Samuelson on the opening page of this chapter is an eloquent expression of the emotional meaning of parenthood in the 1980s.

PROCREATION AND PARENTHOOD: NATURE AND NECESSITY

Childrearing in traditional societies, as we have seen with marriage, tended to be utilitarian; from an early age, children could make material contributions to the family's welfare. A child, however, often came into the world as a liability rather than an asset. For thousands of years people have been trying to break the link between sex and the production of infants.

Far from being a modern preoccupation, the search for some sure, safe way of preventing conception occurs in the oldest records and in the most primitive preliterate groups. The oldest written medical prescriptions for contraception are from ancient Egypt and date from 1850 B.C. They recommend the use of a paste made with crocodile dung to block the vagina (Himes, 1963). Unfortunately such methods do not work very well in preventing conception, nor do the other ancient methods, such as drinking potions, wearing magic amulets, jumping up and down after intercourse, or remaining passive during it. Because abortion until very recently has been a dangerous operation (the abortion laws were originally aimed at preventing the death of the pregnant woman), the leading method of birth control, historically and cross-culturally, has been infanticide.

Around the turn of the century, William Graham Sumner (1960) suggested that if sexual relations were painful rather than pleasurable, human beings would probably have become extinct long ago. Sumner argued that the relation of parent to child is one of

FIGURE 12.1
Ideal Family Size

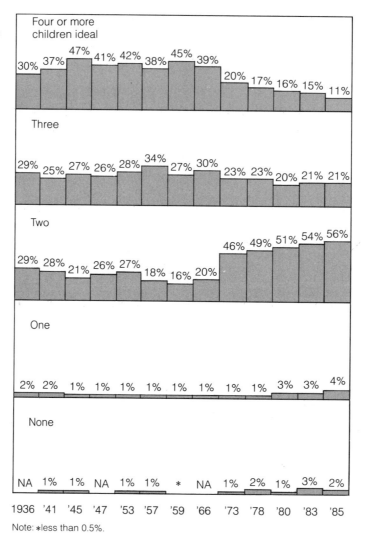

Four or more
children ideal

30% 37% 47% 41% 42% 38% 45% 39% 20% 17% 16% 15% 11%

Three

29% 25% 27% 26% 28% 34% 27% 30% 23% 23% 20% 21% 21%

Two

29% 28% 21% 26% 27% 18% 16% 20% 46% 49% 51% 54% 56%

One

2% 2% 1% 1% 1% 1% 1% 1% 1% 1% 3% 3% 4%

None

NA 1% 1% NA 1% 1% * NA 1% 2% 1% 3% 2%

1936 '41 '45 '47 '53 '57 '59 '66 '73 '78 '80 '83 '85

Note: *less than 0.5%.

From *Public Opinion*, December/January 1986, p. 28.

sacrifice; children add to the burdens of the parents in their own "struggle for existence." That there are compensations for the parents does not alter the fact that "the interests of parents and children are antagonistic."

Now that we do have effective contraception, and raising children is a costly commitment with no economic return, why do people still have them? In the modern world children have an emotional and symbolic value to their parents that has no relation to practical economics.

Studies carried out since the late 1960s demonstrate dramatic changes in attitudes toward family size as well as the continuing appeal of parenthood itself. Thus a 1967

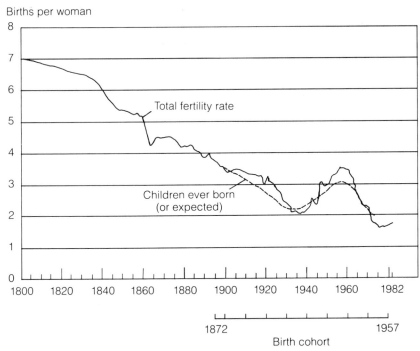

Births per woman

FIGURE 12.2
*Average Number of
Children Ever Born to
(or Expected by) Birth
Cohorts and Annual
Total Fertility Rate,
White Women:
1800–1982*

Total fertility rate

Children ever born
(or expected)

Birth cohort

From A. Thornton and D. Freedman, *Population Bulletin: The Changing American Family*,
a publication of The Population Reference Bureau, Vol. 38, No. 4, October 1983, p. 13.

study of 15,000 college women found a large majority disapproving of large families, defined as three or more children (Westoff & Potrin, 1966). This was a marked change from the 1950s and early 1960s, when three children was the average family size. Public attitudes then favored families as large as the parents could afford, and people with small families were perceived as being selfish.

Most people now favor smaller families, rather than childlessness (see Figure 12.1). One public opinion poll conducted in 1978 (U. S. Department of Commerce, 1979) found that 11 percent of women between the ages of 18 and 34 expected to have no children. Among those who went to college, 14 percent planned no children. While most people want to have children, they want smaller

families than people did during the baby-boom era. The two-child family seems to be emerging as the ideal family size today (David & Baldwin, 1979).

During the late 1970s and the early 1980s, it appeared to many people that a new baby boom might be at hand: the birth rate rose somewhat, and there seemed to be a lot more pregnant women and babies around than there had been before. There has not been a dramatic rise in the fertility rate, however. Some demographers had predicted that the baby-boom generation would produce an "echo" of itself—another huge baby boom when it began to have children. The larger number of babies we are seeing is not an illusion; it is an "echo" of the earlier boom, but the current generation of young women is not expected to have anywhere near the fertility rates of the 1950s. There are, however, so many women of childbearing age now that even if they have fewer babies than their mothers did, they will produce an "echo" in the coming years. It is estimated that in 1980 there were about 20 million women in their prime childbearing years—twice as many as in 1960. This abundance of women in their fertile years will last until about 2000. Thus even if their fertility rate remains at or slightly below the replacement level of 2.1, they will sustain a growth in the native American population for several decades (see Figure 12.2).

Why have fertility rates dropped so dramatically? One reason is the long-term trend we have mentioned earlier: the decline in childbearing over the past 150 years (Cherlin, 1981c). In historical perspective, it was the great baby boom of the postwar era that was unusual. Most demographers believe that the baby boom came about because of an unusual set of social and economic conditions—a generation of people who grew up during the depression and found themselves starting families in a time of great relative prosperity. Thus the behavior of today's young women is not so unusual in historical context. Further, in recent years there have been increases in the factors that traditionally contribute to lower fertility rates: more education for women and the growing expectation among women that they will spend many of their adult years in the labor force. Finally, the economic stresses of recent times, both the inflation that makes two incomes necessary for many families and the recession that makes good jobs relatively scarce, also contribute to lower fertility rates. The United States is not alone in these trends. Most industrialized countries, both capitalist and communist, are experiencing reduced birth rates.

Many people fear that low birth rates signal a "weakening" of family life and a rejection of children. As we have seen, however, most people want smaller numbers of children, not childlessness. In fact, along with providing new contraceptives, medical advances in recent years have made it possible for women who would have been unable to have children in former times to have the children they want. Thus people have more choice in both directions—having children as well as not having them. Further, rather than being "weak" families, small families in many ways are beneficial to children. Even at the same economic level, children from small families receive more care and adult attention and do better in physical and intellectual development than children from large families. From the point of view of the child, growing up in a large family has advantages as well as disadvantages, and being the object of one's parents' intense love and concern can be a mixed blessing. Lowered fertility rates, however, cannot be taken as evidence for "the breakdown of the family."

"Natural" Interpretation of Parenthood

Much thinking about parent–child relations in the social sciences assumes a natural fit between the needs of the parents, particularly the mother, to nurture the child and the need of society to support and encourage the parents. Thus psychoanalysts argue that every woman's deepest instinctual wish is to bear and nurture an infant; the child represents the substitute for the never-to-be-obtained penis, and being a mother represents the fulfillment of the girl's Oedipal wish to replace her own mother.

The more contemporary ego-psychology version of psychoanalysis defines parenthood in terms of the growth of skills and per-

Percent

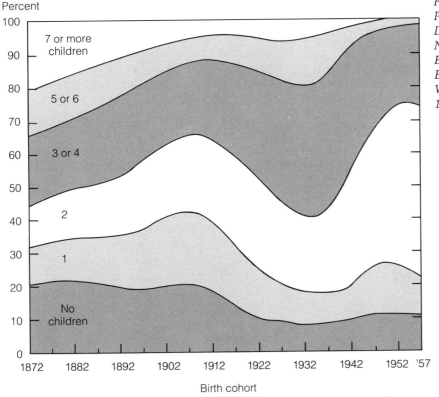

FIGURE 12.3
Percentage
Distribution of
Number of Children
Ever Born (or
Expected), Cohorts of
White Women:
1872–1957

From A. Thornton and D. Freedman, *Population Bulletin: The Changing American Family*,
a publication of The Population Reference Bureau, Vol. 38, No. 4, October 1983, p. 13.

sonality resources. For Erikson (1963), parenthood represents a stage of development in the course of the life cycle. Erikson asserts that the desire to care for very young children is built into the human nature of both men and women.

Erikson and other writers in the psychoanalytic tradition argue that within each society institutions arise that take into account the needs of the very young. Parents provide physical care and teach children what they need to know to deal with the environment and society, and society supports the parents in their efforts because it "needs" stable adults (M. J. Levy, 1965). Sociological

thinking about childrearing also tends to assume an intuitive fit between social patterns and the needs of children. The very term *socialization*, or even *childrearing*, implies that parental behavior toward children is usually dedicated to the child's education and welfare.

Functional sociology interprets reproduction and childrearing in terms of society's need for "social replacement," the production of a new generation to replace the parents. This interpretation tends to assume that every child comes into the world with a fixed, positive value. It does not allow for the possibility that a new mouth to feed may, at a particular time, be dysfunctional for the parent or the community, possibilities seen very clearly by Sumner and still earlier by Malthus and Darwin.

The belief that biology guides and directs parental behavior pervades both popular and "expert" thinking. The older notion of blind instinct has given way to the more sophisticated view that mother and child are genetically programmed to be attracted to each other. An animal infant provides the specific stimulus to release an appropriate response in the mother, which in turn will evoke a further response in the infant and so on in a chain of coordinated behavior. Thus the human child is said to be equipped with an innate tendency to attach itself to a mothering figure early in life. This tendency is said to be matched by a built-in responsiveness on the part of the mother (Bowlby, 1969).

Misuses of biology Both the old and the newer versions of the idea that mothering is a "natural" biological process are seriously flawed. Like arguments about the biological determination of sexual behavior, they underestimate the role of culture and social context. Furthermore, the belief in innate nurturance is based on an oversimplified version of biology and evolution. First, the argument that maternal instincts in animals reveal the biological source of human mothering overestimates the similarities between humans and other species. Further, it presents only one side of animal behavior. As Pohlman (1969) put it:

If research from comparative psychology and anecdotal observation of animal life are cited to try to show innate tendencies toward parenthood, in fairness we should note that some animals, including mammals, will kill and eat their own offspring. (p. 52)

Animal analogies can offer useful and interesting illustrations for understanding human behavior, but they certainly should not be used to define the human condition.

The innateness-of-parenthood argument also rests on a misunderstanding of evolutionary process. It assumes that evolution works on the principle of preserving every individual newborn animal or human. Rather, recent work in primate behavior reveals a variety of "reproductive strategies," some based on individual gain, others based on altruism, and in many species, as Sarah Hrdy (1981) has documented, on a strategy based on infanticide. (Male primates often kill an infant before mating with the mother, which has the effect of increasing the survival chances of their own offspring.) She notes, "In case after case throughout the natural world, animals are caught in . . . evolutionary traps: selection favoring individual gain detracts from the fitness of others, from the general viability or survival of the species, and from what humans might call 'quality of life.' Infanticide simply happens to be a particularly striking and well-documented example of this phenomenon" (p. 94).

The war of the breast It is very well known that women in contemporary society have a great deal of trouble breast feeding their children. The very fact that there are organizations devoted to convincing women to breast feed and to helping them do so indicates how far from automatic nursing is. Nursing difficulties usually are attributed to the hectic pace of modern life, to the fact that women are rejecting their children or are just unwilling to do their motherly duties, or to some combination of these. It is ironic that women are blamed for failing to do something "instinctive." As far as the child is concerned, the prevailing assumption is that the availability of bottles represents a loss for the child.

In spite of the belief that breast feeding has been a problem only in recent times, the

The importance of fathers in the lives of children is increasingly recognized. [Dick Swartz/Office of Human Development Services]

historical records indicate otherwise. The nursing of children has been a matter of serious concern in Western civilization for the past two thousand years. William Kessen (1965), in a history of ideas about child development, wrote about the "war of the breast." He noted that the most persistent theme in the history of the child is the reluctance of mothers to suckle their babies. "The running war between the mother, who does not want to nurse, and the philosopher-psychologists, who insist she must, stretched over 2,000 years" (p. 1).

Margaret Mead's analysis of mother–child relations in early infancy is more consistent with the historical picture than the alternative image of nursing as a mutually beneficial instinctive relationship. She wrote that lactation and early maternal care may be biologically a life-*selecting* process as much as a life-*saving* one. In other words, "nature" is not a benevolent, child-saving force. Rather, the biological factors seem to be arranged to ensure that only the strongest, most vigorous babies will survive, and only if they are born to women with the right physical qualifications to feed them. Far from being a simple process by which any mother can feed any baby born to her if only she wants to, lactation seems to require a specific set of physical and constitutional capacities on the part of both mother and child.

Many babies have individual quirks of temperament that make them hard to feed. Thus there are "rejecting" babies—babies who shortly after birth seem to fight the whole feeding process. There are also babies born with a seemingly innate lack of interest in being fed, as well as babies with breathing difficulties or mouths too small to nurse.

Further complications arise from the shape of the mother's breast. One study found that the suckling response in human infants is elicited by the whole front of the mother's breast filling the entire oral cavity of the child. About one-quarter of mothers do not have breasts of the right shape or elasticity to fill the child's mouth.

Finally, the production of milk is based on a "letting down" reflex that is highly vulnerable to anxiety. When a child sucks well and thrives, a mother has little anxiety and much milk. But if there is some difficulty, such as those just suggested, a vicious circle starts. The child fails to suck well or thrive, the mother is made anxious, her milk supply fails, the infant receives still less food, and soon, if there are no other ways to feed the child, it will die.

Margaret Mead (1957) once argued that breast feeding seems to fit the model of a process designed to eliminate all but the strongest, "fittest" babies. She criticized the ethologist's model of nursing, which pictures every mother as biologically able to nourish every infant she brings into the world, and nursing itself as a chain of mutually beneficial responses.

This, argued Mead, is the "natural" biological fate of an "unfit" infant under survival conditions. She sees a parallel in the maternal behavior of herd animals, such as reindeer, sheep, and goats. Immediately after giving birth, such animals are highly attentive to their infants. The mother will nuzzle the infant, lick it, feed it, try to get it up on its feet. But she will do this only for a certain number of hours. If the baby does not stand up and walk well enough to follow the herd, the mother will no longer recognize it as hers. She will abandon it and go with the herd, because that is the only way she can survive. Mead suggests that the human situation is comparable. The very vulnerability of the mother's milk supply, the ease in which it can be turned off, may have been in evolutionary terms a selective device for ensuring that the mother's energy would not be wasted on trying to rear a child who did not have a vigorous grasp on life.

Thus it is not "nature" but culture that values human life and holds it as an ideal that every infant shall live, the weak as well as the strong, the premature as well as the full-term. And it is not instinct but human inventiveness that found other ways to nurture infants than by the lactation of their biological mothers.

The nurturance gap   The invention of bottles to feed babies illustrates one of the paradoxes of the human condition. The same evolutionary pressures that created a brain able to conceive of inventing something to save infants' lives, and a pair of hands capable of actually making it, resulted in human infants' being born into a nurturance gap: the human infant comes into the world the most helpless of all the primates, and yet its care is less assured than that of any other.

The idea that evolution works by the principle of guaranteed nurturance is at odds with recent studies of human evolution. Mother Nature appears to be more of a trickster than a Lady Bountiful. The trick nature played on humans was to give them the most burdensome infants of all the primates while removing the detailed genetic instructions that guide maternal behavior among other species. The extreme helplessness of the human newborn, its existential plight, results from the same evolutionary pressures that created human intelligence.

Most people know what newborns look like, but our imagery of babies comes mostly from photographs, paintings, and advertisements showing plump, smiling, rosy-cheeked little cherubs. Therefore some parents are disappointed and perhaps even shocked when they first see their scrawny, limp, unresponsive offspring. It takes about 6 months for the child to resemble the cherubic advertising image.

The human infant is, in primate terms, at least 6 months premature at birth, perhaps more; that is, if human infants were born at a comparable point to other primate newborns, they would be like 6-month-olds. The burdensomeness of the human infant is a byproduct of the evolutionary process. Chimpanzee or baboon babies are much more developed at birth. They can, in part, determine their own relationship to the mother, and after weaning they gather their own food.

At one stage in human development, babies were born in such an advanced state. The large human brain developed rather late. Our earliest immediate ancestors—the Australopithecines, the so-called apemen of southern and eastern Africa—were tool-using bipeds with ape-sized brains. The Australopithecines lived 2 million years ago, but proto-

humans did not look like today's people for about a million years. The tool-using, cooperative way of life of these hominids led to the enlargement of the human brain. This is a relatively new version of human evolution; it used to be thought that human beings first acquired the physical form that distinguished them from the apes, then developed culture. It now appears, however, that tool use and cultural life shaped the human body and brain by favoring the survival of those with small teeth and big brains.

Tools, language, and cultural life set human beings apart as a species. Humans are "incomplete" apes or, as Geertz (1965) put it, they are born into "an information gap." The human nervous system evolved in interaction with culture. It cannot direct behavior or organize experience without the guidance of language and other significant symbols.

Beavers build dams, birds build nests, bees locate food, baboons organize social groups, and mice mate on the basis of forms of learning that rest predominantly on instructions encoded in their genes and evoked by appropriate patterns of external stimuli: physical keys inserted into organic locks. But men build dams or shelters, locate food, organize their social groups, or find sexual partners under the guidance of instructions encoded in flow charts and blueprints, hunting lore, moral systems, and esthetic judgments: conceptual structure molding formless talents. (p. 112)

While the brain and head were growing larger during the course of evolution, the human pelvis was (and is) more limited in the size it could grow. Thus the same selection pressures that led to larger brains led to earlier births. The psychological effects of this change in the direction of premature birth were momentous. As Washburn and DeVore (1961) described it:

The psychological consequences of the change from the monkey pattern to the human are profound. . . . When the baby baboon is born, it has its own reflexes and motor development that enable it to help determine its own relationship to the mother. . . . The helpless human infant is exposed to maternal whim, custom, or vagary in a way that is true of no other primate. (p. 42)

The relationship between the monkey or ape infant and its mother is not completely determined by the infant's reflexes and its mother's drives and physiology. Learning and even custom play a role in primate maternal behavior patterns. One study (Harlow, Harlow, & Hansen, 1963) has shown, for example, that female rhesus monkeys raised in isolation do not treat their infants in a "normal" way when they become mothers. They may ignore, reject, or even beat them. They evidently have to learn how to handle infants from living in a social group of other monkeys, although even when the isolation continues, the rhesus mother acts more "normally" when she has a second and third child.

Biological drives and reflexes, however, play an even smaller role in human mothering.

Although female monkeys appear to learn part of their maternal behavior patterns, and older juvenile females hold and carry infants before they have any of their own, the role of learning, culture, and custom in determining the care of the young is vastly greater in man than in any nonhuman primate. (Washburn & DeVore, 1961, p. 42)

In short, the human infant is born into a nurturance gap. Once the large brain had been built, people no longer lived in a world of things, of simple stimuli, but a world of meanings, concepts, and significant symbols. Further, the human consciousness can negate the world, can imagine the hypothetical. A human parent is uniquely capable of imagining the nonexistence of a child. This capacity can lead to a cherishing of the child as an irreplaceable treasure, to resentment, or to a search for a means of birth control. No ape ever tried to invent a contraceptive device. Even supposing an ape had the capacity to think of doing such a thing, it would have no need to. The nonhuman primates are tropical creatures. Each one finds its own food in the rich vegetation. Humans developed as a separate species in response to the food scarcities of the Ice Age. Therefore a human infant can never be considered a bundle of stimulus patterns that can call forth a predetermined response in the mother; each infant comes into the world carrying a very specific set of meanings for that particular mother, at that particular moment, in that particular set of circumstances, in that particular culture. This freedom may have tragic implications.

The analysis of the evolution of human mother–child relations offered by Washburn and DeVore (1961) makes it clear that nothing is guaranteed about the reception an infant will receive on being born. "The helpless human infant is exposed to maternal whim, custom, or vagary in a way that is true of no other primate" (Washburn & DeVore, 1961, p. 39). Everything people do is mediated by language and culture. There is no such thing as "natural" childbirth and childrearing, in the sense of a process unmediated by learning and cultural rules.

Infanticide As mentioned earlier, infanticide has been a leading means of population control in precontraceptive societies. Not only is the infant not guaranteed a warm welcome through natural mechanisms in the mother, but in many times and places a new infant would simply not be allowed to live. When we think of such practices at all, we think of them as barbaric customs existing only at primitive levels of culture, and as incompatible with "civilization." (There is a paradox here in the idea of the maternal instinct needing civilization in order to flourish.) Actually, however, infanticide has been much more widespread in Western civilization than is generally recognized (Shorter, 1973; Trexler, 1973).

Further, one savage practice has flourished during most periods of European history, but has not been reported for other cultures: the maiming and crippling of children to use them as beggars. The fact that such practices now seem horrible beyond belief indicates that our feelings about maimed children, not to speak of adults, have changed drastically.

The historian William Langer (1972) reviewed the history of infanticide as a means of population control in Europe and Britain. He noted that Plato, Aristotle, and other writers of the same period advocated infanticide as a means of regulating the size of the population as well as ridding society of deformed and diseased infants. During later times both the church and governments made infanticide a crime punishable by death. Yet, as late as the last century, infanticide was frequent as well as publicly noticeable. Langer concentrated on the period of 1750–1850, when the population of Europe nearly doubled. He argued that the two major brakes on population growth were celibacy and infanticide, and that without these controls the population of Europe would have outrun the food supply. He noted:

In England as late as 1878 about 6 percent of all violent deaths could be classed as infanticides. . . . In the 18th century it was not an uncommon spectacle to see the corpses of infants lying in the streets or in the dunghills of London and other large cities. . . .
In 1862 one of the coroners for Middlesex county stated infanticide had become so commonplace "that the police seemed to think no more of finding a dead child than they did of finding a dead cat or a dead dog." The Morning Star (June 23, 1863) declared that infanticide "is possibly becoming a national institution"; the Morning Post (September 2, 1863) termed it "this commonest of crimes." (pp. 96–97)

Public attitudes toward infanticide were remarkably lenient, according to Langer. In contrast with the attitudes of most people today and with religious and legal authorities then, public sympathy tended to be on the side of any woman who was charged with killing her child. Very few culprits were discovered anyhow, and very few of those ever reached the courts. One London coroner said he had never known a woman to be punished for killing her baby, "no matter how flagrant the circumstances." Usually the women involved in court cases were destitute workers or servants who had been abandoned by the men involved.

Before recent times it was difficult to draw lines between infanticide, child abandonment, and putting an infant in a foundling home. The mortality rates of the latter tended to be 80–90 percent. Foundling homes were started by reformers, such as St. Vincent de Paul, Thomas Coram, and Napoleon, who were shocked at infanticide. Whenever a foundling home opened, however, it was swamped by more babies than it could handle. Conditions were so bad that foundling homes became, ironically, another form of the infanticide they were designed to prevent.

When Coram's London Foundling Hospital was finally opened in 1741, it immediately became evident that he had underestimated the need. The pressure of applicants was so great that women fought at the hospital gates. . . . In the first four years nearly 15,000 children were accepted. It was impossible to find enough wet nurses for such a number and thousands died in early infancy; only 4,400 of the foundlings lived to reach adolescence. (W. Langer, 1972, p. 96)

Wherever foundling homes sprang up as a way of saving abandoned children, the same tragic irony was repeated. At the height of his power Napoleon decreed that foundling homes be set up in every region of France and if possible in every arrondissement (district). Again the facilities were overburdened and the expenses staggering to local governments. Napoleon tried to make it possible for a baby to be left without anyone seeing the person who was leaving it. The method was so successful that one-fourth to one-third of the foundlings were thought to be *legitimate* children whose parents either could not or would not care for them. The mortality rates led one writer to suggest that the homes put up signs saying "Children killed at government expense" (W. Langer, 1972, p. 98).

Langer's article deals mainly with demographic issues: the factors that led to the population explosion in Europe between 1750 and 1850 and the checks on population growth. He did not deal with the many questions that might be asked about the psychological and social aspects of the situation. How did the factors to which Langer attributed the rise in population—the introduction of the potato and corn from the New World—actually lead to the birth of more children? How did the need for checks on population become translated into individual acts of infanticide? Why were mothers increasingly likely to abandon children until 1850, and why did the attitude toward children change thereafter?

Evidence emerging from the work of Langer and other historians shatters easy notions of an intuitive fit between the needs of children, the inclinations of parents to nurture them, and the functional need of every society to care for infants. Langer's work also illustrates how technological changes enter into the parent–child relationship. Better sanitation and the introduction of smallpox vaccination, for example, seem in part to have been responsible for the rise in population. Malthus had described smallpox as one of the major natural checks on population. Before the vaccination was invented, 96 percent of the population contracted the disease, which was fatal in one-seventh of the cases (W. Langer, 1972). The chief victims of this "hideous illness" were children in the first year of life. The eradication of smallpox and the plague, another epidemic killer, must have tremendously reduced infant mortality. Contraception, however, was not widely known or practiced. Hence the result was a baby glut dealt with by the means just discussed.

THE DARK SIDE OF PARENTHOOD

John Stuart Mill, writing about the Victorian family, argued that one should not judge a social institution by its best examples nor by its worst. One must look at each institution as a system, considering not only the virtues of its best practitioners but also the abuses it allows and encourages. Thus absolute monarchy produced some enlightened kings and queens—truly benevolent despots. The problem with despotism, as Mill put it, was not that most despots were bloodthirsty ogres; rather, the problem was that nothing was built into the system to prevent the ogres from coming to power and carrying out their whims.

Mill found the key to the problem of the family in the distribution and control of

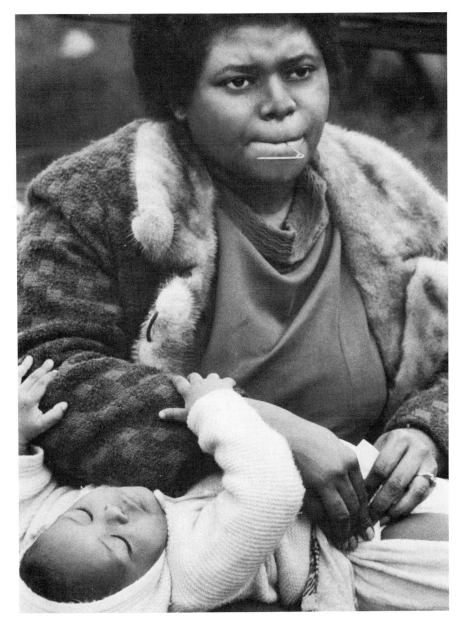

Despite the increased attention being paid to fathers' roles in childrearing, it is still mothers who do most of the "mothering." [Abigail Heyman/ Archive Pictures Inc.]

power. He argued that the Victorian family concentrated enormous power in the hands of the husband–father, made women and children powerless economically and legally, and yet did not do anything to prevent the worst sort of brute from finding some poor woman to marry and doing with her whatever he liked.

Today the most flagrant abuses of the Victorian family have been reformed. Women are no longer legally defined as having a childlike status in relation to their husbands. The official version of childrearing no longer makes a virtue of beating children in the interests of breaking their will and shaping their character. Even parents who believe in strictness and obedience tend to think of spankings more as a last resort than as a good thing in themselves.

Yet the structural problems resulting from the power imbalances in the family remain. These are more subtle but no less real for women, although women are not typically in as much physical danger as in Victorian times. Children, however, do face physical risk, but our system is not structured to prevent child abuse, and may even encourage it. Babies and young children really are weak and dependent—that is, powerless—emotionally, physically, and intellectually. Notions such as permissiveness and the child-centered society obscure the basic inequality with which parent and child confront each other at the outset of the child's life. The basic imbalance is corrected in other societies by the presence of other people in or near the household.

Child Abuse

Researchers point to the difficulty of drawing a line between "normal" discipline and child abuse because the parent is legally empowered to use corporal punishment to enforce rules, no matter how arbitrary they may appear to the child or to others. If a parent should kill a child in the course of administering a "deserved" beating, some states would consider the event as excusable homicide.

It is also difficult to state how abusing parents differ from normal parents. There is a strong tendency to interpret child abuse as the result of some gross psychological abnormality—what sort of parental monsters would abuse their children? Yet the literature on battered children reveals no clear line of demarcation between battering parents and "normal" ones. Nothing sets them off in terms of social class, occupation, IQ, urban/rural residence, or psychopathology. Research has found nothing more striking than a pattern of childrearing merely exaggerating the usual one (Gil, 1971).

Most instances of physical abuse occur when the parent or caretaker gets carried away in anger and goes too far. Some battering parents expect strict obedience from very young children; they possess a marked sense of righteousness, and feel they are encouraging their children to behave and be respectful. Or they may be under severe economic or other strains. For example, B. F. Steele and C. B. Pollock (1968) observed that there seems to be an "unbroken spectrum" of parental disciplinary behavior, ranging from mild pats on the bottom, through severe spankings, through bone-breaking beatings:

To be aware of this, one has only to look and listen to the parent/child interactions at the playground and the supermarket, or even to recall how one raised one's own children or how one was raised oneself. The amount of yelling, scolding, slapping, punching, hitting, and yanking acted out by parents on very small children is almost shocking. Hence, we have felt that in dealing with the abused child we are not observing an isolated, unique phenomenon, but only the extreme form of what we would call a pattern or style of child rearing quite prevalent in our culture. (p. 104)

It is impossible to determine accurately the number of instances of child abuse. About 10,000 cases of serious injury to children inflicted by parents or their caretakers are recorded annually by child-abuse registries. The rate is 9 cases per 100,000 children per year. Researchers in the field assume this to be merely the tip of an iceberg; it is impossible to estimate the number of injuries passed off as accidents or never even reported. An English study of parents whose children were hospitalized for treatment of burns found many instances of what appeared to be willful negligence on the part of parents; for example, the parent was angry at the child and somehow just didn't move fast enough to prevent the child from tipping a pot of boiling soup onto himself.

Accidents constitute the leading cause of death in young children, almost three times more frequent than the next leading cause. Assuming that many of these accidents actually represent cases of child abuse, or willful negligence shading into carelessness, some researchers have suggested that parental abuse and neglect may be the most frequent cause of death to children in the United States today (Fontana, 1964, p. ix).

On the other hand, David Gil (1970), another child-abuse researcher, argued that physical abuse of children may not be the major killer and maimer that others have claimed. Gil argued that individual acts of violence against children within the family may be overshadowed by collective societal abuse through poverty and discrimination:

America has sometimes been described as child-centered; however, any unbiased observer of child life in this nation will find that many millions of children are living and growing up under circumstances of severe social and economic deprivation which tend to inhibit the fullest possible development of their innate capacities. . . . Many of these children lack adequate nutrition, medical and dental care, and educational vocational opportunities. Any serious student of child life in American society would have to con-clude that, however high the prevalence of physical abuse of individual children within their families and homes may be, the abuse inflicted upon children collectively by society as a whole is far larger in scope and far more serious in its consequences. (pp. 15–16)

Although child abuse may not overshadow the child problems caused by poverty and inequality, Gil agreed with other researchers that the propensity toward child abuse is extremely widespread in the population. In a national survey carried out by Gil (1970), about 60 percent of all the adults interviewed thought that "almost anybody could at some time injure a child in his care" (p. 56). He suggested these results show that the infliction of physical injury on children is viewed as an "almost normal occurrence" in the course of caring for a child. His results are all the more striking in that the survey defined as physical abuse only those incidents resulting in actual injuries. Gil noted that if the definition had included attacks that did not result in injury, an even higher proportion of people would have agreed that almost anyone could at times abuse a child in his or her care.

Thus child abuse must be seen as *potential* behavior in many families, but actually may be relatively rare. The research on actual incidents of child abuse suggests that other factors have to be added to this general propensity in order for an attack on a child to occur. One of these extra factors appears to be the experience of the parents themselves as children. Many of the abusing parents who come to the attention of social agencies and researchers appear to have been—or felt—unloved or unlistened to as children. They expect their own children to supply the love they missed when they were children. Such a parent may take a baby's crying, or the failure of an 18-month-old to obey commands instantly, as a sign that the child really doesn't love him or her.

Child-abusing parents tend to find themselves entangled in a complicated web of emotions. They tend to see their children as both their own unloving parents and their bad, needy, childhood selves. When parents hit children, they sometimes seem to be re-enacting a scene from their own childhood. Often parents report feeling as if hitting the child is like hitting themselves (Steele, 1970).

Such psychological mechanisms do not operate in a vacuum. Situational pressures and the social context also contribute to the chain of events leading to physical child abuse. Money worries, unemployment, and illness are some of the other factors that can tip the delicate balance of parental inclinations toward the child one way or the other. Despite our initial horror and indignation when we first learn of child abuse, many of the actual incidents reveal familiar feelings and understandable—if not forgivable—responses to a difficult situation.

The following case of child abuse, for instance, came to my attention. A school counselor in a California suburb told me there were many instances in which she and the teachers in the school suspected child abuse. Most often the children would not "tell" on their parents, but one instance was confirmed. An 11-year-old boy came to school with a broken arm. He said he had fallen out of a tree. The counselor was working with the boy on learning problems, and eventually he took her into his confidence. He said his father had broken his arm, but made him swear not to tell anybody.

The circumstances were as follows: the boy's mother had died shortly before, leaving the husband with four children, of which this boy was the oldest. The father, who was a skilled worker in an aerospace industry, had been struggling to manage the housework and child care as well as keep up his job. One after another, a series of housekeepers had been hired, but they all quit. The incident of the broken arm occurred when the most recent housekeeper walked off. The father had done the wash and asked the boy to hang it on the line. Through carelessness or accident, the whole wash landed in the dirt in the back yard. That was the last straw for the father, and he hit the boy in the arm with a baseball bat.

Reactions to incidents of child abuse are complicated: On the one hand we are horrified and cannot understand how a parent could harm a child; on the other hand, as Gil's statistics indicate, most people feel that almost anyone could abuse a child at one time or another. The following letter from a mother to a child psychologist illustrates both the accepting attitude toward child abuse and the ease with which a conscientious middle-class mother can find herself cast in the role of child abuser.

One Saturday morning, I was rushing to gather the children's clothes, bottles, and diapers, preparing to leave for the weekend.

I was making some hot milk for the girls. While the baby was crying in the high chair and throwing his breakfast on the floor, the milk boiled over. June, my 5-year-old, was giving me her tenth excuse why she didn't want to put on her shoes, even though she was sick and the floor was cold. I blew up: "Do I have to start screaming before you'll listen to me?" (Thinking to myself at the moment—this isn't me—this is my mother yelling.)

June stood there holding her ground. I picked her up in a sweep of anger, dragged her to her room, and heaved her onto the floor yelling, "and don't come out until your shoes are on!" She landed on her stomach and chin and I immediately saw that she was hurt. I ran in, picked her up, and laid her on her bed.

Under her chin was a gash so deep I couldn't see the end of it. I don't remember what I said to comfort her. All I remember is how I felt: I had taken a child who was whole and broken her.

I ran out into the front hall and rang my neighbor's doorbell. He is a doctor. When no one answered immediately I rang another bell. Two neighbors came to the door at the same time. I told them what had happened and they came in to help. The doctor wasn't home but his wife knew what to do. She stopped the bleeding, and told me to get hold of myself. She phoned my pediatrician and told him that June had had an accident and described the wound. The doctor asked for me. I told him the truth. He laughed and said, "It happens in the best homes."

He told me to take her to the emergency room at the hospital and assured me that she would be all right. Both my neighbors told me to forget it. "It was an accident, it happens all the time." The doctor's wife said she had hurt her sons a few times by throwing them against the wall and the other neighbor, a minister's wife, told me that once she had thrown a shoe at her youngest daughter and cut her forehead open.

"Forget it. It was an accident," they all advised. It took six stitches to sew my daughter up. She was wrapped in a sheet like a mummy, and taped down to the table. She kept crying: she was afraid that I would be angry with her because her tights would be dirty from the tape.

I never understood how a parent could hurt a child. I learned that it was very easy, and that it's accepted by friends and neighbors as an accident, as something to forget.

When June got home from the hospital, I held her in my arms and told her that I never meant to hurt her, that I loved her and that we were going to have a new rule in our home: People are not for hurting. (Ginott, 1972)

PARENTHOOD IN CROSS-CULTURAL PERSPECTIVE

As the preceding incidents illustrate, there is something peculiar about American childrearing that has been remarked on by a number of anthropologists. This peculiarity apparently stems from the isolation and privacy of the nuclear family, which leads to intensive parent–child interaction. Thus the isolated family may tend to produce child abuse along with overprotection and other forms of psychological engulfment.

The issue has been stated most bluntly by Jules Henry (1963):

In our culture babies are a private enterprise—everybody is in the baby business as soon as he gets married. He produces his own babies; they are his; only he has a say-so in their management. . . . Pinched off alone in one's house, shielded from critical eyes, one can be as irrational as one pleases with one's children as long as severe damage does not attract the attention of the police. (pp. 331–332)

Henry contrasted this private-enterprise version of parenthood with the social regulation of parent–child relations in other cultures. In primitive cultures or large households many eyes watch what a mother does; she cannot do what she pleases with the child. Of course, this means a mother may have to carry out what she or a medical authority from another culture might consider harmful traditional practices, but the child is shielded from the mother's whims or gross incompetence. Often, as Henry pointed out, the child is thought of as belonging to the clan or whole family as much as to the parents.

The point is further documented by William Stephens (1963) in his cross-cultural survey of family life. Stephens wrote how, in a number of ways, American childrearing practices are "strikingly deviant" from those of other cultures; it seems, said Stephens, that practically the whole world does things one way, while we do it another way. One of the areas of great deviance concerns this matter of the isolated nuclear-family household. In every other society but one, the Copper Eskimo, Stephens found the nuclear family living with or near the husband's or wife's kin. Regardless of the degree to which the nuclear family is thought of as a separate

Taking baby pictures is part of the role of the modern parent. [Abigail Heyman/ Archive Pictures Inc.]

unit, ecologically it is part of a larger household or complex of households.

The chief feature setting American parenthood apart from its traditional counterparts is not so much the loosening of kinship bonds as the absence of what anthropologist John Whiting (1977) has called the "microcommunity." A microcommunity is a group of about twenty or thirty mothers and their children—with or without fathers or their relatives—who live close to one another. All the mothers know the names of all the children. It is the microcommunity, Whiting argued, not the extended family, that serves as the basic support group for parenting in preindustrial societies.

Although something resembling the microcommunity may exist to this day in some small towns and urban ethnic neighborhoods, the mobility of American life,

both social and geographical, and the strong value placed on family privacy have encouraged the separation of the family unit from the surrounding community.

In the microcommunity the child is surrounded by parental surrogates. The influence of the nuclear-family ideology has led to this situation being described at times as a deprivation for the child, as if the child can receive only a fixed amount of love—all of it from the mother or the same amount divided in several ways. Actually, however, the presence of stand-ins and helpers for the mother may increase the amount of warmth and attention the mother can give to the child. For example, one six-culture study (W. W. Lambert, 1971; Minturn & Lambert, 1964; J. W. M. Whiting, 1961) found that the more mother substitutes available, the warmer and more stable the mother was in interacting with the child. Lambert wrote of this as perhaps the most important finding of the study: "It suggests that the mental health, or at least the style of emotional life, of both the mother and her child is enhanced by the availability of acceptable surrogates" (W. W. Lambert, 1971, p. 55). J. W. M. Whiting (1961) reported that the attention and comforting a child receives is roughly proportional to the number of adults living in the household. The more adults there are in a house, for example, the more time an infant is likely to spend in someone's arms, and the sooner he or she will be attended to after starting to cry.

Once the point has been made, it seems rather obvious that the all-your-eggs-in-one-basket system of the isolated family imposes strains on both mother and child. As Stephens (1963) put it, mother's feelings become very important because she is the only mother you have. If she gets angry with you, there's no place else to go, nor is there any place for her to go to rest or to get out of an angry mood. This sets the stage for emotional outbursts, which at the extreme may result in child abuse, but more frequently result in scoldings and complaints, perhaps spankings, sometimes accidents. It's not a matter of villains or bad parents, but rather an ecological one of great demands being placed on limited parental resources of time, energy, and money.

The lack of social regulation of parenthood by the clan or community has many disadvantages for parents even as it increases their power over a child. Again we encounter one of the many paradoxes of freedom: in the tribal family or traditional kin group, children not only do not belong to parents in the same way as they do to isolated modern parents, but also the parents deal with their children according to a script written by the larger culture. The culture's traditional beliefs and superstitions strengthen the par-

ents' position in dealing with children and, again paradoxically, can make the parents more relaxed, warm, and affectionate.

In the old system the parent resembles an administrator in a large bureaucracy, carrying out policies made by higher authorities. Children may disobey or fail to carry out assigned tasks, but they are unlikely to argue with very many of the rules themselves. Even if they do, however, the parents can argue back that it's beyond their power to change the rules. What the parents lose in personal power they more than make up for in institutional backing for their position. By contrast, the American parent is often uncertain about rules because no community tradition exists, and advice from experts may be contradictory and difficult to apply. Whether or not the parent is unsure, the child recognizes the parent as the source of the rules—the parent is the legislator as well as the executive and the judiciary. Thus the stage is set for submission or resentment or rebellion.

No matter what the outcome, it is a two-party conflict between parent and child. Books of advice to parents often suggest that parents state rules impersonally, not in the form of orders. Thus they are advised not to say to their children "Go to bed" but "It's bedtime"; not to say "Pick those toys up off the floor" but "There are some toys on the floor that need to be put away." Parents can even say "I know you want to stay up, but it's bedtime," indicating even further separation of themselves from the rules and a closeness to the child. This technique often does work because it prevents confrontation between parents and children. But it hardly duplicates the situation of the parent in a traditional society. The child usually comprehends that the buck really does stop at the parent, and that there is only a remote authority, if any at all, supervising both the parent's and the child's acts.

The most extreme form of social support for parental authority is the supernatural. Consider the following incident, reported by a Hopi Indian man about his childhood.

I later saw some giantlike Katchinas (masked dancers who impersonate supernatural beings) stalking into the village with long black bills, and big sawlike teeth. One carried a rope to lasso disobedient children. He stopped at a certain house and called for a boy. "You have been naughty," he scolded. "You fight with other children. You kill chickens. You pay no attention to the old people. We have come to get you and eat you." The boy cried and promised to behave better. The giants became angrier and threatened to tie him up and take him away. But the boy's parents begged for his life and offered fresh meat in his place. The giant reached out his hand as if to grab the boy but took the meat instead. Placing it in his basket, he warned the boy that he would get one more chance to change his conduct. (Stephens, 1963, p. 341)

Notice the role of the parents in the anecdote: from the child's point of view they are benevolent protectors saving him from a terrible fate. In the American family system, the frightening giant and kind protector are one person.

MODERN MOTIVATIONS FOR PARENTHOOD

In looking at parenthood as an institution, we have not yet focused on the parents themselves. What is the meaning of parenthood in the lives of parents? Given the burdensomeness of children and the difficulties of being a parent in the modern world, why do people choose to have children?

One reason is that it is still the expected thing for a married couple to do. Although "pronatalist" pressures have lessened in recent years, they have by no means disap-

peared. A 1973 study of more than fifty voluntarily childless couples by sociologist Jean Veevers revealed some of the social pressures toward parenthood that prevailed at the time. All of the wives reported being stigmatized by their decision not to have children. There is, they felt, a widespread stereotype of the childless woman as selfish, abnormal, immoral, and irresponsible. In addition, the childless woman was assumed to be unhappy, unfulfilled, and unfeminine. Many of the women had experienced direct pressures from family and friends: they had been subjected to arguments in favor of having children, as well as more subtle pressures, such as being asked to explain their failure to become parents and being asked when—not if—they were going to have children.

Despite the negative view of childlessness, however, these women were content with their decision. Veevers pointed out that these women were quite well defended against such sanctions. They drew support from their husbands, and they found various ways of "discrediting the discreditors."

But it is of course much more than social pressure that makes people want to have children. As we saw earlier, while children have become expensive and economically "useless," they have become "emotionally priceless" (Zelitzer, 1985). The desperation of many people with fertility problems and the willingness of significant numbers of single professional women to have babies demonstrate the emotional value of children.

Despite all the talk of the declining family, there has been no significant increase in recent years in the percentage of people who prefer not to become parents. In fact, the proportion of young women who say they don't expect to have children is no greater than the percentage of childless women during the baby boom (Thornton & Freedman, 1983). The generations that included the grandmothers and greatgrandmothers of today's young people contained about twice the proportion of childless women. The women of the baby-boom generation are delaying the birth of their first child, and many of them may have difficulty getting pregnant when they try. But they have not rejected the idea of motherhood in significant numbers.

Why hasn't there been a marked increase in voluntary childlessness over the past decade or so? It's an interesting question. Researchers have often offered a demographic explanation of voluntary childlessness: women who are highly educated and/or involved in careers are the most likely candidates. Yet educational and employment opportunities for women in recent years have expanded greatly. Sharon Houseknecht (1982) suggests that the explanation may lie in a widespread social and cultural reaction to the 1970s. As we have mentioned in earlier chapters, in all segments of society there seems to have been a turning away from the free-wheeling, anything-goes, individualistic values of the "me decade." Houseknecht proposes that this response represents a "normative reaction to normlessness" (H. Becker, 1960)—a conscious return to traditional norms when these appear to be threatened. This familistic trend, she suggests, has had two effects on women who might otherwise choose to be childless. They have become more familistic themselves, and find less support for childlessness among people they know and in society as a whole.

The reaction to the normlessness of the 1970s does not, however, explain the longer-term trend that increased children's emotional value as children lost their economic usefulness. The experience of parenthood provides many emotional and symbolic rewards, despite the costs. Life in a modernized society—urban, industrial, bureaucratic, impersonal—as we've observed before exerts paradoxical pressures on the family and on intimate relations generally. They are both

more difficult to sustain and more deeply needed. It is not only love that we crave, but power and influence. As Jerome Kagan (1977) observed:

As modern environments make a sense of potency and individual effectiveness more difficult to attain, freedom from all affective involvements becomes more and more intolerable. Involvement with a family is the only viable mechanism available to satisfy that hunger. (p. 54)

Thus it is not as surprising as it may seem at first glance that there is an inverse relation between social class and fertility—as in the saying that the "rich get richer and the poor get children." The explanation is not simply that poor and working-class people don't know about contraceptives or are careless about using them. Rather, as several studies have shown, lower-status couples may want more children than their middle-class counterparts because children provide satisfactions that cannot be had any other way. For women who lack the opportunity for satisfying work outside the home, the bearing and rearing of children can provide emotional rewards as well as a recognized social role (Luker, 1984; Rainwater, 1960). For the working-class man, fatherhood can provide a source of pride and the opportunity to exercise a degree of power not possible at work or anywhere else but in the family. As Blau and Duncan (1967) observed:

Whereas successful achievers have their status as adult men supported by their superior occupational roles and authority, the unsuccessful find a substitute in the authority they exercise in their role as fathers over a number of children. (p. 428)

It is not only for working-class people that parenthood promises compensatory rewards—that is, gratification to compensate

Despite the family's changing functions, certain jobs still belong to parents—like pulling out loose baby teeth. [Charles Harbutt/Archive Pictures Inc.]

for lacks and deprivations in other areas of life. Many people have children because they want to feel important and needed, or because life seems empty and pointless and children promise excitement. Perhaps the most basic deprivation that leads people to have children is death; having children has always symbolized a kind of immortality. Through children one takes one's place in the chain of generations, linking ancestors with generations yet unborn. Children have assured the continuation of the family name and lineage, as well as the perpetuation of the family farm or business. In recent years, however, people have come to care less about what historian Edward Shorter has called "the posterity business," and more about the psychological rewards of parenthood.

There have been a number of studies dealing with motivations for parenthood, many of which have been summarized by Pohlman (1969). One of the most common reasons people give for becoming parents is that they "like" or "love" children. Sometimes this statement seems to be given as an easy answer when a person is asked why he or she wants to have children. But as Pohlman pointed out, some of the commonsense reasons for liking children are important: "Children provide action and stimulation and change, some of the factors that attract one to raise pets or watch a television program" (p. 60). Adults can relax with children and relive some of their own childish ways by joking, teasing, and roughhousing. They can also hug, cuddle, and kiss their children, thus fulfilling a basic human need for touch that is otherwise hard to express in adult life. In many families, particularly working-class ones with rigid sex roles, the affection provided by children may make up for a lack of closeness between husband and wife.

Further, LeMasters (1970) has pointed to a "romantic complex" surrounding parenthood, as seen in seventeen "folk beliefs" about parenthood that have been popular in American culture. Some examples of these are:

Rearing children is fun.
Children are sweet and cute.
Children will turn out well if they have "good" parents.
Children appreciate all the advantages their parents give them.
Two parents are always better than one.
Love is enough to sustain good parental performance.
All married couples should have children.
Childless married couples are frustrated and unhappy.
Children improve a marriage.
Child rearing is easier today because of modern medicine, modern appliances, child psychology, etc. (pp. 18–29)

THE COSTS OF PARENTHOOD

Although parenthood often brings the satisfactions that people hope for before they have children, there are also costs. In recent years a trend has developed away from the notions of parenthood as fulfillment and of childrearing as part of the grand design of the social system. There is a growing awareness that even wanted and dearly loved children seem to bring heavy costs to parents.

The experience of parenthood varies, of course, with the age of the child. John Clausen (1986) suggests that the following stages of the family life cycle are significant for most families:

1. life as a couple, often with a period of living together before marriage
2. life with children in the home:

   preschool: youngest child under 6
   preadolescence: youngest child 6–12
   adolescence: youngest child 13–20
   unlaunched: youngest child over 20

3. empty nest: couple with no children at home

For many people, the birth of the first child is the most dramatic, demanding transition in the whole life course. Reuben Hill (1949) was the first to suggest that the coming of the new baby would result in a "crisis" for married couples. Despite debate over the term *crisis* (Cox, 1985), several decades of research has shown that the transition to parenthood is a major upheaval in the lives of a couple, and it often sets the stage for increased difficulties in the marriage (Cowan et al., 1985).

One study reported that following childbirth the amount of time the wife and husband converse with each other is cut in half (Feldman, 1962, cited in Pohlman, 1969). The sexual relationship is disrupted and may even be discontinued for as long as 4 months— 8 weeks before birth and 8 weeks after birth while tissues heal. Some women remain indifferent to sex even after their physical recovery from childbirth. The presence of the child looms large, and parental sex may be interrupted by the baby's cries. The exhaustion of the new mother hovers constantly in the background, and at times is overwhelming.

Another of the themes of this literature on the costs of parenthood is the feeling on the part of many parents, particularly fathers, that they are competing with the child for the attention and love of the spouse. In many homes the coming of the first child changes the household from husband-centered to child-centered. Some of the earlier literature on parenthood as crisis saw the crisis as a "normal" one, emphasizing the transitory nature of the problems brought on by the coming of children.

Alice Rossi (1968) took issue with the "normal" crisis idea. She argued that the crisis need not always have a positive outcome: people do not always mature in response to the strains of parenthood, but may suffer deterioration. This is particularly so for women, she notes; the cultural pressure to bear children is so great that many women may have children in the absence of a genuine desire for them or the ability to perform well at the task.

Rossi compared parental roles with those of marriage and work. She argued that the parent role is much more difficult in American society than the other two roles. Marriage and work often involve a long period of preparation, with gradual transition to the role. The transition to parenthood, on the other hand, occurs abruptly and totally, as if a person shifted from being a graduate student to a full professor with little intervening apprenticeship experience of slowly increasing responsibility. The new mother starts out immediately on 24-hour-a-day duty with full responsibilities. Further, in contrast with other commitments, parenthood is irrevocable. Rossi noted that we can have ex-spouses and ex-jobs but not ex-children.

Rossi argued that failures in mothering should be blamed not on individual women but on the isolated nuclear family structure and the failure of society to provide institutionalized substitutes for the extended kin to assist in the care of infants and young children. Pohlman (1969) likewise concluded that because so many women have dreary re-

actions to their first 10 or 12 years of motherhood, a society-wide problem seems to be present, and he calls for a society-wide solution.

It seems illogical that each one of many thousands of mothers should conclude she has some peculiar individual problem, and should go through a period of soul-searching and hostility and repression and guilt in her relations to her children. (p. 153)

Not only the transition to parenthood but also the continuing psychological costs of raising a child have received attention from a number of writers. John and Suzanne Clausen (1973) reported the following findings:

Especially during the early years, children connote broken sleep, noise, confusion, and when there are several, congestion. Mothers of young children put in an inordinately long work week and tend to be confined to the home much of the time. The early years of motherhood are frequently remembered as the period when one constantly yearned for a full night's sleep and for a day free of demands. In our longitudinal data at the Institute of Human Development, mothers with three or more children fairly closely spaced, looking back at the early years of motherhood, from the perspective of the late 40's, are likely to recall those early years as years of extreme exhaustion and discouragement. (p. 7)

Pohlman (1969) noted that many parents find interacting with children, especially over long periods of time, a strain.

Parents want the child to do one thing; the child wants to do another. The battle between wills can prove wearying. Demanding strict and unwavering obedience may be the simplest procedure, but even this is a strain on parents. And many parents doubt whether this is the right approach. . . . They may alternate between permissiveness and irritated punitiveness. If they punish physically, they may feel guilty for this; if they fail to do so, they may feel guilty for the omission. (p. 105)

But the strains of parenthood are not the inevitable battle of wills and the temperamental incompatibilities of adults and children. In part, they are the responsibility of social arrangements that make parents solely responsible for children and fail to provide even minimal assistance for parents as they go about their daily rounds of work and chores.

Moreover, despite the myth of the child-centered society, we are remarkably adult-oriented, with few places where children can be integrated into adult activities. One mother has described the result as follows:

I have three children, 8, 2½, and 1. They are beautiful children, and most times I delight in them. But there are times when I see them as encumbrances, the objects of my frustration and anger. They are welded to me not only at birth, but by a society that sees them as totally my problem, my burden alone. Wherever I move, they move with me: to the drugstore, to the newsstand, the fish market. Where once I moved on two legs, now I move on eight.

As parents, my husband and I are the sole providers, protectors, entertainers, and watchdogs for our young. We have no "extended family" to help care for them, no communal group to share the tasks. . . . When there are errands to be run or places we want to go—even for an hour—the scheduling and logistical arrangements that must be made would spin the most grizzled heads in the Pentagon. (Francke, 1972, pp. 27–28)

For many parents, adolescence rivals early childhood as the most difficult period. Not only do teenagers pose new problems for the parents, but the parents themselves may disagree about how to deal with their problems. Marital tensions often reach a peak at this period (Blood & Wolfe, 1960).

Parent–child relationships have always continued after the "empty nest" period, but in recent years parental involvement in the lives of children often persists into the children's 20s. During the prosperous decades of the 1950s and 1960s, couples married young and often moved far away from their original families. In recent years, this pattern has changed. Young people do not leave home and become independent in the same ways they did in earlier decades. They are delaying marriage, getting divorced more often, and finding it difficult to find well-paying jobs and affordable housing. In a reversal of historical trends, increasing numbers have been returning home to live with their parents for various periods.

One study of the "not-so-empty nest" (Clemens & Axelson, 1985) found that half of the parents involved in such arrangements had expected their children to live away from home after the age of 18, and 80 percent had expected them to do so by the age of 22. The arrangement seemed to work best when the child was younger rather than older and when it was a temporary arrangement. Most parents do not welcome the return of children they had expected to be on their own, and many found it stressful.

Parents as Pygmalions: Prescriptions for Perfection

As we have noted, modern parenthood can be a burden because parents lack the support of kin and community in the daily tasks of rearing children, and also because children have come to be consumers of the family's resources rather than productive contributors to it. But there is another reason why modern parenthood has become burdensome. The modern parent is responsible not only for the child's physical well-being, but also for the child's psychological adjustment. Since the beginning of the twentieth century, the leading psychological theorists and their popularizers have argued that parents play an omnipotent role in their children's psychological development. Only if parents do the right things at the right time will children turn out to be happy, successful adults. Conversely, any flaws in a person's adjustment, even in adulthood, can be traced to a lack of parental love or some other parental failing.

In historical and anthropological perspective, this preoccupation with the psychological consequences of parental behavior is unusual, if not unique. Earlier generations of parents were concerned with the bodily health and moral virtue of their children. In times of high infant mortality and strong religious beliefs, God, Fate, and the Devil reduced the perceived influence of the parents over the child's life. As two anthropologists put it:

For the whole of human history up to the turn of the present century, simple physical survival has been the dominant issue in child rearing: a question not of "How shall I rear my child?" but "*Will* I rear him?" . . . Child psychology is a luxury which only a small section of the world's parents can afford to consider. (Newson & Newson, 1974, p. 55)

A concern with child psychology may indeed be a costly luxury for modern Western parents, but it does not make childrearing any easier. Just as improvements in household appliances have failed to reduce the housewife's working hours, but merely have raised standards of housekeeping, so have child psychology and improved pediatrics raised the standards for childrearing.

Child-development experts—psychologists, psychiatrists, and doctors—have been "worshipped as the high-priests of child rearing" (Pohlman, 1969, p. 102), yet the advice of the experts is often inconsistent and usu-

ally difficult to apply to specific situations. One expert may write, for example, that hugging and kissing is good for babies and children, whereas another writes that physical affection is seductive and disturbing. Some experts favor permissiveness; others argue that children need firm rules and authoritative direction. In a classic article, Martha Wolfenstein (1955) reviewed the changes in advice given in various editions of the pamphlet *Infant Care,* published by the United States government on consultation with the experts in the field. In ten editions issued over 40 years, there have been remarkable alterations in concepts of the child's psychological and physical needs and the kind of parental behavior recommended:

In the earlier period, the mother's character was one of strong moral devotion. There were frequent references to her "self-control," "wisdom," "strength," "persistence." . . . In the 1929–1938 period, parenthood became predominantly a matter of know-how. The parents had to use the right technique to impose routines and keep the child from dominating them.

In the most recent period, parenthood becomes a major source of enjoyment for both parents. . . . The parents are promised that having children will keep them together, keep them young, and give them fun and happiness. . . . Enjoyment, fun, and play now permeate all activities with the child. "Babies—and usually their mothers—enjoy breast feeding," nursing brings "joy and happiness" to the mother. At bath time, the baby "delights" his parents, and so on. (p. 173)

A review of childrearing research by Bronfenbrenner (1958) revealed that middle-class parents seemed to reflect in their actual childrearing practices the swings in expert opinion. During the first half of the twentieth century, middle-class parents tended to be more strict with their children than working- and lower-class parents, but by the

Parent-child relationships shift in many ways as children approach their own adulthood. [Leslie Starobin]

1950s they had crossed over and become more permissive. During the earlier period, for example, middle-class parents tended to wean and toilet train their infants earlier and to keep them on stricter schedules than did working-class parents; in more recent years, however, middle-class parents have swung over to later weaning and toilet training and to more flexible schedules. Ironically, attention to the experts among middle-class people seems to raise anxiety rather than reduce it. Research on middle-class mothers,

such as that conducted by Sears, Maccoby, and Levin (1957), suggests that the more awareness a mother has of the childrearing literature, the more uncertain she feels that she is doing the right thing:

I spend most of my time thinking I am a perfectly lousy mother and I suppose all mothers feel that way. The thing of motherhood brings out my own inefficiencies, my own deficiencies, so terribly, that . . . the outstanding thought in my mind is that I should try to be a better mother each new day." (p. 43)

Such problems as bed wetting or stuttering tend to be interpreted by middle-class parents as a negative reflection of their parenting. In former days, however, parents more often blamed such problems on the child's character or on physical difficulties. Furthermore, working-class parents show relatively more concern for the child's outward behavior than his or her inner states (Kohn, 1963). A concern for the inner life of the child may make things harder for both parent and child.

The notion that parenthood is fun may lead paradoxically to greater strains for parents.

The characterization of parenthood in terms of fun and enjoyment . . . may express a new imperative: You ought to enjoy your child. When a mother is told that most mothers enjoy nursing, she may wonder what is wrong with her in case she does not. Her self-evaluation can no longer be based entirely on whether she is doing the right and necessary things but becomes involved with nuances of feeling which are not under voluntary control. (Wolfenstein, 1955, pp. 174–175)

There is little evidence that the parental mystique that flourished in the 1950s has faded away. Indeed, in some ways the gap between the standards of child care and the realities of raising children has grown wider. Although most mothers are in the labor force and divorce has risen sharply, most of the popular childrearing manuals remain grounded in the norms of the postwar world. One study found that only seven of the twenty most influential childrearing guides gave even grudging approval to mothers working while their children are young (Etaugh, 1980). Most assume, contrary to the research evidence, that nonmaternal care is inevitably harmful to children (Scarr, 1985). As one writer puts it:

In some of its aspects, the culture of the 1950's seems strange but distant. A rerun of *I Love Lucy* is not threatening because most of us recognize the styles and values of the show as a relic from another age. Not so when we come to fifties attitudes towards motherhood and childrearing. The cult of motherhood is alive and well; our standards are still set by the "smother love" of the 1950's. Images of the complete, all providing mother remain powerful enough to furnish women with a bottomless pit of maternal guilt. (Hewlett, 1986)

THE FUTURE OF PARENTHOOD

We have focused so heavily on the dark side of parent–child relations in this chapter because the prevailing views of the subject have been so romantic and unrealistic. It is possible, however, to end on an optimistic note.

As we have emphasized throughout this chapter, the care children will receive when they come into the world is not guaranteed by genes, instincts, or societal necessity. The first requirement for adequate child care is this: children should be wanted by whomever is responsible for them, although loving and wanting children do not guarantee competence in a parent. Anything that reduces the likelihood of unwanted births can only increase the chances that children who are born will be treated humanely. The ability to exercise control and choice about parenthood must mark a milestone in what Erich Fromm has called the "revolution of the child."

Many other ongoing social changes now—the women's movement and the increased acceptability of singleness and of childlessness—can only mean that fewer children will be born as a result of carelessness or social pressure. When parenthood is romanticized, when it is assumed that all women are endowed with maternal instincts and innate competence in caring for infants and young children, any alternative means of child care can only be seen as a deprivation for the child. The prevailing myths of parenthood obscure the possibility that child-care facilities may rescue children from physical and emotional mistreatment and may even improve the relationship between the parents and children. After reviewing the literature on the experiences of women during the first 10 or 12 years of parenthood, Pohlman (1969) suggested that neighborhood child-care and education centers are a vital necessity for the well-being of both mothers and children. He wrote:

We believe that most mothers need to be away from their children for a few hours each day, whether they are employed outside their homes or not. Such a "recess" probably permits a mother to relate to her children with greater zest and effectiveness when she is with them. Many mothers cannot bring themselves to leave their children, because of justifiable concern with the quality of substitute care they will receive. Also many mothers lack even the small initiative needed to arrange to be away from children, under existing circumstances. All of this seems to imply the need for a systematic program of child care and education, a program of excellent quality. (p. 153)

The prejudice against child-care facilities outside the home has become a self-fulfilling prophecy. The relatively few day-care facilities that do exist are woefully inadequate in terms of both quantity and quality. They are conceived to be places in which only a mother in extreme circumstances would consider sending a child. And they are conceived to be total substitutes for family child care—5 days a week, 8 hours a day, all year long.

Such forms of child care are needed, but there is another kind for which the need is even greater—part-time, drop-in child care for parents to use as they go about their business. Pohlman also mentioned the need for visiting nurses or other parent surrogates to help out when parents or children are sick. Such services would relieve the kinds of strains that led the widowed father to break his son's arm in the incident reported earlier in this chapter.

Further, trends within the family itself promise to relieve some of the strains of parenthood, which until now have fallen most heavily on women. In young middle-class families, that segment of the population most sensitive to changes in the intellectual climate, parenthood is coming to be defined more and more as a joint enterprise of both the husband and the wife. The trend seems to be motivated not only by women who are insisting that the men share some of the load, but also by many young professional men who no longer accept as their fate the compulsive male careerism that dominated the 1950s.

Finally, parent–child relations are being affected by far-reaching changes in definitions of both adulthood and childhood. We will consider these changes in the following chapters.

SUMMARY

The prevailing conceptions of parenthood in the social sciences and popular thought have emphasized the naturalness of parenthood and the societal need for children. Early mother–child relations in particular are assumed to be governed by innate processes of mutual attraction, independent of social contexts.

Actually, however, the evolutionary evidence suggests that human infants, in contrast to our primate relatives, are born into a nurturance gap. The same factors that led to the evolution of the human brain resulted in the greater helplessness of human infants and a greater dependency on learning and culture for carrying out maternal activities.

Parent–child relations cannot be understood apart from specific social, cultural, and historical settings. The feeding and care of young children can be a heavy burden or an easily assumed one, depending on the food supply, cultural attitudes toward infants, and the particular circumstances of individual parents. The fact that infanticide has been widely practiced in Western society and elsewhere is evidence that benevolence toward children is not built into human nature and is not a societal imperative.

To understand parenthood in our own society, we must realize how modern kinship and work patterns may make parenthood more difficult than in traditional societies. In most cultures and in our own historical past, parenthood is carried out in the midst of the community and along with economic responsibilities. It is a less self-conscious process because traditional ways can be followed, and the child's future status is already known. Our own society, however, imposes great demands on parents while providing minimal institutional support to replace the kin and community assistance of former times.

CHAPTER 13

The Construction of Childhood

Nature wants children to be children before they are men. If we deliberately pervert this order, we shall get premature fruits which are neither ripe nor well flavored. . . . Childhood has ways of seeing, thinking, and feeling, peculiar to itself; nothing can be more foolish than trying to substitute our ways for them.

Jean-Jacques Rousseau
Emile

There seems little doubt that, in our . . . culture, a contributing factor to the characteristic features of "child mentality" that we have discovered is the positive efforts we make to keep our children childish.

A. Irving Hallowell
Culture and Experience

Americans have long been considered the most child-centered people in the world. Foreign observers throughout our history, as well as anthropologists who have observed other cultures, have commented on the American preoccupation with childrearing. No other group of parents seems to have been so anxious about children or so uncertain about how to deal with them. And no other society has so persistently experienced a sense of crisis over the future of children and the family. For the past century, public concern over children has resulted in wave after wave of reform movements and social policies.

Despite our reputation for child-centeredness, however, American children are now more likely to be poor than any other part of the population. This disparity reflects what many observers have seen as a sharp contradiction between the public and private value of children. Norton Grubb and Marvin Lazerson (1982) noted that while Americans love their own children deeply, they lack "public love" for "other people's children."

IMAGES OF CHILDHOOD

The coexistence of concern and neglect, or worse, in the treatment of children is not unique to our time and place. Perhaps the greatest gap between popular imagery and reality concerning children occurred in the Victorian era when, as Peter Coveney (1967) pointed out, the *myth* of innocent childhood prevailed along with the *practice* of savagery toward children. Coveney referred not only to the exploitation of children in mines and factories, but also to the severe childrearing practices approved by Victorian families.

In addition to the gap between ideal and reality in the treatment of children, our attempts to understand the child's place in society are complicated by contrasting images of the child that not only have succeeded each other but have coexisted side by side. Ideas about children taken for granted in one era come to be regarded as false by the next. In medieval times, for example, children were seen as miniature adults. They wore adult clothing, and when painters gave them adult proportions, no one seems to have noticed that the representations were inaccurate. To later ages such paintings appear quaint and funny.

The image of the child as an incomplete adult was replaced by the demonic child of Calvinism and the Jesuits, a child whose corrupt nature and evil will called for severe discipline, of which whipping was a ritual part, in order to fit the child to be a moral citizen. "Spare the rod and spoil the child" was once a literal prescription for childrearing.

The corrupt child in turn became—for the romantic school of writers, such as Blake, Wordsworth, and Rousseau—a noble savage, whose "doors of perception" and capacities for experiences were not yet deadened by an industrial society. The serious social criticism implied by the image of the romantic child wilted away to become the Victorian cult of the innocent child; childhood became a never-never land of fun and games.

Actually, the image of childhood innocence never entirely replaced the demonic child of the Puritans; particularly in England and America, attitudes toward childhood have been marked by "a curious conflict between childhood as innocence and the grim portrait of an evil being who must be scourged to his salvation" (Kessen, 1965, p. 337). At the end of the nineteenth century Freud revived the image of the demonic child and made it the focus of a new psychology. Freud's theories of infantile sexuality attacked the image of childhood innocence and ushered in the first of the "developmental images" of the child that have dominated twentieth-century thinking about children. Since that time the leading images of the child have been supplied by scientific professionals—psychologists, psychiatrists, pediatricians—rather than by religionists and poets. Thus the child is defined by a place on a staircase of development—the child of ages and stages.

In view of the profound changes that have occurred in our culture's theories of childhood, we can hardly rest assured that we have at last discovered childhood as it really is.

WHAT IS A CHILD?

The enormous variation in the ideas different cultures and historical eras have had about children, their needs, capacities, and the dynamics of growth suggest that the answer is not as obvious as it seems. In this chapter we are going to explore such issues as the following: Is the nature of childhood universal, or do childhood experiences and the characteristics of children vary? To what extent has childhood as we know it been shaped by our family life and other social practices regarding children? Does a society's recognition of the various stages of childhood and youth indicate sensitivity to children's needs? Or does age grading represent a means of segregating children from adult society and exerting greater social control over them?

In trying to define a child, we face many of the same problems we faced earlier in trying to arrive at a definition of the term *family*. The very word *child* carries with it a number of assumptions that get in our way. The term, for example, exists in opposition to another term—*adult*—like light and dark, male and female. Thus our language suggests an opposition, a discontinuity between children and adults, which fits with actual social practice in our society. We tend to assume that children have a separate and distinct nature that distinguishes them from adults: Adults work and are responsible, children play and are irresponsible; adults are controlled and rational, children are emotional and irrational; adults think abstractly, children think concretely; adults are sexual, children are asexual; and so on.

Above all, we do tend to view children through the lenses of the developmental model or paradigm: the assumptions that the child develops naturally by passing through a number of stages, that these stages follow one another in a constant order, that each order is appropriate for a particular age, and that the child has a built-in timetable of development. The essential principles of the developmental paradigm, first elaborated in 1762 by the philosopher Rousseau in *Emile*, continue to guide the field of child study.

In premodern societies, in our own historical past, and in groups outside the middle class, a different concept of childhood has prevailed: children are seen as miniature adults—small or inadequate versions of their parents, often totally subject to traditional or parental authority.

By contrast, the "modern" industrial, middle-class view tends to treat the child as a distinctive social category: children have their own special psychology and their own special needs, patterned processes of growth often elaborated into ideas about developmental states that may postpone advent to "full" adulthood well into a person's 20s, and still later (Berger, Hackett, & Miller, 1972, p. 11). Most professional and popular writings on childhood seem to take for granted that there is a closer fit between the child's special nature and his or her place in modern societies than in the premodern model in which children are treated as little adults.

The prevailing assumption is that when the discontinuities between adults and children are not recognized, the child's nature is being violated. For example, we find the fact that young children work in some cultures both anomalous and distasteful. Even an anthropologist can express surprise at the failure of Indian mothers, for example, to appreciate children's work:

Even those children who did work regularly were not accorded recognition. For instance, Narayan's mother, when asked about her son's chores, reported that he did not do very much work. It would seem that walking an average of 12 miles a day, and carrying a load for 6 to 9 of those miles, might be considered a rather arduous undertaking for a slightly built 7-year-old boy, but his mother was not impressed. (B. Whiting, 1963, pp. 356–357)

Although generally anthropologists have rejected the notion that the norms of child development in Western cultures are the measuring rod against which other cultures are to be judged, the equation of preliterate adult with Western child has been persistent in psychology. Further, psychological concepts of childhood not only are *ethnocentric*—biased in favor of Western culture—but also they may be *chronocentric*—biased in favor of a particular historical period. As Kenneth Keniston (1971a) has put it:

Every epoch tends to freeze its own unique experience into an ahistorical version of life in general. Modern developmental psychology witnesses this universal trend. (p. 332)

THE DEVELOPMENTAL PARADIGM

Childhood became an object of scientific inquiry in the psychology laboratory beginning in the second half of the nineteenth century, although there had been increasing concern on the part of parents, literary figures, and social reformers for about 2 centuries before. Darwin's theories stimulated the rise of scientific interest in the child. It is almost impossible to overestimate the dramatic impact of evolutionary theory on our notions of children as well as on psychology in general. "Development" became the guiding metaphor for theorizing about children. As Kessen (1965) put it, there was a "riot of parallel-drawing" between the mind of the child and what were presumed to be earlier historical stages of the human species.

The irreducible contribution of Darwin to the study of children was . . . in his assignment of scientific value to childhood. Species develop, societies develop, man develops. From the publication of *The Origin of Species* to the end of the nineteenth century, there was a riot of parallel-drawing between animal and child, between primitive man and child, between early human history and child. The developing child was seen as a natural museum of human phylogeny and history; by careful observation of the infant and child, one could see the descent of man. (p. 33)

Although psychology has outgrown its historical origins, evolutionary doctrines continue, in many subtle ways, to influence the study of the child. Contemporary devel-

The mirror becomes an essential tool of self-discovery at adolescence. [Leslie Starobin]

opmental psychology, like psychology in general, is divided into two radically different ways of looking at human nature—the mechanistic approach and the organismic approach. Both reflect, in different ways, the biological frame of reference inherited from Darwinism.

The Mechanistic Approach

The mechanistic approach consists of behavior or learning theories, as exemplified by the work of Skinner, Hull, Dollard and Miller, Bandura, and many others (see Baldwin, 1967; J. Langer, 1969). The intellectual ancestors of these theories were the empiricist or associationist philosophers who assumed that the child's mind was a blank slate (tabula rasa). Where the earlier versions of this position attempted to analyze the contents of the mind into basic elements, current proponents have dispensed with the concept of the mind. The child is shaped not by original nature, but by the environmental contingencies to which he or she has been exposed, just like any other organism from animal to adult human. The Darwinian influence on mechanistic theories is evident in the influence of animal psychology on the study of the child.

At first glance, one might think that mechanistic theories see little difference between adults and children because the same "laws of learning" apply to both. In fact, however, adult and child differ as much in mechanistic developmental theories as in any other kind. Though not qualitatively different from adults, children—along with animals—are assumed to be much simpler organisms:

The animal and the child are imperfect adults for the associationist and imperfect in a critically important way. They can be assumed to have fewer, or more simple, units of behavior than the full man, and their apparent simplicity may permit finding the beginning of the thread that is woven into the inexplicably complicated pattern of adult human behavior. . . . (Kessen, 1965, p. 129)

The Organismic Approach

Mechanistic theories use the term *development* in a general and descriptive sense. Organismic theories use the term in a more restricted way. They define development as a qualitative change of the whole organism from one state or form to another. The organismic approach may be further subdivided into psychoanalytic theories and what J. Langer (1969b) has called "organic lamp" theories. The psychoanalytic theories include the work of Freud and Erikson. By organic lamp theories, Langer meant the work of Piaget and Heinz Werner. Like psychoanalytic theorists, organic lamp theorists assume that innate, biologically rooted functions are the organizing forces that govern development, although they operate in interaction with the environment.

Although each theory selects a different aspect of the child as the key to understanding the process of development, they all agree on several things. First, development is self-propelled and teleological—that is, the "push" to change comes from within the organism, and the endpoint of development is implicit at the beginning. Second, the adult is categorically, or qualitatively, different from the child. The different stages of childhood are also qualitatively different from each other. The endpoint of development is placed in the 20s. The legal designation of 18 or 21 as the age of adult status thus accords well with developmental theories. Finally, developmental theories are organized around specific concepts of adult competence. For Freud the endpoint of development is the genital, heterosexual adult, who is parent to children and has a place in the occupational world. For Piaget the endpoint of development is the stage of formal operational thinking—the ability to think hypothetically and abstractly.

Thus, by definition, these theories set up a polar opposition between child and adult nature. If the adult end of the scale is defined as logical and rational, then the child is by definition autistic, irrational, emotional, and lacking in perceptual and cognitive structures. These qualities are conceived of as being appropriate for children.

Developmental theories claim to be universal. In Freudian theory, development is caused by changes in the body's erotic emphasis. The theory allows for different outcomes depending on how the child's development crises are met, but the psychosexual basics of orality, anality, genitality, and the Oedipal crises are held to be universal. Piaget's progressions are based on maturation of the brain and nervous system along with the child's encounters with the physical and social environment found in all cultures. As J. Langer (1969) put it, "The environment . . . in organic lamp theory is merely the *occasion* for or *scene* of, and not the cause or *agent* of development" (pp. 1–11).

Although both organic lamp and psychoanalytic theories fit the developmental framework or paradigm in both of these senses, they differ in important ways. In some ways the Piagetian image of the child is the polar opposite of the Freudian image. If the Freudian child is a demonic little beast seething with lust and aggression, Piaget's is a scientist bubbling with curiosity. The baby dropping toys out of the crib is revealed to be a little Galileo, observing the behavior of falling bodies. Not only does the Piagetian child exhibit a thirst for knowledge as strong as the sexual urges of the Freudian child— even stronger, because less satiable—but also the child has an active and independent intellect.

In Freud's imagery of the child as well as that of most socialization research, the child is more or less a passive recipient of the demands and teachings of the culture; the only alternative to acceptance is resistance. The choice of weaning and toilet training as the central events in the socialization of the child are significant: these are precisely the areas that allow no room for innovation on the part of the child. All children are eventually weaned and toilet trained; in these struggles the culture always wins, and the child always conforms.

The Piagetian child, however, does not merely internalize the standards of adults as he or she grows up. Piaget's model of development credits the child with more autonomy and creativity than any other. The child participates in his or her own development, and is not the passive victim of either an internal process unfolding on its own or social pressures.

Yet the Piagetian child is not so unlike the Freudian one as may appear at first glance. The child is curious like a scientist, but the capacity to process information is as yet unsophisticated. Thought processes are egocentric, animistic, and easily tricked by appearances: show the child two equal balls of clay, roll one into a sausage, and he or she will tell you there is now less clay in it because it is thinner. The child has a very long way to go before being ready to participate in adult life.

Limitations of the Developmental Paradigm

The problem with all of these images of the child is not so much that they are wrong but that they are limited in a variety of ways, despite the many valid insights they provide. We shall argue here that developmental psychology has overemphasized the view of development as an individual process unfolding from within and has neglected the influence of social and cultural contexts on children and concepts of childhood, and that it has emphasized grand theories and laboratory tests rather than empirical studies of children in their ordinary environments.

One surprising limitation is that most developmental research has little to say about children and their daily lives. American developmental psychology, as Bronfenbrenner (1974) and others have observed, has tended to emphasize laboratory studies in which the child performs an unfamiliar task in a strange situation with a strange adult. It has tended to neglect the study of social settings in which children live and the persons who are central to them emotionally.

As a result of the emphasis on laboratory studies, developmental psychology tends to deal with bits and pieces of the child. The rationale for this approach is that eventually all the bits and pieces can be added together to give a comprehensive picture. It is rare, however, for anyone to try to construct the comprehensive picture. More often, there is a tendency for the bits and pieces to be taken for the real things they represent. Von Bertalanffy (1960) called this the fallacy of the "nothing-but." In the field of child development, the nothing-but fallacy takes the form of assuming that a child is nothing but the developmental stage or test performance typical of that age. Even if the attempt were made to put the pieces together, it is doubtful that they could compose a valid and comprehensive picture of the child. A review of developmental research summed up the problem in this way:

Social scientists, it is sometimes said, are forced to look at small bits and pieces and construct from them a model of reality. In doing this they are often forced into a kind of shorthand. The problem is that this shorthand tends to become a substitute for reality, in interpreting results, in reporting them, and in making recommendations based on them. (Herzog & Sudia, 1973, p. 207)

The grand developmental theories of Freud, Piaget, and Werner, though much richer in their descriptions of children and their behavior than laboratory studies, also fail to portray children in terms of their day-to-day lives. For example, parents who have studied Freud before having children are often surprised to find that the very young infant does not seem to spend all the time being "oral" and that toilet training doesn't occupy most of the toddler's days. Robert White (1960) has written of the discrepancies between theoretical notions of children at different ages and their actual daily behavior. Even in infants, such discrepancies are striking:

Somehow, the image has gotten into our minds that the infant's time is divided between eating and sleep. . . . This is not true even for newborn infants, who show distinct forerunners of what will later become playful exploratory activity.

Gesell notes that at four weeks there is apt to be a waking time in the late afternoon during which visual experience begins to be accumulated. At 16 weeks this period may last for half an hour, and then increase steadily up to one year. Gesell's typical "behavior day" shows an hour of play before breakfast, two hours before lunch, an hour's carriage ride and another hour of social play in the afternoon, and perhaps still another hour after being put to bed. At the age of 12 months, the child is already putting in a six-hour day of play, not to mention the overtime that occurs during meals and the bath. (pp. 110–111)

Piaget's model of the child is as incomplete as Freud's even though it focuses on the very things that the Freudian theories slight: the young child's eagerness to learn, to explore, and to make sense of environment. Piaget's work on the first 2 years of life is rich in detailed descriptions of actual behavior, but the incidents are selected to illustrate the stages of intellectual growth rather than to give a rounded picture of the child in the framework of daily activities.

After the first 2 years, Piaget's writings serve as an even less useful guide to the activities and interests of children than his description of infant activities. He becomes less interested in the child's thinking, especially the limits of the child's conceptual capabilities.

Baldwin (1967) pointed to a gap between the ordinary everyday functioning of preschool children and their performance on Piagetian tests of their thinking. It is surprising, he notes, that sensitive observers of children had never discovered Piaget's findings before he published his research:

Nursery school teachers with years of experience find it impossible to believe that the child thinks the number of objects changes as one spreads them out or clusters them together. For some reason, in an experimental situation where he must deal with the problem in terms of language and engage in conceptual thinking about it, the child reveals weaknesses and defects that are seldom, if ever, manifested in his overt behavior. (p. 584)

A similar point was made by the sociologist Norman Denzin (1970). He found that the actual behavior of children is more complex, both intellectually and socially, than developmental theories would lead one to assume. He summarized his findings as follows:

Children's work involves such serious matters as developing languages for communication; presenting and defending their social selves in difficult situations; defining and processing deviance; and constructing rules of entry and exit into emergent social groups. Children see these as serious concerns, and often make a clear distinction between their play and their work. This fact is best grasped by entering those situations where children are naturally thrown together and forced to take account of one another. (p. 14)

The argument is not that the concept of development is wrong; rather, the concept should be used sparingly and critically. Susan Isaacs (1966), a psychologist who studied cognitive development in preschool children, summed up her findings by noting that the overall impression one gets from her records is that the cognitive behavior of little children, even in the very early years, is not very different from that of adults:

Allowing for the immense difference in knowledge and experience, they go about their business of understanding the world, and what happens to them in it, very much as we do ourselves. . . . If we stress maturation in mental growth too strongly, and treat it too readily as literal, organic fact (of the same order as the facts of embryology), we are likely both to overemphasize the difference between children and ourselves, and to underestimate the part played by experience in their development. (p. 57)

The Recapitulation Hypothesis

Part of the reason for psychology's relative neglect of children in daily life is the emphasis on laboratory methods and the attempt to emulate the experimental sciences. Another reason is the impact of evolutionary theory on developmental psychology. As we noted earlier, modern child study was stimulated by the evolutionary theories of Darwin. The use of biological models of development as lenses for viewing children can be traced to these origins.

One of the most influential concepts to emerge from the new interest in evolution was the recapitulation hypothesis, the notion that the development of the individual repeats the history of the species ("ontogeny recapitulates phylogeny"). The starting point for the recapitulation hypothesis was the development of embryos. Thus it was noted that the human embryo starts out as a single-celled organism, becomes a multicelled organism, then resembles a fish, and so on. Extending this idea, the mental development of the growing child was assumed to repeat the mental development of the human race, reaching its highest point in the adult rational mind of Western man.

G. Stanley Hall's (1904) work is the prime example of how Darwin's biological concepts were translated into psychological ones. Hall is widely recognized as the father of child study in America (see Grinder, 1969; McCullers, 1969). He divided child development into stages corresponding to prehistoric eras in the development of the human race. Thus infancy, the first 4 years of life, corresponded to the animal stage of the human species when it was still using four legs. Childhood, ages 4–8, was supposedly a recapitulation of an earlier cultural era of hunting and fishing, and the period 8–12, which Hall called "youth," was a reenactment of the "humdrum life of savagery" before the higher human traits emerged. (Hall's conceptions of childhood seem to have influenced the founding of the Boy Scouts. Scouting was thought to provide a means of satisfying the various prehistoric instincts, such as hunting, fishing, and gathering.) Adolescence, in Hall's scheme, represented a turbulent, transitional stage in the history of the race after which the highest levels of civilization were attained.

Hall's ideas sound rather farfetched to modern ears; indeed, his highly literal version of the recapitulation theory, based on the inheritance of acquired characteristics, is no longer acceptable scientifically. Yet in some basic ways, Hall's views of human development are retained in much current psychological theorizing. The following are some of the assumptions of recapitulation theory that correspond to those of contemporary views of development: (1) Psychological development consists of a succession of genetically determined stages that are relatively independent of environmental factors; (2) each stage in the sequence is necessary for the emergence of the next; (3) there are direct parallels between child development and cultural development; at the apex of each developmental sequence stands the Western (male) adult. Thus both the development of the individual and the development of the species follow a unilinear progression from lower, simpler, and more primitive functioning to higher, more complex, and more advanced functioning. "Primitive" people now living are the psychological equivalents of both prehistoric man and contemporary Western children.

Almost every major developmental theory today has been shaped by the assumptions of recapitulation doctrine, although this is rarely acknowledged explicitly. McCullers (1969), however, has pointed to important parallels between Hall's ideas and those of five eminent developmental psychologists: Freud, Jung, Werner, Vygotsky, and Piaget. Although most of these men rejected aspects of Hall's thinking and did not consider themselves his intellectual followers, Hall was the senior psychologist of this group of men and had many opportunities to influence them both directly and indirectly. As a group, McCullers observed, these men had a surprising number of things in common: (1) All were evolutionists with some grounding in biology; (2) all found some parallel between racial–cultural development and the development of the individual; (3) all conceived of development as progressing from a primitive to more complex organization through a series of stages or levels, determined by a continuous interplay between what is biologically given and environmental stimulation (McCullers, 1969, p. 1113).

If this analysis of the intellectual origins of developmental theory is correct, then much is explained about current ways of thinking about children as well as human development in general. The metaphor of development, based on embryology, leads one to think of psychological development as an internal process unfolding according to its own laws. It encourages a heavy emphasis on biological maturation in developmental theory, to the neglect of social, cultural, and historical influences. In short, child psychology assumes, as Riegel (1973) put it, that the child grows up in a "sociocultural vacuum" (p. 3).

INDIVIDUAL GROWTH AND SOCIAL CONTEXT

No developmental psychologist disregards entirely the influence of the environment or claims that development is purely a matter of biological maturation. Both Freudians and Piagetians, for example, stress the interaction between internal change and environment. But to emphasize a point made earlier, the environment in these theories is the mere scene of development; it does not cause development to happen or determine its nature or direction. Like the effects of soil and climate on plants, the effects of environment in the prevailing developmental theories are important but limited; growth can be stunted or stimulated, but the nature of the organism remains the same.

Recently, some psychologists have begun to go beyond this limited view of how individual development interacts with the social and cultural context. Rather than looking at development as a process whose outcome is somehow inherent in the child from the beginning, they are arguing that the growth of the individual is inextricably bound with sociocultural conditions and changes.

The paradigm traditionally applied in child psychology pretends that individuals grow up in a sociocultural vacuum. Growth of the individual, as depicted by all the tables and curves in articles and textbooks, is likely to be a mere artifact generated by systematic disregard of historical changes in education, communication, welfare, etc. (Riegel, 1973, p. 3)

Failing to recognize the interdependence of individual psychology and the social matrix may invalidate many research results. Thus findings may be valid for one historical era but not for another. Although anthropologists have for some time argued that many psychological concepts may be *ethnocentric* or biased in favor of Western culture, it is only recently that there has begun to be an awareness of what Keniston calls *chronocentrism*—that is, the possibility that findings may be valid for one historical era but not for another. Also, some psychologists have come to realize that individual change has often been confounded with social and cultural change. It was once regarded, for example, as well-established fact that a person's IQ inevitably declines with aging. This "fact" has turned out to be untrue, however; the seeming decline with age was an artifact of the cross-sectional method of comparing people of different ages to each other. There has been a tendency in the twentieth century for succeeding generations or cohorts to score better on IQ tets. Thus at any one point in time, older adults will score lower than younger adults, but not necessarily lower than themselves at earlier ages.

More far-reaching psychological change may be found in the psychiatric literature. Since the beginnings of psychoanalysis around the turn of the century, psychotherapists have been observing changes in the character structures and symptomatology of the patients who appear for treatment. The pre–World War I patients differed from those of the 1920s and 1930s; the post–World War II patients differed from those of the 1960s and 1970s (Hale, 1971; Levenson, 1972). The most dramatic instance is the disappearance of hysteria as a medical problem (Veith, 1965). For 2,000 years, since the beginnings of recorded medicine in ancient Egypt, medical writers and practitioners were preoccupied with the "disease." Paradoxically, the understanding of hysteria that emerged in the twentieth century may have led to its disappearance.

Writing of developmental psychology in particular, Keniston (1971a) described the problem of chronocentrism:

Despite recent advances in our understanding of human development, our psychological concepts have generally suffered from an historical parochialism that takes the patterns, timetables, and sequences of development prevalent among middle-class children in contemporary Western societies as the norm of human development. (p. 329)

Child laborers in a bobbin factory in the early twentieth century. [Lewis Hine/National Archives]

The Discovery of Adolescence

Nowhere is chronocentrism clearer than in the development of the concept of adolescence. The emergence of this concept illustrates how a set of social and cultural changes that shaped children's lives came to be interpreted as a natural process. The history of adolescence illustrates the relativity of stages of the life cycle, the looseness of the relationship between biological maturation and psychological development, and the interdependence of individual experience and the social and cultural context.

The dramatic physiological changes of puberty are often thought to be the cause of adolescent psychological characteristics, such as storm and stress emotionality. It is important to distinguish, however, between the physiological changes marking sexual maturation and the changes in behavior and social status that may or may not accompany

A farmer's daughter grading and tying tobacco, North Carolina, 1939. [Marion Post Wolcott/ Reproduced from the Collections of the Library of Congress]

them. *Puberty* is a universal occurrence, but *adolescence* can be viewed as a social invention of advanced technological societies. Muuss (1962), for example, observed that the anthropological evidence concerning the relationship between pubescence and adolescence is complicated:

In some instances, the transition from childhood to adulthood is smooth and without social recognition; in other instances puberty rites bring about a transition not from childhood to adolescence but from childhood to adulthood. (p. 62)

In earlier eras of our own society, puberty was not considered the decisively important transition it was later to become. The historian Joseph Kett (1971) argued:

The onset of male puberty failed to coincide with any fundamentally new life experience; boys at puberty simply were not conspicuous in the way they later became. . . . The twentieth century has argued that no matter where the boy is, what he is doing, or what he has been through, with the onset of puberty he becomes an adolescent. In the 1830's, in contrast, popular definitions of youth took their cue more from social status than from physiology. If a sixteen-year-old boy were in district school, he was called a child, and for the most part treated like one. If in college, he was usually described as a youth. Strictly speaking, the same boy could be a child for part of the year, and a youth for the remainder. (pp. 273, 294–295)

Historical evidence from our own culture permits us to observe adolescence in the process of being "invented." Rousseau is generally credited with introducing the concept into Western culture. Describing adolescence as a second birth, he was the first to list the emotional traits that have come to be the hallmark of adolescence: the frequent outbursts of temper, moodiness, and so on. "A perpetual stirring of the mind makes the child almost ungovernable. He becomes deaf to the voice he used to obey; he is a lion in fever; he distrusts his keeper and refuses to be controlled" (cited in Kessen, 1965, p. 93).

Rousseau wrote in the eighteenth century, but the idea of adolescence did not become part of everyday social reality until the dawn of the twentieth century. G. Stanley Hall is generally credited with popularizing the concept. His monumental two-volume work on adolescence not only made the term a household word, but also stimulated a vast amount of scientific investigation.

Rousseau and Hall, of course, did not invent adolescence. Rather, their work reflected social and cultural changes that were transforming human experience. The years between puberty and the achievement of adulthood were coming to have a significance they did not possess in previous eras.

The emergence of adolescence is related to the decline of the working family as the unit of economic production. In stable agricultural societies, where occupations are passed from father to son, one generation quietly merges into the next. The decline of this tradition opened a gap between the experience of parents and children, and transformed the teen years into a time of occupational choice. The prolongation of education and the removal of childhood from the labor market by means of compulsory education and the child-labor laws also contributed to adolescent experience. The age-graded school created a separate world of children and youth. Without such peer groups, the emergence of the "teenager" and youth cultures could not have taken place.

Thus economic, familial, and cultural changes transformed the experience of growing up; adolescence became an important stage of the individual's biography. The opening of a gap between physically and socially becoming an adult led to the psychological characteristics that have come to be known as the adolescent experience: the urge to be independent from the family, the discovery of the unique and private world of the self, the search for an identity, and the questioning of adult values and assumptions, which may take the form of idealism or cynicism—or both at the same time.

There is still debate among psychologists about the precise nature of adolescence—whether it is strictly a social phenomenon or whether it is based on some neurological, if not hormonal, substrate and thus in some sense culturally universal and "natural." Even those who argue for universality, however, recognize the role of environmental stimulation and that the adolescent experience is not inevitable (Kessen, 1965, p. 93). Indeed, some researchers argue that even in contemporary America, much of the population does not experience adolescence, but goes directly from childhood into adulthood without passing through the stage of emotional turbulence, questioning, search for self, and so on (Douvan & Adelson, 1966).

On the other hand, some observers have noted that the adolescent experience is taking longer and longer to come to a close, and that the transition to adulthood is becoming harder to discern. Keniston (1971b) has argued that the same factors that give rise to adolescence are now at work in later decades of life: (1) The extension of education through college and graduate school for masses of the population; (2) rapid social changes making it hard to achieve a settled identity, occupationally or otherwise. Keniston argued that, as a result of these changes, a new stage of life, which he calls "youth," has emerged between adolescence and adulthood.

The Discovery of Childhood

If adolescence may be viewed as a socially constructed stage of life, is it possible that childhood—the years between infancy and adolescence—can also have undergone the same process of social construction? In fact, recent historical work on the history of childhood parallels the findings on adolescence. Phillippe Ariès (1962), the historian who first enunciated this thesis, wrote:

In medieval society, the idea of childhood did not exist: this is not to suggest that children were neglected, forsaken, or despised. The idea of childhood is not to be confused with affection for children; it corresponds to awareness of the peculiar nature of childhood, that particular nature which distinguishes the child from the adult, even the young adult. In medieval society, this awareness was lacking. That is why, as soon as the child could live without the constant solicitude of his mother, his nanny, his cradle-rocker, he belonged to adult society. The infant

who was too fragile as yet to take part in the lives of adults "did not count." (p. 128)

Ariès's work sketches the movement of the infant from a limbo outside society to a central place in the family. The movement of the middle-aged child (the child 7–12 years old), however, was from a place in the adult community to a segregated existence outside the world of adults. Ariès argued that the recognition of childhood was brought about by the emergence of specific social institutions, namely the modern school and the bourgeois family, which created distinct roles for children. Children came to be perceived as not yet ready for life; they needed a sort of quarantine before joining adults.

The solicitude of family, Church, moralists and administrators deprived the child of the freedom he had hitherto enjoyed among adults. . . . But this severity was the expression of a very different feeling from the old indifference: an obsessive love which was to dominate society from the eighteenth century on. (Ariès, 1962, p. 413)

Though Ariès's assertions may seem startling, his thesis that premodern Europe lacked a clearly distinguished concept of childhood was not entirely unprecedented. Anthropologists have often made the same point for non-Western cultures. They have often voiced objection to the assertions of psychologists concerning universal developmental stages and the incompetence of children (Benedict, 1938; Goodman, 1970).

Margaret Mead's (1928) study of adolescence in Samoa was one of the earliest critiques of the notion of adolescence as an inevitable period of emotional crisis. Another supposedly universal stage of development that anthropologists have failed to find in other cultures is that of latency—the period from about six to adolescence that Freud has described as free of sexual drives and interests. In many cultures genital sexual behavior is continuous from infancy through adulthood (Hardy, 1964; Stephens, 1963).

In fact, as Ruth Benedict (1938) has written, our culture is distinctive because of the sharp discontinuities between the behavior demanded of children and that demanded of adults: Children play and are nonresponsible, adults work and take responsibility; children are supposed to be obedient, adults dominant; children are supposed to be sexless, adults are supposed to be sexually active and competent. In few other cultures, Benedict pointed out, do children have to learn one set of behaviors as children and then unlearn or reverse these patterns when they grow up.

Meyer Fortes (1970) made a similar point. In many traditional African societies, he wrote,

the social sphere of adult and child is unitary and undivided. . . . Nothing in the universe of adult behavior is hidden from children or barred to them. They are actively and responsibly part of the social structure, the economic system, the ritual ideological system. (pp. 14, 18–19)

The major contrasts between premodern societies and our own society focus on middle-aged children, those 7–12 years old. In a worldwide and historical perspective, our culture is decidedly unusual in that children of this age are not involved in productive work. Stephens (1963) pointed out, for example, that in nearly all societies, children go to work by the age of 10, after a period of apprenticeship:

Typically, work begins somewhere between the ages of three and six, the load of duties is gradually increased, and sometimes between the ages of nine and fifteen the child becomes—occupationally speaking—a fully functioning adult. (p. 386)

Ariès's (1962) description of premodern European practice is similar:

Generally speaking, transmission from one generation to the next was insured by the everyday participation of children in adult life. . . . Everyday life constantly brought together children and adults in trade and craft. . . . The same was true of the army. . . . In short, wherever people worked, and also wherever they amused themselves, even in taverns of ill repute, children were mingled with adults. In this way, they learnt the art of living from everyday contact. (p. 222)

How do we resolve the contradiction between the "small adult" conception of childhood and the early entrance of preindustrial children into adult life, and psychological theories proposing that children are not ready for participation in adult life until they have completed a series of developmental tasks lasting into their twenties? The issue has rarely been raised explicitly, but it is possible to discern three general approaches to an answer.

The first approach might be called *psychological universalism*. Some psychologists assume that development universally runs its course whether or not children wear adult clothes and take part in adult life.

The second interpretation might be called an *arrested-development approach*. It assumes that the sequence of development is the same everywhere, but the different stages may be reached later or not at all under some circumstances. As we noted earlier, most developmental theories look on the "primitive" adult as psychologically comparable to the Western child. Thus a child in such a society would not have as far to go as the child in an advanced society in order to be fully developed.

The basic flaw in the arrested-development model lies in its choice of the endpoint of development or, more precisely, its failure to observe that a choice is being made at all (Kessen, 1966). The researcher who wishes to study development must choose some conception of adult competence as an endpoint toward which the child will develop. Developmental theories take the modern Western educated adult as the norm of development. Observations of the child are then organized around this concept of competence. As one critic argues, such an approach is

a grandiose, ethnocentric conception that regards the post-Renaissance ways of thinking of Western man, and more particularly the mathematical-physical scientific modes of apprehending and interpreting reality, as the self-evident norm for cognitive development. It elevates one possibility of human nature into the grand design, the secret intent, of biologically given human nature. (Schmidt, 1973, pp. 145–146)

An alternative point of view might be called *cognitive pluralism.* Rather than regard the course of development in middle-class Western children as the unfolding of a "basic human potential," which is everywhere the same, or as the internalization of the only valid forms of knowledge, development can be viewed as the emergence of particular sets of adaptive *skills* that are geared to particular social and environmental circumstances.

If nonliterate peoples are not intellectually retarded, we cannot conclude that their failure to recognize childhood as a separate state of life leads to developmental arrest. But it would be wrong to equate premodern Europe with contemporary underdeveloped societies. Economically, politically, and culturally, medieval society was more developed than contemporary preliterate cultures. Furthermore, the bulk of the historical data pertains to the upper social classes of the

times—people most advanced in such matters as literacy. Thus the pattern described by Ariès and other historians represents an important test case for developmental psychology: the concept of childhood as we know it may not have existed, but the adult forms of competence were similar to our own. The evidence points to the conclusion that, under such conditions, children become competent at earlier ages.

Children in preindustrial Europe not only performed such craft occupations as farming, baking, and shoemaking, they also could be apprentices to lawyers, merchants, pharmacists, administrators, and, of course, the church. The strongest evidence against equating the absence of childhood with developmental arrest is the evidence of precocity in premodern Europe. Young children not only could enter apprenticeship, but also could enter college at the age of 9 or 10 and complete their studies at 13. Ariès (1962) noted that up until a certain time, "whether this [precocity] was the result of talent, as in the case of Descartes, or of forcing . . . precocity implied a superiority which opened the way to a great career" (p. 222). Only later did the idea appear that there was something not quite right about doing adult things or older child things before one was "ready."

Developmental Stages Revisited: The Great Transformation at 5 to 7

At this point the reader may be wondering whether there is anything left at all of the concept of development. In this section we shall argue that the concept is useful, if used carefully, and will advance the hypothesis that there are two major psychological stages of development—infancy and post-infancy—during which time the child comes into possession of essentially adultlike mental capacities. Developmental theorists may have wrongly designed their staircases of growth by making the upper steps as steep as the bottom ones. The historical studies raise the question of whether it is useful and valid to consider the changes from childhood to adolescence, and from adolescence to adulthood, as fully comparable to the change from infancy to childhood.

The historians, as noted earlier, report a transition in the child's social status between the ages of 5 and 7. This same age is often the point of assuming adult work responsibilities in primitive societies; it is also the age of first communion in the Catholic Church, and used to be the age of legal responsibility for crime in the common law. Within psychology also, evidence shows that this age represents a major transition, although the assumption usually is that this is the age when the child becomes ready for school, rather than, as in other periods and cultures, ready for participation in adult life.

Thus Baldwin (1967), in his survey of the major theories of child development, concluded that despite their differences, there is a consensus among the theories that there are two main types of psychological functioning. The first is primitive, direct, impulsive, and noncognitive, or primary process; the second is more controlled, thoughtful, and logical, or secondary process. One is essentially childlike, the other adultlike. Baldwin did not specify the age at which the transition from one type of functioning to the other occurs, but there is remarkable consensus on this point also.

At about the time Baldwin was writing, Sheldon White (1965), a psychologist, published a paper on the significance of the 5–7 period. White was intrigued that different types of learning experiments revealed a marked change in children's performance between 5 and 7, so he looked for more evidence of such shifts. He listed twenty-one behavior changes from age 5 to 7 gleaned from his survey of the research literature.

Perhaps the most striking single item in this list is the finding that the adult IQ can be predicted with a high degree of accuracy at this age. Other changes include the following: Children are becoming more abstract and symbolic, less concrete; they are responding to stimuli less in terms of physical properties and more in terms of the way they are categorized in terms of language; they are learning to string together images of the past and of the future, and so can plan behavior in advance; they are learning to locate themselves in space, and gaining knowledge of left and right and memory of where things are in relation to each other. In practical terms this means that children can get from one place to another and back again without getting lost.

At a more general level, theoretical treatments of child development also describe the 5–7 period as a major turning point. For Piaget this age represents a transitional period between major epochs of thought. For the Russian developmental theorists Vygotsky (1962) and Luria (1961), this is the decisive turning point in behavior. Soviet researchers after Pavlov emphasize language (the second signal system) as the basis for higher human thought. They explain the changes at 5 to 7 as resulting from the internalization of speech; speech becomes the vehicle of thought and the regulator of behavior. For Freud the age between 5 and 7 is a time when infantile sexual impulses are repressed, and parental prohibitions are internalized to form the superego. Finally, for learning theory this is a time when children's responses to stimuli come to be guided by their own mediating responses rather than the stimulus itself.

Sheldon White (1965) concluded:

Perhaps the 5–7 period is a time when some maturational development, combining perhaps with influences in the . . . environment, inhibits a broad spectrum of first-level function in favor of a new, higher level of function. (p. 213)

In White's model of learning processes we have a picture of human development that is fully compatible with the premodern life-style as portrayed by the historians. Both suggest that there is essentially one step up from the childhood to the adult level and that the transition takes place at around 5 to 7.

The conception of two major stages of thought does not imply that there are no important changes before or after this major watershed. Particularly during infancy, important developmental changes occur—for example, the toddler's learning how to talk. But the model does suggest that changes occurring after the age of 5–7 are not as momentous and, further, the basis of development changes. Before this period, maturation plays a major role in developmental change; after, learning and culture become major forces influencing psychological development. Because psychologists, as we noted earlier, typically do not study the effects of the enduring environments in which children live, they have overlooked the possibility that schooling may have a profound effect on psychological development. Actually, the fact that virtually all normal children in America and Europe go to school between the ages of 5 and 7 poses a major theoretical challenge to contemporary psychological theory (Cole, Gay, & Glick, 1971).

School and Society as Developmental Contexts

The institution of schooling in Western societies has had profound effects on conceptions of childhood, as well as on children themselves. It is school, along with the family, that defines the child's place in contemporary Western culture. For us, school is the "natural habitat" of childhood and the schoolchild is the child. The concept of childhood, the emergence of the private, emotionally intense family, and the idea of the school as part of the normal socialization of the child are different aspects of the historical process of modernization.

The assumptions about childhood and education that we regard almost as part of human nature grew up gradually over the past 400 years. We assume, for example, that stages of education should correspond to the age of the student. Thus we take it for granted that all children in a class should be the same age, or close to it. Only in college and graduate school is the connection between level of subject matter and age of the student loosened somewhat. But even here there is an appropriate age for a particular level of work, and a person much younger or older than the standard will be noticeable and perhaps feel out of place.

By contrast, in medieval times and for a while after, school was not associated with age. A person attended school whenever he was ready and it was convenient, regardless of age. A 7-year-old could join a class where most other students were 15 and over. Or a young man could work at a trade during his childhood and begin school at adolescence without spoiling his chances for a higher-level career.

Further, within the early school the child enjoyed the same status as outside—a free adult in a world of other adults. In fact, schoolchildren were frequently armed, and schools established regulations for student firearms and swords.

Old men, young men, adolescents, and children could all be found sitting in the same classroom, learning the same lessons. They turned up for classes, but no one cared about the rest of their lives. Sometimes, as we learn from Thomas Platter's story of his school days in the early sixteenth century, groups of students ranging in age from the early twenties to a mere ten would wander in search of learning from France to Germany and back again. They lived like hippies and wandered like gypsies, begging, stealing, fighting; yet they were always hungry for books. Platter was nineteen before he could read fluently, but within three years he mastered Latin, Greek, and Hebrew. And in the end he became rector of Basel's most famous school. (Plumb, 1972, p. 84)

Only gradually did the following ideas emerge: that the different ages ought to be separated, that there is an appropriate age at which students ought to do a certain grade level of work, that the subject matter should be divided into grade levels, that students need to be protected from the vicissitudes of adult life and subjected to a special discipline to develop their characters. Authoritarian regimes, corporal punishment, and constant surveillance replaced student autonomy. Ariès argued that these changes in education were developed by moralists who should be sharply distinguished from humanists concerned with spreading intellectual ideas and culture.

The new moral ideology stressed by Ariès is but one possible explanation for the growth of schooling. Another is that an emerging capitalist society began to need increasing numbers of skilled and trained men for commerce, law, and diplomacy.

The turning point that gave rise to most of the traits peculiar to our culture is essentially to be found between the eleventh and the twelfth centuries when towns grew in number as well as in size and established their predominance over the countryside. . . .

As an urban life based in the main on trade and manufacture developed, the division of labor grew and social structures became progressively more complex. The needs for literacy and literate persons became . . . obvious. Growth of an urban society and growth of schools and literacy

The creativity of children often creates work for parents. [Dick Swartz/Office of Human Development Services]

were closely related phenomena. The areas that experienced higher rates of economic expansion and more revolutionary social change were also the areas in which schools and teachers were relatively more numerous. (Cipolla, 1969, pp. 44–45)

Imperialism and conquest also increased the demand for skilled manpower.

The great empires—the French, the British, the Spanish, and the Dutch—required men with the habit of authority. The proconsuls of empire had to be stamped with the image of gentlemen, aware of obligations as well as privileges. Discipline, best enforced by regular schooling, proved the most efficacious mold. (Plumb, 1972, p. 84)

Nor was it only the gentlemanly arts of diplomacy and law that required education. In the sixteenth century one had to be literate to be a gunner, to navigate a ship on the open sea, to be a printer, or to be a maker of maps, clocks, and precision instruments. Although schooling and literacy spread in response to social need, they soon began to acquire an independent value. To be illiterate came to be a mark of social shame.

Although schools, as we noted earlier, began by mixing people of all ages, they gradually developed into private worlds of children, distinct from adult life. There began to be a culture of childhood, developed in part by adult regulations of children's dress, reading, and deportment, and in part by the children themselves. Kept out of the adult world, children began to develop their own "lore and language" (Opie & Opie, 1959). Among the European upper classes of the nineteenth century, children were separated from adults even within the home. Children lived in their own section of the house, with nurses, governesses, and tutors, visiting their parents only for short periods: "The difference between the life of a sixteenth- and a late nineteenth-century child is so vast as to be almost incomprehensible. Three centuries had created a private world for children" (Plumb, 1972, p. 84).

Besides their social effects in creating a separate world of childhood, schools may have profound consequences for the thought processes of the individual. A good deal of evidence shows that many of the psychological changes once thought to represent the unfolding of the innate capacities of the human mind may actually be the result of literacy and the experience of going to school. For example, schooling has dramatic effects on cognitive development in nonindustrial cultures. Tribal children or adults with a few years of schooling think and carry out intellectual tasks more like American schoolchildren than like their own unschooled brothers and sisters (Greenfield,

cited in Bruner, Olver, & Greenfield, 1966, pp. 225–256).

All societies educate their children, but those without formal schools do so in the course of everyday adult activities, in which, as we've noted earlier, the children take part according to their abilities. In this type of learning—or "informal education" (Scribner & Cole, 1973, p. 553), as the anthropologists call it—children learn by looking and doing rather than by verbal instruction. In school they learn abstract concepts without any immediate functional use. Even the attempts to make school education more real or interesting for children still proceed at high levels of conceptualization and abstraction. Thus the school environment and the demands it makes on the child push cognitive development in a particular direction:

Many modes of thinking—categorizing, inferring, abstracting, grouping and ordering arrays of information—that we associate with a certain age of child and use as an index of the intelligence or cognitive level of the child may in fact be heavily dependent on Western-type schooling. . . .
It seems likely that without the specific contribution of the Western-type school, . . . the whole direction of the children's cognitive development would be different. (Schmidt, 1973, pp. 145–146)

In our own and other advanced industrial societies, school does not introduce new ways of thought that are discontinuous with daily life outside school. Rather, it extends and elaborates ways of thinking that pervade the society at large, particularly in the middle classes. Sociologists agree that modernization is not merely an economic or technological change but involves profound social and psychological changes also. It changes all aspects of life: physical environment, the types of communities people live in, the way they view the world, the way they organize their daily lives, the emotional quality of family relationships, and on down to the most private aspects of individual psychological experience. Thus children growing up in modern societies face radically different sets of demands from those of children growing up in more traditional societies. These demands, rather than the inherent psychological differences between children and adults, may account for the gulf that seems to separate children and adults in modern societies.

Childhood and Social Reform

Although the history of childhood may not fit the model of uninterrupted progress, changing attitudes toward children were often motivated by genuine concern for children's welfare. The brutal exploitation of children in the mines and mills of nineteenth-century England served as a horrible example to discredit the idea of children working. In 1842 a Commission on the Employment of Young Persons and Children included among its findings a report that children sometimes as young as 5 were employed as beasts of burden in the mines, harnessed to heavy carts that they had to pull through tunnels that were long, low, dark, and wet:

The child is obliged to pass on all fours, and the chain passes under what, in that posture, might be called the hind legs; and thus they have to pass through avenues not so good as a common sewer. . . . By the testimony of the people themselves, it appears that the labor is exceedingly severe; that the girdle blisters their sides and causes great pain. "Sir," says an old miner, "I can only say what the mothers say; it is barbarity, absolute barbarity." Robert North says, "I went into the pit at 7 years of age. When I drew by the girdle and chain, the skin was broken and the blood ran down. . . . If we said anything they would beat us. (A. A. Cooper, 1842, p. 49)

The reaction against this exploitation made it difficult to see anything but deprivation in the image of a child doing real work. Women, of course, were exploited in the factories along with children. Again the reaction against this led reformers, even Karl Marx, to protest against women working outside their homes.

In short, the industrial revolution transformed cultural attitudes toward children and work because it changed the nature of work. Before the rise of factories and other large-scale institutions, as we have noted earlier, there was no separation of workplace and residence. Work went on at home, as part of family life. Indeed, in the early years of industrialization in England, whole families went to work together in factories. During this time, some evidence suggests, factory work was experienced by the workers as less oppressive than it was later (Smelser, 1968).

Another reformist trend that helped shape our current ideas about childhood was aimed at changing schools. One of the reasons that teaching very little children how to read and write fell into disrepute was the harshness of the early schools. Fowler (1962) wrote:

At all levels of the infant (ages 2–7) and grammar school systems, serious deficiencies prevailed which persisted well into the last half of the nineteenth century. . . . Curricula were narrowly restricted to religious dogma and [the three R's]. . . . Authoritarian discipline, enforced by harsh physical punishment, was the rule. Teaching methods were rigid and tedious, being based on rote learning through incessant drills on isolated elements. The lecture system was used freely, making little concession to age differences. Enormous classes were characteristic. Infant schools typically confined immobile for hours from 50 to 200 and sometimes as many as 1,000 undernourished children, crowded into galleries. They were watched over by the petty, severe, and ignorant eyes of monitors only slightly older than the children. Over such a mass only one or two adult teachers presided, who were poorly trained, if at all. (p. 129)

The kindergarten and nursery-school movement arose as a protest against harsh schools. Such reformers as Pestalozzi and Froebel argued that young children would learn best through their own activities, that they needed sensorimotor experiences rather than rote drills, and sensitive understanding rather than harsh discipline. Although some of the leaders of the nursery-school movement invented ways of combining teaching with play—for example, in the form of educational toys—the major thrust of the movement was to define early childhood as a time for play and social and emotional development. Thus the school-reform movement tried to liberate children from harsh, repressive, and really antieducational schools, but it also contributed to the definition of the child as a weak, incompetent, and fundamentally unserious creature. Such institutions as the nursery school and kindergarten widened the gap that separated children from adults.

Thus our present images of the child originated from a complex of trends and conditions. The image of the child as weak and dependent both mentally and physically was constructed by the rise of the bourgeois family, by moralists trying to save the child's soul from original sin, by schoolmasters rationalizing their institutions, and by reformers trying to save the child's body from industrial slavery and the mind from the shackles of rote learning and authoritarian discipline.

All these influences contributed to the image of the child that took shape in developmental psychology. The theories and images of the child put forth by the profes-

sional specialists, however, amplified and specified the differences between adults and children, and between children of different ages. Further, they replaced religious dogma, educational theories, and sentimental notions as the authoritative source of information concerning the child's nature and competence.

The Child's Changing Place

Recently, several social critics have pointed to what they perceive as the "erosion" or "disappearance" of childhood. For example, Neil Postman (1982) argues that as both parents "abandon" the home for the workplace, children become more burdensome, and parents hurry them out of childhood and into adultlike behavior. Postman, along with Marie Winn (1983) and others, argues that parents no longer struggle to preserve their children's innocence and shelter them from adult experience. A worse charge is made by Valerie Suransky (1982): children are being treated as "commodities" to be deposited for the convenience of the parents at inadequate childcare institutions.

Such nostalgic pleas for the restoration of childhood show little awareness of how recent a historic creation the "emotionally priceless" but "useless" childlike child really is (Zelitzer, 1985). Indeed, there is little evidence for the claim that children's emotional value has decreased in recent years. If anything, it seems to have increased. As we noted in the last chapter, rates of voluntary childlessness have not risen with the increase in women's employment. And, because having a child is more than ever a voluntary choice, it seems likely that today's families place an even higher value on children than did those of previous generations.

Yet children's roles have changed in recent years. Zelitzer (1985) suggests that the useful child may be making at least a partial comeback. Changing family structures and new egalitarian beliefs seem to be increasing children's household responsibilities. There is, she observes, no necessary correlation between valuing children emotionally and appreciating their utilitarian worth. Moreover, for some time now scholars from a number of disciplines have been suggesting that the role of the "useless" child is psychologically costly for children themselves.

THE COSTS OF CHILDHOOD

Those who have examined childhood in history and across cultures agree that the roles of children and adults in contemporary Western societies are out of balance. Just as casting the sexes into the roles of strong, breadwinning male and weak, dependent female imposes costs on both men and women, so does a sharp split between child and adult roles take its toll. Economist David Stern and his colleagues (1975) observed that adult work roles seldom allow for the imaginative, growing, and feeling parts of human beings. Dependent children, by contrast, are often given opportunities to play, experiment, and make mistakes, but "they lack power, social standing, and responsibility" (p. 117).

The roles of child and adult, as we have seen in this chapter, have not always been far apart. Ariès's description of medieval culture as "lacking a concept of childhood" may be misleading. The period seemed equally lacking in a concept of adulthood; it was a society lacking age consciousness as an important definer of role, behavior, and status. Today one's age is almost as much a part of one's identity as one's name—for example, people are identified by names and ages in newspaper stories. People in earlier times were not unaware of age differences, but age

consciousness and age grading were simply not that important.

Dependency and Self-Validation

We have heard much in recent years of the costs of children to parents, not only in money, but in freedom and opportunity as well. Very little has been said about the costs to children themselves—and to the adults they will later become—of their prolonged dependency. Although the participation of children in economic life has been the practice in all times and places up until the twentieth century, we persist in regarding the role of the playful, self-indulgent child as the only natural one. One could just as easily argue that industrial society's creation of an extreme discontinuity between child and adult roles is "unnatural."

Arguments about naturalness are seldom conclusive; more significantly, there may be profound psychological consequences arising from the modern child's having to spend the first 2 or even 3 decades of life in a state of uselessness. As women have been discovering, economic dependency can easily lead to emotional dependency and to doubts about one's worth as a person. Women experience these doubts even though they know they are doing vitally important work in the home.

Children, excluded from the workplace, are in a more extreme psychological position. Children's chores, such as taking out the garbage, are regarded by no one, least of all children, as productive work. The persistent restlessness of young people at school indicates that school also is not regarded by them as serious, socially useful work (Panel on Youth, 1974). Perhaps most schoolchildren, particularly older ones, realize that one of the major functions of the school is simply to warehouse a portion of the population that is not needed anywhere, but cannot simply be let loose on the streets. And many of the most dedicated students view their school years as a bureaucratic hurdle they must pass on the way to adult careers, rather than as a time of meaningful work or learning.

By Love Obsessed

Over 4 decades ago, Ruth Benedict (1938) pointed out how the discontinuities between child and adult roles create problems for the individual as he or she progresses from one role to the other; adolescent turmoil can be understood as a result of having to perform in ways that were forbidden to children. It is little wonder, she observed, that many people find it hard to "put off childish things" and so remain "fixated" at immature levels of behavior. Thus the removal of children from productive work roles and, more generally, the dichotomy between child and adult roles may be responsible for much psychological maladjustment.

Apart from the problem of having to bridge the gap between the child's role and the adult's, the prolonged economic uselessness of modern children may deprive them of a major source of self-validation, and make them more dependent on the parental affection and the opinions of other people. Children working on the family farm or as apprentices in a trade could, as Jerome Kagan (1977) pointed out, see evidence of their virtue in the results of their work.

The daily life of the peasant's son or daughter, as we saw in Chapter 5, was hardly idyllic. Such activities as plowing fields, tending to animals, cutting wood, spinning and weaving cloth, and making soap, candles, butter, and cheese, however, provided clear physical evidence of contributions to the family welfare.

By contrast, the middle-class child has historically lacked that advantage, while enjoying many others. Unable to point to any physical product of their labor, middle-class children have had to base their sense of worth on their psychological qualities. "As a result," Kagan (1977) observed, the middle-class child "may have been more uncertain of his value, more dependent on parental communication assuring him of his worthiness, and more preoccupied with parental attitudes towards him" (p. 43).

Kagan's speculations are in line with what we know about the origins of self-esteem. Traditionally social psychologists have emphasized the affection and approval of other people as the source of our attitudes toward ourselves—the well-known "looking-glass self." But researchers recently have become aware that love may not be enough to guarantee self-esteem.

The other major source of self-esteem derives from our own activities—from the feeling of having an effect on the physical or social environment. Seeing the products of our labor, solving a problem, influencing someone, having some control over the events in our lives—these experiences produce a sense of competence and mastery. One psychoanalyst (Silverberg, 1952) has succinctly expressed the difference between the two sources of self-esteem. Both are important, he noted, but the experience of mastery is steadier and more dependable; the opinion of others is always more uncertain:

Unhappy and insecure is the man who, lacking an inner resource for self-esteem, must depend for this almost wholly upon external sources. It is the condition seen by the psychotherapist almost universally among his patients. (p. 26)

It is also the condition that prevails almost universally among contemporary children and youth.

Thus the great emphasis on the power of parental love in contemporary culture may have arisen as a substitute for the self-validation children used to achieve through productive work. Kagan (1977) observed that non-Western cultures, and Western society before the seventeenth century, did not recognize parental attitudes as a source of physical or mental illness. By contrast, twentieth-century society believes that a lack of parental love can have disastrous consequences later on. These beliefs can act as self-fulfilling prophecies: parents believe they will harm their children if they fail to love them enough. Children and adolescents learn of scientific and popular theories relating lack of parental love to unhappiness and psychological illness; and adults interpret their emotional problems as delayed reactions to a lack of love during childhood, rather than, say, fate, witchcraft, or evil spirits.

Our books, magazines, and television dramas all announce the healing and prophylactic power of parental love and the toxicity that follows closely in its absence.

Americans seek out psychiatrists, new love objects, or peers whom they hope will love them and dissolve their anguish. This faith in love is not unlike the faith in the curative power of the potion or the incantations of the shaman. (Kagan, 1977, p. 44)

THE FUTURE OF CHILDHOOD

In view of the profound changes in the social place of children and in theories of childhood that occurred in our culture, it would seem unreasonable to assume that our present conceptions of childhood will remain in force indefinitely. New stages of life have been added to the life cycle. The child's future at birth has changed from one of almost certain death to one of almost un-

limited possibility. In the eyes of parents, the growth and development of the child has shifted from being the object of mild concern or indifference to the major emotional focus of the family. If the nature of childhood and of human development has changed in the past, it is capable of changing again. Although it is difficult to predict the next directions of social change, a new view of childhood may be visible on the horizon. And new stages of development may emerge from these changes.

There is evidence that contemporary social changes are altering the child's place, both inside the family and in society at large. In a variety of ways the norms of conventional age grading appear to be losing their previous decisive influence. Although the adult world is still sharply marked off from the world of the child, there is a certain blurring around the edges. "Adolescence" is spreading at both ends: younger children are absorbing teenage culture and attitudes, and many people in their 20s are refusing to progress to "adulthood." Some of the indicators of separate status used by Ariès, such as dress and amusements, no longer distinguish children and adults as sharply as they once did. Current clothing styles not only are unisex, they are increasingly uniage. Whereas fairy tales once were shared by all age groups, now television is.

The future of schooling as the child's place and hence definitions of childhood itself are being changed by the current crisis surrounding education. As we noted earlier, schools helped to invent childhood by creating places and roles for children. Educational change now in prospect seems to be in the process of unmaking such places. James Coleman (1972) argued that we live in an information-rich society, in which children at young ages begin to have large amounts of vicarious experience through radio, television, and other media (p. 72). The present

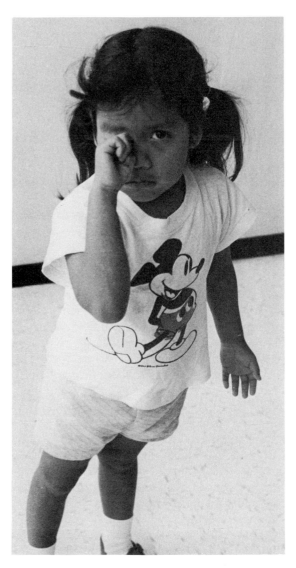

Girl in day-care center. [Leslie Cooper for the Office of Human Development Services]

educational system was designed for societies that were information-poor. Children obtained most of what they knew from direct experience, supplemented by reading. The schools were the community's gateway to information.

Television has altered the ratio between direct and vicarious experience for everyone, but especially for children. Long before they enter a schoolroom, young children have acquired an enormous amount of knowledge about the world. In past ages a child entering school would have the adventure of discovering many simple but exciting facts. Coleman cited the example of a man born in 1870 who wrote in his autobiography of his amazement at hearing in school of a train that could go 60 miles an hour (p. 72). Thus children may have outgrown the schools.

On the other hand, more and more adults want and need to continue their learning over the lifespan. Some have suggested that the schools should be opened to people of all ages, and that children should be integrated into work activities. The distinction between economic and educational institutions would become blurred. Schools might become communities in which children would carry out responsible service activities, but also include time for learning. The White House Conference on Children (1970) suggested something like a revival of the apprentice system: workplaces would be modified to include the young in productive work; they would divide their time between learning and actual work. The life cycle would no longer consist of an early period of full-time school and then full-time work later, but a combination of the two activities over many years.

In short, traditional notions that work is "bad" for children and separation from the adult world is good are being reexamined. The exploitation of children in the mines and mills of the last century may have blinded us to the fact that responsible and productive action may reward children and aid in their development. A series of studies by Mary Engel and her associates (Engel, Marsden, & Woodman, 1967, 1968) produced findings that challenged the prevailing assumptions about child work. These researchers found that child work—defined as working part-time for strangers for pay—is much more prevalent among fourth- to eighth-grade boys than is generally believed. (The study did not include girls.) Nor did they find that only boys from the poorest homes worked: child work was most prevalent in the lower-middle- and middle-class groups. As for the psychological effects of working, these researchers found that having a part-time job not only was not harmful, but also could actually aid in the development of competence and personality. On the other hand, as we observed earlier, the prolonged uselessness of children today may be demoralizing and even debilitating.

Although nobody advocates reversing history and returning to the era of childhood exploitation, there is a growing recognition that the roles of self-denying adult and irresponsible child are frustrating for both parties. The challenge for theorists and policy makers is to devise new kinds of settings that could function in an industrial society to integrate children and adults, and at the same time develop the full range of children's abilities.

SUMMARY

The concept of childhood as a separate stage of life, having its own psychology and requiring separate institutions, is an invention of modern times. In premodern societies, including Western society several centuries ago, children did not live in a separate world from adults. In the premodern pattern, children after the age of infancy participated in the economic life of society. The modern concept of childhood seems to be a product of the process of modernization: a complex occupational structure calls for an educated population.

Schools during the medieval era were for anyone who wanted to learn Latin. There was no sequence of courses and no notion that a person could be too young or too old to study a subject. School was a part of the adult world; schoolboys made their own rules and came and went as they pleased. Precocity, particularly among preadolescent children, was common in school as well as in the professions, arts, and trades.

During this period there was little emphasis on love as the essential ingredient in parent–child relationships. Parent–child relationships were weakened by the practice of apprenticeship, with children often residing and working in other homes by the age of 7.

Over several centuries, definitions of childhood, school, and family changed. Childhood came to include adolescence, being defined as the preparatory stage of life for the not fully socialized. Accordingly, schools became instruments of discipline and character training. The home became a place to nurture children and prepare them for later life. Precocity came to be seen as unwholesome. Adults abandoned the toys, games, and stories they shared with children and became more serious. The work ethic replaced the old sociability, and the nuclear family's importance rose.

In recent years, scholars in a number of fields have pointed out that the sharp contrasts between child and adult roles in our culture impose costs as well as benefits on both sides. Children who must spend at least the first 2 decades as economically unproductive dependents may grow up doubting their own self-worth. Current social trends as well as changes in educational and work policies may, in the not too distant future, reduce the discontinuity between age groups.

CHAPTER 14

Socialization: Generational Politics

Conformity to norms is sometimes said to be the end result of a positive or successful socialization. This is much too narrow a conception. The norms of a language are the rules of pronunciation, spelling, semantics, and grammar. Some who have learned these rules very well—children, poets, the Beatles—elect on occasion to violate them. Others who know them well undertake to reform them: to make spelling consistent, or to strip certain works of ambiguity. Similarly, the moral theory an individual forms by working over his moral experience can lead him to reject some part of the conventional morality. He is likely to argue . . . the change he favors will make the total morality more consistent or . . . will more truly realize the basic values of the culture. . . . Saints and revolutionaries and reactionaries all take some such position. It does not seem correct to consider such persons . . . failures of socialization.

R. W. Brown
Social Psychology

In the ideal societies of the utopian writers, the only recurrent threat to changeless peace arises out of human mortality. People die and new people are born. The social structure is seen as a set of roles that must be filled, like the positions on a baseball or football team. The whole society must be duplicated anew in every generation. Utopian writers from Plato on, therefore, have been preoccupied with the regulation of reproduction, the training of the young, and the assignment of young people to their adult places in society. In the literary utopias these processes are arranged so as to affirm the status quo.

Ralf Dahrendorf (1958) has pointed to striking similarities between sociological theorists and utopian writers. Like the utopians, functional sociologists also have been preoccupied with the problem of generational replacement. They have traditionally conceived of socialization in the same terms as the utopians, as a regular, patterned process that maintains the status quo.

The youth protests of the 1960s were upsetting to then-prevailing assumptions about socialization. They were, as Keniston (1971b) observed, like experiments that fail and therefore refute the hypotheses they set out to test. From the point of view of scientific theory, such experiments are often more useful than those that confirm our expectations. When scientific prediction fails, it is necessary to reexamine the assumptions on which they were based. The emergence of youthful dissent raised fundamental questions about the transmission of culture and social structure from one generation to the next.

Were the student protesters psychological misfits? These campus protesters were the most studied rebels in history—not only psychologists but also commissions of distinguished citizens investigated the various student protests and the participants. There is remarkable agreement in findings of a variety of different researchers as to the characteristics of the student protesters. Activists typically came from the ranks of the better and more serious students (Cox Commission, 1968, p. 41).

It could not be said that the majority of activist students were rejecting the values of their parents and the nation. Rather, as the Cox report and other investigations concluded, they took very seriously the ideals taught in schools and churches; their protests were directed at what they saw as society's deviation from its professed ideals, particularly racial injustice and the war in Vietnam. Thus the traditional explanation for deviance—that there will always be a certain number of misfits who, through faulty childrearing or some inherent defect, will fail to absorb the values of their society—did not apply.

GENERATIONAL CONFLICT AND CONTINUITY

The youthful protests of the 1960s and early 1970s gave rise to much discussion of "the generation gap." A spate of theories defined student protesters as being in rebellion against their own parents and taking it out on school authorities and society in general.

Some writers argued that the generation gap was a myth because lots of parents got along fairly well with their children. Then it turned out that student protesters often agreed with their parents on values although they had experienced conflicts about *actions* at the same time. It was the hippies, it seemed, not political activists, who were more extreme in rejecting the *actions* and *values* of their parents (Keniston, 1971b). Other writers argued that young people could not be neatly separated into political activists or hippies. Margaret Mead (1971) entered the debate by declaring that the generation gap doesn't have anything to do with parents and children at all: "The generation gap is between all the people born and brought up after World War II and the people who were born before it. It's not at all about children and getting on with parents" (p. 50).

In contrast to Margaret Mead's view of the generation gap as something that "happened only once," other observers noted that rebellion has long been recognized as an inevitable part of growing up—a "stage," like the temper tantrums of the 2-year-old. Piaget (1967), for example, has noted that the newly maturing intellectual powers of adolescents make them aware of the general moral rules of the society and enable them to be shocked by the failure of adults to live up to them. Adolescents are idealistic because their limited experience has not yet taught them how hard it is to put ideals into practice (pp. 64–68). As they "mature" further, they will settle down, give up youthful ideals, and become members of the adult society. S. M. Lipset (1967) has pointed out that almost every country has a version of the saying: "He who is not a radical at twenty does not have a heart; he who is still one at forty does not have a head" (p. 58).

A Multiplicity of Gaps

The profusion of contradictory explanations of the generation gap suggests that social scientists were overtaken by events and caught with their theories in disarray. Many social scientists are aware that the prevailing models of socialization don't fit with the complex realities of generational relations in contemporary society, but have not been able to abandon them. Norma Haan (1971) attributed the predicament of developmental psychologists and sociologists in dealing with the generation gap to the persistent notion that the mind of a young person is simply a blank slate:

Parental power and social countervention are still the foci of much research, as if empty-headed children are automatically stamped with effects or simply duplicate their elders. This supposition continues to determine the research design, and in the realm of common sense, leads the older generation to expect that there *should* be a generational replacement, but to their subsequent chronic dismay, there isn't. (p. 260)

On the other hand, the theories of rebellion as an inevitable stage tell us nothing about the rise and fall of youthful protest in particular historical periods; they do not tell us why the college generations of the 1950s were the silent generation, why campuses erupted all over the United States and in many parts of the world during the late 1960s, and why they became quiet in the 1970s and 1980s. Nor do they explain why large numbers of the not-so-young have not settled down on reaching 30 or even 40. Margaret Mead was correct in pointing to the social changes going on in society as a whole as a source of the generation gap, but she seemed to underestimate the complications these changes introduce into parent–child relations. The realities that impinge on families may result from conditions having nothing to do with families, but they affect families in profound ways. If the balanced, homogeneous social system is not a tenable model of society, the idea of socialization as smooth replacement is no longer tenable either. Socialization then becomes problematic: what is the child being socialized to fit into?

If every society contains within it important internal conflicts, then growing children are exposed not to a stable, self-consistent set of social expectations and cultural values, but to social and cultural contradictions. . . . Furthermore, in times of rapid historical change, the societal conflicts to which one generation is exposed will differ from those of the previous generation; partly for this reason, individuals of different historical generations will typically differ from each other in basic personality. (Keniston, 1971b, p. 297)

In short, if we give up the notion that socialization involves the smooth replacement of one generation by the next, we are driven to the conclusion that some sort of generation gap is inevitable. We must also explain, however, why it appears more acute at some periods rather than others. In fact, there seem to be several kinds of generational cleavage, not just one.

Generational Conflict

To most people the term *generation gap* implies conflict between parents and children. Actually, there can be generational conflict without a generation gap, and a generation gap without conflict. Maybe it is because the assumption of generational continuity is so ingrained that little attention has been paid to the variety of ways generational cleavage can come about.

Let us look at generational conflict first. In its purest form generational conflict does not involve a challenge to the social order; it is simply a power struggle between parents and children. The son, for example, may want to take over the father's position, as in a peasant family in which the son remains a "boy" until he has taken over the family farm. In general, it seems that tension and hostility follow patterns of inheritance. Thus R. A. LeVine (1965) noted that in societies with patrilineal inheritance and descent there are antagonisms between father and son; in matrilineal societies in which the son inherits from his mother's brother, tensions occur between uncle and nephew (p. 195). Some societies overtly recognize intergenerational antagonism. Among the Tallensi of northern Ghana, for example, sons eventually do take the places of fathers in the life of the community, and are suspected of wanting to hasten the day when this will happen.

Tallensi themselves make no bones about the matter. "Your oldest son is your rival," . . . the men say bluntly. . . . This candor in fathers is not matched by their sons, who never admit the rivalry. . . .
Tallensi explain the rivalry between father and son by means of the mystical concept of the Yin or personal destiny. There is, they say, an inborn antagonism between the Yin of a father and the Yin of his oldest son. . . . The son's Yin wants to destroy the father's Yin; but the father's Yin wants the father to live and be well and remain master of the house. . . . Therefore it will try to destroy the son's Yin, and if it is the stronger Yin it will cause misfortune and perhaps death to the son. (Fortes, 1949, pp. 225–227)

Freudian writers have emphasized the sexual aspects of conflicts between parents and children, particularly fathers and sons. Although sexual feelings enter into such struggles, an overemphasis on the Oedipal feeling—the sexual rivalry with the parent of the same sex—has obscured the situational realities of power as a source of generational conflict. Thus we have the Freudian explanation of revolutionary activism as a disguised attack on father.

In 1940 Kingsley Davis published a classic article which outlines the sociological reasons why conflict between parents and children is inevitable, and why for most societies in history there has been relatively little awareness of the generation gap. Davis argued that the ingredients for generation conflict exist in any society. In traditional societies, however, these inescapable conflicts between parents and children are counteracted in various ways. Part of the potential for conflict arises out of biological and psychological differences between organisms of differing ages, part from the power relations of child and parents. Davis also saw social complexity and social change as sources of parent–child conflict, but these are best considered separately from the more universal power and organismic differences.

Davis noted that parental power is sociologically one of the most extreme forms of authority. Unlike the authority of boss over worker, for example, parental power is unlimited, personal, and inescapable. In traditional societies, however, the power conflicts inherent in parent–child relations are mitigated in several ways. The authority of the parent is supported by the rest of the kinship group and the community in general. There are no competing authorities, such as schools, the mass media, or peer groups. Another reason for the relative lack of challenge to the older generation in traditional societies is the sense of the unbroken continuity of life—the sureness of all concerned that the lives of the children will duplicate the lives of the parents and grandparents.

Another source of parent–child conflict lies in the contrast between ideals and reality. Parents tend to offer their children idealized versions of the culture during the course of socialization. In daily interaction as well as in more formal teaching situations, the child learns such ideals as: be sincere, don't lie, don't steal, treat other people as you want to be treated yourself, be kind and generous, love your relatives. Because no society ever observed has lived up to its ideal norms, sooner or later the child discovers that the adults don't practice what they've been preaching.

This credibility gap can become a source of conflict between seemingly hypocritical elders and their children. In traditional, slowly changing societies there is what Keniston (1971b) has called the "institutionalization of hypocrisy" (p. 297). Violations of the rules are built into the rules. Children are taught that for certain situations and people the rules don't apply. Or they are told that what appears to be an inconsistency isn't really that after all. Thus the ideal of honesty may be ignored in business dealings, the ideal of kindness may not be extended to foreigners or wartime enemies. In times of rapid social change, however, the institutionalization of hypocrisy may break down. New rules and ideas come into being, and there is a lag in the development of rules to justify hypocrisy. Modern parents trying to follow the latest expert advice on childrearing, for example, may have no rationalization to fall back on when they fail to live up to the new principles. Instead of being able to explain confidently why they departed from the rule, the parents may feel guilty and anxious. In such a situation, the children are likely to "see the emperor's nakedness with unusual clarity" (Keniston, 1971b, p. 297).

Experience Gaps

Social change increases the likelihood that the potentials for conflict inherent in parent–child relations will emerge in consciousness and behavior. But social change need not lead to conflict; it does, however,

Children's "uncivilized" ways can be a joy to adults. [Abigail Heyman/Archive Pictures Inc.]

add an experience gap to the other, more universal gaps.

Social change breaks up this smooth continuity of generations, no matter how it comes about—whether by immigration, revolution, catastrophe, conquest, new technology, or anything that invalidates the experience of the older generation as a model for the young. The parent can no longer use his or her own youth or present reality as a model for the child. The classic example of discontinuity occurs in the immigrant family. The children can easily grow into natives, but the parents forever bear traces of the old country—in their speech, manners, and standards of propriety.

It is remarkable how long the social sciences have viewed growing up as a process of psychological and physical changes in individuals, set against a background of social stability. There is a superficial awareness that we live in a changing world; we are used to a steady stream of innovations in fashion, popular music, intellectual trends, and so forth. But we lack an appreciation of how profoundly social change affects us, and how greatly it differentiates American society from more static ones.

The assumption is . . . that the normal course of a human life would be cast under conditions where all the ancestors had lived for several generations in the same place; where social changes are registered in the living habitats of two generations was slow enough to be easily assimilable by adults, and where young people would in turn grow up to marry others of almost exactly the same background. (Mead, 1947, p. 633)

Margaret Mead and other observers have suggested that today's parents and children are in something of the same position as immigrants. People born before World War II, she writes, are immigrants in time. It is more difficult to adapt to new circumstances when you have to unlearn previous knowledge and attitudes. The parents of today's college students, for example, grew up believing that technology and economic growth could produce limitless abundance and solve all problems. They were taught that new products must inevitably be better than older or less-processed ones. Disposable products were the wave of the future; when people thought about the year 2000 during the 1940s and 1950s, they thought in terms of plastic or paper clothing and furniture, and electrically controlled weather. Energy seemed to be an unlimited resource that could be called upon to do an ever-increasing variety of jobs. For many people who grew up with these attitudes, the new concerns over environmental pollution, ecology, the problems of waste, and the idea that unlimited growth and meddling with nature can lead to catastrophe are hard to grasp emotionally, even when they can be accepted intellectually.

THE PSYCHOLOGY OF SOCIALIZATION

Psychological theories of socialization have absorbed, sometimes inadvertently, sociological and anthropological emphases on the continuity of generations and the social-control features of socialization. Psychological theories are also based on assumptions of social stability. The child presumably grows up to mirror the parents, doing so through two models of socialization: social molding and impulse taming.

The first model emphasizes the plasticity of human nature and stresses the seeming inevitability that infants in any culture, starting out very much like each other, will end up as little replicas of adults of their cultures—talking like them, doing things like them, thinking like them. Stimulus–response or conditioning psychology is one version of a social-molding theory. The rules and prohibitions of the culture become the rewards and punishments the parents use to shape the child's behavior.

The other view emphasizes the control of impulse. The child is not so much a bit of clay, waiting to be shaped, as a willful, aggressive, dirty little animal who must be tamed. Freudian theory provides the most emphatic expression of a basic conflict between biological drives and the demands of organized social life. The key to successful socialization in the Freudian conception is the child's identification with the parent of the same sex as the resolution of the Oedipus complex. Thus the child acquires the roles, values, and morality of the culture as these are embodied in the parent.

In both of these conceptions, socialization is defined as the inculcation of conformity. Although they differ in their estimates of the forces opposing socialization, in both approaches the terms are set by the society and by the family acting as society's agent. One presents an image of human nature easily adapted to any social order, and whose strongest motive is conformity; the other portrays children in the image of the cruel but clever savages of Golding's *Lord of the Flies*. There is no room in either model for legitimate autonomy, dissent, or conflict, no way to conceive of the forces opposed to socialization in any positive way. Both the social-molding model and the impulse-taming model have to define any behavior that deviates from the norms as representing some defect in childhood experience.

Rethinking Socialization

In sum, then, socialization theorists have been faced with the dilemma of choosing between an oversocialized view of human nature on the one hand, or an antisocial view on the other. This impasse is revealed in a striking way in Dennis Wrong's (1961) widely quoted critique of sociological conceptions of socialization. Wrong attacked the (then) prevailing ideas about the nature of society and human motivation. The overintegrated view of society, he wrote, is the counterpart of an oversocialized view of human nature. Thus if one defines society as stable, consensual, and harmonious, one must go on to assume a psychology in which the need to conform is the most important human motive. Wrong argued that socialization theorists have overlooked the "forces in man that are resistant to socialization."

In trying to identify these forces, Wrong could only point to the Freudian id—powerful drives that resist the restraints that civilization places on them. At the time he was writing, there was no other image of human nature that seemed strong enough to compete with the oversocialized models. Further, the turbulence of the 1960s had not yet broken the silence of the previous decade. The years of dissent and protest were to make many observers dissatisfied, as Wrong had been, with the oversocialized, overintegrated view of society and human nature. The idea of bodily instincts as the major force opposing social equilibrium, however, also seemed inappropriate as an explanation of social turbulence. Although some writers tried to explain ghetto revolts and student protest in such terms, others felt that psychology simply had nothing to contribute to an understanding of historical realities.

There was, in fact, however, a new psychological perspective emerging from research and theory, one that was not committed, as the older psychologies had been, to assumptions of social stability and generational continuity.

In the past decade, the field of psychology as a whole, and child development in particular, has quietly been passing through a conceptual revolution (Gardner, 1985). There has been a return to basic psychological questions that have been ignored for half a century—the nature of human thought, language, perception, memory, and imagination. From the 1920s to the 1960s, American psychology had been dominated by ideas derived from behaviorism and psychoanalysis. Freud taught that unconscious sexual and aggressive impulses were the source of human behavior, and that conscious, rational thought was the least powerful and important part of the mind. Watson, Skinner, and other behaviorists argued that people are almost infinitely malleable by the environmental forces of reward and punishment; mental processes were only an illusion.

These psychological models are still alive and well; and both provide valid, if partial, insights into human nature. By the early 1960s, however, the claims of behaviorism and psychoanalysis were shaken by findings in a number of related areas of research—children's play, animal curiosity and exploration, and most important of all, the study of human language. These new findings made it necessary to redefine human beings as active seekers, processors, and users of information, rather than as the passive victims of inner drives or environmental forces.

Another major reason for the new interest in thought and language was the emergence of the computer. Psychologists have always liked to compare the mind to a machine. Before the computer, however, such mechanical models had been very simple ones; the behaviorists had likened the mind to a telephone switchboard hooking up stimuli and responses. Freud had based his model of the mind on nineteenth-century physics. The computer, by mimicking such mental activities as taking in information, storing information in memory, solving problems, manipulating symbols, recognizing patterns, and so forth, provided evidence that such mental acts were real and could be studied.

The insights of the new cognitive psychology suggest a new view of socialization. Instead of defining socialization as the growth of conformity, or as a struggle between the forces of "instinct" and the forces of "civilization," the new vision emphasizes the autonomy and activity of the child in his or her own socialization. Further, the new vision sees both conformity and nonconformity as arising out of the same psychological processes. The nature of human thought and language suggests there may be inherent limits to the prediction and control of behavior.

The Experiencing Child

The traditional views of socialization have tended to assume that what the child experiences can be directly inferred from parental behavior or environmental events. Recently there has been a growing realization that socialization cannot be described without taking into account the point of view of the central character in the drama—the child. The parents' power is limited by the ability of children to interpret their experiences in their own ways.

The most basic generation gap, then, is the gap between the selfhood of the growing child and the attempts of other people to control and define him or her. The prevailing theories of socialization, however, have tended to ignore a conscious "I." They have, as Erik Erikson (1968) put it, deleted "the core of human self-awareness" (p. 218).

Many psychologists, under the influence of Freud's teachings, believed that the decisive events in a person's life occurred in the first few years of life and centered on nursing, weaning, and toilet training. A huge number of studies were carried out to show that different patterns of infant care, such as breast or bottle feeding, gradual or abrupt weaning, or strict versus relaxed toilet training led to differences in adult personality. The results of these studies have been disappointing. It is by now generally conceded that specific practices, in and of themselves, have no demonstrable effects on adult personality (Caldwell, 1964; Schaffer, 1971).

H. R. Schaffer (1971) observed that these studies were based on the assumption that a particular practice must have the same effects on different children:

The nature of the experiencing child, that is, is left out of consideration. . . . It is probably this factor more than any other which accounted for the failure of the above line of investigations and which has now convinced developmental psychologists of the need to pay attention to the experiencing infant. (p. 16)

It is significant that Schaffer, an experimental child psychologist, is writing of the first year of life. Even working with infants at this very young age, Schaffer found he could not make meaningful statements about the child's behavior without taking into account the child's thoughts, feelings, and representations of reality. Even newborns show selective attention. They like to look at certain patterns more than others. Further, the child is now coming to be seen as a socializer of the parents. With the cry and the smile, the infant commands two powerful means of controlling the caretakers. Harriet Rheingold (1969) has described how the infant makes "fathers and mothers" out of "men and women." Even very young infants have the power to reward and punish the parents and to let them know the things that please and displease them. Through fretting sounds of impatience and facial expressions, the infant lets the caretakers know what to continue doing and what to stop.

In general, defining socialization as weaning, toilet training, and the control of aggression and sexuality stresses just those aspects of growing up in which the child is "wrong," the adult is "right," and conformity is the only outcome. Such an emphasis on what the child must suppress in the course of growing up overlooks the staggering amount of learning the child has to do, starting from birth.

Socialization and the Self

All theories of socialization ask the question "How does the helpless infant, apparently lacking a mind and a sense of self, come to be a functioning member of society?" The traditional answer, in both sociology and psychology, is that the child acquires knowledge about itself and the world from its caretakers, usually the parents. The child "identifies" with the parents and "internalizes" the norms of society.

The traditional assumption in both sociology and psychology has been that the young infant's mind, in William James's words, is a "buzzing blooming confusion." In regard to the self, it was assumed that infants have no capacity to tell the differences between themselves, the world, and other people. According to this view, the capacity to make such discriminations grows slowly over the child's first couple of years. Theorists in the psychoanalytic tradition, such as Margaret Mahler (1968), assume that the infant's self is merged with the parent and only gradually emerges as a separate entity.

Sociologists, especially those in the symbolic-interactionist tradition, have placed the self at the core of the socialization process (Gecas, 1979), emphasizing the social nature and origins of the self. Thus, many hold to the notion of "the looking-glass self" postulated by Charles Cooley, a sociologist of the early 1900s. Cooley (1902) stressed that self and society are aspects of a common whole. Other people are the looking glass in which we discover ourselves. The infant, Cooley believed, is unaware of the self or others, experiencing just a simple "stream of impressions." Only gradually does the child discriminate the self from other people and society.

George Herbert Mead (1934/1965), a contemporary of Cooley, elaborated the theory of the looking-glass self. Mead also made use of William James's (1890) distinction between the "me," the self as observed or known, and the "I," the self as observer and actor. Mead, however, emphasized the role of language in the emergence of the self; he believed that the self emerges as a product of language development. Once the child has the ability to communicate in words, he or she can take the role of the other and can perceive the self as an object. The child first discovers itself as "me," the self as object of knowledge, and only then does it discover the other aspect of self, the "I" or subjective sense of self.

As we noted earlier, traditional theories of socialization have been criticized for their "oversocialized view of human nature" (Wrong, 1961, 1976). The concepts of the looking-glass self and the "internalization of norms" offer a view of human beings as passive conformists totally shaped by their social environment. Actually, Mead and Cooley, despite the looking-glass metaphor, recognized the autonomous aspects of the self. Mead, following James, saw the "I" as the unpredictable source of human action. He saw the infant as active rather than passive in the construction of self and selective rather than indiscriminate in responding to events. Yet those who followed Mead and Cooley tended to emphasize the oversocialized looking-glass self.

Wrong and others have argued that it is biological drives, in the Freudian sense, that keep people from being simply "social puppets" (Carveth, 1977). Yet while the body and its urges do provide one answer to the oversocialized conception of human personality, such an answer is incomplete. It does not explain the experience of being an active, thinking agent, rather than a passive object (Gecas, 1979).

The new infant Until recently, theorists could speculate freely about the infant mind, unconstrained by hard evidence. As one researcher put it, infancy was like the dark side of the moon (Bower, 1977). Except for Piaget's pioneering research, there was little empirical evidence about what babies know and when they know it. Piaget's emphasis on the child as active agent in its own development provided an important counterargument to the oversocialized view of human nature. His findings on cognitive development made it hard to think of infants as blank slates waiting to be conditioned by the environment, or as helpless pawns in the grip of raging instincts. Yet Piaget also emphasized the incompetence and egocentricity of the infant and young child. He shared the very strong assumption among psychologists and sociologists that we come into the world with practically no ability to process information, and only gradually come to learn all we know, bit by bit.

In the last 2 decades, there has been a revolution in the study of infancy (Flavell, 1985; Stern, 1985). One result of this revolution has been to reveal that Piaget and other researchers and theorists had greatly underestimated the young infant's ability to process information, including information about the self. The new findings have far-reaching implications for theories of socialization.

Several methodological breakthroughs provided the key to unlocking the secrets of the infant mind. Researchers found ways of exploiting the easily observable infant behaviors that are under voluntary muscle control—looking, sucking, head turning. For example, in one of the earliest of the new studies, a researcher found that newborn infants prefer—that is, like to look longer at—certain patterns rather than others, especially facelike patterns (Fantz, 1963). As a result of the revolution in infancy research, there is now an abundance of evidence suggesting that infants never experience the kind of confusion that had been attributed to them. Instead, infants come into this world prepared to perceive and recognize its "natural categories"—faces, objects, colors, and speech sounds. In contrast to what Piaget and most other writers on infancy had believed, infants do not have to piece together their knowledge of the world from scratch. Further, the new evidence suggests that these abilities enable the infant to establish a rudimentary sense of self in the earliest weeks and months of life.

This is not to say that infants have fully formed conceptions of themselves in the first months. Rather, infants have self *experiences* long before they have self *concepts*. For example, they are born with perceptual sensitivities that enable them to discover the distinction between themselves and the rest of the world. As P. L. Harris (1983) points out, information about the bodily self is specific and directly available. For example, touching an object feels different from touching ourselves, or being touched. By the same token, when we move we feel our movements; we do not feel anything when we see another person move. Contingency—the experience of making something happen—

Parents still play an important role in the transmission of skills from one generation to the next. [Dick Swartz/Office of Human Development Services]

is another clue that specifies the self; infants can make things happen: closing the eyes makes the world go dark, screaming makes a sound, and so forth. Even young infants are highly sensitive to contingency (Watson, 1979).

Michael Lewis and Jean Brooks-Gunn (1979) have analyzed the early development of self and have labeled the first phase as the emergence of the *existential self*. During this phase, the infant develops a sense of bodily and psychological existence. The self is experienced as an active agent, separate and distinct from other people and objects in the world.

Later, during the second year, the child develops a sense of the self as an object possessing certain qualities and belonging to certain social categories. Thus, a little girl would learn that she is a baby or child, not an adult, and is female rather than male. Lewis and Brooks-Gunn refer to this stage as the *categorical self*. It corresponds to James's "me."

Recently, Daniel Stern (1985) used the latest research on infancy to describe the earliest stages of the self in greater detail. Stern suggests there are three "senses of self" that precede the verbal or categorical self. Between birth and 2 months, the sense of self is *emergent.* The infant is beginning to sort the world into basic categories of self, other people, and inanimate objects as well as to connect different experiences, such as the way a nipple feels and the way it looks.

Between 2 to 6 months, the *sense of a core self* emerges. This sense of the self will persist throughout life. During this phase, the infant begins to experience its physical self as "a coherent, willful, physical entity with a unique affective [emotional] life" (p. 26). At the same time, the quality of the infant's interpersonal relations changes. The infant senses that it and the parent are separate entities, physically and psychologically. From the parent's point of view, infants of 2–3 months seem to be very different from their younger selves. There are many behavioral changes, but most significantly the baby now smiles and looks directly into the parents' eyes. This feels to the parents as if their infants have "an integrated sense of themselves" as complete persons, and also regard the parents as persons. Stern refers to this as "core relatedness."

At about 7–9 months, the sense of a *subjective self* emerges. The infant realizes that he or she has a mind, that other people do also, and that mental states can be shared. One clear example of this sharing of experiences is pointing. At about 9 months, babies begin to point to get their parents to look at things. They also look at what the parent points to, rather than at the parent's hand. Even before 9 months, infants follow the mother's line of vision when she turns her head.

Thus, long before language begins, the infant manages to tune in to the attentional focus of another person and get the other to tune in to its own. This communication is one important precursor of language. Another is the child's preverbal requests—signaling the parent that he or she wants something.

At around 15–18 months, language emerges. The child develops what Stern labels a new sense of a *verbal self.* There are many indicators of the child's developing self-awareness after about 15 months. At this age, for example, babies can recognize that what they see in a mirror is their own reflection (M. Lewis and Brooks-Gunn, 1979).

Jerome Kagan (1981) has used a variety of other tasks to document the growth of self-awareness during this period. For example, he has studied the emergence of references to self in the child's speech, distress when the child is unable to imitate an adult's task, and smiling when successfully accomplishing a goal. In general, in the second half of the second year the child becomes concerned with adult normative standards, such as badness or dirtiness, as well as with awareness of the self's actions, internal states, and competencies. At this age also the child establishes a basic gender identity and engages in acts of empathy.

With the emergence of the "verbal" or "categorical" self, the child has attained the kind of self discussed by Mead and Cooley. But this period marks not the beginning of the self, but the reworking and transformation of earlier senses of the self. Nor is this sense of the self simply a reflection of the child's social environment. As Stern puts it, "The fact that language is powerful in defining self to the self does not mean that an infant can be 'bent out of shape' by those forces and become totally the creation of others' wishes and plans. The socialization process, for good or ill, has limits" (p. 229). Paradoxically, language makes socialization possible and increases self-awareness. In short, language both *socializes* and *individualizes*.

Linguistic Development

Recent discoveries in linguistics have made clear that children, in learning to speak their native language, face an enormously complex task. It used to be thought that children learned to speak through a process of trial and error, imitation of and correction by the parents. Bit by bit, according to the same principles that animals learned to perform tricks, the theory went, the child built knowledge of language. The stimulus–response explanation of language learning is not supported by observations of young children. It fails completely to account for the fundamental fact about language: its creativity, the fact that the speaker of a language can understand and produce sentences never heard before. A child learns not words and particular sentences, but a system of rules for translating meaning into sound.

Further, as Jerome Bruner (1964) has pointed out, when children acquire language, they learn not only to represent the world but to transform it. Transformation of reality is built into the grammar of every language.

The transformational rules of grammar provide a . . . means of reworking the "realities" one has encountered. Not only, if you will, did the dog bite the man, but the man was bitten by the dog, and perhaps the man was not bitten by the dog, or was the man not bitten by the dog? The range of reworking that is made possible even by the three transformations of the passive,

the negative, and the query is very striking indeed. (p. 4)

Bruner did not exhaust the possibilities: after all, there is still "the man bites the dog" as another alternative. Indeed, very young children like to play with language in order to "violate the established order of things," as Chukovsky (1966) put it, as in nursery rhymes, nonsense verse, and so forth. Thus the oversocialized view of human nature overlooks more than bodily impulse as a source of nonconformity. It ignores the possibility of using the cultural rules and tools in nonconforming ways.

The Limits of Behavior Control

The new cognitive psychology has important implications for the possibility of predicting and controlling behavior, as well as for socialization. Many people believe, either hopefully or fearfully, that psychologists possess powerful techniques of behavioral control that could change the world if only they were fully unleashed. B. F. Skinner is a well-known proponent of this point of view, which is shared by many other behavior modifiers.

Other people feel that such psychological techniques pose a threat to human freedom. Both the hopes and the fears may be undeserved. As one cognitive psychologist sums up the argument: "The facts of human cognition imply that the psychological manipulation of behavior is bound to fail; it cannot lead to systematically predictable outcomes under ordinary cultural conditions" (Neisser, 1976, p. 177). This is not to deny that much human behavior is predictable. Society could hardly exist if everyone's behavior was random. Nor do the facts of human cognition imply that people's behavior cannot be manipulated in tightly controlled laboratory experiments, or in coercive and closed environments, such as prisons, mental hospitals, prisoner-of-war camps, and the like. There is little evidence, however, that the control techniques used in these settings, such as behavior modification or brainwashing, have predictable or lasting outcomes once the individuals are released.

The question is not whether people can be coerced into behaving in particular ways; people with guns and not much knowledge of psychology can be very successful in manipulating others. Theorists of socialization have always recognized that it's not enough to induce the proper *behavior* in children, but to win their hearts and minds; they are supposed to believe in or, to use the jargon term, to *internalize* the values and attitudes of their society.

The traditional views of socialization, however, have tended to overestimate the amount of internalization that actually takes place in society. They have done so in two ways: by underestimating the role of coercion in inducing compliant behavior and by assuming that conforming, nonrebellious behavior has to imply an inward acceptance of the values and rules of the society.

On the first point, William J. Goode (1971) has noted that most social theories have tended to underestimate the role of force and violence in maintaining social arrangements. They have assumed that because force is not visible, it is not there. But Goode pointed out that the threat of force keeps people in line and creates "a relatively stable, unchallenged set of understandings, behaviors, and imbalances of influence or dominance" (p. 625). Thus many would-be rebellious wives or children do not actually commit deviant acts because they know that the father or husband is stronger, has more economic resources, and can call on outsiders who will support his force with ad-

ditional force. The community will back up traditional family patterns, particularly dominance of adults over children.

But behavioral compliance does not necessarily lead to internal change. Psychologist Gerald Davison (1973), in a discussion of the limits of behavior modification, points to a "Kol Nidre" effect. During the Spanish Inquisition of the fourteenth century, all Jews had to convert to Catholicism or else be executed or banished. Most Jews complied, and many became well known as devout Catholics. Despite their seeming change, however, most did not really convert. Each year, on the eve of the Jewish day of atonement, small groups of "Catholics" met secretly to sing a prayer called "Kol Nidre" and to inform God that, despite their outward behavior the rest of the year, they had not given up their original faith.

Davison argued that much behavioral modification that goes on in institutions is probably the Kol Nidre effect, rather than a change of hearts and minds. He also points out some facts well known to behavior modifiers themselves, but not to the general public. Most people tend to think of behavior modification as a powerful technique that can be applied against a person's will—as, for example, subjecting homosexuals to electric shocks or other "aversive conditioning" in conjunction with homosexual images. In fact, nearly everything that behavior modifiers do requires the active cooperation of the subject. Conversely, the subject can sabotage the procedures. The homosexual who gets electric shocks when shown homosexual images, for example, can imagine heterosexual scenes while undergoing the unpleasant stimulation (Bandura, 1969) and thus reverse the effects intended by the conditioner.

In short, human cognitive processes, such as deciding what to pay attention to and thinking of images and ideas, impose limits on the manipulation of behavior, including that of children.

Indeterminacy and Unanticipated Consequences in Socialization

Thus, despite its dependency, the infant comes into the world with a certain degree of distance and autonomy from other people and the environment. For if the child selectively interprets situations and events, we cannot confidently predict behavior from knowledge of the situation alone. The search for direct and simple cause-and-effect relationships between what the parent does and what the child does is bound to fail.

Parents who turn to "the experts" for advice on how to rear their children are often surprised to learn that the expert may not have very specific advice to offer. If he or she does offer a specific technique, chances are another expert will disagree with the first one. "Children need firmness," says one. "Children need understanding above all," says another. "The worst thing a parent can do is vacillate and be inconsistent," says still another.

Jane Loevinger (1959) suggested that one of the reasons for such disagreement is that none of the theories work. She provided an amusing and insightful account of how "the experiencing child" introduces indeterminacy into the childrearing process. There is no guarantee, she wrote, that when a parent tries to get a disciplinary message across to the child, the child will interpret that message in the way the parent intends. She offered the following illustrative situation: a mother has come upon her 5-year-old son hitting his 2-year-old sister. She wants to teach him that this is wrong. How will she do it?

Some mothers believe in strong discipline. They feel that unless children feel pain for wrong behavior, they will tend to repeat it the next time the impulse arises. Such a mother may spank an offending child. Another mother may feel that a child has to be made to understand why it is wrong to hit a little sister, so she will explain the error of the child's ways. This mother would be following an insight theory of learning, in contrast to the first mother who is following a reinforcement or punishment-and-reward theory. A third kind of mother might believe that the strongest influence on the child is the example or model provided by the parent's own behavior. Such a mother would hesitate to use physical punishment for fear the child would learn that it is all right for a bigger person to be mean to a smaller one.

Thus the inescapable parental dilemma: there is no way for any of the mothers to make sure the child will learn what she tries to teach. This, Loevinger claimed, is the fallacy common to all parental-teaching theories. The mother can decide to spank or not, but she cannot control how the child will interpret her action. Thus the child whose mother spanks for reinforcement may learn according to identification theory that it is all right for a big person to hit a little person if you really feel strongly about something and if nobody bigger is around to get you for it.

The children of the insight- and identification-teaching mothers may learn, according to the reinforcement theory their mothers disavow, that nothing much will happen if you do beat up your little sister. The parent teaches by one theory; there is no guarantee the child will not learn by another.

Thus researchers as well as parents have been frustrated in the search for clear or simple cause-and-effect relationships between the things parents do or don't do and the way children turn out. There are no cookbook recipes for producing a particular kind of child. Although it was widely believed a few years ago that the crucial determining events of a person's life were those that occurred early in infancy, in the ways that the parents handled the infant's oral, anal, and genital impulses, there is little evidence that specific practices such as breast or bottle feeding or early or late weaning or toilet training have any profound influence on later development. The same may be said about different disciplinary practices, such as strictness or permissiveness. Whatever specific techniques the parent may use are influenced by the emotional context—most importantly, whether the parent is relatively warm and loving, or cold and hostile, or ambivalent.

The research literature even documents the idea that certain parental actions may produce quite opposite effects. Wesley Becker (1964), in a review article on the effect of parental discipline, cited studies showing that in boys strict discipline on the part of parents may result either in sons who are extremely nonaggressive or extremely aggressive. Becker also pointed out that all the different approaches to discipline entail certain costs or risks, even if they do result in the very kind of behavior the parent is aiming at. Strictness may foster well-controlled, obedient behavior, but it may also result in children being fearful, dependent, and submissive; further, it may dull their intellectual striving and inhibit their ability to deal with aggression in themselves and others. On the other hand, permissiveness may result in children who are outgoing, sociable, assertive, and intellectually striving, but it may also lead to less persistence and more aggressiveness.

Pearlin (1971) has discovered another paradoxical outcome of parental pressure in a different set of circumstances. He found that working-class parents who want their children to reach a level of occupation much higher than their own often urge their children to work hard to succeed in school. The children, however, are likely to respond to these pressures not by working hard but by cheating.

Another instance of socialization pressures leading to paradoxical effects is found in Jessie Pitts's (1968) description of French family life. The upper-middle-class French child is not supposed to make friends with other children. The extended family is a "total society," and no one is supposed to have any relationships outside it. The child is supposed to find friendship among cousins or among children of adult "friends of the family," who have a familylike status. Nevertheless, the child eventually goes to school and participates with peer groups. This is where the paradox comes in. Because the family does not recognize sociability among unrelated children, whenever peer groups do arise they possess a delinquent, antiadult quality.

By contrast, most American parents, who want their children to be popular and to participate in group activities, such as sports, often encourage and manage their children's social lives. Parents may even take over and run peer-group activities, such as Little League baseball.

Finally, Ronald Laing (1969) has described a common family scenario in which the parent, trying to produce one kind of behavior in the child, actually succeeds in encouraging the opposite. How many times have we heard parents say something like the following to a child?

"I'm always trying to get him to make more friends, but he is so self-conscious. Isn't that right, dear?"

"He's so naughty. He never does what I tell him. Do you?"

"I keep telling him to be more careful, but he's so careless, aren't you?" (p. 81)

Usually the parent is exasperated and confused about why the child persists in being

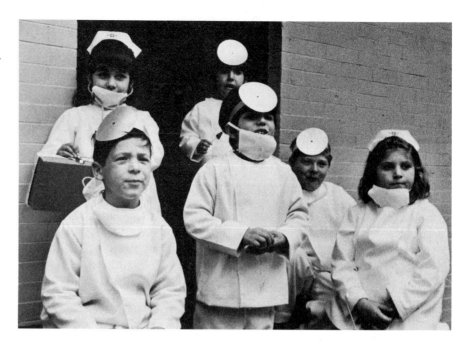

Playing at adult roles is one way children prepare for adulthood. [Abigail Heyman/ Archive Pictures Inc.]

self-conscious, naughty, and careless in the face of such pleadings. Laing argued that such statements as those quoted contain a double message. The child is being told "Do X (the good thing), but you really are the kind of person who does Y (the bad thing)." Being told what you *are*, argued Laing, is a much more powerful message than an order merely to do something. In this way the parents, without realizing it, may be teaching the child to persist in the very behavior they are trying to change.

Conflict and Growth

One reason for the persistence of the idea of the family as a harmonious, balanced social system is a line of thought that goes something like this: (a) the society needs stable adults to survive; (b) stable adults are produced by warm, harmonious, stable families; (c) society is surviving; so (d) families *must* be warm, stable, and harmonious. The

concept of the family as a difficult environment, which has emerged from the study of family interaction, has been hard to accept because of these assumptions.

Recently some writers have suggested that we need to rethink the role of conflict in human development. In looking at an individual or a family, the prevailing assumption of most psychologists has been that conflict was neurotic and undesirable. Now, however, it appears that conflict is not necessarily something of which the less one has the better. Rather, the optimal dose is somewhere in between—not too much, but not too little either. Piaget and other students of cognitive development have argued that intellectual and moral growth occurs as a result of conflict. The child must feel some "perturbation," some sense that something is wrong with the way he or she is thinking.

Intellectual growth occurs not through a smooth process of adding on pieces of knowledge bit by bit, but rather by a constant series of small crises in the way the child looks at the world. The child has a certain idea or interpretation or expectation—the moon follows me, people can see my dreams and thoughts, shadows are a substance, if you pour water into a tall, skinny glass there will be more of it, and so on. If these beliefs were never challenged by experience or other people, the child's reasoning processes would remain at this primitive level. If we think of what kind of environment is most likely to stimulate intellectual skill, it would be one providing some surprise, contradiction, and challenge rather than a merely bland and pleasant one.

There is reason to believe that the same is true of the child's emotional development. The pleasant, conflict-free family atmosphere idealized in the sentimental model of the family may not prove the optimal environment for child development, even in those rare instances in which it occurs. Thus the findings of the new anthropology of the family are not, in the end, as shocking as they seem to be at first glance.

The Uses of Adversity

The image of a troubled adult scarred for life by an early trauma, such as the loss of a parent, lack of love, or family tensions, has passed from the clinical literature to become a cliché of our popular media. The assumption of childhood vulnerability, the belief that only a stable and supportive family life with gentle parents attuned to the child's inner needs can assure a child's personality development, is, however, not supported by the literature. The idea that childhood stress must inevitably result in psychological damage rests on a methodological flaw inherent in the clinical literature—that of starting with adult problems and tracing them backward in time.

Thus many studies trying to document the effects of early pathological and traumatic conditions have failed to demonstrate more than a weak link between such conditions and later development. It is true that whenever the backgrounds of delinquents, mental patients, or psychiatric rejectees from military service are investigated, a large number are found to come from broken or troubled homes, overpassive, domineering, or rejecting mothers, or inadequate or violent fathers. The argument is typically made that these circumstances cause the maladjustment of the offspring. The difficulty, however, is that if "normal" or "superior" people are sampled—college students, business executives, professionals, military officers, creative artists, and scientists—these same pathological conditions occur in the same or greater proportions.

Although such findings have been appearing in the literature at least since the publication in 1949 of Stouffer's massive studies on the American soldier (Stouffer, Star, & Williams, 1949), they have never attracted very much public and professional attention. One of the most thorough studies of the effects of childhood stress on later development was the Midtown Manhattan study by Srole and others (Srole, Langner, Michael, Opler, & Rennie, 1962). Some of the most striking findings concerned the effects of broken homes on mental health. Among psychiatric patients included in the study, 20 percent had reported a history of a home broken in early childhood by death, divorce, or separation. But 35 percent of the nonpatient control population also came from broken homes. This is not to say that having a broken home has no effect at all. The severity of effects seemed to depend on the age of the child, whether the parent lost was the mother or the father, and the social class of the family.

The work of Norman Garmezy (1976, 1983) of the University of Minnesota on the subject of "invulnerables" has received considerable coverage in the press. Garmezy began his work by studying adult schizophrenics and later turned to developmental studies comparing children judged to be at high and low risk for developing schizophrenia and other disorders at a later age. When these children were studied over time, only 10 or 12 percent of the high-risk group became schizophrenic, while 85 to 90 percent did not. He became increasingly fascinated by these seeming invulnerables—children who thrived in spite of genetic disadvantages and environmental deprivations. Through interviews with teachers and principals, he has identified many such children; for example, a 10-year-old facing extreme poverty, with a dying ex-convict father, an abusive, illiterate mother, and two mentally retarded siblings is described as charming, popular with peers and teacher, a good student, and a natural leader.

The striking differences between retrospective studies—starting with adult misfits and looking backward to childhood conditions—and longitudinal studies—starting with children and following them through time—was shown earlier in a study at the University of California's Institute of Human Development. Jean Macfarlane (1964) and her associates studied, through tests and interviews over a period of 30 years, a group of 166 infants born in 1929. The purpose was to observe physical, mental, and emotional growth in average people.

Over the years this study has generated several significant research findings, but the most surprising of all was the difficulty of predicting what 30-year-old adults would be like even after the most sophisticated data had been gathered on them as children. Macfarlane, the director of the project, wrote that the researchers experienced shock after

shock as they saw the people they had last seen at age 18. It turned out that the predictions they had made about the subjects were wrong in about two-thirds of the cases! How could a group of competent psychologists have been so mistaken?

Above all, the researchers had tended to overestimate the damaging effects of early troubles of various kinds. Most personality theory had been derived from observations of troubled people in therapy. The pathology of adult neurotics and psychotics was traced back to disturbances early in childhood: poor parent–child relations, chronic school difficulties, and so forth. Consequently, theories of personality based on clinical observation tended to define adult psychological problems as socialization failures. Psychiatrists, however, see only disturbed people; they do not encounter "normal" individuals who may experience childhood difficulties but who do not grow into troubled adults. The Berkeley method, however, called for studying such people.

The experience of the Berkeley subjects showed the error of assuming that childhood stress must inevitably lead to adult maladjustment, or that similar childhood conditions must affect all children the same way. The adult data showed that early difficulties could be overcome or compensated for. "In fact," as Macfarlane (1964) pointed out,

many of the most outstandingly mature adults in our entire group, many who are well integrated, highly competent, and/or creative, who are clear about their values, who are understanding and accepting of self and others, are recruited from those who were confronted with very difficult situations and whose characteristic responses during childhood and adolescence seemed to us to compound their problems. (p. 121)

The theoretical predictions of the researchers were also jarred from the other direction by the adult status of the children who had seemed especially blessed with ability, talent, popularity, or easy and confidence-inducing family lives. Those who had enjoyed admiration, success, and approval as children failed to live up to the expectations that the researchers, along with everybody else, held for them. As adults they seemed strained and dissatisfied, wondering what went wrong and longing for the good old days. This pattern was particularly strong for boys who had been athletic leaders and girls who had been extremely beautiful and popular in high school.

Summing up the implications of the Berkeley study, Macfarlane noted:

We had not appreciated the utility of many painful, strain-producing, and stressful experiences . . . nor had we been aware that early success might delay or forestall continuing growth, richness, and competence. . . . We need to look at and to try to conceptualize the configurations of what kinds of stress, in what graded doses, with what compensating supports, and what developmental periods, and in what kinds of organisms, forestall maturity and strength or facilitate them. (p. 123)

A more precise explanation of the kind of evidence just described has been presented by Martin Seligman (1975) in his theory of "learned helplessness." Summarizing a vast array of data, including animal experiments, clinical studies, psychiatric case literature, and reports from prisoner-of-war camps, Seligman proposed that the key to whether one copes with difficulty or gives up in despair is the feeling of helplessness—the expectation that our efforts have little or no important effect. The feeling of helplessness can come about through actual experiences of uncontrollable events, simply believing that we have no control over what will happen. The expectation of having some control, not the objective conditions of controllability, is the crucial determinant of helplessness.

The expectation of helplessness can result from being told by someone authoritative that you are helpless, or it can come about through actually experiencing uncontrollable events. Thus, in experiments studying the stressful effects of loud noise, subjects who were told they could turn the noise off if it became too disturbing suffered from less stress than those who were told the noise was uncontrollable. And, in other experiments, children who were given unsolvable arithmetic problems were later unable to solve easy ones.

A key point in the theory is that good events that happen outside our control can produce a sense of helplessness as much as bad ones can. Thus the theory helps explain both of the puzzling findings from the Macfarlane study—not only the positive outcomes of many of the people who had troubled early lives, but the finding that many of those who had had "everything" as children failed to realize their potential later on. The theory of learned helplessness suggests that the experience of controllable stress may be better for a child's ego development than good things that happen without any effort on the child's part.

The statements of Macfarlane's subjects seem to confirm this hypothesis. A central theme running through the accounts of those who successfully coped with difficulty seems to be the perception that their own actions could have some effect on what was going on in their lives. Looking back at their early lives at the age of 30, these individuals convinced the researchers that what had looked like disturbed behaviors were actually ways of coping with difficult situations.

Even at their most troubled periods, they do not reveal themselves as passive victims of circumstance or of uncontrollable symptoms or impulses. Rather they seem to have been trying to deal with difficult situations, to exercise some degree of choice no matter how extreme the situation, to construct a self of their own choosing, even if that meant engaging in behavior that looked bizarre and meaningless to others. For example, a woman who had been seen as a "full-blown schizophrenic" during adolescence, but who turned into a competent adult, said:

The only stabilizing aspect of my life during that period was the undeviating and all-enveloping homicidal fantasies against my mother. I believe they prevented my complete disintegration until I could escape my home and achieve other methods of handling my strains. (Macfarlane, 1964, p. 121)

A man who had been in constant trouble in school, and who was finally expelled at age 15, said:

Granted that my defiance of authority precluded a college education. I desperately needed approval, even if it came from kids as maladjusted as I was. Yet I can see positive results too. To maintain my rebel status called for a commitment that demanded my disciplining *all* of my intelligence and stamina which, I believe, has contributed to my adult strength and to my self-confidence in tackling later tough problems. (Macfarlane, 1964, p. 121)

Another subject who defied expectations was a girl who also spent most of her adolescent energies defying authorities. She too was expelled from school at age 15. At age 30 she was described as an understanding, compassionate mother. She had taken specialized training and was working with physically handicapped people.

The ability to cope does not mean that the child does not suffer; in that sense, the term *invulnerables* is misleading because it suggests an imperviousness to pain. One woman who successfully overcame a childhood marked by the death of her beloved but alcoholic and abusive father and rejection by her mother and stepfather put it this way: "We suffer but we don't let it destroy us." This woman became active in her school and community and sought support from peers, teachers, and other adults. Recent studies of children of divorce show that successful coping seems to imply the ability to function on two levels, to experience one's misery and yet to go on with living (Wallerstein & Kelly, 1980).

Another problem with the term *invulnerables* is that it implies that the ability to cope is a trait, something internal to the child. In the case histories of successful and unsuccessful copers, one often finds external supports that integrated the impact of the traumatic event. Thus in many of Macfarlane's cases, something in the child's environment provided alternative sources of love and gratification—one parent compensating for the inadequacy of the other, a loving sibling or grandparent, an understanding teacher, a hobby or strong interest, a pet, recreational facilities.

Indeed the local community may play an important role in modulating the effects of the home environments on the child. Once at a seminar discussing the life histories of Macfarlane's longitudinal subjects, Erik Erikson, who had worked on the study, was asked how so many of these people overcame the effects of truly awful homes. Without hesitation, he answered that it was the active street life in those days, enabling the child to get out of the house and play with other children when relations with parents got to be too difficult.

SOCIAL CLASS AND FAMILY ENVIRONMENT

If we take seriously the notion that family interaction is difficult, it may be that the various modes of childrearing may differ not

TABLE 14.1   *Two Patterns of Socialization*

"Traditional" or status-centered	*"Modern" or person-centered*
1. Each member's place in family is a function of age and sex status.	Emphasis is on selfhood and individuality of each member.
2. Father is defined as boss and more important as agent of discipline; he receives "respect" and deference from mother and children.	Father more affectionate, less authoritative; mother becomes more important as agent of discipline.
3. Emphasis on overt acts—*what* child does rather than *why*.	Emphasis on motives and feelings—*why* child does what he or she does.
4. Valued qualities in child are obedience, cleanliness.	Valued qualities in child are happiness, achievement, consideration, curiosity, self-control.
5. Emphasis on "direct" discipline: physical punishment, scolding, threats.	Discipline based on reasoning, isolation, guilt, threat of loss of love.
6. Social consensus and solidarity in communication; emphasis on "we."	Communication used to express individual experience and perspectives; emphasis on "I."
7. Emphasis on communication from parent to child.	Emphasis on two-way communication between parent and child; parent open to persuasion.
8. Parent feels little need to justify demands to child; commands are to be followed "because I say so."	Parent gives reasons for demands—e.g., not "Shut up" but "Please keep quiet or go into the other room; I'm trying to talk on the telephone."
9. Emphasis on conforming to rules, respecting authority, maintaining conventional social order.	Emphasis on reasons for rules; particular rules can be criticized in the name of "higher" rational or ethical principles.
10. Child may attain a strong sense of social identity at the cost of individuality, poor academic performance.	Child may attain strong sense of selfhood, but may have identity problems, guilt, alienation.

so much in degree of strain as in what kind of problem they pose for the child growing up in them. Despite the size of the literature on childrearing and the diversity of the populations studied and measures used, two broad patterns of childrearing appear again and again. These two patterns stand as polar contrasts to each other (see Table 14.1). One is organized around sound obedience, the other around the personality of the child. The first pattern is typically called traditional, repressive, or authoritarian socialization; the second is called modern, democratic, or child-centered. The chief characteristics of each style are contrasted in the table. Needless to say, these represent ideal types rather than patterns one can observe in every family. At the present time most researchers agree that the traditional style of socialization tends to be found in the working class, whereas the democratic style typifies the middle classes—or at least those segments of it most influenced by the literature on childrearing advice. In the past, however, the pattern seems to have been reversed, with the middle classes more "repressive" in childrearing (Bronfenbrenner, 1958).

Most writers see the repressive style as creating a less benign environment for the child and as impairing the child's intellectual and emotional development. It appears, however, that both these environments are best seen as problematic for the child, each in its own way. For example, a number of writers have suggested that such predicaments as the double bind may not reflect personality traits of parents so much as the built-in structure of the middle-class nuclear family. To understand how the middle-class nuclear family has such strains built into it, it is necessary to contrast this family form with two different ones: the traditional extended family of preindustrial society and working- or lower-class family patterns in industrial societies. The characteristic of the modern middle-class family that sets it off from both of these others is the emphasis on individualism and autonomy on the part of the child. Paradoxically, individualism represents both the chief glory and the chief source of difficulty in modern middle-class socialization. To the extent that the nuclear family and middle-class values represent the norm to which these other groups will move, the attendant problems will be found in these groups also.

The contrast between socialization in traditional kin groups and in the modern nuclear family has been summarized by Hsu (1961) as follows:

There is . . . [in the nuclear-family system] . . . an inherent tendency to conflict between the generations not known in other types of kinship systems. On the one hand, parents view their children as their exclusive possession, since they are given unbridled authority to order the youngsters' lives. On the other hand, privacy and self-reliance keep parents and children apart even before the latter reach majority in ownership of property, correspondence, relationship with friends, romance, and in the choice of life partners. Therefore, parents often find it hard to let their children go their own way as the youngsters advance in age, while children often find it necessary to reject their parents as the most important sign of maturity and independence. As a result, the parent-child tie is not only terminated legally upon the youngster's reaching majority, it may be socially and psychologically broken long before. (p. 418)

In short, Hsu pointed to a contradiction between the values of independence and self-reliance for children and two other aspects of the nuclear-family system: the actual power of parents and the emotional significance of children in their parents' lives. Thus modern nuclear parents are both more powerful and more affectionate than traditional parents, although their ideology underplays the parental authority as an ideal.

Behavioral Versus Attitudinal Conformity

In traditional societies children depend less on parents alone, and individuality and independence are less valued; children are supposed to conform behaviorally. In middle-class Western society, especially American society, parents don't generally want their children to conform for the sake of conformity. They want them to internalize the rules the parents are trying to teach, to believe in them as the right thing to do. Whereas working-class parents tend to value neatness, cleanliness and obedience in a child, the middle classes tend to value happiness, considerateness for other people's feelings, curiosity, and self-control. They want not only behavioral conformity but attitudinal conformity (Kohn, 1959). The prototypical working-class parent, as he or she emerges from research findings, is happy when the child obeys and does not mind spanking the child for disobedience. The middle-class parent may actually spank the child sometimes, but disapproves of spanking for two reasons: first, he or she believes in the child-centered, psychologically oriented childrearing teaching of the experts (Bronfenbrenner, 1958). Second, having to spank the child is in itself proof that the parent has failed to get the child to internalize the parent's values—to want to do the "right thing" because it is right. Kohn argued that the emphasis on different values in different social classes reflects both the circumstances of life in each social class and the qualities necessary for the advancement of the child. For the working-class child, cleanliness, neatness, and obedience may actually be necessary to attain respectability and success. The middle-class family, however, can take these values more for granted. Further, lower-class occupations stress working with the hands; middle-class occupations involve working with symbols and people. Kohn (1959) has described the "message" of middle-class socialization as follows:

The child is to act appropriately, not because his parents tell him to, but because he wants to. Not conformity to authority, but inner control; not because you're told to, but because you take the other person into consideration—these are the middle-class ideals. (p. 351)

Thus modern middle-class socialization is both more permissive and more demanding than traditional, restrictive socialization. As Bronfenbrenner (1958) put it:

Though more tolerant of expressed impulses and desires, the middle-class parent . . . has higher expectations from the child. The middle-class youngster is expected to learn to take care of himself earlier, to accept more responsibility about the home, and—above all—to progress further in school. (p. 424)

The prevailing emphasis in the literature has been that the middle-class pattern of childrearing is better—and that, in fact, the lower-class pattern is a social problem because it is associated with poor school performance. On the other hand, a number of observers have pointed out the problematic qualities of middle-class socialization. Arnold Green (1946), for example, has contrasted the neurotic tendencies of the middle-class male child and the freedom from guilt of his lower-class peers. The very repressiveness of lower-class parents, Green argued, makes it easier to reject them and assert one's own autonomy.

In a similar vein Rose Coser (1964) has pointed out that the "schizophrenogenic" mother who exposes her child to the double bind of love and hostility is none other than the ordinary middle-class mother caught between contradictory demands placed on her by society. The schizophrenogenic mother is described in the writings of many clinicians as having the following characteristics: She dominates her children and is strongly ambivalent. She is both punitive and overprotective. She shrinks from the children when they try to get close to her, but if they withdraw from her, she tries to bring them closer or else punishes them for implying that she is not a loving mother. The classic example is Bateson's (Bateson, Jackson, Haley, & Weakland, 1956) tale of the mother who comes to visit her schizophrenic son in a mental hospital. He hugs her and she shrinks from his embrace. He withdraws. "Don't you love your mother?" she asks. He blushes. "You mustn't be ashamed of your feelings, dear," she says.

The role models children choose for themselves may not be the ones their parents would choose for them. [Leslie Starobin]

of the immediate situations, but also in terms of their symbolic meaning in regard to attitudes and future development. The scolding phrase, "It's not that I mind you not doing the dishes—I do them myself faster anyway—it's your attitude that I object to" expresses criticism both of the youngster's inability to do the task . . . as well as of his underlying disposition. Such control is aimed at both levels of the personality at the same time. (Coser, 1964, p. 378)

Adding to the magnification of the impact the mother has on the children is a child-rearing ideology in which the raising of perfect children offers the chief justification for the mother's life. Thus everything the children do not only validates or invalidates their own inner worth, but that of the mother.

The child is also exposed to contradictions arising out of the mother's various roles. Being a wife, mother, and house-keeper involves opposing demands and pressures. The traditional, obedience-demanding mother has little difficulty in resolving conflict between household cleanliness and childhood messes, but the modern middle-class mother, faced with finger paint on the walls or a clock broken in the pursuit of intellectual curiosity, may experience personal conflict over whether to scold or praise the child for creativity. Besides the conflict concerning the immediate versus the long-range view of the child's behavior, the mother may also be in conflict between her own interests and what she conceives to be those of the child. The child wants to spend Saturday morning watching those awful cartoons. Should she, in the interests of the child's future development, forbid this? Should she permit it in the name of the child's autonomy to choose his or her own activities? Or should she let the child watch the awful stuff to gain 2 to 3 hours of peace and quiet for herself and her husband?

The role of the father in the modern middle-class family contains paradoxes of

He stays with her only a few minutes; after she leaves he assaults an aide.

Coser argued that double binding results from the mother domination and mother–child ambivalence that are built into the middle-class family. Mom is such a dominant force in middle-class children's lives for several reasons. She is the source not only of affection, but of both attitudinal and overt conformity—that is, she is concerned with both their inner dispositions and the details of their everyday behavior. Because it is the mother's task to supervise all the children's activities, her position of control tends to outweigh the control that a busy and absent father can have over his children.

Being interested in the children's attitudes as well as their behavior, her supervision makes it possible to weigh all their acts not only in terms its own. On the one hand the cultural script calls for the father to be a warm family man, even a pal to his children. The literature comparing the American father with fathers in other cultures shows how much the distribution of authority and affection within the family contrasts with the stereotypical Victorian family. The father is no longer used as the ultimate threat to enforce obedience: "Wait till your father comes home." This means that the middle-class mother can no longer pretend to be the sheltering buffer between child and the father's wrath and power. Thus the figure of "Mom" takes on witchlike proportions in the child's eyes, while "Dad" seems to embody the gentler virtues.

On the other hand, the middle-class father role competes with occupational demands. The highly career-oriented father may be available to his children hardly at all, partly from necessity and partly because he finds that life in the family is mundane when compared with life outside the home, where the responsibility and the power he can command are exciting.

Still another contradictory aspect of the paternal role concerns achievement. Both parents teach achievement values, but father is supposed to embody them more than the mother. Most men in this culture, however, are ambivalent, to say the least, about their work. In general, the system makes failures of many men. They fail if they occupy a low-status job, and in high-status jobs they judge themselves against impossibly high standards of creativity and success (W. J. Goode, 1963). The middle-class father communicates standards that define him as a failure, or else he communicates dissatisfaction with the cultural standards. Thus the middle-class child receives confusing messages about achievement (Flacks, 1971). In the working class, by contrast, the child acquires either a fatalistic attitude—success is all a matter of luck—or else the world of achievement can be held out as a promised land that the child may reach, but the parents may never enter. That world is not discredited through familiarity.

Middle-class socialization may be paradoxical at an even deeper level. The demand that a child internalize a rule, for example, creates a double-bind situation. The point has been made by Sluzki and Eliseo (1971). They gave the following example: a university student in therapy reported that his parents had always stressed the importance of having clean teeth. When he was a child they had emphasized that brushing his teeth regularly, on his own initiative, would be clear proof of his being grown up—that is, independent. Sluzki and Eliseo argued that this example represents in effect a pathological double bind or paradoxical communication: "Do just what we say, but do so on your own initiative." The parental demand to brush one's teeth on one's own initiative is a model of the paradoxical nature of all socialization based on internalization rather than obedience.

In short, middle-class families embody in an acute way the strains in the larger culture. The reason they convey contradictory messages to the child in the course of socialization is that the society itself contains contradictions. Thus, as we noted earlier, the middle-class parent is torn between responding to the child's behavior in the here and now and thinking of its meaning for future development. In the society at large a similar conflict occurs between present and future orientations:

In the schools, the media, and the churches, such contradictory values as self-denial and self-expression, discipline and indulgence . . . are being preached, dramatized, and fostered all at once. On the one hand, television and magazines advocate hedonism, consumption and living it up, while schools and churches continue, uneasily, to embody the Protestant ethic. The economy demands discipline and self-control in order to *make* a living and spending and self-indulgence as a *way* of living. (Flacks, 1971, p. 33)

These contradictions in contemporary values are vividly shown in a survey of 2,000 American families with children under 12. Ironically, the youthful protesters of the 1960s have given rise to a new kind of American parent. According to Daniel Yankelovich (1977), who conducted the poll, the new breed of parent is self-oriented, not ready to sacrifice for their children, questioning of all authority including their own, and scornful of traditional values such as marriage as an institution, religion, patriotism, and material success. They have a "laissez faire attitude that says both they and their children should do as they like" (Yankelovich, 1977, p. 1).

One surprising finding of this poll is the large proportion of parents—43 percent—who fit the new pattern. Another is the finding that the new kind of parents hesitate at imparting their new values directly to their children. They join the more traditional parents in stressing values such as "duty before pleasure," "hard work pays off," "my country right or wrong," "people in authority know best," and "sex without marriage is wrong." As Yankelovich observed, "The upshot of all this at the moment is confusion for both the children and the adults" (Yankelovich, 1977, p. 1).

SUMMARY

Social scientists have tended to look on socialization as a process by which new generations replace their elders; the social system itself remains the same, like a long-run play performed by a succession of different actors. Some social theorists have regarded socialization as a process of shaping and molding; others have emphasized "internalization" as the key: the child takes into his or her own personality the norms and values of the culture. In spite of their differences, however, the prevailing theories have tended to define the end result of socialization as conformity to social norms.

This view of socialization has been undermined by several developments. First there is the rise of a youthful opposition in the United States and the other industrially advanced countries. The wide-scale dissent of upper-middle-class youth could not be accounted for simply as failures of socialization.

The turbulence of the 1960s undermined theories of social stability and consensus as the normal state of social life. If society were not stable and consensual, however, then growing children would be exposed to social and cultural conflicts and inconsistencies. The idea that stable societies are maintained by stable families passing the cultural heritage from one generation to the next becomes increasingly untenable.

The demise of theories of socialization based on stability and consensus brought to the fore a number of concepts that had been anticipated earlier but were analyzed and developed more fully in the 1960s. These include the ideas: that generation gaps are inevitable in any culture; that the child is an active and autonomous agent in his or her own socialization; that the child is an experiencing self that interprets events in his or her own way; and that conflict may be useful for emotional and intellectual development.

Recent psychological research and theorizing suggest that there may be inherent limits to the manipulation and control of human behavior, even in young children.

Rather than being the passive objects of inner impulses or environmental conditions, people are active seekers and processors of information.

Ultimately, patterns of socialization reflect the technology, organization, and dynamics of society. The process should not be regarded as a constant, and new societies may produce socialization patterns for children and adults that are as yet unimagined.

CHAPTER *15*

The Future of the Family: Prospects and Policies

Perhaps some day we will cease to relate to families just as we no longer relate ourselves to clans, and instead be bound up with some new, as yet unnamed principle of human association. If and when this happens, we may also see a world of unisex, multisex, or nonsex.

Suzanne Keller
"Does the Family Have a Future?"

Long after the last reader of this volume has moldered into dust, the vast majority of human beings will continue to be born into a family unit with two spouses, male and female, with or without another child already there. They will live most of their lives entwined closely in family relations and will experience much of their anguish and happiness because of what takes place there.

William J. Goode
Principles of Sociology

We cannot begin to think about what the future of the family is likely to be unless we understand the present. And we cannot really make sense of the present unless we have some idea of what the past was like. So in this chapter, we will at times have to look backward in order to look ahead.

Looking at the same world, contemporary observers of family life see vastly different things. Whatever else the family is, Joseph Featherstone (1979) observed, it is "the great intellectual Rorschach blot" (p. 37). His remark was provoked by a comparison of the family in Mary Jo Bane's *Here to Stay* (1976), which he saw as a "generally sunny sketch" and also "the best sociological summary of the current state of the family," and Christopher Lasch's "gloomy jeremiad on the decay of the American family"— *Haven in a Heartless World* (1977).

The phrase "the breakdown of the family" has become entrenched in the national vocabulary. No social problem can be discussed without the ritual invocation of the phrase. As Gilbert Steiner (1981) has pointed out, many of the problems that cause concern about families have little to do with whether the family is currently "in trouble" or "here to stay" as an institution. Such problems as child neglect, domestic violence, teenage pregnancy, and so on have been on the public policy agenda for the past 3 decades at least. "What is new is the discovery that all these depressing problems can be gathered under the heading 'decline of the family'" (p. 205).

Although in recent years "the breakdown of the family" has come to be taken for granted as a fact, many scholars have argued that the reports of the death of the family are greatly exaggerated. The litany of statistics cited by the doomsayers—the rising divorce rate, the number of single-parent homes—seems convincing enough at first glance, until we remember the number of times in previous eras that obituaries were written for the family. As W. J. Goode (1976) pointed out, for generations people have been observing the breakdown of the family, yet it shows no signs of disappearing. Every major social change in American life generated worry about the future of the family.

For every recent trend that seems to show the family is declining, historians can point to evidence showing that things were no better, and even worse, in the past. Today's divorce rate, for example, seems to provide the most striking statistical indicator of family conflict and instability. As we have seen, however, during some periods in American history, the statistics of marriage and family life were more dismal than they are today.

There is also statistical evidence suggesting that the erosion of the family's childcare role is more myth than fact. Mary Jo Bane (1976), taking issue with those who believe that the decline of the extended family, the increasing number of working mothers, and the isolation and mobility of American life has undermined family life, wrote:

The extended family is not in fact declining; it never existed. Family disruption has not increased but has only changed its character. The proportion of children living with at least one parent has gone up, not down. The increased proportion of children living in single-parent families results mostly from mothers keeping their children instead of farming them out. Mothers have changed the location and character of their work, but there is no evidence that this harms children. Nor is there any evidence that contemporary families have fewer neighbors and friends to call on than in the past. (p. 70)

The debate goes on. In a 1982 article in the *New York Review of Books*, sociologist Andrew Hacker lamented that

all is not well with the family. Far fewer people are willing to accept the constraints and obligations required for family ties . . . now more people want more freedom than family life has allowed. . . . What we call a "strong family" requires a degree of dedication today's adults and children can no longer give. (p. 37)

In the same year, the Middletown researchers described in Chapter 1 (Caplow et al., 1982) reported that while almost everyone in Middletown was worried about the crisis in the family, Middletown families themselves seemed to be in surprisingly good condition. From the 1920s to the 1970s, they observed, the generation gap had grown smaller, marriages had become closer, and Middletowners had grown more religious and less mobile.

Other researchers have questioned the findings and optimistic conclusions of the Middletown researchers. It is true that they place emphasis on the dark side of family life, and the ironies and contradictions that beset even the best of families. The Middletown researchers focus on domestic routines, family rituals, and social harmony in the community more than they do on conflicts of tension and times of confrontation and crisis.

It is interesting to contrast their approach with another study of a midwestern town, *Hometown* by Peter Davis (1982). Davis is a journalist and television producer who, incidentally, produced the PBS television series on Middletown. Davis focuses on the passions and conflicts that divide the town of Hamilton, Ohio, rather than on the more routine aspects of life there. Even though the book begins on a seemingly happy note, with a wedding, Davis reveals that the members of the wedding are haunted by past failed relationships and lost dreams.

In the Middletown book, the authors would emphasize the wedding, not the lost dreams. Nor do we find much about the kinds of families that face the most serious problems today: the poor, the black underclass, single mothers struggling to both support and care for children. Each account may be incomplete without the other—like two different photographs of the same scene that, when viewed together through special lenses, give a three-dimensional view.

The Not-So-Good Old Days

If the emphasis is on the sunny rather than the dark side of family life, it is because the realities of family life in Middletown contrast so sharply with the gloomy images of the family as a dying institution. And because the historical realities of family life in small-town America in the 1920s contrast so sharply with nostalgic images of "the good old days."

In 1924 the Lynds had been impressed by the dreariness and lack of communication between husbands and wives in Middletown, especially in the working class. They did observe a few happy marriages among both working and middle classes, in which they were aware of "a constant undercurrent of sheer delight, of fresh, spontaneous interest between husband and wife" (Lynd & Lynd, 1929, p. 130). Such marriages stood out because of their rarity. Most couples seemed bound together by children, the daily business of living, and community values dis-

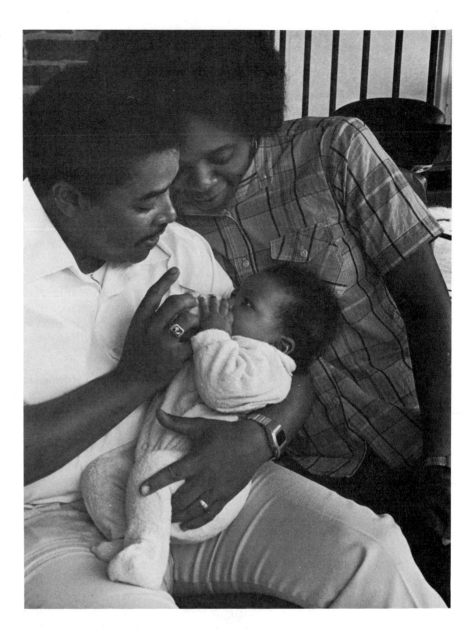

Despite the increasing diversity of life-styles, the nuclear family remains an important family form. [Dick Swartz/Office of Human Development Services]

couraging divorce. They shared a house, each other's bodies, and little else.

The division of sex roles was so sharp that husbands and wives seemed to live in different worlds. There was little information about birth control and there were ta-boos against talking about it. Many working-class women resented their husbands and tried to avoid sex. Prostitution flourished in Middletown during the 1920s. Another indication of the lack of communication between husbands and wives appeared in the answers to a 1924 questionnaire item. When a sample of wives was asked what gave them courage when they were thoroughly discouraged, not a single woman mentioned her husband.

The current Middletown researchers found that the quality of marriage had improved considerably in the course of 50 years. The kind of dismal, noncommunicative marriage the Lynds described as typical in the 1920s was now relatively rare. The division between the sexes was not so great, and the old stereotypes had lost their force, although men's and women's family behavior still showed much of the traditional division of labor. Contemporary wives were no longer afraid to discuss birth control with their husbands, or family finances, which had also been a taboo subject in the 1920s.

The youngest generation of Middletown couples seemed to be the most open and competent communicators. In joint interviews designed to encourage disagreement and the resolution of differences, these couples were the most willing to argue with one another and express hostility, but then come to agreement and end the argument with gestures of affection.

Not all the contemporary marriages were happy. Middletown's divorce rate is in line with the national average. By 1975 a majority of the adult population had experienced one or more divorces in their immediate family—their own or those of parents or siblings. But the high divorce rate is one reason marriages seem so happy in today's Middletown: most of the unhappy ones break up. Divorce has become a viable option for people caught in unhappy marriages.

People in Middletown are deeply ambivalent about divorce. They condemn divorce in the abstract, deplore it among people close to them, and think divorce is now "too easy." On the other hand, they think it good that divorce is no longer scandalous, and do not believe that couples should stay together in unhappy marriages. They would like marriage to be a life-time commitment, but they accept divorce as a normal part of life, and do not expect all marriages to last forever.

The findings about parents and children were also contrary to the image of family disintegration. Parents and children in 1977 spent *more* time together than parents and children in the 1920s. Although there was a generation gap between adolescents and their parents and today's Middletown parents thought it was getting wider, in fact the researchers found the gap was less than it had been in earlier generations.

In the original study, the Lynds had given a detailed description of disagreements between parents and their teenagers—teenagers who were now the grandparents of Middletown's current crop of adolescents. In 1937 they wrote:

It is our impression that no two generations of Americans have ever faced each other across as wide a gap in their customary attitudes and behavior as have American parents and children since the World War. And this disjunction, we believe, has been increased by the depression. (p. 168)

The point is not that the relationship between adolescents and their parents is always the same, but rather that in a changing society children grow up in a different world than their parents did and face very different futures. The Lynds had found a sharp change between 1890 and 1920s. During that era, the major transition from the traditional to the modern family had occurred—from child labor and the transmission of skills from parent to child to the era of prolonged education and work outside the home, from the hand-powered to the machine-powered home, from an isolated, closed community to one opened by the mass media to national and international events and influences.

Looking back on almost a century of change, the current Middletown researchers found that the changes that occurred between 1890 and the 1920s were far more extensive and significant than those that had taken place in the following 50 years. The real continuity was the continuity of change.

THE PAST AS PROLOGUE: AMERICA THE CHANGEABLE

In 1888 James Bryce observed in *American Commonwealth*: "America is change." Change has been the major constant in American life, and there have always been a great many Americans who found it disturbing. Reading contemporary material from almost any era of America's past one finds a sense of uncertainty about the family, a longing for a more stable past, and frequent calls for reform to bring the reality more in line with the image.

Social change often transforms family life. It disrupts traditional roles and breaks up the continuity of generations. No matter what the form of the change—whether immigration, revolution, or new technology—it calls for alterations in the family's way of doing things; parents can no longer use their experience as a guide for the young. In a country based on both immigration and a constantly expanding frontier, there has never been a time when an older generation could pass on to its children a society and landscape exactly like those it had known in its youth.

Concern about loss of parental control over children began early in our history. Although the seventeenth-century settlers did try to "strengthen" and "preserve" the home, as Oscar and Mary Handlin (1971) observe, "it was not an effective instrument of social control in the New World. The laws with monotonous regularity tried to shore up the

institution; the preambles which described the need were a desperate commentary on the failure" (pp. 15–16).

What many viewed with alarm as a loss of social control was a shift in authority relations within the family. The position of the young was strengthened in America. Young people approaching adulthood, unlike their counterparts in Europe, did not have to wait to inherit their parents' land, but could settle on the frontier. "It was a basic part of the New World experience," observes John Demos (1976), "that families should be continually divided, and that at least some elderly people should be left to fend for themselves" (p. 16). The ability to leave the family strengthened the hand of the young within the family as well; they could use the threat of leaving as a weapon in struggles with parents.

Indeed, a surprising degree of looseness in the bonds between parents and children could be found well into the nineteenth century. Many young people in their early teens left home to make their own way in the world. The courts often legitimized these realities by terminating the mutual rights and obligations between parents and the children who had left (Marks, 1975). By the end of the nineteenth century, however, children could no longer be absorbed in an increasingly industrialized economy—they would be "runaways," not young persons in search of work.

If the departure of the young for the frontier created one kind of family drama, another kind of drama was repeated through the whole course of American history in the lives of immigrant families: the young were often more competent in the new environment than their foreign-born parents. In making their way in the New World they would almost inevitably reject their parents' traditions, if not the parents themselves.

Besides the changes brought about by social and geographic mobility, the growth of industry and of cities changed the American way of life, as have accompanying changes in knowledge, education, communication, and government policy. Change in all areas of life is a characteristic of modernized societies, and as historians have recently been putting it, America was "born modern."

To take but one example of the continuity of change in America, consider a man interviewed by the Lynds (1929) as part of their 1924 study of Middletown. When seen by the Lynds, he was one of the town's oldest citizens. He had been a leading local physician in the 1890s, and his memory reached back to the 1840s. Within his lifetime, local transportation had changed from the horse to the railroad and the car, "grain . . . ceased to be cut . . . by thrusting the sickle into the ripened grain as in the days of Ruth, . . . getting a living and making a home . . . ceased to be conducted under one roof, education . . . ceased to be a luxury accessible only to the few" (p. 10).

His own field of medicine had been revolutionized by the X ray, anesthetics, and the germ theory of disease. He had experienced the discovery of electricity and the invention of the telephone, the telegraph, radio, and countless other innovations. This enormous change within a single lifetime was not unique to this man, to his part of the country, or even to his generation. Indeed, much of *Middletown* is a study of changes in progress at the time and their impact on people's lives.

In their first study of Middletown in the 1920s the Lynds found a community in the midst of a sexual revolution that was at least as far-reaching as the one we have known during the 1970s. In fact, as we mentioned earlier, many researchers regard today's changes as a continuation of those that began during the era of "flaming youth." The Lynds witnessed the automobile and the movies revolutionizing small-town society, changing leisure-time activities, and creating new tensions between parents and children. Courtship in the family parlor was replaced by dating, women's clothing styles were designed to emphasize sex, not conceal it, and sex was a dominant theme in the popular literature and the movies.

The automobile freed young people from parental supervision. It blasted its way through such previously unquestioned rules as: "rain or shine, I never miss a Sunday morning at church," "a high-school boy does not need much spending money," and "parents ought always to know where their children are." Many people perceived the home to be endangered when riding in cars replaced the traditional visit in the family parlor as the way unmarried young people got together. Even the Lynds were worried about the future of the family.

Indeed, the worries of many parents were justified. The movies revealed a sophisticated world of sexuality, which the parents of Middletown had tried to keep "out of sight and out of mind," and the automobile gave young people a place to act out their learning.

Another social invention of the period, along with dating, was petting. Petting as behavior was not really new, but its use and meaning changed in the 1920s. Petting included most of the sexual activities couples engage in before intercourse, but it stopped short of actual intercourse. In the 1920s petting appeared as a compromise between traditional morality and the new opportunities for sex, allowing girls to preserve their virginity at least in a technical sense. In the 1980s the line between going very far and going all the way may seem absurdly thin, but it had great symbolic value from the 1920s to the late 1960s (M. Hunt, 1974).

The Lynds also witnessed the coming of assembly-line production and its transformation of the industrial worker from master craftsman to just another part of the machine, replaceable and unskilled. It became possible for a boy of nineteen to turn out a greater amount of work than his 45-year-old father; indeed, it was not unusual for fathers to be laid off during slack times while sons continued to hold jobs. "Whether one is temperamentally well disposed toward social change or resistant to it," the Lynds (1929) concluded, "the fact remains that Middletown's life exhibits at almost every point either some change or some stress arising from failure to change" (p. 498).

The same might be said about almost any other place and time in American history. Despite the pervasiveness of change, Americans have been ambivalent about it. On the one hand, they have had faith in progress, in new technology, and in new ideas. On the other hand, they have often been unwilling to accept the social consequences of change.

For example, at the turn of the century, many people, including many scholars, worried about the fate of the family in industrial society. They feared that when the family "surrendered" its functions to other institutions—manufacturing to the factory, education to the state, health care to the hospital, and so on—it could only wither away.

These anxieties seemed to be confirmed by divorce rates. The divorce rate, as we mentioned in earlier chapters, has been rising relentlessly since the middle of the nineteenth century. There had been 7,000 divorces in 1860; 56,000 in 1900; and 100,000 in 1914. As historian Peter Filene (1975) observed, in an era when "many people believed that a kiss signified engagement and a marriage was forever, divorce was considered an ominous symptom not only of family disintegration, but of moral decay" (p. 37).

The other sign of crisis in the family was the decline in the birth rate. Not only had the overall birth rate declined, but the drop · was greatest among native, white, middle-class families; the birth rate among immigrant women was nearly twice as high. Theodore Roosevelt called it "race suicide."

During the early decades of the twentieth century, other political figures and social scientists, in numerous speeches, writings, and conferences, denounced the breakdown of family life. As late as 1929, a presidential commission reporting to President Hoover 1 month before the stock-market crash, was still sounding the alarm about the crisis in American family life and morality:

Birth control, race riots, stoppage of immigration, . . . governmental corruption, crime and racketeering, the sprawl of great cities, . . . international relations, urbanism, . . . shifting moral standards, . . . the status of womankind, labor, child training, mental hygiene, the future of democracy and capitalism, . . . all of these grave questions demand attention if we are not to drift into zones of danger. (quoted in Hodgson, 1977, p. 14)

The Woman Question

Throughout the nineteenth century, the issue of woman's proper role in the home and in society was a persistent theme. The movement for women's rights, although it had never won over a majority of women, had provoked widespread and often bitter debates. Between the 1930s and the late 1960s organized feminism and the arguments of women's rights virtually disappeared from the social landscape. One reason was that it had achieved one of its major goals: the right of women to vote. Another was the onset of the Great Depression. At any rate, during the period that Peter Filene has labeled "the long amnesia," the arguments on both sides about women's roles were forgotten. As a result, when the women's movement began again in the 1960s and 1970s, it took the country by surprise, as if nothing like it had ever happened before.

Fathers are becoming increasingly involved in the care of young children. [Gilles Peress/Magnum Photos, Inc.]

The feminist movement in America has followed a certain pattern. It began when large numbers of women came to be involved in other kinds of emancipation movements. In fighting against another kind of injustice, they came to understand the injustice in their own position. Thus the first wave of feminism was set in motion in the 1850s by women's participation in the movement to abolish slavery. The second wave took place in the Progressive era, the period of social and intellectual ferment in the period leading up to World War I. The most recent resurgence of the movement was set in motion in the 1960s by women who had taken part in the social movements of the 1960s:

the civil-rights, student-protest, and antiwar movements.

From the very beginning the feminist movement has been concerned with both public and private aspects of women's lives. The central issue at first was gaining women the basic right of citizenship, the right to vote. Looking back, it is surprising how long the struggle was and how bitterly it was fought. All during the nineteenth century, the vote was extended to more and more disenfranchised groups—the propertyless, aliens, and former slaves. But no state granted the vote to women until the 1890s, and it was not until 1920 that women's right to vote was added to the Constitution as the Nineteenth Amendment (Degler, 1980).

The major reason people opposed women's suffrage was that they thought it threatened the family. Underlying all the arguments against giving women the vote was the fear that the granting of legal recognition to women as individuals would force an alteration in the traditional family, create conflict between husband and wife, and violate the basic biological nature of the sexes. As one antisuffrage statement put it, "We believe that men are ordained to govern in all forceful and material matters, because they are men, physically and intellectually strong, virile, aggressive, while women, by the same decree of God and nature, are equally fitted to bear rule in a higher and more spiritual realm" (Degler, 1980, p. 351).

Along with getting the vote, the feminist movement from its earliest days was concerned with the suffocating restrictions that had been placed on women in the nineteenth century. The removal of production from home to factory resulted in a new ideology glorifying and sentimentalizing the home and the woman who maintained it. An enormous outpouring of writings on family life prescribed proper behavior for women and children. The new ideology saw the world as sharply divided between a chaotic, threatening public world and the home as a private retreat. The woman's role was to provide perfect peace, emotional comfort, and moral uplift to husband and children. The early feminists, observed John Demos (1976), "despised all this adoring rhetoric on woman-in-the-home; they sought to expose this myth of domesticity for what it really was" (p. 21).

Other important issues that concerned the women's movement of the time were the right to work, the right to a college education, and—trivial as it sounds—the reform of women's dress. In the 1850s, feminists provoked a furor by rebelling against the restrictive clothing styles that symbolized women's status. Instead of the conventional way of dressing with its tight corsets and hoop skirts, they proposed a "bloomer" outfit consisting of pantaloons and tunic.

The passage in 1920 of the Nineteenth Amendment, granting women the right to vote, marked both the highest achievement and the beginning of the end of the feminist movement that had begun a century earlier. A number of reasons have been advanced for the decline of feminism: having achieved its major goal, the movement lost its purpose; the conservative political climate of the 1920s did not support social-protest movements.

Perhaps a more fundamental reason was that feminism was undone by the sexual revolution that began in the 1920s. Most feminist women had been Victorians in their sexual attitudes, despite the presence of a few well-publicized advocates of free love in their midst. The majority had assumed that sex was unpleasant, that celibacy did not imply deprivation, and that being a spinster was an honorable role.

By the 1920s these attitudes had changed. A new kind of rebellious woman appeared in the figure of the flapper—girls with "bobbed hair and powdered noses, with fringed skirts just above the knees and hose rolled below, with a cigarette in one hand and a man in the other" (Filene, 1975, p. 134). Flaming youth and its smoking, drinking, jazz, and petting became a major topic of public and private debate; the new generation outraged both feminists and traditional Victorian conservatives. Although the majority of women did not model themselves on the flapper, the new sensuality she represented spread from the far-out fringe to the middle-class center.

As the Kinsey reports were later to document, the incidence of premarital intercourse among middle-class women did rise sharply during the 1920s. Thus the 1920s destroyed one of the basic hopes of nineteenth-century feminism and Victorianism in general: that there could be a single standard of morals compelling men to be as chaste as women. This proved unworkable. The 1920s showed, as William O'Neill (1969) observed, that "if men and women could not be equally chaste, they could at least be equally promiscuous" (p. 4).

The feminist movement that had been an important part of American public life died in the crash of 1929. Despite the movement's loss of momentum in the 1920s, the issues were still being debated. Magazines carried articles about equal marriage, cooperative nurseries, and combining work and career. The crash and the Great Depression that followed ended the debates about sexual equality and made the other "new woman," the flapper, irrelevant.

In the struggle for economic survival, the needs of the male breadwinner came first. One out of four men were unemployed, and millions more feared losing their jobs. Public opinion turned with a vengeance against women who seemed to be taking jobs away from men and their families. In fact, most women in the labor force, as today, were in female occupations, and the majority of male occupations hired few or no women.

Also, just as today, most women worked out of necessity to support their families with or without a husband in the home. Despite the economic realities of women's work, her place was still in the home.

World War II brought an even greater discrepancy between women's work and the ideology of women's roles. Women moved in record numbers into every level of factory work and business. Rosie the riveter became a popular image of women's contribution to the war effort, and almost 200,000 women put on uniforms and joined the WACs and the WAVEs. The federal government provided day-care centers for the children of working mothers, although there were never enough places to meet the need. All this changed behavior, however, did not result in changed attitudes; once again, women's work was defined as a temporary expedient.

It was not always defined that way by women themselves, however. Surveys taken at the time showed that a majority of women wanted to continue with the work they had done during the war (Degler, 1980). Neither the government nor labor nor the men returning to their old jobs, however, were eager to see women remain on the job. The government, fearful of another depression and worried about employment problems of returning veterans, ended its child-care programs and in other ways encouraged women to withdraw from the labor market. Social scientists, the mass media, and such groups as the Child Welfare League and the Family Service Association joined in the task of mobilizing women to return to the home.

Women did leave the niches they occupied in the male world, but many continued to keep a hand in the world of work, in the women's jobs they had traditionally occupied. Working or not, however, most women of childbearing age contributed to the baby boom. The traditional role as housekeeper and childbearer was joined to the newer ideas about sex. The long amnesia had finally snuffed out the memory of both feminist protests and the fear of family disintegration that had haunted earlier generations.

Back to the Present

In the 1980s, women are in transition, caught between competing models of female roles and demanding new social realities. The situation of American women is a complex mixture of constancy and change, significant improvement, and shocking deterioration.

The prevailing image of the modern American woman is summed up by the line from the cigarette commercial: "You've come a long way, baby." In many ways, women have come a long way. The nation's consciousness has been raised. Despite the failure of the Equal Rights Amendment, the principle of gender equality has won wide acceptance, not just in the United States but around the world. American society has changed dramatically from the "long amnesia" of the 1940s and 1950s when the position of women was rarely considered as a public issue and the "feminine mystique" dominated public and private life. It is truly a long way from Marilyn Monroe and *I Love Lucy* to Mary Tyler Moore and *Cagney and Lacey.*

In the past 2 decades, changes in women have transformed public and private life in America. The number of women working has doubled since 1960. The streets of American cities are crowded with career women with their briefcases, business suits, and running shoes. The pages of *Fortune* and other magazines run stories on glamorous women executives with six-figure incomes. Apart from these superwomen—some of whom are also "supermoms"—large numbers of women have entered the previously male worlds of law, medicine, and police work. The consciousness of the nation has been transformed. Even a highly conservative

president, opposed to most of the aims of the women's movement, appointed a woman to the Supreme Court.

Yet despite the progress women have made, inequality continues. The gap between men's and women's wages remains what it was in 1939; women make 64 cents to a man's dollar (U. S. Department of Commerce, Bureau of the Census, 1985). For many women, recent years have brought changes for the worse, a trend that has been labelled the "feminization of poverty" (Pearce, 1982). Two out of every three adults living in poverty are women. Rejecting the view that American women have never had it so good, economist Sylvia Hewlett argues that they are locked into a "no-win situation":

They have lost the guarantees and protection of the past—marriage has broken down as a long-term and reliable source of financial security—and at the same time they have failed to improve their earning power as workers in the labor market, for the wage gap between men and women is as wide and as stubborn as it ever was. Modern women are squeezed between the devil and the deep blue sea, and there are no lifeboats out there in the form of public policies designed to help these women combine their roles as mothers and as workers. (1986, pp. 49–50)

Nevertheless, despite the new problems women face, 71 percent of women in a 1986 Gallup poll said the women's movement had improved their lives (*Newsweek*, 1986). Further, a majority consider themselves feminists. Talk of a "postfeminist" era thus seems misguided. The worth and dignity of women are taken for granted, even if they are accorded only lip service. Many problems stem from the fact that the revolution has become stuck in the middle: women have achieved equality in principle but not in economic or social reality. The present imbalance is responsible for a great deal of strain now felt by women and the rest of the family; it is likely

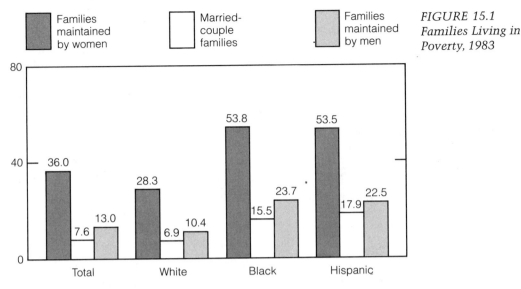

FIGURE 15.1
Families Living in
Poverty, 1983

Families
maintained
by women

Married-
couple
families

Families
maintained
by men

From U.S. Department of Labor, Office of the Secretary, Women's Bureau, *The United Nations Decade for Women, 1976–1985: Employment in The United States,* July 1985.

that these strains will make the family become an even more central issue on the public agenda.

THE FUTURE OF THE FAMILY

As Andrew Cherlin (1981c) has observed, every change in family life since the Depression has taken scholars by surprise. Worried about the falling birth rates of the 1930s, none foresaw the postwar baby boom. During the era of the baby boom and the feminine mystique, no one foresaw the steep rise in the divorce rate and the other recent changes.

Events of the past 2 decades should also worry anyone who would dare to predict social futures. Those who foresaw a continuation of the public turbulence of the 1960s turned out to have been as mistaken as those who thought of the tranquility of the 1950s as the permanent and natural state of an advanced technological society. Nobody foresaw

the economic crisis of the 1970s. Nevertheless, in the near future, it seems reasonable to expect some current trends to continue.

The major reason is that these trends—in life-styles, behavior, and attitudes—are not simply fads based on personal whims. Rather, they are reflections of and reactions to American society and its institutions—its economy, its occupational structure, its values.

Much of the turmoil in family life today stems from a series of social revolutions with direct impact on the family. These have been discussed at various times in this book:

1. The subtle revolution. There has been a steady increase of women in the paid labor force, and a majority now work outside the home, while the traditional full-time housewife represents a minority of women.

2. The sexual revolution. Despite the new mood of restraint, sexuality for most people is no longer bound to marriage and

childbearing. The ancient double standard, in which virginity was expected of the bride but not the groom, has been laid to rest.

3. The longevity revolution. For the first time in history, most people in our society will live to be old. Aside from the transformation of the individual life course, and the obvious economic issues raised by a graying society, the change has important implications for marriage, divorce, and kinship. Four and even five generations of many families are alive at the same time, resulting in relationships and family types never known before (Riley, 1986).

4. The divorce and remarriage revolution. The high divorce rates and changing divorce laws of recent years have transformed the meaning of marriage in our society. People still marry with the hope they will stay together permanently, and they suffer when marriages break up. But divorce and remarriage have become common events, part of the normal vicissitudes of life.

5. The transformation of parent–child relations. Parenthood has become voluntary; children have been transformed from economic assets to economically useless but emotionally "priceless" love objects. The result is an asymmetric relationship between generations (Caplow et al., 1982) in which parents make heavy financial and emotional investments in children who will become independent of parental authority at adolescence.

6. The psychological revolution. Over the past several decades in the United States and other advanced countries, people have come to define their satisfactions and problems in psychological, relational terms. This cultural change is most pronounced among the highly educated, but it has spread to all sectors of society. People increasingly tend to define themselves less in terms of external qualities such as social status, income, and the outward signs of success and more in terms of inner experience and the warmth of their relationships. Thus, the qualities people value in marriage have changed; traditional marital roles, such as being a good provider and a good homemaker, count for less and emotional sharing and expressiveness count for more.

7. The postindustrial revolution. Since the 1950s, the United States and other highly modernized societies have been experiencing a complex set of technological, economic, and social changes. The term *postindustrial* is most often used to describe the change, but there is also talk of "the information society" and "the service society." Alvin Toffler has popularized the notion of "the third wave" (1980), the first wave being agricultural society and the second industrial society.

As Raymond Williams (1983) observes, however, the shift is not so much away from industrial society as to new forms of industry. The computer is the symbol of the new era, just as the steam engine was the symbol of the first stage of industrialism. But satellite broadcasting, videocassette recorders, CAT scanners, and genetic engineering also symbolize some of the new technologies.

Despite the disagreement about how to label it, observers agree that a major societal transformation is in process and that it has profound implications for personal and family life. Some futurists have painted a rosy vision of postindustrial society, centered on the "electronic cottage." Homes would once again become workplaces and schools, healing the split between men and women, parents and children that came with the indus-

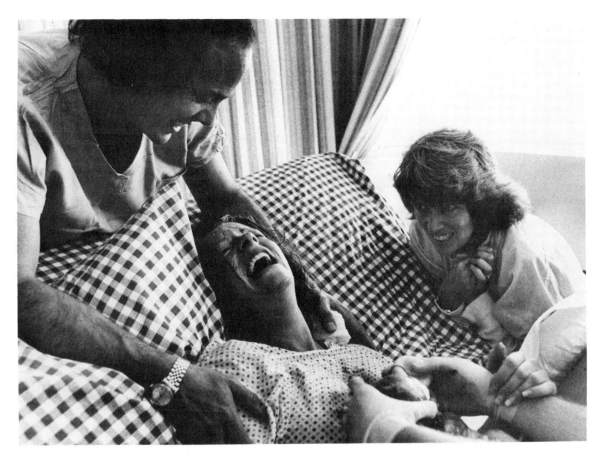

Many people have come to feel that birth should be treated as a major but normal family event, rather than as an illness or operation. Some hospitals are trying to create homelike settings for birth so that mothers and babies can have the best of both worlds. [Hella Hammid/Photo Researchers, Inc.]

trial revolution. The electronic cottage, in turn, could restore community life as people seek friendship and fellowship outside the home.

In the meantime, however, the blessings of the changes now in progress have been much more mixed. Any period of rapid social and economic change, as noted earlier, means changes, often disruptive, in family life. The closing down of whole industries and the economic decline of whole sections of the country are even more damaging to families and communities. Whatever the eventual outcome of the current changes, it is clear that we are in the midst of an unsettled transitional period between the old industrial age and the new one. The family will be in transition also.

Based on these trends, the following are some of the major changes in marriage and family arrangements in recent years that seem to be here to stay, at least for the immediate future. Two cautions are in order. First, the trends are not intended to describe everyone. They describe emerging tendencies, not necessarily statistical majorities. Second, in the long run things may look very different. If, as we have repeatedly seen in this book, the family is a product of its time and place, when and if social conditions change drastically the family will change also.

Increasing Symmetry in Sex Roles

Women are likely to spend a substantial portion of their lives doing paid work outside the home. As we have seen, this is a long-term trend that began decades before the women's movement of the 1960s. It is likely to continue for a variety of reasons. First of all, the evidence is that women like to work. They work because they have to, but would still want to be employed even if they did not need the money (*Newsweek*, 1986). Second, women are living longer and are having fewer children closer together than in the past. These changes in the life cycle mean that women will have more time to spend working even if they stay home until their children are married—an increasingly rare choice. If they stay home only until their children reach school age, they can work 80 percent of their adult years (Bane, 1976).

Finally, women are likely to work because of strong economic pressures. As we noted in an earlier chapter, with the likelihood of divorce approaching 50 percent, it is reckless indeed for any woman to assume she will be supported for life by a man. Further, most men's jobs do not pay enough to support a family at a standard of living most Americans would consider good. As more families come to have two earners, those with non-working wives will be at a competitive disadvantage. As Ross and Sawhill (1975) observe:

"It is difficult enough to keep up with the Joneses under normal circumstances, but when both of them are working, it becomes virtually impossible" (p. 171).

Sexual equality is likely to be pursued if not achieved in the next decade. The backlash to the women's movement—such as the so-called Moral Majority and the "total woman" movement—is not the most important obstacle. Women's continuing economic handicaps and the persisting difficulties of combining family life and a career pose more significant difficulties.

Most women continue to do traditional "women's work"—teaching, clerical work, sales, and so on—although increasing numbers are beginning to pursue male careers, such as law and medicine. Apart from the problems of job discrimination and segregation, most jobs are designed for men who can work long hours without attending to child care and other family needs.

As long as women continue to bear major responsibilities for child care and housework, they will have a hard time achieving economic equality. Many of the early feminists resolved this dilemma by remaining single, but later generations were unwilling to trade marriage, maternity, and domesticity for careers. Although the options to remain single, or childless even if married, are readily available, relatively few people will choose them as lifetime patterns. Sooner or later, however, business and government will have to adapt to the fact that most women work, including the mothers of young children. Even the current Secretary of Labor recognizes the problem and describes as "incredible" the lack of adaptation to the feminization of the work force (*Newsweek*, 1986).

In this time when public services of all kinds are being cut back, it is useful to remember that the United States has always been behind other advanced nations in providing supports and services to families. We have no national policy to provide child care to those who need it, no national policy of providing maternal and/or paternal leaves, or flexible working hours for parents. While the proportion of working parents has gone up, the United States has been spending less on child-care programs than it did a decade ago.

There are some profound ideological reasons why there is such resistance to child care and other family services—fears of undermining the traditional family, fears of creating dependence, or "federalizing" children—but Western European countries who share our political and cultural values do not have such ideological obstacles. They regard family services, such as child care, as public utilities—like education or electricity—that should be available to all as a matter of course.

Although working wives and mothers still carry the main burden of child care and housework, there is some evidence that men are beginning to contribute more. In a survey carried out in 1981, a large majority of both men and women—62 percent and 65 percent, respectively—said they preferred "an equal marriage of shared responsibility in which the husband and wife cooperate on work, homemaking, and child raising" to a traditional marriage in which the man is the provider and the woman the homemaker (*Public Opinion*, Aug./Sept. 1981, p. 26).

In a study of how husbands and wives allocate time to paid work and family work, Joseph Pleck (1985) came up with some complex and surprising findings. On the one hand, he found that employed wives still suffer from "role overload"—carrying the major burden of family work in addition to their jobs. Further, many men have little desire to do more housework. On the other hand, looking at trends over time, the evidence suggests that men's time in the family has increased over recent years. The increase is small, but it is accompanied by a decrease in the time women devote to family work. Thus, men and women are moving in the direction of convergence, even if it will be a long time before they reach equality. Moreover, men's involvement in the family has increased even when their wives do not work. Pleck concludes that there has been a value shift in our culture towards greater family involvement by men, especially in their role as fathers.

Continuing Fragility in Marriage

No one expects the divorce rate to go down in the near future. Several trends seem to be making marriages harder to sustain. First, the prevalence of divorce itself reduces the pressure on couples to remain in unsatisfactory marriages. Second, the new roles for women not only make women less dependent on marriage, but women's new demands and expectations, plus the changes in family living that come about when a woman works, also may contribute to marital tensions and conflicts.

Eventually, after the period of transition, as the new patterns become institutionalized and husbands and wives enter marriage with similar expectations, tensions arising out of women's new roles may subside. On the other hand, two-worker marriages may always be more complicated than the more traditional kind. And when men's and women's roles are more symmetrical, spouses can be less dependent on one another.

Another source of marital instability stems from the new set of demands placed on marriage by the ideal of finding personal growth and self-fulfillment in intimate relations. Most Americans, however, remain deeply committed to the ideal of permanent marriage, even though they accept divorce as a normal hazard of marriage today.

Ironically, by creating new expectations, this new romanticism in marriage creates new sources of discontent as well. In the past and in traditional families even today, married people seemed to require very little from each other except a bit of compatibility. Marriages were held together by practical necessity, moral commitment, and community opinion. Even today, in working-class and ethnic communities, husbands and wives often lead rather separate lives; the wife may be intensely involved with her kin, the husband with his work, friends, and relatives. When marriage becomes more intense and intimate, it also becomes more difficult. In traditional societies, as Philip Slater (1968) observed,

spouses are not asked to be lovers, friends, and mutual therapists. But it is increasingly true of our society that the marital bond is the closest, deepest, most important, and putatively most enduring relationship of one's life. Therefore it is increasingly likely to fall short of the demands on it and to be dissolved. (p. 90)

More Fluid Individual Life Cycles

People live much longer than they used to, and fertility patterns have changed so that women spend a smaller portion of their time bearing and raising children. These changes create new problems as well as new opportunities. Husbands and wives have many more years alone together; on the average, couples born in the 1930s will live two-thirds of their married lives without the responsibilities of young children at all in the home (Bane, 1976). It is little wonder then that the personal relationship between the spouses has taken on so much importance in recent years.

Not only has the marital life cycle changed, but the individual life cycle has also. The idea of development, once applicable only to growing children, is applied to adults, as new stages of adult life are "discovered." The link between a person's age and his or her family and work roles has been dramatically loosened in recent years. Instead of following an age-graded ladder of roles, people make changes in their commitments all through the life cycle. Schooling lasts longer, and is no longer confined to early youth. People leave school and continue their education at some later point. Older people move to new careers or drop out for a while to explore new possibilities of self-realization.

All of this change and possibility of change creates new sources of stress. People experience a heightened awareness of time's passing and a sense that all commitments are fluid and open to redefinition and renegotiation. The awareness that options remain open creates sensitivity to the inner self and to its wishes and potentials. This fluidity of self and its commitments contributes to the instability of marriage and other family ties.

Diversity of Life-Styles

For the first time in history it is becoming legitimate to choose from a number of family and life-style options: singleness, living together, single parenthood, custom-designed marriage contracts, and dual-career marriage, as well as traditional marriage. The diversity of family life today has been widely recognized in mainstream American life. The generally conservative magazine *Reader's Digest* announced a new magazine about families with the following advertisement:

Today's family is:

—Mom, Dad, and 2.4 kids
—A couple with 3 kids: his, hers, theirs
—A 26-year-old secretary and her adopted son
—A divorced woman and her stepdaughter
—A retired couple raising their grandson
—All of the above.

The trend toward living together—what used to be called "living in sin"—has emerged as the most persistent and widespread legacy of the sexual revolution of the 1960s. Between 1970 and 1980, according to the Census Bureau, the number of unmarried men and women living together in a single household had tripled—from 523,000 to 1,560,000 (U. S. Dept. of Commerce, 1981). Undoubtedly, these figures underestimate the actual number of cohabiting couples, but the very fact that the Census Bureau is counting them shows that this way of life has become an important part of the social scene.

The change occurred with remarkable speed. In 1968 a Barnard College sophomore became front-page news when she was almost expelled from college for living with a man. Today few colleges place restrictions on student living arrangements. And the people who live together are not only college students, but also adults of all ages, including senior citizens for whom marriage often means the loss of social-security benefits. Today, cohabitation has become a widely accepted living arrangement and has gained increasing legal recognition (Skolnick, 1981b).

The other major change in family lifestyle has come about because of the increase in divorce. New kinds of family ties are emerging as a result of divorce and remarriage. The formerly married, particularly those who have children, continue to maintain relationships as part of what Daniel Bell once described as "the ex-kinship" system, and various kinds of "blended" families and step-relatives are being produced in vast numbers by the high rate of remarriage.

In the third chapter of this book, I noted that anthropologists have had trouble coming up with a definition of the family that would fit all societies. In recent years the same problem has come to plague those who would define the family in our own society. One think-tank group concerned with the current state of the family defined a family as "any two or more biologically related or legally related people" (*McCall's*, 1977, p. 63). The limitations of this definition—it seems to exclude a long-term living-together couple from being a family, and it doesn't say whether biologically related people have to live together to be a family—only illustrate the complexities of family life today. Some people have suggested that we stop talking about *the* family and talk about families instead.

Deepening Commitments to Intimate Relationships

The concern with personal growth, awareness, and self-fulfillment is often viewed only as a threat to the family. According to its critics, the new narcissism leads to mindless self-indulgence and living for the moment. It encourages people to avoid commitments to love and friendship, and to treat all relationships as casual encounters, to be enjoyed while they last, and then replaced by later models.

As in all caricatures, there is some truth in this one. But by exaggerating the dark side of the new concern with personal development, it completely overlooks the positive aspects. It sees the possibility for viciousness and psychopathology in the new values, just as the advocates of self-realization exaggerate their morality and mental-health potential. Every personality style or ethical stance has its vices and weakness, but also its virtues.

Thus the new ideology of self-fulfillment can lead to a greater fragility in relationships, but it also encourages a deeper emotional involvement between people. The new awareness of self goes along with an increased sensitivity to others and a greater capacity for sharing and caring.

A "blended" or reconstituted family; such families are increasingly common as divorced parents remarry. [Helen Nestor]

Sexuality and Commitment

Surprisingly, recent changes in sexual behavior provide a good illustration of the two-sidedness of the new ideology. When we think about the liberalization of sexual behavior and attitudes in recent years, we are likely to think of casual or unconventional sex. Sexual liberation, however, may have had its greatest impact for most people within marriage itself. Thus in his survey of sexual behavior in the 1970s, Morton Hunt (1974) found that "a dramatic and historic change" has taken place in the practice of marital sex in America.

Hunt's data reveal a great increase in marital eroticism in recent years: married people of all ages are having sex relations more often, they are spending more time in both foreplay and intercourse, and they are engaging in formerly taboo activities, such as oral sex. Further, women appear to be equal, rather than reluctant, participants in this increased eroticism. Thus many more women report having regular orgasms than they did in the past, and only a tiny fraction complain that their husbands are too demanding sexually, in contrast with the large majority who previously made that complaint.

It would be a mistake, however, to think that the sexual revolution has brought nothing but uninhibited joy. Although for many people it has permitted the enjoyment of long-denied pleasures, for others it has brought new burdens and anxieties. Lillian Rubin (1976), for example, has written of the difficulties experienced by blue-collar couples as they try to explore the new sexual options. For wives caught between the new standards for sexual performance and previous training to be "good" (that is, asexual), orgasms and experimental sex can be just another chore in a life full of chores. Middle-class women, on the other hand, may worry about being neurotic if they fail to live up to their own "liberated" standards.

In spite of these complications, however, both men and women are becoming more concerned with their partner's gratification as well as their own. Lillian Rubin argued that if working-class men ever were the boorish, insensitive studs they have been portrayed to be in both literature and social science, they no longer are. In line with Hunt's findings, she noted that men at all educational levels have become more sensitive to women's sexual needs, with the most increase among high-school educated men.

The new sexuality also implies greater attention to the sexual and psychological needs of adults. It reflects the new definition of adulthood as a time of growth and change. As Ann Swidler (1981) observed, in American culture sex used to belong to the young,

and was played down, if not renounced, in adulthood. But "the new clinical approach to sexual fulfillment, which seems lacking in romance, may be seen as an attempt to keep sexuality gratifying for people who are not in the first blush of romantic involvement" (p. 33).

Some writers have worried that the sexual revolution and the increase in divorce will lead people to avoid permanent commitments and to treat all relationships as casual encounters. There is little evidence for this view. Despite the increased eroticism within marriage—and the marked increases in premarital sex—the new permissiveness does not seem to have blurred the difference between marital and extramarital sex.

Extramarital Sex

Extramarital sex, suggests James Coleman (1984), is the Bermuda Triangle of marriage: Many marriages have been reported lost there, but it remains a mystery. Researchers disagree about its extent; estimates of the number of marital partners who have extramarital sex range from 30 percent to 60 percent (Blumstein & Schwartz, 1983; Ramey, 1977). Traditionally, extramarital relationships were judged by a strict double standard: they have been tolerated in men, and condemned in women.

In recent years, researchers have found some evidence of convergence in men's and women's behavior as well as less of a double standard. Although Hunt's survey (1974) did find that extramarital intercourse is three times as frequent among wives aged 18–24 as it was in Kinsey's time, the percentage of women engaging in it is only 24 percent, still below the incidence for males in that age bracket. Furthermore, Hunt found little evidence of an increase in extramarital sex for men. Blumstein and Schwartz (1983) found that for couples married 10 years or more, the incidence of nonmonogamy was 30 percent for husbands and 22 percent for wives. Nevertheless, the vast majority of couples strongly held to monogamy as a moral ideal. Thus in spite of all the talk about open marriage, affairs, and "swinging," there has not been a sharp break with the traditional sexual norm of marriage. What has changed is the double standard: the pursuit of extramarital sex is no longer confined to husbands.

The majority of married people interviewed by Hunt expressed the feeling that extramarital sex could be damaging to the marriage and would be emotionally devastating to the spouse. They were also more aware, however, of their own extramarital desires and the various possibilities of permissive or nonexclusive marriage than people in previous generations. As a result of all the talk, Hunt observed, many people tend to overestimate the amount of the extramarital sex actually going on, and come to wonder if their own reluctance to engage in it is a sign of some neurotic hangup.

Other researchers have come to different conclusions about the possibilities for reconciling marital commitments with extramarital relations. A number of studies suggest that in many instances, such relationships can actually bolster the marriage. Cuber and Harroff (1965) found that many mature couples with good marriages could have outside relationships as a matter of principle. In general, couples following such nontraditional life-styles do not seem to lose sight of the difference between the primary, committed relationship with spouse and outside relationships.

Despite their differences as to the incidence and emotional implications of extramarital sex, these writers all agree that the marital relationship remains central to contemporary Americans, even to those engaging in sexually variant life-styles. In sum, then, the sexual liberation of recent years

does not appear to have led people to abandon marital commitments in favor of casual sex and a search for kicks.

A variety of other evidence supports the contention that commitments to family relationships are not being abandoned wholesale. Especially in middle-class families, for example, divorce does not mean the end of parental involvement in the lives of their children, although there is a sharp gender difference. The vast majority of divorced mothers have their children live with them, while most divorced fathers gradually become disengaged from their children's lives (Furstenberg, Peterson, Nord, & Zill, 1983; Weitzman, 1985). In the not-too-distant past, mothers who lost their husbands through death or divorce were likely to send their children to live with relatives or in orphanages (Bane, 1976). Another area in which increased choice seems to have led to increased commitment is childbearing. Despite the availability of contraceptives and legal abortion, many young women are choosing to give birth to, and keep, their "illegitimate" babies. They are less inclined than women in the past to give up a child they have borne to adoptive parents—an inclination that is often a mixed blessing, or worse, for the child if the mother herself is very young.

An even more striking development of recent years is unwed motherhood among professional women in their 30s and 40s. A small but increasing number of economically comfortable women, facing the waning of their fertility without a father for their future children, are going ahead and having them anyway, through both childbirth or adoption.

Other evidence for increased commitment may be found in the mass movement of women to change the way hospitals and the medical profession handle childbirth and the care of the newborn and the mother. Many women are pressing for birth practices that

Population in thousands

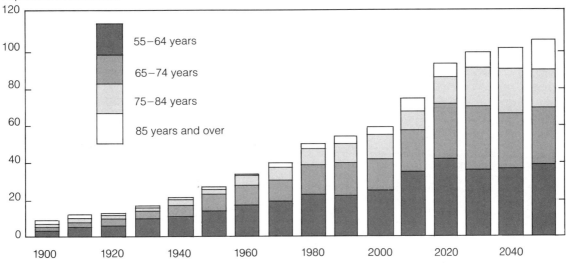

From U.S. Department of Commerce, Bureau of the Census, Current Population Reports, *America in Transition: An Aging Society*, Series P-23, No. 128, 1983.

FIGURE 15.2
Population 55 Years and Over, by Age: 1900–2050

are more child centered; they want fewer anesthetics and "nonviolent" handling of the child. In addition, many women also want encouragement for breast feeding and increased contact between mother and child during the postpartum period.

The Graying of the American Family

The United States has traditionally been a youth-oriented society, but the aging of the population in the next several decades seems destined to change that tradition. In 1979 the median age in the country passed 30 for the first time, after remaining constant for decades. By the year 2000 it is likely to be 35. Between now and the turn of the twenty-first century, the original baby-boom generation will enter middle age.

Family life has already been profoundly affected by the extension of life expectancy in the twentieth century. As we mentioned earlier, contrary to the myth of the extended family as the typical family of the past, it is only in this century that grandparents have become a regular part of children's growing up. The most novel result of the longer life expectancy among the aged is the emergence of the four-generation family. Many people became grandparents today while their own parents are still alive. Ethel Shanas (1980) found that over half of all persons 65 and over have great-grandchildren. Very little research has been done on these families, but the evidence so far suggests that the grandparent generation may experience considerable strain dealing with obligations not only to children and grandchildren, but to their own parents. One researcher has labeled this the "generation crunch" (Hagestad, 1979).

There are some widespread misunderstandings about the relationships between the elderly and their families. One is the myth of a Before and After in the history of

FIGURE 15.3
Life Expectancy at
Age 65: 1900–2050

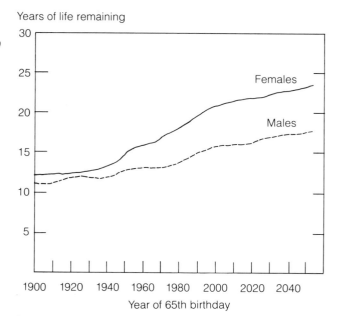

From U.S. Department of Commerce, Bureau of the Census, Current
Population Reports, *America in Transition: An Aging Society*, Series
P-23, No. 128, 1983.

FIGURE 15.4
Expectation of Life at
Birth, by Race and Sex:
1900–1980

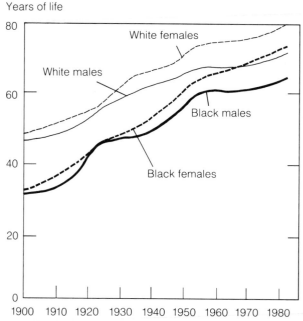

From U.S. Department of Commerce, Bureau of the Census, Current
Population Reports, *America in Transition: An Aging Society*, Series
P-23, No. 128, 1983.

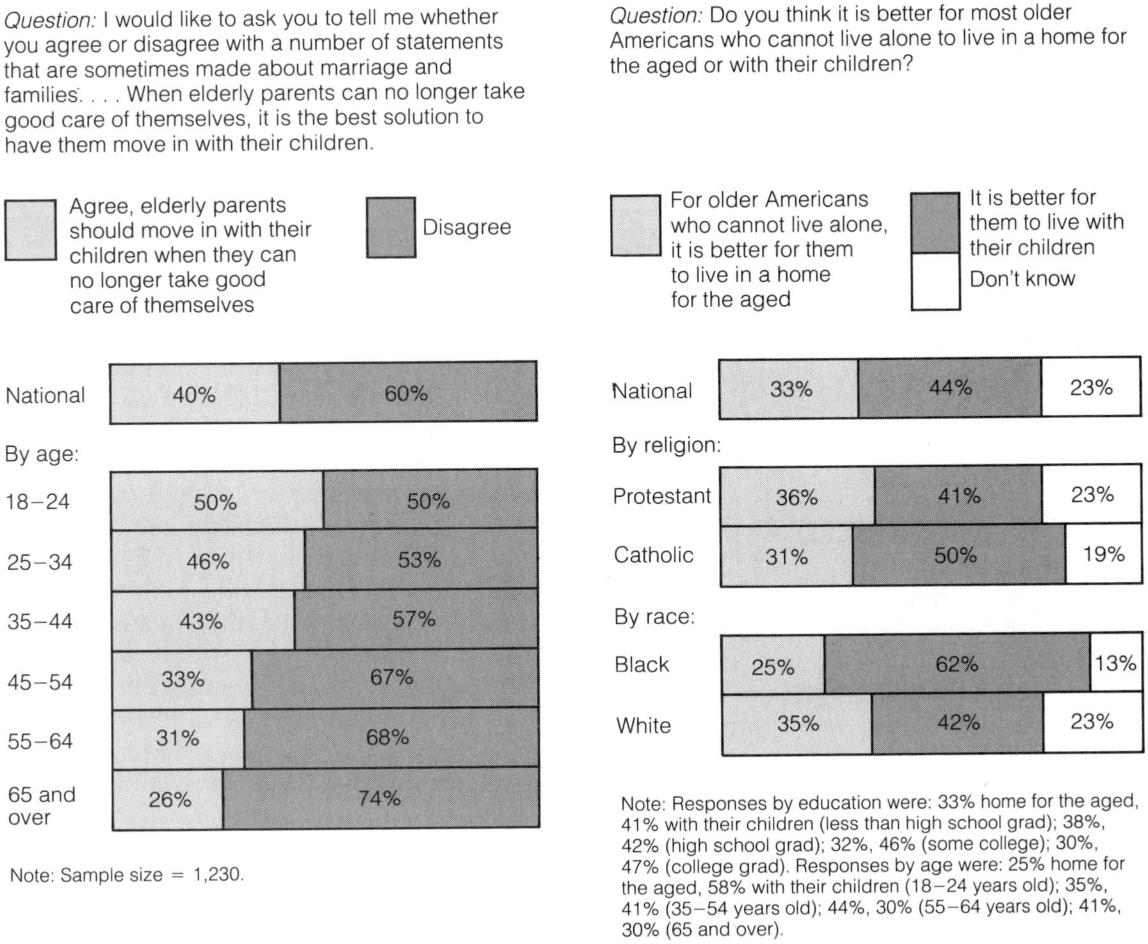

From *Public Opinion*, December/January 1986.

Question: I would like to ask you to tell me whether you agree or disagree with a number of statements that are sometimes made about marriage and families. . . . When elderly parents can no longer take good care of themselves, it is the best solution to have them move in with their children.

☐ Agree, elderly parents should move in with their children when they can no longer take good care of themselves

▨ Disagree

National	40%	60%

By age:

18–24	50%	50%
25–34	46%	53%
35–44	43%	57%
45–54	33%	67%
55–64	31%	68%
65 and over	26%	74%

Note: Sample size = 1,230.

Question: Do you think it is better for most older Americans who cannot live alone to live in a home for the aged or with their children?

☐ For older Americans who cannot live alone, it is better for them to live in a home for the aged

▨ It is better for them to live with their children

☐ Don't know

National	33%	44%	23%

By religion:

Protestant	36%	41%	23%
Catholic	31%	50%	19%

By race:

Black	25%	62%	13%
White	35%	42%	23%

Note: Responses by education were: 33% home for the aged, 41% with their children (less than high school grad); 38%, 42% (high school grad); 32%, 46% (some college); 30%, 47% (college grad). Responses by age were: 25% home for the aged, 58% with their children (18–24 years old); 35%, 41% (35–54 years old); 44%, 30% (55–64 years old); 41%, 30% (65 and over).

FIGURE 15.5
Elderly Parents: Family Ties

old age (P. Laslett, 1976). Before was a golden age when older people were loved, revered, and powerful, and lived full, happy lives in the bosom of the family. In the After, forces of change—modernization, industrialism, political revolution—displaced the aged from their former status. Historical research has cast serious doubt that there ever was a golden age of aging in Western societies (P. Laslett, 1976; Anderson, 1980), and recent anthropological work casts doubt on the no-

tion that the aged are uniformly well treated in today's traditional societies. Two factors seem to explain the treatment of the aged: the balance between the costs of their maintenance and the contributions they make, and the degree of control they exercise over valuable resources, such as land and money (Amoss & Harrell, 1981).

A corollary to the myth of the Before and After is what researchers in the field of aging and family relations term "the myth of abandonment": the notion that today's old people have been neglected and abandoned by their own children. There is no research evidence to support this notion that older people are isolated from their kin, although they rarely share a household with their children. Every study of the subject has found that the overwhelming majority of old people are in regular contact with their children, see them often, and turn to them in times of difficulty. Part of the reason for the myth of abandonment may be that today's older population came of age during the Depression, which affected their family formation patterns. About 27 percent of people born between 1901 and 1910 never married or had children (Bane, Rainwater, & Rein, 1980). About half of the population of elderly living in nursing homes have no living children. The other half, who do have children, have typically been placed there as a last resort, after their families have undergone severe personal, social, and economic stress to provide alternative care (Brody, 1978).

In a review of the literature on aging and the family, Andrew Cherlin (1981b) comes to the conclusion that relations between the elderly and their adult children are emotionally closer when neither generation is directly dependent on the other. In the historical past, the young were dependent on the old, and in the more recent past, before Social Security, the older generation was dependent on the younger. Thus, the conditions for emotionally satisfying relationships exist more today than they did in the past. The research clearly indicates that both generations prefer to be financially independent of one another, and "intimate, but at a distance." Alvin Rabushka and Bruce Jacobs (1980) summed it up this way:

Most elderly [people] want love and attention from their children, but not necessarily their

help with money, housing, or other charitable gestures. Indeed, some prefer to do things for their children and grandchildren, rather than be on the receiving end of things. (p. 47)

Politics and the Family

Since the election of Ronald Reagan, conservatives, especially the New Right, have dominated public discussion of family issues. Proposals for new policies seem irrelevant. Existing government services are being reduced or dismantled, and the rhetoric of "getting the government off our backs" seems to be carrying the day, except in such matters as abortion and sex education.

It is hard to say, however, how long the influence of the New Right will continue. Although the New Right groups are extremely well organized and effective politically, they do not represent the mainstream of American public opinion. Public opinion polls have consistently been reporting that while the family remains a preeminent value in the lives of most Americans, family norms have also been changing. As we saw earlier, a large majority favors a more egalitarian type of marriage, in which both spouses do outside work as well as family work inside the home, to the more traditional kind of marriage. Similarly, opinion polls reveal a majority of people are against the outlawing of abortion, and tolerant of such alternative lifestyles as single parenthood, premarital relationships, and so on (Clark & Martire, 1979).

The changes we have witnessed—the emergence of the two-worker family, rising divorce rates, lowering birth rates, and so on—are found in other highly modernized societies, including the Soviet Union. In the United States these represent long-term trends that were interrupted during the post–World War II period. The 1950s family pattern that many Americans idealize as

Physical and social environments have profound effects on individuals and families. [Charles Harbutt/Archive Pictures Inc.]

the normal, typical family was, as Andrew Cherlin (1981c) puts it, a "historical aberration." He goes on:

We can no more keep wives at home or slash the divorce rate than we can shut down our cities and send everyone back to the farm. (p. 10)

Sooner or later, it seems likely that policymakers and the public will be ready to address the realities of current family life: the economic hardships of single parent families, the inequities of divorce, the difficulties faced by working parents. Indeed, there are beginning to be signs that public at-

tention may be moving away from highly divisive symbolic issues like abortion toward these more practical matters. If so, the almost-forgotten 1980 White House Conference on the Family offers some grounds for hoping that some degree of consensus may be possible. Despite the battle between conservatives and liberals, the delegates did manage to agree on a set of recommendations on family-oriented workplace policies: flexible working hours, better leave provisions to enable parents to care for infants and sick children, more shared and part-time jobs. There was also consensus about the importance of economic well-being for family life; by large majorities the delegates called for public and private support for full employment.

However the political battle over families turns out in the near future, the family will remain a central issue for American public policy and a potent symbol of anxiety and hope.

THE DILEMMAS OF INTIMACY

There is good reason to believe that some dilemmas of the family may never be solved. As we have emphasized in previous chapters, there are some cogent reasons for believing that social life in general is never in a steady state of conflict-free equilibrium. There is always change, conflict, disagreement over means and ends, and gaps between ideal norm and the activities of everyday life. Rather than being the exception to the general state of social life, the family is best seen as a model of conflict, change, and ambivalence. Indeed, as Freud and Simmel have argued, the more intimate social relations are, the more likely they are to give rise to conflict. The norms that people bring to family life cannot be left out of the picture, however. The struggles between the sexes and the generations cannot be understood as power struggles pure and simple. Even the most extreme instances of physical violence between family members usually arise from a complex mixture of hate and love rather than cold, uncaring hostility. Indeed, as Freud has taught us, love and hate are closely linked—we do not love or hate, but love and hate.

David Schneider (1968) has noted that when kinship is stripped of its economic and political functions, it remains as a symbol of a particular quality of human relationship. Kinship ties symbolize love, or in sociological jargon, "enduring diffuse solidarity":

They symbolize those kinds of interpersonal relations which human beings as biological beings must have if they are to be born and grow up. They symbolize . . . a special kind of trust which is not contingent and which does not depend on reciprocity. (p. 116)

It is significant that no revolutionary movement, however opposed to conventional forms of the family, has dispensed with the symbolism of kinship as an ideal form of human relatedness. Revolutionaries may wish to abolish the family, but only in the name of brotherhood or sisterhood.

In a very real sense the family has stood for the best in human feeling between people. Marx, for example, took the natural relation between man and woman as the ideal model of human relatedness. Brotherhood, sisterhood, motherly love, fatherly concern—we still use family terms when we want to describe good relationships between people, even though these terms have often been abused. A most striking example of this paradox is found in David Cooper's *The Death of the Family* (1970). Cooper proclaimed "the end of the age of relatives" and declared that a family is a trap, an ideological conditioning device of an exploitive society, and a destroyer of all autonomous initiative and spontaneity. Yet he dedicated the book to his brother and sister-in-law and their children, who, during a mental and physical crisis that occurred while he was writing the book, treated him with "immense kindliness and concern . . . just as a true family should."

The need for intimacy and commitment seems to persist after the traditional assumptions about the family have lost their validity. Each model of the family has its own set of virtues, but also a set of liabilities. Thus it is currently popular to romanticize the traditional extended family, but when this form of the family prevails it is experienced by many of those in it—especially by women and young people—as highly oppressive. In looking at extended-family systems in other societies, Western observers tend to be highly impressed by their benefits and to overlook their strains. The extended family is seen as providing care for the aged, the sick, and the unemployed. It seems to provide security for all its members, ensuring that no one will have to face life's troubles alone. As anthropologist Robert LeVine (1965) noted, however, a growing body of anthropological evidence indicates that extended families confer not only benefits on family members, but considerable fear and hostility as well:

We hear of the frequency of suicide among the desperate young married women of traditional China seeking to escape their tyrannical mothers-in-law. From North India it is reported that young wives develop hysterical seizures when marital obligations force their return to residence with their husbands' families. Assassins are hired to help settle internal family quarrels in Egyptian villages. Fraternal tensions within domestic groups are extremely widespread from China to West Africa. . . . Accusations of witchcraft and sorcery—a common medium for the expression of hostility—tend to be concentrated among kinsmen in East African societies. Parricide is a marked phenomenon in at least one Uganda tribe. . . . The burden of such disparate fragments of data is that the very structures which entail kinship obligations beyond the nuclear family engender antagonisms which may ultimately be registered in homicide, suicide, litigation, and other forms of interpersonal conflict. (p. 189)

In general, then, it appears that the tensions that arise in family systems are not separate and distinct from their benefits. The intimate environments of the extended family provide security because of each member's life-long obligation to the other members, but these very commitments often give rise to intense conflicts that cannot be expressed in an open and direct way. If conflict does occur it often takes an explosive and disruptive form, such as witchcraft accusations.

In short, the search for some ideal form of the family may be futile. Every principle of family organization, whatever its benefits, entails certain costs. The anthropologist Paul Bohannan (1971) has stated the point in terms of household structure. Every family system, he noted, must solve the problem of how to organize households. There are a variety of problematic side effects. Bohannan examined three types of household structure: the household in which the father–son relationship provides the cornerstone, as in the Tiv; the mother–daughter-based household that prevailed among the Iroquois Indians in the eighteenth and early nineteenth centuries; and finally the American nuclear-family household, grounded on the husband–wife relationship.

We have already noted structural problems of the nuclear-family household: it places a great burden on the marital relationship and it is vulnerable to disruption through divorce and death. By contrast, among the Tiv, both parenting and spousing are highly diffuse activities, leading to a seemingly idyllic stability, continuity, and calm.

The security and continuity provided by the extended-family household, however, also entail certain costs not immediately evident in an idealized version of extended-family life. In Tiv and Iroquois societies, parent–child conflicts are not expressed rectly; instead they emerge in the form of preoccupations with witchcraft.

LAST WORDS

All fixed, fast-frozen relations, with their train of venerable prejudices and opinions, are swept away, all new-formed ones become antiquated before they can ossify. All that is solid melts into air, all that is holy is profaned, and men at last are forced to face with sober senses the real conditions of their lives and their relations with their fellow men. (Marx, quoted in Berman, 1982)

In these words Marx described the destruction, by the modernizing forces of capitalism, of the myths that had sustained traditional society. It is a description that few students of "modernization" would dispute.

What a chilling prospect—to face the real conditions of life and our relations with others with sober senses! The other side of liberation from the constraints of religion, family, hereditary status, and small community has been described as alienation. As Peter Berger (Berger et al., 1974) pointed out, the alienation or "homelessness" of modern social life is most clearly seen in the fate of religion in the shift from traditional to modern society. For most of human history, religion has provided an "overarching canopy" of symbols that explained the meaning of life, death, suffering, and one's place in the universe. Religious beliefs in traditional societies are experienced as certain and real because they are taken for granted by everyone. In modern societies religion is pluralized and certainty is lost. The individual encounters others who do not share his or her beliefs. Religion is no longer socially given, but becomes a matter of individual choice or preference. Although religion in modern society suffers from a "crisis of plausibility," the experiences that called for the comforts of religion are still with us, however—sickness, death, loss, and pain.

Much of the same sort of analysis can be applied to the family today. For most of human history, intimacy and community were the byproducts of kinship systems and economic necessity. Families were economic units, and they monopolized, albeit imperfectly, the supply of sexuality. The freedom to choose one's spouse was the first step in the liberation of personal life from these restraints. In our own day we are witnessing a further pluralization: one chooses not merely a spouse, but whether to marry, or have children, at all. Individual men and women are no longer dependent on the family for economic support or for the fulfillment of sexual needs. Only children, the very old, and the ill remain unable to fend for themselves. But the ability to live as isolated individuals does not mean that most people will *want* to live that way. Like death and sickness, the need for intimacy and enduring commitment has outlasted the social institutions that provided for them in the past.

The idea that the family today is in an unprecedented state of crisis or collapse is not well founded, however. Almost no generation has passed through history without some public concern about the state of the family or morality, and almost every period has shared a belief in some golden age of family harmony in the near or distant past. The one possible exception to this general trend is the period from the Great Depression of the 1930s through World War II to the postwar years of prosperity, suburban togetherness, and the feminine mystique—the period that historian Peter Filene called "The Long Amnesia."

To deny the existence of some past golden age, however, is not to deny the reality of the tensions and strains many people are experiencing in their family and private lives. We are living through a time of normative change when old rules and accustomed patterns of behavior no longer apply. There are more choices in family life than ever before: whether to marry, whether to have children, whether to have an abortion. The responsibilities of family members to one another now have to be negotiated. We have lost the ease, as well as the constraints, of traditional, taken-for-granted patterns of behavior.

All of this is happening at a time of great economic dislocation. In retrospect the 1960s were an incredibly optimistic period. Both Left and Right agreed that progress was possible, that problems could be solved, and that economic growth was limitless. No one foresaw that the late 1970s would dramatically reverse this optimism and the social and economic conditions that had sustained it. Instead of limitless abundance and an end to scarcity and poverty, we began to speak of lowered expectations, lifeboat ethics, and zero-sum economics. The unsolved problems of the 1960s—poverty and inequality— were joined in the 1970s and 1980s by unemployment and inflation, which cut across class lines. In the 1980s, the worst recession since the Great Depression was followed by an uneven economic recovery that bypassed millions (Serrin, 1986). For the first time in more than a generation, middle-class youth can no longer count on those basics of middle-class family life, a good job and a single-family home. For the first time in history, Americans have had to face the prospect that their children would not lead better lives than themselves.

These changing and uncertain times have had contradictory effects on family life. Surveys reveal that more than ever people are turning to family and private life as a source of meaning and self-worth. On the other hand, the very lacks in community and work life that encourage this turn toward domesticity put strains on close relationships. There is a powerful yearning for close and lasting bonds that often takes the paradoxical form of loneliness, emptiness, disconnectedness, and nostalgic longings for a happier past. Social trendwatcher John Naisbett (1984) talks about the "high tech/high touch" connection: the postindustrial trendy attachment to old-fashioned styles— "country" furniture, Amish quilts, ceiling fans, Victorian houses.

However appealing these relics of the past, there is no point in giving in to the lure of nostalgia. There is no golden age of the family to long for, nor even some past pattern of behavior and belief that would guarantee us harmony and stability if only we had the will to return to it. Family life is bound up with the social, economic, and ideological circumstances of particular times and places. We are no longer peasants, Puritans, pioneers, or even suburbanites circa 1955. We face conditions unknown to our ancestors, and we must find new ways to cope with them.

Ackerman, N. (1958). *The psychodynamics of family life: Diagnosis and treatment of family relationships.* New York: Basic Books.

Adams, B. N. (1968). *Kinship in an urban setting.* Chicago: Markham.

——— (1980). *The family: A sociological interpretation* (2nd ed.). Chicago: Rand McNally.

Allen, W. R. (1978). The search for applicable theories of black life. *Journal of Marriage and the Family, 40,* 117–130.

Almond, G. A., N. Chodorow, and R. H. Pearce (Eds.) (1982). *Progress and its discontents.* Berkeley: University of California Press.

Amoss, P., and S. Harrell (Eds.) (1981). *Other ways of growing old: Anthropological perspectives.* Stanford, Calif: Stanford University Press.

Anderson, C. H. (1975). *The political economy of social class.* New York: Prentice-Hall.

Anderson, M. (1980). The relevance of family history. In M. Anderson (Ed.), *Sociology of the family* (2nd ed.), pp. 33–63. New York: Penguin Books.

Anthony, E. J., and T. Benedek (1970). *Parenthood: Its psychology and psychopathology.* Boston: Little, Brown.

Ariès, P. (1962). [*Centuries of childhood: A social history of family life.*] (R. Baldick, Trans.) New York: Knopf.

——— (1981). [*The hour of our death.*] (H. Weaver, Trans.) New York: Knopf.

——— (1985). Love in married life. In P. Ariès and A. Bejin (Eds.), *Western sexuality: Practice and precept in past and present times,* pp. 130–139.

Arnesberg, C. M., and S. T. Kimball (1968). *Family and community in Ireland* (2nd ed.). Cambridge, Mass.: Harvard University Press.

Auletta, K. (1982). *The underclass.* New York: Random House.

Baldwin, A. (1967). *Theories of child development.* New York: Wiley.

Ball, D. W. (1972). The "family" as a sociological problem: Conceptualization of the taken-for-granted as prologue to social problems analysis. *Social Problems, 19*:3, 295–307.

Bandura, A. (1969). Social-learning theory and identificatory processes. In D. A. Goslin (Ed.), *Handbook of socialization theory and research,* pp. 213–262. Chicago: Rand McNally.

Bane, M. J. (1976). *Here to stay.* New York: Basic Books.

———, L. Rainwater, and M. Rein (1980). Filling the cracks. *The Wilson Quarterly,* Summer, pp. 136–146.

Barone, M. (1985). Welcome to the age of restraint. *San Francisco Chronicle: This World,* Sept. 29, p. 5.

Barry, H., I. L. Child, and M. K. Bacon (1959). Relations of child training to subsistence economy. *American Anthropology, 61,* 51–63.

Bart, P. (1970). Mother Portnoy's complaint. *Transaction, 8,* 69–74.

Bateson, G., D. D. Jackson, J. Haley, and J. Weakland (1956). Towards a theory of schizophrenia. *Behavioral Science, 1,* 251.

Beach, F. A. (1956). Characteristics of masculine "sex drive." In M. R. Jones (Ed.), *Nebraska symposium on motivation, 1956,* pp. 1–32. Lincoln: University of Nebraska Press.

Beauvoir, S. de (1968). Cited in A. Memmi, *Dominated man.* New York: Orion.

Becker, H. (1960). Normative reactions to normlessness. *American Sociological Review, 25,* 803–810.

Becker, W. C. (1964). Consequences of different kinds of parental discipline. In M. L. Hoffman and L. W. Hoffman (Eds.), *Review of child development research* (vol. 1), pp. 169–208. New York: Russell Sage.

Bell, D. (1976). *The cultural contradictions of capitalism.* New York: Basic Books.

Bellah, R. N., R. Madsen, W. M. Sullivan, A. Swidler, and S. M. Tipton (1985). *Habits of the heart: Individualism and commitment in American life.* Berkeley: University of California Press.

Bender, D. R. (1967). A refinement of the concept of household: Families, co-residence, and domestic functions. *American Anthropologist, 69:* 5, 493–504.

Benedict, R. (1938). Continuities and discontinuities in cultural conditioning. *Psychiatry, 1:* 2, 161–167.

Berger, B., B. M. Hackett, and R. M. Miller (1972). Childrearing practices in the communal family. Unpublished progress report to the National Institute of Mental Health.

Berger, P., B. Berger, and H. Kellner (1973). *The homeless mind: Modernization and consciousness.* New York: Random House.

Berkner, L. K. (1972). The stem family and the developmental cycle of the peasant household: An eighteenth-century Austrian example. *American Historical Review, 77,* 398–418.

Berman, M. (1982). *All that is solid melts into air.* New York: Simon & Schuster.

Bernard, J. (1964). The adjustments of married mates. In H. T. Christensen (Ed.), *The handbook of marriage and the family,* pp. 675–739. Chicago: Rand McNally.

———— (1972). Paper presented at symposium on sex role learning in children and adolescents. American Association for the Advancement of Science Meetings, Washington, D.C., December 1972. Reported in *Science, 177,* 1973, 1128.

———— (1975). Adolescence and the socialization for motherhood. In S. E. Dragastin and G. H. Elder (Eds.), *Adolescence in the life cycle,* pp. 227–252. New York: Wiley.

Berscheid, E. (1982). Attraction and emotion in interpersonal relations. In M. S. Clarke and S. T. Fiske (Eds.), *Affect and cognition.* Hillsdale, N.J.: Erlbaum.

———— (1985). Interpersonal attraction. In G. Lindzey & E. Aronsons (Eds.), *Handbook of social psychology. Vol. II: Special fields and applications,* pp. 413–484. New York: Random House.

———— , and J. Fei (1977). Romantic love and sexual jealousy. In G. Clanton and L. G. Smith (Eds.), *Jealousy.* New York: Prentice-Hall.

Billingsley, A. (1968). *Black families in white America.* Englewood Cliffs, N.J.: Prentice-Hall.

Birdwhistell, R. L. (1966). The American family: Some perspectives. *Psychiatry, 29,* 203–212.

Blake, J. (1979). Structural differentiation and the family: A quiet revolution. In A. H. Hawley (Ed.), *Societal growth: Processes and implications.* New York: Free Press/Macmillan.

Blau, P. M. (1964). *Exchange and power in social life.* New York: Wiley.

———— , and G. D. Duncan (1967). *The American occupational structure.* New York: Wiley.

Block, J. (1976). Debatable conclusions about sex differences. *Contemporary Psychology, 21:* 8, 517–522.

Blood, R. O., Jr., and D. M. Wolfe (1960). *Husbands and wives: The dynamics of married living.* New York: Free Press.

Blumberg, P. M., and P. W. Paul (1975). Continuities and discontinuities in upper class marriages. *Journal of Marriage and the Family, 37,* 63–78.

Blumberg, R. L., and R. F. Winch (1972). Societal complexity and familial complexity: Evidence for the curvilinear hypothesis. *American Journal of Sociology, 77:* 5, 898–920.

Blumstein, P., and P. Schwartz (1983). *American couples.* New York: William Morrow.

Bohannan, P. (1963). *Social anthropology.* New York: Holt, Rinehart & Winston.

———— (1971). Dyan dominance and household maintenance. In F. L. K. Hsu (Ed.), *Kinship and culture,* pp. 42–65. Chicago: Aldine.

Boone, P. (1958). *Twixt twelve and twenty.* Englewood Cliffs, N.J.: Prentice-Hall.

Bott, E. (1957). *Family and social network.* London: Tavistock.

Bottomore, T. B. (1966). *Classes in modern society.* New York: Pantheon.

Bouvier, L. F. (1980, April). America's baby boom generation: The fateful bulge. *Population Bulletin, 35(1),* 1–35.

Bower, T. G. R. (1977). *A primer of infant development.* San Francisco: W. H. Freeman.

Bowlby, J. (1969). *Attachment and loss.* New York: Basic Books.

Brehm, S. S. (1985). *Intimate relationships.* New York: Random House.

Brenner, H. (1976). *Estimating the social costs of national economic policy: Implications for mental and physical health and criminal aggression.* Joint Economic Committee, 92nd Congress, October 26, 1976. Washington, D.C.: U.S. Government Printing Office.

Brody, E. (1978). The aging of the family. *Annals of Political and Social Science, 438,* 13–27.

Bronfenbrenner, U. (1958). Socialization and social class through time and space. In E. E. Maccoby, T. M. Newcomb, and E. L. Hartley (Eds.), *Readings in so-*

cial psychology (3rd ed.), pp. 400–425. New York: Holt, Rinehart & Winston.

—— (1974). Developmental research, public policy, and the ecology of childhood. *Child Development, 45*:1, 1–5.

Brown, D. G., and D. B. Lynn (1966). Human sexual development: An outline of components and concepts. *Journal of Marriage and the Family, 28,* 155–162.

Brown, R. W. (1965). *Social psychology.* New York: Free Press.

Bruner, J. S. (1964). The course of cognitive growth. *American Psychologist, 19,* 1–15.

——, R. R. Olver, and P. M. Greenfield (1966). *Studies in cognitive growth.* New York: Wiley.

Burgess, E. W. (1926). The family as a unity of interacting personalities. *The Family, 7,* 3–9.

——, and H. J. Locke (1945). *The family: From institution to companionship.* New York: American Book.

——, and P. Wallin (1953). *Engagement and marriage.* Philadelphia: Lippincott.

——, ——, and G. D. Schultz (1953). *Courtship, engagement, and marriage.* Philadelphia: Lippincott.

Caldwell, B. M. (1964). The effects of infant care. In M. L. Hoffman and L. W. Hoffman (Eds.), *Review of child development research* (Vol. 1), pp. 9–87. New York: Russell Sage.

Campbell, A. (1975). The American way of mating: Marriage, si; children, maybe. *Psychology Today,* May.

——, P. E. Converse, and W. L. Rodgers (1976). *The quality of American life.* New York: Russell Sage.

Capellanus, A. (1968). The art of courtly love. Excerpted in W. M. Stephens (Ed.), *Reflections on marriage,* pp. 39–46. New York: Crowell.

Caplovitz, D. (1979). *Making ends meet* (Vol. 86). Beverly Hills, Calif.: Sage Library of Social Research.

Caplow, T., and H. M. Bahr, B. A. Chadwick, R. Hill, and M. H. Willemson (1982). *Middletown families: Fifty years of change and continuity.* Minneapolis: University of Minnesota Press.

Carver, R. (1982). *What we talk about when we talk about love.* New York: Vintage/Random House.

Carveth, D. L. (1977). The disembodied dialectic: A psychoanalytic critique of sociological relativism. *Theory and Society, 4,* 73–102.

Cernea, M. (1970). *Changing society and family change: The impact of the cooperative farm on the peasant family.* Stanford, Calif.: Center for Advanced Study in the Behavioral Sciences.

Chafe, W. H. (1986). *The unfinished journey: America since World War II.* New York: Oxford University Press.

Chamblis, W. J. (1973). *Sociological readings in the conflict perspective.* Menlo Park, Calif.: Addison-Wesley.

Cherlin, A. (1978). Remarriage as an incomplete institution. *American Journal of Sociology, 84,* 634–650.

—— (1981a). A sense of history: Recent research on aging and the family. In B. B. Hertz and K. Bond (Eds.), *Leading edges: Recent research on psychological aging.* Essays prepared for White House Conference on Aging, N.I.H. U.S. Department of Health and Human Services.

—— (1981b). How to help the family. *Newsweek,* July 27, p. 10.

—— (1981c). *Marriage, divorce, remarriage.* Cambridge, Mass.: Harvard University Press.

—— (1983). Family policy: The conservative challenge. *Journal of Family Issues, 4*(3), 427–438.

Chesler, P. (1971). Patient and patriarch: Women in psychotherapeutic relationships. In V. Gornick and B. K. Moran (Eds.), *Woman in sexist society,* pp. 362–392. New York: Basic Books.

Chodorow, N. (1978). *The reproduction of mothering.* Berkeley: University of California Press.

Christensen, H. (Ed.) (1964). *Handbook of marriage and the family.* Chicago: Rand McNally.

Chukovsky, K. (1966). [*From two to five.*] (M. Morton, Trans. and ed.) Berkeley: University of California Press.

Cipolla, C. M. (1969). *Literacy and development in the West.* Baltimore: Penguin.

Clark, R., and G. Martire (1979). Americans, still in a family way. *Public Opinion,* Oct./Nov., pp. 16–19.

Clausen, J. A. (1986). *The life course.* Englewood Cliffs, N.J.: Prentice-Hall.

——, and S. Clausen (1973). The effects of family size on parents and children. In J. Fawcett (Ed.), *Psychological perspectives on population.* New York: Basic Books.

Clemens, A. W., and L. J. Axelson (1985). The not-so-empty-nest: The return of the fledgling adult. *Family Relations, 34,* 259–264.

Cohen, R. (1971). Brittle marriage as a stable system: The Kanuri case. In P. Bohannan (Ed.), *Divorce and after,* pp. 205–239. Garden City, N.Y.: Doubleday/Anchor.

Cole, M., J. Gay, and J. Glick (1971). *The cultural context of learning and thinking.* New York: Basic Books.

Coleman, J. (1984). *Intimate relationships, marriage, and family.* Indianapolis: Bobbs-Merrill.

Coleman, J. S. (1972). The children have outgrown the schools. *Psychology Today, 5*:9, 72–75, 82.

Coles, R. (1971). *The middle Americans.* Boston: Little, Brown.

———, and G. Stokes, (1985). *Sex and the American teenager*. New York: Harper & Row, Colophon Books.

Collier, J., M. Z. Rosaldo, and S. Yanagisako (1982). Is there a family? New anthropological views. In B. Thorne and M. Yalom (Eds.), *Rethinking the family: Some feminist questions*. New York: Longman.

Collins, R. (1971). A conflict theory of sexual stratification. In H. P. Dreitzel (Ed.), *Family, marriage and the struggle of the sexes*, Recent Sociology, No. 4. New York: Macmillan.

Comfort, A. (1967). *The anxiety makers*. New York: Dell/Delta.

Conger, J. (1981). Freedom and commitment: Families, youth, and social change. *American Psychologist*, 36, 12, 1475–1484.

Cooley, C. H. (1902). *Human nature and the social order*. New York: Scribners.

Cooper, A. A. (1842). A speech before the House of Commons, U.K., June 7, 1842. Reprinted in *Speeches of the Earl of Shaftesbury, K. G.*, pp. 31–58. London: Chapman & Hall, 1968.

Cooper, D. G. (1970). *The death of the family*. New York: Vintage.

Coser, R. L. (1964). Authority and structural ambivalence in the middle-class family. In R. L. Coser (Ed.), *The family: Its structure and functions*, pp. 370–383. New York: St. Martin's.

Coughlan, R. (1956). Changing roles in modern marriage. *Life*, Dec. 24, pp. 109–111.

Coveney, P. (1967). *The image of childhood*. Baltimore: Penguin.

Cowan, C. P., P. A. Cowan, G. Heming, E. Garrett, W. S. Coysh, H. Curtis-Boles, and A. J. Boles, III (1985). Transitions to parenthood: His, hers, and theirs. *Journal of Family Issues*, 6(4), 451–481.

Cox, M. J. (1985). Transition to parenthood. *Journal of Family Issues*, 6(4), 395–408.

Cox Commission (1968). *Crisis at Columbia*. New York: Vintage.

Cozby, P. (1973). Self-disclosure: A literature review. *Psychological Bulletin*, 79, 73–91.

Crozier, B. (1935). Constitutionality of discrimination based on sex. *Boston University Law Review*, 723, 727–728. Cited in L. Kanowitz, *Women and the law*. Albuquerque: University of New Mexico Press, 1969.

Cuber, J. F., and P. Harroff (1965). *Sex and the significant Americans*. Baltimore: Penguin.

Dahrendorf, R. (1958). Out of Utopia: Toward a reorientation of sociological analysis. *American Journal of Sociology*, 64:2, 115–127.

D'Andrade, R. (1966). Sex differences and cultural institutions. In E. E. Maccoby (Ed.), *The development of sex differences*. Stanford, Calif.: Stanford University Press.

David, H. P., and W. P. Baldwin (1979). Childbearing and child development: Demographic and psychosocial trends. *American Psychologist*, 34, 866–871.

Davis, K. (1940). The sociology of parent-youth conflict. *American Sociological Review*, 5, 523–535.

——— (1972). The American family in relation to demographic change. In C. F. Westoff and R. Parke, Jr. (Eds.), *Commission on Population Growth and the American Future, Research Reports 1: Demographic and Social Aspects of Population Growth*. Washington, D.C., U.S. Government Printing Office, pp. 246–247.

Davis, K. E. (1985). Near and dear: Friendship and love compared. *Psychology Today*, Feb., pp. 22ff.

Davis, M. (1973). *Intimate relations*. New York: Free Press.

Davis, N. (1971). The reasons for misrule: Youth groups and charivari in sixteenth-century France. *Past and Present*, 50, 71–75.

Davis, P. (1982). *Hometown*. New York: Simon & Schuster.

Davison, G. C. (1973). Counter-control in behavior modification. In L. A. Hamerlynck, L. C. Handy, and E. J. Marsh (Eds.), *Behavior change: Methodology, concepts, and practice*. Champaign, Ill.: Research Press.

Degler, C. N. (1980). *At odds*. New York: Oxford University Press.

Demos, J. (1970). *A little commonwealth*. New York: Oxford University Press.

——— (1972). Demography and psychology in the historical study of family life: A personal report. In P. Laslett and R. Wall (Eds.), *Household and family in past time*, pp. 561–569. London: Cambridge University Press.

——— (1976). Myths and realities in the history of American family life. In H. Brunebaum and J. Christ (Eds.), *Contemporary marriage: Structure, dynamics, and therapy*. Boston: Little, Brown.

Denzin, N. (1970). The work of little children. *New Society*, July, pp. 13–15.

Deutsch, H. (1944/1945). *Psychology of women* (vols. 1 and 2). New York: Grune & Stratton.

Deutscher, I. (1967). The quality of postparental life. In B. L. Neugarten (Ed.), *Middle age and aging*, pp. 263–268. Chicago: University of Chicago Press.

Dickstein, M. (1977). *Gates of Eden*. New York: Basic Books.

Dinnerstein, D. (1976). *The mermaid and the minotaur*. New York: Harper & Row.

Donohue, K. C., and R. G. Ryder (1982). A methodological note on marital satisfaction and social variables. *Journal of Marriage and the Family, 44*(3), 743–747.

Douvan, E., and J. Adelson (1966). *The adolescent experience.* New York: Wiley.

Downs, A. (1977). The impact of housing policies on family life in the United States since World War II. *Daedalus,* Spring, pp. 163–180.

Duesenberry, J. (1976). *Income, savings, and the theory of consumer behavior.* Cambridge, Mass.: Harvard University Press.

Duncan, G. J. (1984). *Years of poverty, years of plenty.* Ann Arbor: University of Michigan, Survey Research Center, Institute for Social Research.

Dutton, D. G., and A. P. Aron (1974). Some evidence for heightened sexual attraction under conditions of high anxiety. *Journal of Personality and Social Psychology, 30,* 510–517.

Edmonds, V. H. (1967). Marriage conventionalization: Definition and measurement. *Journal of Marriage and the Family, 29,* 681–688.

———, G. Withers, and B. DiBatista (1972). Adjustment, conservatism, and marital conventionalization. *Journal of Marriage and the Family, 34:* 1, 96–104.

Ehrenreich, B. (1983). *The hearts of men: American dreams and the flight from commitment.* New York: Anchor/Doubleday.

Elder, G. H. (1981). History and the family: The discovery of complexity. *Journal of Marriage and the Family, 43,* 489–519.

Engel, M., G. Marsden, and S. Woodman (1967). Children who work and the concept of work style. *Psychiatry, 30,* 392–404.

———, ———, ——— (1968). Orientation to work in children. *American Journal of Orthopsychiatry, 38,* 137–143.

Erikson, E. H. (1963). *Childhood and society* (2nd ed.). New York: Norton.

——— (1964). Inner and outer space: Reflections on womanhood. *Daedalus,* Spring.

——— (1968). *Identity: Youth and crisis.* New York: Norton.

Etaugh, C. (1980). Effects of nonmaternal care on children: Research evidence and popular views. *American Psychologist, 35,* 309–319.

Fantz, R. L. (1963). Pattern vision in newborn infants. *Science, 140,* 296–297.

Farber, B. (1964). *Family organization and interaction.* San Francisco: Chandler.

——— (1966). *Kinship and family organization.* New York: Wiley.

Farnham, M., and F. Lundberg (1947). *Modern woman: The lost sex.* New York: Harper & Bros.

Featherstone, J. (1979). Family matters. *Harvard Educational Review, 49,* 20–52.

Feldman, H. (1962). Unpublished research. Cited in E. H. Pohlman, *Psychology of birth planning.* Cambridge, Mass.: Schenkman, 1969.

Ferguson, T., and J. Rogers (1986). The myth of America's turn to the right. *Atlantic Monthly, 257* (May), 43–53.

Ferrar, J. W. (1977). Marriages in urban communal households: Comparing the spiritual and the secular. In P. J. Stein, J. Richman, and N. Hannon (Eds.), *The family: Functions, conflicts, and symbols,* pp. 409–419. Reading, Mass.: Addison-Wesley.

Filene, P. (1975). *Him, her, self: Sex roles in modern America.* New York: Mentor.

Fincke, H. T. (1891). *Romantic love and personal beauty: Their development, causal relations, historic and national peculiarities.* London: Macmillan.

Flacks, R. (1971). *Youth and social change.* Chicago: Markham.

Flandrin, J. L. (1979). *Families in former times: Kinship, household, and sexuality.* Cambridge: Cambridge University Press.

——— (1985). Sex in married life in the early Middle Ages: The Church's teaching and behavioural reality. In P. Ariès and A. Bejin (Eds.), *Western sexuality: Practice and precept in past and present times,* pp. 114–129. Oxford: Basil Blackwell.

Flavell, J. H. (1985). *Cognitive development,* 2nd ed. Englewood Cliffs, N.J.: Prentice-Hall.

Fontana, V. J. (1964). *The maltreated child.* Springfield, Ill.: Charles C Thomas.

Ford, C. S., and F. A. Beach (1951). Human sexual behavior in perspective. In C. S. Ford and F. A. Beach, *Patterns of sexual behavior.* New York: Harper & Bros.

Fortes, M. (1949). *The web of kinship among the Tallensi.* London: Oxford University Press.

——— (1970). Social and psychological aspects of education in Taleland. In J. Middleton (Ed.), *From child to adult,* pp. 14–74. Garden City, N.Y.: Doubleday/Natural History Press.

Fowler, W. (1962). Cognitive learning in infancy and early childhood. *Psychological Bulletin, 59:*2, 116–152.

Fraiberg, S. (1959). *The magic years.* New York: Scribner.

Framo, J. L. (1965). Systematic research on family dynamics. In I. Boszormenyi-Nagy and J. L. Framo (Eds.), *Intensive family therapy,* pp. 407–462. New York: Harper & Row.

——— (1972). *Family interaction: A dialogue between*

family researchers and family therapists. New York: Springer.

Francke, L. (1972). Tot lots: Integrating children into everyday life. *Ms., 1:1,* 27ff.

Frazier, E. F. (1948). *The Negro family in the United States* (abridged ed.). New York: Dryden.

Freed, D. J., and H. H. Foster, Jr. (1969). Divorce American style. *The Annals, 383,* 75.

Freud, S. (1898). *The future of an illusion.* Garden City, N.Y.: Doubleday/Anchor, n.d.

Friedan, B. (1963). *The feminine mystique.* New York: Dell.

—— (1981). *The second stage.* New York: Summit Books, Simon & Schuster.

Fromm, E. (1970). *The crisis of psychoanalysis.* New York: Holt, Rinehart & Winston.

Furstenberg, F. F., Jr. (1981). Conjugal succession. Reentering marriage after divorce. Draft of chapter for volume 4 of P. B. Baltes and O. R. Brim, Jr. (Eds.), *Life-span development and behavior.* New York: Academic Press.

——, T. Hershberg, and J. Modell (1975). Family structure and ethnicity: The black family. *Journal of Interdisciplinary History, 6:2,* 211–233.

——, J. L Peterson, C. W. Nord, and N. Zill (1983). The life course of children of divorce: Marital disruption and parental contact. *American Sociological Review, 48,* 656–668.

Gagnon, J. H. (1965). Sexuality and sexual learning in the child. *Psychiatry, 28,* 212–228.

——, and B. Henderson (1975). *Human sexuality: An age of ambiguity,* MagaBack Social Issues Series, No. 1. Boston: Little, Brown/Educational Associates.

Gallup Poll (1985). 50 years of American opinion. *San Francisco Chronicle,* Oct. 21, p. 2.

Gambino, R. (1975). *Blood of my blood.* Garden City, N.Y.: Doubleday/Anchor.

Gardner, H. (1985). *The mind's new science.* Cambridge, Mass.: Harvard University Press.

Garmezy, N. (1976). Vulnerable and invulnerable children: Theory, research, and intervention. Document MS 1337, American Psychological Association. Washington, D.C.: Journal Supplement Abstract Service.

—— (1983). Stressors of childhood. In N. Garmezy and M. Rutter (Eds.), *Stress, coping, and development in children,* pp. 43–84. New York: McGraw-Hill.

Gartner, A., and F. Reissman (1974). *The service society and the consumer vanguard.* New York: Harper & Row.

Gecas, V. (1979). *Beyond the "looking-glass self": Toward an efficacy-based model of self esteem.* Paper presented at the annual meeting of the American Sociological Association, Boston.

Geertz, C. (1965). The impact of the concept of culture on the concept of man. In J. R. Platt (Ed.), *New views of the nature of man,* pp. 93–118. Chicago: University of Chicago Press.

Gelles, R. J. (1972). *The violent home.* Beverly Hills, Calif.: Sage.

—— (1976). Demythologizing child abuse. *The Family Coordinator, 25:2,* 135–141.

Gibson, G. (1972). Kin family network: Overheralded structure in past conceptualizations of family functioning. *Journal of Marriage and the Family, 34:1,* 13–23.

Gil, D. G. (1970). *Violence against children.* Cambridge, Mass.: Harvard University Press.

—— (1971). Violence against children. *Journal of Marriage and the Family, 33:4,* 637–648.

Gilder, G. (1981). *Wealth and poverty.* New York: Basic Books.

Gilford, R., and V. Bengston (1979). Measuring marital satisfaction in three generations: Positive and negative dimensions. *Journal of Marriage and the Family, 41,* 387–398.

Gilman, C. P. (1903). *The home: Its work and influence.* New York: McClure Phillips.

Gilmartin, B. G. (1977). Swinging: Who gets involved and how? In R. W. Libby and R. N. Whitehurst (Eds.), *Marriage and alternatives: Exploring intimate relationships,* pp. 161–185. Glenview, Ill.: Scott Foresman.

Ginott, H. (1972). Being a parent. King Features Syndicate. Reprinted in *San Francisco Sunday Examiner and Chronicle,* Feb. 11, 1973.

Ginzberg, E. (1976). Quoted in Women at work. *Newsweek,* Dec. 6, p. 69.

Glendon, M. A. (1977). *State, law and family.* Amsterdam-New York-Oxford: North Holland.

Glick, P. (1980). Remarriage: Some recent changes and variations. *Journal of Family Issues, 4,* 455–479.

Goethals, G. W., R. W. Steele, and G. J. Broude (1976). Theories and research on marriage: A review and some new directions. In H. Grunebaum and J. Christ (Eds.), *Contemporary marriage: Structure, dynamics, and therapy.* Boston: Little, Brown.

Goffman, E. (1959). *The presentation of self in everyday life.* Garden City, N.Y.: Doubleday.

Goode, W. H. (1982). *The family* (2nd ed.). Englewood Cliffs, N.J.: Prentice-Hall.

Goode, W. J. (1959). The theoretical importance of love. *American Sociological Review, 24,*.38–47.

—— (1963). *World revolution and family patterns.* New York: Free Press.

—— (1964). *The family.* Englewood Cliffs, N.J.: Prentice-Hall.

—— (1971). Force and violence in the family. *Journal of Marriage and the Family, 33:4,* 624–636.

—— (1976). Family disorganization. In R. K. Merton and R. Nisbet (Eds.), *Contemporary social problems,* pp. 511–554. New York: Harcourt Brace Jovanovich.

—— (1977). *Principles of sociology.* New York: McGraw-Hill.

Goodman, E. (1985). *Keeping in touch.* New York: Summit Books.

Goodman, M. E. (1970). *The culture of childhood: Child's eye views of society and culture.* New York: Teachers College Press.

Goody, J., and I. Watt (1962). The consequences of literacy. *Comparative studies in society and history, 5,* 304–326, 332–345.

Gordon, S. (1974). *Lonely in America.* New York: Simon & Schuster.

Gough, K. E. (1971). The origin of the family. *Journal of Marriage and the Family, 33:4,* 760–771.

Gove, W. R., and J. R. Tudor (1973). Adult sex roles and mental illness. *American Journal of Sociology, 78:4,* 812–835.

Grazia, S. de (1962). *Of time, work, and leisure.* New York: Twentieth Century Fund.

Green, A. W. (1946). The middle-class male child and neurosis. *American Sociological Review, 11,* 31–41.

Greenfield, J. (1982). Looking for a happy marriage on TV? Forget it! *TV Guide,* April 17.

Greenfield, S. J. (1969). Love and marriage in modern America: A functional analysis. *Sociological Quarterly, 6,* 361–377.

Greven, P. (1970). *Four generations: Population, land and family in Andover, Massachusetts.* Ithaca, N.Y.: Cornell University Press.

Grinder, R. E. (1969). The concept of adolescence in the genetic psychology of G. Stanley Hall. *Child Development, 40,* 355–370.

Griswold, R. L. (1982). *Family and divorce in California, 1850–1950: Victorian illusions and everyday realities.* Albany: State University of New York Press.

Grubb, N. (1977). Families and the economy. Unpublished manuscript. Childhood and Government Project, University of California Law School, Berkeley.

——, and M. Lazerson (1982). *Broken promises.* New York: Basic Books.

Gurin, G., S. Veroff, and S. Feld (1960). *Americans view their mental health.* New York: Basic Books.

Gutman, H. G. (1976). *The black family in slavery and freedom, 1750–1925.* New York: Pantheon.

Haan, N. (1971). Moral redefinition in families as the critical aspect of the generational gap. *Youth and Society, 2:3,* 259–283.

Hacker, A. (1982). Farewell to the family? *New York Review of Books,* March 18.

Hagen, E. E. (1962). *On the theory of social change: How economic growth begins.* Homewood, Ill.: Dorsey Press.

Hagestad, G. O. (1979). Problems and promises in the social psychology of intergenerational relations. Paper presented at the Workshop on Stability and Change in the Family. National Academy of Sciences, Annapolis, Md.

Hale, N. (1971). *Freud and the Americans.* New York: Oxford University Press.

Haley, J. (1963). *Strategies of psychotherapy.* New York: Grune & Stratton.

Hall, G. (1904). *Adolescence: Its psychology and its relations to physiology, anthropology, sociology, sex, crime, religion, and education.* New York: Appleton.

Hallowell, A. I. (1955). *Culture and experience.* Philadelphia: University of Pennsylvania Press.

Hamilton, R. F. (1972). *Class and politics in the United States.* New York: Wiley.

Handbook on women workers (1976). U.S. Department of Labor, Bulletin No. 297, Chap. 1, Sect. 8.

Handel, G. (Ed.). (1967). *The psychosocial interior of the family.* Chicago: Aldine.

Handlin, O., and M. F. Handlin (1971). *Facing life: Youth and the family in American history.* Boston: Little, Brown.

Hardy, K. R. (1964). An appetitional theory of sexual motivation. *Psychological Review, 71,* 19–26.

Hareven T. (1971). The history of the family as an interdisciplinary field. *Journal of Interdisciplinary History, 2:2,* 399–414.

—— (1978). The dynamics of kin in an industrial society. In *Turning points: Historical and sociological essays on the family.* Supplement to *American Journal of Sociology, 84.* Chicago: University of Chicago Press.

—— (1982). American families in transition: Historical perspectives on change. In F. Walsh (Ed.), *Normal family processes,* pp. 446–466. New York: Guilford Press.

Harlow, H. F. (1962). The heterosexual affectional system in monkeys. *American Psychologist, 17,* 1–9.

————, M. K. Harlow, and E. W. Hansen (1963). The maternal affectional system in infant monkeys. In H. J. Rheingold (Ed.), *Maternal behavior in mammals.* New York: Wiley.

Harrington, M. (1981). *The next America: The decline and rise of the United States.* New York: Holt, Rinehart & Winston.

Harris, M. (1968). *The rise of anthropological theory: A history of theories of culture.* New York: Crowell.

Harris, P. L. (1983). Infant cognition. In P. H. Mussen (Ed.), *Handbook of child psychology, Vol. II: Infancy and developmental psychobiology* (4th ed.), New York: Wiley.

Hauser, P. M. (1970). Comments in *The Millbank Memorial Fund Quarterly, 48:*2, Part 2.

Hawks, J. (1963). *Prehistory.* In *History of mankind: Cultural and scientific development* (Vol. 1, Part 1). New York: New American Library/Mentor.

Heer, F. (1962). *The medieval world.* New York: Praeger.

Heller, P. G., G. M. Quesada, D. L. Harvey, and L. G. Warner (1981). Familism in rural and urban America: Critique and reformulation of a construct. *Rural Sociology, 46*(3), 446–464.

Henry, J. (1963). *Culture against man.* New York: Random House.

———— (1971). *Pathways to madness.* New York: Random House.

Hershberger, R. (1948). *Adam's rib.* New York: Pellegrini Cudahy.

Herzog, E., and C. E. Sudia (1973). Children in fatherless families. In B. M. Caldwell and H. N. Ricciuti (Eds.), *Child development research* (Vol. 3), pp. 141–221. Chicago: University of Chicago Press.

Hess, R. D., and G. Handel (1959). *Family worlds.* Chicago: University of Chicago Press.

Hewlett, S. A. (1986). *A lesser life: the myth of women's liberation in America.* New York: William Morrow.

Hill, M. S. (1985). The facts: Changing structures of the American family. *Texas Humanist, 7*(4), 11.

Hill, R. (1949). *Families under stress.* New York: Harper.

Hilliker, G. (1976). Quoted in W. F. Mondale, Government policy, stress, and the family. *Journal of Home Economics, 68:*5, 14.

Himes, N. E. (1963). *Medical history of contraception.* New York: Gamut.

Hochschild, A. R. (1975). Attending to, codifying, and managing feelings: Sex differences in love. Paper presented at a meeting of the American Sociological Association, San Francisco.

Hodgson, F. (1977). *America in our time.* Garden City, N.Y.: Doubleday.

Hoffman, L. W. (1972). Early childhood experiences and women's achievement motives. *Journal of Social Issues, 28:*2, 129–155.

Hooker, E. (1965). Gender identity in male homosexuals. In J. Money (ed.), *Sex research.* New York: Holt, Rinehart & Winston.

Houseknecht, S. K. (1982). Voluntary childlessness: Toward a theoretical integration. *Journal of Family Issues, 3*(4), 459–471.

Howe, L. K. (1977). *The pink collar ghetto.* New York: Putnam.

Hrdy, S. B. (1979). Infanticide among primates: A review, classification and examination of the implications for the reproductive strategies of females. *Ethology and Sociobiology, 1,* 13–40.

———— (1981). *The woman that never evolved.* Cambridge, Mass.: Harvard University Press.

Hsu, F. L. K. (Ed.) (1961). *Psychological anthropology.* Homewood, Ill.: Dorsey.

Hulbert, A. (1984). Children as parents. *The New Republic,* Sept. 10, pp. 15–23.

Hunt, M. (1959). The natural history of love. New York: Knopf.

———— (1969). *The affair.* New York: World.

———— (1974). *Sexual behavior in the 1970's.* Chicago: Playboy Press.

Institute of Life Insurance (1974). *Youth.* New York: Institute of Life Insurance.

Isaac, G. (1978). The foodsharing behavior of protohuman hominids. *Scientific American,* April.

Isaacs, S. (1966). *Intellectual growth in young children.* New York: Schocken.

Jackman, M. R., and R. W. Jackman (1982). *Class awareness in the United States.* Berkeley: University of California Press.

James, W. (1890). *Principles of psychology,* (Vol. 1). New York: Holt. (Reprinted 1983, Cambridge, Mass.: Harvard University Press.)

Jeffrey, K. (1972). The family as utopian retreat from the city: The nineteenth-century contribution. In S. TeSelle (Ed.), *The family, communes, and utopian societies,* pp. 21–41. New York: Harper & Row.

Kagan, J. (1977). The child in the family. *Daedalus,* Spring, pp. 33–56.

———— (1981). *The second year: The emergence of self-awareness.* Cambridge, Mass.: Harvard University Press.

Kaledin, E. (1984). *Mothers and more: American women in the 1950s.* Boston: Twayne.

Kanowitz, L. (1969). *Women and the law: The unfinished revolution.* Albuquerque: University of New Mexico Press.

Karl, F. R. (1983). *American fictions 1940–1980: A*

comprehensive history and critical evaluation. New York: Harper & Row.

Katz, J. M. (1977). Discrepancy, arousal, and labeling: Towards a psychosocial theory of emotion. Unpublished manuscript, York University, Toronto.

Keniston, K. (1971a). Psychosocial development and historical change. *Journal of Interdisciplinary History*, 2:2, 329–345.

—— (1971b). *Youth and dissent: The rise of a new opposition.* New York: Harcourt Brace Jovanovich/Harvest.

Kephart, W. M. (1967). Some correlates of romantic love. *Journal of Marriage and the Family*, 29, 470–479.

Kerr, M. (1958). *The people of Ship Street.* London: Routledge.

Kessen, W. (1965). *The child.* New York: Wiley.

—— (1966). "Stage" and "structure" in the study of children. In W. Kessen and C. Kuhlman (Eds.), *Thought in the young child*, pp. 65–82. *Monograph of the Society for Research in Child Development*, No. 83.

Kett, J. (1971). Adolescence and youth in nineteenth-century America. *Journal of Interdisciplinary History*, 2, 283, 294–295.

Kilpatrick, W. (1975). *Identity and intimacy.* New York: Dell/Delta.

Kinsey, A. C., W. B. Pomeroy and C. E. Martin (1948). *Sexual behavior in the human male.* Philadelphia: W. B. Saunders.

——, ——, —— (1953). *Sexual behavior in the human female.* Philadelphia: W. B. Saunders.

Kirschner, B. F., and L. R. Walum (1978). Two-location families: Married singles. *Alternative Lifestyles*, 1:4, 513–525.

Klein, M., and J. Riviere (1964). *Love, hate and reparation.* New York: Norton.

Klemesrud, J. (1971). Happy duos aren't so rare. *San Francisco Chronicle*, June 8. (Copyright 1971, N.Y. Times News Service.)

Knapp, J. J., and R. N. Whitehurst (1977). Sexually open marriage and relationships. In R. W. Libby and R. N. Whitehurst (Eds.), *Marriage and alternatives: Exploring intimate relationships.* Glenview, Ill.: Scott Foresman.

Kohlberg, L. (1966). A cognitive-developmental analysis of children's sex-role concepts and attitudes. In E. E. Maccoby (Ed.), *The development of sex differences*, p. 91. Stanford, Calif.: Stanford University Press.

Kohn, M. L. (1959). Social class and parental values. *American Journal of Sociology*, 64, 337–351.

—— (1963). Social class and parent-child relationships. *American Journal of Sociology*, 68, 471–480.

Komarovsky, M. (1962). *Blue-collar marriage.* New York: Vintage.

König, R. (1974). Sociological introduction. In A. Chloros (Ed.), *International encyclopedia of comparative law* (Vol. IV). Rockville, Md.: International Publishing Co., Sijthoff and Noordhoff.

Krauskopf, J. M. (1977). Partnership marriage: Legal reforms needed. In J. R. Chapman and M. Gates (Eds.), *Women into wives.* Beverly Hills, Calif.: Sage Publications.

Ladd, E. C. (1981). Opinion roundup: Americans at work. *Public Opinion*, August/September.

Laing, R. D. (1969). *Self and others.* Baltimore: Penguin.

—— (1971). *The politics of the family.* New York: Random House.

Lambert, H. H. (1978). Biology and equality: A perspective on sex differences. *Signs*, 4:1, 97–117.

Lambert, W. W. (1971). Cross-cultural backgrounds to personality development and the socialization of aggression: Findings from the six-culture study. In W. W. Lambert and R. Weisbrod (Eds.), *Comparative perspectives on social psychology*, p. 433. Boston: Little, Brown.

Lancaster, J. B. (1985). Primates. In A. S. Rossi (Ed.), *Gender and the life course*, pp. 3–27. New York: Aldine.

Landis, P. H. (1955). *Making the most of your marriage.* Englewood Cliffs, N.J.: Prentice-Hall.

Langer, J. (1969). *Theories of development.* New York: Holt, Rinehart & Winston.

Langer, W. L. (1972). Checks on population growth: 1750–1850. *Scientific American*, 226, 93–100.

Lasch, C. (1965). *The new radicalism in America.* New York: Vintage.

—— (1977). *Haven in a heartless world. The family besieged.* New York: Basic Books.

—— (1978). *The culture of narcissism.* New York: Norton.

Laslett, B. (1973). The family as a public and private institution: A historical perspective. Unpublished manuscript, University of Southern California, Los Angeles, September 1972. Published in shortened version in *Journal of Marriage and the Family*, August 1973, 35, 480–494.

Laslett, P. (1965). *The world we have lost: England before the industrial age.* New York: Scribners.

—— (1972). Introduction: The history of the family. In P. Laslett and R. Wall (Eds.), *Household and family in past time*, pp. 29–34. Cambridge: Cambridge University Press.

—— (1976). Societal development and aging. In R. H. Binstock and E. Shanas (Eds.), *Handbook of aging and the social sciences*, pp. 87–116. New York: Van Nostrand.

——— (1977). Characteristics of the Western family considered over time. *Journal of Family History*, 2:2, 89–115.

———, and R. Wall (Eds.) (1972). *Household and family in past time*. Cambridge: Cambridge University Press.

Lawton, A. (in press). *Adultery* (manuscript in preparation).

Lee, R., and I. DeVore (1968). *Man the hunter*. Chicago: Aldine.

LeMasters, E. E. (1970). *Parents in modern America: A sociological analysis*. Homewood, Ill.: Dorsey.

Lennard, H. L., and A. Bernstein (1969). *Patterns in human interaction*. San Francisco: Jossey-Bass.

Lenski, G. (1966). *Power and privilege: A theory of social stratification*. New York: McGraw-Hill.

Le Play, F. (1866). *La réforme sociale*. In C. C. Zimmerman and M. E. Frampton (Eds. and trans.), *Family and society*. Princeton, N.J.: Van Nostrand, 1935.

Levenson, E. A. (1972). *The fallacy of understanding: An inquiry into the changing structure of psychoanalysis*. New York: Basic Books.

LeVine, R. A. (1965). Intergenerational tensions and extended family structures in Africa. In E. Shanas and G. F. Streib (Eds.), *Social structure and the family: Generational relations*, pp. 188–204. Englewood Cliffs, N.J.: Prentice-Hall.

——— (1970). Cross-cultural study in child psychology. In P. H. Mussen (Ed.), *Carmichael's manual of child psychology* (3rd ed.), pp. 559–612. New York: Wiley.

LeVine, S. (1966). Sex differences in the brain. *Scientific American*, *214*, 84–90.

———, and R. A. LeVine (1985). Age, gender, and the demographic transition: The life course in agrarian societies. In A. S. Rossi (Ed.), *Gender and the life course*, pp. 29–42. New York: Aldine.

Levinger, G. (1974). A three-level view on attraction: Toward an understanding of pair relatedness. In T. L. Huston (Ed.), *Foundations of interpersonal attraction*. New York: Academic Press.

Levison, A. (1974). *The working-class majority*. Baltimore: Penguin.

Levitan, S. A., and R. S. Belous (1981). *What's happening to the American family?* Baltimore: Johns Hopkins Press.

Levy, M. J., Jr. (1955). Some questions about Parsons' treatment of the incest problem. *British Journal of Sociology*, 6, 277–285.

——— (1965). Aspects of the analysis of family structure. In A. J. Coale, L. A. Fallers, M. J. Levy, Jr., D. Schneider, and S. S. Tomkins, *Aspects of the analysis of family structure*. Princeton, N.J.: Princeton University Press.

Levy, R. I. (1973). *Tahitians: Mind and experience in the society islands*. Chicago: University of Chicago Press.

Lewis, C. S. (1958). *The allegory of love: A study in medieval tradition*. New York: Oxford University Press.

Lewis, H. (1968). Child rearing among low-income families. In L. Ferman, J. Kornbluth, and A. Haber (Eds.), *Poverty in America* (rev. ed.). Ann Arbor: University of Michigan Press.

Lewis, M., and J. Brooks-Gunn (1979). *Social cognition and the acquisition of self*. New York: Plenum Press.

Lewis, M., and M. Weinraub (1979). Origins of early sex-role development. *Sex Roles*, 5, 135–154.

Lewis, O. (1951). *Life in a Mexican village: Tepoztlan restudied*. Urbana: University of Illinois Press.

——— (1965). The folk-urban ideal types. In P. M. Hauser and L. F. Schnore (Eds.), *The study of urbanization*, pp. 491–503. New York: Wiley.

Lidz, T. (1963). *The family and human adaptation*. New York: International Universities Press.

Liebow, E. (1967). *Talley's Corner*. Boston: Little, Brown.

Light, D., Jr., and S. Keller (1982). *Sociology* (3rd ed.). New York: Knopf.

Linton, R. (1936). *The study of man*. New York: Appleton-Century-Crofts.

Lipset, S. M. (1967). *Student politics*. New York: Basic Books.

———, and R. B. Dobson (1972). The intellectual as critic and rebel: With special reference to the United States and the Soviet Union. *Daedalus*, Summer, pp. 137–198.

Litwak, E. (1965). Extended kin relations in an industrial democratic society. In E. Shanas and G. F. Streib (Eds.), *Social structure and the family: Generational relations*. Englewood Cliffs, N.J.: Prentice-Hall.

Loevinger, J. (1959). Patterns of child rearing as theories of learning. *Journal of Abnormal and Social Psychology*, 59, 148–150.

Luker, K. (1984). *Abortion and the politics of motherhood*. Berkeley: University of California Press.

Luria, A. (1961). *The role of speech in the regulation of normal and abnormal behavior*. New York: Pergamon.

Lynd, R. S., and H. M. Lynd (1929). *Middletown: A study in American culture*. New York: Harcourt, Brace.

———, ——— (1937). *Middletown in transition: A*

study in cultural conflicts. New York: Harcourt, Brace.

McCall, M. M. (1966). Courtship as social exchange: Some historical comparisons. In B. Farber (ed.), *Kinship and family organization,* pp. 190–200. New York: Wiley.

McCall's Magazine (1977). How the government affects family life. May, p. 63.

McCloskey, M. E., and S. Glucksberg (1978). Natural categories: Well-defined or fuzzy sets. *Memory and Cognition, 6,* 462–472.

Maccoby, E. E. (1980). *Social development.* New York: Harcourt Brace Jovanovich.

——, and C. N. Jacklin (1974). *The psychology of sex differences.* Stanford, Calif.: Stanford University Press.

McCullers, J. C. (1969). G. Stanley Hall's conception of mental development and some indications of its influence on developmental psychology. *American Psychologist, 24,* 1109.

Macfarlane, J. W. (1964). Perspectives on personality consistency and change from the guidance study. *Vita Humana, 7,* 115–126.

McKinley, D. G. (1964). *Social class and family life.* Glencoe, Ill.: Free Press.

Macklin, E. D. (1980). Non-traditional family forms: A decade of research. *Journal of Marriage and the Family, 42:4,* 175–192.

Mahler, M. S. (1968). *On human symbiosis and the vicissitudes of individuation.* New York: International Universities Press.

Malinowski, B. (1913). *The family among the Australian aborigines.* London: University of London Press.

—— (1930). Parenthood, the basis of the social order. In V. F. Calverton and F. D. Schmalhousen (Eds.), *The new generation,* pp. 113–168. New York: Macauley.

—— (1944). *A scientific theory of culture.* Chapel Hill: University of North Carolina Press.

Mander, J. (1969). In defense of the 50's. *Commentary,* Sept.

Marks, F. R. (1975). Detours on the road to maturity: A view of the legal conception of growing up and letting go. *Law and Contemporary Problems, 39:3,* 78–92.

Marks, S. (1986). *Three corners: Exploring marriage and the self.* Lexington, Mass.: D. C. Heath.

Martin, M. K., and B. Voorhies (1975). *Female of the species.* New York: Columbia University Press.

Martin, W. (1985). Two cheers for the moral majority. *The Texas Humanist, 7(4),* 12–14.

Marx, K. (1950). *Selected works.* Moscow: Foreign Languages.

Masnick, G., and M. J. Bane (1980). *The nation's families 1960–1990.* Boston: Auburn House.

Masters, W. H., and V. Johnson (1970). *Human sexual inadequacy.* Boston: Little, Brown.

May, E. (1980). *Great expectations: Marriage and divorce in post-Victorian America.* Chicago: University of Chicago Press.

Mead, G. H. (1965). *Mind, self, and society.* Chicago: University of Chicago Press. (Originally published 1934.)

Mead, M. (1928). *Coming of age in Samoa.* New York: Morrow.

—— (1935). *Sex and temperament in three primitive societies.* New York: Morrow.

—— (1947). The implications of culture change for personality development. *American Journal of Orthopsychiatry, 17,* 633ff.

—— (1949). *Male and female.* New York: Morrow.

—— (1957). Changing patterns of parent-child relations in an urban culture. *International Journal of Psychoanalysis, 38,* 369–378.

—— (1971). Future family. *Transaction,* Sept., pp. 50–59.

Memmi, A. (1968). *Dominated man.* New York: Orion.

Merton, R. (1976) *Sociological ambivalence and other essays.* New York: Free Press.

Middlebrook, P. (1974). *Social psychology and modern life.* New York: Knopf.

Miller, D. T., and M. Nowak (1977). *The fifties: The way we really were.* Garden City, N.Y.: Doubleday.

Miller, M. (1954). Quoted in D. T. Miller and M. Nowak, *The fifties: The way we really were.* Garden City, N.Y.: Doubleday.

Miller, S. M., and F. R. Reissman (1964). The working class subculture: A new view. In A. B. Shostak and W. Bomberg (Eds.), *Blue collar world: Studies of the American worker.* Englewood Cliffs, N.J.: Prentice-Hall.

Mills, C. W. (1959). *The sociological imagination.* New York: Oxford University Press.

Minturn, L., and W. W. Lambert (1964). *Mothers of six cultures: Antecedents of child rearing.* New York: Wiley.

Mitchell, G. D. (1969). Paternalistic behavior in primates. *Psychological Bulletin, 71,* 399–417.

Mitchell, J. (1974). *Psychoanalysis and feminism.* New York: Random House/Vintage.

Modell, J., F. Furstenberg, and T. Herschberg (1973). Social change and transitions to adulthood in historical perspective. *Journal of Marriage and the Family, 35,* 467–478.

———, ———, and D. Strong (1978). The timing of marriage in the transition to adulthood. Continuity and change 1860–1975. In J. Demos and S. S. Boocock (Eds.), *Turning points*, Supplement, *American Journal of Sociology, 84,* 5120–5150.

Money, J. (1961). Sex hormones and other variables in human eroticism. In W. C. Young (Ed.), *Sex and internal secretions.* Baltimore: Williams & Wilkins.

———, and A. Ehrhardt (1972). *Man and woman, boy and girl.* Baltimore: Johns Hopkins University Press.

Moore, B. M., Jr. (1958). Thoughts on the future of the family. In *Political power and social theory.* Cambridge, Mass.: Harvard University Press.

Morgan, D. H. J. (1975). *Social theory and the family.* London, Boston: Routledge and Kegan Paul.

Morison, E. (1958). *The American style.* New York: Harper & Bros.

Morris, J. (1974). *Conundrum.* New York: Harcourt Brace Jovanovich.

Moynihan, D. P. (1965). *The Negro family: The case for national action.* Cambridge, Mass.: M.I.T. Press.

Murdock, G. P. (1949). *Social structure.* New York: Macmillan.

Murillo, N. (1971). The Mexican American family. In N. Wagner and M. Haug (Eds.), *Chicanos: Social and psychological perspectives,* pp. 97–108. St. Louis: Mosby.

Murphy, R. F. (1971). *The dialectics of social life: Alarms and excursions in anthropological theory.* New York: Basic Books.

Murstein, B. I. (1971). A theory of marital choice and its applicability to marriage adjustment. In B. I. Murstein (Ed.), *Theories of attraction and love,* pp. 100–151. New York: Springer.

Muuss, R. E. (1962). *Theories of adolescence.* New York: Random House.

Myrdal, J. (1968). *Confessions of a disloyal European.* New York: Pantheon.

Naisbett, J. (1982/1984). *Megatrends: Ten new directions transforming our lives.* New York: Warner Books.

Negrea, A. G. (1936). *The sociological theory of the peasant household.* Bucharest: 1936, p. 45. Cited in M. Cernea, *Changing society and family change: The impact of the cooperative farm on the peasant family,* p. 114. Stanford, Calif.: Center for Advanced Study in the Behavioral Sciences, 1970.

Neisser, U. (1976). *Cognition and reality: Principles and implications of cognitive psychology.* San Francisco: W. H. Freeman.

Newson, J., and E. Newson (1974). Cultural aspects of childrearing in the English-speaking world. In M. P. M. Richards (Ed.), *The integration of the child into a social world.* London: Cambridge University Press.

Newsweek (1984). The year of the yuppie. Dec. 13, pp. 14ff.

——— (1986). A mother's choice. March 13, pp. 46ff.

Nimkoff, M. F., and R. Middleton (1960). Types of family and types of economy. *American Journal of Sociology, 66,* 215–225.

Norton, R. (1983). Measuring marital quality: A critical look at the dependent variable. *Journal of Marriage and the Family, 45,* 141–152.

O'Neill, N. (1977). *The marriage premise.* New York: Evans.

———, and G. O'Neill (1972). *Open marriage.* New York: Evans.

O'Neill, P. (1959). The only rebellion around. *Life,* Nov. 30, p. 114.

O'Neill, W. L. (Ed.) (1969). *The woman movement.* Chicago: Quadrangle.

Opie, I., and P. Opie (1959). *The lore and language of school children.* London: Oxford University Press.

Oppenheimer, V. K. (1979). Structural sources of economic pressure for wives to work: An analytical framework. *Journal of Family History, 4,* 177–197.

Orwell, G. (1946/1953). The art of Donald McGill. In *A collection of essays,* p. 107. New York: Harcourt, Brace. (Originally published 1946).

Otto, H. A. (1970). *The family in search of a future.* New York: Appleton-Century-Crofts.

Otto, L. (1975). Class and status in family research. *Journal of Marriage and the Family, 37,* 315–332.

Panel on Youth of the President's Science Advisory Committee (1974). *Youth: Transition to adulthood.* Chicago: University of Chicago Press.

Parish, W. L., and M. Schwartz (1972). Household complexity in nineteenth-century France. *American Sociological Review, 37,* 154–173.

Parker, R. (1972). *The myth of the middle class.* New York: Harper & Row/Colophon.

Parsons, T. (1949). *Essays in sociological theory: Pure and applied.* Glencoe, Ill.: Free Press.

——— (1951). *The social system.* Glencoe, Ill.: Free Press.

——— (1955). The American family: Its relations to personality and the social structure. In T. Parsons and R. F. Bales, *Family socialization and interaction process,* pp. 3–21. Glencoe, Ill.: Free Press.

——— (1965). The normal American family. In S. M. Farber, P. Mustacchi, and R. H. L. Wilson (Eds.),

Man and civilization: The family's search for survival, pp. 31–50. New York: McGraw-Hill.

——— (1971). Kinship and the associational aspect of social structure. In F. L. K. Hsu (Ed.), *Kinship and culture*, pp. 409–438. Chicago: Aldine.

———, and R. F. Bales (1955). *Family socialization and interaction process*. Glencoe, Ill.: Free Press.

Patzer, G. (1985). *The physical attractiveness phenomenon*. New York: Plenum Press.

Pearce, D. (1982). *Women in poverty. Justice and economic opportunity*. New Brunswick, N.J.: Transaction.

Pearlin, L. I. (1971). *Class-context and family relations: A cross-national study*. Boston: Little, Brown.

———, and J. S. Johnson (1977). Marital states, life strains, and depression. *American Sociological Review, 42*, 704–715.

Petchesky, R. P. (1984). *Abortion and woman's choice: The state, sexuality, and reproductive freedom*. Boston: Northeastern University Press.

Piaget, J. (1967). *Six psychological studies*. New York: Random House.

Pilbeam, D. (1972). Evolutionary anthropology: Review of *The brain in hominid evolution* by P. V. Tobias. *Science, 175*, 1011.

Pilpel, H. F., and T. Zavin (1964). *Your marriage and the law*. New York: Macmillan/Collier.

Pineo, P. C. (1961). Disenchantment in the later years of marriage. *Marriage and Family Living, 23*, 3–11.

Piotrowski, C. S. (1978). *Work and the family system: A naturalistic study of working class and lower-middle class families*. New York: Free Press.

Pitts, J. (1968). The family and peer groups. In N. W. Bell and E. F. Vogel (Eds.), *A modern introduction to the family*. New York: Free Press.

Pleck, J. H. (1985). *Working wives/working husbands*. Beverly Hills, Calif.: Sage Publications.

Plumb, J. H. (1972). The great change in children. *Intellectual Digest, 2*, 82–84. (Originally in *Horizon*, Winter 1971.)

Pohlman, E. H. (1969). *Psychology of birth planning*. Cambridge, Mass.: Schenkman.

Poster, M. (1978). *A critical theory of the family*. New York: The Seabury Press.

Postman, N. (1982). *The disappearance of childhood*. New York: Laurel.

Preston, S. H., and J. McDonald (1979). The incidence of divorce within cohorts of American marriages contracted since the Civil War. In *Demography, XVI*, 1–25.

Proxmire, W. (1975). Quoted in National Science Foundation funded projects controversy: Senator William Proxmire vs. social scientists. *Wisconsin Sociologist, 12*, 72–86.

Queen, S. A., R. W. Habenstein, and J. S. Quadagno (1985). *The family in various cultures*. New York: Harper & Row.

Rabkin, R. (1970). *Inner and outer space: Introduction to a theory of social psychiatry*. New York: Norton.

Rabushka, A., and B. Jacobs (1980). *Old folks at home*. New York: Free Press.

Rainwater, L. (1960). *And the poor get children*. New York: Quadrangle Books.

——— (1974). *What money buys: Inequality and the social meanings of income*. New York: Basic Books.

Ramey, J. W. (1977). Alternative life-styles. *Society, 14*: 5, 43–47.

Rapp, R. (1977). Gender and class: An archaeology of knowledge concerning the origin of the state. *Dialectical Anthropology, 2*:4, 309–316.

Reich, C. (1964). The new property. *Yale Law Journal, 73*, 733.

Reiche, R. (1971). *Sexuality and class struggle*. New York: Praeger.

Reik, T. (1944). *A psychologist looks at love*. New York: Lancer.

Reisman, D. (1960). The oral and written traditions. In E. Carpenter and M. McLuhan (Eds.), *Explorations in communication*, pp. 109–124. Boston: Beacon.

Reiss, I. L. (1960). *Premarital sexual standards in America*. Glencoe, Ill.: Free Press.

Reusch, J., and G. Bateson (1968). *Communication: The social matrix of psychiatry* (2nd ed.). New York: Norton.

Rheingold, H. L. (1969). The social and socializing infant. In D. A. Goslin (Ed.), *Handbook of socialization theory and research*, pp. 779–790. Chicago: Rand McNally.

Ricoeur, P. (1973). Psychiatry and moral values. In S. Arieti (Ed.), *American handbook of psychiatry* (2nd ed.). New York: Basic Books.

Riegel, K. (1973). An epitaph for a paradigm. *Human Development, 16*, 1–3.

Riley, M. W. (1986). The family in an aging society: A matrix of latent relationships. In A. S. Skolnick and J. H. Skolnick (Eds.), *Family in transition* (5th ed.), pp. 498–509. Boston: Little, Brown.

Robinson, H., N. Robinson, M. Wolins, U. Bronfenbrenner, and J. Richmond (1973). Early child development and care. *International Monographs on Early Child Care, 4*:3.

Robinson, P. (1976). *The modernization of sex*. New York: Harper & Row.

Rodman, H. (1965). The textbook world of family sociology. *Social Problems, 12*, 450.

Rogers, C. (1972). *Becoming partners: Marriage and its alternatives.* New York: Delacorte.

Rollins, B. C., and H. Feldman (1970). Marital satisfaction over the family life cycle. *Journal of Marriage and the Family, 32,* 20–28.

Rose, S. (1986). *The American profile poster.* New York: Pantheon.

Rosen, R. (1982). *The lost sisterhood: Prostitution in America 1900–1918.* Baltimore: Johns Hopkins University Press.

Rosow, I. (1965). Intergenerational relationships: Problems and proposals. In E. Shanas and G. F. Streib (Eds.), *Social structure and the family: Generational relations,* pp. 341–378. Englewood Cliffs, N.J.: Prentice-Hall.

Ross, H. L., and I. V. Sawhill (1975). *Time of transition: The growth of families headed by women.* Washington, D.C.: Urban Institute.

Rossi, A. (1968). Transition to parenthood. *Journal of Marriage and the Family, 30,* 26–39.

——— (1977). A biosocial perspective on parenting. *Daedalus,* Spring, pp. 1–31.

Rougemont, D. de (1956). *Love in the Western world.* New York: Pantheon.

Rousseau, J. J. (1762). *Emile, or on education.* London: Dent, 1911. (Original French edition 1762.)

Rubenstein, C. (1985). What's become of the American family? *Family Circle,* Oct., pp. 24ff.

Rubin, L. B. (1976). *Worlds of pain.* New York: Basic Books.

——— (1983). *Intimate strangers.* New York: Harper and Row.

Rubin, N. (1982). *The new suburban woman.* New York: Coward, McCann and Geoghegan.

Rubin, Z. (1970). Measurement of romantic love. *Journal of Personality and Social Psychology, 16,* 265–273.

——— (1973). *Liking and loving: An invitation to social psychology.* New York: Holt, Rinehart & Winston.

——— (1977). The love research. *Human Behavior,* Feb., pp. 56–59.

Ryan, W. (1976). *Blaming the victim.* New York: Random House/Vintage.

Rybczynski, W. (1986). *Home: A short history of an idea.* New York: Viking.

Ryder, R. G. (1970). A topography of early marriage. *Family Process, 9,* 385–402.

Ryle, A. (1967). *Neurosis in the ordinary family: A psychiatric survey.* London: Tavistock.

Sahlins, M. (1968). The original affluent society. In R. Lee and I. DeVore (Eds.), *Man the hunter.* Chicago: Aldine.

Samuelson, P. A. (1967). *Economics: An introductory analysis.* New York: McGraw-Hill.

Samuelson, P. J. (1986). In praise of children. *Newsweek,* Jan. 13, p. 49.

San Francisco Chronicle (1977). Big increase in men who live alone. Sept. 26.

Satow, R. (1979). Pop narcissism. *Psychology Today,* Oct., pp. 14–17.

Scanzoni, J. H. (1970). *Opportunity and the family.* New York: Free Press.

——— (1972). *Sexual bargaining: Power politics in the American marriage.* Englewood Cliffs, N.J.: Prentice-Hall.

Scarr, S. (1985). *Mother care/other care.* New York: Basic Books.

Schacter, S. (1964). The interaction of cognitive and physiological determinants of emotional state. In L. Berkowitz (Ed.), *Advances in experimental social psychology* (Vol. 1), pp. 49–80. New York: Academic Press.

Schaffer, H. R. (1971). *The growth of sociability.* Baltimore: Penguin.

Schmidt, W. (1973). *Child development: The human, cultural, and educational context.* New York: Harper & Row.

Schneider, D. M. (1968). *American kinship: A cultural account.* Englewood Cliffs, N.J.: Prentice-Hall.

———, and R. T. Smith (1973). *Class differences and sex roles in American kinship and family structure.* Englewood Cliffs, N.J.: Prentice-Hall.

Schudson, M. (1984). *Advertising: The uneasy persuasion.* New York: Basic Books.

Schulman, A. K. (1977). The war in the back seat. In P. J. Stein, J. Richman, and N. Hannon (Eds.), *The family: Functions, conflicts, and symbols.* Reading, Mass.: Addison-Wesley.

Scribner, S., and M. Cole (1973). Cognitive sequences of formal and informal education. *Science, 182,* 553–559.

Sears, R. R., E. E. Maccoby, and H. Levin (1957). *Patterns of child rearing.* Evanston, Ill.: Row, Peterson.

Seligman, M. P. (1975). *Helplessness: On depression, development, and death.* San Francisco: W. H. Freeman.

Sennett, R., and J. Cobb (1974). *The hidden injuries of class.* New York: Random House.

Serrin, W. (1986). Growth in jobs since '80 is sharp but pay and quality are debated. *The New York Times,* June 8, p. 1.

Shaefer, L. C. (1964). Sexual experiences and reactions of a group of thirty women as told to a female psychotherapist. Unpublished Ph.D. thesis, Teachers College, Columbia University. Cited in E. M. Brecher, *The sex researchers.* Boston: Little, Brown, 1969.

Shaffer, J. B. P. (1970). Review of recent books on marriage. *Harvard Education Review, 40,* 165–174.

Shainess, N. (1971). "New" views of female sexuality: A book review of *Female sexuality: New psychoanalytic views* by J. Chasseguet-Smirgel with C. I. Juquet-Parat. *Psychiatry and Social Science Review, 5:4,* 13–19.

Shammas, C. (1980). The domestic environment in early modern England and America. *Journal of Social History, 14:1,* 3–24.

Shanas, E. (1980). Old people and their families: The new pioneers. *Journal of Marriage and the Family, 42,* 9–15.

Shanley, M. L. (1979). The history of the family in modern England. *Signs, 4* (Summer), 740–750.

Shaver, P., and J. Freedman (1976). Your pursuit of happiness. *Psychology Today,* Aug. pp. 26–29.

Shorter, E. (1973). Infanticide in the past: A review of *Slaughter of the innocents* by David Bakan. *History of Childhood Quarterly, 1:1,* 178–180.

——— (1975). *The making of the modern family.* New York: Basic Books.

Shostak, A. B. (1969). *Blue-collar life.* New York: Random House.

Siegel, F. F. (1984). *Troubled journey.* New York: Hill & Wang.

Silverberg, W. V. (1952). *Childhood experience and personal destiny.* New York: Springer.

Simmel, G. (1950). In K. Wolff (Ed.), *The sociology of Georg Simmel.* New York: Free Press.

Simpson, G. (1960). *People in families.* New York: Crowell.

Skolnick, A. (1981a). Married lives: Longitudinal perspectives on marriage. In D. H. Eichorn, J. A. Clausen, N. Haan, et al., *Present and past in middle life.* New York: Academic Press.

——— (1981b). The social contexts of cohabitation. *American Journal of Comparative Law, 29:2,* 339–358.

Slater, P. E. (1963). On social regression. *American Sociological Review, 28,* 339–364.

——— (1968). Some social consequences of temporary systems. In W. G. Bennis and P. E. Slater, *The temporary society,* pp. 77–96. New York: Harper & Row.

——— (1974). Parental role differentiation. In R. L. Coser (Ed.), *The family* (2nd ed.), pp. 259–275. New York: St. Martin's Press.

Sluzki, C. E., and V. Eliseo (1971). The double bind as a universal pathogenic situation. *Family Process, 10:4,* 397–410.

Smelser, N. J. (1963). *Social change.* Englewood Cliffs, N.J.: Prentice-Hall.

——— (1968). *Essays in sociological explanation.* Englewood Cliffs, N.J.: Prentice-Hall.

———, and E. Erikson (1981). *Themes of love and work in adulthood.* Cambridge, Mass.: Harvard University Press.

Solomon, R. C. (1981). *Love, emotion, myth and metaphor.* Garden City, N.Y.: Anchor/Doubleday.

Sorensen, R. C. (1973). *Adolescent sexuality in contemporary America.* New York: World.

Spanier, G., and R. A. Lewis (1980). Marital quality: A review of the seventies. *Journal of Marriage and the Family, 42,* 825–840.

Spencer, H. (1946). *Essays on education.* New York: Dutton. (Originally published 1858.)

Spiegel, J. (1971). *Transactions: The interplay between individual, family, and society.* New York: Science House.

Srole, L., J. S. Langner, S. T. Michael, M. K. Opler, and T. A. C. Rennie (1962). *Mental health in the metropolis: The midtown Manhattan study.* New York: McGraw-Hill.

Stack, C. B. (1974). *All our kin.* New York: Harper & Row.

———, M. D. Caulfield, V. Estes, et al. (1975). Anthropology (review essay). *Signs, 1:1,* 147–159.

Staples, R. (1971). Towards a sociology of the black family: A theoretical and methodological assessment: *Journal of Marriage and the Family, 33,* 119–135.

———, and A. Mirande (1980). Racial and cultural variations among American families: A decennial review of the literature on minority families. *Journal of Marriage and the Family, 2,* 157–173.

Stark, R., and J. McEvoy III (1970). Middle class violence. *Psychology Today,* Nov., pp. 52–65.

Stearns, P. (1980). Modernization and social history: Some suggestions and a muted cheer. *Journal of Social History, 17:2,* 189–209.

Steele, B. F. (1970): Parental abuse of infants and small children. In E. J. Anthony and T. Benedek (Eds.), *Parenthood: Its psychology and psychopathology,* pp. 449–477. Boston: Little, Brown.

———, and C. B. Pollock (1968). A psychiatric study of parents who abuse infants and small children. In R. E. Helfer and C. H. Kempe (Eds.), *The battered child.* Chicago: University of Chicago Press.

Stein, P. J. (1977). Singlehood: An alternative to marriage. In A. S. Skolnick and J. H. Skolnick (Eds.), *Family in transition* (2nd ed.). Boston: Little, Brown.

Steiner, G. (1981). *The futility of family policies.* Washington, D.C.: The Brookings Institution.

Steinmetz, S. K., and M. A. Straus (1974). *Violence in the family.* New York: Dodd, Mead.

Stephens, W. N. (1963). *The family in cross-cultural perspective.* New York: Holt, Rinehart & Winston.

Stern, D., S. Smith, and F. Doolittle (1975). How children used to work. *Law and Contemporary Problems*, 39 (Summer).

Stern, D. N. (1985). *The interpersonal world of the infant: A view from psychoanalysis and developmental psychology.* New York: Basic Books.

Sternberg, R. (1985). A triangular theory of love. Paper presented at meeting of the American Psychological Association, Los Angeles.

—— (1986). A triangular theory of love. *Psychological Review, 93*(2), 119–135.

Stone, L. (1960). Marriage among the English nobility. *Comparative Studies in Society and History, 3,* 182–206.

—— (1964). Marriage among the English nobility. In R. L. Coser (Ed.), *The family: Its structure and functions.* New York: St. Martin's Press.

—— (1977). *The family, sex, and marriage in England, 1500–1800.* New York: Harper & Row.

—— (1981). Family history in the 1980s. *Journal of Interdisciplinary History, 12*(1), 51–87.

—— (1985). Sex in the west: The strange history of human sexuality. *The New Republic,* July 8, pp. 25–37.

Stouffer, S. A., S. A. Star, and R. M. Williams (1949). *The American soldier: Studies in social psychology in World War II.* Princeton, N.J.: Princeton University Press.

Straus, M. A., R. J. Gelles, and S. K. Steinmetz (1980). *Behind closed doors: Violence in the American family.* New York: Anchor/Doubleday.

Sullivan, H. S. (1953). *The interpersonal theory of psychiatry.* New York: Norton.

Sumner, W. G. (1960). *Folkways.* New York: New American Library/Mentor.

Suransky, V. P. (1982). *The erosion of childhood.* Chicago: University of Chicago Press.

Sussman, M. B. (1965). Relationships of adult children with their parents. In E. Shanas and G. F. Streib (Eds.), *Social structure and the family: Generational relations.* Englewood Cliffs, N.J.: Prentice-Hall.

Swidler, A. (1981). Love and adulthood in American culture. In N. Smelser and E. Erikson (Eds.), *Themes of love and work in adulthood.* Cambridge, Mass.: Harvard University Press.

Tavris, C. (1976). The Cory complex. *Psychology Today,* Aug., p. 32.

Teele, J. E., and W. M. Schmidt (1970). Illegitimacy and race: National and local trends. *Millbank Memorial Fund Quarterly, 48*:2, 127–144.

Tennov, D. (1979). *Love and limerance: The experience of being in love.* Briarcliff Manor, N.Y.: Stein & Day.

Terman, L. (1938). *Psychological factors in marital happiness.* New York: McGraw-Hill.

Thomas, L. (1982). The art of teaching science. *New York Times Magazine,* March 14.

Thompson, E. P. (1963). *The making of the English working class.* New York: Random House/Vintage.

Thornton, A., and D. Freedman, (1983). The changing American family. *Population Bulletin, 38*(4), 1–43.

Tilly, L. A., and J. W. Scott (1978). *Women, work and family.* New York: Holt, Rinehart & Winston.

Toffler, A. (1980). *The third wave.* New York: Bantam Books.

Tomkins, S. S. (1965). The biopsychosociality of the family. In A. J. Coale, L. A. Fallers, M. J. Levy, Jr., D. M. Schneider, and S. S. Tomkins, *Aspects of the analysis of family structure.* Princeton, N.J.: Princeton University Press.

Trexler, R. C. (1973). Infanticide in Florence: New sources and first results. *History of Childhood Quarterly, 1*:1, 98–116.

Troll, L. E. (1969). Issues in the study of the family: A review of *The psychosocial interior of the family,* G. Handel (Ed.), *Merrill-Palmer Quarterly, 15*:2, 221–226.

Trumbach, J. (1978). *The rise of the egalitarian family: Aristocratic kinship and domestic relations in 18th century England.* New York: Academic Press.

Turnbull, C. (1961). *The forest people.* New York: Simon & Schuster.

Turner, R. H. (1976). The real self: From institution to impulse. *American Journal of Sociology, 81*:5, 939–1016.

Udry, J. R. (1971). *The social context of marriage* (2nd ed.). Philadelphia: Lippincott.

Uhlenberg, P. (1980). Death and the family. *Journal of Family History, 5*:3, 313–320.

U.S. Department of Commerce, Bureau of the Census (1979). *Fertility of American women: June 1978.* Current Population Reports, Series P-20, No. 341. Washington, D.C.: U.S. Government Printing Office.

—— (1981). *Marital status and living arrangements: March, 1980.* Current Population Reports, Series P-20, No. 365. Washington, D.C.: U.S. Government Printing Office.

—— (1982). *Statistical abstract of the United States, 1982–83.* Washington, D.C.: U.S. Government Printing Office.

—— (1985). *Money, income, and poverty states of families and persons in the U.S.* Current Population Reports, Series P-60. Washington, D.C.: U.S. Government Printing Office.

Valentine, C. A. (1968). *Culture and poverty: Critique and counterproposals.* Chicago: University of Chicago Press.

Veevers, J. (1973). Voluntarily childless wives: An exploratory study. *Sociology and Social Research,* April, 356–365.

Veith, I. (1965). *Hysteria; The history of a disease.* Chicago: University of Chicago Press.

Veroff, J., G. Douvan, and R. A. Kulka (1981a). *The inner American: A self-portrait from 1957–1976.* New York: Basic Books.

———, R. A. Kulka, and G. Douvan (1981b). *Mental health in America: Patterns of help-seeking 1957–1976.* New York: Basic Books.

Vinovskis, M. A. (1981). An "epidemic" of adolescent pregnancy? *Journal of Family History,* 6 (Summer), 205–230.

Viorst, J. (1977). Confessions of a jealous wife. In G. Clauton and L. G. Smith (Eds.), *Jealousy.* Englewood Cliffs, N.J.: Prentice-Hall.

Vogt, E. Z. (1969). *Zinacantan: A Maya community in the highlands of Chiapas.* Cambridge, Mass.: Harvard University Press.

Von Bertalanffy, L. (1960). General system theory and the behavioral sciences. In J. Tanner and B. Inhelder (Eds.), *Discussions on child development* (Vol. 4), p. 155. New York: International Universities Press.

Vygotsky, L. S. (1962). *Thought and language.* New York: Wiley.

Waller, W. (1938). *The family: A dynamic interpretation.* New York: Dryden.

Wallerstein, J. S., and J. Kelly, (1980). *Surviving the breakup: How children and parents cope with divorce.* New York: Basic Books.

Walster, E. (1971). Passionate love. In B. D. Murstein (Ed.), *Theories of attraction and love,* pp. 85–99. New York: Springer.

——— (1973). Equity theory and interpersonal relations. Paper presented at American Sociological Association, New York.

———, V. Aronson, D. Abrahams, and L. Rottman (1966). The importance of physical attractiveness in dating behavior. *Journal of Personality and Social Psychology,* 4, 508–516.

Washburn, S. L., and I. DeVore (1961). In S. L. Washburn (Ed.), *Social life of early man.* Chicago: Aldine.

Watson, J. S. (1979). Perception of contingency as a determinant of social responsiveness. In E. Thomas (Ed.), *The origins of social responsiveness.* Hillsdale, N.J.: Erlbaum.

Watt, I. (1957). *The rise of the novel.* Berkeley: University of California Press.

Wattenberg, B. J. (1985). *The good news is the bad news is wrong.* New York: Simon & Schuster.

Weiss, R. S. (1973). *Loneliness: The experience of emotional and social isolation.* Cambridge, Mass.: M.I.T. Press.

Weisstein, N. (1971). Psychology constructs the female. In V. Gornick and B. K. Moran (Eds.), *Woman in sexist society: Studies in power and powerlessness,* pp. 207–224. New York: Basic Books.

Weitman, S. R. (1973). Intimacies: Notes toward a theory of social inclusion and exculsion. In A. Birenbaum and E. Segarin (Eds.), *People in places: The sociology of the familiar.* New York: Praeger.

Weitzman, L. J. (1977). To love, honor, and obey: Traditional legal marriage and alternative family forms. In A. S. Skolnick and J. H. Skolnick (Eds.), *Family in transition* (2nd ed.), pp. 288–313. Boston: Little, Brown.

——— (1981a). The economics of divorce: social and economic consequences of property, alimony, and child support awards. *UCLA Law Review,* 28, 1181–1268.

——— (1981b). *The marriage contract: Spouses, lovers, and the law.* New York: Free Press.

———, and R. Dixon (1980). The transformation of legal marriage through no-fault divorce. In A. Skolnick and J. H. Skolnick (Eds.), *Family in transition* (3rd ed.), pp. 354–367.

Weitzman, L. (1985). *The divorce revolution.* New York: Free Press.

Westoff, L. A. (1977). *The second time around.* New York: Viking Press.

Westoff, C. F., and R. H. Potrin (1966). Higher education, religion, and women's family size orientations. *American Sociological Review,* 31, 406–496.

White, G. (1977). Inequality of emotional involvement and jealousy in romantic couples. Paper presented at meeting of the American Psychological Association, San Francisco.

White, R. W. (1960). Competence and the psychosexual stages of development. In M. R. Jones (Ed.), *Nebraska symposium on motivation,* pp. 97–141. Lincoln: University of Nebraska Press.

White, S. (1965). Evidence for a hierarchical arrangement of learning processes. In L. P. Lipsitt and C. C. Spiker (Eds.), *Advances in child development and behavior,* pp. 184–220. New York: Academic Press.

White House Conference on Children (1970). *Profiles of children.* Washington, D.C.: U.S. Government Printing Office.

Whiting, B. B. (1963). *Six cultures: Studies in child rearing.* New York: Wiley.

Whiting, J. W. M. (1961). Socialization process and personality. In F. L. K. Hsu (Ed.), *Psychological anthropology.* Homewood, Ill.: Dorsey.

———— (1977). Cross-cultural perspectives on parenthood. Paper presented at Groves Conference on Marriage and the Family, Grossinger, N.Y., May.

Whyte, W. (1956). *The organization man.* New York: Simon & Schuster.

Williams, R. (1983). *The year 2000.* New York: Pantheon.

Willie, C. U. (1981). *A new look at black families* (2nd ed.). Bayside, N.Y.: General Hall.

Wilson, W. J. (1978). *The declining significance of race.* Chicago: University of Chicago Press.

Wilson, S. (1955). *The man in the gray flannel suit.* New York: Simon & Schuster.

Winch, R. F., and R. L. Blumberg (1968). Societal complexity and familial organization. In R. F. Winch and L. W. Goodman (Eds.), *Selected studies in marriage and the family* (3rd ed.). New York: Holt, Rinehart & Winston.

Winn, M. (1983). *Children without childhood.* New York: Pantheon.

Wittgenstein, L. (1953). *Philosophical investigations.* Oxford: Basil Blackwell.

Wolf, M. (1972). *Women and the family in rural Taiwan.* Stanford, Calif.: Stanford University Press.

Wolfe, T. (1976). The me decade. *New West Magazine,* Aug. 30, p. 31.

Wolfe, L. (1981) *The Cosmo report.* New York: Arbor House.

Wolfenstein, M. (1954). *Children's humor: A psychological analysis.* Glencoe, Ill.: Free Press.

———— (1955). Fun morality: An analysis of recent American child-training literature. In M. Mead and M. Wolfenstein (Eds.), *Childhood in contemporary cultures,* pp. 169–178. Chicago: University of Chicago Press.

Wright, E. O., C. Costello, D. Hacher, and J. Sprague (1982). The American class structure. *American Sociological Review, 47,* 709–726.

Wrigley, E. A. (1972). The process of modernization and the industrial revolution in England. *Journal of Interdisciplinary History, 3:2,* 255–260.

Wrong, D. (1961). The oversocialized conception of man in modern sociology. *American Sociology Review, 26,* 183–193.

———— (1976). Postscript 1975. In D. Wrong, *Skeptical sociology,* pp. 47–54. New York: Columbia University Press.

Yankelovich, D. (1977). Quoted in A new kind of parent. *San Francisco Chronicle,* April 21.

———— (1981a). *New rules.* New York: Random House.

———— (1981b). New rules in American life: Searching for self-fulfillment in a world turned upside down. *Psychology Today,* April, pp. 35–91.

Young, M., and P. Willmott (1973). *The symmetrical family.* New York: Random House/Pantheon.

Zaretsky, E. (1976). *Capitalism, the family and personal life.* New York: Harper & Row/Colophon.

Zelditch, M., Jr. (1964). Cross-cultural analyses of family structure. In H. T. Christensen (Ed.), *Handbook of marriage and the family,* pp. 462–500. Chicago: Rand McNally.

Zelitzer, V. A. (1985). *Pricing the priceless child: The changing social value of children.* New York: Basic Books.

Zelnick, M., J. F. Kanter, and K. Ford (1981). *Sex and pregnancy in adolescence* (Vol. 133), Sage Library of Social Research. Beverly Hills, Calif.: Sage Publications.

Zimmerman, C. C. (1947). *The family and civilization.* New York: Harper & Bros.

Canterbury Tales, The (Chaucer), 231
Capitalism
  and individualism, 232–233
  new capitalism, 44–45
  and self-awareness, 130
Career women. *See* Working women
Categorical self, 377
Centuries of Childhood (Ariès), 117–118
Chicano families, 178–180
Child abandonment, 317
Child abuse, 15, 320–323
  accidents as, 321
  continuity in, 98–99
  by premodern parents, 97
  and unemployment, 169
  see also Infanticide
Childbirth, 329, 416–417
Child care services, 411
Childhood, 337–364
  changing place of child, 359–360
  costs of, 360–362
  dependency of children, 360–361
  developmental paradigm of, 340–346
  discovery of, 351–353
  emotional value of child, 359
  5–7, ages of, 353–355
  future of, 362–364
  nature of, 339–340
  recapitulation hypothesis, 345–346
  school and, 355–358
  small adult conception of, 352
  social context of, 346–360
  and social reform, 358–359
  see also Adolescence; Child abuse; Infants; Parenthood; Socialization
Child labor, 22
Childlessness, 326–327
Childrearing. *See* Parenthood
Child support, 281
Chinese families, 64
Christianity and sex, 203
Chronocentrism, 347
  and adolescence, 350
Cities
  and black families, 177
  inner-city environment, 1960s, 37–38
  and Mexican American families, 178–179

Civil rights protests, 35–36
Class. *See* Social class
Clinical sociology, 100
Cognitive-development model, 199–200
Cognitive pluralism, 353
Cohabitation, 258–259
  current trends in, 413
  inventing relationships, 274–275
  marriage compared, 275
  and sexual bargaining, 265–271
  terminology of, 263
Cohorts, 26
Colonial family reconstruction, 107–108
Communicational psychiatry, 100
Communications model of marriage, 288–291
Communication theory, 99–100
Competent husband/incompetent wife pattern, 295
Complexity, 95–103
  and family form, 126
Computer dance study, 244
Conflict
  in family, 146–148
  marriage as, 285–286, 292
  models of, 84–85
  socialization and, 382–383
Conflict-habituated marriage, 292
Conformity, 388–392
  in 1950s, 34
Conjugal family, 120–121
Consummate love, 240
Contingency, 375–376
Contraceptives, 217
  history of, 307–308
  Middletown study on, 399
Contradiction in family, 146–148
Conundrum (Morris), 197
Conventionalism of marriage, 283
Cooperative model of marriage, 286
Coresidence, 71
Core self, 377
Corrosion in marriage, 298
Cory complex, 46
Cosmopolitan, 236
Counterculture, 43
Counterfeit decade, 29–30
Counternorms, 88
Couple culture, 234
Courtly love, 229–230
Courtship, stages of, 266–268
Cox Commission, 366

Credit, 44
Critical theory, 85
Cultural symbol, family as, 64
Culture of poverty, 172, 173
Custody of children, 281

Death
  and divorce rates, 261
  see also Mortality rates
Death of the Family, The (Cooper), 422
Declining Significance of Race, The (Wilson), 177
Deference societies, 113–114
Delay of gratification, 173
Demographics
  postwar era and, 49–55
  and sexual attitudes, 217
  transitions in, 125
  trends in, 2–3
Depression. *See* Great Depression
Desertion, 261–262
Development, 121
Deviance and family, 87
Devitalized marriage, 292
Disciplinary practices, 380–381
  see also Child abuse
Disenchantment in marriage, 298
Disengagement in marriage, 298, 299
Displaced homemakers, 269
Dissent, trends in, 45–46
Divorce, 18
  age, rates by, 259
  annual divorce rates, 50
  coping with, 386
  and definition of family, 60
  1860–1982 rates, 49
  financial circumstances after, 269
  first marriage divorce rates, 256
  and importance of marriage, 9
  law of, 280–281
  and mental health, 383
  Middletown study and, 399
  mortality rates and, 21–22, 261
  no-fault divorce, 275, 281
  normalization of, 259–263
  1,000 persons, rates per, 22
  and parental involvement, 416
  in postwar era, 50–51
  porportions of marriages ending in, 51
  reasons for, 281–282

Gallup Polls, 9
Game theory and marriage, 285–286
Gender, 184–185
    and body, 200–202
    identity, 199
Generation crunch, 417
Generation gap, 366–371
Genitor, 72
Gentrification, 43–44
Geographic mobility, 400
Goods News Is the Bad News Is Wrong, The (Wattenberg), 8–9
Grandparents, 60
Great Depression, 154, 155, 167
    and women, 405
Great Society program, 38
Greece, ancient
    love in, 229
    sexuality in, 203
Greensboro, North Carolina protests, 35–36
Groucho Marx effect, 243
Group marriage, 111

Happiness ratings, 46
Haven in a Heartless World (Lasch), 396
Hearts of Men, The (Ehrenreich), 34
Here to Stay (Bane), 396
Hermaphrodites. See Intersexed persons
Herpes, 39, 216
Heterosexual knots, 190
Hidden injuries of class, 167
Hippies, 367
Hispanic American families, 178–180
History, 96–97
    of childhood, 358
    of childhood sexuality, 210
    of feminism, 404–406
    of homosexuality, 202–203
    of industrialism, 122, 124–125
    of infanticide, 316–318
    of marriage, 255, 258
    new history of family, 107–109
    of parenthood, 306–307
    sex in, 202–204
Hometown (Davis), 397
Homosexuality
    in history, 202–203

in 1950s, 29–30
    see also AIDS
Hormones and sex roles, 193–194
Households
    definition of, 71–72
    family distinction, 67–68
    inclusions in, 69–71
    in preindustrial times, 70
    residence pattern variations, 68–72
    and universal nuclear family, 161
Housewives, full-time, 271
Housework in 1950s, 32–33
Housing
    in cities, 37
    in 1950s, 35
Humor and marriage, 276–277
Hunting and gathering societies, 110–112
    modern societies compared, 126

Iatrogenic malady, 204
Id, 372
Identification teaching method, 380
Illegitimacy, 60
    and black women, 177–178
    irrelevance of, 269
    sexual freedom and, 121
    and teenage pregnancy, 213–214
    trends in, 416
    and value judgments, 75–76
Impulsive husbands, 295
Incest, 15
Independence as value, 388
Indeterminacy, 380–382
Individualism
    affective individualism, 97, 127–128
    and love, 232–233
    and modern family, 125–126
    and rationality, 129–130
Industrialism, 116, 122, 124–125
    and children, 358
    and familial texture of society, 131–132
    and importance of family, 136
    and labor force, 145–146
    and women, 120–121, 145–146
Infant Care pamphlet, 332
Infanticide, 97, 307, 316–318
    in primates, 312
Infantile sexuality, 93
Infants, 314–316

socialization and, 374, 375–378
    theoretical notions of, 344
Inflation, 160
Inner American, The (Veroff, Douvan & Kulka), 41
Inner-city environment, 1960s, 37–38
Innocent child myth, 338
Insanity, 99–102
    and married women, 269, 271
    and masturbation, 205, 207
    see also Schizophrenia
Insight theory of learning, 380
Institution, defined, 274
Institutionalization of hypocrisy, 369
Institutional marriages, 303
Instrumental father, 137
Internalization
    concept, 87–88
    of norms, 374
Interpersonal psychiatry, 100
Intersexed persons, 197
    sex roles of, 200–202
Intimacy model of marriage, 283–285
Intimate Strangers (Rubin), 287–288
Intrinsic couples, 294
Invulnerables, 384, 386
IQ, 387
    5–7 years, prediction at, 354
Irish peasant family study, 114
Isolation
    emotional isolation, 234
    of family, 137–138
    fear of, 233
Israeli communes, 69

Jealousy, 246–250
Jokes about marriage, 276–277

Kingdoms, 115
Kinsey reports, 208, 405
Kinship
    in agrarian society, 113
    ascriptive friendship, 140
    in Blue Ridge mountain families, 141
    isolation of family from, 137–138
    as matriarchal, 64
    meaning of, 72–73
    primary-kin-oriented families, 141, 142

in slavery system, 176
see also Extended family
Kol Nidre effect, 379

Labor force
adolescents in, 23
children in, 358
and industrialization, 145–146
see also Unemployment; Work;
Working women
La familia, 179
Language
development of, 378
therapeutic language of relation-
ships, 245–246
Latchkey children, 12
Learned helplessness, 385
Legal system. *See* Family law
Legitimacy principle, 75–76
Leisure activities, 163
Life cycles, 412
Life-cycle servants, 70
Life expectancy figures, 418
Life-styles, 412–413
Lifetime income patterns, 162
Liking scale, 238–239
Limerance, 221–226
Literacy, 130–131
Literature, 230
Little Hans, case of, 94–95
Living arrangements, chart show-
ing, 7
Living together. *See* Cohabitation
Loneliness, 233–234
and single people, 237
of spouses, 296
Longevity revolution, 408
Looking glass self, 361, 374
Loose connection in marriage, 297
Lord of the Flies (Golding), 371
*Lore and Language of School-
children* (Opie & Opie), 210
Love, 219–252
and children, 228, 361–362
and conflict, 250–251
criticisms of, 245
cross-cultural perspective,
226–234
as emotion, 223–224
instability of, 224–225
jealousy and, 246–250
and labeling, 227–229
and loneliness, 233–234

mixed emotions of, 242–243
in modern world, 234–241
necessity for, 232–233
process of, 241–242
reciprocity and, 224
research findings, 238–241
ritual declarations of, 228
romantic love, 221–226
and single persons, 236–238
symbols of, 231–232
terminology of, 241
two-part theory of, 227
in Western culture, 229–232
Love scale, 238–239
Lower class
household boundaries, 67–68
middle class distinguished, 157
in 1960s, 37–38
and working class, 159
Lower middle class. *See* Working
class

McCarthyism, 29
Maccoby and Jacklin review,
187–189
Machismo, 179
and jealousy, 248
Maiden names, 279
Mainstream standard package,
159–160
Making of the Modern Family, The
(Shorter), 128–129
Male, use of term, 197
Male roles. *See* Fathers
Man in the Gray Flannel Suit
(Wilson), 34
Man's Fate (Malraux), 246
Marital quality, 282
Marital satisfaction, 299–300
Marriage, 253–272
advantages of, 270–271
ambivalence about, 275–277
bargaining and, 265
cohabitation compared, 275
as conflict, 285–286, 292
continuity and, 263–271
conventionalization of, 283
cross-cultural ambivalence, 277
dual aspect of, 274–281
expectations of, 282
and finances, 164–166
fragility of, 411–412
future of, 301–304

humor and, 276–277
in hunting societies, 111
institution of marriage, opinion
on, 261
jealousy in, 247–248
and kin groups, 60–61
later marriage, trend to, 258
legal images of, 277–280
life cycle and, 298–301
models of, 281–297
in nineteenth century, 255, 258
norms of, 40–41
open marriage, 274, 284
patriarchal marriage, 119–120
payoffs in, 268–269
permanent availability model of,
265–266
Puritans and, 231
rates of, 18
self influences in, 296–297
sex in, 414–415
sophisticated humor of, 277
spiritual marriage, 251
statistics on, 255, 256–257
strains in, 146–147
trends in, 254–263
types of couples, 291–297
utopian marriage, 282–285
see also Households; Remarriage
Marriage Premise, The (O'Neill),
249, 274
Masculinity, 197, 199
Mass consumption, 44
Masturbation, 194
and insanity, 205, 207
as sin, 206
Materialism, 157
Mate swappers, 248
Matriarchy
and black families, 174
and kin systems, 64
Mechanistic approach to childhood,
341–342
Me decade, 4, 9, 38–48
Medicaid, 158
Medical model of pathology, 91–92
Medicare, 158
Mental illness. *See* Insanity
Mexican American families,
178–180
Michigan studies, 41–43
Microcommunity, 324
Middle Ages, 117–118

Middle Ages *(continued)*
  antifemale humor in, 276
  legal rights and marriage,
    278–279
  love in, 229–230
  marital sex in, 203
  school in, 355
Middle Americans, The (Coles), 163
Middle class, 154–155, 160–162
  affective individualism in, 97
  black families, 171
  children in, 361
  father, role of, 390–391
  and gentrification, 43
  lower class distinguished, 157
  message of socialization, 389
  mother, role of, 389–390
  in 1950s, 29
  in 1960s, 38
  and parenthood, 333–334
  and sexual freedom, 215
*Middletown Families: Fifty Years
    of Change and Continuity*
    (Caplow et al.), 9–11
Middletown studies, 9–11,
    397–400
  and sexual revolution, 401
Mid-life crisis, 301
Midtown Manhattan study, 383
Minorities. *See* Ethnic families
Mixed-motive model of marriage,
    286
Modernization, 121–122
  and childhood, 357–358
  and industrialization, 125
Modern Woman: The Lost Sex
    (Farnham & Lundberg), 29
Modified extended family, 139–140
Money. *See* Economic resources
Monkeys. *See* Primates
Moral Majority, 8, 410
Mortality rates, 21–22
  and divorce, 21–22, 261
  and extended family, 124
  at foundling homes, 318
  in industrializing countries, 125
  and parental attachment, 97
  and sexual attitudes, 217
Mother substitutes, 324–325

Naked-ape school of writing, 191
Narcissism, 4, 40
Negative carry-over, 166
Negro Family: The Case for Na-

tional Action, The (Moynihan),
    170
New capitalism, 44–45
New Family morality, 96–97
New Right conservatives, 5, 7–8,
    39, 420
1984 (Orwell), 83
No-fault divorce, 275, 281
Normalization of divorce, 259–263
Normative system, family as,
    64–66
Norms. *See* Social norms
Nothing-but, fallacy of, 343–344
Not-so-empty nest, 331
Nuclear family. *See* Family
Nursing children, 312–314
Nurturance gap, 314–316

Oedipal hostility, 209
Older people
  family ties with, 419
  plight of, 148–149
  poverty among, 158
  trends among, 417–420
  see also Retirement
Open Marriage (O'Neill & O'Neill),
    249, 274, 284, 303
Organic lamp theories, 342
Organismic approach to childhood,
    342–343
Organization Man, The (Whyte),
    34
Orgasms, 195–196, 208
Orientation, family of, 60
Oversocialized view of human na-
    ture, 372

Palimony cases, 254, 266–267
Pamela (Richardson), 231
Paradise Lost (Milton), 231
Paradox, marriage, as, 288–291
Parenthood, 305–336
  and conflict, 325–326
  costs of, 329–334
  cross-cultural perspective on,
    323–326
  dark side of, 318–323
  and financial problems, 163
  as fun, 334
  future of, 334–335
  and generational conflict,
    366–371
  in hunting societies, 112
  innateness of, 312

in Mexican American families,
    179
  motivations for, 326–329
  natural interpretation of,
    310–318
  psychological consequences of,
    331–334
  revolution in, 408
  romantic complex about, 329
  stages of, 329
  strains of, 330–331
  supernatural support for, 326
  see also Childhood
Passion, 242
Passive-congenial marriage,
    292–293
Passive males, 32
Pater, 72
Patriarchal family, 113–120
  change and, 120–121
  idealization of, 116–118
  marriage in, 119–120
  modern family compared, 123
  strains in, 118–119
Peer groups and sexuality, 212–213
Penis envy, 31
Permanent availability model of
    marriage, 265–266
Person-centered view of sex, 217
Petting, 401
Pink collar ghetto, 31
Platonic love, 222
Playboy, 236
  in 1950s, 34
Politics and family, 420–422
Polyandrous society, jealousy in, 248
Polygamous family, 63
Positive carry-over, 166
Postindustrial revolution, 408
Postwar era, 26–27
  demographics of, 49–55
  family in, 27–35
Poverty
  and black families, 170–171,
    172–173
  culture of, 172, 173
  discovery of, 154–155
  divorce revolution and, 281
  and extended family, 124
  feminization of, 281, 406
  1983, families in poverty, 407
  official poverty line, 158
  social psychology of, 159
Pregnancy in teenagers, 213–217

Premarital contract, 280
Primary-kin-oriented familism,
    141, 142
Primates
    infanticide among, 312
    infants of, 315–316
    sex-role behavior in, 191–192
Prisoner's Dilemma game, 286
Private family, 143–145
Procreation, family of, 60
Prostitution, 11, 398
Psychiatry, 91–95
    interpersonal psychiatry, 100
Psychoanalysis, 87–88, 342
    model of marriage, 283–285
    parenthood, defined, 310–311
Psychology
    of family life, 127–129
    and Freud, Sigmund, 92–95
    interface, 166
    and love, 221
    revolution in, 408
    of socialization, 371–386
    universalism, 352
Psychology of Sex Differences, The
    (Maccoby & Jacklin), 187–189
Puberty, 348–349
Public housing projects, 37
Puritans and love, 231

Rating-and-dating complex,
    243–244
Reading, effect of, 130–131
Rebellion, theories of, 367–368
Recapitulation hypothesis, 345–346
Reciprocity and love, 224
Reconstituted families, 60
Reds, 43
Rejecting babies, 314
Relationships, commitments to,
    413
Religion, 424
    and family, 59
    and sex, 203
Remarriage
    divorce rate for, 262
    rates of, 256–257
    revolution in, 408
Repression, 93
Republic (Plato), 83
Residence pattern variations, 68–72
Retirement, 48
    communities, 37
Richard Cory complex, 46

Rise of the Novel (Watt), 231
Role concept, 89–90
Role metaphor, 90
Role stage of love, 241
Rome, ancient
    family in, 116–117
    love in, 229
Romantic fashion, 296–297
Romantic love, 221–226
Romantic male, 240–241
Romantic view of sex, 216
Roots, 169
Roots, 176
Rumanian peasant family study,
    114–115

Sanctity of family, 59–60
Scenes from a Marriage, 251
Science
    and sexual attitudes, 217
    teaching of, 58
Schizophrenia
    and family, 86–87
    coping with, 101–102
    features of, 100–101
    socialization and, 384
    studies of families, 99
Schizophrenogenic mothers,
    389–390
School. *See* Education
Secrecy
    and family, 59–60
    and sexuality, 208–209
Seduction fantasies, 94
Segmented families, 66
Self-esteem of children, 361
Self-fulfillment, 39–41
Self-transformation, 46
Serial marriage, 262
Sex-change operations, 196–197
Sex characteristics, 198
Sex roles, 184–218
    ambivalence about, 287
    biology and, 187–196
    cognitive-development model,
        199–200
    cross-cultural research and,
        192–193
    Freud, Sigmund on, 189–190
    hormones and, 193–194
    infancy, learning in, 202
    and intersexed children, 200–202
    Maccoby and Jacklin review,
        187–189

in Middletown study, 398
    and peer groups, 212–213
    natural behavior, 192
    social learning model, 199
    symmetry in, 410–411
Sexual arousal, 195
Sexual bargaining, 265–271
Sexual development, 196–202
Sexual revolution, 407
    and love, 235
    Middletown study, 401
    of 1920s, 404–405
    and single people, 237
Sexuality
    changes in attitudes, 2
    childbirth and, 329
    in childhood, 209–210
    and cohabitation, 258–259
    commitment and, 414–415
    dissatisfaction with, 215–216
    and Freud, Sigmund, 93
    and generational conflict,
        368–369
    in history, 202–204
    in hunting societies, 111
    images of, 186
    and jealousy, 248
    learning in family, 211–212
    and Middletown studies, 10–11
    in 1950s, 32
    paradoxical messages and,
        290–291
    and peer groups, 212–213
    process of, 194–196
    prudery and, 185–186
    and secrecy, 208–209
    and single people, 238
    social context of, 207–217
Sexual monism, 189
Sexual politics, 277
Single persons
    childrearing by, 76
    and love, 236–238
    McCarthyism and, 29
Singles bars, 244
Sixteenth century society, 106
Slavery-specific hypothesis, 176
Small pox, 318
Social class, 153–181
    and black families, 171–172
    and environment of family,
        386–392
    hidden injuries of, 167
    kin systems of, 65

Social class (*continued*)
in medieval society, 117–118
new family pattern, origination of, 129
review of, 156–159
see also Lower class; Middle class; Working class
Social conflict models, 81, 84–85
Social exchange theory
of family, 80–81
of marriage, 285–288
Socialization, 311, 365–393
adversity and, 383–386
conflict and, 382–383
indeterminacy and, 380–382
psychology of, 371–386
and self, 374–378
social class and, 386–392
two patterns of, 387
Social-learning model, 199
Social norms
and behavior, 88–91
changes in, 53
and illegitimacy, 76
see also Values
Social puppets, 375
Social reform, 400–406
and childhood, 358–359
and New Right, 7
in 1960s, 38
Social role theory, 80
Social System, The (Dahrendorf), 84
Social Security, 158
Sociocultural vacuum, 346
Sociology
of family, 19
of parenthood, 311–312
Solitude, fear of, 234
Spiritual marriage, 251
Standards of living, 159–160
Stern husband pattern, 295
Stimulus stage of love, 241
Strangers on a train phenomenon, 250
Strategy model of marriage, 285–286
Structural-differentiation model, 146, 149
Structural-functional approach, 80–83
Subjective self, 377
Subordination patterns, 114
Suburbs, 1960s, 36–37

Suffrage for women, 404
Superwomen, 406
Swinging groups, 249
Symbolic interaction theory, 81
Symmetrical Family, The (Young & Willmott), 302
Symposium (Plato), 222
Systems approach to marriage, 288–291

Teenagers. *See* Adolescence
Television, 207–208
and children, 363
happy marriages on, 255
Therapeutic language of relationships, 245–246
Tipping points, 54
Togetherness ideology, 32
Tomboyish girls, 201
Total marriage, 294
Total woman movement, 410
Traditional family. *See* Patriarchal family
Traditional rationality, 129–130
Transsexualism, 196–197
Tribes, 115
True self, 41

Underclass, black, 172
Underclass, The (Auletta), 172
Unemployment, 160
effects of, 167–169
Universal nuclear family, 62–63, 141
Unmarried persons. *See* Single persons
Unstable family, 117, 134
Utopian marriage, 282–285
Utopian visions, 83–88

Values
and behavior, 88–91
and family, 18–20
and patriarchal family, 121
Value stage of love, 241
Vecindad, 144–145
Verbal self, 377
Veteran's Administration housing loans, 35
Victorian era
childhood in, 338
family in, 318, 320
morality in, 204–207
Vital marriage, 293–294

Violent families. *See* Domestic violence
Virginity
and adolescents, 52
declines in, 51–52
ideology of, 268

War on Poverty, 158
Weak male stereotype, 32
Wealth and Poverty (Gilder), 7
Wealthy families, 158
Welfare state, 7
White House Conference on Children, 1970, 363
White House Conference on the Family, 1980, 5, 421–422
Wife beating. *See* Domestic violence
Women
black women, 170
changing role of, 2
and courtly love, 230
and extended family, 150
in family economy, 120–121
and industrialism, 120–121, 145–146
in 1950s, 30–32
and patriarchal marriage, 119
social change and, 402–407
suffrage for, 404
see also Family law; Feminism; Working women
Work, 166–167
of children, 361, 363–364
psychology of, 166–167
separation of home and, 145–146
strains of, 149–150
see also Labor force; Unemployment; Working women
Working class, 154–169
black families, 171–172
careers of, 162–163
finances of, 162–164
inappropriateness of term, 157
and lower class, 159
in 1950s, 31
in 1960s, 38
parenthood and, 327–328
passive-congenial marriages in, 293
sexual freedom and, 215
working women in, 164
Working women, 12
in 1950s, 30–32
and parenthood, 334

participation rate of married
women, 17
role overload, 411
working class wives, 164
and World War II, 405

youngest child, participation by
mothers by age of, 23
World War II
and women, 405
see also Postwar era
Writing, effect of,130–131

Young Intellectuals, 43
Yuppies, 26–27, 155–156

Zen Buddhism, 34
Zinacantecos, family of, 63